Fatal Flaws

The Historical Web From WWI to September 11, 2001

Book 3

Fall 1975 - September 11, 2001

Capt. Richard A. Meo   Ret. FDNY

Other Books by Richard A. Meo

My Turn on the Firelines:
A 22 Year Manhattan Firefighting Journey

Fatal Flaws: Book 1

Fatal Flaws: Book 2

Website
firelines-fatalflaws.com

Fatal Flaws: Book 3

Copyright © 2019 by Richard A. Meo

Richard Meo
Fatal Flaws: Book 3
786 pgs
ISBN 978-1-935795-58-2 softcover

All Rights Reserved. No part of this book may be reproduced, stored in a retrieval system, or transmitted in any form or by any means, electronic, mechanical, photocopying, recording, or otherwise, without permission in writing from Michael Ray King Publishing.

MRK Publishing
PO Box 353431
Palm Coast, FL 32135-3431
www.gowriteandyouwontgowrong.com

Printed in the United States of America

Introduction

My first book, *My Turn On The Firelines* **1980-2003**, came out originally in 2009 and was updated in 2014. That work detailed my twenty two plus years in the FDNY. Among the numerous events was the terrorist bombing at the World Trade Center in February 1993, when **The War Against America** actually began, and ended after the (preventable) attacks of September 11, 2001 had occurred. Mistakes within the City Command and Emergency Structure contributed to the extreme losses we in the FDNY and the civilians suffered on that September morning. Sadly many of the most vital lessons were never absorbed.

As hard as it is to believe the FDNY still does not have a helicopter unit. America's largest city, with the most Hi-rise buildings in the nation cannot provide for its citizens because those in power do not wish it. **Dozens of civilians trapped on the upper floors of Tower 1 could have been saved if the FDNY had their own helicopter unit.**

Our losses would also have been reduced if we had a helicopter staffed with Firefighters. They could have observed the weakening of the Towers, the same way the NYPD helicopter people did. **The PD crew wisely radioed out warnings of the deteriorating South Tower 10 minutes before the buildings came down.** Hundreds of PD personnel escaped, but the FDNY operated on different radios and were never told of the pending collapse. The same failure happened with the North Tower.

As someone who is a history buff I felt driven to continue the story of September 11, 2001 with a series of books titled ***Fatal Flaws***.

My research worked backwards in time from the attack. As I moved from source to source it became clear that all of the terrorist attacks were interrelated to historical events from decades before. *No one teaches History as an interconnected web, it is taught as a linear line of time/events.* In most cases the historical trials appear to be a foregone conclusion, but that is wrong on both counts.

World events are always interrelated and always complex. For examples no one could have known what the post WWI breakup of the Ottoman Empire would result in, any more than if the June 1944 invasion of France would succeed. It turned out that the breakup of the Ottoman Empire had deep worldwide consequences that are still being felt, one of which was the attacks of September 11, 2001. As for the invasion of France, numerous planning and operational failures among the senior WWII commanders and leaders such as Churchill, Eisenhower, Montgomery and the Air Corps commanders nearly resulted in the invasion at Normandy collapsing on the beach. Fallout from their many mistakes and the numerous additional strategic failures during the war needlessly prolonged the fighting in Europe. **Those mistakes were a vital part in the creation of the Cold War.**

In writing the *Fatal Flaws* series I tried to rectify the ongoing teaching failures by highlighting many world events, decisions, non-decisions, mistakes, lies and failures that were seen and unseen by the general public. Inside these pages are events as described by other authors, researchers and video documentaries. All of the information is based on those facts, with insights added in. I tried to present these interrelated events in sequence, to show the reader the numerous issues happening at the same time. **It was during those prior decades that the story of 9/11 actually began.**

Thanks to the fine work by numerous authors and videographers, it has been revealed in some detail the failed Clinton presidency and the dozens of missed chances that could have prevented the 9/11 attacks and the trials that followed.

For a deeper look into history one must read and watch the hundreds of outstanding books, articles and videos that are available. In the Index I listed the ones that I feel everyone should read or watch in bold print.

(Hopefully I did not make too many mistakes jumping from source to source in an effort to convey this story..)

I did not use chapters in the first two books of the *Fatal Flaws* series because that implied a separation between events, and History is a continuous flow. For ease of distinction, this book is separated by presidential administrations, but the events are continuous.

Prologue

Most people look at History as just a boring series of dates and events from the past. But history is all around us and the events of today were predicated on decisions, errors and occurrences of yesterday. And those defining events were also shaped by their immediate past forming a historical web that never ends. That is why it is so vital that Americans understand History, and choose "leaders", not politicians or useless lawyers for high office. It was, and is their failures that have, and will again cost hundreds of thousands of lives and untold suffering.

*The clearest examples of their **Fatal Flaws** were the world leaders ignoring Japan's invasion of Manchuria in 1931, the appeasing Hitler in the mid-1930s,, FDR's inane give-aways to Stalin, President Truman's disarming of America in 1946 and his abandoning of our ally Nationalist China. Truman's mistakes set the stage for the Cold War, the Communist takeover in China and new wars in Vietnam and Korea.* Each of those issues are historically interrelated, and all had far reaching effects that are still felt today.

I have read over 600 history books during my adult years. Ninety percent of those covered our century, from 1900 to 2000. What becomes evident as you delve into the past are the numerous political and military mistakes that have occurred. Those errors have been caused by prejudice, stupidity, cowardice, lack of information, or of reaching the wrong conclusions from some intelligence source or prior events. **It is those mistakes, as much as our successes that have shaped our world.**

FATAL FLAWS Book 1 1914-1945

I tried to highlight the broken world of post WWI and the takeover of the Communists in Russia. In the early 1920s the Communists began conquering most of the neighboring nations. While the Western World worried about this expansion and aggression by this dangerous political entity, foreign policy failures by Colonial England and France in their administration of the defeated and disbanded Ottoman Empire laid the groundwork of the world's future enemy, **Islamic Fundamentalism**.

Before the world had caught its collective breath WWII began in Asia in 1931 when Japan invaded Manchuria. During that decade numerous chances came and went to avoid the next World War. *Appeasing* became a new and common word in the world of the 1930's, and as you will read here it would occur again in the 1990s. Those weak attempts to avoid a painful issue would result in far worse, as war would still occur.

As the war-weary Western European nation feared, Communist Russia expanded greatly in the early 1920s to become a major political threat. Watching the European powers sitting idle, the Bolsheviks observed Japan's invasions of Manchuria and China, Fascist Italy and Nazi Germany's aggressiveness, and joined forces with Germany. Russia coldly invaded neighboring Poland as World War II "officially began". Two months later Stalin ruthlessly invaded Finland in another quest for easy gains. Then in 1941 backstabbing Russia was suddenly invaded by the Nazis, and the treacherous Stalin reluctantly become allied with the Western Powers to fight the fascists of Germany and Italy.

In America Franklin Delano Roosevelt was an outstanding domestic politician, but poor in the world of foreign affairs. **His first major foreign policy decision in 1933 was to renew diplomatic relations with the Communist Soviets.** That unleashed a flood of Russian spying and recruitment inside the U.S., which would have vast and detrimental consequences worldwide. FDR's first ambassador to Russia was Joseph Davies, a "progressive" and a Stalin admirer. Both men continuously and arrogantly believed that they could "make deals" with Stalin despite a plethora of anti-freedom actions by the iron-fisted Russian ruler. FDR's Vice President Henry Wallace was another ardent supporter of Stalin and Russia.

As the years went by FDR became ill and was clearly dying. *In the summer of 1944 Wallace was taken off the election ticket because the Democratic party bosses knew that FDR would die in office. They did not want a Socialist becoming president, and unfamiliar Senator Harry Truman was picked as the Democrats vice-president for the 1944 election!*

FDR favored Stalin far above our ally the French, and his "ill advised" decisions at Tehran and Yalta ceded major territorial and political concessions to the Soviets at the expense of many sovereign states and allies. FDR died soon after and Truman took over. (FDR died on April 12, 1945. The next day his aide Harry Hopkins sent a personal message to Stalin, that "Russia has lost her greatest friend in America".)

When the war ended in September 1945, Stalin's Russia was a military powerhouse thanks to U.S. aid and FDR's mistakes. Russia now controlled most of central and eastern Europe. Stalin had told Marshall Tito and his Yugoslav delegation that "This war is not as in the past. Whoever controls a territory imposes on it his social system, it cannot be otherwise."

As had occurred after WWI, the peace treaty of WWII did not bring peace. Only the atomic bomb of the United States prevented Stalin and his Communists from conquering all of Europe and Asia in 1946.

FATAL FLAWS Book 2   1945-1975

This work examines the Cold War which grew from President's Roosevelt's and Truman's many policy failures. While the post-WWII western nations fought the Communist subversions in Greece, Turkey, and Indochina, our vital WWII ally in the Pacific, Nationalist China, was stupidly abandoned and then lost to Mao and his Communists. Large amounts of military and economic aid was needed and given from America in order to save Europe, but Asia went ignored.

Unseen during those years was the continued growth of the Islamic Fundamentalists. They had joined forces with Hitler in the hopes he would drive the French and British out of the Muslim world. But with his defeat they had to wage that war on their own.

The major points in Book 2 were:

1. Pres. Truman's pullout from China in May 1945 and his unilateral disarmament after WWII allowed the Communists to takeover China and threaten western Europe.

2. Soon after the loss of China full scale wars occurred in Indochina and Korea. Though S. Korea was saved from the Communists, French control of Indochina ended in their defeat. With China turned, Mao and his forces had greatly aided the Communists in Northern Vietnam in their war against France. Pres. Eisenhower refused to intervene, and France was defeated in 1954 with N. Vietnam becoming a Communist state.

3. At that same time deadly Communist led uprisings were also occurring in Indonesia, the Philippines, Burma and Malaya.

4. As a result of those repeated wars the world became completely polarized in a Communist vs Non-communist line. All policy efforts in the West, and especially those in America were concentrated on stopping them.

5. The Islamic nations despised the United Nations and their 1948 inspired Israeli homeland formed in the territory known as Palestine. (Which was actually ancient Judea.) Pres. Truman readily recognized Israel, and America joined the Islamists enemy's list. As the years went by the Islamic world fought the Israelis unsuccessfully many times. Similar to the West's concentration on Communism, the Islamic world devoted decades in a vain effort to destroying Israel. In the process they damaged themselves and their futures.

6. With the Western powers concentrating on Communism, *Islamic Nationalists* began seizing political power in the Islamic world, first in Iran in 1951 and then in Egypt in 1953. Within their power base were the *Islamic Fundamentalists* and *Islamic Extremists* who sought to end all "corrupting western influence" in their world. Unable to compete militarily, the Islamic rebels turned to terrorism and economic blackmail by using their main commodity oil.

6. Communist N. Vietnam would soon threaten all of the neighboring countries, while the Democrats rigged the election in 1960 and put JFK and LBJ into office. John Kennedy decided to fight the N. Vietnamese in mid-1961, but after he was murdered Lyndon Johnson took over and his poorly run war effort turned into a disaster. The war in Vietnam was polarizing our nation, and in November 1968 Richard Nixon won the presidency.

Nixon had tons of liberal enemies from his work on the Alger Hiss spy case back in 1948, and their hatred followed him all his life. *(Most people do not know this but every year that JFK and LBJ were in power Nixon was audited by the IRS in the hopes he could be charged with something. And JFK and LBJ both had Nixon's phones illegally tapped as were the phones of his running mates.)*

After Nixon won, it took until June 1969 for the stunned and obstructionist Democrats to approve the last of his cabinet choices. *All of their efforts were directed to hurting his administration, and had nothing to do with helping our nation.* (Just like with Donald Trump after his win in 2016.)

During his first years in office Nixon worked tirelessly to end the Vietnam War with the most favorable strategic circumstances possible. For months Henry Kissinger met with the intransient N. Vietnamese representatives in Paris as they hashed out the final details. After accomplishing that feat, Nixon won a landslide victory in 1972. But with no warning a month later the N. Vietnamese decided they were not going to complete the peace agreement. Nixon cautioned them to comply, but they refused. He then renewed an intensive bombing of N. Vietnam.

For two weeks the Communists were struck continually losing most of their military infrastructure. They finally gave in and signed the peace treaty. Our POWs (prisoners of war) were returned to us, brutalized, injured and starved. (They knew they would be freed when the bombs started destroying the North.)

Liberals and the elitist pundits are always happy to exclaim that we lost the war in Vietnam, but that is not true. **When we left S. Vietnam they were still a viable country. Tragically our eleven year effort did not end in victory, but in a stalemate.**

As a result of the Watergate affair Richard Nixon resigned from office in August 1974, leaving Gerald Ford in charge. Nixon definitely was wrong for trying to protect his mid-level staffers over the Watergate break-in.

But the real scandal of Watergate was the collusion and conspiracy during the investigation. Illegal leaks from Hoover's FBI insured the Watergate scandal took hold and progressed. Then the prosecutors and judges involved in the hearings and trials hatched illegal back room deals to bring Pres. Nixon and his administration down.

Unelected to office, Gerald Ford could not influence the Congress on any national issues, especially in helping S. Vietnam. The Democratic run Congress wanted no part of the world, and the Communists took advantage of our absence as all of Indochina would fall.

At the same time Islamic terror attacks were increasing in severity and in numbers. Those terrorists were becoming better organized, and Lebanon would be their first test case in taking control.

While most of the western world desires peace, the majority of the planet does not. There are many nations and leaders who want war, and a chance for power.

For there Are Tigers in This World, (2)

And They Are Always Watching

Give me your time and I will reveal and unravel how the past has led us to these trials. You may not like the information that you will read, but all of it is true.

And it all started with WWI.

Our age must learn the lessons of WWII, brought about when the democracies failed to understand the designs of totalitarian aggressors. But we must also remember the lessons of WWI when Europe, despite the existence of a military balance, drifted into a war no one wanted, and a catastrophe no one could have imagined. Military planning drove decisions, bluster and posturing drove diplomacy, and the Leaders committed the cardinal sin of statecraft;

They lost control of events. (2A)

Henry Kissinger, *Years of Upheaval*

"You know full well that when strategic-political matters are discussed by practical people, the standard of justice depends on the equality of their power.

The strong will do what they have the power to do, and the weak will accept whatever they have to accept!"

(Thucydides, History of the Peloponnesian War)

Sections

1. The Ford Years - A Time of Dejection

   August 1974- January 1977

   Pages 13-47

2. The Carter Years - Decline and Despair

   January 1977- January 1981

   Pages 48 - 147

3. The Reagan Years - Renewal and Rebuilding

   January 1981 – January 1989

   Pages   148- 297

4. The Bush Years - Freedom and Strength

   January 1989 – January 1993

   Pages 298 - 452

5. The Clinton Years - Appeasement and Subversion

   January 1993- January 2001

   Pages 453-678

6. The Bush 43 Presidency   Page 677-731

7. September 11, 2001   Pages 698-731

Fatal Flaws   Book 3   1975 - September 11, 2001

Section One   August 1974- January 1977

The Ford Years   A Time of Dejection

As bad as things were in Vietnam with the Communist victory, in Cambodia it was far worse. The Communist Khmer Rouge had been fighting for final control of the country since early 1974. Into the new year the battles had continued. With the end of all U.S. aid the Khmer Rouge had encircled the capitol of Phnom Penh four months earlier. During the heavy fighting they killed multiple thousands of innocents as they inexorably advanced. On April 16, 1975 the defenses of the city finally collapsed. By then Phnom Penh itself had been mostly destroyed by the communist artillery. As usual, the Communists killed and wounded multiple thousands of innocent civilians. Once inside the city, anyone who was educated, was from the military or government were quickly and ruthlessly eliminated. *But that was the good news.*

Pol Pot, the demented leader of the Khmer Rouge had decreed that the entire population of the city, some two million plus souls were to be forcibly moved to the country. And this happened in every city and large town. Cambodia was to be transformed into an socialist agricultural state, and all "Class Enemies" would be weeded out and executed. To cajole the citizens to leave their homes the Khmer told them that it was just for a few days and they should take only what they could carry. Even the hospitals were emptied, as new mothers with babes, the lame, sick and dying were all kicked out. Anyone who protested was shot. Anyone who fell behind was shot. The rifle fire was endless.

To save ammunition the Khmer was forced to turn to "other methods" of eliminating "the unworthy". The results were catastrophic as columns of city dwellers succumbed to the unending forced marches into the hot countryside. They endured meager rations, limited rest or water, and back-breaking labor. The marches went from days into weeks. Eating without permission meant death, as did the stealing of any scrap of food. In their weakened states families became separated, children were missed, forgotten or abandoned on the side of the road. Their pitiful cries echoing past the lines of marchers until they were silent.

Any type of human connection was broken by the Khmer rules, or by violence. All public records were destroyed and all commerce was ended. Any modern contraption such as phones, record players to microscopes were shattered. As the economy of the once vibrant nation collapsed, starvation which was previously unknown in Cambodia began with a vengeance. Bodies lay everywhere as the demented orgy of death continued unabated. Between one to two million Cambodians were murdered, sickened or starved in that first year. Three million died by the time it ended.

This was the time known as the Killing Fields. (3)

"It was a on a scale of biblical proportions, but it most definitely was not a natural disaster." (4)

(The movie *The Killing Fields* did a fine job highlighting the horrors of the period, but it was a shameless liberal lie over why it happened and what was done about it. Most of the media and the liberals of that time glossed over the slaughter, and many outright lied about. They still do.)

Such was the barbarity inside Cambodia, that over 250,000 souls desperately crossed into recently conquered Vietnam trying to find refuge. Another 100,000+ crossed into Thailand before the Khmer closed the borders. Thousands upon thousands died or were murdered unseen in the dark forbidding jungles. Along with their insane genocide, border clashes became common with all of Cambodia's neighbors.

Pres. Ford appealed to the Congress to restore aid and help the Cambodians. He was derided for his concerns. *Democrats led by Bob Carr, Tom Downey and Chris Dodd were adamant that no help would be given from the Congress.* It was just too bad for those people. However some help was secretly given.

Hidden from public view and the uncaring media, another of those unseen and unstated U.S. humanitarian operations began. This one was a food program initiated by the U.S. Ambassador to Thailand Morton Abramowitz. *Despite the world's abandonment of the Cambodians, Abramowitz saved dozens of thousands of Cambodians by sneaking foods across the border to the starving masses.* *(5)

To continue this life saving assistence, his work was done in the shadows. The Democrats in Congress were not informed.

To Cambodia's east, the other SE Asia humanitarian crisis grew in scale as hundreds of thousands of civilians were also fleeing Vietnam. **This was more fallout from the loss of South Vietnam to the Communists of the North.**

Our Democratic controlled Congress had cut the funding to S. Vietnam from $2.1 billion in 1973 to $1.1 in 1974 to just $700 million in 1975. With Nixon gone the Democrats saw no reason to support the South, and this cut in funding had come in just as the price of oil was skyrocketing from the Arab boycott.

Unable to afford the costs of modern war the South was forced to ground their aircraft and most of their transport vehicles. Amply supplied by the Soviets, the N. Vietnamese did not have that logistical issue. Their overpowering and multi-axis armored forces ran amok.

Once the South was defeated, the Communists from the North pushed aside all of the Viet Cong leaders. The northerners took control, once again showing the world that this was not a civil war. (The VC had been used as puppets.)

With the fighting over our liberals and many Democrats in our government crowed over the North's win. They callously ignored the reports of the arrests and the forced re-education camps that were being organized. Anyone who had worked for the South, any former military personnel, anyone educated, and even protesting former VC found themselves taking the long walk into the jungles. Estimates range from 200,000 to over a million people were sent to the "re-education camps".

The larger number was probably correct as the Communists were never really good at keeping records like those.

Overcrowding in their prisons was extreme as eighty prisoners were crammed into cells built for twenty. There was little water or sanitation, and only one small air vent was allowed. Prisoners subsisted on just 200 grams of rice a day. But the ones in the prisons were the lucky ones, as their sentences had limits. Those sent to the "re-education camps" deep in the countryside were sentenced to a lifetime of hard labor.

Lifetime being a relative term.

Reliable reports put the number of Southerners who were executed at 65,000. "But that does not include those killed or those who died while at or on their way to the camps and prisons." (The last prisoners would not be released until 1986.) (6)

As always our liberals refused to see these truths and callously lied about everything in the media, in books and to the Congress over what was happening. Even after the undeniable truth came out they disingenuously blamed America for the crisis instead of the Communists. Only William Shawcross of the *Sunday Times* admitted his gross error in not seeing the reality of the Communists. *But it was years too late to save the ones they had condemned.*

Fallout from this typical Communist doctrine was relatively quick. Best guesses believe over 800,000 S. Vietnamese (plus Cambodian refugees) took to the sea to try to escape. Fishermen from numerous countries began reporting on this looming crisis. Naval vessels from the U.S., England, Australia and even Israel began pulling refugees from the sea. Many of their civilian craft were unseaworthy and dangerously overcrowded. Casualties were constant.

Pres. Ford again went to the Senate to plead the case for taking in some of the growing mass of humanity that were desperately trying to escape. Few in the post-Watergate Congress wanted to help. Their close-sighted mission was to fight all of the factors that had caused Vietnam. Led by Democratic Sen. Clairborne Pell of Rhode Island, he derisively suggested sending them to Borneo as the climate there is the same as Vietnam and they have need of "anti-communists". Pell was another of those shameless liberals. *(Despite the films and photos of Hue in 1968, Pell "doubted the N. Vietnamese had murdered anyone". Yet mass graves found outside the city held over 5,000 residents murdered by the NVA.)*

Ford angrily shot back that our nation has always accepted those oppressed by war and it should be no different this time. More hostile voices spoke out in the Congress. Pres. Ford eventually won the day with help from Rep. Peter Rodino of NJ, some stalwart Governors, Jewish groups and even some trade Unions. Because of those few, thousands of destitute Vietnamese refugees were eventually saved and taken in. By December 1975 the last of those relocated few entered their new land across the sea. Hundreds of thousands had died ignored and unseen in their frantic attempts to escape.

The United Nations, that corrupted world body that complained so often over America's actions in SE Asia, refused to condemn N. Vietnam and the Communists for their far worse actions and latest atrocities. Not until 1983 did the U.N. even address the genocide in Cambodia!

Conservative columnist William F. Buckley pointedly observed that far more S. Vietnamese had died trying to save their nation from the Communists, than the French had suffered fighting Hitler. (7) (One sardonic joke states, "How many Frenchmen does it take to defend Paris? No one knows, it has never been tried.) (7A)

To the north Laos finally fell to the Communists in mid-August 1975. Their coalition government had been established two years earlier, but as everyone knew would happen it was dissolved as the Communist Pathet Lao gradually took over.

As shown in *Fatal Flaws Book 2*, the CIA had wrongly insisted during 1969 that the Laotian guerrilla army (we were financing), be converted into regular ground troops. Those indigenous Hmong-Meo tribal people could not make that transition, and it cost them as their small population suffered increasing casualties fighting the communists toe to toe. When the CIA and America pulled out from SE Asia in 1974 those tribal people were callously left to their fate, with most disappearing in the dense jungles. With this final collapse of Laos, only a few thousand Hmong-Meo tribesmen were able to escape to the U.S.

With that country's fall all of French Indochina was now Communist. **Harry Truman's failure to support Chiang and the Nationalists in China in 1945/46 had finally born its full measure of poisoned fruit.**

Neighboring Thailand began to brace for their war. Fortunately, they had watched and helped fight the Communist efforts the past thirty years. Because of their proximity to those fights, Thailand had been the first SEATO nation to send troops to the war in Vietnam. They had committed 11,000 troops fighting in South Vietnam and 16,000 committed to helping in neighboring Laos. Their air corps had been trained by our people during the war and they had a good grasp of the tactics needed to survive. The Thais were combat savvy and prepared. Unlike the former French Indochina colonies, Thailand had a long history as an independent and proud nation. Their people were not the easy marks the other colonized nations had been.

Historical Note: As shown in *Fatal Flaws Book 2 1945-1975*, the 1960 presidential election had been rigged by the corrupt Democrats in Illinois and Texas. That allowed JFK and LBJ into office. JFK was addicted to drugs and constantly used his elected office for sexual encounters even with prostitutes. *(8a)*

During his years Kennedy repeatedly made poor decisions that affected the world. Among them were strategic crisis with the Communists at the Bay of Pigs in Cuba, then Laos, Vietnam, and the Cuban Missile Crisis.

Kennedy had made multiple operational changes prior to the Bay of Pigs operation causing its failure. At the following summit meeting with Khrushchev in Vienna in June 1961, JFK timed the trip to give him a visit to a French bordello where they found a Jackie look-alike. Khrushchev however came prepared, and was aggressive in berating the young president on multiple subjects which included Cuba. After the meetings ended the media kept a lid on the disaster, but Kennedy was stunned.   *He realized that Khrushchev had verbally beaten and humiliated him, and Kennedy resolved to "make our power credible".*

The place we would do that would be Vietnam. *(8)

Every idea and decision the JFK and LBJ Administrations made about Vietnam was wrong, and the Vietnamese and our citizen-soldiers paid the terrible price for that election fraud. At home our country was polarizing and falling apart as evidenced by the riots in Chicago at the 1968 Democratic Party Convention. Nixon was elected in that terrible time, but could not end the Vietnam War on our terms until late 1972.

When we left S. Vietnam in early 1973 they were still a viable entity, and Nixon promised them we would return if the North invaded as they tried in April 1972. South Vietnam had been spared from a Communist takeover, if only for a little while.

As the Watergate issue deepened the Democrats smelled political blood and were pushing for Nixon to resign or face possible impeachment. It was vital to have a new vice president in place. Some of the left wing Democrats led by Bella Abzug from Queens, NY did not want Speaker Albert to approve anyone, as they were actually hoping to stage a political coup. If no replacement vice president was approved by them, and Nixon was ousted or resigned, the Speaker of the House, Albert was next in line and would take over. Thus the Democrats could regain the White House using subterfuge. (A feat they could not attain by vote after two humiliating losses to the hated Nixon.)

Congressman Ford was grilled for days by the Democrats in an effort to discredit him. They failed and he became the new appointed Vice President, the first time in our history.

Jerry Ford had actually been Nixon's second choice as the replacement Vice-President. (VP Spiro Agnew had resigned for not claiming some questionable income on his taxes.) Nixon had initially wanted John Connelly, the former Democratic Governor had been shot in Dallas with John Kennedy in 1963. But years later Connelly switched over to the Republicans as he realized that the Democratic Party was the enemy of our nation. (Vietnam).

Democrat Speaker of the House Carl Albert let it be known that the Democratic controlled Congress would never approve of the "turncoat Connelly", but they would approve of Gerald Ford. He was chosen, and those conspiring Democrats rejoiced in having "picked the next president".

Gerald Ford was from Michigan, and had a typical mid-western upbringing that was disciplined, conservative and family oriented. Many believed when he was growing up that America should be isolationist, as George Washington had warned. Ford excelled at school and sports, and was enrolled in Law school when WWII began. Like JFK and Nixon, Ford served in combat with the Navy in the South Pacific. When he returned home from the war he had changed his isolationist political views.

America had to stay involved with the world to prevent this from ever happening again! In 1948 he was elected to the Congress and served there until he became vice-president.

Because of the increasing hostilities and anger over the senseless Watergate affair, VP Ford stayed away from Washington and the hearings. He traveled the country seeing and learning on what was happening to our citizens. At every press conference he was grilled by the media over Watergate and Nixon. For the most part he was able to deflect and avoid the media's shrill cries for Nixon's head. Inside the White House Nixon's staff and advisors counseled him it was time to resign, and he did in August 1974. Gerald Ford had to assume the vital role as president, but he was an unelected official. (That was the first time that had happened.)

In his inaugural address Gerald Ford simply stated that our national nightmare was ended. It was time to get to work to fix our myriad problems. On Nixon he simply said, "For Richard Nixon who had brought peace to millions, hopefully he can find some peace for himself".

As Ford took to the office the world's problems continued unabated. He had to find ways to solve them, and that meant fighting with the Democrats who at that point were only looking to the 1976 presidential election. They would fight Ford over everything. (Same as they're doing with President Trump).

Fresh from their win over Nixon the Democrats wanted more. In the U.S. Senate Democrat Frank Church's 1975 commission began a political witch-hunt against the FBI and CIA. The intent of those leftists in the Congress was to weaken and place severe restrictions upon the nation's intelligence and law enforcement agencies. NY Democrat Otis Pike and Michigan's Lucien Nedzi were doing the same thing from the House.

Incredulously the Democrats blamed Vietnam on the CIA, and felt them to be a threat. *Yet it was the Democrats who had created and controlled the CIA, and gave them their ability to act. It was Truman who lost Asia to the Communists, and Vietnam was one facet of his failures.* And JFK had committed us to fight there. But again those failuers were never brought up in the hearings.

It was the Democrats, JFK and LBJ who had used the CIA, the FBI and IRS for their own political objectives throughout their years in office. Kennedy had the FBI plant the most illegal wiretaps during his three years in office, while LBJ planted second most during his five years! *(Dr. Martin Luther King was one of their main targets for illegal wire taps. Those facts were also covered up by the Democrats and the leftist media.)*

Over time Nedzi was not considered liberal or anti-CIA enough, so he was eventually replaced by Pike. Fallout from those committees was the end of the CIA's intelligence gathering, and soon after the FBI shuttered its domestic security apparatus.

Yet during those years domestic terrorism was still occurring to the tune of dozens of attacks and incidents. Leftist terrorist entities like the weather underground, political activists like the Puerto Rican separatists (FALN) and anti-Israel terrorists were all striking inside America murdering and wounding dozens. By not being able to intercede against those groups while they were planning attacks, the FBI, police and first responders were forced to deal with the them after their attacks had occurred. Their terrorism furthered the malaise that was growing in our nation, and encouraged our enemies that we were collapsing.

("Bill Ayers and his wife were members of the terror group the weather underground. They set bombs off in NYC Police headquarters 1970, the U.S. Capitol building 1971, and the Pentagon in 1972, plus other targets murdering and wounding a dozen people. Ayers stated he did not regret setting the bombs, his regret was that we did not do more." *(9)* *This murderous domestic terrorist scum was later pardoned by Democrat Bill Clinton.)*

Foreign Affairs

In Central America left-wing radicals seized twenty civilians at a 1975 Christmas Party in Managua, **Nicaragua**. President Somoza who had been in the U.S. rushed home to face the crisis. Martial Law was declared as the left-wing *Sandinista rebels* were becoming a dangerous force. Their communist ideals were being spread with Cuba's help, which is exactly what all had feared when Castro came to power. As had happened in S. Vietnam and Cambodia, Pres. Ford was powerless to intercede as the Congress refused to give any anti-Communist aid to Somoza.

In late 1974 a Communist inspired coup occurred in **Portugal**. The ruling junta quickly announced that Portugal would end all of their colonial rule. Though this ending was long past due, this news created a power vacuum which meant those nations would be at risk for subversion.

As a vital NATO member, Portugal was slowly becoming a Socialist nation. In their 1975 election the Socialists took 38% of the seats while the Communists took another 12.5%. With Portugal's government now neutralized, this was an opportunity by the Soviets, and they quickly stepped up their support to the MPLA (Popular Movement for the Liberation of Angola), Communist rebels in Angola. Communist supporters in the Portuguese army had been helping the Cubans and Soviets ship weapons into Angola for years, but now they had a chance to take direct action.

On January 16, 1975 Portugal's government officially ended their colonial rule of the resource rich colony of Angola on Africa's SW coast. A ten-month transitional government would be formed from the three rival liberation movements that had been struggling for over a decade for independence. (The other two groups that had been fighting the Portuguese these past years were FNLA National Front for the Liberation of Angola and UNITA The National Union for the Liberation of Angola)

During March a right-wing counter-coup succeeded in taking power in Portugal, but they could not reverse the transition process. The rival governments being established in Luanda and Huambo set the stage for conflict. As was expected, the two political sides were based on a communist model or a more western one. As usual the Soviet backed MPLA was way ahead of the western backed forces. And as they had done in Vietnam, the Communists setup safe staging areas across the border with the Congo. Training centers had also been established near Brazzaville, as Soviet air and sea units delivered arms shipments weekly. All the CIA could do was send $300,000. The Congress would not send any anti-Communist aid to Angola.

With the political fall of America becoming apparent, the Soviets became outright aggressive by sending Cuban troops to

join the fighting in Angola during May 1975. Equipped with all types of Russian weapons the Soviet trained Cubans were able to speedily turn the tide to the Communist rebel side. On July 9, 1975 a full scale offensive was made driving the UNITA and FNLA forces from the Angolan capitol of Luanda.

Democrats in the U.S. Congress held hearings over the growing crisis in Angola. They passed the Clark Amendment to prohibit any more U.S. military aid. America would not get involved in the third world again. Their vote did not stop the fighting as the Communist bloc was actively promoting the war. But their amendment did guaranty that the Communists would emerge victorious. (Perhaps that was the plan all along.)

Knowing the Communists were going to take over their neighbor, S. Africa sent military units in to try to stop them. In Moscow the Politburo decided to raise the stakes as they airlifted in additional Cuban troops to fight the S. Africans and their ally the UNITA forces. Sec. State Kissinger became actively involved in trying to alert the Congress to this extreme danger as Portugal could be turned too if we stayed away from this emergency.

Pres. Ford directed the CIA and DoD get aid into the region. The small amount of funding we sent ($25 million) allowed the Western backed UNITA forces to hire mercenaries as a way to get trained soldiers into the fight. CIA's Colby was asked to get more aid into the region which aroused fierce opposition in Congress. *Word was "leaked to Seymour Hersh at the NY Times, and soon after the Senate stepped in and stopped all U.S. aid to Angola.*

Neighboring Zaire and Zambia supported the anti-communist forces. Joseph Mobutu agreed that we could use Zaire as a base for the FNLA forces, while Zambia's Kenneth Kaunda used his country to help the UNITA forces. By the fall of 1975 South Africa had sent several thousand of their troops to fight against the communists. MPLA leader Neto then asked the Soviets for more troops, and was told to approach Castro, who agreed to send more men. *To insure their side would win the Soviets shipped in tons of additional arms and ammunition worth over $200 million dollars. Soviet ships sea-lifted more Cuban troops in, and their numbers rose to over 20,000.* Castro was determined to become a major player in the Communist world.

(At a press conference on the growing Communist subversive wars in Africa, Sec. State Henry Kissinger sarcastically joked that the one place there are no Cuban troops was in Cuba.)

Portugal ended their efforts in Angola on November 11, 1975. **The United Nations again did nothing, and with each failure to combat the Communists, it emboldened them to continue.**

Historical Note: Castro and his ally Che Guevara were serious practitioners of Communism, and both were cruel and ruthless towards any anti-communists. *After they took over in 1959 Guevara opened Cuba's first forced labor camp, while Castro closed all media outlets, religion was suppressed and all schools were shut down. Former allies and non-believers were tortured and brutally murdered if they did not quickly embrace Communism.* (Guevara was killed in Bolivia trying a revolt there.)

Over on the east coast of Africa, Ethiopia also erupted into civil war. During February 1975 Ethiopian troops were battling two rebel groups, the Eritrean Liberation Front and the Marxist Popular Liberation Front. Both of them were being financed by the Soviets and the nearby Arabs nations. Those groups were equipped with communist built weapons, and were trained by Communist advisors. *As had happened in every previous rebellion, the Marxist side was winning.*

And after the U.S. Congress stopped all aid to Angola, the Soviets knew they would have a free hand in the Horn of Africa for at least two years due to our election cycle.

Months later Emperor Haile Salassie was deposed in a coup.

After the coup, Salassie was kept under house arrest until he was murdered in August 1975. One of his finest quotes was; *"Throughout history it has been inaction by those who could have acted, indifference by those who should have known better, and silence from the voice of justice when it mattered most that made it possible for evil to triumph."* * (10)

Historical Note; Selassie was as most autocratic rulers are, corrupt, and had squandered vast sums of wealth during his 58 year reign while his country struggled with abject poverty. Throughout his reign Salassie had remained pro-Western in his foreign policy, even though the League of Nations had not helped him fight off the Italians back in 1937. After Italy was defeated the Allies reinstated Salassie in 1944, and he met with FDR in early 1945 to discuss world affairs and his country's place in it. Like many rulers in those post-WWII years, he had been a stopgap to Soviet ambitions. Salassie had ruled Ethiopia for decades, unlike many other nations in Africa that had constant turnover.

To help the Soviets and to ensure the U.S. did not get involved in this latest subversive war, the Democratic controlled Congress passed specific legislation preventing any CIA involvement in Ethiopia.. They also passed a War Powers Resolution to stop any potential military action by the president. Sec. State Kissinger was stunned at how fast our Congress was abandoning the world to the Communists. It would get much worse.

The most senior Soviet to ever defect was Arkady Shevchenko. He wrote that the Soviet leaders were overjoyed at this ignominious end to American involvement in world affairs. That meant their total victory was near. * (11)

Nearby in the Middle East continuous trials within the oil producing countries was becoming alarming. During the days when Britain ruled the seas and the sun never set on the British Empire, England had maintained control of that region.

Historical Note: Since the early 1800s it was the Royal Navy who prevented pirates from controlling the trade routes. It was England and her military who stood watch over the small sheikdoms they had created in Aden, Oman, Qatar, Kuwait, Iraq, Bahrain, and the area that was called the Pirate Coast, the United Arab Emirates. Included in their former empire were Singapore, Malaya, Burma, India, Ceylon, Suez, Kenya, South Africa, New Zealand, Australia, Micronesia and Diego Garcia. With the stability and protection offered by the British, large companies began operating in the region, trade could flourish and the region's cities and populations grew and prospered. (But not always fairly.)

Back in 1900 the small islands of England with a population under 40 million ruled an empire greater than Rome. They controlled fifty countries with a landmass of 11.9 million square miles and a combined population of 345 million souls. This constituted a quarter of the world's landmass and population. However the seeds of her destruction were already at hand, the Industrial Revolution. Dozens of decades ago British timbers were solid and strong and had enabled Great Britain and the Royal navy to rule the waves and in many cases the lands of others. But mass produced steel would be the great equalizer.

In 1901 oil had been found in commercial quantities in the Persian basin by Russian teams. At that time oil was not the primary energy source it is today coal was, *and England controlled much of the worlds coal.* But tensions quickly increased over who would control this new energy source. Some of the bright sparks in the British Navy and Intelligence sent a spy named Sydney Reilly to investigate. He returned months later with the entire report on the Russian findings. His actions alerted England to the value of the oil, and of the potential conflict with Russia over controlling it.

Two years later Reilly was sent to France to "convince" an Australian mining engineer who was developing an oil field in Arabia to sign a commercial pact with England instead of France. *The new energy company that was formed would be called BP, (British Petroleum), and Winston Churchill was one of those bright sparks.*

To ensure that this increasingly vital commodity would be delivered safely the British maintained firm control over the "oil area" and that included the British built Suez Canal. At that time the Islamic Ottoman Empire was still holding on, though it had shrunk by over half from its earlier glory. When the Great War began in 1914 the Ottoman leaders wrongly sided with Germany. From their defeat, all of their lands were remapped and ruled by European Colonial governors. **The Muslim world fell into chaos.**

More tragedy befell the world's nations with a second World War. In the aftermath the Jewish state of Israel was formed from what had been an area in the Ottoman Empire called Palestine. Violent resistance and wars followed which further inflamed hatred and retribution.

England would be bankrupted by the two World Wars, and the nation reluctantly began to shed her costly empire. Tragically the new independent Islamic states they created would mostly be ruled by corrupt governments and rulers. *(For the Islamic extremists of the 1980s their rallying cry was that "they had been oppressed by decades of European Christian rule".)*

With Britain leaving the region another dangerous power vacuum ensued, one that the Communists began to fill. The region turned extremely violent, and by default America had to step in to hold the line. But it was not a task we were mentally prepared for, or even wanted to do. As a result our efforts were centered on following what the English had done, and try to maintain the status quo. One event that occurred was the ill advised effort helping the British in a 1953 Iranian coup. The plan was to keep the Shah of Iran in power instead of the leftist leading voter elected government. The fallout from that day was twenty-two plus years of an ally in the region, but a calling card for the Islamists to rally behind.

Britain maintained an ever shrinking presence in the region until 1971, when they released their last colony. Right up to that time the British had continued fighting Communist insurgents in Oman in an effort to keep the Soviets out.

To maintain a Western military presence, America began using the small British base at Diego Garcia as a hedge against a Russian naval force that was on permanent duty in the Indian Ocean since 1968. Though America was still tied up in Vietnam, Pres. Nixon and his State Dept. decided to help the local powers shore up the region primarily in Iran and Saudi Arabia. Arms and military training were given to try to keep this vital region safe, but things were getting worse as each year went by. Islamic Fundamentalists and extremists were vying for power, terrorist attacks against the West were increasing, and it seemed the world of the early 1970s was falling apart. *The Soviet Union played the major part in promoting that anarchy.*

The Communist Threat

At the end of WWII the Soviet Union was the "other global power". Though they had been ravaged by the war, losing over 15% of their population and half of their economic infrastructure, they had the most powerful army in the world thanks to America and Lend-Lease aid. With the terrible political mistakes by FDR the Soviets controlled over half of Europe, and had made inroads into Asia which foolishly included Manchuria. The Cold War between the West and Communism was soon a reality, and became the dominating political event in the post-WWII era. **Had it not been for economic and atomic power of the United States, the entire world would have turned Communist.**

Back in the spring of 1950 Truman's National Security Council investigated world events and came up with a warning called **NSC-68**. Their report was a history lesson, and the blueprint for the Cold War. *They warned that since 1900 five dominate old world empires had fallen apart, Spain, The Czar's Russia, The Ottoman Empire, The Kaiser's Germany, and Austria-Hungary. Two others were almost gone, Great Britain and France.* During the decades past those "Old World" Empires had kept each other in relative check. **But in the span of just 50 years all were gone.**

Only two real powers remained, America and the Communists.

Echoing Truman's 1947 anti-communist speech, the NSC warned that those two systems were diametrically opposed to each other and could not coexist. One operated under laws and freedom, the other under slavery and force of arms. The NSC warned that if the Soviets continued to expand unchecked eventually the forces of freedom would not be able to defeat them. *The Communist world must be contained if our way of life and freedom was to be maintained. Allies were needed across the globe, even if they were not up to our political or social standards.* (Rome was not built in a day, and it was hoped that the lesser nations could watch and learn from us, and Democracy would eventually take over.)

Yet in just twenty five years since that policy was formulated the Democrats of the mid-1970's were abandoning all previous ideas and promises on freedom. They were preparing to give up the fight.

Lebanon and the PLO

In mid-April 1975 civil battles finally exploded inside of Lebanon. This Christian-Muslim nation sat on the eastern edge of the Mediterranean Sea, and harbored deep internal problems, fallout from post-WWI French control. Being a Christian nation France had installed the minority population of Maronite Christians, who were 2/5 of Lebanon's population, into most of the political positions. This was the same tactic the French had tried in Vietnam, but in Lebanon renewed religious tensions were the cause of violent hostilities and skirmishing began.

Historical Note: The areas of Syria and Lebanon were also part of the old Ottoman Empire. Their populations were comprised of Phonecians, Greeks, Arabs, Armenians and Jewish people. In 1921 Lebanon was officially formed and became a French protectorate. In 1926 Lebanon became a separate Republic, and in 1943 an independent Christian run nation. The Islamic populations took great umbrage at this "new crusade", and trouble was constant. When WWII ended De Gaulle attempted to re-assert France's control, which caused even more hostility. In 1956 Eisenhower had to send in the Marines as a show of force and the situation reduced to a slow simmer.

Their religious divide became fatal with the growing and ever hostile presence of the PLO, Palestinian Liberation Organization operating in Lebanon. The PLO was established in 1964 with Nasser's help as a way to "address the Israeli problem" without involving Egypt directly. The PLO was anti-Israel and anti-West. They became a voice for disenchanted Palestinians who had waited two decades for the Arab states to help them end the 1948 U.N. establishment of Israel. The PLO were primarily based in Jordan, though their refugees also lived in Egypt, Iraq and Syria.

Al-Fatah was the terrorist arm of the emerging PLO and their first operation against Israel was an attempted bombing of Israel's water supply in January 1965. The tougher minded Lebanese government of that time arrested every Al-Fatah squad that entered Lebanon and disarmed them. They did not want to be caught up in that struggle, and only a few Palestinians had relocated to Lebanon because it was Christian run.

During that time the PLO's defacto leader was one Yassir Arafat who was born Abed a-Rachman al-Husseini, was a nephew of the Gran Mufti Amin al-Husseini, a descendent of the prophet Mohammed. Arafat's family was political, and many members belonged to the **Muslim Brotherhood**, the first of the Islamic movements dedicated to ending European colonialism in the Middle East. As shown in *Fatal Flaws Books 1&2,* the Muslim Brotherhood began in the 1920s to fight the colonial powers that controlled the Middle East after WWI. In the 1940s and 50s they were led by **Sayd Qutb** who was fiercely anti-west, again fallout from the creation of Israel. *He had a particular hatred for the U.S., which he highlighted in a 1951 article that "American Jazz was the creation of Negros to satisfy their primitive desires."* * (12)

Within the PLO numerous well-organized subdivisions were formed and directed to promote terrorism or political action and lobbying. Many separate splinter groups broke off from the original subdivisions. By the late 1960s the PLO and its spin-offs were operating from Jordan with impunity, and attacking into Israel often. The Israeli's finally reacted in late 1968 by crossing the border and striking the PLO at their main regional base in Karameh. Loss of their Jordanian border outposts ended Arafat's dream of ringing Israel with hostile Palestinian bases, as Arafat and a few other leaders barely escaped. (He would turn that defeat into the chairmanship of the PLO.)

Even though they had been forced out of Jordan many Al-Fatah members hid out among the numerous Palestinian refugee camps that existed there. They began threatening King Hussein for not helping them fight the Israelis. Fighting between the PLO and Hussein's Bedouin army quickly grew worse, and over 6,000 PLO fighters would be killed. As shown before *in Fatal Flaws Book 2,* the King grew tired of their aggressive actions and he expelled all of the Palestinians. But his actions had an unexpected and tragic down side.

When King Hussein expelled the increasingly hostile and dangerous PLO in 1970-71, they relocated into southern Lebanon. The strong willed Lebanese government of 1964-65 was gone, and the Lebanon of 1971 had a weak coalition government. They wrongly allowed the heavily armed PLO into their country, and placed no controls over them.

Over the next years the PLO began annexing areas of southern Lebanon and in short order they had created a separate state. Throughout that time the terrorist minded PLO had been constantly striking into Israel from their new bases, and they also continued their attacks against Jordan. Jordan's Prime Minister was murdered, their ambassador to London was wounded and King Hussein survived at least seven attempts on him.

In addition to the localized fighting those new Lebanese- PLO base-camps were used as training stations for every terrorist organization in the world! *That list included, Italy's Red Brigade, the Irish Republican Army (IRA), France's Direct Action, Germany's Red Army Faction, Japan's Red Army,* **Iran's Revolutionaries** *and a host of groups from Latin America which included* **the Sandinistas** *from Nicaragua!!*

Similar to future terror leader Osama bin Laden, Yassir Arafat made a lot of money in a construction business. As he moved around the Middle East he became an admirer of the Algerian separatists that were fighting the French and was able to meet up with many of the leading regional figures, many of them extremists. One of those was the **Ayatollah Khomeini**, the spiritual leader of the anti-Shah forces in Iran. Khomeini was an active enemy to the Shah and had been jailed and banished. Khomeini grew close to the terrorist inclined *Devotees of Islam*. He maintained those ties during the 1960s as the Iranian clerics and other special interest groups turned against the Shah's secular and modernized rule. (After watching what Nasser had done in Egypt, and Ataturk's rule in Turkey, the Iranian clerics decided they needed to rule Iran to protect their power.)

At the time of the Arafat-Khomeini meeting the cleric was based in Najaf, Iraq. *For Khomeini, Arafat and the PLO were perfect partners to help him foment trouble inside the region, but especially for the Shah.* His agitators would willingly do the bidding of the Islamists, without realizing what was coming.

(Ironically this was the same technique the clerics had used back in 1953 when Khomeini had been one of the followers of the Ayatollah Kashani, a leading cleric in Iran and a Muslim Brotherhood member. Their following was conservative and anti-communist, and was one of the main reasons Eisenhower agreed to participate in Churchill's misguided coup against the leftists.)

Arafat also met with the Shah in late 1969. The modern thinking Shah quickly developed a strong enmity for Arafat and his Palestinian group. Arafat and the PLO felt the same for him. *In short order PLO terrorists attacked Iranian targets as often as possible, and were helping to train home-grown Iranian terrorists for Khomeini's needs.* Many future Iranian revolutionaries such as Mustafa Tzamran and Sadegh Ghotbzadeh were trained in PLO terrorist camps. **(Illuminating that the Iranian Revolution was not brought on by its citizens.)**

During the 1973 Middle East War the PLO cleverly stayed in the background and consolidated their new territory in Lebanon. The 1973 Arab oil embargo and the 1974 Arab summit further inflamed the strains between the West and the Islamic world, which also helped the PLO and the Ayatollah in their overall efforts. The oil embargo caused prices to double which enabled the oil kingdoms to spend lavishly. (That same price spike crippled S. Vietnam's war effort.)

In Saudi Arabia their overall budget went up over $ 9 billion by 1974. **King Faisal** spent all of their extra income on sumptuous furnishings, palaces and unwise civil projects. Like many rulers in that time he attempted some westernization of his country, and was quickly beset with protests and violence from their **Wahhabi Fundamentalists.** *Back in 1962 the Muslim World League was founded, a vast collection of the Islamic conservatives.* Practicing out in the open these "rightists" were able to organize and spread without fear of the local security forces. (The Saudis even gave them funding.)

"Ironically when King Faisal assumed power in 1964 he had encouraged the growth of their Wahhabist religious sect as a way to counteract Nasser and his growing Socialism."*[13] But on March 25, 1975 Faisal was murdered by a Fundamentalist cousin who was infuriated with his attempts at modernizing. Faisal was replaced by his son **Prince Khalid**. Another son **Prince Turki** left his position in England and returned home to begin his future in the Saudi Intelligence, the GID.

Inside Lebanon their Christian communities were against all of the problems the PLO was causing. A right wing group called the *Phalangists* eventually took up arms against the better equipped PLO in an effort to fight for their country. In the first week of violence over 100 people had been killed, and by September 1975 a full scale civil war had broken out.

By late January 1976 hundreds of additional fighters from the PLA, (Palestine Liberation Army) crossed from their secret training grounds in Syria into Lebanon.

This "civil war" was as usual, secretly being supported by the KGB station in Beirut. Since 1968 Soviet activity in the region had been constant as the Communists sent arms to the PLO and every Muslim nation it could sway. (*Moscow had even invited Arafat to set up a PLO bureau in Russia in the mid-60s.*) During this time frame of détente with the West, Romania was used as the "secret supplier" to the PLO sending two cargo planes of supplies a week. Additional communist arms went to S. Yemen to help those leftist rebels fight against the Saudis.

(After the fall of Communism in 1989, Czechoslovakia's President Vaclav Havel admitted that **the Communists had shipped 1,000 tons of the odorless explosive Semtex-H to the Islamic terrorists in the region during the1970s-80s**. Their efforts were non-stop in trying to destabilize the region.)

Russian support of Lebanon's leftists and terrorist groups worked to shred the Government's control over their port cities and the strategic Bekaa Valley. Vast areas were being ruled by the PLO and Communist war supplies could be easily transported in.

In addition to that problem Prime Minister Karami was a Muslim. He did not want to send in the mostly Christian Lebanese National Army against the brother Muslims of the PLO. But by not acting against them, he was setting the stage for the destruction of his nation.

Within Beirut rival factions began fighting over neighborhoods and streets. The city that had been called the "Paris of the East" was subjected to this continuous urban warfare and was becoming a lawless land. Westerners were particularly at risk by Muslim fighters as it became routine for them to kidnap and ransom people right off the street. Western women who were despised by the Islamists would be raped and brutalized before their release, or else they were murdered. Lebanese Christians began to panic for no one knew what would be the result of this civil breakdown. *They asked for U.S. assistance, and warned that the Russians were operating inside their country.*

Within Lebanon **the various leftist factions** had come together to form the LNM, **Lebanese National Movement**. Their stated claim was to end *all Christian and Western influence* in Lebanon, and form a "pure Arab state". Since the PLO was the best trained and equipped of the various terrorist groups they had been given the task of striking any enemy targets.

In the south of Lebanon Israeli warplanes continued to fly in to strike at the PLO bases in that part of the country. (Retaliation for the constant terrorist attacks directed at them.) PM Karami then made another fatal mistake by asking Syria to help stop the Jewish air attacks. Syria's Assad was only too happy to send his forces into Lebanon, 40,000 of them. Naively all of the LNM groups believed that after their goals had been reached the Syrians would exit and leave the PLO in charge of Lebanon.

Once the Syrians came in they refused to leave.

What no one in the LNM or PLO knew was that Syria's Assad had already secretly contacted the Israelis to establish "zones of influence" inside Lebanon. In Assad's plan, Syria would control Lebanon north of the Litani River while Israel could do the same south of the river. That would protect Israel and greatly benefit Syria. *According to Assad, Syria had sent their forces into Lebanon to "stop the civil strife", and they had insulated the Christian community from the LNM and PLO.*

When word got out about Syria's duplicity Arafat decided to strike harshly. On June 16, 1976 U.S. Ambassador Francis Meloy, his advisor Robert Waring and their turncoat driver Zohair Moughrabi were forcibly abducted at a security checkpoint near E. Beirut. Hours later all three were found shot to death on the waterfront in West Beirut. Those murders prompted the State Dept. to advise all Americans to leave the country. Days later the ambassador's car was seen being driven around southern Lebanon by members of the PLO's Force 17, Arafat's bodyguards. Unhappy with that PLO action, additional Syrian troops "entered the country", and began taking over the transportation system. That strategy would enable them to control all movement within the nation.

Despite those events America and the Western World remained absent. After the effort in SE Asia no one wanted to get involved in another hot spot, and that included England and France which had created the maps of the present day Middle East.

(Syria had always claimed Lebanon as part of their original lands from during the Ottoman Empire. Both nations had been remapped by the French after the WWI defeat of the Ottoman's. It was time to end all of that.)

At this time Pres. Ford was in a tight electoral race against Democrat Jimmy Carter and he decided not to try to act against the PLO. (Perhaps he would have after being elected to office.) That inaction may have sent a further message of weakness to the Islamic terrorists, for there were additional attacks against the Americans in the region.

At the U.N. headquarters in Manhattan the Arab nations were able to get a resolution passed that equated Zionism, (Jewish homeland), as a form of racism. Ambassador Daniel Moynihan decried the act as a pervading state of anti-Semitism, but at that point in time the United Nations had been corrupted into political blocks and most were now openly hostile to America. As always, Communism was the major agitator.

The U.S. Congress began their move to a standard human rights policy by passing legislation that any foreign or military aid we administered was to be decided based on information from the recipient country. The State Dept. was delegated to collecting this information on "human rights", and supplying that information to the Congress. They would determine if a country could get aid from us. *Though on paper the policy and requests seemed to be noble, in reality what the Democrats were doing was stacking the deck against any rightist / conservative leaning government.*

Most of our allies in the "Third World" were conservative, and many were fighting Communist and leftist subversions. As a result most had jails full of those suspects. By pretending to "oversee our national foreign policy efforts via human rights", **the Democratic run Congress was setting up a legal way to stop any support to and precipitate the fall of any governments the Democrats did not approve of.**

The two nations most in jeopardy were Iran and Nicaragua. (The Communists did not care about anyone's rights, so they never reported any types of violations. And once they took over the reports stopped because those societies were closed to outsiders.)

By mid-1976 world events had completely changed the strategic balance of power. Vietnam, Laos and Cambodia had all fallen to the Communists, and America had not intervened as Nixon had promised. Serious proxy wars were ongoing in Africa, and Lebanon was collapsing. It promised to be a good year for Moscow.

In addition to those subversions, the Soviets looked upon the political savaging the Congressional committees were giving to the FBI and CIA as proof that the United States was falling. Soviet Ambassador Anatoly Dobrynin sternly told Henry Kissinger; **"Any nation that can't protect their own intelligence agencies is not to be taken seriously."** (14)

Iraq

Since the 1950s Iraq had been getting weapons from Russia as a counter to the U.S. supplied Iran. *By 1975 Soviet advisors were virtually running the country.* It was Russian experts and work teams that were drilling for oil and water, and it was the Russians who were running the infrastructure and training Iraq's military. Their price for all of that help was the demand that Iraq back them diplomatically and that the Iraqis stick together. The former was not a problem, but the latter still was.

As shown in *Fatal Flaws Book 1,* when Iraq was formed by Churchill and the Colonial Office in 1921 the British Foreign Office warned that the three divergent religious groups in this new country would never unite. Kurds, Shia and Sunni Muslims made up the majority of Iraq's population and each hated the other. The only way the land stayed together was from the harsh rule of Britain's governors and then Iraq's hard rulers.

One brutish Iraqi named Saddam Hussein finally decided it was his time as President Ahmad al-Bakr was little more than a figurehead. Saddam who ran Iraq's security service was determined to make bloody war with his rivals for power, many of whom were members of the Iraqi Communist party. Starting in 1974 Saddam went after the Iraqi Kurds, a favored people of the Soviets. Russia stopped all deliveries of ammo and spare parts. That kick was a bitter experience, and Saddam vowed to never let that happen again. Hussein traveled to France knowing of their greed and easily swayed commercial ties. He was going to use France as seperate weapons market in case the communists shut off the flow again.

On September 5, 1975 Jacques Chirac, France's youngest Prime Minister, met with this secretive visitor in Paris. Saddam Hussein the strongman of Iraq's Socialist Ba'thists Party had come to finish a yearlong project. France was selling Iraq tons of arms and technology, and they wanted to sell more. Hussein stayed at the Marigny Palace and dined with French upper crust citizens including Pres. Valery Giscard d'Estaing. This "marriage of reason" hinged on France getting solid access to Iraqi oil, a hard to get commodity in the hostile times of the 1970s.

(Oil's price had quadrupled in the year 1973-1974.)

During the next fifteen years Saddam would spend over $20 Billion on French arms. Among the regular weapons France sold to Iraq was the advanced F-1 Mirage fighter, a better model than the ones Israel had. This aircraft was close in performance to the U.S. built F-16 which was equipping NATO as well as America. France's arms bazaar went so well for Saddam, that the French also sold him desalination plants, radars, housing units, defensive electronics systems, car assembly plants, a new airport etc, etc. Those sales gave him freedom from any more Soviet interference, and he hoped military superiority over his soon to be enemies.

Sec. State Henry Kissinger viewed this French-Iraq deal as a better arrangement for Iraq than the ten year deal they had signed with the Soviets back in 1972.

But what should have set off alarm bells in France was the Iraqi "need for" and purchase of a bacteriological laboratory. It would only take some modifications to turn the lab into a program to build relatively inexpensive biological weapons. Saddam was determined to chase all of the usurpers out of the Middle East, leaving him as the regional ruler.

Soon after Saddam decided he also wanted a nuclear power industry, something a nation with the world's second largest oil reserves should not have needed. *France decided to sell one of their Osiris nuclear research reactors to Iraq anyway.*

French nuclear-electrical reactors were called "breeder reactors because they produced bomb grade plutonium as a byproduct of electrical production. Selling this type of reactor to Saddam insured him a supply of weapons grade fuel, just as it did for the French. This purchase was a good opening point for Iraq, but would not give them "large amounts" of plutonium immediately in case he was trying to build atomic bombs.

However the wily Saddam insisted that France give them a four year supply of fuel in advance, which was enough to arm two Hiroshima type bombs immediately.

French Commissariat 'a l'Energie Atomique, (CEA), director Andre' Giraud went a step further to complete the deal, and wanted to sell Saddam all types of equipment that would have made Iraq nuclear independent. Giraud (a leftist) actually felt that the more nuclear weapons in the world the weaker the superpowers became. That would enable France to have more say in world affairs.

On November 18, 1975 a treaty was officially signed, and in June 1976 the public actually learned all about it. Knowing of Saddam's hatred of the Jews, the French never batted an eye to what they were doing. To hide their work from America and the world the French quietly manufactured nuclear fuel for Iraq. **After those nuclear deals were signed Saddam told a Lebanese paper that now we have the first step to an Arab atomic weapon.** Not until late 1980 did the French wake up to the monster they were creating. The Israeli's however did not miss the point.

U.S.-Soviet Foreign Affairs

Back in the early 1970s the CIA promoted a report stating that the Soviet Union was not involved in a centrally-directed civil defense effort. That report was prepared to help the State Dept. in their arms treaties negotiations. *But the Air Force which controlled our satellite reconnaissance systems had thousands of photos showing the 1972 CIA report was untrue.*

Our photo recon efforts clearly showed that since 1955 every apartment house built in Russia was equipped with a nuclear bomb shelter. So were their factories. Complementing those shelters were dozens of secret tunnels linking those sites creating an underground network of conduits where their people could live and work. Photo-interpreters also found seventy-five command sites in massive bunkers covered by parks and wooded areas. They also uncovered a large ABM (anti-ballistic missile) radar installation placed near their Abalakova SS-11 & SS-18 ICBM installations in Siberia. Had the radar been defensive in nature it would be sited along a border area instead of protecting just their offensive missiles as an ABM system would.

What all of this information unveiled was that the Soviets were prepared to fight and survive a nuclear war. And as part of their overall war-planning effort, the Soviets had quietly returned to Cuba and were building a submarine base at Cienfuegos. At that same time Syria backed by Russia invaded Jordan who we supported. Nixon handled the breech of the 1962 Cuba agreement quietly, and the Soviets ended the sub-project. They also stopped Syria's invasion of Jordan before it turned into another superpower problem.

Pres. Richard Nixon had begun the process of superpower arms control with his SALT I program (Strategic Arms Limitation Talks). Pres. Ford had continued the program, and in late 1974 had gone to Vladivostok to meet with Russian leader Leonid Brezhnev. To the surprise of many, Ford emerged with a framework for a SALT II treaty. A ten year nuclear agreement appeared to be just months away. *Though the treaties were far from perfect, the SALT talks were the only way to try to control the nuclear weapons issues between the superpowers.*

(As with the SALT I treaty the details favored the Soviets.)

Back in 1971 CIA's William Colby had left SE Asia and returned to Washington. He became the executive director-comptroller, (#3 in the agency) and oversaw the increasingly complex organization. He learned of our vast space based recon satellites, electronic sensors, infrared photography and more, becoming dazzled by the agencies growth. (Lyndon Johnson had boasted that by 1967 we had spent $35-40 Billion on the "Space Program".) For America this eye in the sky capability had far reaching implications enabling us to monitor Soviet military systems and movements. *Many in power, which included Colby, (but not the military leaders), felt we could proceed with weapons treaties because "we could see" what the Russians were doing.*

Colby became the Director of the CIA in 1973, but was maligned by the leftists and subversives within our country and government for his successful **Phoenix Program** used in Vietnam. *As shown in Fatal Flaws Book 2, the Phoenix program targeted VC (Viet Cong) suspects for arrests and interrogations.* Many of the VC suspects were killed while trying to arrest them or in retaliation by the S. Vietnamese. However the program was designed to capture and interrogate them. That part was vital in tracking and shutting down their extensive network. **Phoenix was so successful, that by 1972 the VC had been beaten which allowed S. Vietnam to stabilize even as the last of the U.S. troops departed!**

After he took over at the agency Colby tried his best to control the savaging to the CIA that the post Vietnam Democrats and leftists insisted upon. (More to follow.) To prevent another potential 1976 election issue to Pres. Ford, Colby was replaced by George Bush in November 1975. (Colby would die under suspicious circumstances in 1985.)

Another foreign affairs bright spot during the year was the continued cultural exchanges that were crossing the Iron Curtain. Included in those "friendly" meetings was an increasing economic flow. Each deal or investment meant more personal contacts between our worlds, and those prisoners of Communism could see and hear of the world outside of their dark and isolated one. (Radio Free Europe was a huge help in reaching those trapped behind the Iron Curtain. Even the Soviets could not block the airwaves.)

West Germany took the lead with an emphasis on improving ties with E. Germany. Due to their location and increasingly pacifist attitude Europe was at the forefront in this new period of détente. But as always the Communists had an ulterior motive for all of the easing of tensions. They were trying to separate western Europe from NATO and America. If nothing concrete happened, possibly Europe would become neutral.

(NATO's first Secretary General had been Britain's Lord Ismay. *His stated feeling on the creation of NATO was to keep the Russians out, the American in, and the Germans down!*)* (15)

Historical Note: The Europeans had actually broken the ice between our two worlds back in 1969 when they had proposed arms talks. Pres. Nixon had greatly advanced those ideas and furthered the West-Communist rapprochement with his trips to China and Russia in 1972. *No one in the West understood how deep the Soviet fear of China was. Nixon's secret and shocking trip to China, and our increasing ties with them prompted Russia into increasing their commercial and diplomatic exchanges with us.*

Despite the superpower tensions from the 1973 Yom Kipper War, détente, (easing of tensions), continued to be sought after and additional meetings and talks were held through 1974. Pres. Ford and his administration continued that work throughout 1975, and he promoted, (against a lot of opposition), the follow on Helsinki Accords. Most of our political leaders felt his work on the Human Rights Agreement was just window dressing, and of no real value.

But **Compliance on Basic Human Rights** was inserted into the wording at the work-shops, and a treaty was finally established in an effort to prevent any further barbarity to our species. Normally the Soviets would never have agreed to any such wording on anything, but they desired allied participation at the Conference on Security and Cooperation in Europe (CSCE). *That group worked to "finalize the national borders from WWII".*

When Pres. Ford went to Europe (Helsinki) for the signing of the new treaty on August 1, 1975, he made side trips to Poland, Rumania and Yugoslavia to show those trapped behind the Iron Curtain they were not forgotten. *Editorials from numerous U.S. media outlets like the NY Times called his trip "misguided and empty."*

As always, the slanted liberal media missed the major point. Pres. Ford's work had allowed Pandora's Box of human rights to open up behind the Iron Curtain

Human Rights Activists setup operations throughout Europe and even in the Soviet Union. Every time the Communists acted against those treaty protocols or arrested political Dissidents, attention and outrage quickly followed. A follow-on conference in Belgrade furthered the process by creating a review process and penalties for violations. Dissidents could now protest publicly and be "relatively safe".

The first place it would be tested was in Poland.

In 1976 Polish citizens organized the *Movement in Defense of Human and Citizen Rights*. This was a non-communist organization that was created inside the Iron Curtain. This was unprecedented, and had occurred because of the fine work by those European leaders and presidents Nixon and Ford.

Not long after Poland had flared up, East Germany also began having dissident problems. CIA reported that E. Germany's Eric Honecker was complaining to the Soviets about these "new problems". The Communist rulers were unsure how to respond, and by the summer of 1976 the CIA was reporting on the increasing worries those dissidents were causing. Many saw them as a threat to their rule.

Pres. Ford was maligned by many over his insistence on signing the accords, and possibly lost the election because of it. But history clearly shows that he was spot on with his beliefs and actions. *Lech Walesa the future leader of Poland's Solidarity Party stated that Helsinki gave them the freedom to reach out and press for change.* Though they paid a fearsome price behind closed doors, those brave dissidents were going to change the world!

Unknown by the West, the Soviets post-war economic expansion was coming to an end just as they were achieving their goal of strategic military parity with America. At the end of 1976 the Soviets had 1,556 inter-continental missiles to our 1,054. Four new Soviet missiles were being developed and deployed with greater MIRV (multiple independent re-entry vehicles) capability. They had almost 800 submarine based missiles on 60 submarines, while we had half that number on just forty subs. And they were launching six new boats per year, and all were much more capable than the previous class, etc.

No one in the West knew of their economic issues at that time, though suspicions were raised when the Soviets began buying large amounts of U.S. grains. To further promote the reduction in super-power tensions, Pres. Nixon had allowed the Soviets access to the U.S. Export-Import Bank, additional U.S. ports and a new trade bill. Senator Jackson from Washington State added an amendment that required the Soviets to allow Jewish emigration to Israel. The Soviets agreed, and reciprocated with some ease of access to their cities too, such was their need for foods and trade.

As shown earlier the reduction of superpower tensions was called Détente, and was greatly desired by the increasingly pacifist West. Nixon used the effort to help us in SE Asia and to try to keep a lid on the Soviets. *The Soviets saw détente as a way to help with their overall strategy of world domination.*

For them, Peace was a relative term.

Historical Note: Most people never realized that in the fallout from Nixon's surprise visit to China in February 1972, the Soviets had become much more accommodating to talks on weapon reductions. The Soviets truly feared a U.S.-China pact, and felt if they made some accommodations they might keep **us apart**.

Nixon visited Russia in May 1972, and besides the SALT I treaty an Anti-Ballistic-Missile (ABM) agreement was also passed. Each side was allowed to protect their national capitol and one offensive missile field only. Both sides knew if ABM systems became the norm each side would just build larger numbers of offensive weapons to overwhelm the defenses. Thus the ABM agreement was a large part of the reduction in offensive missiles. The Soviets also signed a treaty to end bio-weapons.

But when Nixon left office, and our political weakness evident, the Soviets saw no need to follow any past treaties, not unless they were forced to.

Pakistan had been the middle-man in arranging the thaw with China. They became involved in a brutal civil war in 1971 when east Pakistan demanded their independence, and was backed by India. Pakistan and India soon began fighting again, Pakistan lost, and Bangladesh was formed from East Pakistan creating a new nation. The Democrats were incensed that Nixon supported Pakistan during that time, and they made many negative headlines against him. **Everyone was stunned when Nixon suddenly visited China, especially Russia. Which was just the way Nixon and Kissinger had planned it.**

Angola

In early February 1976 the Communist Popular Movement for the Liberation of Angola, MPLA, supported by Cuban troops and weapons took two seaport cities which virtually closed off the country. *Soon after a new Communist government was established in the oil rich former Portuguese colony.* Superpower tensions quickly renewed and our cooperation ebbed. Pres. Ford went to the Congress to get them to react to this blatant Communist incursion, but the Democrat controlled Congress refused by a large margin claiming this was just a new Vietnam. *(Ironic since it was the Democrats who got us into Vietnam and then ruined the effort with their poor strategy and policies.)*

Those Democrats had unilaterally decided that we would no longer police the world. Sec. State Henry Kissinger quickly warned that this Angolan action was a dangerous precedent for the Soviets to have taken. They had aggressively moved a large military force, (Cuban), over a long ocean distance to impose a hostile regime on a non-threatening nation.

Never before had they strayed so far outside of their power base. This was the first time since WWII, (Poland & Finland), **that America had failed to respond to a direct Soviet threat. If this pattern is not broken now we will face increasing Soviet pressures and harder choices later.*** (16)

Soviet leader Brezhnev happily wrote, *"The general political crisis in the capitalist states continues to deepen." Russia's victories in the "Third World" and our improving strategic and military position constitutes a real chance for overall victory. This is concrete evidence of the inherent superiority of socialism over capitalism.* * (17)

Under his direction, Soviet-backed Communism was insinuating itself into every corner of the world as the death toll climbed into the millions.

New York

Since early 1975 New York City was facing a catastrophic financial crisis. Massive payouts for the welfare state requirements enacted in the 1960's and poor fiscal operations had created huge budget deficits. At the same time rampant drug use fueled major outbreaks of violent crime, and there was an unprecedented epidemic of arson. Those problems cost billions in lost jobs and lost tax revenue, and greatly increased the city's costs of social care, policing, fire service, courts and jails.

However New York City and State were not alone with those issues as most of the northern states with large urban populations and extensive social programs had budgets in the red. Faced with those repetitive deficits and the ever increasing social requirements and costs, most of the local governments began raising taxes and cutting services. Those measures began driving even more of the small and mid-sized businesses out of the cities. As they moved out the lower skilled job opportunities went with them, creating even more dependency on welfare and social programs by the un/under-educated masses.

All across the nation mayors were seeing the hard truth that the Republicans had warned about in 1965. Once those welfare programs started it would ruin the nation's work ethic and the numbers of people on welfare would soar as would the costs.

It was clear that the Democrats of the 1960s had created a perfect storm of economic and social chaos that was forcing more and more citizens into permanent economic stagnation and dependency. America as a whole was still reeling from the immense costs from the war in SE Asia, and inflation was rising from the large federal budget deficits. Pres. Ford refused to simply bail out NY City, offering a loan instead. (His fear was that if the Federal Government bailed out NYC other urban centers would certainly follow suit.)

In addition to the above social/economic issues the 1970 U.S. Census reports had been fully analyzed. It revealed that a large population shift was beginning to show itself as our citizens were abandoning the increasingly expensive and crime ridden Northern cities and states for the open, safe and vastly less taxed South and Southwest.

And there was the terrorism.

On January 24, 1975 Puerto Rican extremists from the FALN (Fuerzas Armadas de Liberacion Nationale) planted a bomb in a hallway of the landmark Fraunces Tavern at the Battery near the tip of Manhattan. Their bomb was the equivalent of ten sticks of dynamite and the large explosion murdered four and wounded over fifty more. No one was ever caught.

At LaGuardia Airport near the TWA baggage terminal another bomb exploded. It was the equivalent of twenty-five sticks of dynamite, and that larger explosion murdered 11 and wounded over 70. Again no one was ever caught. This time period was a heightened period of terrorism in the U.S. as even Pres. Ford narrowly escaped assassins twice that year.

On September 10, 1976 Croation Nationalists hijacked TWA Flight 355 from NYC to Chicago. Those terrorists were demanding a release of compatriots in jail and they also planted a bomb at Grand Central Terminal. Bomb Squad members were able to get the device to the Bronx to set it off, but when they tried one officer was killed in the explosion. Again no one was ever caught.

By this point NYC had turned into a cesspool of garbage, crime and arson. Companies were leaving the city in droves.

The Cold War

On the Cold War front the recon aircraft the SR-71 was absolutely the best aircraft in the world. During July it set the (still standing) speed record of 2,194 mph at the incredible altitude of 85,000 feet. (The true flight ceiling was over 100,000 feet.) Unknown to the designers, the shape of the SR-71 gave the aircraft "stealth characteristics " making it even harder to track. This secretive recon platform was impervious to all of the Soviet defensive measures as it flew through their airspace taking photos and signal intelligence. Soviet fighter pilots were often scrambled to intercept, but were always left in its wake. Soviet defector Lt. Viktor Belenko landed in Japan with his new Mig-25 interceptor in September 1976. He told his interrogators the frustration of chasing but never even getting close to the Blackbird to get off a shot. (His aircraft's capabilities were fully examined.)

But recon aircraft were not our only assets. As mentioned earlier, we had invested heavily with our space program and satellite technology and had dozens in orbit. Despite the arms talks and détente, Soviet Spetznaz commando teams routinely landed in Sweden, (starting in 1962), to infiltrate, plan and prepare to take out NATO's northern allies. Norway was a key cog in the NATO anti-Soviet submarine defenses, and in our **Satellite Signal Centers**. *Destroying those centers would be a vital move to defeating NATO when war came.*

In the southern hemisphere we had bases and satellite centers in Australia that were doing the same vital work. But there it was much harder for the Soviets to infiltrate into the outback, though local Communists were always present and a threat.

Then in 1977 two Americans, Andrew Lee and Christopher Boyce joined the long list of American traitors and became paid Soviet spies. **During the time they were active they gave our enemy thousands of pages of documents on our impressive satellite technology and capabilities. Prior to their acts the Soviets did not understand how well we were keeping tabs on them.** They were shocked when they realized our capabilities.

At this point in time we also used recon aircraft like the KC-135, U-2 and SR-71, low earth orbiting satellites, medium altitude ones from 1,000-10,000 miles high, ocean recon satellites and geo-synchronous units based 22,300 miles up to try to keep watch on the communist enemies. But watching was not always knowing as human spies were extremely hard to come by, especially behind the Iron Curtain.

Historical Note: One spying-secret kept from the public eye was the fact that many of our ultra-secret communications systems had been lost in the past few years. The first ones were grabbed by the Russians when the N. Koreans overwhelmed and stole the *USS Pueblo* back in 1968. More were lost in the unexpected collapse of S. Vietnam in 1975, and during the 1973 Yom Kipper War when Syria overran an outpost placed there. Those losses and the information from spies enabled the Soviets to decipher our most secret naval codes and cryptography. Many in the military were certain the Soviets were reading our mail.

Jimmy Carter

During the 1976 Presidential campaign the Republicans chose Pres. Ford over conservative former California Governor Ronald Reagan. The Democrats picked former one term Georgia Governor and peanut farmer Jimmy Carter. Carter had tried to get on the McGovern presidential ticket in 1972 but was quickly refused for having no qualifications. To increase his "resume", in 1975 David Rockefeller picked Carter as a representative in his Trilateral Commission to promote trade. It was there that Carter cultivated contacts and learned the "strategy to get elected". He would emphasize work, family, religion and patriotism.

A review of and Democratic polls of the political history of the past decade convinced many in the Democratic party that the next presidential candidate needed to appear to be an outsider, and promise "change from the stale politicos".

(Ironically Obama followed many of the same premises for his 2008 campaign such as promising change. And like Carter he would be a complete failure.)

During the campaign Pres. Ford was battling the shadows of Watergate, Vietnam and his pardon of Richard Nixon. Continued calls for nonsensical legal issues and lawsuits were plaguing every minute of Nixon's life. Based on his deep religious beliefs about forgiveness, Ford granted a pardon to put the non-issue to rest. For that act he was vilified by the media and liberals.

Though he had done well in office during the past year and a half, he was consistently caricatured by the press as a stumbling fool. His poor showing in the debates were highlighted often as the liberal media was actively promoting the Democrat. *Coverage of Carter was so one sided he rose from being an obscure figure to president elect in just nine months!* (Just like Obama in 2008.)

In actuality Carter had limited domestic experience outside of Georgia politics, and most of his foreign policy experience was based on trade trips. As had been planned by the party politicos, Carter ran a straddle the fence type of campaign. He was against

Washington politics, Watergate and Vietnam. Carter was portrayed by the left-leaning media as a political outsider, though he was not.

He spoke on how all of "our policies needed to mirror our beliefs of being open, honest, unselfish and compassionate". Yet none of those characteristics would apply to American liberals or even to him. He was quite religious, but his moralistic stance was actually a fatal weakness. *Though he would continue championing the worldwide effort for human rights, he was unable to recognize or to stand up to the reality of Soviet totalitarianism and ambitions. He also ignored every instance of Soviet treachery and genocide, going back to their beginnings.*

Like so many on the left, Carter totally overlooked all of the good things our allies had accomplished in the Third World. He was going to change everything.

Historical Note: As a civilian Herbert Hoover who later became president began a humanitarian mission to feed the millions of starving people in Russia in the first years of the Bolshevik takeover. Those famines were orchestrated by Lenin and his communist followers, and by 1922 five million peasants had starved to death. No Democrat ever condemned them for their murderous actions to take power. None of the Republican presidents would recognize the Bolshevik-Soviet Regime, and that included Herbert Hoover who had worked there twice trying to prevent mass starvation. But FDR did in 1933 after he defeated Hoover. FDR unleashed the Soviet espionage machine that stole the Manhattan Project, and still threatens us today.

Similar to FDR, Carter's political idol was "Democrat-progressive" Woodrow Wilson. That group of liberal Democrats felt a world body should run the world, not European countries or America. Those "Progressives" were the ones who gave us income taxes, big government, the Federal Reserve system, (unelected), which actually controls our money, public schooling controlled by government bureaucrats, the Antiquities Act that allowed the Federal Govt. to usurp citizen property rights, and the 17th Amendment making the Federal Government all powerful. They also got us into both World Wars, and then lost China which resulted in the first Indochina War, the Korean war and then the second Indochina War.

Historical Note : Wilson in 1916, FDR in 1940 and Johnson in 1964 all campaigned on how they "kept us out of that foreign war". Yet within months of their election both Wilson and Johnson sent our citizens to fight in WWI and Vietnam respectively. FDR quietly maneuvered us to aid Great Britain, and his Japanese policies helped push Japan into war with us with their December 1941 attack at Pearl Harbor. An attack many believe he knew was coming as coded radio intercepts and tips from observers came in.

Jimmy Carter like all Democratic candidates was duplicitous. He appeared in public as a moral and righteous person, but his former Lt. Governor Lester Maddox was quoted as saying; " Jimmy Carter was the most dishonest man I've ever met".* (18)

Author Gary Fink described Carter's governorship as a surface picture of moral and ethical high ground, but a secretive style based on exaggeration, disingenuousness and at times outright deception. He tried to paint a saintly picture of himself similar to what JFK had done, but he was seriously disliked by most in the Georgia legislature. * (19)

Days after Jimmy Carter won the election, his church suddenly and quietly ended a ban on black parishioners! The major media never reported on that aspect of his life.

Historical Note: Most people have forgotten that the Democrats, the party of Andrew Jackson, were also the party of the slave owners in 1860. They had fought all efforts at ending the vile practice which led to the Civil War. Republican Abraham Lincoln was elected president in 1860, and wanted to give citizenship and voting rights to the slaves after the Civil War ended.

To prevent that scenario, Lincoln was murdered.

Democratic Vice-president Andrew Johnson replaced Lincoln, and he quickly repealed the land grant that Lincoln had given to the just freed black people. Johnson then implemented a different plan for the Reconstruction of the South that did not include any rights or benefits to the freed slaves. He also pardoned all of the former Confederates and repudiated all of their debts!

Because of those nefarious moves, the same southern Democrats of the 1860 mindset remained in political power and became the post Civil-War obstructionists who passed anti-black laws to keep the freed blacks powerless. In many states the freed blacks outnumbered the white southern Democrats. It was vital for the southerners to enact Jim Crow, Poll Taxes, etc, and to form and use the KKK to keep the freed blacks down. (It turned out that too many blacks were winning political office.)

The 13th Amendment was passed in the Congress in January 1865 outlawing slavery. All of the northern states ratified it as did most of the border states. **100% of Republican legislators voted for it while only 23% of Democrats did.**

The 14th Amendment passed in 1868 and was bitterly contested by the southern states. That amendment gave citizenship and equality under the law to freed blacks. For the Southern States to regain their representation in the Congress they had to ratify it. **Again 100% of Republican legislators voted for it, while 100% of Democrats voted against it. Pres. Johnson the Democrat led their refusal.**

The same bitter fighting happened over the 15th Amendment (1870) which prohibited states from denying voting rights to the freed blacks. Deadly riots occurred in Memphis and New Orleans to stop blacks from voting. Southern Democrats also passed and enforced restrictive local laws based on economic restrictions, literacy tests, etc, that worked to prevent most blacks and poor whites from voting. As the Democrats hostility towards freed blacks increased The NRA, National Rifle Association was actually formed to help blacks defend themselves against the KKK and other violent groups. Decades after the Civil War little had changed in the south.

In 1913 incoming President Woodrow Wilson, another southern Democrat, wanted and directed all of his Administration department heads to stop the ongoing integration of blacks into our society and to promote segregation to stop it. It was Wilson who demoted blacks into second class citizens, even in the military where blacks had advanced to higher ranks. Wilson set back Black advancement by fifty years. During WWII the famed Tuskegee Airmen, (most were college graduates) had to jump through hoops (with support by FDR) to get the obstructionist Democrats to allow them to become fighter pilots and serve their country. As had happened with the Japanese Americans illegally sent to concentration camps (by FDR after the attacks at Pearl Harbor), the Tuskegee airmen and the Japanese -American 442 Regiment were two of the most decorated units in the U.S. Army. Still the racism persisted.

The modern Civil Rights crusade began in the 1950s. **It was the Republicans who pushed for and signed the Civil Rights acts during those years. And after signing them into law, Pres. Eisenhower,** (Republican), **used federal troops to enforce the new laws onto the Democratic run states who refused to follow them.**

In 1960 more Republicans voted for that Civil Rights law than did Democrats! The same thing happened again in 1964!

During the previous decades most blacks voted Republican, and even Dr. Martin Luther King supported them. Yet in the 1960s they were somehow turned into Democratic lemmings. It is mind boggling on how conniving the Democrats were and still are, being able to trick so many people into believing they are the party looking out for black citizens. (Or any of us for that matter.)

Section Two January 1977- January 1981

The Carter Years Decline and Despair

Jimmy Carter narrowly won the 1976 election with 50.1% of the vote to Ford's 49.9%. In the electoral college he won by a 5 vote difference, with Hawaii being the deciding state.

On January 12, 1977 Carter and his transition team met with General George Brown chairman of the Joint Chiefs of Staff. They were together to discuss SIOP, the Single Integrated Operational Plan which covered the president's overwhelming responsibilities in the event of a Soviet nuclear attack. *Carter shocked everyone by instructing Gen. Brown to begin studies of cutting our nuclear arsenal down to 200 or so missiles.*

Carter was thinking of unilaterally disarming.

Gen. Brown and everyone else around were speechless, what was this man thinking? *But Carter and most of the Democrats of that time believed we were wrong for fighting Communism.*

Carter opened his inaugural address with a classy statement praising Ford for getting America past Watergate and the loss of confidence in our government. But then he droned on for an hour turning the event into a sermon. At his inaugural dinner Carter or his staff insultingly placed Democratic House Speaker Thomas Tip O'Neil and his family at the table farthest from the president. They had words the first time they met, and it got worse with every meeting. In short order Carter's behavior alienated most of the people with whom he was expected to work with. He also declared the White House and all environs "Dry", but then expected drinks before church service.

On his first official day at work Carter made everything far worse. **He gave a blanket pardon to the one million citizens who had illegally evaded the draft, those who were military deserters, those who went into exile and the those who took a dishonorable discharge to end their military service.**

This was an egregious act that ignored the laws of that time and was a terrible affront to those who did serve and suffered. Claiming he was healing the nation, (as Ford had done with Nixon), Carter's pardon only further divided it. (As Andrew

Johnson had in 1865.) Few of the millions of draftees had wanted to serve or to go to Vietnam, but they went.

During his years in office Richard Nixon had strongly opposed any such move, as the actions by the draft dodgers were criminal offenses. President Ford tried to soften the divisive issue with a limited pardon. But he insisted that any offer of amnesty for the *draft dodgers* could only be made with a 24-month commitment to public service as a penance for their crime. Only 6% of the 350,000 active draft offenders accepted his terms.

None of those citizen-criminals died, suffered wounds or even lost a moment in their lives. Yet here they were being given a free ride while those who did serve lost much more. *All of those offenders had knowingly made their choice. They should have been convicted and faced whatever punishment was handed down.*

And those who were for the pardons failed to grasp this one essential factor; *Because the draft dodgers and other categories escaped their military service, some other mother's son went to Vietnam in their place.*

(My feeling is this; if a person won't serve this country when called they should lose all access to Federal programs such as school loans, welfare, mortgages, jobs etc.)

Historical Note: One of those pardoned draft dodgers was William Clinton from Arkansas. In complete arrogance and mendacity, *Clinton had finished Law School because he evaded his military service.* He then worked for Democrat George McGovern's 1972 Presidential campaign even though he was legally a wanted criminal. After that electoral failure, (McGovern lost in a landslide to Nixon), Clinton ran unsuccessfully for Congress in 1974 also losing badly. In 1977 the recently pardoned draft dodger tricked enough people to become Attorney General for the state of Arkansas. (Sad and ironic.) He would eventually become another corrupt Democratic governor and president.

By the time of Carter's 1977 inauguration the Democratic party was splitting into two factions. The old wing of anti-communists who believed in freedom like JFK, Henry Scoop Jackson, etc, and the emerging new wing on the left that felt American power was bad and must be stopped. That list included George McGovern, Jimmy Carter, Frank Church, Otis Pike, Paul Warnke and most of the incoming politicos. Those latter Democrats refused to remain aligned with any allied governments like Pres. Thieu in South Vietnam, Anastasio Somoza in Nicaragua, Ferdinand Marcos in the Philippines or the Shah of Iran. For those **"new ideologues"** it no longer mattered if someone had been solid allies or friends, now they would be outcasts and abandoned by the U.S.

Warnke was one of the last of McNamara's failed Pentagon whiz kids from the 1960s. His abridged thoughts were similar to the failed British liberals of the 1930s. They foolishly believed if you disarm yourself your enemies would too. Warnke had been against any upgrading of our military forces with the B-1 bomber program, the Trident submarine or their improved missiles, building submarine launched cruise missiles, the AWACS aerial radar program, mobile ICBMs similar to what the Soviets used, MIRV technology (multiple re-entry vehicles for warheads), improvements to our ICBMs, improved warhead design, or even getting a new tank for the army!

He was for large reductions in military spending, manpower and nuclear munitions, regardless on if the Soviets reciprocated. Unfortunately Warnke was able to exert a solid hold on the administration's outlook and policies, and that failed ideology would be quickly evident.

Senator Frank Church had always sided on party lines with everything LBJ wanted with no regard as to verifying the information the Administration was providing. After things turned bad in Vietnam in 1968 with the TET offensive, Church turned against LBJ's foreign policies. He later became a rabid anti-intelligence bureaucrat who would head the committee on our Intelligence services. His report on the CIA was so negative and one-sided, it appeared that the CIA had started the Vietnam War instead of the Democrats and Communists. *Church recommended and was able to pass laws and rules placing severe restrictions upon the CIA.*

Carter and his Administration were all "suspicious and distrustful of the CIA. He had campaigned against the agency, and accepted all of the unsubstantiated leftist propaganda about the them. His vice-president Walter Mondale had been a member of the Church committee that cut back on the CIA. (The issues that William Colby tried to fight off before he was let go.)

To insure that all of their new restrictions were followed Carter picked his old classmate Admiral Stansfield Turner as the CIA Director. His ordered mission was to change the CIA from an actionable governmental office to one that collected and analyzed data only! *Dozens of senior positions were filled with party loyalists determined to break up the CIA.* (Clinton would do the same thing when he got in, resulting in 9/11.)

Enno Knoche had become the interim CIA Director when Carter took over, as Republican George Bush was quickly dismissed. To forestall their further destruction Knoche attempted to highlight the agencies accomplishments by showing Carter some of their satellite photos during their first meeting. Carter was unmoved, and when Turner officially took over Knoche and 800 others were fired from the CIA. That one move tore apart the Operations Directorate and eliminated most of the old hands and seasoned agents.

Historical Note: One of the most visible issues the Founding Fathers faced when creating our national government was the subject of political parties. Most of them did not want such entities because they knew that "political parties" would interfere with rational thinking and pragmatism. Having a party would create the condition where "party loyalists" would cling to "party lines", instead of acting for the good of the nation. That is never more true than watching the Democrats in action. No matter what benefit or detraction something is for the nation, they always vote as a block on that issue, and they always follow the party line.

New York City

Upon taking office Carter announced that he would not let NYC go bankrupt. He would arrange for more loans to help them stabilize their finances. (Ford had given in on some loans, but the city had to layoff 40,000 workers which included Police, Sanitation and the Fire Dept.) By 1977 NYC was an economic basket case. The city's economy which had prospered so well in the post-WWII decades was collapsing as more and more jobs fled the high taxes and rising crime. Illegal drugs was one of the main culprits in the crime problem.

Historical Note: As shown in *Fatal Flaws Book 1,* Prohibition was not only a foolish law, it spurred the creation of organized crime due to the vast profits it created to the bootleggers. When it was repealed in 1932 those criminals owned vast fleets of trucks and small boats which enabled them to corner many transportation markets. They were also well organized thanks to Lucky Luciano and the Italian gangsters in NYC, and they quickly branched out into new enterprises which included the labor unions. By the 1950s Organized Crime had begun bringing in large amounts of heroin which caused a synergistic crime wave as the addicts needed money to get their next fix. By the 1970s that drug-crime issue was an epidemic.

As the lower level jobs disappeared more and more of the poor and undereducated young people turned to drinking and taking drugs. *Welfare rolls climbed to over 1 million in NYC alone.* Tenants could not or would not pay rent, and hundreds of buildings fell into disrepair each year. Arson for profit became commonplace. In the post-WWII economic heyday most FDNY fire companies responded to 1500-2000 calls a year. Most calls were for actual fires, and the majority of them were considered normal fires. But by the late 1950s the FDNY was responding to hundreds of serious fires a year. *This was the start of the "FDNY War Years", a period (1959-1979) of unfathomable fire duty that claimed hundreds of lives and thousands of viable buildings.*

By 1977 dozens of FDNY units were responding to over 7,000 calls each year! To try to handle this insane number of calls some units had second sections opened up. In no time they too were responding to 5000-7,000 calls per year. Serious fires were an everyday occurrence in many infamous neighborhoods, such as Harlem, the South Bronx, Bedford-Stuyvesant and the Lower East Side. Some sections of our city resembled Berlin in 1945.

As the financial problems caused cutbacks in city services, the streets were filled with garbage. Kids played in piles of trash, abandoned and burnt out cars littered the streets, and thousands of vacant buildings and empty lots became obscene playgrounds where fine buildings once stood.

Racial tensions were always present in NYC as each ethnic group was in competition with the next one for jobs, neighborhoods and the daily struggles to advance. Carter naively felt ethnic neighborhoods were wrong, that it invited racial tensions. But in reality each ethic group shares social and lifestyle issues in common, hence each immigrant always sought solace in living with your own kind. (My family grew up on an Italian block, and I sought the same neighbors when I moved around during my early adult years.)

Strikes by union workers were also commonplace and added to the city's misery. The latest one was a long garbage strike. Piles of trash eight feet high covered the city's streets and created a stench that filled the air.

On July 13, 1977 all of those social issues came to a head. The past week had been another scorcher in the northeast. In NYC temperatures were over 100 degrees and Con-Edison was strained trying to provide electrical power. An electrical storm around 9PM caused one power line to fail north of the city. Unable to restore that line, within an hour all of NYC went dark. An hour after that widespread looting began in many sections of Brooklyn and the Bronx.

The first wave of looters were the criminals who took advantage of the darknes and the lack of police on the streets. Storefronts were forced open and everything of value was stripped and stolen. A second wave of looters arrived a little later, the local citizens. They took whatever was there, and in many cases the stores were "picked clean".

In addition to the appalling looting, over 1,000 major fires occurred that night! Arson was the new way of showing frustration, and settling any "scores". Because of the prior cutbacks, the already strained FDNY was overwhelmed by the nights rapid and heavy arson-fire disaster. *The city was not losing a few buildings to these fires, they were losing blocks!*

(I joined the FDNY in 1980, and worked with many of those veteran firefighters of that time. They told us youngsters of pulling up to an intersection and having heavy fire conditions on all four streets. When they called the dispatchers requesting help they were told your company is all you got. Do the best you can.)

By morning the situation had stabilized, but many neighborhoods had been destroyed. Towers of smoke covered the skyline and the streets were littered with debris, destruction and refuse. The neighborhood called Bushwick in northern Brooklyn never recovered from the wonton devastation. July 14, 1977 was the lowest of the low points for a dying city. And sadly we were not the only one facing these issues.

(In 1991 Los Angeles would suffer this same disaster.)

France

As shown in ***Fatal Flaws Book 2***, in the early sixties France's Charles de Gaulle was completely against "our war" in Vietnam. Pres. De Gaulle was extremely upset that America sent troops into Vietnam when JFK and LBJ decided too, but not in 1953 when the French wanted our help to hold off defeat. **Two of the most vocal critics of our getting involved back in 1953 were *John Kennedy and Lyndon Johnson.***

In 1965 De Gaulle demanded that he have control of any U.S. weapons based on French soil. LBJ refused to give that kind of control to him and soon after de Gaulle pulled France out of NATO and kicked America out of France! Operation FRELOC, Fast Relocation, was conducted in early 1966. It was a daunting mission of relocating 70,000 U.S. personnel, 400 military facilities which included 30 major bases, and a NATO HQ. We had spent hundreds of millions building and equipping those bases in our effort to protect France from the Soviets. As our troops were forced to depart, anything we could not take was broken in spite. Relations between our countries fell to an all time low.

Besides his action in 1965, De Gaulle created a serious economic issue for us in 1970 when he hoarded dollars and then traded them in for U.S. Gold. That move forced Pres. Nixon to take us off of the Gold monetary standard in 1971 which further stressed our economy and still does. (It seemed every chance he could de Gaulle worked to hurt America, even in WWII.)

De Gaulle had once stated that any nation that does not have an atomic bomb could not consider themselves an independent nation. They eventually created their own atomic weapons, but even into the early 1970s France was still behind every one else in their military-atomic program. They had but thirty six crude gravity bombs that had to be delivered to the attack site by aircraft. Any war with the heavily armed Soviets was virtual suicide for their pilots. Not until 1972 did their first missile capable submarine take to the sea, and their feeble ICBM base north of Marseille was still incomplete.

Pres. Nixon and Henry Kissinger had gotten the 1972 SALT agreement with Brezhnev for "nuclear parity" between the superpowers, and a worldwide nuclear test ban. That position upset the French for they could go no further in their nuclear programs without more tests. *De Gaulle arrogantly wanted nuclear help from America in order to catch up!* Condescendingly he insisted that France receive the same benefits as we had provided England since the mid-1950s. **Nixon refused.**

Once de Gaulle was no longer in power Nixon and Kissinger decided to give in and provide France with nuclear support. Three years later French ICBMs had caught up to our standards saving the French $Billions in R&D costs. Those upgrades gave the Soviets a serious strategic issue, as they realized that they could be now be destroyed just with the French nuclear weapons which only France controlled. With France as an independent power the Soviets could never be sure what the French might do if a war broke out. That factor may have put a damper on Soviet actions in Europe and helped us strategically. (Which is most likely the reason Nixon decided to help them. Out of all of our presidents of this century, he is the one who most understood the synergy of world power and world politics)

It was known for a while that the French CEA, Commissariat a` l`Energie Atomique was dominated by pro-Soviet leftists, and penetrated by Soviet moles. Their officials had often publicly stated that France "would never attack Russia". (Which was one reason why we had not shared many atomic secrets or improvements with them in years past.) After Ford became president he continued the reduction of our anti-French sentiments, and Pres. Carter further increased our aid to them.

During 1977 Carter secretly decided to sell France state of the art Cray supercomputers. Those computers were so powerful they could do thousands of complex computations in minutes. Despite the fact no one could be sure that the Soviets would not benefit from this move with the many pro-Soviet leftists inside the French government, Carter made this secret sale. **So surreptitious was this technology transfer that not until 1985 did the U.S. Senate even learn of it!** (This issue was then covered up.)

Soon after France announced that they would sell nuclear technology to Pakistan! In an act of incredible shallowness the French Government gave no thought to nuclear security or the long term view. All they were interested in was making money. Pakistan was an unstable Islamic nation that had had many fights with its neighbor India. This move, like their many questionable projects in Iraq would only add to the regional instability.

Africa

During the last few years the Soviets had been aiding the Eritrean rebels who lived in the northern most province of Ethiopia along the coast, as well as rebels in Ethiopia and Somalia. The new ruler in Somalia, Siad Barre began seizing territory from Ethiopia that it claimed as theirs. Ethiopia then turned to the Soviets for more help. Violence again flared up and seven government leaders were killed in early February 1977. By the end of April the leftist leaning junta in Ethiopia ordered all U.S. officials and missionaries out of the country. (*We had been allied with Ethiopia and Haile Salassie for decades.*)

To insure that this "Ethiopian rebellion" would succeed the Soviets transported 25,000 Cuban troops plus crew served weapons to this war zone to support the leftist Mengistu regime. The Soviets committed over a $ Billion in arms to this takeover, and their supply aircraft landed in Addis Abba every twenty minutes! Soviet and Cuban officers actually led many of the front line battles. Once the leftists took over in Ethiopia proper, the Soviets suddenly turned their backs on their former friends the Eritreans, and the communists were soon fighting against them. (Why fight for one small area when you can control the entire country.)

The addition of the Cuban forces allowed the Ethiopians to send even more troops to fight in Eritrea which caused their defeat.

The Soviet's had also been allied with neighboring Somalia for over a decade. But once Ethiopia was turned the Soviets moved away from Somalia too. That created the bizarre condition of Soviet advisors fighting other Soviet advisors across the border. For the Soviet long-term plans, Ethiopia was far more important strategically. Their peculiar machinations and their aggressive Communist imperialism were ever changing.

But the key to the Soviet efforts was their ability to look at everything in the long-term view.

By not having to face an electorate or a complaining media, the Soviet leaders could do whatever they wanted, anytime they wanted, to whomever they wanted as they moved towards their goal of worldwide Communism. To ensure the Ethiopians would stay in their sphere, over 10,000 Ethiopians attended Soviet schools to learn the fine art of Communism and subversive warfare. Castro was brought in to try to mediate any disputes, and create a union of East African socialist states. But Somalia's Barre wanted no part of their scheme. He kicked the Soviets out in November 1977, and was soon fighting Russian and Cuban forces.

While the fighting mentioned above was ongoing the U.S. under Ford had been aiding the Sudan as a last-ditch bulwark against the Communists. With the recent change of events in the Horn of Africa, we began aiding Eritrean rebels in their desire for independence.

Then in May 1977 the Somali's also asked for our help. *But Carter refused to send any U.S. military forces or additional aid to the region. This crisis in the Horn of Africa became a flashpoint within the Administration.*

A few principals like Brzezinski and some of the Democrats running Congress finally realized that when they allowed the Communist takeover of Angola in 1975 it had been a bad idea. The Communists were not stopping at the Angola border, and their efforts were spreading across Africa. (Go figure.)

Zaire (formally the Belgian Congo), had been a key ally of the western backed fighters in Angola. They too had opposed the Cuban proxy troops and MPLA Angolan Communist rebels. Zaire was soon targeted, and in March 1977 the Communists attacked into Zaire's Shaba province. Brzezinski felt this was a Soviet test of the new administration, not just an attempt to hurt Zaire. We had to get involved and we had to link all of these crisis to any arms talks or detente.

On March 19 the Congo's President Ngouabi was killed by a suicide bomber.

On April 4, Zaire broke off diplomatic ties with Cuba over their proxy troops invading their outlying province of Shaba.

Some arms then went to help Zaire fend off the rebels attacking them from Angola, but despite the warnings, no U.S. aid went to the Ethiopians, or the Somalis..

At this point in time over 40,000 Cuban troops were fighting in Angola, supplied by three massive airlifts of weapons, ammo and supplies from Russia.

Incredulously Carter's Sec. State Cyrus Vance saw the growing East vs West war in Angola as America's fault.

Carter's U.N. Ambassador Andrew Young claimed that the presence of Cuban troops offered a "certain stability and order to the region."??! Both were members of the "blame America club". Like most of the Western liberals of that time, Ambassador Young also downplayed the recent Soviet trials upon their dissident citizens. *The Soviets claimed the trials for treason did not show repression, but a gesture of independence.* Young concurred.??

Across the jungle on the south-eastern side of Africa were Rhodesia and Mozambique. They too were involved in border clashes, and again Communist agents worked to insure that those resource rich nations were in a constant state of turmoil. *By keeping the fighting going the Communist agents prevented any economic development and political stability.* Once the unschooled native populations had bled themselves long enough, and the fighting had caused dozens of thousands of others to flee, the Communists expected to quickly take over.

By the fall of 1977 numerous states in Africa and the Middle East which included Egypt, Sudan, Iran and Saudi Arabia were pressing the Carter Administration for action over the hostile Communist takeovers. **Sudan's president wrote to Carter complaining about the passivity from America while the Soviets implemented their "sinister grand plan" over Africa!**

Not until January 1978 did the secretive Administration begin briefing the media over Soviet and Cuban actions in Africa. Even though these wars were a clear and present danger to western interests, most in the administration wanted no action taken.

But Africa was not the only continent in turmoil.

Nicaragua was a small country in Central America that was ruled by an autocratic conservative dictator named Anastasio Somoza. Like many who ruled in Latin America he was not a popularly elected democratic leader, and threats to his regime were harshly put down. His main attraction for the U.S. was he was anti-communist.

Since the 1961 Bay of Pigs disaster in Cuba, Nicaragua had been under the gun from Communist rebels. Cuba was actively helping to foment dissent in many countries in Latin America, but especially in Nicaragua since they had been the base area for the Cuban exiles who came ashore at the Bay of Pigs.

In late January 1977 a newspaper editor who had been critical of Somoza had been killed. Protests against the regime appeared quickly, and all were well organized. (Which suggested that the killing was staged as a way to prompt these well planned protests.) In short order violence appeared countrywide resulting in martial law. Fighting was soon occurring in many areas and the leftist rebels were growing in their scope of activity. During March the Nicaraguan National Guard commander was assassinated, another warning of the trials soon to come.

America

As stated before Carter's pick to run the CIA was Adm. Stansfield Turner. He performed as was requested in "reforming" and choking off the agency. **Turner fired 820 agents within the Operations Directorate and their official termination notices were sent out on Halloween, Oct 31, 1977.** Those massive and unwarranted cuts devastated the Clandestine Service as the dedicated agents read, "Your services are no longer needed." *This dismissal of almost all of the veteran agents eliminated most of our worldwide human intelligence capability at the same instant.* And this void would quickly show itself as troubles were brewing across the globe.

This Administration and the Democratic Congress were demanding America leave the world stage. But in doing so it was our enemies who would take over the void. It appeared that JFK's 1961 speech on "bearing any burden" to insure our safety was just that, an empty political speech.

Détente was not bringing the Soviets into a period of harmony with the world, they were expanding their seditious operations. At this same time Carter continued to alienate the Congress in trying to balance the budget by eliminating favored Democratic pork barrel programs. Ted Kennedy was incensed that Carter had rejected his favorite wasteful program of a **national health insurance plan.** Carter also broke many of his campaign promises and he refused to compromise on anything. The Democrats had bemoaned the eight prior years of Republican control of the White House, and had hoped to advance more of their favorite social and urban spending programs with a fellow Democrat sitting there signing everything they passed. But Carter refused.

In addition to Carter's governing problems the national economy continued to get worse. The Dow Jones index of stocks fell 16% during 1977. At the same time inflation continued to go up, rising to 6.7 % . That reduced the purchasing power of the citizens, and during 1978 inflation hit 9%. In 1979 it rose to a strangling 13.3%! During this same time the nation's unemployment rate hit 10% of the workforce, and Carter's picks to run the nations finances were all failures who were forced out of office. It was becoming quite obvious that his administration was in serious jeopardy.

Historical Note: Senator Ted Kennedy should have gone to jail over the 1969 death of Mary Jo Kopechne. She was in a car Kennedy was driving, and died when the car went into a pond. Kennedy left the scene, went to a hotel and did not report the accident. He was casually having breakfast the next morning when the police pulled his car from the water finding the young woman dead in the back seat. Despite witnesses stating he was drunk, he was never charged for that or for vehicular homicide. It was all covered up.

Foreign Affairs

But Carter's problems were not just domestic or Communist directed. Islamic terrorists and other terror groups were still active. Many of them were supported by the Soviet Union, and that included Carlos "The Jackal", Japan's Red Army, Italy's Red Brigade, the PLO, Germany's Baader-Meinhof gang, France's Action Direct and the PFLP, Popular Front for the Liberation of Palestine. The objectives of those groups was chaos, and the fall of the present governments.

On Jan. 1, 1976 Mideast Airlines Flight 438 from Beirut to Abu Dhabi was destroyed by a bomb in the forward cargo hold. Eighty one were murdered. No one took responsibility.

On March 9, 1977 three local governmental buildings in Washington DC were seized by twelve Muslim terrorists. Led by Hamas leader Abdul Khaalis, the Hanafi terrorists, (an offshoot from the Nation of Islam) took 149 hostages. Two hostages were murdered with seven wounded. Islamic emissaries were able to end the 39 hour standoff.

Lufthansa Flight 181 was hijacked on Oct. 13, 1977 by PLO terrorists. Commandos stormed the aircraft killing the attackers, but five more civilians were wounded. No one had a clue on what to do about this airline hijacking problem.

January 7, 1978 Italian left-wing terrorists attacked in Rome murdering three in the Acca Larentia Massacre.

February 1, 1978 Arab terrorists from the Arab Revolutionary Council poisoned oranges with mercury injuring five children.

February 4, 1978 Columbia's Communist FARC terrorists ambushed an army column murdering ten.

Carter had come into office insisting that Israel must be defended. For the Democrats that was a key voting bloc, the Jewish vote. But after taking office Carter began expressing his criticism of Israel's policies. His sympathies were for the Palestinians in the West Bank and Gaza, and he relinquished our monopoly on Middle East peacemaking that Nixon and Kissinger had worked so hard on. *Carter invited the Soviets to join in the peace process as he declared his intention to seek Israel's withdrawal of all occupied territories from the 1967 war. He also pledged to legitimate Palestinian rights!*

Israeli PM Begin was stunned at this political reversal, while Egypt's Sadat was appalled that Carter would invite Syria, the Soviets and the Palestinians into any negotiations. Pres. Sadat had begun making his own moves to promote peace, as he opened secret contacts with the Israelis. His advances were met with open arms, as Israeli Prime Minister Menachem Begin felt the same. They began making quite inroads, and under his government Israeli soldiers forcibly prevented new Israeli settlements from being erected in disputed areas.

Incredibly on November 21, 1977 Egypt's President Anwar Sadat not only traveled into Israel, he addressed the Israeli Knesset in a surprise speech and promised them peace and security. "Israel is welcome in the region but must give back the lands they had captured and recognize the rights of the Palestinians". This was a major opening for peace, and there was no American involvement. The Mid-East leaders were making progress on their own.

By mid-December Israeli PM Begin traveled to Egypt and agreed to give the Sinai back to Egypt, (captured in the 1967 war.)

For his peacemaking efforts Sadat was maligned by the other Arab leaders and Egypt became a diplomatic pariah.

Instability in the Horn of Africa was increasing. During February 1978 Somalia began mobilizing for a full war with Ethiopia, and that meant fighting Russia and Cuba too.
   As those war worries increased Sec. of State Vance stated that the U.S. would not send arms to help Somalia, and we would remain neutral. That weak response basically told the Soviets to do whatever they wanted. For any nation to have any chance to fight off the Communists would require aid from America.

During the 1976 presidential campaign a political action group innocuously called *the Institute for Policy Studies, IPS* was becoming a growing left-wing entity. They supported Carter, but only if he followed their entire political platform of supporting Left-wing regimes, ignoring any conservative ones even if they were allies, and by making large reductions in the U.S. military. *This group exerted a strong influence on this Administration and caused irreparable harm to our world.*
   Both Carter and his Vice-president Walter Mondale, (a Hubert Humphrey protégé`) had surrounded themselves with many disciples of the IPS platform. Some of the others that came aboard were first-timers in positions of immense importance. This was eerily similar to JFK's senior picks who had failed him and nation in the 1960s. Among the crowd of newcomers were Warren Christopher and Anthony Lake. (Both would be recycled in the 1990s when another failed Democrat took over the White House, Bill Clinton.)
   Sec State "Vance was so far to the left from reality he stated to Time magazine in 1978 that Carter and Brezhnev shared similar dreams and aspirations for the future of the world".* [20] (Was he was implying that Carter was in on the Soviet plans.) Those post-Vietnam leftists truly believed that all of our Cold War actions were groundless and based on our paranoia of the Communist utopia.
   Historical Note: It is truly hard to understand the feelings of liberals when it was a known fact the Bolsheviks used starvation in the 1920s killing millions of innocents as a way to force the masses to accept their rule. Stalin's follow-on reign of terror during the 1930s killed almost 10 million more, and his invasions of Poland and Finland were nothing more than blatant acts of aggression, greed and butchery. Mao's insanity in China killed 65 million

people, and he supported the war in Korea killing over a million there. China and Russia both supported the communists in SE Asia losing over a million in that fighting, and the more recent horrors after they took over. Communist efforts for proxy-takeovers were occurring in Angola, S. Yemen, Grenada, Ethiopia, Mozambique, Nicaragua, Rhodesia and Afghanistan. What more did those Democrats need to see?

"One senior Carter official tried to put a nice face on things by stating that all of the developing countries at risk were just searching for viable forms of government capable of managing the process of modernization." * (21)

(And you thought the Politically Correct nonsense started in the 1990s.)

The people in those countries were not involved in choosing their government, it was being forced on them from the barrel of a gun. A Communist gun. But Vance and the Carter Administration did not see it that way. Vance felt it was just the inevitable march of history as capitalism / democracy collapsed.

The truth of the matter is simple. No nation or people on this planet has ever chosen in a truly free election to be ruled by Communists. Each time they were either conquered, overrun or forced into it. To make their takeover look presentable, the people were made to vote. The only catch was there was just one slate of candidates, Communists. * (22)

The war in the Horn of Africa was brutal with thousands being killed. As usual the Soviets supplied the weapons which included MiG fighter-bombers, and the Cubans supplied the trained fighters. Realizing that our staying neutral had not worked to prevent that war the Carter Administration warned the Soviets that SALT II was in jeopardy if they did not desist. Their diplomatic efforts also failed to reign in the communists. The war went on, and the Cubans continued advancing. Carter needed some positive headlines via the SALT II talks, and he backed down on his threat.

One unintended fallout from the crushing Arab defeat in the 1967 War was that the future of the Arab world was in turmoil. Millions of disgruntled citizens had been devastated by the rout they had suffered, and political tumult soon followed. There was a marked rise of Islamic extremism, and several regimes turned left-leaning nationalist. Assad took over in Syria, Qaddafi overthrew the king in Libya, Jaafar Numieri seized power in the Sudan and the Baath Socialist party rose up in Iraq. Most were backed by the

Soviets. Soon after Qaddafi took over in Libya he was threatening Egypt, the Sudan and Chad with war. And his forces were in Uganda helping Idi Amin in his takeover.

When the British withdrew from Aden (South Yemen) in 1967 the Soviets had stepped right in. The pro-Soviet group called the National Liberation Front, NLF operated unopposed in South Yemen and had purged all of their opponents by 1970. They turned S. Yemen into a Marxist state called (as every Communist state does), *The Peoples Democratic Republic of Yemen*. Not long after the Soviets tried to create an insurrection in Oman by using their S. Yemen client state. It took three hard years of fighting to seal and secure that border using their SAS forces. Stopped from getting to Oman, the South Yemini Marxists changed directions and began attacking into N. Yemen and Saudi Arabia.

Historical Note: Our part in this tangled story began back in 1961 when JFK sided with Egypt's Nasser, undoing Eisenhower's previous Mid-East policy of non-alignment. Kennedy was quickly beset with complaints from Oil companies, anti-communist groups and Britain over his policy change. The CIA prepared an NIE (National Intelligence Estimate) for him warning that the present and growing militant Arab Nationalism from Egypt was a great danger to the region and the Saudis.

To show gratitude to Kennedy for his policy change, in 1962 Nasser and his allies acted and overthrew the government of Yemen. They then began threatening the Saudis when Nasser sent thousands of Egyptian troops into Yemen. The Saudis quickly funded the Yemeni monarchists in opposition, and large battles soon began. Britain was still in control of Aden (S. Yemen), and their government still despised Nasser from the 1956 Suez Crisis. MI-6, Mossad, the Saudi GID and even Iran's SAVAK added their support to the Saudi effort to oppose Nasser's plans.

If Nasser could create an ally in Yemen he could control the Red Sea. During the fighting in Yemen Nasser also continued his harsh rhetoric and subterfuge against Jordan and the Saudi's. *Kennedy was forced to send in naval forces in November 1963 to protect Riyadh from collapsing.* By the wars end in 1970 over 200,000 had died including Nasser, (cancer).

In 1970 Nixon was president and he continued our support of Jordan and the Saudi's. *But the Middle East he inherited from the Democrats was a tangled disaster of war, hatred and superpower tensions.* Nixon and Kissinger made good diplomatic progress in the region, but the Soviets had become "the champions of the Arab nationalists". As usual they inserted Communist subversives into those groups as they built them up militarily for the next war. When the 1973 fighting went against Syria and Egypt and they were near collapse, the Soviets prepared to join in. Nixon was able to warn the them off just as it appeared that a superpower battle was going to start in the Middle East. (And the tangled web of history continued with the current issues of 1978.)

By mid-1978 the Soviet subversion in the horn of Africa had officially moved into the Arabian Peninsula. The NLF in S. Yemen launched a "civil war" against North Yemen which was being supported by the Saudis. As usual a convenient coup had killed N. Yemen's President Al-Hamdi resulting in political chaos. This war was a dire problem for the Saudi's as N. Yemen supplied much of the labor force for the oil Princes. They also shared a common and porous border, and it was well known that Saudi Arabia had a small and weak military. They would not hold out long to a determined and well trained foe.

U.S. Military and Intelligence officials worried that the Cubans would soon show up as they were just a few dozen of miles away in Ethiopia.

Inside Saudi Arabia their renewed and dangerous form of Islam called **Wahhabism** was taking over. That strain follows strict Islamic Fundamentalist guidelines as all reformers or modernizers must die. Wahhabism was named for an Islamic scholar named Muhammad al-Wahhab. His ideas began spreading through the region about two hundred years ago, but were initially controlled by the rule of the Ottoman Empire. *Wahhabism was the religion of the al-Saud family when they were picked by the British to rule the Arabian Peninsula after WWI.* The al-Saud family unified the Arabian tribes, and the kingdom of Saudi Arabia was formed.

To promote their strict policies the Wahhabists used their new-found stores of oil money and Islamic banks to build Islamic schools and mosques all over the world. In that way they could ensure that only their Wahhabist teachings would be taught and the young would be indoctrinated in their ideals. (Similar to the mandatory liberal-politically correct teachings going on in our schools and colleges.) *A young student named Osama bin Laden was raised in that sect in the 1970s.*

"To spread their beliefs beyond Saudi Arabia the **Muslim World League** sent out "missionaries" to speak, help out, print propaganda and fund local construction projects." (23) Regional CIA agents realized and reported on the consequence of the Muslim League in advancing this strict Islamic renewal and influence, but none of the principals in Washington saw anything worth their time. Even the Soviet proxy war being fought in Yemen could not wake the Carter Administration.

During June 1978 the president was briefed by the Intelligence Community. Their topic was the Soviet Union, Goals and Expectations. *This group now recognized that the Soviets were determined to expand their control, particularly in the Third World.* A massive Soviet military buildup had been ongoing since the Cuban Missile Crisis, while we had been tied up in SE Asia. The Soviets were surpassing us in many military capabilities, and were capable of aggression anywhere. And by using their recently upgraded Cuban proxy troops, the Soviets could avoid a direct conflict with the West. The Vance State Dept. did not agree with this intelligence assessment, and they delayed any types of actions insisting their diplomacy would rectify the problems.

Brzezinski began a national policy review, while Carter decided to seek out human rights issues and economic competition. In any event nothing concrete would be done before 1979.

During that same time the administration had also learned the Soviets had secretly returned to Cuba shipping in the latest variants of their MiG-23 fighter-bomber. Those aircraft could carry nuclear weapons and were in violation of the 1962 treaty. Unlike when Nixon was president, this Administration argued about this issue into 1979, but could not get the Soviets to back down. The MiG's stayed in Cuba, as Carter and his administration came away looking even more weak and ineffectual.

Iran

Back in 1953, the Cold War was still hot, and the Iranian Communist Tudeh party was at its peak. Leftist Mohammed Mossadegh was elected as Prime Minister by their Parliment. He soon dissolved the Parliament, and began breaking with the prior treaties that had greatly benefitted Great Britain. Winston Churchill convinced Eisenhower to wrongly intercede, and the CIA and other allied Intelligence Services gave aid to the coup mentioned earlier. They succeeded in stopping Iran's turn towards the leftists as Mossadegh was removed and placed in house arrest. (Kermit Roosevelt, grandson to Teddy was one of the coup conspirators.)

The young Shah was returned to power while Mossadegh died under house arrest. (Ironically Iran's strict clerics approved and helped with that effort.) Mohammed Reza Pahlavi, became an invaluable ally to the West. To help him get on track with his *White Revolution,* (a program of internal redevelopment), Pres. Eisenhower approved aid to expand the Iranian railways, air transport, education, dams, irrigation and roads. Reza was following Turkey's hero and brilliant founder Kemal Ataturk's 1920s policy of a secular government.

Because of Kemel's efforts, Turkey, unlike the other Islamic states, had grown and developed from a broken part of the old Ottoman Empire into a modern, moderate, semi-democratic state. The Fundamentalists hated and feared them.

As thanks for our help, the Shah paid back the West by settling numerous territorial disputes in the area and using his military to shore up the northern tier of countries such as Iraq, Turkey and Pakistan from Soviet interference. Iran joined the Baghdad pact in 1956 with England and America to ensure the region's security from the Soviets. When Great Britain finally withdrew from the Persian Gulf in 1971, it was the Shah's forces who occupied the islands in the vital Strait of Hormuz to prevent any terrorists or Communists from trying to. In 1973 it was the Shah who sent forces into Oman's Dhofar province to help battle the Marxist guerrillas operating from South Yemen.

It was the Shah and his army that kept the large and powerful Iraqi army out of Kuwait when they threatened to invade them in 1961, and again in 1973. During the 1961 Iraq-Kuwait incident the British and the Arab / Persian coalition forced the Iraqi's to back down. In 1973 the Iraqi forces actually took over some of Kuwait, but were forced to settle the issue peacefully or risk war with Iran.

During the Mideast wars of 1967 and 1973, the Shah was the one voice of reason. *And his threatening military strength kept a lid on Iraq, which prevented them from joining the fight against Israel in 1973. That action quite possibly saved Israel and the region.* Facing a potential defeat and massacre in 1973, Israel was about to use the few atomic weapons they had to stave off their demise. (Those humiliating events were all part of the reasons why Saddam Hussein was so intent on attacking Iran after the Shah was toppled.)

Back in 1972 Pres. Nixon had made a point of visiting Iran and working with the Shah to continue our good relationship. Nixon was known to the Iranians since his days as the Vice President, and as was his passion he had worked hard to cultivate solid relationships with as many foreign leaders as possible.

From that 1972 trip new foreign policy formulations were made and dubbed the "**Nixon Doctrine**", which he based on **his Two Pillars philosophy.** *Nixon was prepared to overlook some human rights failings by foreign governments, if they were a vital "pillar" in keeping the Communists at bay.* Which Iran was. (That policy was the exact opposite of Carter and his Administration.)

At their meetings the Shah and Nixon spoke for hours on the issues facing the world. Iran was still needed to shore up the Persian Gulf, and Nixon was prepared to give them the best equipment and training we could to bolster Iran's military. (It included starting a atomic powered -electrical reactor.) The Shah was eager to fulfill that need, and to play a role in the Indian Ocean where the Soviets had based naval ships since 1968. *Over $10 billion in military equipment sales and training were made ensuring Iran's safety and ability to project regional power.* With our relations cemented, the Shah kept our naval forces supplied with oil, and he alone supplied Israel with oil.

Historical Note : Captured German documents from 1945 had shown that when the Russians and Germans signed their non-aggression pact in 1939, **Stalin had specifically written down his desire to control the Persian Gulf and all of those nations.** It had been decided at Yalta that Iran would remain free, but after the war the Russians remained in the country and Truman had to warn Stalin in 1945-46 to leave Iran. Russian agents however stayed in the shadows waiting for a chance to strike.

And as shown before, *after the tide had turned in the 1973 war the Soviets were threatening to join that Mid-East conflict.* The Shah refused to grant the Soviet Military over-flights when the Russians threatened to commit their forces. The Soviets could not attempt any flights over Turkey because they were a member of NATO, so any attempts by them to get into the fight had to go via the Mediterranean. That made them vulnerable to intervention by NATO and U.S. forces. **Nixon was able to warn the Soviets off, because they knew he would fight.**

Throughout 1978 it was the Shah who was actively helping the Afghan's pull away from their dependence on the Soviets. Because of his efforts they wanted him gone. **To make that a reality the Soviets helped stoke the fires of Islamic discontent in Iran by providing money and training to get the protestors started.** Russia realized that if they were successful their actions could change the world.

During his twenty plus years in power the Shah had enacted domestic reforms which included a massive land reform campaign.

Prior to that change most of their land was held by 1% of the population. His reforms included a divestiture of some of the Crown lands, as well as forcing the wealthy landowners and Moslem clergy to give their holdings back to the people. *Those reforms earned him the enmity of both influential groups.*

Way before our efforts, the Shah had enacted profit sharing for workers and stock investments as a way to encourage their labors. He began an Iranian type of Peace Corp., and sent them to the impoverished countryside to help alleviate the problems faced by the rural population. The number of schools in Iran skyrocketed as did national literacy. Better educated people led safer and more hygienic lives, and Iran's population benefitted greatly. In the Shah's Iran, medical care was free for all and well funded.

With his financial help, over 40,000 of their best students were sent abroad to receive higher degrees in the fine universities of the West. They then returned and became the next generation of Iranian leaders which further advanced their nation with needed infrastructure and civil engineering projects. *Women were given full civil and political rights despite bitter opposition from the Fundamentalists of the Islamic world.* This last group had been fighting a long campaign to destroy any Western influence in their world and they were not done. Russian aid was a great help.

During the late 1970s Iran's economy was growing at 9% a year, even before the extra wealth of the oil crisis was added in. His economic plan at times bordered on socialism as he tried to provide for the have not's. *But the key point was that he tried to help his people unlike most of the other autocratic rulers, especially those in the Arab nations!*

The only area in which the Shah did not excel was in the area of political rights. Iran as in much of the non-western world never had a history of democracy. Most of those old world's nations were ruled by one ruler, a Premier, King, Prince, Chieftain, Emperor or Sheik. Governing in that fashion was a common entity known as autocratic rule. That type was not necessarily good or bad as it depended on the ruler.

But in all cases the ruled had little or no say in their fates. If the ruler was a tyrannical despot the population would be in for a harsh existence. However as shown above the Shah was not of that mindset or he would not have done as much for his people and his nation as he did.

Stanford University had actually done a study and found the Shah's rule was exceptional in benefitting Iran's people! In comparison to all of the other regimes in the Middle East the people of Iran had the best life. *And they actually had more* political and human rights than 75% of the world's people! Only in the Democracies of the West were the average people treated better. (The vast sum of souls suffering under Communism dwarfed those thriving under Democracy.)

Still like most autocratic rulers his rule was law and political opposition could be treated harshly. And in the leftist mindset of the Carter Administration human rights was the only meaningful entity. That was why they did not follow any of Nixon's well based foreign policies. *Carter and his people made horrible mistakes, and it would cost the world and the U.S. dearly.*

For the nearby Saudi's the Shah's reign had proved extremely beneficial. Like their neighbors in Kuwait and the U.A.E., Saudi Arabia is vastly under-populated by its own citizens. They must import hundreds of thousands of Palestinians and other Arab workers to meet the business and commercial needs of the country. That weakness means that the Saudi's and their neighbors are very susceptible to sabotage and undermining by revolutionaries. *During 1978 S. Yemen was again trying to destabilize Oman and N. Yemen. The Saudi's faced the possibility of being surrounded by hostile leftist regimes.*

As the fighting intensified in the new year the Carter Administration asked the CIA for alternatives. In March 1979 the CIA advised that it was too late for any type of counter-insurgency effort in S. Yemen. But we needed to stop any advances into the rest of Arabia. It was decided to work with the Saudis to come up with an interim policy.

Then a terrible sequence began to destroy what the Shah had worked so hard to make. Reza Pahlavi was sickened by cancer. At that same time Islamic militants and Fundamentalists worked tirelessly, (assisted by their Communist Tudeh Party), to undermine his regime. *Their well trained subversives assigned militants to provoke clashes with Iran's security forces. Their efforts were designed to gain negative publicity as the Shah's security people unleashed harsh tactics and retaliatory policing.*

The Fundamentalists also used terror and sabotage to frighten the Shah's supporters, disrupt the country, provoke additional civil clashes and incite the western media who always had something negative to say about the Shah. (This same procedure is happening currently in America with our subversive leftists.)

As always the naive, liberal, western media turned on the Shah because he did not "live up to western ideals". (Just like they did to

Diem in S. Vietnam.) During that period the NY Times was still the number one media outlet in America. The BBC was the same in Britain, and other leftist entities served similar functions in Europe. Those entities did (and still) exert a great control over the day to day thoughts by controlling what was seen and what was heard by the masses. All of their reporting was negative, and every time the Shah did something the corupted western media did not like they attacked him. *As had happened in S. Vietnam in the 1960s, Iran was in turmoil because of subversive outside forces.* What the Iranians did in their quest for security was for them to work out, not for apologetic, idealistic fools to condemn and undercut his regime. But that is just what the media and the Democratic Administrations did in 1963, and again in 1978. Carter never spoke up for the Shah, and his State Dept. was filled with left-leaning Arabists who did not support Israel or the Shah's Iran.

France were still quite active and well placed inside Iran, and playing both sides at the same time. *They had warned the Shah a few times that he had to react to the increasing threats from the fundamentalists or he would lose the nation.*

Yet France allowed the **Ayatollah Khomeini** to remain in their country and have a live audience each day. French media outlets presented fuzzy and warm coverage of the Ayatollah, while the BBC became a primary voice for him. *None would speak up for the Shah.*

Over the past years the Fundamentalist protests and propaganda had made inroads among the young and naïve Iranians. Even though their best and brightest had gone off to the schools in the West to become better educated, they too foolishly joined the forces of those against the Shah. None had lived during the harsh times before the Shah, so they did not have a clue as to how lucky they were. Some of the protestors wanted a return to a constitutional monarchy, some a socialist/communist government, while the Shia mullahs wanted an Islamic republic.

Few understood what that would mean.

Pahlavi's regime like most autocratic rulers lived a lavish lifestyle, and as in most of the world, the majority of the nation's wealth was controlled by a small percentage of its people. And as in the West a large percentage of their citizens struggled to make ends meet. Those easily influenced young people listened to the preaching's and stories from the Ayatollah Khomeini that were being broadcast. Some of the media outlets came from as far as Libya. Tragically they turned away from the Shah's progressive view of Iran, and like lemmings they followed the siren song of those promising change. One can only guess how many of them survived after the Fundamentalists took over.

(This propagandizing of the young is exactly what is happening here with the liberal lies and scamming of our young people. They hastily follow the Democrats and their liberal viewpoint, voting for Obama who "promised change". But all America and the world got was eight more years of liberal failures and lies. And during those years our enemies grew stronger and more dangerous.)

Carter and his administration's main foreign policy goal was "human rights" for all. A fine goal to be sure, but America's version of those rights is not the same as other countries. It takes dozens upon dozens of years of fine tuning to get the government you want. In following Carter's lead the liberal western media became obsessed with changing the world's opinion of the Shah from a champion of modernization, to a monster of human rights abuses. (Which were not true.)

At a November 1977 visit to America, Iranian dissidents were foolishly allowed access to the Shah and the Carter retinue. Harsh protests began which caused the unprepared Secret Service and local law enforcement to use tear gas on the unruly crowd. Had they wanted to, those protestors could have charged into and killed all of those officials who were assembled.

Back in 1775 America was blessed with hundreds of learned and dedicated citizens who had suffered a restricted and regulated life as colonists under English rule. Tired of that existence they risked all to create a Declaration of Independence from England. **It then took twelve years to formulate a Constitution that all could agree to. They setup a extraordinary and revolutionary government that was to be run by the governed. A monarch or ruler would not decide their fates, the people would.** America had only existed for 200 years by the time of Jimmy Carter. Iran had had only 25+ years of the Shah and his social advancements. That further democratic reforms may have come to his land we will never know.

It is a bizarre and sad twist of irony that the liberals of the world who profess to be such caring and tolerant of earth's citizens, are also the most intolerant, impatient, sanctimonious and narrow minded.

As shown before those same "liberal minded people" had turned against S. Vietnam's Diem which prompted JFK's 1963 coup and Diem's murder. South Vietnam fell into chaos and Communist regimes eventually took over all of French Indochina resulting in millions being ruthlessly murdered, killed, imprisoned and exiled. Now in the late 1970s those same leftists were echoing similar sentiments about Iran and Nicaragua. In the latter case they were actually undermining the Somoza regime to the enhancement of the encroaching Communists.

(If one looks at the biased and wrongful work of the media since 1960 it is easy to conclude that our media have been working to destroy Western Civilization.)

To try to intercede with the unknowing and worrisome Carter, and to help their "public image" with western media, the Shah enlisted some confidants to come up with a PR plan. Research into the situation produced two reports that instead of helping him, anticipated Iran's fall into chaos. One report cautioned Iranian Jews to flee the country and seek refuge elsewhere. Iran had the largest Jewish population in the Middle East, and hundreds heeded the warning and left.

Reza Pahlavi had had a longstanding friendship with the Republicans. He had been upset at the anti-Shah American election propaganda, and with the end results of the election in 1976. In his view the Democrats had been doing and saying anything to win that election with no thought given to Iran or America's long term interests. Now in 1978 his reign was in deep trouble, and no help was coming.

In addition to his perception problems in the West, the Shah had greatly antagonized the Islamic leaders of his country. His secular type of government excluded the Shia religious leaders from power. His land reforms took titles from the clerics and gave it back to the people. And his emancipation of Iranian women was threatening the traditional way of Muslim life as they were the most educated and free of any women in the Islamic world.

He stopped the use of the Islamic calender and sharia law. And in accepting aid and advice from the mostly secular America and the West, the Shah was allowing their pollution to affect Iran's way of life. All of the Shah's policies were an anathema to the Islamists, and they were dedicated to removing him, before "they lost all control over their societies the way the West had".

Since the end of the 1940s a new type of Fundamentalist was appearing, the Islamic Extremists. Those radicals existed for only two ideals, a return to strict rule by Sharia Law and the elimination of Israel. One of their main philosophers was Egyptian Sayyid Qutb. Originally a free thinker who traveled greatly, he had once lived in America and was appalled with our freedoms. When he returned to Egypt he joined the Muslim Brotherhood and became the senior advocate for Islamic Radicalism as the remedy for American self-indulgence and failings. Qutb also opposed Nasser, and died in 1966. (Khomeini was one of his followers.)

Like the Communist totalitarians, the fanatics in Iran used all of the anti-Shah groups to assist their efforts in deposing the present government. Once the Shah fell they would step in and take over imposing their version of Islamic law. Anyone who was against their agenda would be removed. (Sharia Law is based on an eye for an eye punishment. Drinking and gambling are punished by the whip, adulterers are stoned to death. Men can strike women for any offense, homosexuals are to be killed, and any insult to Islam is punished with death.)

Instead of realizing their dream of an American or European style of Democracy, the other anti-Shah protest groups would be subjugated under an Islamic Dictatorship.

As shown earlier expelled Iranian cleric Ayatollah Khomeini, (Ruhollah Khomeini) had initially been agitating against the Shah from Najaf, Iraq. He was assisted by the Iraqi's at first, but then his Shia followers inside Iraq began causing troubles in the Sunni ruled nation. Khomeini was expelled again and ended up in France. **Since the 1960's his efforts had been financed by the Soviets who were also dedicated to bringing down the Shah.**

Khomeini had millions of like minded followers who worked for him for years. Khomeini may have been the one who perfected the practice of using clerics and mosques as the secretive and primary way to establish his network. He and his principal supporters had agents in every village and neighborhood, spying on the locals and making their lists of who was on what side. One of their favorite methods of communicating was to use smuggled cassette tapes from Kurdish Iraq that had the clerics speeches or instructions for his confederates. *Hidden among their ranks were Khomeini's followers.*

(Ironically the Shah had previously helped the Iraqi Kurds with their desires for independence, and he allowed them to travel freely through Iran.)

Like all who can sway the masses, Khomeini was a good orator. And similar to the Communist charlatans (who he actually despised), he appealed to the poor and even convinced the Mujahedeen-e-Khalq and the Marxist Fedayeen-e-Khalq fighters to join his ranks. They became a vital part of his "muscle needs" to seize power. (But after they succeeded in deposing the Shah both groups were put down to prevent them from rising up against the Ayatollah and his restrictive Islamic rule.)

And the PLO added their trained terrorists to the mix.

The Soviets were not silent during this time. Their well funded and re-organized Communist Tudeh party worked with Soviet propaganda units to foment as much unrest and turmoil as possible. Chaos in Iran was definitely in Russia's best interests for they were looking to maintain control of Afghanistan, (initially).

Meanwhile the Carter Administration was vacilating, one day professing support for the Shah and the next day they were in contact with the opposition groups. Gradually the unrest began to take over and with Iran falling into turmoil Iraq was free to become aggressive in an area that holds most of the worlds oil supply.

Lebanon and Syria

In nearby Lebanon there was little warning when Syrian armored forces swept through the nation attacking the Lebanese Christian militia strongholds and defeating them.

Westernized Lebanon was to be remade into a Syrian run Islamic state, and become the main residence for the PLO. Israel was targeted daily with attacks from that broken land. As a result of the Syrian takeover there was no end in sight for the terrorism or strife. (Lebanon had become a refuge for all kinds of terrorist groups hiding out in the chaos that was once a peaceful country.)

On March 11, 1978 PLO terrorists staged the coastal road massacre in Israel. Their attack was timed to stop the ongoing and infuriating peace talks between Egypt and Israel. Thirty eight were killed including 13 children. Over 70 were wounded. Faced with those recurring attacks, three days later Israel invaded southern Lebanon. Once again the news flashes showed daily scenes of war and suffering. The Carter Administration was silent.

In an effort to hurt Syria and the PLO, Israel and Jordan ironically had a growing relationship with the Muslim Brotherhood. Syria's Hafez Assad was another secular ruler, and a member of a religious minority called the Alawites. They were a quasi-Shiite sect that was not liked by orthodox Sunni Arabs of the Muslim Brotherhood. They hated the Alawites calling them false Muslims, and since 1976 they had been actively fighting with Assad. Syria had been repeatedly struck with car bombings and assassinations that targeted Assad family members and even his Soviet advisors. A new Mideast war was starting.

America

September 16, 1977 became a watershed day, as that was the day the first American steel plant closed. Over 5,000 steel workers were laid off, and within months sixteen more plants closed at a cost of 40,000 jobs! Secondary effects were immediate as local stores went out of business and vibrant communities quickly became ghost towns. The Rust Belt crisis was beginning across middle America. Union workers organized petitions and sent busloads of protestors to Washington demanding an end to the cheap steel imports that were saturating our markets. Even with Democratic Senator John Glenn in attendance, Carter ignored their efforts.

Over the following months our serious economic decline continued, and in April 1978 President Carter warned America that they must treat the most recent oil crisis like a war. Carter wanted stringent conservation efforts, penalties for wasting fuels and higher fuel prices. Most of our continental oil recovery efforts were slowly dwindling, and unless America woke up the 1980s could be catastrophic.

One of Carter's first decisions concerned shifting our electrical generation facilities from burning oil to using domestic coal. That action was beneficial in two ways, it provided much needed jobs to our coal producing states and the railroads that transported it, and it reduced our dependence on foreign oil. On the down side it increased the air and water pollution.

By the end of June the Trans-Alaska oil pipeline, an engineering marvel was completed and began sending oil on its thirty day journey from the Arctic to Valdez, Alaska. But rather than ship the oil to our refineries in the Gulf of Mexico, it was cheaper to just sell much of the oil to Japan. (Most of the refineries on the West Coast had been closed by our environmentalists.)

Carter was also looking to make far reaching changes to Social Security and the national tax system. One of his major proposals was to increase our payroll taxes by a factor of 300%. This would be the largest tax increase ever conceived in peacetime. In effect America would have become a socialist country with most of your wages and business profits going to the government for them to spend as they saw fit. Business leaders were outraged by his plan, which did not pass. His complicated energy plan also fell apart.

The one act Carter did pass was an $18 billion tax reduction for wealthy individuals and corporations.

Then Carter decided he wanted to "turn over the Panama Canal" to Panama twenty years before it was required by treaty. This measure was also met with much negativity by Republicans and conservatives, as he was giving away a vital national security resource that was built and paid for by America.

Historical Note: Back at the turn of the century the U.S. had offered to purchase a "Canal Zone" from Columbia. The agreement was rejected by the Columbian Senate as giving too much control to the U.S. Soon after a small revolution occurred, (supported by our government), giving the neighboring Panamanians their sought after freedom with a new country. Theodore Roosevelt's administration quickly recognized the new nation, and then purchased the same Canal Zone area in 1903 for the exact offer that had been made to Columbia the year before, $10 million outright and $250,000 per year. It was also agreed that the Canal zone would be transferred over to Panama in 1999.

It had taken years of effort and 5600 lives, (Malaria and Yellow Fever), but a canal was created that linked the Pacific Ocean to the Caribbean Sea / Atlantic Ocean. This incredible feat of engineering had cost the French (when they tried and failed twenty years earlier) tons of money and over 22,000 lives. When the U.S. built Canal opened it revolutionized oceanic trade and travel cutting weeks off of voyages between the oceans. It also saved huge sums for consumers and shippers. Prior to the Panama Canal the railroads had joined our large continent into a working entity. Now a trans-ocean sea trade would join the effort.

During 1921 incoming Republican Pres. Harding gave Columbia a $25 million dollar indemnity for what had been done to them, and the yearly rental fee to Panama was increased substantially. As America prospered our navy became larger and the Canal was a key component in joining the fleets together if need be. To protect this now vital waterway, numerous U.S. military bases were established in the region and proved needed especially during WWII. A Two Ocean War had to be fought and the Panama Canal was a key factor to our logistic and naval might.

But despite the follow on wars in Korea and Vietnam, Carter was convinced he was right in giving away the Canal as a way to gain favor in the perpetually unstable Latin America. Many feared that Cuba would soon have a say in the control of the canal as Panama's Gen. Omar Torrijos' was considered a tin-pot dictator and a Communist sympathizer. But Carter signed the treaty with

Torrijos on September 7, 1977. The Democratic controlled Senate ratified the new pact (by one vote) in April 1978.

What most Americans do not know, was that Gen. Torrijos had objected to a paragraph in the new treaty that allowed the U.S. to intervene in the Canal Zone if needed. *Carter allowed him to rewrite that amendment for his country's version of the treaty, but never mentioned that fact to the Senate.* He then duplicitously presented the Senate with the first written version for them to vote on and pass. **The Senate never realized that there was a second treaty version altered by Torrijos.** Because of Carter's duplicity and illegality, the two countries never ratified the same treaty!

Throughout 1979 the final passage of the paperwork was completed. On October 1, 1979 the United States handed over numerous military bases, equipment, over 7,000 buildings, rail lines and trains, hundreds of vehicles of all types and all manor of equipment to the tune of over a billion dollars. The U.S. Government offices and services all had to close down and the U.S. employees lost their jobs. Any Americans remaining in Panama had to register as workers and guests. The Russians were stunned at Carter's foolishness.

Soviet Subterfuge

With little warning progressive Afghan President Mohammed Daoud Khan was killed in a coup with most of his family in late April 1978 by leftist rebels. They quickly setup a new government and called themselves, the Democratic Republic of Afghanistan. *A revolutionary council was organized to govern, run by the head of the Afghan Communist party, Nur Muhammad Taraki. He had been arrested by Khan the year before because of his communist activities.*

The Soviets immediately recognized the new government, but that is not surprising since it was Russia that helped provoke the coup. Within a short time every Afghan government ministry and army unit had Soviet Advisors attached to it. Those advisors came from Soviet Central Asia and were Tadzhiks, a people who speak a dialect that the Afghans can understand. Those moves clearly threatened Pakistan and Iran, since both nations had common borders and tribes.

In the U.S. the reaction from the Administration was again indifferent, and bewildered. The NY Times ran an appeasing editorial titled, "Keeping Cool About Kabul."

However inside Afghanistan, Taraki's harsh rule and the Communist inspired purge were causing many local tribes to began a guerilla war against them. Hafizullah Amin was the number two in the Afghan party and he too became disillusioned with Turaki. As events grew worse Turaki asked the Soviets to intervene which they initially refused. Plans needed to be made.

With the end of all Western colonial rule in Africa the dark continent was ripe for subversion. **There were five separate Communist insurrections happening at the same time in Africa. It was clear to most that the Soviets were determined to gain control of the continent, and if that had happened the West was doomed. Besides their natural resources, Africa had millions of potential soldiers, potential communist soldiers.** Add to that the large numbers of ports and the easy access to S. America and the Middle East even a neophyte could see the strategic implications.

To help their efforts the Communist rulers in Angola had been aiding rebels infiltrating into S. Africa. Their mission was to destabilize the western-capitalist segregationist government that was under increasing worldwide hostility for their racial social policies. In May 1978 troops from S. Africa crossed the border to fight the SWAPO communist guerrillas. Again there was no reaction from the West, America or the U.N.

To the north in Zaire, French and Belgium paratroops had dropped into the besieged town of Kolwezi located in the southern part of the country. Over 3,000 civilians were trapped by the advancing Communists, with dozens of civilians found to have been massacred by the Katangese rebels.

Pres. Carter finally decided to act, and sent eighteen USAF planes to aid in the evacuations. That move constituted the Administration's first military action since taking office over sixteen months ago. Carter tried to make a show of his commitment to countering the Soviet and Cuban forces that were backing the rebels. But the only things his actions demonstrated was that the U.S. was assisting the evacuation of non-communists as the West retreated from the region.

In the Middle East yet another coup in N. Yemen was staged as the new President Al-Gashmi was assassinated on May 24, 1978. Then on the 26th the leader of S. Yemen was suddenly executed and replaced by pro-Soviet ruler Ali Nasser. Every day the western world was being beset by communist agents and forces. And as each day went by nothing was being done in Washington to rectify it.

America

Alexander Solzhenitsyn, one of a group of famous Soviet protestors who had spent decades in the Soviet Gulags, was invited to speak at Harvard's graduation. Solzhenitsyn like the other protestors had become media darlings for their bravery and honor. If anyone knew about the horrors of Communism he was one to tell the tale. But in his speech he chided the increasingly liberal west for their societal declining, for losing their way and their courage. He also chastised them for losing their religion, for it was a guiding light that was instrumental in keeping the oppressed going. *Overnight* Solzhenitsyn *went from a media star to an outcast. He was suddenly ignored and fell from the public eye. That was the price for telling the truth to the elitist liberals.*

By mid-1978 U.S. military expenditures were down to just 5% of the nations GDP. Not since 1948 had our military shrunk to such low levels, and morale in our military forces plummeted. Our military decline was exacerbated by this inane and indifferent Administration. The same thing had happened before, with another Democrat named Truman.

Historical Note: Conservatives around the world had been against Communism since it had been founded. That attitude continued into the 1920's with the Red scare, and into the 1930s during the worldwide depression. They renewed their case when Germany and Russia signed their 1939 non-aggression Pact. The world was stunned again when they proceeded to invade Poland in Sept. 1939. Soon after Russia invaded neutral Finland with the intent of conquering and inserting a Communist regime.

Journalist Herbert Matthews wrote that Fascism and Communism were the same enemy, just on different sides of the political world. (24)

Once we entered the war in Europe, FDR went out of his way to support Stain and Russia. He gave into all of Stalin's needs throughout the war in material, finances and land grabs! (Our aid was titled Lend-Lease. But Stalin never leased anything to us!) After the fighting ended serious political problems arose among the former allies.

In September 1945 our military force was so strong we could have ruled the world. But in late 1945-46 America's immensely powerful military machine was unilaterally disarmed and then emasculated by Pres. Harry Truman. His mindset was to bring the boys home, but Truman did not understand that there was no going home. There were only two dominating powers left on the globe, America and Russia. *Someone had to stay in control for there is no such thing as a power vacuum in this world. As soon as one empire falls a new one takes over.*

As shown in *Fatal Flaws Book 1*, after he took office in April 1945 the unknowing Truman made many correct calls to end the war. **But then he lost the peace, and his worst failure was abandoning Nationalist China.**

Nationalist China had been fighting the Japanese since 1936 when Japan invaded them. (The start of the Pacific side of WWII.) FDR began assisting them in 1938 with the creation of the infamous Flying Tigers led by Col. Claire Chennault. That small air unit was instrumental in keeping Chiang kai Shek and his Nationalists in the war. Without this help and our supplies, it was possible that the defeat of China would have occurred by 1940. *Had China been defeated, it would have freed up multiple Japanese armies, hundreds of aircraft and dozens of naval ships. Those forces could then have taken India and /or Australia in 1941.* It was also possible that the freed up Japanese would have invaded Hawaii causing monumental strategic issues for our Pacific War effort.

Before the war in the Pacific had even ended Truman cast off our long time ally Chiang kai Shek and the Nationalists by disbanding the 14th AAF, (the Flying Tigers) in May 1945. After the surrender of Japan in September 1945, Truman refused to have our troops help our ally in their fight against their Communists led by Mao Tse-tung.

(Mao was greatly aided by Stalin during that time.)

To make those grievous mistakes worse, during that same Chinese civil war Truman interceded twice forcing a ceasefire on Chiang's forces. Both stoppages cost the Nationalists their momentum just as they were within range to defeat the Communists.

The whole purpose of the 1947 Truman Doctrine was to help Greece and Turkey fight off the encroaching and subversive Communists. The 1948 Marshall Plan was used to rebuild Europe to keep the Russian Communists from infiltrating and taking over in the devastation that was now Europe.

In fact Truman had stated that the Truman Doctrine existed because any victory for the Communists meant a defeat for non-communists everywhere! But inanely Truman and his administration's anticommunist outlook only applied to Europe.

(Was it racism or was he tricked by Communist subversives in our government.)

By not helping Chiang and the Nationalists win, China fell to Mao and the Communists. Communist China then began helping Ho Chi Minh and his Communists in northern Vietnam, and the French could not defeat them. During February 1950 China and Russia signed a Friendship Pact. Soon after Communist North Korea invaded South Korea. **Faced with a crisis he had actually created, Truman then committed our military forces to fight in Korea without consulting Congress.**

When the war in Korea landed upon us in June 1950 the greatly reduced and untrained U.S. Army was a hollow shell of its former self. Only the solid generalship of Matt Ridgeway in 1951 and James Van Fleet saved it from defeat and returned it to functionality. (The underfunded USMC fought fine on their own.) *A pyrrhic victory was obtained in Korea, with the South remaining free, but the Communist North constantly threatened war and tied up vast U.S. resources to keep them at bay.*

Truman's failures in China again reappeared when the French forces were finally defeated in Indochina in 1954. In the peace treaty that followed, Cambodia and Laos were granted their freedom and Vietnam was partitioned (as had Korea in 1945). That set the stage for our next war against Communism, trying to protect S. Vietnam. As shown in the first pages of this book, in 1975 the Communists eventually defeated the S. Vietnamese and Cambodia, and took over all of Indo-China. (And the web of history goes on.)

As a result of all of those previous failures, our flawed national leaders of the 1960s inadvertently destroyed our army in the war in Vietnam. By 1974 few troops would re-enlist, and without solid leadership at the squad and platoon level our army was collapsing. Future general Barry McCaffrey who was stationed in Germany in the 1970s wrote, there were gang rapes in the barracks, and officers carried loaded pistols for protection. Drugs and racial strife were the norm. America had to build a new military, one that was based on volunteers, and we had to work quickly for the Russians saw our weakness.

General Creighton Abrams had fought in Europe in WWII, taken over for the disgraced Westmoreland in Vietnam in 1969, and became Chief of Staff of the Army in 1973. To try to save what was left of the army Abrams began discharging thousands of undesirables. McCaffrey recalled that units were thrilled as the "draftee bums" were being dismissed. Soon after Abrams would fall from cancer and Gen. William DePuy would step in. He continued to rebuild the U.S. Army and senior officers made additional vital changes. Training was revolutionized and realistic field exercises improved unit operations. Advanced training grounds with laser weapons insured the "live-fire" training seemed real. Our volunteer soldiers quickly saw who lived and who did not, and efficiency went up. Candid discussions were finally allowed among the officer ranks and it was hoped the scamming and ticket punching for commands would end. (It did not.)

The one thing that most needed to be changed in the Army was the poor generalship. Sadly that escaped intact as did the old boys club that advanced favored careers remained.

Gen. DePuy instituted five major new weapons systems, the Abrams M-1 computerized tank to replace the aging M-60 Patton's, the Bradley Fighting Vehicle to replace the APC troop carriers, the Apache attack helicopter would replace the Cobras, the Black Hawk transport helicopter would replace the Huey, and a new mobile anti-aircraft system to give the troops some protection from Russian aircraft. All of this equipment would be computerized and required educated and dedicated troops to man them. Costs were anticipated to be high, and the disinterested Congress of the 1970s fought against them.

From the White House Carter also fought against the Department of Defense requests and many of their new strategic weapons programs such as the B-1 bomber, the Trident Submarines, the ERW enhanced radiation weapon commonly called the neutron bomb and the MX strategic missile system. In 1977 he cut the DOD budget, which was low to start with, by another $6 Billion. During June of that year Carter cancelled the B-1 bomber and told Sec. State Vance to cancel the Trident Submarine program completely if a SALT treaty seemed possible. In April 1978 Carter shut down the ERW - Neutron bomb program against the wishes of many of his principal advisors. He also called for troop reductions in S. Korea and talked about ending our nuclear triad of launchers. (His initial disarmament plan had been stopped by the Congress, but he was still trying to weaken us.)

Of the four main programs he opposed, the dismissal of the ERW was his worst decision. The Neutron bomb was a smaller nuclear weapon and would have been devastating against any invading Russian tank-infantry formations. It was a low yield munition and its smaller explosion would spare the European countryside from nuclear devastation. *That was the one weapon program that could have stopped and prevented any potential Soviet invasion saving millions of lives.*

The Soviets had been very unhappy over that weapon system as it rendered their entire land strategy obsolete. To help defeat it the KGB had manufactured large protests in Europe. Carter was bothered by the protests, and unilaterally cancelled ERW. *(Carter secured nothing from the Soviets in return. At the least he could have used the ERW as bargaining chips.)*

During Carter's years he wrongly subordinated our security policies to achieve his moral and questionable arms control objectives, rather than shaping his arms control agenda around our security needs. Senator John Tower was in Moscow a short time after Carter cancelled the B-1 bomber program. Tower asked Russian arms negotiator Alexander Shchukin what the Soviets would reciprocate with. The Russian smiled and said, "I am neither a pacifist nor a philanthropist." You did that on your own. * (25)

As the arms control talks continued Administration negotiations over SALT II failed to reign in the latest Soviet missile designs of the SS-18s, SS-19s or their new Backfire bombers. One conciliatory side statement the Russians gave was that they would build only thirty of the new bombers per year. But our satellite photos picked up twice that rate of production, yet again a Soviet lie. At that rate of production their bombers would overwhelm us in an attack when they struck. European fears of Carter and his policies appeared quickly.

On May 22, 1977 Carter lifted the ban on Americans traveling to Cuba or N. Korea. Strangely Carter had a cordial relationship with N. Korea's Kim Il Sung, and after the 1976 campaign ended he wanted to pull our troops from S. Korea.

In a speech given on May 22, he stated he was ashamed that Americans had such an inordinate fear of Communism.

It appeared that Carter was actually surrendering. * (26)

(Days after the speech Castro sent additional troops to fight in Ethiopia.)

In late 1977 the Soviets began deploying their new medium range nuclear missiles the SS-20 to threaten Western Europe and Asia. At that time the West had no counter system to that threat except the ERW munitions. Similar to Britain and pre-WWII Prime Minister Neville Chamberlain, Carter wanted to be known as a peacemaker. But as was seen in the 1930s that character trait led to war.

Facing an increasingly hostile Soviet Union, many European leaders demanded an American response to the recent Soviet actions. But all that they saw was weakness. Carter's indecisions, vacillations and poor decisions was inducing serious doubts inside Europe's capitols. Was America going to abandon them too? (Germany's Chancellor Helmut Schmidt met with the other European leaders in London in the fall of 1977. All who attended were urging the U.S. to respond.)

Conservative California Governor Ronald Reagan was out of office since 1975, and the Democrats had taken over. Soon after that political change Californians saw an incredible rise in their state taxes. Almost all of it was due to the massive social programs that were instituted and sucked up vast amounts of revenue but gave almost nothing back to the municipality. (Versus money used for Fire, Sanitation or Police costs.) *When the June vote was tallied two thirds of the state voters approved the measure cutting property taxes by 57%.* The result was a sharp cut in municipal services in the poorly run state, but not to the social programs. California voters passed Proposition 13 on June 6, 1978 to try to stop the runaway taxes that were crippling their state.

Carter had previously approved the Federal Government giving NYC a $2 billion bond to keep the city going. Though Mayor Koch and the financial overseers had made a lot of fiscal progress since 1975, the city was still ailing. As shown before massive welfare requirements were draining the municipality. One example of that extreme cost; the city had built and tried to maintain at great cost hundreds of large housing-project buildings to house the one million citizens on public support. But vandals and criminals infested those structures causing millions of dollars in damages each year. As shown earlier out of control crime, drugs and arson were constant occurrences as the city slowly died. Unless the national economy turned around bankruptcy was just around the corner.

One of the "unseen fallouts" from the crime and arson epidemic that was sweeping the nation's urban areas was the secondary decrease in tax revenue. Each building that was destroyed by fire falls off of the municipality's tax rolls, thus less tax money is collected. In the case of commercial buildings the result is magnified many times since each structure could house multiple companies which all pay numerous taxes to the city via payroll, sales taxes, fees and licensing etc. If a large commercial building is severely damaged or destroyed by fire those jobs are lost as was all of that tax revenue. And following close behind are the secondary tax loses in food service, local subcontractors, shipping, transportation, etc. After a severe fire it can take years for some of those businesses to recover, if they return at all.

As the municipality's tax base falls inevitably the bean counters look to cutting services to reduce their debt. (Like California did.) Most times that foolishly included cuts to the Fire Service which at that time in NYC was already stretched to its limit by the arson wave and social/crime issues. More cuts to the Fire Service meant more losses to the flames, and a tragic cycle was repeated until you have a sight such as NYC in the late 1970s or Detroit, Michigan as it still exists today. (What was once a vibrant and large urban center of commerce and manufacturing in Detroit has now become a ghost town of empty lots and burned out/abandoned buildings.) Our nation was sinking into a deep despair.

(I was sworn into the FDNY in 1980 and would witness all of the above not just as a citizen but also as a firefighter. A great read on that time period would be *Report From Engine Company 82* by Dennis Smith who was based in that unit in the South Bronx. His book runs from 1968-1975. My book on the FDNY, *My Turn on the Firelines 1980-2003 is a solid follow up covering stories from the Lower East Side to Times Square to Washington Heights and September 11.*)

Foreign Affairs

On August 19, 1978 **Islamic terrorists** set fire to the Rex Cinema in Abadan, Iran murdering over 475 people. The Islamists were trying to weaken the rule of the Shah, and naturally the propagandists blamed his government for the flaming massacre. Only one newspaper the *Sohhe Emruz* boldly pointed the finger at the Islamic militants. That paper was quickly besieged by the terrorists and their allies, and swiftly shut down.

(That same nefarious style of thought control is currently in place within the U.S. Anyone or any entity that deviates from what the liberals deem "appropriate" is quickly attacked en-mass in an effort to silence and scare them off. Our First Amendment has been stolen by the leftists in their guise of political correctness as they seek to take over and ruin our country.)

In Nicaragua leftist rebels seized the National Palace on August 22-24, 1978 and took hundreds of government workers, legislators and Somoza family members hostage. The rebels, known as the Sandinista National Liberation Front, (a reference to the 1930's leftist rebel Sandino) had grown to a dangerous level in their quest to depose Pres. Anastasio Somoza. He was another hard-line ruler who the Democrats hated and the Communists wanted to replace. *Similar to Truman's inane demands on Chiang kai-Shek in China in 1946, the Carter Administration urged Somoza to negotiate with the Sandinistas even if it meant his resigning!*

To save the hostages Somoza paid a large ransom and released dozens of FSLN rebels from prison. Panama's leftist leader Torrijos sent a plane to Managua and flew the Sandinista rebels to Panama. Torrijos had been a major supporter of the Sandinistas from the beginning of his rule, and after a short rest and refit in Panama, Torrijos returned all of those insurgents to Nicaragua. Well supplied with arms from Cuba, Venezuela and Panama, those rebels were well trained by the Cubans. *Their "civil war" was turning into a conventional one, and the Communists were again winning.*

To help them succeed, Carter cutoff all military aid to the Somoza regime even though his country had free enterprise, religious freedom, an open press and semi-democratic elections. Carter's action gave full support to the Communists who offered none of those things.

His Administration was so jaded with left-wing politicos that an Israeli ship carrying military supplies bound for Somoza's Nicaragua was forced to turn back. All arms markets were closed to Somoza's government, and even the IMF, International Monetary Fund was directed as off limits to Nicaragua. **Under Carter' inane policies the IRS was instructed to allow donations to the Communist Sandinistas as a U.S. tax write off!** * (27)

In neighboring Guatemala nationwide strikes paralyzed that country as leftist rebels sought to expand their influence. They too were under increasing communist agitation, and to many it seemed as if we had lost the Cold War.

Egypt's Pres. Sadat, Israel's PM Begin and Pres. Carter met at Camp David in Virginia for a peace conference on September 5, 1978. For thirteen days the negotiating teams stayed at the task to get a peace proposal. They met with the hope of achieving a military stand down in the Sinai, the elimination of Israeli settlements in the West Bank and Gaza Strip, and an agreement to return to the pre-1967 war borders. For Israel to agree to those terms it would require a serious trade off from Egypt.

Carter wanted the Egyptian-Israeli negotiations to include the future of the West Bank and Gaza. His interference was not welcome by Egypt or Israel, and the peace that was obtained was not a result of his actions, but in spite of them. Carter also tried to impose the Soviets into the negotiations. Sadat harshly objected, but Carter continued this inane line of operating and tried to bring in Syria and Jordan too. Despite all of Carter's strange interference the peace process that had been started by Sadat and Begin in 1977 continued. (The last thing Sadat wanted was for the Soviets to get involved. He knew personally how they operated, and they were not there to make peace but to foment dissent.)

For some strange reason Carter picked that time to approve the sale of F-15 fighter bombers to Saudi Arabia. Those were our newest and best aircraft, and Israel had recently purchased both the F-15 & F-16s. With this latest sale Carter was allowing them to go to an enemy of Israel, and naturally the Israelis were outraged. Congress reluctantly approved the deal with the Saudi's, but only if the aircraft were modified with limited flying ranges.

When the parties signed the Camp David Accords Israel agreed to leave the Sinai completely and to exchange normal ties with Egypt. Egypt agreed to end their negative and hostile press coverage of Israel. *The United States served as guarantor of the agreement and provided $Billions in aid to both nations annually.* A five year period of Palestinian autonomy would be followed by talks on territorial status and statehood, but all terrorism must end. Televised coverage of the Camp David Accords insured the world saw the peace process unfolding. But in the Islamic world there was shock to see such bitter enemies cooperating, and many of their leaders were highly critical of Pres. Sadat.

Anwar Sadat had been a member of the Muslim Brotherhood in the 1940s, and joined up with Nasser's left-leaning government in the 1950s. He rose through the ranks and took over after Nasser's death. Sadat worked hard to eliminate the leftists and kicked the Soviets out of Egypt in 1972. To aid him in his efforts he had re-joined forces with the ultra-conservative Muslim Brotherhood. But Sadat realized after Egypt's defeat in the 1973 War that the Arab states could not defeat Israel.

(Supplied with tons of arms and weapons from Russia, Egypt and Syria launched a well executed surprise invasion and gained the upper hand the first two days. But the Syrians were poorly led and motivated, which squandered their forces and gave them defeat. The Israelis then turned their attention to the strung out Egyptians and routed them too.)

As shown earlier Pres. Sadat had contacted Pres. Nixon back in 1971 and both wanted to mend fences. During Pres. Nixon's June 1974 foreign policy trip they finally met and Nixon promised that a new beginning could be started if Sadat wanted to. He did, and U.S. aid was soon given to Egypt. Nixon also visited Syria, Jordan and Saudi Arabia that June, and was met with enthusiastic crowds for his help in ending the Yom Kipper War and saving Egypt and Syria from total defeat. Nixon explained his foreign policy proposals simply, **"We wanted peace for the Middle East, while the Soviets wanted the Middle East".** * (28)

It was from those prior dealings in June 1974 that set the stage for the momentous events at Camp David in 1979.

(Most people do not know this, but Morocco's King Hassan II was the active go-between for Israel and Egypt. His help was vital to securing this peace, and he placed himself at great risk. Like many rulers in the region he was worried about the growing Islamic radicalism that was occurring in Egypt and in his country. Hassan astutely warned all of the parties of this increasing danger in their midst's, but with the Russians aggressively expanding across the globe no one listened.)

The photo-op on the White House lawn in March 1979 did not last long. The Egyptians never ended their latent hostility, relations did not normalize and the Palestinian issue remained unchanged. For his attempts at making peace Egypt was boycotted by the other Arab nations, and Sadat would be murdered.

One special Historical Note on this seemingly endless problem:

The area of land listed these past decades as Palestine was originally called Judea, the home of the ancient Jews. They have a true claim to that land. It was the ruling Romans who changed the name of that land to Syria et Palestina, the name of the original enemy of Judea, the Philistines. That name change came in the *second century* as a result of the horrific casualties the Romans had suffered in the Bar-Kokhba Jewish revolt. With the rise of Catholicism, Christians, Jews and the desert Bedouins shared the lands for centuries under the rule of the Roman Empire.

Islam became a religion in 610 AD when Mohammed organized it. One major practice of Islam is that they recognize no other religions. Mohammed and his followers took over Arabia by 635 AD, and began spreading (forcing) their religion around the region and into Africa. They conquered the area of Judea/Palestina around 1090 AD. Soon after the period of the Crusades was waged in an effort by the Christian world to retake the "Holy Lands" from the Islamic invaders. They failed and the entire region was ruled by various Muslim rulers, 1095-1291. Throughout that time the same populations lived on that land.

In 1295 the Ottoman Empire was formed and ruled over much of the Middle East extending into Europe. At their peak the Ottoman Empire covered all of present day Egypt, Iraq, Syria, Lebanon, Israel, Sinai coastal N. Africa into Algeria, the Balkans, and into the Ukraine. **Yet even when the Ottoman Empire ruled Judea/Palestina (1300-1922), that land was always inhabited by multiple religions and populations.**

As shown many times the Ottoman Empire was broken up after their defeat in WWI. Separate states were formed from that former empire, and in effect the Ottoman Empire was de-colonized. Even then all of the previous populations and religious groups remained in place.

As the Colonial Governors of England and France redrew the maps of the region and instituted their political/military control, they garnered intense hostility. For their help in WWI, talks were begun of re-creating Judea. Again intense hostility followed stopping it. Economic depression and World War II fell upon the world, and many of the nations in that area aligned with the Nazi's in the hope the French and British would be defeated and forced out. But Germany lost, and it was the post-WWII United Nations that decided to create a Jewish State as a place for the displaced European Jews to have a true homeland. (Many Muslim countries had joined that world body.)

There was never any thought to evicting the other religious or tribal groups from the land, and Israel granted all of those residents citizenship if they stayed. Most of the Muslims who were there refused to live under Jewish rule, and they left the land becoming voluntary refugees. Wars and suffering became normal conditions, with the last war being fought in 1973.

By 1978 Israel's population was only 2% of the total in the Middle East, and its land mass was less than 1%. There were over 1.6 billion Muslims worldwide, while there was only 40 million Jews. Yet for over forty years the only thing any of the Arab nations could fixate on was the creation of Israel. All during those past decades none of the Arab nations accepted the U.N. ruling even though they had signed up to join that world body and its decisions.

And none of those nations set aside any land to give to the Palestinian people as a homeland for those who refused to live inside the nation of Israel. During the past decades the Arab rulers spent billions on armaments to make war, instead of spending a tenth of the money and working together to create a nation for the Palestinians who voluntarily left that land.

Anwar Sadat recognized that issue, and agreed it was time for change. With Henry Kissinger's follow on diplomacy under Pres. Ford, Egypt's hardline stance was ended. War would not solve the problems between their nations, it was time to use their money and resources for better purposes. U.S. aid began the healing process as Egypt turned away from the Soviets. The Western world was pleased as it seemed peace in the Middle East might be possible, but again that is not what the Islamic extremists wanted to hear. They wanted to rule.

Carter-France-Iran

Iran and France had had close commercial ties for decades. Yet they continued to allow Ayatollah Khomeini to setup an "Iranian Government in exile" outside of Paris and have access to the western media and money. This never-ending blitz increased the appeasement pressures from the West on the Shah.

(It made no strategic sense for French Pres. Valery Giscard d'Estaing to have allowed this enemy to Iran and western interests a safe haven.)

Khomeini had a bass toned voice that was considered serene and moving. Even the social and intellectual elite in Iran were enthused by his words. (His speaking ability was almost as good as Adolph Hitler.)

As France's philosopher Voltaire` would write, "Those who can make you believe in absurdities, can also make you commit atrocities." * (29)

Carter naively thought of the Ayatollah as a religious figure, while the senior people at Vance's State Dept. thought he would be a "model of human rights concerns".

But Khomeini actually had a long history of terrorism. During the 1960s into the 70s he was noted by the CIA of working closely with the Islamic Terrorist group *Mujahedeen-e-Khalq,* and he was listed as an extremist. Khomeini had issued decrees for all Shia to support his efforts against the Shah and for the faithful to provide them with funding. Money was raised in bazaars and funneled to Khomeini who gave it to his agitators/ terrorists to keep their anti-Shah attacks going. During June 1973 two U.S. army officers in Iran were murdered by the *Mujahedeen-e-Khalq,* and in August 1976 three U.S. civilians were.

While he resided in Najaf, Iraq, Khomeini had, (mentioned previously) met with PLO leader Yassir Arafat. **They joined forces to work against Israel, America and the Shah.** Both routinely operated with various Marxist entities and terrorists. Anything that needed to be done was done to further their goals. In May 1978 organized bloody riots erupted in most of Iran's cities. Evidence was eventually obtained that those well planned riots **had utilized trained Palestinian extremists** to spark the furor.

Religious fervor was becoming the new norm in the country as "Iranian insurgents" demanded the closing of all theaters, bars, nightclubs, television and ending the emancipation of Iranian women. Soon after those initial staged events had occurred, the previously mentioned savage August theatre fire-bombing was setoff killing hundreds of innocents.

Khomeini and his supporters which included the PLO decided to force their religious proposals through by the use of terrorism. With the continuing turmoil inside Iran martial law was finally imposed. That drew complaints from liberal groups about the "heavy handed tactics" being used by the Shah's security forces to maintain order.

The next round of trouble in the well formulated insurgent plan was to use organized strikes in the oil fields and industrial plants to shut down the economy. To assist his forces in trying to control the rioters, the Shah asked to purchase U.S. issued tear gas, riot gear, and small arms ammunition. Many in the Carter Administration were fiercely opposed to any such sales because of "potential human rights abuses". Lawyers were conveniently provided to all of the Iranian agitators arrested in their riots to insure "their court cases were handled fairly".

(However no lawyers would be present after the "Ayatollah's kangaroo courts" were in session. "The guilty" were quickly executed. Case Closed, Next.)

Despite this clear and present danger the Carter administration continued to double talk the Shah during those tense months. *In October 1978 Carter sent Theodore Eliot Jr. from the State Dept. to speak with Khomeini and his entourage.* Khomeini showed no interest, but Carter continued to placate him. Carter also sent a military liaison of Generals Haig and Huyser to Tehran to try to shore up the Iranian military so they could take over. (Carter's plan to remove the Shah.)

All the while Iranian security and intelligence officials were warning that the Soviets were becoming more active in the region. The Shah even wrote a letter to Carter alerting him

that Russia had aggressive plans for Afghanistan. Still Carter refused to support his rule. (None of the previous Democratic presidents had supported Iran, and Carter followed that line.)

On November 6, 1978 the Shah reluctantly placed the military in charge of his troubled country. *Moscow then issued a warning to Carter not to interfere with the internal troubles inside Iran as serious security issues would arise!* The State Dept. gave a weak response that nothing would be done to interfere in Iran.

Ayatollah Khomeini lived in a Paris suburb and was on television and in the press everyday demanding an end to the Shah's rule. As with all good liars, the Ayatollah would routinely deny that his new Islamic Republic would be run by the mullahs. (When he was in Iraq his face was never shown on Iranian TV.)

France has a strange passion for harboring Islamic revolutionaries. After WWII ended they harbored the "mufti of Jerusalem", Haj Amin el-Husseini who was a wanted war criminal for siding with Hitler. (Both Husseini and Khomeini were fascists.) France also built up the military and industrial capability of Iraq's Saddam Hussein and Libya's Momar Qaddafi. (Qaddafi had overthrown King Idris in 1969 and closed the U.S. base. Soviet arms and advisors soon poured into the region, and with it came new subversive wars.) And it was France that had turned Yassir Arafat into a "world figure" even though he was a known terrorist.

In 1978 French leaders naively believed the Ayatollah would be grateful for their years of assistance. Carter also foolishly believed the Ayatollah would be glad if we withdrew our support for the Shah. He thought that appeasing the Islamists would avoid any civil conflict, and he secretly wanted the Iranian military to seize power to prevent one. *His moralism was so extreme he completely discounted the strategic implications for the region.* Throughout his one term Carter's State Dept. continued to complain about Iranian human rights abuses no matter how trivial, which added to the turmoil and negativity inside the Shah's Iran. *Yet once the Ayatollah took over Carter's State Dept had nothing to say on his rule. Carter and the French would be proven fatally wrong with their decisions. But they did not suffer from them.*

During January 1979 a private meeting was held in Guadalupe. Present were Carter, France's Giscard D'Estaing, Germany's Helmut Schmidt, and Britain's James Callahan. All three Europeans were deadly serious, the hot breath of the Russian bear was upon Europe's neck and a deterrent had to be found to keep them at bay. During the past year tensions between the West and Communism had escalated dramatically. Russia had continued emplacing their medium range SS-20 nuclear missiles throughout Eastern Europe, and the Communist Warsaw Pact units ran extensive military exercises and war gamed constantly. America's military and political demise from Vietnam was still in full swing and obvious to all. Many of the world leaders feared a Soviet led Communist invasion of Europe was coming.

To try to gain some footing in the event war did come, (and save themselves), *France made a secret pact with the U.S. to allow us access to their ports and rail networks.* As shown before America had been banned from France by De Gaulle back in 1966, but with the latest Soviets actions "we were now being invited back." This secret pact was the only way to save Europe if the Soviets made a conventional armored attack. With their huge advantage in conventional weapons the Soviets would overrun the northern European ports quickly. Southern France was the only alternative.

At that time America was completing the research and development (R&D) of the Pershing II medium range missile and a nuclear tipped cruise missile. They were the Allies best choice in a tit for tat move against the deployments of the newest Soviet weapons. However it was decided not to deploy them yet, just announce that they were ready for deployment if need be. As usual with Democracies there were dozens of hurdles and a lot more talking needed before a final plan was drafted on December 11, 1979. To placate the Soviets, the peaceniks and the liberals in Europe it was announced that those newer missiles would just replace older ones, and 1,000 older warheads were being removed from service.

While in Guadalupe, Carter surprised those leaders by stating it was time for a political change in Iran. He had met with the Shah back in January 1978 claiming our loyalty, but had changed his mind. **Even though a mid-1978 French intelligence report warned the CIA about Khomeini's intentions, and a CIA report dated November 20, 1978 warned that Khomeini was xenophobic and a danger to the West, Carter was backing the cleric.** French President Valery Giscard d'Estaing privately cursed Carter for his callous abandonment of a man all had supported for so long.   *(29a)

With the populace becoming more militant and uncontrollable the Shah reluctantly went into exile in January 16, 1979. The NY Times and most of the other leftist media were pleased that the Shah was out of power. Pres. Sadat of Egypt welcomed his friend, and felt the fanatical Khomeini would do drastic harm to Islam and

Iran. The West lost an invaluable ally who had stood by them whenever he was needed. **Once again a Democratic President had abandoned a former friend. It would not be the last time.**

On January 19, 1979 the CIA prepared a special report on Khomeini and his aides Abolhasan Bani-Sadr and Sadegh Ghotzbadeh. Both men had ties to Palestinian terrorists, though the CIA had tried to recruit Bani-Sadr once. Khomeini was considered an anti-communist, but those around him might not be. The CIA warned that serious trouble could develop in Iran.

With the Shah gone people poured into the streets of Iran in celebration. Iranian Prime Minister Shapour Bakhtiar assumed control of the government and he reluctantly allowed the Ayatollah Khomeini to return from exile. Bakhtiar had initially refused to allow him back because of Khomeini's insistence on forming an alternative government. He pleaded with the Ayatollah that they needed more time to restore order, but he was forced to back down under clouds of protests by the "militants that were now everywhere".

For the Ayatollah fifteen years of exile ended on February 1, 1979 when Khomeini returned to Tehran. Fearing an attack or sabotage, Khomeini and his supporters rented a charter Air France flight with a volunteer crew. *They "welcomed more than one hundred journalists" to come aboard and witness his return to Iran.* What those naive 120 civilians did not realize was that they were there as human shields to prevent any action upon the jet.

(Khomeini left his wife and extended family behind just in case the "insurance policy of western journalists" did not work.)

Everything in the nation had stopped functioning. Iran's military, especially the air force had been built up to a high level, but they had been breaking up over the past weeks amid months of political turmoil. Khomeini and his minions had worked especially hard on them with intense propaganda the past two years. His plan worked out just the way the Islamists wanted, the Iranian air force was not there when things turned bad.

South East Asia

In the years since America had left Southeast Asia, Cambodia had become a client state of China, while Vietnam sided with the Soviets. It was estimated that two to three million had been killed in the chaos the "Democratic Republic of Kampuchea" had become. Their economy had collapsed completely, and famine purposely swept the land. Reports from refugees told of how stealing a banana was an immediate death sentence. Couples could only visit each other twice a year to conceive, and flirting was a death sentence as was any public displays of affection or laughing. It is enlightening that each communist leader watched and learned from the earlier ones, and would integrate some of the previous lessons onto their particular *criminal enterprise*. "Cambodia's Pol Pot learned his Marxist ways in Paris during the 1950's, when French philosophers were vainly trying to explain how terrorism-ala-Communist ideology would lead to humanism." (30)

But Pol Pot's Communist Khmer Rouge were the worst of the worst. One out of every seven Cambodians had benn killed in the lawless and mindless slaughter of their own citizens. It was apparent to all who cared to see just how demented their Communist indoctrination programs were.

(Lenin had stated to his followers decades before, murder and terrorize the people until they give in and accept Communism. Lenin called the masses "noxious insects")

In January 1977 Pol Pot began sending Khmer raiding parties into Laos, Thailand and Vietnam. They would routinely plunder and burn any unfortunate villages they ran across and murder everyone present. The Khmer plot for Vietnam was to depopulate the area along the Mekong River and "retake" what was theirs from centuries ago. *By December 1978 conditions inside Cambodia had fallen into such a maelstrom of death and suffering, and the Khmer border raids had reached such a serious intensity, that Vietnam decided they had to invade and stop them.* (At the Vietnamese village of Ba Chuc over 3,000 were slaughtered.)

The Vietnamese Communists decided the demented Pol Pot and his Communists had to go, and a government run by their forces would be installed. To accomplish that objective Hanoi committed over 120,000 troops to the invasion of Cambodia!

Bloody battles began between those SE Asia Communist neighbors on December 25, 1978. (For many of us that was a fine holiday gift.) After just a few weeks of heavy fighting the Vietnamese forces gained control of Phom Penh. By January 1979 all of southeast Cambodia was under Vietnam's control. Their attacks continued, and by February 1979 the proficient Vietnamese Army forced the Khmer Rouge into complete collapse. Khmer survivors escaped into the jungles along and across the border with Thailand to try to regroup. Pol Pot had also escaped there with some loyalists and their remaining forces. But the Khmer Rouge were never able to return, and the Vietnamese Army remained in control of Cambodia until 1989.

Former Khmer Rouge leader Heng Samrin was one of a few who did not agree with Pol Pot or his polices. His sector of control did not employ the *killing fields* as a way to enforce their takeover. Disturbed with what he was hearing Samrin had led an unsuccessful coup against Pot in 1976. He was quickly defeated and forced to escape into Vietnam. When the Vietnamese invaded Cambodia, Samrin fought with them and was directed to run the eastern section of Cambodia. Once the Khmer forces were driven out of the entire country the Vietnamese installed him as the new President of Kampuchea. *But the war had a new chapter coming.*

Senior NVA General Tran Van Tra command the Vietnamese forces when they invaded and defeated the insane Khmer Rouge. (He had been the commander of all Viet Cong forces during the Vietnam War, while NVA General Van Tien Dung was the commander of all NVA, North Vietnamese Army forces. Their superior throughout the war General Vo Nguyen Giap.)

After the fall of South Vietnam, Gen. Tran become the commander in the occupation of Saigon. It was he who oversaw the harsh post-war relocations and re-education of the city's residents. Gen. Tran would retire in1981 and wrote a military volume that was critical of the NVA strategy and tactics, especially during TET in 1968. As a result of that truthful work, *(always a bad idea around liberals and Communists),* he would be purged from the Party in 1982, dying alone in his home confinement. In the world of Communism, the Party is always right.

China

On January 1, 1979 America severed all diplomatic ties to the Nationalists on Taiwan. Full diplomatic relations were established with (Red China), the People's Republic of China. Deng Xiaoping became the new leader of the most populous nation, and was making great strides in modernizing post-Mao China. His agricultural reforms allowed the peasants to sell their products on the open market, instead of the produce being confiscated by the party. *Farm production soared.*

To compensate the Party their farmers paid the Chinese State rent for any land they tilled. As the farmers made extra money on their produce itt enabled them to build better housing for themselves and purchase more and better farm tools to further increase their yields. *This new farming model was in great contrast to the underfed Russian and European Communists, and it was a lesson that would soon spread to them.* Even the hardiest Communist could see the cause and effect relationship on farm production, and the infusion of rent-money greatly benefitted China's bottom line. That allowed them to purchase U.S. weapon systems, and then figure out how they worked to make their own.

(Again this reconciliation between us and China was giving the Soviets nightmares. Russia depended on their massed armies to defeat the West. But they knew that *even they* could be defeated by China's massed armies. Having China aligned with America buying and using American arms was a severe danger to them.)

A Chinese delegation arrived in Washington for the official diplomatic ceremony and meetings on January 29-30, 1979. Deng was there and asked for a semi-private meeting with Carter and staff. *Behind closed doors Deng alerted the White House that China was preparing to "put a restraint on the Vietnamese and teach them a lesson".* * (31) Carter cautioned moderation, but stated we would not interfere in that situation.

At a follow on meeting the outspoken Chinese ruler criticized the Carter Administration on all of the current U.S. actions and agreements that were being made with the Soviets. **Deng stated that Carter's policies in foreign affairs were prompting the Soviets into taking direct action, and sternly warned National Security Advisor Brzezinski that all of your agreements with the Russians are the product of U.S. concessions, not actual negotiations!** It was dangerous to continue down that path.

Historical Note: One feature that is often overlooked when people think of China is the fact they have a history spanning millennia. No matter who rules or for how long, China is always there. *Thus the Chinese look at everything in the "long term".* Only a small number of Europe's nations have a history of a few hundred years, some are as young or younger than America.

To showcase the Chinese way of thinking; when Henry Kissinger first spoke with Chinese premier Chou En-Lai back in 1972, he asked the hard core leader what he thought of the French Revolution of 1789? Characteristically Chou thought for a moment and then replied, *"It is too soon to tell."* * (32)

Within days of those meetings fourteen Chinese army divisions were setup on the northern border of Vietnam. A second echelon was also approaching the border areas. CIA warned that with this massive force it was possible China would invade and go into Hanoi. They also warned that the Soviets could intervene, but would probably stay out of the issue unless the Chinese threaten to take over Vietnam.

China and Pol Pot had a history of supporting each other, and as the Vietnamese invasion continued China had attempted to reign them in. But Vietnam refused any negotiations.

To try to support their collapsing client state, Red China invaded Vietnam on February 17, 1979. Over 200,000 Chinese swarmed across their common border. It seemed as if all of the Asian Communists would kill each other as a second large war progressed.

Upset with this invasion the Soviets again warned the Chinese to end it before it was too late. But the Soviets stayed out of the war, and sent only ten flights of arms and supplies to Vietnam. (They had sent one flight every to Ethiopia every twenty minutes for three months! Apparently even Communists lose interest.)

Ironically by March 5 the Chinese had to stop their invasion and begin retreating. They too found the Vietnamese a tough adversary as over 10% of their force had become casualties in less than two weeks! When they finally exited Vietnam, the Chinese had suffered over 26,000 killed and 37,000 wounded. (This was the first large scale fighting the Chinese military had been involved in since Korea in 1953, and they were relearning many lessons the hard way.)

By the end of March all of the Chinese units had crossed back to their side of the border, bested by the Vietnamese Army they had helped to create. Many nations of the world condemned Vietnam for their invasion of Kampuchea. But even Carter and his bizarre State Dept. were highly critical. *(Why would anyone in our government be upset that the suffering and murdering in Cambodia was being stopped??!)*

There was one unnoticed strategic fallout from those two wars. With Pol Pot's Khmer Rouge and China's defeat, China was no longer able to flank Vietnam via Cambodia. For Vietnam that was a potential life saver. As had happened to S. Vietnam in 1975, the Communists running Vietnam in 1979 knew they would not be able to defeat Chinese armies coming at them from two sides. To gain a strong ally, Vietnam opened their door to the Soviets and they began using our old naval base at Cam Ranh Bay. The Soviets also constructed a large SIGINT center in Vietnam similar to the one they had built at Lourdes, Cuba. (Their target from the base in Vietnam obviously was China.)

Iran

Back in Iran the return of militant cleric Khomeini had been greeted by millions at first. But in just days revolutionary fervor was unleashed by the extremist Shiite rulers. Khomeini told his supporters that he would cleanse Iran of all undesirable elements. "Our final victory will come when all foreigners are out of our country".

One of Khomeini's long-time supporters was Mustafa Ali Chamran. Like so many young students he left Iran in 1957 to get a degree in physics from Berkley. With that done Chamran moved to Lebanon and married a Palestinian woman. *While living there he became indoctrinated in PLO goals and he oversaw the training of any Iranians that went to PLO camps. But his specialty was smuggling PLO terrorists and arms into Iran.*

It was learned that PLO terrorists were the organized rioters that had caused most of the violence and damage inside Iran the past months!

Soon after Khomeini returned, the Israeli embassy in Tehran was ransacked and set on fire. The PLO took over the building, and Yassir Arafat traveled to Iran to preside over the ceremony of taking over the Israeli embassy. **In his speech he gloated on how the PLO had trained 10,000 Iranian revolutionaries to make this day possible!**

(Over 1,300 Israeli diplomats, engineers, instructors, scientists and business people were still in the country. Most made a harrowing escape from the mullahs and their execution squads.)

Arafat also told the world how the PLO provided weapons and hundreds of their fighters to help the "Iranian Revolution" succeed. **Khomeini agreed, and thanked Arafat for the PLO assistance. He promised to return the favor and send Iranian volunteers to help the PLO drive Israel from the Middle East!**

(That ceremony was proof that the Iranian rioters were not mere "students", and that their revolt was not home-grown. It was orchestrated by professional non-Iranian agitators. **Carter, his foolish Administration and the voices from the left had perpetrated one of the worst Foreign Policy disasters in our history.** Only Truman's failure in China was worse. *"NY Senator Patrick Moynihan declared that Carter was incapable of distinguishing friend and foe."*) (32A)

Khomeini declared the government of Bakhtiar was illegal and all would be arrested if they did not step down. Khomeini's subterfuge was working overtime, and Bakhtiar's interim government collapsed on February 11, 1979. The next day the Ayatollah Khomeini and his followers seized all power. Once in control, the Ayatollah became just another ruthless despot as he invoked Sharia law onto the foolish and gullible masses.

Khomeini's muscle was his Revolutionary Guards, and their thousands of fanatics obeyed every whim from the Ayatollah. *They had been trained in PLO camps in Lebanon and Libya, and had appeared in Iran's cities months ago causing widespread problems.* Similar to Hitler's Brown-shirts and Lenin's Chekka, the Guards were there to brutalize, torture, savage, and murder anyone who disagreed with the party line. (As the years went by they grew into their own organization making $Billions from stolen businesses and products such as oil.)

Work in Iran's oil fields had already been curtailed from their earlier violence, and after their takeover oil exports from Iran stopped. Oil prices worldwide jumped up again and long lines formed up in America as people waited an hour to get some gas. Fuels were scarce even inside Iran, but Khomeini cared not. He had a nation to conquer and millions to re-educate.

(Unable to remain in Egypt the Shah and his family took forced refuge in Morocco.)

Khomeini appointed Mehdi Bazargan to head his new government. Bazargan had been arrested many times before by the Shah, so that meant he must be someone on Khomeini's side. *Carter was so eager to establish a rapport with the new regime he gave a fawning approval of this ruling group as "Western-educated and cooperative".*

Khomeini severed all Iranian ties to Israel, and used his "new government" to pacify the military to buy time for his plan to take hold. Iran's Army had become divided over religion, and was now ineffectual. Senior military members were told at a special meeting that everything was fine. Stay in your positions and continue to work. Thinking that things were safe most returned to their assignments and then went home.

That night they were all arrested in their beds. Most were killed. (Many commanders had wisely sent their families abroad as a precaution. Their forward thinking saved hundreds of innocent women and children.)

On February 14, 1979 the American Embassy in Tehran was aggressively attacked. Well trained snipers provided covering fire for groups of armed "students" (insurgents) who carried everything from rifles to machine guns. They cut off the water and electricity and quickly breeched the outer wall firing on the embassy itself. From inside the building USMC guards returned fire with shotguns using "birdshot", so as to not be lethal. They were ordered to stand down by Ambassador Sullivan. After that order the assailants entered the building and ransacked the East wing destroying furniture, communications equipment, windows and anything they could find. Sullivan's calls to the Khomeini regime went unanswered for over an hour. At one point many of the staff were held at gunpoint by the *Fedayeen* fighters. Iranian police eventually evicted the "student demonstrators".

Sullivan wrote a scathing report to the State Dept. highlighting how well trained the terrorists were. He felt they were directed by the Popular Front for the Liberation of Palestine. Sullivan outlined how the *Fedayeen* group had infiltrated the embassy using local workers to scout out the building. He stated that PFLP and similar terrorist groups were based in Oman and Yemen, and were Communist controlled. He also stated that their funding comes from the PLO and Libya. *(Earlier reports from the Shah's SAVAK warned that many of the new terrorists in Iran had received training in Cuba.)*

When the Embassy was attacked on the 14th two "students" had been killed by the Marine guards while two Americans were wounded. As the days went by more threats followed. The Administration had been caught completely by surprise, even though Khomeini had warned of their intolerance for foreigners.

Carter and his Administration rejected using any "show of force over this incident". *And they never increased the protection of the embassy, nor did they think of evacuating the U.S. citizens working there!* A day after the attack the State Dept. **began working on a low-profile plan** for evacuating the thousands of Americans who lived and worked in the country. "We just have to wheedle them out the best we can".

Few who were living in Iran could understand the speed with which the Administration had turned on the Shah. Carter and his people readily accepted this Islamic radical who was against anything from the West. Somehow all of Khomeini's beliefs and past hostility was "overlooked". Khomeini often referred to America as the Great Satan, a superpower that must be brought to their knees. To achieve that goal blood would need to flow through the streets of Tehran.

(Ironically the Ayatollah's first ride in Iran was in a Chevy, and a U.S. made helicopter was used to ferry him around.)

A short time later the Pahlavi family was no longer welcome in Morocco, and they sought refuge in Britain, France and then Mexico. They were not welcomed anywhere, and even Carter's promise of asylum in America was reneged on.

One crucial issue that was never reported by the Administration to the public was that Americans in Iran were already being taken captive! Even with this unprecedented capture of U.S. citizens by a foreign government Carter and his principals did not react to the situation militarily or even to put them on alert. And no new security changes were made.

Khomeini hurriedly opened a training center for terrorists and his Revolutionary Guards. *North Koreans and Syrians were brought in as training staff for his new center.* (That site was to have been a University for Girls. Later when Iraq invaded Iran that site was used to indoctrinate the 15-18 year old boys who were to be used as sacrificial lambs on the front lines. "Special work was done" at the center on any Iranians who had returned to Iran from the West. They were required to recant the decadence of the West, especially in America. After they were cleansed of all western corruption they too were sent into the minefields to set off the explosives with their bodies.)

Strangely Khomeini decided not to allow the PLO to train there, though the PLO was allowed to setup bureaus in many Iranian cities.

Khomeini would quote, "Islam says whatever good there is exists thanks to the sword, and remains only because of the sword. People cannot be made obedient without the sword, and the sword is the key to paradise which is only open to true Holy Warriors." *(33)

"The foolish and discontented men and women in Iran broke their old chains, only to forge new ones. They had demolished the rule of the one man who had tried to help them, and then submitted to the tyranny of another who cared not."   *(34)

Days later the Islamic death squads appeared all across the nation. Hundreds of officials who had worked for and backed the Shah were simply lined up and executed. Many of those murdered were military officers and members of the secret police. Cagily the Ayatollah's followers "enlisted some of the more *politically* *correct"* members of those services to remain on duty. But only if they would serve this new master. The smart ones quickly said yes.

(Torture was commonly used at the infamous Evin Prison. Dissidents to Khomeini's revolution were left freezing on the ground, their legs shattered by bats or clubs. Even into the 1990s the mullahs ruled Iran with an iron fist.) *(35)

As they seized control of the nation, Khomeini's minions were getting into every facility they could locate. Untold treasures were being found, and then they discovered the Shah's (U.S. based) intelligence sites located along the Caspian Sea. *America and Iran had been listening to and recording dozens of Soviet communication channels and telemetry data from their missile launches. That intelligence was a windfall for the U.S., and we had provided state of the art equipment for those sites.*

For the Islamic revolutionaries those finds and the knowledge about them convinced the new rulers that all electronic communications could be tracked by America. They would need to be secretive and careful. They also discovered Iran's extensive western backed nuclear-electrical program, but they had new plans.

The Ayatollah saw his takeover in Iran as the first step in his Islamic revolution. He felt that the time was right for Islam to sweep the globe, but it was vital for the U.S. to fall. Only then would all of the Western world submit to Islam. Under his guidance a Muslim theocracy would be established in every corner of the world. For Khomeini, what was happening in Iran was not victory, but a prelude to an Islamic Shia triumph!

Khomeini even outfoxed the Communists in the Tudeh party. He used them in the resistance to the Shah, but banished them once he took over. To the Ayatollah those few dozen thousand "Communist believers" could not hope to overrule the 30 million Persians who had revolted in the name of Islam.

On March 10, 1979 over 15,000 Iranian women marched through the streets protesting the new governmental policies. The Ayatollah had just required that women were to return to the traditional Islamic dress codes, no makeup and covered head to toe. Life in Iran was changing all right, for the worse.

(Just like Obama promised in 2008.)

A referendum was sent to the people and gave them two choices, vote Yes for an Islamic Republic, or No to reject it. A green ballot meant a yes vote, while a red one meant no. *The vote was overseen by his Revolutionary Guards, and the smart ones voted yes.*

There were some political protests over this "national vote". Moderates who had joined the Khomeini bandwagon to get more freedom were unhappy that their New Constitution did not resemble the earlier proposals. They also protested that Khomeini was now Iran's guardian for life. Most of them were soon in prison.

The rule of law in Iran was now Islam.

Everything was permitted, except when it was contrary to Islamic law. And almost everything in the modern world was against Islamic law. Iran was regressing to the Middle Ages.

By the early summer of 1979 almost 75% of the Shah's military officers had been executed. Of the eighty top generals, more than seventy had been tortured and then executed. Khomeini had deviously appointed Islamic mullahs to be the military court prosecutors. Bakhtiar and a few of the other civilian leaders protested the often grisly executions, and the follow-on arrests of 15,000-30,000 civilian leaders and protestors.

But their words were of no use to those who held rifles.

By the end of the year the ranks of Iran's military had been reduced by 100,000. Similar to how the Communists performed their takeovers and indoctrination, Khomeini was removing any potential leaders who might lead an uprising. Influential people, potential leaders and visible protestors were removed first. The masses would get theirs in short order.

Seeing the grim reality Bakhtiar wisely fled Iran for Paris. He attempted to replicate the Ayatollah's cassette tape method to create a movement to unseat the cleric, but it was already too late. *Like all tyrants, Khomeini's fast moving efforts at control had already succeeded.* (Bakhtiar escaped death more than once, but he was finally murdered with his secretary by Iranian or PLO assassins in 1991.)

In his book on Jimmy Carter, author Mike Evans states on page 174 that the Carter Administration had been secretly giving money to Khomeini to the tune of **$150 million dollars!**

Carter so misjudged Khomeini and his intentions that one CIA operative said Carter should have been tried for treason.

His Administration was equally inane. Carter's ambassador to Iran since 1977 was William Sullivan, and he compared Khomeini to Mahatma Gandhi, while Andrew Young at the U.N. foolishly called the radical cleric a "twentieth century saint!" *(36) (During his term Carter and his Administration also gave $500 *million in aid to the Muslim Brotherhood, referring to them as "freedom fighters" for their hostility to Israel.!!)*

Over the border in neighboring Iraq was a desert local called Tuwaitha, just fifteen miles south of Baghdad. At this solitary site a nuclear complex was being built by French companies. Growing yells of protest emanated from Israel, Britain, Saudi Arabia, Syria and America. France's Pres. d'Estaing tried to quiet the criticism by offering a low yield fuel that was not "convertible for bomb making". However Saddam Hussein refused to accept that proposal and threatened to cancel the many other lucrative civilian projects that France was enjoying. *A quiet deal was reached between them.*

France's CEA had just completed the construction of the reactor cores and was preparing to ship them to Iraq. A few days later in April 1979, seven commandos covertly went to southern France and destroyed the cores with explosives. **Israel's Mossad had struck, saving the world from a nuclear nightmare.**

To expedite a new core delivery Saddam sent extra oil to France. His effort was well conceived as France needed the oil to replace what was lost when Iran's revolution cut supplies. And to further sweeten the pot, France was informed that they were in the running for an upcoming naval contract worth almost $2 billion more. For France, Iraq was the best game in town.

During July 1979 Saddam Hussein became the president of Iraq. *He then executed one third of the Revolutionary Council in a sweeping purge of the Ba'ath Party.* Like Russia's Stalin, no one was safe from his maniacal outbursts. And the wily Saddam was not just using France to get his atomic bomb. His agents were trolling the world in search of parts and fuel. China, Brazil and Germany were all eager to sell for the right price.

Nearby North and South Yemen were again involved in a border war. The communist run South was again actively working to destabilize the North. On March 7 the Carter Administration reluctantly decided to send arms and advisors to Yemen. They were beginning to realize the region was imperiled because of all of the recent Soviet actions, and we had to slow them down.

Carter's Fall

At home Jimmy Carter was facing his worst domestic crisis. The energy disaster that he had hoped to avoid exploded in his face. Back in 1973 the Arab boycott saw the price of oil go from $3 per barrel to over $13. Pres. Nixon understood our Achilles heel as our domestic production had already peaked in 1970. Nixon launched *Project Independence* in early 1974 to try to make us energy independent by 1980. To counter his plan OPEC ended their first oil boycott in March 1974. That stabilized the price and "ended the need for Nixon's energy policy changes". Pres. Ford signed off on the 1975 U.S. Energy Policy and Conservation Act, which set 1985 as our goal for energy independence. Since he was an unelected Republican, the Democratic run Congress stopped it.

When Carter took over in January 1977 the price of oil had stabilized around $15 per barrel. Over the next two years worldwide oil prices slowly continued to rise, and then the markets reacted to the situation in Iran. Oil prices again jumped.

On June 30 at the quarterly OPEC meeting in Geneva the members set the price of oil 16% higher than their last meeting. **With that increase Oil would be 50% higher than it had been just a year ago, almost $40 per barrel!**

Gas lines formed all over America as the worldwide supply of oil was reduced. And with those rising energy costs our economy sank into a deep recession as everything cost more. For a nation that had grown dependent on oil and their autos, this was a devastating shock. (In the short period of 1975-1979 Saudi Arabia's annual income had grown to $142 Billion per year!) *For over a week Carter hid out at Camp David trying to come to grips with this crisis he had helped cause.* (Carter's CIA director Stansfield Turner felt the CIA had served the president well during his term, but failed him over Iran.)

It was decided the president needed to speak to the American people, and Carter's televised "malaise speech" chastised Americans for their overindulgent lifestyle. They had to make sacrifices, and the U.S. would strive to find alternative sources of fuel from our shores. This would include gasohol, coal, oil shale, new oil and gas deposits and solar energy. It would take time for these upgrades to occur, and Americans just had to make do.

His speech was one of the worst ever, and Americans were furious that this had happened again. Weeks later a major cabinet shakeup occurred as five of Carter's staff resigned. The rats began leaving the sinking ship. *(Robert Gates wrote in his fine work From the Shadows on how dejected he was working in the Carter White House. He called it, "a very screwed up place."* * (37) It took Gates nine months to get out, and he ended up working for DCI Turner at the CIA. Another man who most people in the Intelligence community detested.)

Historical Note: Had the Nixon-Ford energy programs been started when proposed, the oil shock might not have been as severe as many of those same ideas were already planned. In playing their usual political games the Democrats had shot themselves in the foot, and again hurt our nation and citizens.

Latin America-The Carribean

As shown earlier, the State Dept. followed Carter's left-leaning foreign policies and cut all U.S. ties to the Somoza Regime in Nicaragua. During that time the Communist rebels had been increasing their terrorist attacks, and were causing additional civil unrest which was paralyzing that country. (Just like Iran.) But to the Carter Administration, Somoza should have overlooked all of that and negotiated.

For the Carter Administration human rights concerns were only voiced for conservative regimes. Those ruled from the left, and many of them were terrible regimes, were given a free pass. Somoza rightfully rejected any mediation with the Communist Sandinistas, which upset the pacifists and leftists at the State Dept. so they had cut him off from all aid. With the active backing by the Administration, the OAS, Organization of American States issued a call to replace the Somoza regime.

The Sandinistas "pledged to implement the democratic reforms" demanded by the OAS, including holding elections. They just never said what kind of elections.

(All of this was eerily similar to what Truman had forced upon Chiang and his Nationalists when they were fighting Mao and his Communists.) (see *Fatal Flaws Book 2 1945-1975*)

In neighboring Guatemala the police fired on a leftist group protesting in San Salvador. This group was called the Popular Revolutionary Bloc, and they had occupied the cathedral and the Costa Rican and French Embassies.

Not too far away the Caribbean Island nation of Grenada was also beset by a leftist insurrection. Socialist Maurice Bishop seized power in a coup (with Cuban help), on March 13, 1979. Bishop had been close to Castro for years, and began changing the Grenadian government into a socialist entity. On April 14 a Cuban ship docked and unloaded trucks filled with weapons, ammunition and at least 50 advisors. Strangely Carter asked the CIA if a covert effort could be mounted in Grenada.

In July, the Senate Intelligence Committee was briefed on their plans, and reacted negatively. The CIA ended all thoughts over Grenada, and by September 1979 over 400 Cuban troops were on the island. During December hundreds of additional Cuban advisors, and dozens of tons of weapons and ammo had also arrived. Work began on a military airstrip at Port Salinas.

The Administration was finally getting worried about Cuba. Their proxy wars in Africa, their subversive activity in the region and the increased Soviet activity on Cuba warned of future problems. *As shown before the Soviets had shipped in new MiG-23 fighter-bombers, Soviet submarines and ship traffic arriving in Cuba had tripled, and Soviet troops were stationed and training in Cuba.*

That summer the administration tried to influence Cuba by dangling the end of our embargos. Castro sent two emissaries to NYC to listen to the administration proposal, but after two hours they dismissed the pathetic attempt. *Everything was going their way, there was nothing America could offer.* Vance tried a few more times to get Cuba to turn, but all were similarly refused.

Carter-Russia

Carter's governing was based on his liberal and religious ideology, but he was also unduly influenced by Soviet sponsored disinformation and propaganda campaigns. As shown earlier Carter ended the *U.S. Neutron Bomb project* which affected people, not buildings. Russia had no answer or counter to those weapons, and they would have instantly made obsolete the planned massed attacks of army formations they had built up (at great cost), over the decades of the Cold War. A vital part of the Soviet propaganda effort to defeat the Neutron bomb was that "they pledged not to be the first to use nuclear weapons in Europe". Thus those U.S. weapons were not needed. *However the Russians never said they would not invade Europe!*

The anti-nuclear and peacenik groups which were active and vocal in the West were all partly funded by the Soviets. Those citizens foolishly embraced the Communist lies and propaganda, and fought against all of NATO's efforts to protect Europe.

(After the collapse of communism in Eastern Europe, copies of the Warsaw pact War-Plans were found in East Germany. **They had specifically planned for the early use of tactical nuclear weapons and all varieties of poisonous gases in Europe.** Their battle plan was designed to quickly defeat NATO's front line forces before reinforcements could cross the Atlantic from America. Those Communists felt certain that once the European civilians witnessed the destruction of their frontline defenses, it would convince the survivors to give up and sue for peace.)

Strategically the late 1970s was similar to the weakened state the U.S. had fallen into during Truman's post-WWII years. The Soviets did not disarm back then, we did.

As the Soviets continued to get stronger and placed their medium range SS-20 nuclear missiles throughout Eastern Europe and the Pacific. Fear became a big motivator. *Russia was trying to swing Germany into neutrality as a way to breakup NATO. They even promised them a separate détente for Western Europe if NATO was ended.* The Soviets felt that the European's reluctance to base medium range missiles in their homelands was a true test of European pacifism, they were ready to surrender.

Carter's poor negotiations with Russia were so bad Democratic Senate leader Henry Jackson called his June 1979 SALT II agreement, "appeasement in its purest form". (38) Liberals and defeatists to the end, Sec. Vance and Paul Warnke were the most vocal proponents of this failed premise and treaty. Had it been passed by the Senate it would have insured the Soviets had strategic nuclear superiority fordecades.

Carter had placed so much administrative effort on the SALT II treaty that he could offer the nation little else. Their negotiations were so poorly done SALT II was a serious threat to America's future. For that reason Paul Nitze the long serving senior civilian administrator (since FDR) resigned from the SALT committee. Nitze even testified against the SALT treaty in the Senate hearings giving dire warnings of our coming demise. With his defection from the Democrats, most felt the SALT II treaty had no chance to pass as it required a 2/3 vote in the Senate.

Carter was so desperate for some "good news" he was tempted to use Executive action to try to force the treaty through. Trying to make a deal, he approved the MX missile program, the Stealth aircraft technology, and the Trident Submarine came back on the table, as did some missile improvements. But it would be years before any of those weapons would come out, and none could affect what was happening now.

Henry Kissinger would succinctly state of those past months; *"The Carter Administration has managed the extraordinary feat of having accomplished at the same time, The worst relations in history with our allies, The worst relations in history with our enemies, and creating the most serious upheavals in the developing world since WWII."* *(39)

Historical Note: Nitze was not the only major defector from the defeatist Democrats. Jean Kirkpatrick was a well educated research analyst who had worked for years in various Democratic Party committees and DOD research efforts. Unhappy with their turn to the left she began writing intensely negative articles about Carter and his Administration. She especially became vocal over the loss of Iran and Nicaragua to known entities that were intensely harsh and autocratic. *She wrote on how there would never be any chance for democratic opportunities with those new rulers, and she like so many others could not fathom why they were the new choice of the Democratic Party.* Kirkpatrick decried how these new Democrats blamed America for the world's ills, instead of those who were truly to blame. She would later be hired by Ronald Reagan as the first U.S. woman Ambassador to the United Nations, and officially gave up on the Democrats in 1985.

Iran

On May 25, 1979 the Ayatollah blamed America for an attack on one of Khomeini's top officials. Protestors filled the streets of Iran with hate speech and calls for action. Claiming that the "superpowers were against their revolution," the Ayatollah and his backers had sparked the protests in an effort to keep the people agitating against someone else. Continuing the pursuit of their fundamentalist revolutionary goals, alcohol was banned as well as men and women playing tennis together. Women who did not wear the traditional burkas were being stoned and cursed by lines of Fundamentalists and Revolutionary Guards. Their attacks were clearly designed to intimidate the masses and force their ideology on the country. (Sound familiar?)

The first citizen group that was demonized by the Mullahs was the Shah's entire family. Their executions were ordered by Ayatollah Sadegh Khalkhadi, Khomeini's most vile henchman. The second group that was put down was the Iranian military, and the third were the Iranian communists. The next group to be deemed a scapegoat were the Iranian Kurds. They too had been used by Khomeini to get into power, but at this point they were declared enemies of the Ayatollah and his Shia Islamic Republic. It was open season on Iranian Kurds.

Farah Pahlavi, the former Iranian Queen spoke out about the state of her nation, and the former complainers like Jimmy Carter who had pushed the Shah out. *"What happened to those who cared so much for human rights? How come when the Shah left Iran the Iranian people no longer had any civil rights?*

What has happened to our women, floggings, stoning, amputations, insults and beatings are the new normal for Iranian women. Wonton killings run into the thousands, and that includes anyone who goes outside to demonstrate peacefully. Overwhelming oppression exists in the nameof Islam, and now rules our country.

What happened to all of those who pretended to care? *(40)

General Alexander Haig the Supreme Commander of NATO made a simple statement about Iran. "It did not take long for the world to realize that the Shah was an enlightened liberal compared to the bloody reactionary regime that just took power. **The Ayatollah and his followers executed more people in their first three months in power than the Shah had in thirty years"!** *(41)

In the nearby Arab kingdoms much worry began to resonate. Would the U.S. turn on them the way it had with a long-time ally such as the Shah. The Saudi's were particularly apprehensive as they were the obvious next target. They were a "unified country" only because of the hard rule from the Saudi princes. With the fall of Iran that rule would now be questioned by the Fundamentalist masses living inside their own borders. Should the mullahs control Saudi Arabia, they controlled the flow of oil worldwide.

From the Carter Administration there was nothing.

The Christian world was deeply saddened when Pope Paul xi suddenly died on August 6, 1978. The worlds one billion Christians were horrified when his successor, Pope John Paul I, a reformer, also "died" on September 28, 1978!

A new Pope was chosen, but breaking with tradition, he was Polish. His name was Karol Wojtyla, a humble man who was beloved in his homeland. The Communists were horrified at the choice. Yuri Andropov the head of the Soviet KGB was outraged. He angrily asked the head of the Polish section how they could have let this happen?

The Communist rulers in Poland refused his entry in May 1979 fearing his visit would coincide with another Polish celebration and result in control problems. After he did arrive the Communists tried every trick and lie they could to keep the people away from the Pope's events, but again they were unsuccessful. The Pope spoke to large crowds of the faithful inspiring the citizens, praising their religion and giving them hope and purpose. It was clear that he was becoming a huge threat to the rule of the Communist oppressors. *Something would have to be done.*

Nicaragua Falls

Back in the late spring the Sandinistas had launched large scale offensives against Somoza's Nicaraguan government forces. The Carter Administration knew full well the extensive support Castro gave to the Sandinistas, and also knew that at least 24 Cuban military advisors were in Costa Rica leading that insurgency. The Administration did nothing. *But Cuba was not the only sponsor of the Sandinistas as they were also being aided by many Communist groups including some from Europe.*

On June 6, 1979 Pres. Somoza declared a state of emergency. Still he could get no help from America. (Pres. Carter's approval rating at that time was down to 30%, once again proof that the people do know right from wrong.)

On July 19, 1979 it was all over for Nicaragua.

Somoza went into exile as the Communist rebels continued their "civil war". This latest fighting wasn't about Somoza as he had exited, now it was for total control. During those final weeks neither the Carter Administration nor the Congress gave any support to the regime that replaced Somoza. They wanted it to fail. **Within a month a second ally had been toppled by a hostile insurgent force.**

(Inanely on July 20 the Administration decided they should loosen their strict human-rights requirements in Central America, and Carter felt the CIA should *look at* covert actions to counter the Soviet-Cuban activity.)

Though his regime was far from perfect, Somoza had been an anti-communist voice in a region beset with insurgency. At that point several thousand people had been killed with over 500,000 refugees forced from their homes. *And as had happened with every "revolution", the business owners who had sided with the rebels realized their mistake within days of the Communist takeover.* But by then it was too late.

During August a communications network was established linking Managua and Havana. That revealed who was in charge. In October 1979 the Sandinistas began nationalizing the country's economic base beginning with the insurance companies. In November the mining industry was taken over.

*__Yassir Arafat__ then showed up, and again was given the former Israeli embassy as a gift for all of the **PLO's** help during the past decade! The PLO had supplied tons of arms and supplies, and more than two hundred Sandinistas had gone to PLO camps in Jordan and Lebanon to be shown the fine art of terrorism.*

Naively Carter believed in the prior promises from the Sandinistas, and granted them **$118 million** in aid as soon as they took over. His administration also negotiated an additional **$262 million in aid** and arranged financing for **$500 million** in private bank debt. This was more aid than we had given to the anti-Communist Somoza in the past four years!!

Carter even welcomed Daniel Ortega, the new ruler to the White House. *All of the administration principals backed and supported the Sandinistas even though their ideological position was clearly leftist.* Deputy Sec. State Warren Christopher testified to the Congress that all was well in Nicaragua and that they wanted good relations with us. (Castro warned the Sandinistas to be secretive about their Marxist beliefs. Allow the capitalists to finance our socialism.) *(42)

While in exile Somoza would write a book titled, **Nicaragua Betrayed.** In those pages he highlighted the active role that Jimmy Carter had played in allowing the Communist Sandinistas to take over.

"My country and my people were betrayed. That betrayal does not rest with the American people, but with their president Carter. My prayer is that those who lead the U.S. will not betray humanity. **If that happens, God help us all. For then it would be the entire free world and not just Nicaragua that was betrayed."** *(43)

(Shortly after that book was released in 1980 Anastasio Somoza was assassinated. His co-writer Jack Cox and his publisher Larry McDonald were also killed when Korean Air Flight 007 was shot down by the Soviets in 1983.)

In El Salvador a coup removed Pres. Romero and installed a civilian-military junta. After watching what had happened in Nicaragua their leaders were taking drastic action to try to stop the leftist rebel inspired violence in their country before it became worse. Right wing militias were actively hunting for the rebels, and in the U.S. our leftist media portrayed them as "death squads." Media coverage was so one sided it appeared that they were rooting for the communists.

As stated before the Carter Administration was in disarray. During June 1979 U.S. Ambassador Andrew Young was speaking at a conference in Bonn, West Germany. He foolishly stated; *"There was no sense in trying to cast blame or condemn anyone for the ongoing atrocities practiced by the Communist governments in Vietnam and Cambodia. Those events could be* *traced back to America's prior Indo-China involvement."* His statement and all that were similar were then and today, nothing more than self-serving nonsense. Those "political elites" were trying to **rationalize their failures,** and close the world's eyes to the reality that "those leaders" had caused when they turned their backs on those in need. *(44)

Young next gave a ridiculous speech at the U.N. and stated praise for the Ayatollah Khomeini. He even nominated him for sainthood. Incredulously he also claimed that the Cubans fighting in Africa were providing security in those nations, and the Soviet trained guerillas were liberation forces. Young would be one of those let go.

Like so many of that new breed of leftist apologists he was glad that America was failing and that "the rightist dictators of the world were falling". What he and so many of his anti-American kind failed to grasp was that the new dictators they were endorsing were far worse than the old rulers who at least were anti-communist. And all of the new dictators were rabidly anti-America. **The NY Times portrayed those "revolutionaries as successful alternatives to freedom".**

(It is a stunning revelation that so many within our own country, government and media were happy that America was being destroyed. They have not changed their treasonous ways, they have the same mindset in this time of 2019.)

Afghanistan

U.S. Ambassador Adolph Dubs had been kidnapped and murdered in Kabul on February 14, 1979. Amin had refused to negotiate with the rebels as the Carter Administration wanted. During the "rescue operation by Afghan and Soviet forces" the killings occurred which included the ambassador and three of the four rebels. One rebel had clearly been alive after the raid, but "expired" a short while later. He was "unable to be interviewed", and Carter did nothing over this "incident".

In the city of Herat an uprising in March 1979 led by an Afghan army captain resulted in over a dozen of the godless Soviet advisors and their families being slaughtered and their bodies placed on pikes. In retaliation Soviet planes flying from Kabul flew endless missions bombing the city into ruble and killing over 20,000 civilians! KGB Chief Yuri Andropov advised the Politburo we will be labeled as the aggressors, but we must not lose Afghanistan. *(One of his protégés was a young Vladimir Putin.)*

Former Premier Alexei Kosygin flew to Kabul to meet with Pres. Nur Taraki. Islamic sayings covered most of the buildings, a clear warning of the growing religious fervor. Kosygin was told that over half of the Afghan Army officers trained in the USSR had defected to the rebels.

On September 16, 1979 Communist Afghan Pres. Taraki was murdered in another coup. Premier Hafizullah Amin took over, increasing their reliance on Russia. He also conducted his own purge of the officers to ensure their loyalty. Desertions and casualties were wrecking the Afghan army as troop levels fell from 100,000 to less than 50,000. Afghan rebels were gaining control of many areas, and at the present rate of desertions their Communist regime was going to fall.

No one in the Kremlin could understand why this was happening. For nearly two decades Russia had been funding and nurturing the communists in Afghanistan. Hundreds of Soviet advisors were housed in Afghan cities and towns in an effort to organize communist style factories, communist run schools and communist run villages. All the while the requisite secret police were directed to use propaganda and terror on the population to ensure their compliance. Posters showing Soviet girls going to school had been placed everywhere, but they were constantly being ripped down. Those same tactics had always worked before. Decades earlier they were used in the central Asian Islamic states of Tajikistan, Kazakhstan and Uzbekistan when the Soviets invaded and converted them back in the 1920s.

But this Afghanistan was different.

Their religion was too important, the population almost illiterate and inured to hardship, and their economy too backward to appreciate socialism. Great Britain had tried to control Afghanistan a century earlier to thwart any potential Russian activity that might threaten India.

Most Brits of that day felt the Afghans were charming, martial, semi-civilized and completely ungovernable. (Two common but sardonic jokes were; "If you had two Afghans in a room you had three factions, and in Afghanistan every man could be king".) (45)

To force these Afghan peasants to adjust their position the Soviets had (through Taraki's rule) launched a terror campaign against their clerics and social leaders, imprisoning over 12,000. Systematic executions soon followed in the usual Communist effort to eradicate any challenges to their rule.

Still they resisted, and the masses turned even more towards the Islamic Fundamentalists. To the KGB Amin appeared to be turning towards the Islamic right too. Like America, the Soviets did not understand this new Islamic creature nor the effects from Iran's revolution.

England

Across the pond Great Britain was still in economic stress and social unrest. Their Labour Party had gotten into power over 20 years before and destroyed their national economy with liberal-socialist programs which included Nationalized industries, socialized housing, medical care, overregulation of all aspects of life, poor financial decisions and an enormous and expensive welfare state.

In 1950 Britain's share of worldwide production was at 9%. Their Labour Party under Clement Atlee took over and began changing the country with his "peaceful social revolution". By 1979 their share of worldwide production had fallen to just 4%, and their percentage of world trade in that same time frame went from 20% down to just 8%. They had no money left to spend on anything. Unlike the 1940's, we could not bail them out.

Back in 1973 at the height of the first oil embargo, Britain's Coal Miners struck for higher wages. Their actions led to serious nation-wide power shortages which further damaged the economy. Inflation ran as high as 26% during 1975, and Britain was forced to go to the IMF for a loan to stave off bankruptcy. Companies began leaving looking for economic safety and profits. As jobs left the unemployed swelled the roles of those on public support. Not until 1979 did the North Sea oil start to flow which alleviated their energy problems, but it was too late to stop their collapse.

Close by European rival and former mortal enemy Germany had become an economic powerhouse. And so was Japan. "Henry Kissinger called Japan's economic revival the most farsighted and intelligent process of any major nation since WWII." (46) Even France placed far ahead of the Brits. A country that once had one of the highest standards of living was falling off the edge.

On their latest election billboards it was sarcastically exclaimed, that the Labour Party "doesn't work". Their citizens agreed, and they elected their first women Prime Minister, Margaret Thatcher in a landslide. Her Conservative Party won a decisive victory in the October 1979 elections, and Mrs. Thatcher promised to keep the government out of the lives of the people. **"Free choice is what life is about."**

Her arrival was a welcome change to a country that was falling into socialism and despair. She started with deregulation, reduced their high rate of taxation and she cut governmental spending. Her actions were so well devised that in a short time they were rewarded with their economic miracle as Britain began recovering. Thatcher would be reelected in 1983 and again in 1987.

(By 1990 Britain's unemployment rate had fallen to just 6%! Proof again that Conservative policies are better than the liberal-socialist ones.)

U.S Embassy Attack

With his illness getting worse the Shah sought to go to NYC for treatment. On October 19, 1979 Carter made the decision to admit Reza Pahlavi into the U.S.. (By this point all of our citizens had escaped Iran, except those working in the embassy.)

Administration discussions over the Shah revealed worry that the Iranians might just take the embassy and hold the staff hostage. One staffer suggested that the Shah stay out until the embassy was reinforced. Other ideas mentioned keeping a rescue force in the Azores (if they let us), having the 82d Airborne Division on pad alert, or using the British base at Diego Garcia as a staging area. **Asst. Sec State Warren Christopher stopped the idea of evacuating the embassy, "as there was no "indication of danger".** But nothing was implemented by this disjointed administration.

Iran was still divided politically with actual student demonstrations protesting the direction of their revolution. Iran's middle class was dejected and disheartened by the social and economic upheaval, and the educated and political activists crestfallen over the imposition of Islamic law. Even Prime Minister Bazargan was in open rebellion with his mentor over the strict Islamic laws.

Sensing that his revolution was not being accepted by the masses, Khomeini decided to begin a new purge on October 28. He called all of his opponents traitors, and he announced that all must be eradicated. More executions were carried out.

Khomeini also needed a diversion to keep the masses busy, and the perfect present had just arrived. On October 23, the Shah landed in NYC to begin his medical treatments. Days later a call was put out in Tehran to stage a large protest at the U.S. embassy for November 1, 1979. P.M. Bazargan was able to divert the "demonstrators" that day, but with the Shah staying in NYC for medical treatment the Ayatollah was able to launch a fanatical diatribe that "inspired his followers".

On November 4, 1979 "Iranian students" suddenly stormed the U.S. Embassy in Tehran and took the embassy staff and Marine guards hostage. According to their propaganda the "students were angry" over the decision to allow the Shah to enter the U.S.. They wanted him returned for crimes against Iran. *In reality those "students" had been trained by Libyan and Soviet experts just for this mission. These were the same experts who had been so helpful in overthrowing the Shah.*

Leading the attackers was a large group of female protestors dressed in black chadors. Their diversionary tactic allowed another group of armed "students" to enter the embassy through an unsecured basement window. There were still only thirteen mostly lightly armed Marines in the Embassy for security. They were unprepared for the attack and again told by the Ambassador not to return fire. The embassy was quickly overwhelmed and everyone taken prisoner.

Because of Warren Christopher, the Administration had not evacuated or reduced the staffing at the embassy after the previous attack and threats. Nor did they strengthen the embassy's security to prevent this scenario from happening even though this exact situation had been discussed at the White House. Contact with the embassy was lost at 4:57 am est. All of the staff, employees and Marine guards were hooded and paraded around the streets as encouraged hatred raged around them. Most would be held captive for 444 days.

(After their release in early 1980 Marine Sgt Rodney Sickmann stated that they had been ordered by the Ambassador not to return fire. If they fought back in all probability they would have died, but so would a hundred or more of the attackers. Public outrage would have forced Carter to respond militarily.) *(47)

With the muted reaction by Pres. Carter, every hostile group and individual could see the weakness in our country and its leadership.

That next morning protests in NYC occurred at the hospital where the Shah was being treated. But instead of being comprised of hostile Iranians, the protestors were American students with signs, *"Take Carter, we'll keep the Shah."* A day later however large, loud anti-Shah protestors arrived on those same streets. Stupidly they were allowed to get close to the hospital and disrupt the block. *As directed, No arrests were made.*

Again the inept Carter Administration was completely surprised by the embassy takeover, and after a week of humiliation nothing had been done about it. Carter's first effort at diplomacy over this attack was coldly turned down by Iran, and the U.S. staff sent back empty handed. Carter never appeared more useless. And to make this crisis situation even more grim the civilian government of P.M. Mehdi Bazargan was dissolved giving all power and authority to the Ayatollah and the clerics.

France tried to help in getting the hostages released, but the Ayatollah refused all diplomatic attempts and continued to back the "students" actions. He warned that the hostages would be destroyed if America attacked. **"Our youth should be confident that America cannot do a damn thing. America is far too impotent to interfere in a military way. If they could have interfered, they would have saved the Shah. Why should we be afraid, we consider martyrdom a great honor."** *(48)

Takeover of an Embassy was and is considered, and an international treaty made it an act of war. Carter should have immediately sent military forces into the country. But his indecisiveness and moralistic viewpoint hampered his thoughts. Carter's only actions were freezing all Iranian assets in the U.S. and an embargo was placed on Iranian oil. (Little was being produced anyway.) The American people were stunned at the barbaric actions by the Iranians. Days turned into weeks of cruelty, duplicity, and violation of human and diplomatic rights.

Carter wrote two letters to interim civilian leader Abolhasan Bani-Sadr but the attempt backfired as he was ignored. The only good news was the release of most of the female and black hostages on November 19th. Thirteen were freed, with the remaining hostages held in captivity.

(Yassir Arafat actually played a major role in talking Khomeini into it. Arafat wanted Carter's support against Israel.)

Empress Farah Pahlavi wrote in her journal, Is this the start of the Third World War?

The CIA learned that after the Embassy seizure the Soviets prepared contingency plans to invade and occupy northern Iran if the situation became a threat to Russia, or if the Americans attempt to intervene militarily. Continuing into 1980 Soviet forces were placed at forward positions, and war-training increased just across the border of NW Iran. A special NIE was prepared in August 1980 stating that it was obvious and alarming that the Soviets were developing contingency plans for Iran.

Months later the CIA learned that the Soviets planned a two pronged invasion with units going as far south as central Iran, and taking the Persian Gulf ports and oil terminals. Carter and Administration principals were appraised of that intelligence, but did again nothing. *(49)

Middle East Trials

Around dawn on November 20th 1979 the Grand Mosque in Mecca, Saudi Arabia was seized by Iranian - Shiite extremists. Numbering 400-500, those terrorists included women and children used as porters and spies. They wore red headbands to identify themselves as they carried coffins filled with weapons into the mosque. Their leader Abdullah Qahtani claimed to be the Mahdi, the great redeemer of Islam. (That title was required in order to begin the return to original Islam. Khomeini wanted to claim that title too.)

Qahtani's followers had repudiated all things Western, and they demanded the expulsion of all non believers from the region. They also insisted that the Saudi's ban music, television and women holding jobs. In the early hours of this affair the Saudi's did not respond. The Saudi's never like negative press so the Royals said little of the attack. But across the Islamic world rumors and fragmented information inflamed the easily excitable Muslim masses. (Our embassies were warned to be on guard.)

Local security forces attempted to regain the Mosque but were repelled with heavy losses by the well trained terrorists. Days later a small Saudi military force tried a three way assault which was also repulsed. Snipers caused heavy casualties to the poorly trained troops, and many of the hostages were massacred. Forces pulled back and a siege situation developed. (During the takeover and the siege hundreds of the poorly trained Saudi troops died fighting the well trained and prepared extremists.)

The militarily weak Saudis needed help from outsiders which would include troops from Pakistan. It would take weeks for them to arrive and organize. (Somehow in those weeks many of the terrorist leaders "escaped". Their writings got out to the masses, and reached Egypt inspirng the murder of Pres. Sadat.) To assist the Pakistani's in retaking of the mosque, *The Bin Laden Brothers Contracting Industry* supplied their updated blueprints so the troops could visualize the layout. A well devised plan was made and implemented retaking the Mosque.

Historical Note: In another piece of tragic irony, Pres. Eisenhower's desire to build up Saudi Arabia to hold back the Russians meant a lot of our money flowed into the country to help . The Bin Laden Family was given a contract to build a railroad to Mecca for the annual pilgrims. That initial contract and successful venture led to the family fortune and bin Laden's future path.

After the Mosque was retaken sixty-three of the captured rebels were beheaded. Those terrorists who could not get away from the final assaults were so concerned with keeping their identity a secret that they burned and mutilated the faces of their dead. The Saudis tried to claim that only 26 had died in this attack, but most accounts put the death toll at over 1,000. And after this disaster the fearful Saudis did not crack down on the increasingly vocal dissidents. That failure resulted in an increase in the power and allure of the Islamists, and months later many of their strict religious and anti-western rules were being emplaced in the Kingdom. (Women's hair salons were all closed, women could no longer appear on television and all women's education was ended.)

Investigations of the attack were conducted and it was found that the terrorist leaders had been trained in South Yemen by Russian advisors. Their cover story was the one claiming the religious demands listed above, but the real purpose was political, to undermine the Saudi's. **Soviet Russia helped them because they knew that if the West lost their oil supplies the world was theirs for the taking.**

As shown before with the increasing funds coming in from their oil Saudi gross revenue had gone from $9.2 Billion in 1974 to over $142 Billion during 1979. Carter's Sec. of the Treasury William Miller flew to Riyadh to comfort the Saudi Royal's, lest they remove the $30 Billion they had on deposit in U.S. banks. A generation ago the land was comprised predominately of nomadic tribesmen. Now many of them had an income higher than most nations.

The Saudis needed to be protected, now more than ever. Prince Turki oversaw an increasing budget at the Saudi GID, Government Intelligence Department. But they were not accomplishing much as evidenced by the well orchestrated attack in Mecca. In Jeddah the CIA station decided they had to upgrade the Saudi intelligence capabilities for their own good. Prince Turki and many of the GID seniors went to Langley to learn and study our methods and systems. He fit in well with all of the Americans he worked with and was a serious student. *And his large income, both legal and* shady enabled him to "influence" dozens of people in high governmental positions across the globe, especially in London and Washington DC.

But Iran and Saudi Arabia were not the only trouble spots in the region. **Our Embassies in Islamabad, Pakistan and in Tripoli, Libya were also overrun and destroyed by Islamic Fundamentalist extremists.** Again Carter did nothing over these attacks. With the continued tensions in the region the State Dept. urged all Americans to leave the ten listed Moslem countries that were "now deemed unsafe", Libya, Yemen, Pakistan, Iran, Iraq, Syria, Lebanon, Algeria, the Sudan and Jordan.

Young CIA case officer Gary Schroen who spoke Farsi was on duty in Islamabad, Pakistan. It was not considered a dangerous posting until after the Iranian Revolution, then you could feel the hostilities and tensions every time you were out. *After our embassy in Iran had been stormed, sources in Pakistan warned that "Islamic students" were preparing demonstrations there.*

On November 21, 1979 dozens of buses pulled up next to the U.S. embassy and hundreds of rioters jumped off and began the attack. Wave after wave of armed attackers charged the grounds and buildings as additional buses pulled up as if on holiday. Hours into the fight one hundred-thirty nine trapped American and Pakistani employees were hoping for salvation from the Pakistani Army, which conveniently went missing.

British observers from their embassy estimated **15,000 attackers were involved!** Unhappy that they could not get access to the U.S. staff, the rioters began setting dozens of fires. Embassy lawyer David Fields forbade the Marine Guards to shoot. All they could do was use tear gas to try to keep the attackers at bay.

Some of the local Pakistanis spirited away individual hostages and protected the embassy school, but Pres. Zia's armed forces remained conspicuously absent. By late afternoon clouds of black smoke covered the U.S. compound and was seen from miles. A Pakistani helicopter flew past and reported no one could still be alive, so Zia decided there was no sense getting involved. Hours later the Islamists got bored and left on their own. Only then could the one hundred plus make their escape from their holding area. *Soon after the Pakistani army showed up.*

Our embassy compound had cost over $20 Million to build and was a total loss. Five of our personnel had been murdered, and three hundred nine were quickly evacuated back to the U.S. *Pres. Carter and his Administration callously lied through their collective teeth as they gave thanks to Pres. Zia for his prompt assistance.* Those told to remain in country like Schroen were stunned at how coldhearted the Carter Administration was towards all of them.

Lebanon had been a friendly, stable and pro-Western anchor on the eastern shores of the Mediterranean. But by 1979 that nation was gone, lost in the "civil war" created by the PLO and expanded by Syria. Iranian Islamists began exporting their brand of fundamentalism into Lebanon via Syria, their ally.

Though Israel's recent cross-border attacks had overwhelmed the terrorist camps in southern Lebanon resulting in an uneasy quiet, a new terrorist organization showed up. It was organized and funded by the Ayatollah's Iran, and *was called* **Hezbollah**. Flush with cash, fighters and arms they worked tirelessly to destroy what was left of Lebanon and return the PLO to the attack. (As the Ayatollah had promised.) Their leader was **Hussein Massawi.** He described their philosophy as such; "**We are not fighting the Western world so that you will offer us something, We are fighting to eliminate you.** *(50)

On July 3, 1979 Carter reluctantly signed a directive approving covert non-military assistance to the anti-communist rebels in **Afghanistan.** Pakistan and Saudi Arabia agreed to distribute the limited U.S. humanitarian supplies so the effort would go unnoticed. (An NIE was prepared for Afghanistan in late spring and warned that the Soviets could cross into Afghanistan to support their puppet regime. That would cause sharp problems with Pakistan, and what would the U.S. do then?)

Security Advisor Brzezinski and the CIA warned Carter that this effort to provide aid might provoke a Soviet response including an invasion of Afghanistan, possibly even into Pakistan as they were adamantly opposed to the Communist run regime in Afghanistan. In fact Pakistan was actively aiding the rebels who were called the *Mujahedeen*. Pakistan President was Mohammed Zia-ul-Haq, a British trained army officer. During the 1947 civil war between India and Pakistan the religious violence and the brutality was staggering, and seared him and most of the Muslims for life. Pakistan had been formed so their Muslim people could have their own homeland. (Isreal was formed soon after.)

Pakistan's first leader was Mohammed Ali Jinnah, and he wanted a secular nation like Turkey, not an Islamic one. But over the years one failed civilian government followed the next which led to a series of military coups. General Zia decided to try his luck at control in 1977, but unlike his predecessors, he desired an

Islamic State. *With the increasing tide of Islamic Nationalism and Fundamentalism, he seemed to have picked the winning side.*

Historical Note: During 1956 Eisenhower wrongly refused to help the Afghans when the British pulled out. They turned to the USSR for aid. *It was Pres. Nixon who recognized their need, and he began our earliest efforts to help the Afghans during 1973.* At that time it was the Shah's Iran and America working together trying to weaken the Soviet position, but it was too late to get the entrenched Communists out. The Soviets continued their quest for proxy control during the rest of the decade.

After weeks of diplomacy Saudi Arabia's Intelligence chief Prince Turki al-Faisal agreed to match our Afghan bound supplies dollar for dollar. General Zia then cagily insisted that since everything had to pass through his country to get to Afghanistan, it had to pass through their hands first. Pakistan would control who got what. The Administration wrongly agreed to that rule. (We would not know who got what or when.)

For practicality the Fundamentalists fighting the Communists did benefit the most. But Zia and their ISI siphoned off great quantities of money and supplies so they could continue Pakistan's never ending fight with India. (And U.S. taxpayers paid for it!)

Historical Note: During the 1971 Indo-Pakistani war the aggressive Pakistan was hammered losing half of their navy, over a third of their army and a quarter of their air force. India captured over 5,500 square miles of territory, which they later gave back. In the peace that followed East Pakistan was granted their independence and went on to form the new nation of Bangladesh. (That weakened Pakistan's threat to India.)

Two of the most noteworthy Afghan rebels at that time were **Gulbuddin Hekmatyar,** an Islamist and a brutal anti-communist whose group was the largest and had the best fighters. And the Saudi's favorite rebel **Abdul Rasul Sayyaf**, the Afghan Muslim Brotherhood leader. *Both men would become major players in the militant, terrorist organizations that would follow the Soviet invasion.* And both would also become close to a young Saudi rebel named **Osama bin Laden**. (Sayyaf would be killed and martyred, and his name was used for the al Qaeda terrorist spinoff that bin Laden would later setup in the Philippines.)

As the weeks went by the Afghan rebels were gaining more control from the Communists. Russia had invested heavily in the harsh land with roads and infrastructure projects. After twenty plus years of effort and $ Billions invested economically and militarily, they were committed to keeping this country under their control.

KGB reports noted the increasing humanitarian aid coming from America and other nations. They felt the intention of this effort was to defeat the Soviet Union and allow the Muslims to recreate a New Great Ottoman Empire, which could include the southern Soviet Republics! That end must not be allowed.

(A further worry pushed by the KGB was if Afghanistan fell away from Communism the West would place missiles and bases there. They had to hold onto the country.)

During the Shah's reign, the Afghan Shiites were a minority in Afghanistan. They had been assisted by the Shah, and wisely kept to themselves. But once Khomeini took over his Shia Revolutionaries tried to enforce their brand of Islam into the Afghanistan Shia. With this Fundamentalist fanaticism spreading the Soviets had seen enough, and decided to end it before it spread into their own Muslim provinces. In late November the Soviet Politburo decided Pres. Amin would be have to be assassinated and replaced by Babrak Karmal who was in exile. That first week of December 1979 Soviet military and KGB agents began infiltrating into the country.

On December 7 Babrak Karmal was brought in with a retinue of Soviet paratroops and KGB assassins. The CIA was aware of the growing Soviet activity in and around Afghanistan, (and Iran). CIA director Turner warned all on December 19 that the buildup had crossed a significant level. Three days later his deputy Bobby Inman called Brzezinski and Sec-Def. Harold Brown warning that a Soviet invasion was just days away.

Claiming that their communist client state needed their help, the Soviets suddenly invaded Afghanistan on December 26, 1979. With little warning, (though French Intelligence also knew it was coming), Russian transport planes landed at every Afghan airport dropping off highly trained troops. Long road convoys crossed the border and within days 40,000 Soviet troops were in the country. KGB agents in Afghan uniforms had infiltrated the palace killing Amin and 200 palace guards as the Russians quickly installed Babrak Karmal.

Not since Prague in 1968 had the Soviets attacked another nation. In two weeks over 85,000 Russian troops had stormed across the border, with them were 1,800 tanks, 2,000 BMPs, and dozens of helicopters. Deliberate Soviet attacks wrecked villages killing thousands of civilians. Survivors became refugees, joining the escaping residents from the major cities in seeking safety. Iran and Pakistan were quickly overrun, with dozens of thousands forced to living in caves. To increase the terror of their operations the Soviets dispersed thousands of "butterfly mines" from the air. Their intent was killing and maiming unwary women and children.

Though they knew of the CIA reports describing the weeks long Soviet troop buildup, their road clearing operations, and the roadway improvements along the border areas, the Carter Administration was again caught unprepared by the invasion. Jimmy Carter finally woke up and saw reality. He stated that this invasion had utterly changed his view of the Soviets, and told the Senate to delay any SALT treaty ratifications. He offered more U.S. aid to Pakistan, recalled our Soviet ambassador, boycotted the 1980 Olympics, reduced commercial sales and contracts and instituted a limited grain embargo. He next required all 19 and 20 year old males to register for a possible military draft.

Some in the U.S. which included Brzezinski wanted to help stoke the fires of Islamic Fundamentalists as a way of hurting the Soviets from within. The entire tier of southern states in the Soviet Union was Muslim, and no matter how hard they tried the Soviets could not quash that deep religious control. Brzezinski saw a parallel of this new war with us in Vietnam. It was possible we could hurt the Soviets by aiding the rebels. But he warned that the Soviets were not encumbered by a conscious the way we were. *They would probably act decisively and crush the Afghan resistance quickly.*

A plan to aid the rebels had to be organized. Meanwhile fierce fighting was occurring between the armor equipped Russians and the poorly equipped rebels. Because of their armor the Russians controlled all of the roads, but they fared poorly when they had to fight in the hills and valleys. Pakistan was actively arming the rebels against the Soviets. Even the U.N. voted 104-18 deploring Russia's invasion, but as usual nothing more was done.

Despite the planned attack on our embassy and Zia's abandonment of the trapped staff, Zia and Pakistan were going to benefit from this invasion as we now had a common enemy. *That is the world of international and strategic politics. None of us like it, but it is what it is.*

George Keenan the author of our Cold War policy of Containment wrote that a major superpower conflict seemed imminent. It would be a war which could not end for any of the parties involved in anything other than disaster. **"Not for thirty**

years has the political tensions reached so high a danger point as it has now. Not in all that time has there been such a high degree of misunderstanding, suspicion, and fear." *(51)

In reality though this was a normal foreign policy crisis for a nation falling into military / political / economic weakness and despair. The Soviets had been testing the waters since Nixon left office. They had observed no reaction to any of the Communist victories in SE Asia or their incessant proxy wars which were centered on Africa and Central America. They watched as long time ally Iran was abandoned and fell to Islamic extremists without a shot being fired by America. And this new Iran was an aggressive enemy to the West, but especially America. Nicaragua had also been abandoned by the U.S., and lost to Soviet-Cuban sponsored Communists who were threatening two more nearby nations. There had been no reaction from America when three of our embassies were attacked, and the one in Iran seized. Even America's "security services had been shut down by their own political leaders.

To the Soviet Politburo, America was collapsing, and no nation would or could interfere in their "expansion". In their eyes it was time to strike, just as Stalin had done when he gave his blessing to North Korea's invasion of South Korea in June 1950.

For There Are Tigers in this World, (2)

And They Are Always Watching.

Across the Iranian border the Ayatollah and many of his cohorts grew worried. With their purge of their military they had nothing with which to stop the Soviets if they should decide to invade Iran too. (Which was being planned and practiced.) Khomeini decided to dangle the U.S. hostages as bait to see if Carter was prepared to accept him and his Islamic revolution. He would trade the hostages if Carter released Iran's funds and the weapons and supplies the Shah had previously paid for.

America and Foreign Affairs

In America a fundamental awakening was finally occurring. Citizens and leaders were facing up to the fact that Soviet led Communists were attacking our interests all over the globe. This was the Brezhnev Doctrine, formulated in the late 1960s and now bearing fruit. **Rather than confront us directly and risk nuclear war, the Soviet goal was to drown us in never ending subversive wars until we gave up.**

The past four years had been very promising for the Communists. North Vietnam's third and successful invasion of South Vietnam in the spring of 1975 was their *first victory*. Cambodia's fall was *the second*, Laos *was third*, Angola was *the forth*, Ethiopia *was fifth*, Nicaragua was *the sixth,* and Grenada was *the seventh.* More battles were occurring in Africa, while the events in Central America were progressing nicely. And with Russian forces now invading and occupying Afghanistan, *(eighth),* they began rapidly building airfields in SW Afghanistan.

The threat of Soviet based bombers and fighters closing off the oil flow from the Arabian Gulf was becoming a real scenario. They would be just 300 miles from the Strait of Hormuz, the main choke-point that most of the oil from the Persian Gulf had to pass. Just a forty minute flight, from Afghanistan and Ethiopia!

Historical Note: The 1966 Brezhnev Doctrine was actually an offshoot of Khrushchev's 1961 policy. He threatened the JFK administration by "**Aiding leftists in all wars of national liberation**". As shown in *Book 2*, Kennedy had secretly decided in 1961 to confront and fight the Communists in Vietnam. By late 1963 he had sent over 22,000 advisors to S. Vietnam, but would not "start the actual war until he was re-elected in 1964".

Leonid Brezhnev replaced Nikita Khrushchev in 1964 when he was voted out by the Communist Party Central Committee. In 1966 he formulated his plan, and the 1967 Mideast War created a perfect scenario for Brezhnev to begin. Soviet ships were re-supplying the defeated and humiliated Arab nations with newer arms and weapons, and hundreds of Russians came in as advisors. All of their efforts were directed to fight again, defeat Israel, and hurt the West. As payback for their armaments and aid the Soviets opened a KGB base in Egypt to further their subversions in the region. They had enjoyed a nice run of luck since Brezchnev. So far only Sadat had kicked the Russians out, thanks to Nixon.

That the world had been bloodied over and over, and was in a much more dangerous condition in December 1979 than it was in November 1976 can be laid at the Carter Administration's doorstep and no other. **At that point in time there were twelve regional wars being fought on four continents. There were also five active revolutions.**

Democratic Senator Frank Church announced the "discovery of the Soviet combat units" based in Cuba. Those units were already on the radar, and Carter did not want that to turn into another crisis as he tried to "reassure the public" that all was well. He did not pursue it in hopes it would fade from view.

The year of 1979 was a catastrophe for the Carter Administration and the world. At this point in time Soviet imperialism was controlling or threatening to control about half of the world's population. The most obvious strategic threat was in and around the Middle East and East Africa. Worldwide eight countries were totally dominated by the Soviets, six were Soviet proxies and eighteen were now significantly influenced by them. The pandering and appeasing that had been the hallmark of our government since 1976 had to change and quickly.

"Harvard Sovietologist Adam Ulam remarked that the Soviet's expanding empire could not be stopped unless they faced a strong and determined power that could make their expansion too risky or too expensive." *(52)

In Central America, Columbia suffered another serious attack by leftist rebels as they seized the embassy of the Dominican Republic. About 80 people were taken hostage including 14 Ambassadors. A similar attack on the Spanish consulate in Guatemala was broken up the month before resulting in 36 deaths. All over the region the leftist rebels were becoming more aggressive as they tried to rapidly subvert all of the existing conservative regimes in their quest to install Communist ones. Still the Carter Administration was absent, just as the Soviets expected. **It would all be over soon.**

Even in Africa their people realized what was happening strategically. Somalia and Kenya agreed to give U.S. military forces access to base areas in February of 1980. (Naturally U.S. foreign aid helped those nations to reach their decision.) Small outposts began opening up, (in Oman too), though none had any real combat power or capability.

Democratic Senator Sam Nunn who was a leading figure in our defense committees responded to the Carter failures in a 1980 lecture. Nunn stated how America had lost strategic superiority to the Soviets, who despite arms control talks have deployed numerous upgraded nuclear weapon systems such as the SS-18 & SS-19 missiles. And with the Soviet deployment of their medium range SS-20 missiles, the Soviets have nuclear superiority over Europe. *At present NATO is questionable on if it could still maintain a conventional defense.* There is a continuous shortfall of equipment and ammunition, and our sealift and airlift capabilities are too small to maintain a major war. As a committee chairman he knew that our naval power, our sealift and airlift shortfalls were so bad we could not even cope with a medium size conflict in the Indian Ocean region, the Middle East or Africa. Our being able to conduct operations in other undeveloped areas were questionable at best. Chronic shortages in training, operations, and maintenance have plagued all of our military services this past decade. That has reduced our readiness and capabilities. And the West's manpower mobilization base is inadequate in the event of war in Europe. Our dwindling navy is inadequate for the many requirements it faces. We could not fight the Russians even if we chose to!

This senior Democratic Senator was worried that in early 1980 we would lose any type of war against the Soviets.

He was not alone.

Due to the deteriorating worldwide situation Libya became the fifth major oil exporter to raise their oil price in a week, further escalated the devastating inflation that was crippling the western and developing world's economies. By early summer the 13 OPEC members desired the price to be raised to $42 per barrel.

Most people do not know this, but there was talk in the mid-1970s after the first oil shock of invading and occupying Saudi Arabia as a way to protect the worlds oil supplies. Henry Kissinger was one of the main proponents of this desperate scheme, such was the fear of an economic collapse from an oil cutoff. After the Iranian revolution and this latest oil crisis, the idea had resurfaced. But now we had no bases or assets in the region to undertake such a plan! With the Soviet invasion of Afghanistan (and their preparations for invading Iran), Carter was forced into increasing our defense budget. He ordered the (last ditch) creation of the RDF, Rapid Deployment Force. The idea was to air-drop the 82nd Airborne Division into the region as a way to try to protect the world's oil supplies. Most of the military minds considered the attempt a mere speed bump, and those troops doomed to be sacrificial lambs. **But again we had no other options.**

With this new crisis Brzezinski convinced Carter to go with his idea to help the Afghan rebels, and he directed the CIA to get arms to them. Since the Soviets had come out to do battle, now was the time to turn the tables on them, and use an insurgent war in the ever hostile and tortuous terrain of Afghanistan. *Brzezinski's thought was to tie up and bleed the Soviets in Afghanistan as a way to delay them from invading Iran and or entering the Persian Gulf.* Many in the administration including some senior CIA officials were against this idea as too risky, but in reality that was our only option, such was our military weakness. (This was the lowest point in American military capability since the fall of Corregidor and the loss of the Philippines in early 1942.)

Despite approving National Security Advisor Brzezinski's idea, Carter and his administration were boxed in by his and his party's destruction of the CIA. There were few agents left who were capable of initiating such contact or in directing any type of Covert War. And since the liberals in Congress had placed such severe restrictions upon the CIA, if any hearings on the subject were held it would mean our covert action was not covert.

To make things happen the Administration had to turn to the Saudi's. And the Saudi's now realized that by hurting America economically, (using oil), they had set themselves up for destruction. It could come from the Iranian revolutionaries, or it could come from the Soviets, but it was on the horizon. *They needed America to revive and save their bacon.*

Brzezinski flew into Islamabad, Pakistan in January 1980. His mission was to support the Afghan freedom fighters by establishing guidelines with President Zia al-Haq. Pakistan had long been an ally to America. With this Russian invasion their situation was becoming dire. Should the Soviets win in Afghanistan, Pakistan would be trapped with Afghanistan to the north, China to the east and pro-Soviet India on its southern border. Zia's decision to help was made quickly.

The Communists had used Laos and Cambodia to fight us in Vietnam. Pakistan would do the same for our side now. It had been decided by Zia that all arms and supplies had to pass through Pakistani hands. It was vital that the suppliers, America, Great Britain, Israel, Egypt, Saudi Arabia and (even China) maintained silence over their roles, lest the Soviets invade Pakistan too. To maintain that illusion it was easier to hide the truth if the supplies came in by air instead of by ship. Unmarked planes would land at least twice a week. By supplying in this compact method Gen. Zia was trying to keep plausible deniability for the Russians, and to keep tight control on everything coming in. (It did not work out in either case as the KGB were everywhere.)

Over the next months tons of supplies, arms and even CIA training manuals were distributed from holding warehouses. A lot of that aid was stolen and ended up in Islamic battle sites far removed from Afghanistan, such as in Bosnia, the Philippines and Lebanon. Many of the early fighters in Afghanistan were actually Palestinian, and they would soon bring their new skills back to Lebanon to fight Israel. But we had no control over who went there to fight.

America

In the U.S. the 1980 election year politicking began with earnest as America the superpower seemed to be fading away. Ronald Reagan was the lead candidate for the GOP with former U.N. Ambassador George Bush in 2nd place. The GOP message of prosperity and strength was welcomed news for the citizens as our recession deepened and foreign problems abounded.

To try to stimulate our economy Carter deregulated the U.S. banking industry. New financial products would be allowed and many rules were removed. Though this allowed growth in that industry, it also set the stage for the banking collapses that would follow in the 1980's. Carter also positioned himself to the left of the political realm to distance himself from the Republicans. He still desired to be thought of as a candidate of peace, and tried to force the Senate to ratify his sellout SALT II in an effort to achieve that goal. But with the present problems with Russia that treaty was dead.

Noted columnist and thinker George Will wrote that despite all of the arms negotiations that had occurred the past decade, the immense Soviet arsenal had grown quantitatively and qualitatively. "In this same time we have seen an unparalleled period of Soviet aggression worldwide. **We can plainly see that the Liberal fascination with arms controls does not result in any, only a policy of apologetic retreats!"** *(53)

Throughout the campaign Carter and the main-stream media tried to portray Reagan as a reckless cowboy, a dangerous man who would bring war. This was the same mendacious strategy Wilson used in 1916, FDR used in 1940, and LBJ and the Democrats used against Barry Goldwater in 1964. All of those Democrats won their elections, and Americans were fighting in foreign wars just months after.

Carter next tried to resurrect the energy independence theme with his Energy Security Act. He established the Department of Energy which was tasked to oversee our nation's energy needs. His Synthetic Fuels Corporation was directed to providing two million barrels of synthetic oil a day from U.S. coal. (Germany had pioneered the effort in WWII.) Renewable energy sources were to be expanded, and energy tax credits were used to spur R&D and domestic sales. Carter's failed energy plan was four phone books thick, filled with pork barrel spending and federal bureaucrats to oversee it. His creation of the cabinet position of Department of Energy had a budget that rivaled the profits of the major energy companies.

(None of those ideas have worked out these past 35 years. Renewable energy was at 7% in 1981. In 2007 it was only 6.7% of our total production. In 2017 it was 7.4%)

While America stagnated, Germany and Japan were becoming economic giants. Over half of our auto sales were imports from those two countries. Detroit the home of our automotive industry had totally missed the boat in producing fuel efficient or reliable vehicles. The arrogance from our own companies was costing thousands of American jobs monthly, and our trade deficit grew worse turning us into a debtor nation. By 1979 Japan was producing as much steel as America did! Germany's GDP had progressed from $32 billion in 1952 to $600 billion by 1979! And Germans had a higher average income than Americans did, $10,800 vs $9,600. As the European Economic Community began to coalesce into a common market, it appeared that America would fall into a permanent position of second place. The combined production from Europe was more than the U.S. had generated since 1960. America was collapsing right in front of our eyes. (And it appeared that the Axis Powers had won the war after all.)

After his medical treatment ended the Shah left the U.S. and took a brief exile in Egypt, courtesy of Pres. Sadat. His illness was now terminal, and he died in July 1980. *His funeral was held in Cairo, and shamefully no one from the U.S. Government went!* Former Pres. Richard Nixon alone went to the service, incredulous at how callous and empty the Carter Administration was to a man who had been one of America's best strategic allies for the past thirty years.

Poland

As shown earlier the new Roman Catholic Pope was **Karol Wojtyla.** Born in 1918 he was among the first of the young children born into the post-WWI renewed nation of Poland. For the previous one hundred plus years Poland had been dominated by the Russian, Austrian and Prussian empires. Those empires worked tirelessly to dissect and destroy Polish culture, but their people had an intense belief in Catholicism which gave them strength and prevented that from happening.

Poland was reborn from the fires of WWI, and Karol was fortunate to grow of age in a vibrant and happy nation. Unable to accept that fact, in 1921 Russia's Lenin attempted to invade and "reclaim that land". **But his Red Armies were defeated at the**

Miracle of the Vistula, a battle that has been ignored by history. That shattering defeat actually saved Europe from Russian Communism! Had the Bolsheviks won in Poland, they had easy access into the weakened state of post-Kaiser Germany and beyond. (The world would be a very different place had any of that that happened, and no one would have heard of Adolph Hitler.)

During the 1920's intensive political changes occurred in Europe and Asia. Mussolini and his Italian fascists rose to power, and in a few years Adolph Hitler and his Nazi's would do the same in Germany. Japan had been taken over by those who wanted an empire, and Stalin seized power in Russia after Lenin died.

The 1930s were a time of fear as those nations geared up for war. Japan and Italy struck first, and their conquests were tragically allowed by a world weary of war. *Pres. Hoover wanted allied support to confront Japan in Manchuria, but no one came forward to join his effort.* In Europe England and France closed their eyes to the illegal military buildup in Germany, and their leaders used appeasement to try to reign in Hitler and Mussolini. They failed, and new fascist conquests soon occurred in central Europe and Africa. Still there was no reaction from the world powers. (Just like Carter.)

Poland's turn on the fire soon came, and she was invaded by Germany and Russia in September 1939. That event finally sparked the European part of WWII. Set upon by enemies from two sides, fate again worked to destroy the Polish nation. Both of the invading rulers were evil tyrants, and both murdered and enslaved millions of Polish citizens. Karol Wojtyla was forced to work in a Nazi chemical plant under terrible conditions. **He witnessed first hand the depredations of the Nazi's and the Communists, and knew they were the enemies of humankind.**

FDR sold out the Polish people at Yalta in order to get Stalin's help against Japan. Though he tried many times, Churchill was unable to sway FDR or Harry Truman to save the Polish nation, and they were forced to suffer under the harsh rule of Communism for decades. Because of those failures, Poland was lost twice.

After WWII ended Karol became a Catholic priest and his work promoting and managing Poland's faithful became his cause. Religion was an anathema to the Communists, for them the party was the only thing that mattered. Every nation they took over they tried to stamp out religion using lies, spies, terror and deceit. But they always failed.

Wojtyla rose through the ranks of the Church becoming a Bishop and then Cardinal. He was chosen as the new Pope in 1978, an event that stunned the world. Poland was overwhelmed with joy and pride in their home-grown son. And all across Eastern Europe religion became more open and the people were becoming defiant, thanks to Pres. Ford and the Helsinki Accords.

In the Kremlin they realized they had made a serious mistake in not crushing Wojtyla decades ago. *They had all of the Security chiefs from every nation in their sphere attend a meeting to discuss contingency plans. They also plotted and succeeded in penetrating the Vatican.*

Poland's attempts at protesting their fate had failed during 1970-1971, and they suffered serious losses to Communist guns. But the Helsinki Accords in 1974 had opened the doors to "legal protests". Coupled with this Pope's work and the spiritual world of the Roman Catholic Church, it began sparking an awakening for Polish freedom. Present day Polish workers began demonstrating over price increases on foods and the lack of most consumer goods. The economic and social stagnation under Communism was brutal. *Life consisted of nothing but shortages, standing in long lines to purchase anything, and a bleak existence.* Only 1 in 3 homes/apartments had an indoor bathroom, the same ratio for central heat. To get into an apartment was a five-year wait, to build a house was a twenty year wait.

That was what Communism-Socialism offers the people.

Poland and her citizens were becoming increasingly restive as the months went by. In August 1979 striking workers were able to win some concessions from the Polish government, and because of his failures Communist leader Gierek was ousted. He was replaced by Kania who was told to tighten up the government rule. Rumors of Soviet military intervention were picked up, and that caused the members of NATO to warn that any Russian action would end détente. Sec. of State Muskie (who had replaced Cyrus Vance) hailed the pronouncement as a way to convince the Russians that their troop buildup along the Polish border was not welcome. Sanctions would certainly be applied upon any Soviet invasion.

Then in August 1980 at a shipyard in Gdansk a women worker was fired. Her fellow workers went on strike, 20,000 of them. Outside the gates supporters crowded the streets chanting and praying. A day later strikes began occurring across the nation. *Within a week millions of Polish workers walked out to demand economic reforms and a five day work week.* The nation became paralyzed as less than 20% of its workers showed up at their jobs. This was an astonishing event in a communist run nation. For the Polish government there was a great fear that the Russians would attack in retaliation for allowing the workers to unite like this. *(A workers paradise where the workers revolt, how enlightening.)*

An unemployed electrician became one of the strike leaders, and this man named **Lech Walesa** agreed to end the work stoppages if twenty-eight Polish dissidents were released from prison. By the end of September a new union called *Solidarity* was created, and they continued protesting garnering world attention. Meetings were held with the Polish Government and a deal was offered to Solidarity. Walesa wisely refused the deal, unless all of Poland was included in the meager benefits. **Solidarity for all**.

Polish workers and citizens stood strong in the face of constant arrests and attacks. **One of their main strengths was their Christianity.** Masses were held at the sites of strikes, and prayer vigils became a common sight. Inside the Kremlin plans were being made.

After witnessing the recent Russian brutality in Afghanistan Saudi Prince Turki returned home and worked with the Saudi rulers to ensure the Afghan cause was addressed. The Organization of Islamic Conference was held in Saudi Arabia in the resort town of Taif to condemn the Soviet invasion and motivate the regional nations to supply fighters and aid. Afghan **Abdurrab Rasul Sayyaf** spoke passionately to those assembled. Money was collected and distributed by the Saudi-GID. Hundreds of young Saudi's joined the war effort, which included a student named **Osama Bin Laden**.

China also benefitted from the Afghan war as Sec-Defense Brown went to China to get their permission to fly in aid from their country. They readily agreed, and China also allowed us to build two electronic listening posts near the Soviet-Sino border to replace the ones we had lost in Iran. *In return, and despite their horrendous record of fighting us in Korea and Vietnam, plus being guilty of the worst human rights violations in the world, Carter and the Democratic Congress conferred upon China the status of "most favored nation." That enabled them to have quick and easy access to our goods and services, and opened our markets to them. Soon after dual-use technology was being sold to Communist China with Administration approval!* *(54)

Terrorism

London was a victim of another violent terrorist bombing on January 17, 1980. PLO offshoot the *May 15 Movement* announced its presence to the world with a strong bomb on the fifth floor of London's Mount Royal Hotel which caused extensive damage. One of the bombers, a 22 year old Palestinian was killed when one of their other bombs exploded prematurely. Back in July those same terrorists had used hand grenades in an attack in Antwerp murdering one civilian with twenty wounded.

In NYC the bright sparks in law enforcement decided that they had to get better organized to stop the constant low-level terrorist attacks we and the world had been suffering from. The FBI and NYPD formed a Joint Terrorist Task Force, dedicated to anti-terrorism, **the JTTF**. During the next few years they arrested and broke up a who's-who of terrorist groups including the weather underground, the BLA, Black Liberation Army, NAAF and others. Their work saved dozens of innocents as each of those groups was planning multiple attacks. This was just beginning.

Hostage Rescue

After months of failure over Iran, Carter reluctantly approved a military rescue plan to try to bring out the U.S. hostages who were still being held captive. But the erosion, cutbacks and malaise of the last few years meant the military would be hard pressed to perform this mission. As they planned *Operation Eagle Claw* a serious issue became evident. With the loss of the Shah and Iran, America had no bases in the region from which we could operate. Britain had allowed us to use their base at Diego Garcia in the Indian Ocean at various times, but not for this mission. *Pres. Sadat of Egypt graciously allowed us the use of his country as a forward staging base. Without him no rescue could have been attempted!*

A complex plan was created in which the U.S Army's Delta Force and Army Rangers would fly in a C-141 cargo plane from Egypt to the island of Manzirah off of Oman. From there smaller C-130s would fly the rescue force deep into the Iranian desert some 200 miles from Tehran. Some of the Rangers would remain at that site to secure and prepare this initial position called *Desert One*. Then eight Sea Stallion helicopters would fly at night from the carrier *Nimitz* to Desert One. Once there they would be refueled and fly the Delta troops to a holding area outside of Tehran. CIA agents would hire trucks to take the attack force to the Embassy and Iran's Foreign Ministry. The hostages would be grabbed, trucked to the helicopters and flown to the airfield at Manzarieh which was secured by another Ranger team. Carter and his Administration were briefed on the difficult plan and gave their approval.

(Israeli Generals Yitzhak Segev and Dan Shomron were asked for some operational advice. First off they recommended capturing

the Ayatollah. It was easier to pull off grabbing one man vs one hundred plus, and we could use him as a ransom for the other hostages. They also warned that a minimum of ten helicopters should be sent in case something broke down. Both ideas were rejected by the Carter Administration.)*

On April 21, 1980 the force moved secretly into Egypt. On the evening of the 24th *Desert One* was successfully setup inside Iran. Then the problems began.

One of the eight helicopters had equipment problems en-route and had to turn back. A second had mechanical trouble and was forced down in the desert. This mission used Air Force helicopters instead of the more durable USMC or Navy versions. Those units have a dust separator that would have failure, kept the delicate engines clear of the gritty sand. *(Sand that was everywhere on this mission.)*

The Administration had insisted that no replacement helicopters be been planned for to cover potential problems like this, to keep the numbers of personnel down. The remaining six helicopters arrived 90 minutes late when yet another one was found to be leaking hydraulic fluids and also forced out.

At that point the mission commander Col. Beckworth (from the Son Tay Raid in Vietnam), reported that the mission had to be scrubbed. He was told by administration bureaucrats he had to continue on, but he refused. Pres. Carter then approved the withdrawal. During the refueling operation one of the helicopters crashed into a C-130 loaded with fuel. In the explosion both aircraft were destroyed with eight crewmen killed. The rest successfully exited the country. By morning the Iranians were at the smoking site and filmed it to show the world. America was never so inept.

As a result of the failed mission the hostages were moved around and split up so no follow on raids could be mounted. Carter's already low approval ratings fell to historic lows. Inflation which had been 4.8% in 1976 was now 13.3%. Companies were closing weekly and millions of people were out of work. To make things worse for Carter, Ted Kennedy was campaigning hard against him for the democratic nomination. NY Governor Hugh Carey wanted both uninspiring men to drop out so the delegates could find a better candidate. Neither one did, and Carter narrowly won at the August convention. His four years of failure was a hard thing to run on, as even the civilian staff at the White House disliked Carter. On the Republican side Ronald Reagan was steadily moving ahead and would gain the nomination.

Our Defensive problems were not limited to tactical operations like Iran. *In 1980 we suffered three computer failures that could have had serious consequences.* The first failure involved NORAD tracking what appeared to be a single Soviet missile heading towards Oregon. Senior military commanders debated the strange attack long after they should have alerted the Sec-Def and the White House. The incident was analyzed as a computer glitch.

The second incident involved notification that 220 Soviet missiles were heading our way. Brzezinski was awakened with this emergency report. With this type of attack the president had only 3-7 minutes to launch a counter-strike! Brzezinski directed his assistant Odem to find out if SAC had our bombers airborne. *He was then told 2,200 missiles were coming in, an all out Soviet attack that would kill everyone in the U.S.* Just as Carter was to be notified, Odem heard that no other warning stations had picked up any Soviet missiles. **It turned out that someone had mistakenly installed our war-exercise tapes into a defense computer. Whoever that idiot was, they almost created a nuclear war.**

The third incident was an alert system computer failure. What was life-threatening over these three events was that those computers were the best we had, and still things went wrong.

As always the KGB learned of those proceedings and reported back to Moscow. *In their convoluted thinking, they convinced themselves that these events were staged, to create the impression our equipment had failed.* They actually believed the evil Americans were trying to lull the Soviets into a false sense of security, that U.S. computer failures were a common issue. *That would give the U.S. a cover story for their real surprise attack!*

On May 4, 1980 President Tito of Yugoslavia died. Yugoslavia was the only Nation in WWII that defeated the invaders by themselves, and Tito was the only Communist leader in Europe who was able to keep the Soviets out of his country. He had accepted their aid during the war, but staffed his borders with well armed forces to ensure the parasitic Russians out. He was a strong ruler who kept the many warring ethnic populations of Yugoslavia under control, and his passing was not welcome news in that volatile region.

Tito had been an early advocate of the idea of nonalignment among the smaller nations. He did not want his country to be beholden or captive to any one type of political / economic philosophy, especially Russian. Following his lead was Nehru of India and to some extent Nasser of Egypt. All three proved adept at angering the world powers, and each nation rightfully moved on their own axis. Unfortunately Nasser provoked war as a way to control internal dissent, which changed the strategic picture.

Historical Note: After Nasser took power in Egypt, Allen Dulles tried to get him to join an anti-Communist alliance with the U.S. Nasser told him, "The Soviets are over a thousand miles away, and have never been a problem for us. But your friends the British certainly have."* Nasser refused to join in, and America found new allies in Iran and Pakistan as we continued our foreign policy effort of Containment. *(55)

But two major differences existed for America versus what the Europeans had had. *We had to pay for the effort of having allies, and we were not ruling those countries to maintain our political position and bases.* Those former colonial powers taxed and used local resources to maintain their governing presence, and they worked non-stop for multiple decades to keep control. We had no control over anything, and as seen with the Carter Administration there was no long term view either.

Iran-Iraq War

After the failed Iranian rescue mission France tried to assist the CIA by smuggling an agent into Iran. This agent and his French counterpart learned that the Ayatollah frequently went to a home in Iran's holy city of Qom. That neighborhood was quiet and close to an open field. Those agents worked out a plan to seize the Ayatollah and deliver him to a navy ship. "Carter was intrigued but refused to allow the mission because the Ayatollah was a religious figure and he was elderly" *(56)

With his election poll numbers falling fast the Administration hatched another last ditch plot. National Security Advisor Zbigniew Brzezinski went to Amman, Jordan in July 1980 to meet with Jordan's King Hussein. The King was Saddam Hussein's closest confidant in the Middle East, and had learned that Saddam wanted to attack Iran in response to coup offers from Loyalist Iranian Officers still inside Iran. They were plotting an uprising which was directed by former Prime Minister Shahpur Bakhtiar. Now that everyone had awakened to the true nature of the Ayatollah and his followers, many factions had come together to overthrow them. The plotters were secretly operating from Baghdad and at a training camp in the Kurdish town of Sulimaniyah when Brzezinski arrived. Their plot was far along and they were confidant of success. *Unknown to those men the*

Ayatollah and his followers had learned of the plot from Soviet agents operating in France and Latin America. *(57)

Days after the Brzezinski's meetings Iranian leaders gave the arrest orders for six hundred pro-Bakhtiar officers still in uniform. Bakhtiar and many of the loyalists fled to France and exile.

With Iran under his domination, Khomeini wanted to unleash his brand of Islam across the Middle East. With over 100,000 Russians fighting in Afghanistan they were off his list. By default Saddam Hussein and his Ba'thists became Khomeini's next target. Iraq has a large Shiite population, over 55% of their total. At that time Saddam's Sunni minority was still in power, but with the takeover by the Ayatollah in neighboring Iran, the Sunni's were having increasing trouble holding on. Khomeini's mullahs were spreading their Fundamentalist word and attacks, raids and sabotage were spreading.

Iraq's large Shia population had always been a problem for the Sunnis controlling Iraq. (In 1921 the British Colonial Office warned Churchill it was folly to create Iraq with those hostile populations.) During 1980 the hostile Shia group the Da'wa attempted to assassinate Iraq's foreign minister Tariq Aziz. As usual Saddam reacted harshly, and ordered the execution of their leader the Ayatollah Muhammad al-Sadr, and drove the rest out of them from the country. Some sought refuge in Lebanon while others went to Iran. This event actually helped set the stage for Iran's major influence in Iraq afterwards. Those refugees became well trained agents for Iran, and retained their pent up hatred for Saddam and the Sunni's. (In late 2003 they returned for their vengeance. And the web of history goes on.)

On the other side of the story, Hussein and his Iraqi Army had been trying to steal the oil rich province of Khuzestan, (a part of ancient Iraq), from the disjointed Iranians. He had hoped to exploit their internal problems and believed the coming coup would give him his chance. Capture of that area would also shut the flow of weapons into Iraq, and stop the Iranian Shiite sponsored rebellion that was threatening his own rule. Over the last few weeks planes had been shot down on both sides, and in September 1980 Iran lost eight gunboats in a naval clash. Their recent fighting caused the Iraqi's to shut off Iranian oil exports from their common border.

The one factor that had always kept Saddam in check was the large and well armed Iranian Air Force. That unit had been built up and trained by U.S. advisors over the many years of friendship and it was a potent force of U.S. made jets and weapons.

But as shown above the many months of national torment since the Ayatollah seized power those Air Force officers loyal to the Shah had finally reached their limit. Their country was being destroyed by the extremists and was in danger of fighting with America or Russia. Those officers, most of whom were pilots decided to plan and stage a coup. Numerous flights would secretly leave three air bases and bomb the residences of the Ayatollah and his highest aides. Then the army would strike out from their bases and take over the country. *Just as they were finishing the last steps of their coup word got out because of the Russian spies.* Before the pilots could suit up Revolutionary Guards stormed the air bases. Everyone was arrested with hundreds being executed. All of them suffered severe tortures and those not shot were imprisoned under brutal conditions.

With that fortuitous turn of events Saddam's main stumbling block to invading Iran was now gone. His highest officers rushed their earlier made war plans into final completion. Saddam's spies knew the Arab people of the Iranian province of Khuzestan were not happy with the new Persian-Shiite fundamentalist rule, and had been quietly working with Iraq's agents getting things organized.

On September 22, 1980 the Iran-Iraq war began along an 800 mile front! Iraqi units attacked into seven areas initially and their armored units advanced deep into Iran. (Similar to the German advances into Russia in 1941.) Iraq's Soviet supplied weapons proved quite effective at first, and in the southern zone Iraq lay siege to three coastal cities in an effort to close Iran off from the Shat el-Arab waterway. That would prevent them from selling any oil while Saddam often used Kuwait as his middleman.

Initial Iraqi air attacks had struck the Iranian airfields damaging the runways but their poor pilots did not destroy enough of the Iranian planes. Iraq's army was gaining ground and almost freed the province of Khuzestan, but then Iran's Revolutionary Guards mass attacked the Iraqi's dying by the multiple thousands. As had happened to the Germans in WWII, Iraq had attacked too many places at once and was soon stopped at all of them. Having a lot of weapons does not mean proficiency in war, and Iraq's command and logistical weaknesses were revealed. Strong Iranian counter-attacks and a few well placed air attacks checked the Iraqi advances, and then the Iranians used artillery to bleed the stationary Iraqi units.

One unforeseen fallout of this attack was the unification of Iran to fight off the Sunni Arab invaders. (Again similar to what happened in Russia in WWII.) Perhaps in time the Iranian rebels may have hurt or beaten the Mullahs, but with Iraq's inept war that rebellion ended. Their battlefields soon turned into the trench warfare reminiscent of WWI, and it also threatened the world's oil supplies. Prices increased again.

By this point even Khomeini realized that it could take decades for his Islamic theocracy to conquer all of Iran. He could see that the people were unhappy with "his dream". Up to his death, he believed his vision of strict Shia Islam was the correct path for the Islamic world.

The Western media never gave the war a lot of coverage, but the brutal battles were vital to the world's economy and a potential disaster in that weapons of mass destruction, WMD's were being used. Unable to defeat the Iranians using conventional weapons Saddam Hussein had an accelerated program in place to develop his chemical and nuclear weapons. And Saddam's deputy and Foreign Minister Tariq Aziz was in Paris demanding the French make good on all of their prior promises on military aid. However the French were now alarmed. They had not counted on a war breaking out, and they feared that Iran would destroy Iraq's oil export terminals shutting off much of the oil France needed and depended on. After strong-arming the French and threatening to shut off their oil, Saddam received his updated weapon systems. They also provided 12.5 kilograms of enriched uranium for his Osirak reactor. **It was enough to build one atomic bomb.**

Cuba and Central America

As shown before during July 1979 it came to light about that Soviet army unit being based in Cuba. The Administration principals attempted to explain away the find as Carter was desperate to save his SALT II program. Upon investigation it became evident that one Soviet unit had been based there a long time. (Actually since JFK's time.) They were there to prevent the U.S. from invading Cuba, and tensions over this issue increased as the weeks went by. The Soviets refused to remove any of their units. Carter made a small speech that September trying to dismiss the incident, but again it did not work with the voters.

Two unwanted issues arose over those Soviet troops. First it highlighted the increased Soviet-Cuban subversive efforts in the Caribbean, something the Administration wanted kept quiet. Second it also brought out the fact that over 40,000 Cuban troops were still advising and fighting in Africa.

Then during April 1980 thousands of people flocked to the Peruvian Embassy in Havana when a rumor started saying that the embassy was offering visas to get out. *Mobs of Cubans demanded asylum and permission to leave, scaling the embassy walls and overwhelming the guards.* Castro cagily allowed those dissatisfied Cubans to board airplanes for a quick flight to Costa Rica and then onto Peru. Part of his rational was to get the dissenters and malingerers out of his hair as quickly and quietly as possible. He also infiltrated some operatives into the exiting crowds. (Once again those oppressed people were as Lenin had said, "Voting with their feet".)

Days later more people were demanding to leave and an angry Castro opened the port of Mariel near Havana. Anyone wishing to leave could. News of this quickly went out and flotillas of small craft exited Cuba with some 125,000 escapees. Most landed in nearby Florida in a eccentric version of the Dunkirk evacuation. Pres. Carter stated that the U.S. would take in only 3500 of the initial refugees and our Navy and Coast Guard were instructed to send the vessels back out to sea. But it became politically impossible not to take in those suffering souls and thousands came ashore each day.

Not long after the *Mariel boatlift* began Castro saw another rainbow and emptied his prisons and psychiatric hospitals. Boat operators were told they had to take those extra passengers or they would not be permitted to leave.

Between April and September 1980 almost 150,000 Cubans left the island. Most of those refugees landed in southern Florida forcing the unprepared Carter Administration to intern the refugees at southern military bases. Again Carter was unable to address the situation, and it happened just before the election. (This same thing is happening today in Europe with the Syrian civil war refugees and along our southern border. Most are innocents attempting to stay alive, but there are thousands of terrorists and criminals entering the Western nations too. And Obama had thousands of Syrians flown into our country each night in secret.)

Castro and all of the Communist states knew the situation in Cuba was a severe slap at Communism as a whole, but he did get rid of a lot of headaches. To put a smiling face on things Castro allowed some liberalization on the farms, (as Deng had done in China), and opened Cuba to families of expatriates who wanted to visit loved ones. *Their price for admission was to bring dollars and goods for sale that Cuba did not have. The regime made a profit on all sales.* (Communists make such good capitalists.)

Close by San Salvador was again rocked with trouble as twenty people were slain at a rally for a leftist leader who was killed days before. Three American nuns were also killed, and by that point over 9,000 had been killed in the fighting with the FMLN leftists who were being aided by the Sandinistas. *Once again the liberals in America were siding with the Communist guerrillas.*

Carter had suspended all aid to the country months before to stop the regional conservatives from fighting back. But now Carter had a big problem, he was way behind in the election polls. To get some good press and slow the violence, Carter stopped our aid to the Communist Sandinistas in Nicaragua and he resumed aid to El Salvador. *His actions were cold, calculating and disturbing. They were not done to help the people fight off the Communists, but to get reelected.*

Within weeks of taking over in Nicaragua the Sandinistas who were still allied with the PLO began harassing and intimidating their small Jewish community. Businesses were seized and the main Synagogue set on fire. After a few weeks of this terrorism all of the Jewish residents in Nicaragua fled. Christian leaders, even those who had backed the Sandinistas were next in line for torment. Many were arrested and beaten time and again. Religious radio programs were ended, their schools closed and the teachers forced to educate the children on Marxism. Even the impoverished native Moskito Indians were forced into re-education camps taught by Cuban instructors. Prison space was expanded and over 6,000 political prisoners were held and tortured. Tomas Borge the head of their Secret Police spoke of their prisons and conditions, "The revolution can tolerate no exceptions." *(58)

All of this social upheaval and terrorism resulted in the one byproduct that is common to all Communist takeovers, refugees. Ninety-five thousand refugees fled to Costa Rica, and additional thousands made it to Honduras and the U.S.

In addition to the listed issues above thousands of Nicaraguans were pressed-ganged into Sandinista-military service. By 1980 their upgraded militia force was double the size that Somoza had had!! By 1985 the Sandinista army reached 75,000 men. Their conscripts were trained and overseen by over 3,000 Cuban, Soviet and East Bloc advisors. To insure the success of "The Nicaraguan Revolution", the Soviets sent 350 T-55 tanks, 12 transport and 6 attack helicopters, as well as artillery, patrol boats and airplanes. They also built a new military airfield at Punta Hueta with a 10,000 foot long runway. It was capable of handling any aircraft in the Soviet arsenal. At this rate of success it would not be long before Soviet bombers and fighters began using Nicaragua as a "way-station", and closing off the Panama Canal.

By August 1980 the CIA had compiled a report on Cuban activity in Nicaragua. It stated that the Cuban advisory unit was increasing their numbers with an estimated 3,400-4,000 troops in Nicaragua. Cubana airline was making a daily round-trip flight into Managua delivering Soviet bloc weapons and supplies. Hundreds of Sandinistas were in Cuba receiving military training, and seventy are in flight training for MiG jets. CIA expected increased Soviet influence in the region, using Cuba as the primary entity. They expected the Sandinistas to have complete control of the country in months. *And since 1978 Cuba had also trained over 500 Salvadorans in insurgency and military tactics.*

(Whatever weak or nonexistent covert action Carter claimed he approved was accomplishing absolutely nothing. That fall another CIA report stated that the Soviets continued to expand their support of left-wing regimes in the region, all would fall.)

Poland

Poland was still in wonder of their Solidarity movement. Even though the union was under constant scrutiny and threat from spies and infiltrators from State Security forces, they were still active and protesting. On May 3, 1980 members of the Young Poland Movement and the Movement in Defense of Human Rights were arrested. Lech Walesa and others began a public campaign demanding freedoms and an overhaul of their dysfunctional economy. Tensions rose, and in July the CIA warned of trouble.

With the 1980 summer Olympic games being held in Moscow senior Communist leaders decided to allow TV antennas in every village and town. That allowed the citizens behind the Iron Curtain to watch the games. What the Communists did not realize was that those antennas could be turned to pick up signals from any direction. People in Hungary and the other East Bloc states could and did watch Polish TV, and they learned of the struggle for freedom going on there. (They also picked up some Western TV signals enabling them to see our world.)

In the fall additional strikes broke out and began spreading across Poland. U.S. trade unions got involved with the cause and made offers of financial support. Soviet forces were put on alert, and the Carter Administration went into panic mode worrying that our Union's efforts might just provoke a Soviet response. By November 1980 the CIA felt the situation was at a crisis point. Soviet propaganda had hardened as they pressured Kania to act.

On December 1, 1980 Soviet military exercises began near Poland. They were unannounced, and border closures with their neighbors were put into effect. The White House meetings became tense as no one knew what to do. A Hot-Line message was drafted by Brzezinski and agreed to by the principals to be sent to Brezhnev warning of grave consequences if the Soviets acted militarily. (We would end all commercial contracts.) Other Western world leaders were asked to submit similar messages to avoid a massacre of the unarmed civilians.

At a Warsaw Pact meeting on December 5 Party Secretary Kania asked the other Communist leaders for more time. They complied, and the situation slowly wound down. But the CIA still expected the Soviets to strike.

(After the fall of Communism the truth of that time came out. **Kania was supposed to have been "removed" at that meeting. Fifteen Soviet, two Czech, and one E. German Division would invade Poland. An additional 9 Soviet Divisions would arrive days later. Poland and her people were to be crushed.)** *(59)

America

By election day our economy and federal budget were in terrible shape. The overall deficit had gone from $709 billion to over $914 billion. Inflation was almost 20%, and unemployment went to 12% and rising fast. To strengthen the GOP electoral ticket the second place candidate and former CIA Director, Ambassador to China and the U.N., George Bush was named as the candidate for Vice President. They were a tough team to defeat.

As the world's events continued to turn against America's interests and beliefs Jimmy Carter would lose the 1980 election in an electoral landslide. His was a worse defeat than Hoover had suffered to FDR in 1932, though our economy was not yet in a depression. Ronald Reagan had told the crowds during the campaign, *"A recession is when your neighbor loses his job, a depression is when you lose yours, and a recovery is when Jimmy Carter loses his."*

Carter was devastated by his defeat, especially to a man he intensely disliked. Unlike other candidates who lost, every chance he could Carter would publicly criticize Reagan's policies and he interfered constantly in diplomatic matters. In every instance he was on the wrong and losing side.

Hours before he was to leave office, Carter secretly transferred 7.9 $Billion to Iran! *(59a)

Former Democratic Senator Eugene McCarthy succinctly said it all,"Carter was the worst president we ever had". * (60)

Section Three   January 1981 – January 1989

The Reagan Years   Renewal and Rebuilding

Former California Governor Ronald Reagan was 69 when he won the Presidency, the oldest person to hold the office. He was considered a *Hawk* ever since he left the Democratic Party in 1960, and was not liked by most of the media or the Democrats. (Like so many of us Ronald Reagan became disillusioned with the leftist and destructive tilt of the Democrats, and he changed parties becoming a successful Republican Governor of California.)

As a young adult during WWII and then throughout the Cold War, Reagan saw and despised what the Communists were doing. He was determined now that he was president to rebuild America and stop the subversions. His presidential campaign promised to put America back to work, reduce our taxes and get our military capabilities back on track. (Trump followed the same script when he followed another Democratic disaster, Barak Obama.) Despite being caricatured as a reckless cowboy by the leftist media, his platform called for positive non-military means to rollback the growth of Communism.

Reagan came in on a tide of patriotic fervor which completely surprised and chagrined the liberals and Democrats. He felt his mission was to stop the fall of America and keep us safe.

The new President gave a short and upbeat twenty minute inaugural speech that was in complete contrast to Carters in 1976. *Reagan stated that government was not the answer to solving the country's ills, on the contrary the government was the main problem.* His first official act was to order a federal hiring freeze. Reagan correctly wanted to cut taxes to spur investment and return many governmental functions to the states instead of having them entwined within the federal bureaucracy.

(Back in 1960 the Congress had 6,800 staffers which cost the taxpayers $129 million a year. By 1988 that number would swell to 19,500 and cost almost $2 billion, a 1400% increase. And that was just one small part of the Federal bureaucracy.)

Minutes after Ronald Reagan was sworn in the Iranians released the U.S. hostages. They had been captives for 445 days. Pres. Reagan did not mention the hostages during the inaugural speech, it was better served to get them free and away from Iranian airspace. Once that was done they were under the protection of Navy fighter jets. Rumors abounded that the hostage release was no coincidence. Liberals suspected that Reagan had somehow made a "deal" with the belligerent Islamic clerics, while conservatives speculated that a massive military strike was going to be used if they were not released. The latter had it right.

Chief of Staff Edwin Meese had gone to the Iranians in secret and delivered a simple message from the president elect a week before his inauguration. *Meese told them "The Iranians should be prepared that this country will take whatever action is appropriate, and they should think very carefully the fact that it would be to their advantage to get the hostages back now."* This was a thinly veiled reference to Newton's Third Law of Physics, for every action, there is an equal and opposite reaction. (61)

(This was also similar to Ike's threats to end the Korean War in 1953, and was clearly illustrated by Nixon's actions in December 1972 which forced the N. Vietnamese to end the Vietnam War.)

After the hostages returned home one of Carter's own staffers lamented that had the Democrats won the election the hostages probably would not have been released.

(And possibly the Europeans would have given up and disbanded NATO. That would have changed everything.)

Within weeks of taking office Pres. Reagan and his team ran through the various departments and made it clear the previous way of doing things was over. *The Soviets were to be challenged everywhere, and they planned out a $32 billion increase to the defense budget.* The idea was to engage the Soviets in continual proxy fighting and an arms buildup that would bankrupt their struggling economy. At the same time it would restore America's failing military. Both factors would work in tandem to control and stop the Soviets from winning.

"Pres. Reagan was adamant in this outlook. His unwavering determination to reverse the negative flow of recent events was the lynchpin of his foreign policy." *(62)

For those who can think critically, there is a huge and dangerous difference between winning a war and deterring one. Winning a war involves many unknowns such as up to date intelligence and equipment, no bad luck, well trained forces, good commanders and a winning strategy.

In Deterrence one seeks to persuade an enemy that they are bested before a shot is fired. To do that you must have a credible military force, and the will to use it. **Deterrence can be expensive to maintain, but vastly less so than fighting a war. And definitely not as costly as losing a war.**

Historical Note; It was clear to every strategic thinker that the global disarmament by the democracies in the years following WWI had allowed the totalitarian states to institute war as a foreign policy a decade later. It took years (WWII) of incredible effort, millions of lives lost and battered, and enormous expense to right those prior failures. Sadly those same disarmament mistakes were repeated in 1945-48, and led to the loss of China to the Communists in their "Civil War", a Communist insurgent war in Greece, Indochina, Malaya and an outright Communist invasion in Korea. Only the reactionary Truman Doctrine and the Marshall Plan saved Greece, Turkey and Western Europe from Communist domination and control.

As a result of those post-WWII crisis's the strategy of **Containment** was formulated. Truman's decision to fight in Korea was reactionary, and not voted on by the Congress as required by law. He simply ordered our forces in Japan to intercede and fight to save Korea. But then Truman placed political constraints on the war, which created the stalemate conditions of 1952-53. Eisenhower threatened the Communists with a nuclear cannon in early 1953, and they decided it was time to stop.

During the Cold War the West was unable to roll back the Communist gains. With Russia making atomic weapons, **Deterrence** became the foundation for Pres. Eisenhower's New Look Strategic Review. We built up a punishing nuclear force as a Deterrent, to stop overt Communist advances. For Eisenhower the best defense was based on a good nuclear offense. That stopped any new Communist invasions such as happened in Korea.

Both Khrushchev and Chou En-lai made guarded references to the Eisenhower-Dulles atomic policy of *MAD, Mutual Assured Destruction*. Both leaders were quite nervous of what would happen to them had we attacked.

Khrushchev even admitted that Russia was facing barefaced American atomic blackmail. Even so, that policy had to be reckoned with because Russia did not yet possess the ability to strike back. **Both Communist countries avoided another direct conflict with America while Ike was in office.**

*However Ike's Deterrence strategy was not well suited for stopping Communist **inspired insurgencies** such as was happening in SE Asia.* After an extensive review Eisenhower refused to be drawn into the French-colonial war in Vietnam. After the peace treaty was signed he sent a small advisory force to help the fledgling state of S. Vietnam learn how to defend itself. But Ike repeatedly ignored good advice from his WWII peers, and chose poor leaders to lead our effort there. *His six year endeavor produced no effective military or political power.*

During the 1950s we began an intensive buildup of strategic forces to fight the Russians if need be. Eisenhower did not rebuild the Army, and they were unprepared for Vietnam. He also committed the U.S. to more foreign entanglements with the creation of SEATO to protect SE Asia, and CENTRO to protect the Middle East. Unlike NATO, both were controlled and funded by America. Eisenhower unleashed the CIA abroad on covert Cold War missions. And despite being told that the Soviets could shoot down one of our U-2 recon planes, Ike approved of the mission where Gary powers was shot down and captured. Russia's Khrushchev used the effort for maximum propaganda and Eisenhower eventually owned up to the missions.

A scheduled meeting with the Soviet leader was canceled, and a dejected Eisenhower rode out his last year in office. *(Tragically had that super-power meeting occurred in 1960 the peace intuitive Ike sought may have come about, gaining enough votes for Nixon to have won the election despite the Democrat's voter frauds.)*

Meanwhile Russia's 1957 launch of **Sputnik** presented a dangerous realization that our nuclear deterrent was no longer dominating as Russian missiles could now strike us. Arms control was a desired focal point by Eisenhower and presented as a possibility by Khrushchev. But for the militarily resurging Russians of the late 50s, arms control was just propaganda. They felt they were pulling ahead of us in missile technology, and talk of peace was just another weapon in their political struggle to undermine their enemies and take over.

During Ike's two terms the only gains for Communism was in the lost cause of French Indochina and in the poorly governed nation of Cuba. A temporary peace was obtained with the French exit from Indochina, while Fidel Castro, the Cuban rebel had fooled most with his pre-takeover ideas and rhetoric. He did not admit his true politics until after 1959. Once that reality was unleashed, Cuba's Communists began dismantling the country. Ike directed the CIA to find a way to get him out.

Around that time a new strategic thinking was being banded about by the eastern leftist mindset. Eisenhower's policy of MAD was irrational, and "limited wars" like Korea were considered acceptable. (Especially since none of them had to fight in one.)

That was the view of JFK and his Administration when they took office in January 1961, (after fixing the election.) Kennedy prepared for what he felt would be a "low-level war in Vietnam". **He quietly increased the military advisors in the South from the few hundred Ike had sent to over 24,000 by 1963! Those advisors were there to do the setup work for the war Kennedy wanted to fight in 1965, after his re- election was over.** Unfortunately he was murdered in November 1963 and no one can say how he would have run the war he planned to fight. (Hopefully he would not have run it as poorly as LBJ and McNamara did.)

As shown before, the Vietnam War had devastated our military. So much was spent in Vietnam that there were few upgrades done on our equipment, planes and ships. New aircraft like the F-16 & F-14 & F-15s started coming out in the late 70s, and a few new ships arrived, but not in the quantity they could have had we not fought in Vietnam. All of those factors weakened our forces.

For the incoming Reagan administration the 1980 disastrous failed rescue mission in Iran had highlighted how bad things really were within our post-Vietnam military services. If your best units have such trouble what are your regular forces capable of? He and his incoming team needed to rebuild every branch of the U.S. Military, and Carter's defense cuts would be rescinded. (Pres. Reagan's foreign policy game plan seemed to have come from former Pres. Nixon's outstanding 1979 work *The Real War*.)

One of our most pressing problems was in the Navy which had lost hundreds of active duty ships and received few replacements. Reagan desired a 600-ship navy that could contain the growing and advancing Russian fleets which were sailing everywhere. The Russians now had ships operating from our former base in S. Vietnam at Cam Rhan Bay, threatening the sea lanes around Australia and the Philippines. The "Navy is the Shield of our Republic", and had to be rebuilt. *(63)

In order for the U.S. to challenge and deter the incessant Soviet-Communist imperialism (the Brezhnev Doctrine), Pres. Reagan officially ended Détente. At his first press conference Pres. Reagan told the reporters that the Soviets only objective was what would advance their interests.

"Their morality is to lie, to cheat, and to commit any crime that they feel is effective. The Soviets do not subscribe to our sense of morality, such as in God, an afterlife or a religion in general. They fund terrorists and work to subvert democratic governments.

All they recognize is what will advance the cause of worldwide socialism". *(64)

The liberal media and reporters, (many of whom were Socialist supporters) were mortified that anyone especially the President would dare to speak so bluntly. Even the European leaders who had wanted Carter to act were afraid of the effect Reagan's talk would have upon the Soviets. Reagan was worrying everyone, but that was just what was required to have an impact on the Soviets.

(Sadly those political issues Reagan listed were the same ones George Kennan had brought up in 1946 with his famous telegram. His warnings were ignored by Truman until mid-1947. But by then China had been lost to Mao and his Communists.)

Central America

Pres. Reagan's team and many other world leaders were convinced (correctly) that all of the recent troubles in Latin America were Soviet-Communist inspired, and they setout to correct it. In mid-February 1981 the incoming State Department which was now headed by General Alexander Haig announced that the fighting in El Salvador was a textbook case of communist subversion. *Our actions would be to thwart them wherever they were operating. Unlike Carter, we would not sit on the sidelines and observe.*

To counter this growing Marxist threat Reagan sent an additional 35 advisors and $25 million in aid to El Salvador. The CIA would be the lead agency in rectifying the previous failures. *The United States and the West were moving from limited defense to an aggressive offense.*

Sandinista Minister of Interior, and the head of their *Secret Police*, Tomas Borge had recently proclaimed from Nicaragua; **"This revolution goes beyond our borders,"** a clear warning they were going to spread their poison. Sandinista Minister for defense Humberto Ortega told the Nicaraguan people before their first election; **"Keep firmly in mind that these elections are to consolidate revolutionary power, not to place it at stake."** Sergio Ramirez another member of the ruling junta said; **" The Nicaraguan people will get to choose and vote for one candidate, the Revolution."** *(65)

Leftist leaders in El Salvador issued a statement that their struggle has the brilliant example of Nicaragua to look to for guidance. Our struggle in El Salvador is far advanced, the same is happening in Guatemala, and Honduras is also progressing. **Soon all of Central America will be one revolutionary entity."** *(66)

On March 25, 1981 leftist rebels armed with RPG's attacked the U.S. Embassy in El Salvador. It was the forth attack in a month by the rebels who were protesting the increasing U.S. aid to the country. The Democrats in Congress began complaining that all of the recent activity appeared similar to what had happened in Vietnam. (That was true, the Communists did not want us to interfere in Central America or in Vietnam.)

After that latest attack Pres. Reagan directed that all U.S. economic ties to communist run Nicaragua be cut. If the communists wanted the country so badly, they had to pay for and support it themselves. Naturally his actions were condemned by our nations liberals as uncaring. (Why were we still trading with or aiding them at all??)

By the end of April the growing battles in Latin America resulted in the closing of the borders of Honduras and Nicaragua. Liberals and Democrats were in a frenzy over the Administration efforts. NY Congressman Jack Kemp gave a simple explanation for their inane attitudes. *"Democrats are not soft on Communism, they are soft on Democracy".* *(67)

Unlike the Democrats, the Republicans do not seem to have any trouble calling things as they are; Truman calling the Korean War a "Police Action, LBJ refusing to call for a declaration of war in Vietnam, and in our time, Obama refusing to call the war on Islamic Terror, a war on Islamic Terror. Every official in the Reagan Administration was told to be harsh with the Soviet officials they met with and emphasize that America would no longer tolerate the aggressive policies of the Soviets or their client states Cuba and Libya. Soviet officials were warned that Poland must be sparred from any Soviet aggression or there would be consequences.

Reagan's Attorney General Edwin Meese wrote about the Carter administration's inability to correct even Libya's trouble making. Back in 1979 Muammar al-Qaddafi declared a one hundred mile exclusion zone around his nation. Carter directed that all U.S. naval activity was to be ended and our ships and planes had to stay away. The results of that weakness were more Libyan directed terrorist attacks in Europe and in Africa.

(America had had military bases and workers in Libya from their liberation in WWII until 1970 when we were told to leave by the ruling leftist junta.)

Poland and America

During 1981 Polish money became worthless, foods hard to find and the people were again protesting. Polish Party Secretary Stanislaw Kania had barely avoided a Soviet military intervention in December, and was again on the hot seat. To prevent a Soviet invasion the Poles had to crack down themselves, and hard. (We were blessed with the defection of a Polish Army office who had seen enough of the horrors of Communism. Colonel Ryszard Kuklinski was on the Polish General Staff. At great risk to himself he was providing almost real time updates on the situation there.)

The only good thing the dangers in Poland provided was that it strengthened NATO and the Western alliance. *Everyone could see that despite the talking about détente, the Russians had not changed their spots.* And with Reagan and Thatcher providing solid leadership the rest of NATO knew we had their back. Though Reagan was portrayed as a war-monger by the leftists, he was anything but. All of our retaliatory responses to the Polish issue were economic and political.

Polish Premier Pienkowski was replaced by General Wojciech Jaruleski on February 10, 1981. That move and the harsh speeches and orders being issued gave evidence of what was about to happen if the Polish unions did not back down. Solidarity leaders read the tea leaves, and embraced a ninety day grace period. During that quiet period Jaruleski was preparing his orders for martial law, under Soviet review of course.

In March a crackdown on Solidarity members created the next round of tensions, and on the 28th strikes began again. Soviet officials did not like Jaruzelski's plans, they wanted them to be harsher. The Soviets also insisted that every Polish unit had to have Soviet officers at all levels. Polish leaders rejected that issue, and it seemed that a war might break out between Poland and Russia.

NATO leaders met in Brussels to discuss our response. Contingency plans were prepared which included a buildup of U.S. forces, active and reservists. Reagan was prepared to go on TV to explain the situation, and to enlist American support for Solidarity and the Polish people. At the last minute Walesa and Solidarity won some concessions from their government and called the strikes off. The Polish crisis was on hold, but then we had our own.

On March 30, 1981 an assassin slipped in near the White House photographers and shot Pres. Reagan almost killing him. Though suffering a serious chest wound Reagan made jokes and was in good spirits. (Three others were also wounded.) His wound was almost fatal, though the reports of his injuries were kept secret. Days later he was able to resume some work and keep the pressure on the Soviets. *(Had Ronald Reagan not survived, the world would be a much different place than the one people enjoy today.)*

On April 9 CIA Director William Casey, (who served in our WWII OSS ranks), prepared a report showing the intense pressure the Soviets were applying to the Poles. They could not tolerate this breakdown in control lest it spread. The Polish Catholic Church was a key player in these issues, reporting that extremists in the population were preparing for violent confrontations. Casey met with the Pope in Rome and was appraised of the problems. He advised that the unions had to hold back to avoid catastrophe. Word was passed around and Walesa and Solidarity stepped back to hold onto the gains they had already gotten.

Live today, fight again tomorrow.

But the Kremlin was not yet done.

On May 13 Pope John Paul II the extraordinary Polish Pope was seriously wounded by an assassin in St. Peters Square. The Pope had been blessing a small girl when the attack happened. Initial reports claimed the shooter was a Turkish criminal. **It was soon revealed that he was a well trained Bulgarian agent sent by the Soviets.** They had hoped that by eliminating the Polish Pope it would quell the growing unrest inside Poland and the rest of the Eastern Bloc. Instead of reducing tensions it increased them and further inflamed the Polish people.

(Eliminating a problem Pope was not new, anti-Fascist Pope Pius "died in 1939, anti-Communist Pope Paul and reformer John Paul I in 1978".)

Though not revealed at that time, the Vatican under Pope John Paul II, along with Pres. Reagan, the CIA and other western intelligence services led by Britain's Thatcher and Germany's Kohl were actively aiding the Poles.

It was known that all of the Communist economic systems were poorly managed and unfunctional. To hurt the Communists economically, Reagan ended all discussions on helping "Poland with their debts". That included use of the IMF or U.S. loans. He also stopped all agricultural trade with them, ended Polish airlines from entering America, and Polish fishing vessels from operating in U.S. waters.

In addition to those cutbacks scientific exchanges with the Soviets were ended, Russian airlines could no longer land in the U.S., and he also stopped technology sales and future grain sales. *Reagan had called Brezhnev on the Hot-Line and warned him not to intervene in Poland.* "It could unleash a process which neither you nor we could fully control". *(69)

Pres. Reagan wrote, " The great dynamic success of Capitalism has given us a powerful weapon in our battle against the Communists, **money**. The Russians could never win an arms race, for we could outspend them forever". *(68)

Again he was alone in that belief, but again he was correct. The current Soviet economy had run the extent of its abilities and was failing. They had seen the political and military weakness in America and struck out to conquer, Their aggressive expansion into the third world these past five years was putting a serious strain on them. Pres. Reagan needed our allies to close ranks and cut the Soviets off economically and technologically.

That was the way to stop them.

Inside the Kremlin their aging leaders knew what a danger the unleashed American industrial might was capable of. (Just as Yamamoto had warned the Japanese leaders in early 1941.) *They had to stop his efforts, and propaganda was their key.*

Iraq

For the past months French pilots and technicians had been trying to get their Iraqi counterparts up to speed on how to fly and maintain the new jets they had sent. French pilots flew in the back seat of the jets doing everything except pulling the triggers. Iraq was also acquiring the French made Roland-2 air defense batteries, and advanced anti-tank and anti-ship missiles. France also built up Iraq's national air defense system to a high standard.

Despite the hundreds of millions Saddam had spent on French weapons his uninspired troops were still being mauled on the battlefield. Iran had acquired large amounts of U.S. military equipment during the many years of our friendship. Our artillery systems were hammering the hapless and leaderless Iraqis. To try to even the score Saddam purchased the latest French cannon, and another $1.6 billion changed hands. (Their cannon was quite effective and bested many Iranian units.)

At Osirak the rebuilt Iraqi reactor was being installed and was soon to go on line. It was expected the reactor would be operating by July, but instead of producing electricity Saddam had ordered his scientists to use the French uranium to irradiate hundreds of tons of uranium yellowcake purchased secretly from Niger, Brazil and Portugal. **That process would produce plutonium, enough to make dozens of atomic bombs. Saddam expected to be a nuclear power in two years.**

Iraq's atomic program had been greatly helped by Italian Maurizio Zifferero, who had aided in the design and installation of key components. The IAEA (International Atomic Energy Agency) conducted an "inspection of the Osirak reactor" in the spring of 1981 and declared that Iraq was using the system peacefully. IAEA chief Hans Blix was rewarded for his "fine efforts" by being made the director for two separate agencies to insure Iraq's compliance.

However Robert Richter also of the IAEA disagreed completely with the impropriety, and reported to the U.S. Senate that additional facilities had been secretly built close to the "normal" ones. *They had not been allowed to inspect those facilities, and he warned the Senate that Iraq could have an atomic bomb by 1983.* Incoming French President Mitterrand was also warned by his own people what Saddam was up to, but it was too late to stop him. (After the Gulf War in 1991 Zifferero would become a top official at the IAEA, which would oversee the dismantling of Iraq's atomic bomb program.)

During April 1981 Israeli Prime Minister Menachem Begin also learned of the pending atomic hazard. Israel wasted no time in deciding to destroy the reactor. France had built Israel's nuclear reactor at Dimona, and the Iraqi one under construction was a close cousin. That would be a huge help in planning their attack. Similar to the Japanese in 1941, Israeli pilots practiced their bombing runs using their reactor as the target. Their pilots had been picked not just for their flying skills, but also for their linguistic skills.

Terrorism

At a New Years Eve Party at the Norfolk Hotel in Nairobi, Kenya the PLO's May 15 group struck again with a bombing that murdered sixteen and wounded eighty-seven.

On March 28, 1981 Indonesia Flight 206 was hijacked by Islamic terrorists. Commandos stormed the jet killing the terrorists but six passengers were also killed with two wounded.

On May 1, 1981 the Austrian Socialist party leader Heinz Nittel was killed by Iraqi agents in Vienna. His continued support of Israel was used as justification for the murder.

In May 1981 Libyan ruler Mommar Qaddafi declared his support for Iran's revolution. He directed large mobs of protestors to attack and destroy the U.S. embassy in Tripoli. Reagan then closed Libya's diplomatic annex in Washington and banned Libyan oil imports. Qaddafi then claimed all U.S. ships must stay away from his shores. Reagan naturally sent some of our ships to test that rule leading to an air battle in which two Soviet built Su-22 fighters were shot down.

Around this same time Iran's revolutionary guards attempted a hostile takeover in nearby Bahrain. Bahrain had been the site of a small British base during their glory days, and for that reason was quite westernized. Luckily this plot was uncovered and stopped, but it highlighted the growing worries about Iran and their fundamentalists.

On May 15 Islamic terrorists struck the El Al offices in Rome. During August they again struck, in Rome, Athens, and Vienna. All of those attacks used explosives murdering and wounding dozens of civilians.

On June 28, 1981 Iran was rocked with multiple bombings as those opposed to the Iranian Islamists began fighting back. The worst explosion occurred at the Hafte Tir bombing which killed 73 high ranking Iranian Fundamentalists.

August 29, 1981 a Vienna Synagogue was attacked by Islamic terrorists using automatic weapons and grenades. Two were killed and thirty wounded.

On August 31 A Red Army Faction made a successful car-bomb attack at Ramstein Air base in W. Germany wounding seventeen.

Foreign Affairs

France was undergoing a political schism as the scandal plagued government of centrist Valery Giscard d'Estaing was ending. The current form of the French Democracy was formed back in 1958 when Charles de Gaulle returned to office. He called it the Fifth Republic.

In May 1981 Socialist Francois Mitterrand won election as President in a coalition with France's Communist Party the PCF. As was normal in their political system, Mitterrand dissolved the National Assembly and called for new Parliamentary elections. Communist Party leader Georges Marchais was eager for the new elections as his Communists had recently won over 15% of the assembly seats. Mitterrand's Socialists had agreed to work with the communists, and Marchais now demanded numerous Ministerial positions in the new government.

This was the first time since 1947 that the Communists would hold such power in France. Unlike many of the European Communists, the French Communist party did not turn away from Russia after their brutality in Czechoslovakia in 1968. France was packed with Stalinists, including Marchais.

One of the most coveted positions was the Ministry of Transportation. That ministry controlled all road, rail, airport and sea access in and out of France. *Being in command of of that Ministry meant that the Communists would be in position to prevent or delay the recently approved military reinforcement plan allowing the U.S. military to use France as a supply base in case of war in Europe.*

As soon as he was placed in charge, PCF member and the new head of the Ministry of Transportation Charles Fiterman rushed to the office safe to "read" the just completed NATO mobilization plans. Aware of what they were doing and what they were going to do, Mitterrand had wisely ordered the Top-Secret plans removed before they could be seen by the PCF.

(V.P. George Bush had met with and warned Mitterrand of our fears and intentions soon after their election. Mitterrand must have concurred and took the plans out of the safe.)

Mitterrand's win was a huge surprise to the Western world's conservatives, (but not to the French communist party which had worked hard to get him in.) During the campaign Mitterrand had pledged to nationalize their banks and insurance companies, and to place a high tax on the wealthy. He also pledged to restore full employment by using the government to "hire any extra workers".

By the end of June four known Communists were rewarded with important seats in his new cabinet, including Fiterman. That news sent shockwaves through NATO, and the Reagan administration. To many it appeared that France was finally moving into the Soviet orbit. But Mitterrand (like Nixon) was a pragmatic man, and he recognized the many dangers threatening the globe and especially Europe. He did not want to alienate the powerful enemy that was just a days ride away, especially with America in the poor political and military shape they were in.

All of the Western leaders knew that Reagan was refusing to knuckle under to the Soviets or turn the other cheek as Carter had. *And even though Reagan was in the White House no one in France was sure if the Democrats in Congress would support Reagan's policies if a war came.* They were hedging their bets.

During July 1981 Henry Kissinger arrived in France to continue the conversations about Communism. High on the list was Cuba, the Sandinistas of Nicaragua and Russia. Kissinger told Mitterrand that those first two "issues" Pres. Reagan was going to challenge behind the scenes. However in the case of the Soviet Union, they were having economic troubles and once again their harvests had been light. Reagan wanted to hurt them indirectly, and one way was for the U.S. to support the Mujahedeen in Afghanistan with arms and weapons. The other was a new arms race. *One facet of that race was the positioning of American medium range missiles in Europe. It was time to make a decision on those weapons.*

(Henry Kissinger was a teenage Jewish refugee from Nazi Germany. Unlike most of the world, he well knew what bad looked like, and how beneficial the Western world and Democracy worked in saving the world from disaster.) *(70)

In **Afghanistan** the Soviet forces were destroying every village that might house rebels. Civilian casualties meant nothing as they depopulated the areas they invaded. Torrents of additional refugees flooded into Iran and Pakistan. Because of Soviet control the true story of the suffering seldom got out. Only when refugees made it to Pakistan did the West realize what was happening.

Soon after he took office Reagan renewed and expanded Carter's order to aid the Afghan rebels, **but now we would supply weapons.** To hide our involvement in this arms trade *the CIA purchased communist bloc weapons from Czechoslovakia and smuggled them into Pakistan.*

As shown before Carter had agreed that Pakistan's ISI, (Inter-Service Intelligence Agency) took control of all of the aid and supplies coming into their country. That meant there were limited U.S. controls on where anything ended up. Because of that requirement the Saudi's, which included bin Laden, began using private Islamic charities to funnel their aid in. *In that clever way they would control were the weapons and money ended up.*

Hundreds of thousands of old British Enfield rifles (bolt action) were sent over along with RPG's from China and Egypt. Those RPG's (rocket propelled grenades) could knock out the Russian tanks and armored vehicles that were running amok killing everyone in their path. By late 1981 those additional weapons (and Afghan courage) enabled the rebels to operate in nearly all of the twenty-nine Afghan provinces. They were frequently ambushing Soviet armored units and striking Communist controlled towns escaping into the darkness.

(*At the same time Afghan heroin was finding its way into America. The Afghan warlords and criminals in America saw their profits go up.*)

We gave the Afghans about $30 million in aid during 1981. By 1984 it would grow to over $200 million, matched by the Saudi's. That number paled to the $Billions the Russians were spending each year in their side of the war. CIA agents in the field were excited about their successful work against the communists, while at the higher levels many worried that the Russians might strike at Pakistan to end the supply lines. (It was fairly obvious that the aid was not getting in from Shia Iran.)

At a private meeting with Pres. Reagan, Pakistan's Gen. Zia assured him that the tough Afghans would fight the Russians with their bare hands if it must come to that. Reagan assured Pakistan's President that it would not come to that. His rhetoric, speeches and conservative cabinet all appeared to threaten war with the Soviets, but Reagan shrewdly knew where to draw the line. He would fight this renewed Cold War as an exercise in symbolism and ideas, well removed from actual battles. *(71)

Reagan also promised a total of $3.2 Billion in aid to Pakistan which would include F-16 fighter jets that had only been available to NATO and Japan. (And the Saudis thanks to Carter.)

From their side of the line Zia too worried greatly over Soviet reactions and intentions. But he also about any American interference. *He told his ISI Chief Akhtar Rahman to "lure the CIA and America in", but keep them away from Afghanistan and the Afghans.* No close contact would be allowed between the Americans and the Afghans, or any of their ISI people.

Zia told him, "The water in Afghanistan must boil, but at just the right temperature." *(72)

The Saudis also insisted that the CIA could not interact with their GID agents inside Pakistan. All meetings were to be supervised, and major ones had to take place in Riyadh or Langley. With our recent past of abandonment of our allies in the Carter years, no one wanted to get too close to our people. (However some contact and cross border recon did occur between Americans and Afghans.)

CIA agent Howard Hart slipped into Afghanistan a few times meeting with one of their true warriors Abdul Haq. And Hart often conferred with ISI chief Rahman in private talks where he was warned that the Indians did not like America. Hart was also the agent who had brought in the first Enfield rifles, and he expanded his arms trade to include Chinese mortars, RPG's, heavy machine guns plus tons of ammo. Even Polish military officers were secretly aiding the Afghans by stealing Soviet weapons to send over. Everyone in the CIA thought it was great that Soviet bloc weapons were being used to fight Russian soldiers. Even at this early point in the war the Russians had already suffered over 17,000 casualties, lost some 50 aircraft and 2500 vehicles.

Unknown to most of the world, the wanton killing of the Afghan civilians was prompting an unusually aggressive tone among Reagan's Administration. *Casey's CIA was even helping the Afghan rebels to conduct raids inside Soviet Central Asia as payback for those mass killings.* (Many of his deputies were against those raids for obvious reasons.)

Senator Patrick Moynihan asked Hart during a visit on how he could justify helping those poor people when the Soviets were just going to exterminate them anyway? Hart quoted Winston Churchill from 1941, "Give us the tools and we will do the job." *(73)

(On the down side of our aid effort corruption and payoffs colored every aspect of the system. The Pakistani's went so far as to load a Malaysian ship with their old weapons and ammo, sail it over the horizon and then back a few days later pretending the ship came from overseas. They gave the bill to the CIA.)

During his work Hart learned of the Pakistani efforts to build an atomic bomb despite assurances from Zia that they were not doing so. The Administration was torn over the feeling that we should cut our aid since they had lied. But since Russia was the more strategic threat, our help continued.

The Pentagon understood that to even hope to defend the Persian Gulf and surrounding nations the U.S. had to acquire base rights in the region. Negotiations were held with Egypt, Bahrain, Kuwait, Oman, the United Arab Emirates, (UAE), Qatar and Saudi Arabia. *None of those nations (except the Saudi's) wanted to offend the Soviets, in case the U.S. collapsed as it had appeared to be under the Carter Administration.* And none would allow us to have true bases on their soil. But "access agreements were made in case we were needed".

The Saudi's "allowed us to create new facilities" that were much larger than their small military could use. It was called "overbuilding", and we could "pre-position our military infrastructure there in case". As a result thousands of Western civilian contractors and military staff moved around the kingdom which caused much resentment by the Islamists in the region.

Also improved was the old British coaling station in the western Indian Ocean called Diego Garcia. Their small airfield was lengthened to be B-52 capable, and tons of pre-positioned war material was soon based there.

The removal of most of the old line Communists in **China** allowed a planned shift in ideology to allow small private businesses and farms. By 1978 China's new land policy had increased food production 300%, and farm income increased 1500%. China's leaders were well aware of just how far behind their regime and country was to the more modern economies, and western business leaders were only too happy to help as their sales and profits soared. But China had ulterior motives.

Their leaders realized that for China to become a true world force their country must modernize, similar to what Japan had done in the end of the last century.

Historical Note: Back then Japan had changed quickly from a feudal society to an industrial, modern one. That was one of the reasons they were able to dominate their half of the Pacific so quickly. By watching and learning from the old colonial powers, Japan's leaders led by Yamagata Aritomo had pushed for deliberate military expansion as the only way to defend Japan itself. Their Imperialism and Militarism was their way of joining the "colonial club", and became a proven strategy when they defeated the Russians in the 1904 Russo-Japanese War.

That was the first time a non-European nation had defeated a European one in a large war. It convinced the Japanese leaders that it was time to expand. (That Russian defeat also began the downward spiral of the Czar's rule, and was the reason for Stalin's post WWII Pacific game plan that FDR foolishly agreed to at Tehran and Yalta.)

Japan began building her empire from that 1905 peace treaty as they acquired Russian areas on the lower half of Sakhalin Island, the Liaodong peninsula which gave them de-facto rights in Manchuria, and gave them control over all of Korea. Japan joined the allied effort in WWI with their long view of empire building. When Germany was defeated Japan gained most of the German colonies and islands across the Pacific, setting the stage for their conflict with everyone in WWII.

Unlike many nations who simply copied present technology, Japan went out and created many of their own innovations which totally surprised the western powers in WWII. CMD. Minoru Genda was the head planner for the Japanese attack at Pearl Harbor. He argued for Japan to take the Hawaiian Islands when they attacked us in 1941 to prevent any American military recovery, and to have an advance base to threaten us if we tried to fight back. That failure and many others is what led to their defeat in WWII. (Incredibly he survived the war and later became the head of Japan's Air Defense Force.)

Though Japan had become an economic giant by 1980, they had no real military, and thus no Real Power. This new China was going to learn from those Japanese errors. *They would create an industrial nation that had the military means to expand and protect their desired empire.* The Americans and the West would as Stalin had said so long ago, "Sell us the means to destroy them".

Increased fighting in **Lebanon** was occurring between Israel and the PLO and Syria. Iranian money and fighters were adding to the turmoil, as retaliatory missile strikes and air to air battles were again threatening a larger Mid-East war.

Inside Syria the Muslim Brotherhood continued attacking, and even stealing control of the northern third of the country from Assad's forces. Syria's foreign minister denounced Jordan's King Hussein for allowing the Brotherhood to operate freely from his nation. In one attack a bomb was thrown into Assad's offices killing a guard but just missing him. Conditions were getting so bad their Russian advisors were forced to drive around Syria in armored cars. CIA agent Robert Baer was unhappy over the approved Jordanian arrangement. He felt that if Assad was removed from Syria the Brotherhood would takeover and things would get a lot worse under their Fundamentalist mindset. (Jordan was simply getting back at Assad for their attacks.)

America

Back at home Pres. Reagan had recovered from his wounds and was continuing his domestic agenda by trying to enact welfare reform and work programs. Those changes were not welcomed by the Democrats, and the Republican controlled Senate inanely shot down two Social Security reforms that Reagan wanted enacted. Warnings had been springing up from fiscal managers that the present Social Security program was underfunded, (thanks to LBJ and the Democrats), and would cause massive problems when the Baby Boomers begin retiring. To shore up the system changes needed to be made soon. But the fiscal changes the Administration wanted were being fought over because the politicos were only interested in being re-elected, not in taking care of the nation's needs. (Not much has changed in 35 years.)

Historical Note: The baby boomers were a huge population surge of 76 million born between 1946-1964. We forced the growth of the suburbs as the county needed housing outside of the already overcrowded cities. With that need came demands for all sorts of infrastructure including roads, schools, housing, stores and colleges. When I went to Oswego College in 1975 it was common to find three lads forced into each dorm room. Another unobserved effect of our large numbers was the vast increase of additional cars that hit the roads when we came of age. That greatly increased our gas consumption, and need for oil. And the increase in young adults from our age group greatly increased the need for housing and consumer goods which also added to our need for oil.

If the reader remembers from *Fatal Flaws Books 1 & 2, when FDR introduced Social Security in 1935 it was a Ponzi scheme only open to white males in certain high end professions. Basically the poor and middle class workers were being used to subsidize SS pensions for those who already had enough money to retire on. (The whites only requirement was to get the Southern Democrats to sign on to the plan.)*

By 1938 changes were made to include all workers, but in reality the low income workers were hurt twice. The new taxes needed to fund the program took a greater percentage of their pay versus what the wealthy paid, and the poorer workers did not live as long and seldom collected anything anyway. (Those facts are never mentioned by the Democrats or the leftist media.)

At that time the life span of an average citizen was only to age 65. It was expected that most of the retirees would collect for a few years of retirement and then pass away insuring the system stayed solvent. With the U.S. economy booming during and after WWII, large surpluses were built up in the Social Security Trust Fund, and it seemed the program was a sound one. Once the early baby boomers began working additional tax revenue poured in. With their anticipated retirements far off vast surpluses built up. By 1965 the Fund had grown at a fair rate to almost $900 Billion.

Then came The Great Deceiver LBJ, the War in Vietnam and his "Great Society social programs. **Costs were in the billions.** *In 1967 the money that was in the Social Security Trust Fund was quietly transferred (stolen) to the general fund by LBJ and the Democrats.* They needed those funds to pay for the War and his substantial social programs, without raising taxes prior to the next election in 1968.

In place of the money were government issued IOUs. That inanity had continued, and in 1981 it was realized that those IOUs would be coming due in spades in just a decade. Reagan and the

Republicans knew something had to be done and higher taxes were enacted and directed to the Social Security and Medicare programs. Had Reagan not insisted on a fix for those problems none would have been offered by the Democrats until the system collapsed. *(The secret of why this fix was needed in the first place continues to this day.)*

On July 29, 1981 Pres. Reagan scored his first major domestic victory when the Congress enacted a 25% reduction in the tax rates for individuals and businesses. Reagan's economic plan expected that these savings would translate into increased research and development, increased consumer spending, hiring and small business openings. In this way the "market and economics" would spur growth and the government would stay out of their way.

On August 3 the labor union which represented the nation's air-traffic controllers began a foolish strike which grounded over 7,000 daily flights. The air traffic controllers were and are a vital entity for flight operations, air-traffic safety and our overall economy. At that time the members pay averaged about $80,000 per year, and one could get $10-20,000 in overtime. Their union wrongly demanded more pay, a 20 year retirement and a shorter work week. The government refused and the strike began.

A federal judge ordered them back to work and to continue the contract talks, but the controllers union refused. Sec. of Transportation Drew Lewis warned the head of the union that the President would not countenance an illegal strike nor negotiate while one was in progress. Still they refused to return to work. On the 6th Reagan fired the all of the strikers and Military air controllers replaced the civilians. A terrible anti-union precedent began, and continues to this day.

Historical Note: Unions were and still are a vital part of our economic infrastructure. *It was the unions that improved worker safety, pay, time off and other benefits, not the businesses or the owners.* They never wanted any advancements for the lowly workers. All they wanted was their massive profits, lifestyles and perks. The infamous triangle shirtwaist fire in NYC in 1911 killed 146 mostly poor young women because of greed and stupidity. Those deaths spawned a huge movement for safer buildings and working conditions, and unions became the workers voice and power.

Without the unions arguing for firefighter safety, the FDNY where I served might never have been given forty hour work weeks, overtime, air-pacs and bunker gear. Some of the old-timers who broke me in educated me that prior to 1968 the FDNY had a policy of no overtime pay. If a fire started near the change of tours the Chiefs could keep the outgoing and incoming crews to fight the fire. Since there was no overtime, there was no cost! Guys would be kept on duty for hours, putting themselves at great risk for no income. It was a crazy system that was not changed until 1968.

Part of the problem between management and labor is the refusal of management to negotiate. Unions use strikes and threats of labor strikes to force the issue. As a member of the FDNY, I witnessed and lived trough many such episodes in which the City managers would refuse to negotiate fairly or promptly. We were forbidden to strike by law, and as such were powerless to effect the proceedings. Many a contract was completed two or more years late, and the city would refuse to make any back pay.

In 1980 a probationary firefighter such as myself was making the grand sum of $17,500 dollars per year. A 1st grade senior firefighter was making just $26,000, risking life and limb. I felt then and still feel today that the air controllers were unjustified in striking in 1981, and their actions hurt all of the unionized labor force.

In a speech that September Pres. Reagan announced to the nation that our national debt had actually risen to the astonishing figure of one trillion dollars. **"Only once in the last twenty years has our federal budget been balanced". Most of this debt was incurred from Vietnam and LBJ's Great Society debacles.**

Another part of the budget problem was that the Democrats had taken "Impoundment" away from the office of President in 1973. That power enabled the president to impound any funds he felt were causing a budgetary issue. As a result of their action the president is unable to stop any wasteful spending. *Only the Congress has the ability to control spending, but they were only interested in spending your tax money to buy votes and favors.*

Reagan stated; "There are three basic ways to cut the deficit: Decrease Government spending, Increase taxes, or print money to cover the debt. The latter causes inflation. (What Obama did for eight years.) For conservatives increasing taxation is bad since it strangles the economy by removing money from the private sector and wasting it within the bloated government bureaucracy.

Cutting spending was a proven way of reducing the deficit.

(And the way most of us manage our households.)

Congressional critics of the President quickly claimed that he was making the debt worse with his defense buildup and his tax cutting. *Led by Democratic Speaker Tip O'Neil, the Democrats running Congress arrogantly refused any thoughts to cutting spending, and in fact they continued their deficit spending.*

To assist him in his efforts Reagan enlisted the help from NY business leader Peter Grace, who along with other business leaders were tasked to find ways to help cut spending. (Since nothing useful was coming out of the Congress, Reagan went to the private sector to find the solutions.) Those business leaders formed the Grace Commission, and used their proven business knowledge to find ways to cut costs. Their multi-month endeavor found and listed over 2,000 ways to save taxpayer money.

But the Democratic run House enacted less than ten. And so the debt crisis continued, and increases to this day.

(All of us will suffer deeply for Obama's eight years in office. The U.S. deficit more than doubled from 9 to $20 Trillion. In eight years he spent and lost more money than had 230 years of his predecessors.)

One way to force the Congress to cut spending is to change the way spending bills are passed. Normally a sought after law such as clean water starts the process. Then the scheming politicos add in hundreds of unneeded appropriations that get passed with the main feature. In that reckless way it is impossible to stop the waste. *To force the Congress to stop spending, all bills must be passed one at a time or only in a common group.* If you want clean water, only appropriations promoting clean water can be added. In that way the wasteful "pork barrel" nonsense can be averted, such as bridges to nowhere.

Pres. Reagan met with France's Mitterrand in Ottawa to discuss what we knew and what he wanted to do about Russia. Soviet spies were stealing our military R&D at will, making their military a constant threat. Because of that factor the West was never able to stay ahead of them technologically to the point the Soviets would stop the insanity. Mitterrand agreed and told Reagan that the Soviets have a large spying operation in place. He also told him that they had a source high up in the Kremlin, and he was willing to share the information.

Colonel Vladimir Vetrov was an engineer by trade and assigned to evaluate all intelligence stolen by the Soviets. Vetrov like so many had realized that Communism was a failed system. Having once served in France, he decided to spy for them. From April 1981 until he was arrested in February 1982, Vetrov delivered 2,997 pages of the sensitive documents. *In those pages were the* names of Soviet spies operating in the West and of traitors in the West who were working for the Soviets.

Also highlighted were the types of intelligence and technology most sought after by Russia. In a meeting with VP George Bush, CIA Director William Casey and FBI Director William Webster, the Americans learned what a gem the French had found. Within this new intelligence they all realized that the Soviet Union was totally corrupt and bankrupt spiritually and ideologically. They existed only because of their spying. *The Soviets were not innovative and productive, they were just thieves.*

Thanks to Vetrov's brave work over 200 KGB agents worldwide were arrested in one day. Many senior Intelligence officers in France were upset that Mitterrand had revealed so much about Vetrov's position. They believed that he was betrayed because of Soviet moles hidden inside the CIA and FBI. Soviet spy Vitali Yurchenko defected three years later and told the CIA that Vetrov had been executed.

(Only Gorbachev did more to end Soviet Communism.)

But Vetrov did not die in vain as the Reagan Administration was able to quietly shut down large segments of the high-tech pipeline that was keeping the Soviets afloat. In a separate operation U.S. gas pumping equipment that had been "aquired" by the Russians was actiually rigged to fail, resulting in a massive explosion seen from space. Anything to hurt the Soviets.

Islamic World

On June 7, 1981 the Israeli Air Force secretly and expertly bombed and destroyed the Iraqi nuclear reactor near Baghdad. Their jets took off before dawn on Sunday and flew into Jordan. Their pilots conversed in a Saudi dialect and claimed they were lost. The Jordanians did not challenge them. Flying over Saudi Arabia the Israelis switched to a Jordanian dialect and told the Saudi's they were lost. Again they were not challenged. Crossing the southern Iraqi border the flight continued eastward and then turned back towards Baghdad. In that way they approached the reactor from the east so the morning sun would be in the eyes of the Iraqi gunners. Using the precision weapons introduced at the end of WWII and made effective near the end of the Vietnam War, the Israeli's blew a hole in the dome of the reactor. Additional bombs followed in destroying it.

France's Mitterrand complained quickly over the raid but it was just lip service. Israel's Begin had warned him what was coming, and the French technicians were quietly told to hold their Sunday Mass service "away from the reactor". Mitterrand then tried to end any further French weapons sales to Iraq.

In America Pres. Reagan also condemned the raid publicly, but was grateful in private. The world was scary enough without Saddam having nuclear weapons. **Israel was wrongly condemned for the raid, but they may well have stopped a nuclear holocaust in the Middle East.**

Iraq was still deadlocked in Saddam's unwise war as Iranian artillery and human wave assaults by suicidal fighters forced the Iraqi's into fixed defenses. Iranian air attacks were hammering Iraq's forward units and even striking into Baghdad. To get around Iraq's defenses small fast boats were used around the Basra area striking the Iraqis and any shipping found. To counter that strategy Iraq started using their chemical weapons and the new French artillery. Both kept the Iranians from winning.

To help their overall situation **Iran** supplied arms and supplies to Iraqi Kurds to continue their quest for freedom. They tied up 30,000 Iraqi troops. In retaliation Saddam used chemical weapons on the Kurds. With his nuclear ambitions squashed for now, Saddam's chemical weapons programs became even more important. Hussein took extra steps to hide those weapons from prying eyes, and Saddam started firing Scud missiles into Tehran.

As mentioned earlier one unforeseen fallout of Iraq's invasion was the unification of Iran to fight this Arab threat. Thousands of posters were paraded weekly through the streets of Tehran in honor of their "martyrs". They had been able to regroup their military after Iraq's early victories, and were holding their own. Part of the reason for the Iranian turnaround was the fervor of the Iranian Revolutionary Guard and its minions. For them death was and is welcomed on the battlefield. Iran's Fundamentalists were propagandizing the battles and losses to the extreme. Young boys were continually sacrificed in suicidal head-on attacks against prepared Iraqi positions, and in known minefields.

(That same zeal was used in WWII by Stalin in motivating the peasants to fight for Mother Russia against Germany, and in Japan with their suicidal banzai charges, kamikazes, kaitens and baku bombs they used on our forces in the Pacific.)

But Iran was edging towards civil war as more bombs were being setoff nationwide. The latest one on June 29th claimed 72 lives. Some of the attacks were being done by those opposed to the extremist clerics, but it was probable that Iraq may have been involved. Khomeini lost many of his major backers and colleagues in those latest bombs. Rebels vowed to overthrow the Shia Fundamentalists, however the Islamists were not sitting still.

Since June over 1,000 of the rebel supporters and ranks had been executed by Khomeini's death squads. In another case of tragic irony, those Shia Fundamentalists had protested against the Shah for the few executions he had done per year, yet here they were showing their true colors as they savagely struggled to stay in power. (Just like the Communists.)

Amnesty International reported that since July 1981, **over 1,800 additional executions** had been carried out in Iran. *(More than the Shah's secret police had executed in 10 years!)* Iran would close off their world and conduct their cleansing behind a veil of darkness. Multiple thousands more would be eliminated, with no one knowing. Their violent actions succeeded in holding onto power. *(And as stated before, no lawyers or liberals were there to protest those arrests or executions.)*

The *Muslim Brotherhood* had been a political force within **Egypt** since the 1920s. After the failed 1973 war with Israel, Anwar Sadat had met with Pres. Nixon and a rapprochement began. But Sadat was having trouble at home with the Communists and Socialists who tried to end his rule. To gain allies he renewed his alliance in the Muslim Brotherhood. (The Brotherhood had a natural inclination against both superpower political groups, but especially the Communists.)

In 1974 the Brotherhood led by **Abdullah Azzam** issued a declaration commanding their members to support Anwar Sadat. Their help stabilized Sadat's rule, and the appearance of Islamic banks in Egypt, (bloated by petro-dollars) insured financial freedom from the West and helped spread the Brotherhood message of strict Islam. They and the Islamic banks were pro-capitalism, but strangely they would not support the poor or disenfranchised. Western banking institutions jumped at the chance to give advice, training and technical expertise to the fledgling Islamic banking industry. As always profits increased.

The European based IMF, International Monetary Fund required strict changes to national economies if the recipient nation wanted their aid. That caused much resentment in the third world, especially the Muslim World who did not want any non-believer influence. Thus the secret society and Islamic banks of the Brotherhood spread through the Middle East, keeping the Western economic requirements out.

The Brotherhood's influence became dominating, and was joined with Wahhabism from the Saudis to create a true political threat. Saudi run banks would dangle petro-dollar loans to the poorest nations and insist they turn more Islamic and conservative. All did. By the mid-80s the Saudi's would spend over $70 Billion to spread their Wahhabist Fundamentalist religious sect worldwide. (Ironically it was the vast infusion of petro-dollars that made the oil producing nations co-dependent on the Western world. Flush with money, they spent it on huge projects, bringing in even more westerners to teach them how to build and maintain their equipment. And that infuriated the Fundamentalists even more.)

Islamic schools are run by the clerics, even the universities. Schools in Saudi Arabia picked up 85% of their students from other Islamic states (including Egypt). That placed the student bodies under the direct influence of their Fundamentalists. Inside Egypt, the Brotherhood recruited freely at the al-Azhar University in Cairo and their membership swelled with young men. During the late 1970s this increasing Islamic nationalism was also being influenced by the hostile speeches and actions from the Ayatollah Khomeini and his supporters. It became a torrent after the Shah was forced out.

Egypt had been given $1.5 billion in U.S. loan guarantees, and that infusion of money allowed Sadat to create public works projects to help his impoverished land and people. After the war in Afghanistan began, Sadat assisted in sending aid and fighters. To help that effort, the DOD and CIA were secretly in Egypt using special forces troops to train the Egyptian volunteers. That earned Egypt another $2 Billion in U.S. aid and Egypt even purchased F-16 fighters.

(Those same U.S. trainers gave Sadat's security detail additional instruction because of the constant threats he was getting. CIA's William Buckley was one of those senior trainers. He would be kidnapped in Lebanon and killed by Hezbollah in 1984.)

When Pres. Sadat signed the peace accords with Israel at Camp David his former allies inside Egypt became bitter enemies. They were well ingrained inside his government and the Egyptian military. Some of them had morphed into a violent terrorist group known as **Egyptian Islamic Jihad, (EIJ).** They were not going to sit by and allow this peace with Israel to happen.

During February 1981 Egyptian police arrested some of the **EIJ** members and learned of a large plot that was taking shape. Pres. Sadat acted quickly to shut them down before Egypt suffered Iran's fate, and ordered 1500 more arrests. One of those jailed was a blind cleric named **Sheik Omar Abdel-Rahman**. In addition to his extremist views, he was a violent anti-westerner and refused to talk even in the harsh prison conditions of Egypt. Rahman was the spiritual leader of EIJ, and by 1981 they were strong enough to attack their own government. One cell of their terrorist group was missed in that latest crackdown, and it was they who continued planning that attack.

Pres. Sadat's wife had been following in the westernized footsteps of the Shah's wife with their "Family Protection Act" and in pushing for more privileges for Islamic women. That was the last straw for the Islamists as they violently protested. During Sadat's last months incessant security missions were run ferreting out his adversaries. He had to withdraw his support for the Brotherhood, and the extremists in their ranks saw his actions as treason against Islam.

On October 6, 1981 at a military parade in Cairo, Pres. Anwar Sadat and eleven others were murdered in a well-planned attack by those Islamic radicals. (They also attacked other sites in the country and the city of Asyut was taken over.)

Those extremists were against all of the peace initiatives Pres. Sadat made with Israel, his alignment with the U.S. and his recent crackdown on their activities. They hoped that with his death and the many others an Islamic theocracy could be installed in Egypt.

(Sadat's wife Jehan had pleaded with him to wear a bulletproof vest for the upcoming military parade which ironically was celebrating the failed 1973 Mid-East War. The Islamists struck at just the right moment killing him. Pres. Sadat's death was a great loss for peace in the region, and a clear warning of what could happen to any and all of the rulers in the Islamic world if the Islamists got their way.)

When the wounded Egyptian Vice President Hosni Mubarak recovered he took over the nation and stated that all of Pres. Sadat's gains would live on. Hundreds of additional suspects were arrested, unfortunately most were released after a few years. **Among those released were the blind cleric Omar Rahman and a doctor named Ayman al-Zawahiri. Both would be deeply involved in the future attacks against America.**

Palestinian cleric **Abdullah Azzam** had been an important figure in the Muslim Brotherhood of the 1960-70s. His radical teachings exhorted violence against Israel and the West, and was met with as much fervor as had Khomeini's speeches among the

Shia. One trademark slogan he used was; *"Jihad and the rifle alone. No negotiations, no conferences and no dialogues."* *(74)

Since the 1979 Iranian Revolution, Islamic Fundamentalist groups were springing up all over the region. Terrorism was increasing, and all of those groups were becoming more militant in their views and actions. All called for revolution throughout the Islamic world. It was time for them to takeover the region.

July 22, 1981 PFLP terrorists use a bomb to kill two women in Athens at a travel agency.

August 29, 1981 Two of Abu Nidal's terrorists attacked a synagogue in Vienna murdering two and wounding 17.

September 12, 1981 Islamic terrorists used a grenade attack on a group of Italian tourists in Jerusalem murdering one and wounding 28.

On October 20, 1981 a truck bomb was used in a Synagogue attack in Brussels. Three were murdered and one hundred six were wounded in yet another savage attack against civilians.

With no warning, on December 15, 1981 the Iraqi embassy in Lebanon was destroyed in a suicide car bombing. Sixty one were killed and one hundred ten were wounded as Iranian agents struck back for their recent troubles. In retaliation Saddam Hussein ordered a crackdown on pro-Iranians in his country. Dozens were killed and imprisoned as thousands more Iraqi Shia fled into Iran.

On December 20, 1981 the Greek passenger ship *Orion* was attacked by the PLO's May 15 group as it approached the Israeli port of Haifa. Two were murdered and two others injured in the bomb attack.

On January 9, 1982 the El Al office in Istanbul was bombed by the PLO's May 15 group. On the 15th they next bombed the Mifgash-Israel Restaurant in West Berlin. During the past months increased skirmishing with the PLO was happening all along the Israeli border with Lebanon.

The Cold War Resumes

To counter the growing threat of a Soviet invasion the Polish Central Committee had placed General Wojciech Jaruzelski as Premier. (The former office holder was seen as too weak in the face of the continued workers strikes.) This General Officer like all of the ones behind the Iron Curtain had been "trained in Russia". He was considered a hard liner, and was directed to "restore order.

Wojciech Jaruleski was a true survivor. His Polish parents had been deported by Stalin to a labor camp in Siberia in 1941, and both died there. *Orphaned, which is what the communists wanted, he was raised in Soviet schools inside Russia's brand of Communism. With no family or church to get in the way of their propaganda, young Jaruleski complied, advanced and became a party member.* Now he had to perform.

During October 1981 tensions again reached a high point, and martial law proclamations were being printed in Russia. Col. Kuklinski had reported that the Soviets were taking control of most things inside Poland. In November the decision had been made for Martial Law. On the night of December 12, 1981 after more strikes occurred it was implemented and the arrests began. At least seven were killed when Polish tanks and soldiers maneuvered into the cities. Water canon were used to breakup any large formations of protestors with hundreds being arrested, including Lech Walesa. To stop any further unrest Poland's regime smashed the Solidarity trade union arresting and imprisoning all of the leadership. Throughout those trials their religion gave the Polish people hope.

Pres. Reagan blasted the actions and placed restrictions on Polish diplomats in the U.S. Trade with Russia was also cut as Cold War tensions mounted. *Since the military force used was Polish, our response was muted.* Our AFL-CIO unions and the CIA were still assisting the Vatican in sharing information, and getting financial, communications and political resources into the country. (Colonel Kuklinski was rescued in November and escaped to the West. His help had been invaluable.)

Inside Europe anti-Americanism was growing among the peaceniks and other social-liberal groups, spurred on by Communist support. Anti-U.S.-missile protests had begun in early 1980 before the American election was even held, but they were growing larger with Pres. Reagan's recent actions. By late 1981 Reagan and his Administration were worried over the near completion of Soviet medium range nuclear missile deployments. They had been emplacing the mobile SS-20 missiles at the rate of one per week. Each carried three MIRV warheads. No one was sure what would happen once they were all in. (Spurring the better to be Red than Dead philosophy in Europe.)

The Soviets had decided that the larger cities and military bases of Western Europe would be destroyed within minutes of a war by those newer weapons. Their overall plan was to prevent any type of response from NATO. And with the lower flight paths of the cruise missiles, the available warning time from radar would be greatly reduced. Civilian losses in the target areas would be extreme. (Intercontinental missiles fly into the stratosphere which increases their flight and radar warning time. But without a defensive system to shoot them down that point is moot since your destruction is still en-route.)

Throughout the past months intense negotiations with Russia had been going on using the renewed Nitze group. Various proposals were submitted with the purpose of stopping *all of the missile deployments*. As was always the case with the Communists, they sparred and lied and obstructed at every turn in an effort to wear the negotiator down. If any agreement was to be reached, they sought to have the dominate position. Naturally the Reagan Administration did not agree, and Paul Nitze and his staff refused all of their proposals.

With their deployments almost complete the Soviets suddenly withdrew from the INF negotiations. Pres. Reagan's response was to deploy our 108 Pershing medium missiles, and 464 ground launched cruise missiles within the NATO countries as a counter force. In that way if an attack occurred the NATO nations could respond in kind against the Soviet Bloc countries. The political leaders in Europe still had no policy alternatives, which was why they had asked Carter to do something about this dangerous Soviet policy over three years earlier.

In Europe the Green party, peaceniks and other leftist groups were stridently opposed to Reagan's retaliatory placement policy. Their demonstrations were growing in size and noise, and naturally the leftist media gave maximum exposure and coverage in a transparent attempt to undermine Reagan's proposal. The Soviets were fanning those flames using propaganda and other "active measures".

Communist money and agitators were an integral part of all of the peace group's efforts. For three years the Soviets and their client states made a major effort to infiltrate, manipulate and install propaganda into the anti-nuclear-peace movements. The Soviets used local Communist parties and front groups for most of their efforts. East Germany sent $2 million per month into W. Germany for their protests, while Denmark uncovered a $100,000 cash transfer through their Communist party. As they had stated, the Communists also forged documents to arouse anti-nuclear anger and violence.

In London on October 24, 1981 over 150,000 peaceniks protested. A month later 250,000 protested in Bonn. As before the liberal media of Europe and America insured that those groups received plenty of air time and sympathetic coverage. Again it was quite clear that the media wanted those groups to succeed in stopping any anti-Soviet actions. But the question that needed to be asked was why? The only outcome from not placing our weapons was surrender to the Communists.

(In our time of 2019 trained leftist agitators are routinely being used inside the U.S. to intimidate and stop free speech from anyone but them. And the media approves of their efforts.)

As the world watched those "peace protests", Pres. Reagan counter-proposed a **Zero Option** for all European missiles in late November. The U.S. would forgo the previously approved missile deployments if the Soviets would destroy their SS-20s, SS-4s and SS-5s currently emplaced in E. Europe and Asia. That option was quickly refused by the Soviets.

(They had a clear advantage so why give it up.)

Reagan's proposal actually surprised the liberals, and was well received all across Europe. For a while the peace movement quieted down which surprised and irritated the Soviets. (This proposal was promoted by Richard Perle a former aide for Senator Henry Jackson of Washington State on defensive matters. He had done his homework and learned that just 50 of those new Soviet missiles could decimate all of NATO.)

The older SS-4 & 5s were the same missiles that had been shipped to Cuba in 1962. They were not accurate enough to take out military targets, so they would strike the cities of Western Europe. The SS-20's and cruise missiles would go after the military targets. As always, one of the main obstacles to Reagan's peace proposal was getting verification that the Soviets would actually comply. And it would require neutral observers who were free to inspect behind the Iron Curtain, impossible to ensure.

One result over this latest Cold War predicament was that Pres. Reagan was convinced (as JFK did in 1961) that the principal premise of MAD, (Mutual Assured Destruction), was wrong and suicidal. No one could win in such a destructive war, and he desired to end that protocol despite the objections of some of his advisors.

The way he would make it happen would be based on a defensive shield that would be able to protect our nation and allies from enemy missiles. (Instead of relying on the threat of a counter-attack to prevent an enemy from risking nuclear war.)

Unfortunately in the early 1980s the computer and missile capabilities had not caught up to the president's vision. Much extensive and expensive R&D needed to be conducted, but that was alright as long as we worked to develop that shield now. If Europe turned pacifist and NATO was ended, or if they gave up and became Socialists, America would be placed at great risk with few allies. We had to plan ahead and prepare for the worst.

Unknown to most there was a separate but critical issue that also prompted Pres. Reagan into wanting a defensive shield. **That issue was the complete change to Soviet missile submarine operations.**

During the early years of the Cold War Russian subs were patrolling around the globe and we could easily track and attack them because they were noisy. However by the late 1970s it was noted that the Soviets began keeping their missile boats closer to their shores for safety. They also began using their attack submarines as bodyguards for the missile boats. And the Russian subs were getting much quieter. **(Why now?)**

Russia hoped those initial changes would prevent us from sinking their missile subs giving them a second strike capability. To the Soviet mind that capability would checkmate us into surrender. (More than likely we would all be dead anyway.) *This complete alteration in tactics and operations worried the Intelligence community because it implied the Soviets might actually be thinking of launching a first strike and winning.*

Another alarming change was that by the early 1980s the Soviets had learned how to use the perfect hiding zone of the Arctic Ocean. Submarines were almost impossible to track in that noisy sea and the launch time to destroy America could be as low as twenty minutes. And adding to the Administration's war fears was the knowledge that the Soviets were producing a new missile boat, the massive Typhoon Class. They were one and a half times as large as our Trident submarines, and each carried 20 of their large SS-N-20 nuclear missiles. Each missile had ten independent warheads, which totaled to 200 warheads per sub. One of those subs could destroy our entire country. **If just one missile made it through many of America's major cities would be destroyed.**

Those deadly parameters were all part of the critical reasons why President Reagan wanted his defensive plan enacted. It would be called the **Strategic Defense Initiative- SDI,** and it became a center piece of Pres. Reagan's foreign /domestic policy goals. The pacifist charlatans who wanted to just give up and disarm had no way of knowing what the final result of our surrender would be, chains for all, a new holocaust?

Unlike them Pres. Reagan wanted to protect our people and nation from ever being hit, and SDI was the program to do so.

Echoing what had happened in France, Greece elected a Socialist Government ending 35 years of pro-Western rule. Their younger voters had forgotten (if they ever knew) about how bad things had been during WWII, the post-War communist attempted take-over and Civil war, or Greece's salvation thanks to the Truman Administration programs. Like our recent issues with France it was hoped that our relations with Greece would remain solid for a while. (When I was young our family dentist had emigrated from Greece. His family was machine-gunned next to him as they tried to escape from the Nazi's in 1941.)

On December 1, 1981 Pres. Reagan signed an order to authorize covert support to the **Nicaraguan Contras**. A force of 500 fighters would be raised and trained as part of Reagan's desire to confront the Soviets everywhere.

During March 1982 the Sandinista regime suspended all civil rights in Nicaragua. Daniel Ortega the head of the regime and a virtual clone of Castro even down to his wardrobe claimed that his country was being "imperiled by aggression from America". In reality the citizens of Nicaragua had been rioting to protest the Marxist regime and its rulers. Like so many before them, the Nicaraguans realized their mistake after the Communists came to power. Now they needed our help to chase them out.

On March 9, 1982 the media was invited (in a rare move) to see and learn of the Soviet bloc buildup that was ongoing in Nicaragua. Multiple dozens of images were shown to prove the Administration claims that the Communists were using Nicaragua as their entry point into the region, which included the strategic Panama Canal. For some of the old hands that briefing brought back images of the Cuban missile crisis as images showed new Soviet aircraft and crew served weapons at recently completed base areas built in the Cuban model.

At that time there were fifty Nicaraguan pilots training in Cuba and Bulgaria on the MiG-17 and MiG-21 fighters. There was no purpose in having offensive aircraft unless the owners planned on using them. *Visible on the images were two large airbases being built, one with a 14,000 foot runway and the other with 12,000 feet. Those runways could handle the largest Soviet bombers.*

The freighter *Bukuriani* was scheduled to leave the Russian port of Nikolayev on the Black Sea. Stacked nearby were twelve large crates that were carrying MiG aircraft. Pres. Reagan warned Brezhnev not to send any fighters to the region. Their ship purposefully sailed into the south Atlantic and around Cape Horn into the Pacific Ocean, to avoid passing through the Panama Canal and possible inspection. That freighter was "escorted" by U.S. ships and aircraft as it neared Nicaragua, and upon unloading four Soviet patrol boats and a few helicopters were photographed. (Apparently Reagan's warning not to send the MiG's had worked.)

Then in April 1982 Eden Pastora, one of the Sandinista heroes defected to the West. He openly denounced the Communist regime and what they were doing to his country. Supplied with U.S. arms, Pastora would fight back from Costa Rica on the southern border of Nicaragua.

Democrats Dodd from the Senate and Boland in the House were livid over Reagan's anti-Communist decisions and actions. What he was doing was against the laws they had passed back in 1975, and they argued that new laws would be coming.

To help the Sandinistas hold onto power the PLO increased their shipments of arms, advisors and training. They taught Nicaraguan intelligence people how to track the Contras, and assisted in getting arms shipments in from Libya.

The PLO was able to make contact with every leftist group in the region, including the one operating in El Salvador. *Fifty Salvadorans went to PLO camps for terrorist training.* As the leftist subversive efforts in El Salvador continued, in a recent clash four Dutch newsmen were killed by those rebels.

Neighboring Guatemala underwent a coup as charges of election fraud threatened their nation.

By the fall of 1982 the CIA had trained more than 3,500 Contras, plus 900 Miskito Indians. Operating out of Honduras on the northern border were another 2,300 fighters, and Pastora had his 500 operating from Costa Rica. The Sandinistas were not going to have an easy rule, and they declared the regions bordering Honduras and Costa Rica as military zones. Battles in the region continued as fifty abducted Guatemalans were found murdered. (Incredulously our ally France then decided to **sell arms** and send advisors to communist Nicaragua to teach them how to use them.)

Determined to help the Communists succeed, on December 8, 1982 the Democrats passed the Boland amendment in the House. **The Democrats prohibited the CIA from overthrowing the Communists in Nicaragua.**

Casey was furious with their action, because if we could not defeat a Soviet insurgency in our own backyard, where should we. He was determined to fight the Soviets everywhere, and that included Yemen, Libya and the new trouble spots in Oman and Morocco.

To counter-act the Democrats desire for the Communists to take Central America, Pres. Reagan announced a foreign policy plan for economic investment in the Caribbean. (Similar to what Pres. Eisenhower had done in 1956, and JFK tried when he copied a Brazilian proposal in 1961.) His goal was to help those poor nations build up their economies so they could reject Communism. *Despite the Democrats, "The revolutionaries in Managua would face their own insurgency,"* *(75)

Britain and France

On April 2, 1982 Argentina suddenly invaded the Falkland Islands in the far south Atlantic. Those islands had been claimed by Great Britain for 149 years, and most of the islands residents were British with the majority living as fishermen and sheep herders.

Argentines call the islands the Malvinas, and claimed that they belonged to them. Their invasion galvanized the British into action as conservative P.M. Thatcher stated that Great Britain would fight to reclaim their territory. (Pres. Reagan gave covert assistance to aid the Brits.) Despite being militarily unprepared and fighting from an extreme distance, the small British Naval force was soon engaged in a two month long sea-air-land battle with the Argentine forces. The modern weaponry being used for the first time was proving to be extremely effective and lethal. Ships would be wrecked by one missile strike, whereas in WWII it could take dozens of shell hits to do the same. By mid-June the fighting ended when Argentina surrendered. (Their tactics were extremely poor as they failed to use the islands as forward airfields.)

Soon after socialist France signed a major natural gas contract with Russia. However the Soviets needed Western help to build the gas pipeline from their Siberian gas fields to Western Europe. Russia desperately needed the income, and Europe wanted the natural gas as a way to reduce Mid-east oil imports. *However Pres. Reagan was against this pipeline because it would help the Russians stay afloat economically.* He also saw this gas pipeline as a potential means of blackmailing Europe into submission. Once Europe became dependent on the Russian gas supplies the Soviets could threaten to shut the flow (in the dead of winter) to force a political end, just like OPEC had done with their oil.

Since Russia needed our equipment, technicians, expertise and capital to build the pipeline, Pres. Reagan insisted on a trade-off.

We would help on the pipeines, if the Soviets removed all of their medium range nuclear missiles. That offer was refused by the Soviets, and our NATO partners!!

They needed this 3,300 mile long pipeline to move the product, and they would need forty-one pumping stations to maintain the pressure. Reagan's next plan was to block U.S. companies from providing any commercial assistance. It was felt that the Soviets would finally give in to his disarmament demands to make the sale. *But in the blink of an eye companies in Germany and France stepped up to provide the needed components!!* Mitterrand even approved their sales efforts despite prior NATO agreements not to.

Political leaders in Washington hit the roof. Just as we had something to hurt the Russians our allies bent over backwards to supply the enemy with technology and capital instead of pushing them over the economic edge and into disarmament. At stake was not just some jobs and income, but the future shape of the Cold War. Alas even conservative Margret Thatcher told Reagan to back off as the British also wanted in on the economic action. (This was after our help in the Falklands.)

It was soon learned that France had also sold machine tools to Russian aircraft plants so they could make advanced jet turbines, something the Russians were incapable of doing themselves. And France also sold milling machines to Leningrad shipyards to produce advanced ship propellers. The list of inanity went on and on. France knew just what the Soviets needed, and how bad they needed it. But security was last on their list, jobs and profits were first. (It would be three more years before we learned why the Russians wanted to make new propellers.)

Richard Perle and others in the Administration decided we should end our nuclear aid to France. *What was the sense in our spending $Billions in military R&D and sharing it with them, when the peaceful means to defeat the Soviets was right in front of everyone's eyes.* It took weeks of high level meetings to turn our allies around.

All the while Socialist Pres. Mitterrand was continuing his campaign to nationalize the country with the takeover of several large banks, electrical, aluminum and synthetics companies. While most of Europe was cutting costs to escape from the worldwide recession, France was doing just the opposite. The result would be a stagnant economy and increased dependence on government programs that still affects them to this day.

But France was not the only difficult NATO partner as most of the European countries declassified as much advanced technology as possible in order to sell it before the next guy did. *(Stalin had long ago told Levantin Beria the head of Russia's secret police that the capitalist West would sell us the means to destroy them.)*

The Middle East

Despite their continued attempts to take as much wealth as possible from the developed countries OPEC was holding an emergency meeting to come to grips with a new phenomena, falling oil prices. In the past few weeks oil had fallen $5 per barrel. Global conservation measures and a slowed world economy were creating an oil glut. In the U.S. the years of high oil prices had forced consumers to conserve fuel and to buy fuel efficient vehicles, most of which were foreign imports. Those conditions had resulted in a 10% reduction in gasoline sales since 1980, and the "market" was reacting to the supply-demand equation and setting the price.

The Ayatollah decided to send some of his Revolutionary Guard troops into Lebanon. Their mission as declared by Iranian General Ataollah Saleh was to drive all Americans from the country. With Lebanon abandoned the Muslims would take over and destroy Israel next. From May and into June Israel's military began actively fighting with PLA (Palestine Liberation Army) forces operating from southern Lebanon.

On June 3, 1982 three PLO terrorists attempted to murder the Israeli ambassador in London. Shiomo Argov survived the attack but never recovered from his wounds. That attack was the last straw. **On June 6, 1982 Israel invaded Lebanon.**

Operation Peace in Galilee was started as a limited operation to clear the terrorists and the PLO out of southern Lebanon. Over the past six years the once beautiful and vibrant nation of Lebanon had been turned into a war torn and lawless shell as some 100,000 Lebanese had died thus far. (While in college in 1975, we watched this disaster unfold on TV every night, and wondered why it was allowed to happen.)

During the Lebanese "civil war" the PLO and Syrians used the strife to terrorize the Lebanese as well as northern Israel. They took over control of civilian services and ejected or eliminated anyone who got in the way. Entire towns had been cleared out, and wealthy citizens were often times held hostage for ransom. Any resistance from Christians or Muslims was met with violence. In effect the PLO had setup a state within Lebanon, similar to what they had tried but failed to do in Jordan.

At the same time Syria and their Soviet advisers had built up the PLA (Palestine Liberation Army) forces into organized battalions of 1,500 fighters. *Military upgrades included artillery, rocket units, companies of Soviet-built T-34 tanks from Hungary, and supply depots filled with communist bloc weapons and ammunition.*

Soviet support for the PLO was so extensive that it would take the Israeli army units 4,300 truckloads to backhaul the captured munitions and weapons out of the bunkers they would uncover! The Israeli's removed 6530 tons of ammunition, 1,300 armored vehicles which included tanks, 1,300 anti-armor weapons, 82 artillery pieces, 215 mortars, 62 Katuysha rocket launchers, 196 anti-aircraft cannon, 33,000 small arms and ton after ton of ammunition. All of those weapons had come from the Soviet Union, the Warsaw Pact countries, Communist China, N. Korea or Communist Vietnam. Once again providing proof that the West was still at war with the Communist world.

(This extensive Communist supply effort was similar to the NVA supplies uncovered in Cambodia during the U.S./ARVN effort in 1970. Liberals claimed we had expanded the war.)

Zehdi Terzi the PLO's representative to the U.N. casually stated, **"Our boys go to the Soviet Union for training and education. There is no secret about that."** *(76)

A majority of the PLO /PLA officers had received at least some military training in the Soviet Union or other Communist country. Typical PLA units of 194 officers and men arrived in Simferopol in the Crimea to begin their advanced training. *And terrorists from Fatah, PFLP, DFLP and other sub-units were all present.* Soviet training included production of incendiary devices, preparation of electrical charges, bridge destruction, river crossings, all types of sabotage as well as atomic and chemical warfare.

This extensive training was given to all of the Arab nations that had PLO contacts, which furthered Soviet penetration of the Middle East. In repayment for all of that largess, Arafat and the PLO parroted all of Moscow's policies including their invasion of Afghanistan. (But once Reagan took office all of the direct Soviet involvement in the region was reduced, and the schooling was "farmed out to Soviet bloc nations or proxies such as Cuba and Syria".

(Large reductions in Communist aid to the PLO would occur after Gorbachev took power. **Only then** did the PLO decide to "talk about peace" in order to get funding from the West.)

In addition to the PLO fighters in Lebanon, there were major Syrian Army units based there too. When the Lebanese government wrongly asked for help Assad committed some three divisions of Syrian troops to the effort. When the Arab League sponsored a ceasefire in Lebanon, Assad kept his troops there "as part of the Arab peacekeepers". Incapable of defeating the Israelis back in 1973, they forced themselves on the poorly protected Lebanese. *By 1977 Syria had 40,000 troops in the country. They actually considered Lebanon as a "breakaway part of their country from the Ottoman Empire days".* (Similar to Iraq's obsession with Kuwait, they wanted it back.)

Syria's military was firmly in the control of Hafez al-Assad who had taken over in the previously mentioned coup. A year ago the Muslim Brotherhood had staged a rebellion in the city of Ham`ah where they killed hundreds of Syrian soldiers and Ba`athist officials. Assad was infuriated with that latest Brotherhood threat, and assembled his best forces under his brother Rifaat. Over 12,000 Syrian troops entered the city and crushed the Brotherhood killing some 20,000. As had happened in Egypt, this violent response ended the Brotherhood's hold.

By mid-1982 over 70,000 of Syrian troops were occupying Lebanon. *Most were in the vital Bekaa Valley or inside Beirut. They were not there to keep the peace, but to destabilize Lebanon for Syria's benefit.*

Well trained Israeli units (IDF) had crushed the PLO border defenses in **Lebanon,** and began advancing north towards the Litani River. After a few days Israel had grown weary of the constant PLO skirmishing and IED's. They used firepower with reckless abandon as any target or potential target was blasted away. (One of the problems that popped up between Israel and America was that the Israelis were using our latest and more powerful munitions in the civilian areas of the Lebanon.)

IDF units advanced on three axes, intent on destroying the PLO once and for all. Any Palestinian units that were cutoff by the armored spearheads were attacked and attrited by follow on infantry forces. Tough fights occurred in Tyre and Beaufort Castle. Syrian army units began to get in the way of the advancing Israeli's in an effort to protect the PLO. They were openly challenged as diplomatic messages came and went from both countries.

On June 8 fighting started with the Syrians.

In one air battle six Syrian jets were shot down by the proficient Israeli pilots. It took the Israeli Air Force just a few hours to destroy almost all of the Soviet built surface-air missile batteries, and shoot-down 29 more Syrian jets over the Bekaa Valley. During the three day air battle the IAF destroyed 82 of the Soviet supplied jets without a single loss. Intelligence from the fighting again showed that the Russian weapon systems were no match for the Western ones. (But their massed armies were.)

By June 10th Israeli columns moving along the coast were just a dozen miles from Beirut. One town they entered had been a Christian enclave, but it had been ravaged and occupied by the PLO since 1976. It too fell after some bitter fighting. Nearby the Beirut-Damascus highway was the scene of a tank to tank fight with the Syrians. As had happened in 1973, the Syrians quickly lost over 150 of their tanks.

With this obvious strength in the "enemy units", Israel decided to continue on to Beirut itself. Defense Minister Ariel Sharon openly stated his desire to link his forces with the Christian Phalanges in north-central Lebanon and take over control of the country. That would end the PLO, and the terrorism would hopefully stop.

(Unknown to Sharon the first full units of the Iranian Revolutionary Guard troops were crossing the Syrian border and setting up in a town called Baalbek to continue the carnage.)

Additional Syrian counter-attacks occurred along the roadways, and all were beaten, though the Israelis did take a lot of casualties. And despite their dreams of defeating Israel on the battlefield, the PLA (Palestine Liberation Army) units were no match for the IDF. Attacking PLA units that had been built up with great cost were all quickly defeated. Surviving PLO and PLA units took refuge in and around Beirut and were soon besieged.

Israeli P.M. Begin wanted to crush the PLO and take away all of their weapons, but international pressures and threats from the Soviets caused the Israeli's to stop their advance. Even Pres. Reagan warned P.M. Begin it was time to stop before Russia joined in. (With Reagan's election Israel was looked upon as an ally in the fight against communism and Islamic militants. A direct contrast to the Democrats attitude.)

Upon taking office Pres. Reagan had increased our presence and aid in Oman, Bahrain and Egypt. It was common to find U.S. personnel and ships working in and training personnel in those countries. To maintain this good will the Israeli's had to stop their Lebanon incursion. Reagan tried to impose a ceasefire on the 11th, but as always new fighting broke out. Not until the June 24 did a true ceasefire happen.

That one lasted until July 14 when a proposal from the U.S. allowing the Israelis to keep the peace in Lebanon was agreed upon by the Lebanese. *However Syria and the PLO did not concur and the fighting resumed.*

To protect U.S. citizens and designated foreign nationals the U.S. Navy had been called in. Sixth Fleet ships sailed into the eastern Mediterranean and with them were the five ships of the Marine Amphibious Ready Group. On board those ships were the 1,800 Marines of 32d Marine Amphibious Unit. Staffs were warned that they would be evacuating anywhere from 300 to 5,000 civilians. Battalion Landing Team, BLT 2/8 was given the mission of going ashore, protecting the civilians, starting the evacuation and taking care of any "contingencies" that popped up.

Units landed at the Christian town of Jounieh, which at that time was still untouched by the war. Flashes and thumps of distant gun and shellfire alerted the mostly untried marines and sailors that battles were occurring just miles away. Only 581 civilians decided to take this safe way out, and the two day mission became a routine of checking IDs and searching for weapons. A few miles away the Israeli forces (IDF) was becoming weary of the cat and mouse fighting with the PLO and Syrians. They decided to go in for the kill.

With their increasing casualties Arial Sharon ordered the use of massive aerial and artillery bombardments upon any enemy fire. Whole neighborhoods in West Beirut were flattened as the bombardments went on for days. Despite taking hundreds of casualties among his PLO-PLA forces and innocent Lebanese caught up in the fighting, PLO chief Yasir Arafat refused to surrender. *It was a common tactic of the PLO, Communists and other terrorist groups to hide themselves behind curtains of innocents.* Coverage of this fighting and the carnage echoed what had happened in Vietnam, and was watched on nightly television. After all of the years of strife most people wanted no part of the Middle East.

All that summer as the Israeli's advanced into Lebanon the Iranians were furious. The Sunni Arab countries had not mounted an oil boycott over this "aggressive Israeli action". For them everyone and anything not Muslim was to be chased out of Lebanon or killed. In late July **Imad Fayez Mughniyah** sat with **Sheikh Hossein** a Shia leader at a house in Baalbek. Hossein was laying the groundwork for Hezbollah's private war against the West, specifically America and Israel.

Back in October 1979 Khomeini had pledged support for the PLO cause, and Arafat did the same for Iran's revolution. Mughniyah would be given a commission in the Revolutionary Guards to oversee security. No one was to learn of their plans, only cash would be used for purchases or pay, and no radios or phone calls would be made. Runners would convey any messages. Additional fighters and money would come in from Iran, but again it was paramount that no one would ever know.

Their new cover title would be called **Islamic Jihad, IJO**, and they would recruit fighters from the ranks of the PLO, PLA and Lebanese Shia. There were always plenty of young men willing to die for Islam.

In an effort to stop the bloodshed Pres. Reagan offered to use U.S. forces to escort the PLO out. Naturally Arafat derided the help, but Reagan responded by saying that this was a standing offer good at any time. Needless carnage continued.

Finally during the first week of August 1982 Arafat and the PLO began to whimper from their besieged quarters in Beirut. They had wanted the "U.N. to handle their evacuation" but Israel refused that request as the U.N. had become anti-Israel over the past twenty-five years. To solve the issue and end the fighting, France, Italy and the U.S. formed a **Multi-National Force the MNF**, to interpose themselves between the Israelis and the PLO.

Once again our people were being used to safeguard someone else. In this case it was Muslims, and that included the terrorist Muslims of the PLO. Arafat worried about the thousands of Palestinian civilians being left behind in refugee camps at Sabra and Shatilla. He wanted a written guaranty from America that they would be safe. Ambassador Philip Habib complied telling Arafat that U.S. troops would stay up to thirty days to insure everyone could get out. **But those few political successes did not stop the Islamic terrorists.**

On August 9, 1982 Palestinian terrorists used explosives and gunfire in an attack at the Goldenburg restaurant in Paris. Six were murdered and twenty two wounded.

On August 11, 1982 Pan Am Flight 830 from Tokyo to Hawaii was severely damaged by a bomb placed on board. Abu Ibrahim and Mohammed Rashid from Jordan had placed a bomb under a seat killing a 16 year old boy. (Rashid was not found and arrested until 1988.)

On August 25 a bomb was found under a seat on a Pan Am Flight that had flown from Miami to Rio de Janeiro. That explosive was identical to the one that had detonated on the

Hawaii flight. This one luckily did not go off or it was possible the aircraft could have been lost and all aboard killed.

Those highly sophisticated suitcase bombs were becoming the normal attack on airliners by the Islamic terrorists. Most of the suitcases used had the name Valigeria, and came in a variety of shapes, sizes and colors. The explosives were Czech made Semtex, called PETN. (A British created explosive from WWII.) Plastic explosives can be rolled out to form a thin sheet and placed inside the lining of a suitcase. The detonator and batteries were usually hidden in the handle of the bag and at that time were invisible to x-ray machines. To get through as check-on bags, and to prevent a thorough check, soft-sided bags were used to trick inspectors. **Some of those bombs used barometric detonators, others used timers, but all were made so that they would detonate after takeoff, insuring mass casualties.**

In late August BLT 2/8 returned to Lebanon for peacekeeping duties. Views of Beirut took on the appearance of Berlin in 1945 as the streets were filled with fighting and destruction. Firing was still close by as this latest round of evacuations began. Lebanese Armed Forces, (LAF) began trucking PLO evacuees to the Marine checkpoints, as armed soldiers and marines were everywhere. Evacuated Palestinians were allowed to keep their empty rifles and pistols, but no munitions like grenades or RPGs. They rode in U.S. made trucks to the safety of the harbor and the ferry that would evacuate them. Within ten days the last of the PLO fighters (over **14,000)** had been allowed to safely leave the city and nation they had dominated for over a decade, and destroyed with their political strife and terrorism. (Had they not agreed to leave peacefully they would have been crushed by the Israelis.)

As those large groups of PLO-PLA troops minus their major weapons were allowed to leave some went to Cypress and others to South Yemen or Syria. Surprisingly Tunisia's President Habib Bourguiba offered the battered PLO sanctuary in his country. The quiet coastal town of Hammam el-Shat was given over to the PLO and the local residents were forced from their homes and businesses. Thousands of militiamen and PLO staff streamed into the town to re-organize their political and military headquarters. A growing number were unhappy with Arafat and his supporters.

With the PLO now driven out of Lebanon all of their remaining terrorist camps had been shut down, searched and emptied. Intelligence was picked up and revealed what the PLO had been up to. *With the loss of their hideaways the PLO also lost most of their income which had come from drug trafficking, ransoms, taxes and fees forced upon the Lebanese.* For a while the criminal enterprise-PLO was out of business.

Inside Beirut there were the dozens of thousands of rounds of ammo and munitions laying all over. Mines, booby-traps and IEDs were a constant menace in addition to the danger of having thousands of armed individuals in the area. As the port evacuation neared completion an overland repatriation of Syrian troops and their sponsored PLA units also began. Over 6,000 additional PLA fighters were trucked out from Beirut with the premise that they stay out of Lebanon. *However they silently returned to the Syrian fighting positions in the nearby hills of the Bekaa Valley.*

Yassir Arafat tried to orchestrate a similar clandestine return of the PLO to Lebanon in early 1983, but his effort was blocked by Assad. Syria was now in the prime position inside Lebanon, and they no longer needed or wanted Arafat or the PLO to interfere in his plans. The country was his for the taking.

But even after their safe evacuation they were brutal enemies.

On September 8, 1982 Lebanese President-elect Bashir Gemayel was murdered along with many of his staff in a massive truck bomb. The recent election of the Christian Gemayel, who had agreed to a peace accord with Israel infuriated the Muslims. Bashir had also demanded the pullout of everyone from Lebanon, Israeli, PLO and Syrian forces.

It was well known that the cause of Lebanon's seven years of horror was due to the PLO. Getting rid of all of them was a necessary event, just as Jordan's King had done years earlier to save his nation. But with Gemayel's murder all hopes for peace quickly faded. (Bashir was replaced by his younger brother Amin, but it was not a good substitution.)

Though Pres. Reagan was saddened with this second murder of a moderate Arab leader, he publicly (and wrongly) stated that America had no strategic interest in Lebanon. He also said he would not leave our forces in the country indefinitely. On September 10, 1982 the Marines work was done and they returned to their ships.

During the night of September 16, 1982 Beirut became a killing ground as hundreds of Palestinians were shot down inside the refugee camps. The killings went on for two days and it was believed that Christian Phalangists had entered the camps as payback from the terrorist bombing of Pres. Gemayel. *Some of the dead, (around 400), were actually PLO members who were hiding out among the refugee civilians.*

Naturally Israel was blamed for not defending the camps, and Defense Minister Ariel Sharon the hero of the Yom Kipper War was forced out.

Historical Note: Few realized how desperate the Israeli situation was in the 1973 surprise attacks by Syria and Egypt. Soviet supplies poured into both Arab countries throughout the fighting while Israel was running out of needed war material. Pres. Nixon insisted they must be saved and he authorized *Operation Nickel Grass* which sent 300 heavy lift supply jets to Israel with 22,000 tons of ammo and supplies. Those supplies enabled the Israelis and Sharon to fight back and win the war.)

As fighting resumed in Lebanon it was decided with a request from Amin Gemayel that the MNF, Mult-National Force troops from France, Italy and U.S. should return and be used as peacekeepers. Though it wasn't discussed openly, those nations sent troops in as a joint NATO military operation, and Britain joined in. (After the massacres it was felt that using NATO forces would insure a better peace.)

Pres. Reagan sent the Marines back into Beirut, (though the Pentagon objected), to keep watch until the final pullout of the Syrian and Israeli forces could be worked out. That would also give time to the LAF, Lebanese Armed Forces to buildup and assume security for their country.

Unfortunately Pres. Reagan had miscalculated the value of placing our people over there. Those Islamic terrorists were not going to be scared off. Our hurried effort had no game plan on what to do or how best to keep the peace. *In fact the Marines were not allowed any to carry ammo or to fire at anyone firing at them.*

One of the few episodes of discord in this administration was in the use of our military. Sec-Def Casper Weinberger wanted to insure we had no more inane deployments like LBJ and the Democrats had done in Vietnam. He insisted we follow six standard guidelines before committing our people.

First was the principal that our troops were only committed to defend a vital interest, *Second*, our civilian administrators must be certain what the issues are for us to commit to, *Third*, our objectives both political and military must be fully laid out, *Forth*, our government must monitor and assess continually if we are achieving our vital purpose, *Fifth*, before our forces are committed the president must have the support of the people and the Congress, and lastly all diplomatic alternatives must be exhausted before we fight.

Sec-State George Schultz did not agree completely. *His argument was based on Von Clausewitz's premise that war and diplomacy are used to achieve the same goal.* For Schultz diplomats do their best work when backed by armor and aircraft. **"Power and Diplomacy always go hand in hand"**. Diplomats who are not backed by strength will be ineffectual at best. *(77) The clearest example of that fact was England's Neville Chamberlain during the 1930s.

After listening to their arguments Reagan agreed with Weinberger's ideas, but he still committed the Marines as peacekeepers. Someone had to do something to help the people of Lebanon. *(Since 1975 the Democrats in Congress and then Carter stayed completely out of Lebanon, and never once tried to get the United Nations to act. This war was the result of their inaction.)*

To the convoluted minds of the Islamists those western troops were sent to shore up the Lebanese Christians in the secret desire to re-unify the nation under Christian rule. Those Islamists were determined to drive every non-Muslim out and change Lebanon into an Islamic State. All part of their master plan.

In addition to the Syrians and the PLO-PLA, the Iranian backed Hezbollah terrorist forces were growing in numbers. Their leader was **Immad al-Haj Mugniyeh** a devoted Fundamentalist who regularly directed their guerilla tactics to continue the seemingly mindless violence. But now their attacks would also included aggressive strikes against the French paratroops and U.S. Marines. Hezbollah people mixed easily with the crowds, and assisted the movements of PLO Force 17 terrorists in and around West Beirut. With our limited intelligence on the various forces inside of Lebanon this peace- mission was a recipe for problems.

(Iran's leaders were impressed with the zeal and security Hezbollah used. They knew that if a direct link was found back to Iran, America under Reagan would strike back. *In a forerunner to future al Qaeda operations, their forces were only given the information they needed for that unit's mission. Even if someone was captured nothing could be traced past that cell!)*

As the MNF staff work began it was decided to partition the operating zones of the city into three sectors. The French requested the port area and West Beirut, while the Marines wanted the open area of the airport. The Italians by default were given the center zone, which contained the refugee camps. They were diligent in providing security and were welcomed by the Palestinians.

East Beirut was the sector under the control of the Christian Phalange, and needed no outside help. That was also where the IDF relocated to in an effort to lower the tensions. While the press highlighted the aura of stability the MNF gave, it was the massive and well armed IDF that controlled most of the area. Every time the Muslims started a fight the IDF responded with overwhelming force.

Special consideration was afforded the new Lebanese President in an effort to show that he was in charge. Civilians were allowed into the airport as a way to get life back to normal, even though infiltrators were able to get in disguised as civilians.

Only 1,200 Marines and support troops of BLT 2/8 had returned to Lebanon on September 29, 1982. They took up positions around Beirut's airport while the Battalion CP was setup at the University. Col. Mead was initially worried over the tons of unexploded ordnance lying around and the isolated acts of terrorism. Trained Explosive Disposal units had to be flown in, but even so casualties continually occurred. At that time the threat level was considered low so no effort was made to secure the airport on a full 360 degrees.

With their limited deployment only three USMC rifle companies had been sent in. After their landing they setup checkpoints to try to keep the peace, but they were too few to be everywhere. One company was moved eastward to take the high ground near the Lebanese University. That enabled them to monitor the main routes in and out of the airport and keep watch on the Shiite Moslem quarter of Hay-es-Salaam.

Wrongly all of the USMC air and armor assets remained aboard the ships. Thus the peacekeepers consisted of only light infantry. BLT 2/8 (Battalion Landing Team) was rotated out at the end of October and BLT 3/8 moved in. They too were not allowed any armor or air assets.

On October 9, 1982 the Great Synagogue in Rome was attacked by Palestinian terrorists using grenades and automatic weapons. One civilian was murdered with thirty-seven wounded. (Thanks for all of the good work the Italians had done in Lebanon.)

In Tyre, Lebanon the IDF headquarters was abuzz with their morning routine. So far all of their objectives were being met and the local Lebanese who were Shia seemed happy that the IDF was kicking out the Sunni PLO. *Then around 8am on November 11, 1982 a 15 year old boy drove a small van into the eight story IDF HQ. It exploded seconds later killing 75 IDF troops and 14 Arabs* who were close by. This was the first of dozens of suicide bombers they would use over the next few years. Even the Israeli's were stunned at the barbarity of this type of attack. (Hezbollah identified the boy as Ahmed Qasir in 1985.)

Strategic Issues

At their previous meeting OPEC decided they had to cut oil production as a way to bolster the price of crude oil. Again it failed to stop the price decline as worldwide demand continued to fall.

Throughout Iran more opposition leaders were being murdered by the clerics. And in their continuing war with Iraq, Iran was able to recapture over 1,200 square miles of territory in the Khuzestan region. To assist their ally Iran, Syria closed the Iraqi oil pipeline that ran through their country to the Mediterranean Sea. Loss of the oil pipeline forced Iraq to rely on the Gulf as their only major way to export oil. And oil tankers are an easy target for modern weapons. *In return for their support, the Iranians sent hundreds of additional fighters to Syria to help them in their overall plan for Lebanon.*

Back on May 9, 1982 President Reagan spoke at his alma mater, Eureka College. Reagan declared war on the Soviet efforts in the Third World, pledging the U.S. would support people fighting for freedom against Communism. His statement became known as the **Reagan Doctrine**. *(78)

With the growing problems inside Poland Pres. Reagan signed a secret order, **National Security Decision Directive 32.** The order directed U.S. agents and efforts to destabilize the Communist regime in Poland. That effort would involve helping and working with the Pope to funnel aid to the Solidarity Union. CIA would be the lead agency and would use the National Endowment for Democracy, secret Vatican bank accounts, and Western Trade Unions to get aid into Poland.

On June 8, 1982 Pres. Reagan gave one of his best speeches. *"Of all of the millions of refugees the modern world has seen, their flight is always away from the Communist world and towards freedom. Today our NATO forces face East, to prevent a possible invasion by the Communists.*

On their side of the line the Communist forces also face East, to prevent their people from escaping." * (79)

That October German Premier Helmut Schmidt lost an election to Hans Vogel, an anti-nuclear pro-Soviet pacifist. *Vogel even went to Moscow to confer with Soviet leaders.* Anti-everything demonstrations were becoming larger and more violent, and those in Holland and Germany were the most volatile. In Britain their Labour Party made unilateral disarmament their political cornerstone. Even in America the "nuclear freeze movement" was gaining ground, with support from key Democrats in Congress. Large protests occurred in NYC, as future presidential candidate *Jesse Jackson and his following joined forces with the CPUSA (Communist Party USA) and others to demand that America disarm unilaterally.*

During December 1982 Sec. State George Schultz went to Europe to meet with all of the heads of state. He was there to convince those leaders it was time to deploy the 572 U.S. Pershing medium range missiles and cruise missiles. Pres. Reagan was adamant about deploying them as a hedge against the Soviets, but it would be a hard sell in the leftist political climate of Europe.

To ensure the West stayed cowed during that time, Soviet Defense Minister Dmitri Ustinov launched a scare offensive of dire war warnings just before Sec. Schultz's European trip. And Russia had completed their deployments in Eastern Europe and Asia. But Sec. Schultz brought in a doggedness to the meetings, and convinced our allies that they had to step up now. "To sweeten the pot", he convinced Pres. Reagan to end the sanctions on the Soviet gas pipeline so the Europeans could profit.

As shown earlier intelligence was coming in that the Soviets could be preparing to start a war. In October the National Intelligence Council had completed a classified assessment of Soviet Ballistic Missile Defenses. **Though they had signed the 1972 anti-ABM treaty with Pres. Nixon, the Soviets had as usual, lied. They were engaged in a massive program to develop and deploy such weapons.** If they were successful the NIC felt the Soviets could be immune to our nuclear counter-attacks. They believed if that came to pass, as soon as the Russians felt ready they would probably initiate a war to take Europe.

In Moscow Yuri Andropov the head of the KGB had recently taken over for the dying Leonid Brezhnev. Andropov was another hardliner who promised a renewed confrontation with the West. He was also the two-faced Soviet ambassador to Budapest back in 1956 when the Soviets crushed their uprising for freedom. And he was the one who had approved the harsh crackdown in Poland the past fall. His KGB forces tortured and killed with impunity, especially in the media poor Third World. And inside secretive Russia, political detainees were "held" for years as they suffered greatly in the unseen gulags of Siberia.

But despite those brutal credentials, the liberals in America fawned over him. Andropov clearly saw and understood Reagan's plan to roll back their advances, and he was equally determined to prevent it. (Though no one inside the KGB including him foresaw the fierce anti-communist revolt that had occurred in Afghanistan.)

What only a few realized at that time was that the Soviet gains the past years were now becoming liabilities. With Pres. Reagan challenging them everywhere, Soviet costs were running rampant. Costs they could no longer afford. (Andropov wanted to make some economic reforms to stave off their collapse, but he too fell ill before they could be instituted.)

Into this charged atmosphere came an unusual speech by France's Mitterrand. As stated earlier France had upgraded their nuclear forces with help from America, but they also provided the Soviets with advanced equipment and technology causing much anger from the Administration.

But Mitterrand went to Germany and told a surprised German Bundestag and their Chancellor Vogel that there could be no division within NATO. France and Germany belonged to the same alliance, an alliance that had kept them free from the Russians since it had formed. Nuclear weapons had been the guarantor of that peace, but there must be parity between the superpowers to maintain such a peace.

There are now 243 Soviet medium-range missiles threatening entire regions of Europe. None of our nations have a defense against those Russian weapons.

While all of us want the disarmament talks to succeed, we must have solidarity toward each other to make those negotiations a success. *He reminded the Bundestag that the French Second Army was stationed in Germany to protect them, not France.*

His message was clear, the U.S. missile deployments must be allowed in order to maintain the peace

Mitterrand also told all that the French nuclear weapons would not be part a of the current disarmament talks in Geneva. Those discussions were centered on America and Russia only. (A clear warning to Russia that France could bite back.)

In Washington the speech was startling, and appreciated. With the recent political turn in Germany it was feared the country would descend into full scale pacifism wrecking NATO and dooming Europe. More than likely the Europeans would have surrendered soon after to avoid a war with Russia. But Mitterrand's speech was so effective that Germany's Vogel would be voted out as the Christian Democrats under Helmut Kohl won a majority.

As the countdown to the installations drew near, the KGB launched an all out "peace offensive" using multiple front organizations. (Even Hollywood joined that effort, producing two disturbing movies about nuclear war.)

Soviet defector Stanislav Levchenko would later state that all of their efforts to promote discord were all directed at the NATO nations to stop the U.S. missile deployments. * (80)

With their missiles in place the Soviets had a trump card over the Europeans, and they wanted to use it.

With the continuing protests ringing across western Europe Mitterrand would icily remark, **"The missiles targeting Europe are already in the East, while all of the Pacifists are in the West"** * (81)

Asst Sec-Def Richard Perle remarked that in reality the duplicitous Mitterrand sacrificed nothing over this episode. He simply made a political judgment that if Germany fell so too would France. His interests were only for France.

That statement may have been true, but Mitterrand stood up when he had too, and because of him Pres. Reagan and his anti-Communist policies would win the Cold War.

Soviet Ambassador Anatoly Dobrinin's memoir *In Confidence* was written a decade later. He too admitted that it was the Soviets who increased the superpower war dangers with their SS-20 missile deployments, not Reagan's action over the Pershings.

What the Soviets wanted was a visible and overwhelming military capability over Europe. *They knew the Europeans were close to falling apart. The Soviet Politburo felt that their new weapons could be the intimidating factor that caused NATO's end.* Once the American military was gone it was inevitable that the Europeans would be peacefully turned, or conquered.

Had that happened the Soviet Union would not have collapsed, the West would have!

Dobrinin also wrote that Brezhnev's diplomatic efforts in détente was not a true call for peace, it was simply another way of waging their struggle against the West. Their plan was to ease superpower tensions while working to surpass America's declining militarily. Then they could checkmate us. By 1980 the Soviets were ahead of us in strategic forces of missiles and bombers by a ratio of 1.63 to our 1, they also had way more nuclear warheads, 3.68 to our 1. In conventional forces we were far behind in all categories except naval aircraft carriers. *(82)

Dobrinin also admitted that during the past decade the Soviets had used the anti-nuclear, anti-war pacifists to further their goal of defeating the weak-willed West without a war.

They almost succeeded, except for Ronald Reagan.

Democracies are the only form of government that are responsive to the needs of the people. But Democracies are subjected to the ambiguity of those who get elected. Though wars are fought by them, the democracies are more likely to act defensively, than the aggressive and impetuous totalitarian types of governments. But a democracy cannot long survive without an effective military to protect it and its interests, * (83)

For There Are Tigers in This World, * (2)

And They Are Always Watching

At this time the President was also sending more aid to Central America to stop the growing Communist tide. His policies were designed to "stress the Soviet economy and their military forces". Analyst Richard Clarke produced a series of papers on what the cost was to the Soviets for their proxy wars in El Salvador, Nicaragua, Mozambique, Angola and the war in Afghanistan. Even low-end guesses showed a huge drain on the feeble Soviet economy. *His work verified the Administration's agenda, that the best way to stop the communists was to confront and counter them economically, not militarily.*

Throughout the Cold War the Soviets had never sent large numbers of personnel into direct combat against the West. Their preferred method was to fight the West via proxy as shown with the wars in Greece, Korea and Indochina.

With the political and military weakness visible in America in 1979, the Soviets had finally acted directly by invading Afghanistan. *This was the first Soviet war since WWII.* Thirty five years had passed since their armies had faced a determined foe. They too were re-learning many lessons the hard way as battlefield losses were high and progress slow.

By 1983 the Soviets decided to "pacify" the entire country rather than just the major cities. Their effort would require a larger deployment of their conscripted divisions. But that decision highlighted a serious weaknesses in the communist system, the lack of battlefield motivation and leadership. Every time they increased their forces, their casualties became heavier as the Mujahedeen fighters attacked them constantly.

To counter those guerilla fighters Russia was forced to send in their well trained Airborne and Special-forces units. Once those units arrived with their mobility and capabilities, the war returned to Russia's favor. *The Soviets also used chemical weapons and air attacks on the civilians in their effort to crush the local fighters. And they laid 30 million mines throughout the country!*

The continued strategic threat of the Soviets was realized when Air Force Recon photos picked up "dump trucks" exiting a large Russian building that showed no other signs of construction. **Surveillance of the site over a period of months revealed that a massive and secret underground site was being readied to enable the Soviets to fight and survive a nuclear war.**

To cover up their communications effort the Soviets used special electronic channels that even the NSA (National Security Agency) did not know of. America's forced reliance on getting intelligence from electronic sources instead of the human ones underscored a potentially fatal weakness in our security. That reliance was even more one-sided since the destruction to the CIA ordered by Pres. Carter in 1977. More disasters would follow.

Lebanon and Iran

Back in Lebanon BLT 3/8 continued their missions of patrolling and trying to keep the peace. Christian areas north of Beirut were still in pristine condition and considered safe areas. Around the rest of Beirut most of the Muslim residents were pleased that the MNF was keeping their word and them safe.

LAF (Lebanese Armed Forces) patrols entered the Christian areas to show the flag. To bring the LAF up to speed, Marine NCOs worked as training officers teaching them how to act and react to enemy fire. Physical training was a big part of the mission and in short order "Lebanese Marines" were shouting cadence on their morning runs. Their tactical improvement was noticeable.

On February 14, 1983 BLT 3/8 rotated out and BLT 2/6 came ashore. Patrol areas had been expanded. At that time there was little violence because winter was making life difficult for everyone. Many times USMC patrols were involved in saving Lebanese who became caught in heavy snows. Training and healthcare missions became routine and it appeared that the MNF had accomplished its main goal, keeping the peace. But as always looks were deceiving.

On March 16 a grenade attack was made on a USMC patrol. LAF aggressively searched the area and arrested one suspect who was sentenced to death. Close by the terrorists watched it all, learned and waited. A mile away the IDF (Israeli Defense Force) was growing unhappy with their continued role of occupiers, and troubles between the factions began anew.

At home Pres. Reagan had to justify our continued involvement in Lebanon to the Congress as required by law. It passed.

Iran had been giving much aid to the PLO and their new terrorist group Hezbollah, and Syria supported Iran's efforts against Iraq. Assad and Iraq's Saddam were both Ba'thists, but they were also unforgiving rivals for control of the political movement. Despite their animosity in 1979 Saddam had joined with Syria in condemning Egypt's peace with Israel. (Politics are the same all over the globe.)

Iranian army units recaptured the port city of Khurramshahr, the last major area that Iraq had taken almost two and a half years ago. The Arab world was still divided in their outlook on the war. Some countries glad to see the violent Hussein humbled while others feared the Fundamentalist Iranians more. The Saudis were in the latter group, and they were helping to fund Saddam's war.

With the turn of fortunes of war going against him, Saddam began to worry. What if Syria joined military forces with Iran? Saddam toned down his virulent anti-West attitude and speech. (His need for allies may have had changed his attitude, but not his ambitions.) Looking for a way to bleed and destabilize Iran the Reagan Administration made overtures to Saddam. The enemy of my enemy is a friend.

Reagan's Policies

Libya was becoming more of an issue. After the Gulf of Sidra fight in August 1981 Qaddafi demanded revenge. CIA picked up several reports of Libyan hit teams who were after Reagan, Bush, Sec-Def Weinberger and former Sec-State Haig. Security was greatly increased, and barricades were erected around prime targets and installations.

On January 21, 1982 another KH-8 recon satellite was launched from America. Unlike most of its predecessors, this one was placed on an axis to fly over N. Africa. Its target was Libya, and the border areas with Chad and the Sudan. Chad, the neighbor south of Libya was still on Qaddafi's target list. Over the past months Qaddafi's troops were observed massing on the borders, backed by **Soviet Tu-22 Blinder bombers**.

The Administration quietly let it be known that any Soviet military action there would not go unchallenged.

Since the Administration viewed Libya as a Soviet surrogate, here was a chance to hurt both. The Democratic run House Intelligence Committee did not like any U.S. action anywhere, and they did not approve of anything. But Pres. Reagan sent aid went to Chadian Defense Minister Hissen Habre anyway.

By early 1983 the small nations of Latin America found themselves embroiled in a political firestorm. Armed rebels were becoming more aggressive with each passing month. It was normal in the decades past for power struggles to occur among the military rulers. But these battles involved the civilians, and the struggle was ideological of left vs right.

This Communist inspired violence could be traced back to the overthrow of Somoza four years earlier. El Salvador and Guatemala were fighting serious leftist insurgencies, while Honduras was helping the U.S. fight against the Sandinistas. The regional death toll from just the last year had hit 15,000. Sec. of Def. Weinberg proposed sending $110 million in aid to El Salvador.

Pres. Reagan again stated that the Nicaraguan Contras were freedom fighters who were legitimately opposing the communist Sandinistas who had forcibly took over in 1979. Thus the Contras have the right to regain their nation, and America as the bastion of freedom had to help them. (As we were doing in Afghanistan.) Those Contras consisted of abused peasants, former Sandinistas, Somoza supporters and even the indigenous Moskito Indians, all of whom wanted the Communists out.

Despite the aid given to the Communists by the Democrats, the Contras had increased their numbers to over 12,000 by the end of the year. And even though Pres. Reagan had made a solid case for helping the Contras, the hostile Democrats were still fighting his efforts. *They controlled the Congress as they won large majorities in the November 1982 mid-term election. They also passed the second Boland amendment which sought to stop any covert aid to Latin America by the CIA or the DOD.*

On March 8, 1983 Pres. Reagan gave a speech in Orlando, Florida giving a list of social problems that were ruining our nation. Leftist ideas were undermining our families, schools and social structure. The worst issues were Teen pregnancies, abortion on demand, and drugs. We must work and pray to undo those issues if we want to regain our national strength.

(All issues the Muslim clerics observed here and despised.)

On the international front Reagan called the Soviet Union an **Evil Empire,** dedicated to conquering the West. He stated how the Communists continued to bring war and instability to the world in an effort to destabilize it and takeover. Echoing Whittaker Chambers, (the original Communist whistleblower), the President stated that the Cold War would not be decided by arms, but by our belief in God. Our strength is not material, but spiritual. Reagan was challenging the legitimacy of the Soviet Union.

Those on the left had accepted the existence of Communism as a real political system, even though they always took power from the people by using violence. *Incredulously even in 1983 liberals did not rate Communism as something to fear.* *(84) His speech was again assailed by the media, academics and the Democratic politicos. But it also caused much worry in the Kremlin, as his blunt language called the Soviets "outlaws" .

But Reagan was correct, the Communists were criminals. Their political system was akin to an obelisk sitting on a giant platform. Those in the obelisk of the Communist Party lived well, while the masses in the slab slaved for them without gain. Unlike Capitalism, there was no hope for advancement by the masses, and no one could protest against the party without pain.

One of Ronald Reagan's best quotes is; *"Freedom is never more than one generation from extinction. It is not passed down to our children in a bloodline, but must be fought for, protected and handed over to the next generation."* * (85)

During this time the Soviets were mounting a massive campaign to stop the deployments of our INF weapons. Casey and his analysts documented all of it, and passed a report throughout our government and to our allies.

For the Politburo, their decision to press the stakes and deploy their SS-20 missiles was coming back to haunt them. **Instead of checkmating the Europeans, they had awakened the sleeping giant.** If our missile installations went forward, all of the East Bloc cities could be destroyed within minutes. And the Soviets had no ABM defenses against that.

On March 23, 1983 Pres. Reagan went on TV to discuss the numerous problems with the Soviets, and he formally unveiled his **Strategic Defense Initiative (SDI)** initiative. This technologically difficult and expensive program was needed to counter the massive nuclear threats from Russia, and potential threats from rouge nations or groups. Russia had continued their previously banned ABM - Anti-Ballistic Missile system, so they had protection. **SDI would do the same for us.**

Reagan simply stated, *"Let me share with you a vision of the future which offers hope. With this system in place we can counter the Soviet nuclear threat with measures that are defensive. Thus free people can live secure in the knowledge that their security did not rest on nuclear retaliation."* *(86)

No one knew about this aspect of his speech in advance, and it had great shock effect on everyone, especially the Soviets. (Their worst nightmare come true.)

During a campaign visit to NORAD in 1979, military officers had highlighted to candidate Reagan of a dangerous hole in our national defense. **We had no way to stop an enemy missile attack. Even a rogue state could destroy us with just a few nuclear armed missiles.** That information had been a wakeup call for Ronald Reagan, and he had planned on doing something about.

With **SDI** in place we could destroy enemy missiles as they flew towards us. Two panels of experts were convened to discuss the scientific and technological needs of his program. Also examining this proposal were numerous legal minds.

After their legal investigation was done they insisted that this system was not prevented under the existing 1972 ABM treaty. Though the non-stop Soviet efforts certainly were!

The Soviets had consistently denied they had any ABM programs, and the liberals in the West went along with them. But our satellite photos showed that the Soviets were lying. **They were able to defend most of their major urban and military areas from our weapons by using an extensive ABM system.** They also had a nationwide system of radar warning stations, and a nine radar system to help aim their ABM missiles. (Radar guided)

Russia's extensive R&D program employing some 10,000 scientists and engineers, just on ABM research. And missiles were not the only weapons they were testing.

Russia was far ahead of us in lasers, EMP (electromagnetic-pulse) weapons, directed energy systems such as particle beams, and space based weapons.

All of this intelligence had been presented to the Democratic Congress the past months.

Still they derided and fought Reagan's SDI safety plan.

(After the fall of the USSR former Foreign Minister Eduard Shevardnadze admitted that the radar installations at Krasnoyarsk were in direct violation of the ABM treaty.)

Though the leftist pundits and most of the Democrats in the Congress belittled Reagan's proposal, Soviet Premier Andropov and future Soviet leaders Chernenko and Mikhail Gorbachev were horrified. Most in the Politburo understood that America possessed the capitol and technical prowess to make this system work. **And that would mean that all of the Soviet weapons and efforts these past decades would be worthless.**

In an effort to inspire the western liberals and defeatists to stop Reagan, the Soviets complained loudly that America was "militarizing space". In actuality, the Soviets had already done so with their dozens of military satellites already in orbit. *Many carried nuclear weapons.*

(When Gorbachev took over the Soviet Union in 1985 his main strategy was to undermine SDI and change the evil empire view of the Soviet Union. His sly approach would be called *Perestroika,* and again the western leftists loved him.)

Back in 1946 writer George Orwell identified the qualities that a totalitarian state would need to have and use in order for them to get into and stay in power. Ironically those same qualities would make it difficult for them to maintain control as the people would eventually revolt over those qualities. Such a system would demand a continuous alteration of the past, and a disbelief in the very existence of truth. It would also need a schizophrenic system of thought in which common sense and exact sciences would be disregarded, all in the needs of the state. *(87)

(He was describing the nature of Communism, and liberalism.)

Around this time NYC was enjoying a revival of building and growth as the U.S. economy was improving under Pres. Reagan's economic plan. This increase in jobs meant that instead of people leaving the city, they were moving back. Residential construction renewed and prices for housing increased. Mayor Koch created tax subsidies to attract large real-estate developers. They would benefit greatly from those tax abatements, and commercial construction began to increase. Thousands of jobs returned in the construction trades, suppliers, trucking, services and supply houses, and increased the city's tax revenue.

Another major growth engine to the City, NY State and Federal tax revenues were the sizable tax receipts created by the resurgent stock market. One of the most beneficial laws passed in 1981 by the Reagan Administration was the creation of **IRA's, Individual Retirement Accounts.** The idea was to get the normal citizen to invest in the stock market by offering tax credits for retirement accounts. As the economy grew and millions of people were added to the work roles. A lot of personal savings was placed into those IRAs. (Me included.) Buoyed with large amounts of new cash the stock market began a steady climb in sales volume and in prices. Companies provided with this monetary infusion from their stock sales began investing in R&D and hiring more workers. That kept the growth going, and resulted in increased consumer spending and tax collections from sales and payroll taxes.

When Pres. Reagan proposed his SDI missile defense system critics sanctimoniously called it Star-Wars. The NY Times and other liberal-defeatist entities said it was "utopian and inconceivable". His plan envisioned a weapons defense system that could protect our country. If SDI was successful it would give America a multifaceted defense of lasers, particle beam weapons and missiles that would shoot down enemy missiles before they reached our shores. As bids for that and other defense related work progressed, that too spurred on the economy. **The boom times were just beginning, just as Ronald Reagan said it would.**

Historical Note: The Dow Jones index rated the 30 best stocks in the country. In 1956 it topped 500 points for the first time. On November 14, 1972 it reached 1,000 for the first time. For the next years it rose and fell as world and economic events dictated never reaching the next milestone. The recession under Carter drove the Dow well below 1000, but after the IRA law was passed the stock market doubled to 2,000 in 1983. In 1991 it would reach 3,000 and in 1995 it surpassed 5,000! Under Pres. Trump and his economic plan the Dow hit 27,000. *None of that future growth would have been possible without Reagan's economic plan. And it includes the internet which was created from that R&D.*

Lebanon

Unknown to the MNF, Iran's Hezbollah terrorists were ready to strike a major blow. Around 1300 hours on **April 18, 1983** a nondescript pickup truck carrying about 2,000 pounds of explosives entered the U.S. Embassy compound. Few took notice of the truck as the driver had pulled up to the main building, and then detonated the bomb. It destroyed the building murdering sixty three and wounding over one hundred twenty. Most of the CIA personnel in Lebanon were killed in the blast which included Robert Ames the agency's top Middle East specialist.

(Ames had taught CIA Director Casey a great deal about Soviet methods in their never ending imperialism. Ames explained how the Soviets manipulated the education of the young in the schools of S. Yemen to create model socialists for the future. Reducing Islamic religious influences was a vital part to achieve their overall goal of indoctrinating the young to do their bidding.) (Sound familiar??)

It was uncovered that a Lebanese employee who worked in the kitchen had heard of the special meeting with Ames that was to be held at the embassy. He passed on the information to the terrorists. *It was Mughniyah who directed the attack on that specific day and time.* It was also learned that a Christian Lebanese Forces commander had been bribed to allow the bomb-truck to pass his checkpoint. (Though it was unclear if he knew what was in it.)

Three Islamic groups claimed credit for the bombing, Islamic Jihad, the Iranian cover for Hezbollah in Syria, the unheard of Arab Socialist Union, and the Vengeance Organization of Sabra and Shatila Martyrs. The terrorist animals who attacked our embassy did so in a callous and self-serving act. Their reason was simple, to drive us out of Lebanon.

The Islamists did not want peace and stability, they wanted to take over Lebanon, and we were in their way.

This extensive blast should have galvanized the Administration and the Senior Commanders in the Lebanon theatre to strengthen the defenses of all of our positions. It was obvious there was inadequate security around the Embassy and it had been exploited. (Similar to the VC embassy bombing in Saigon in 1962.)

This repeated use of suicide bombings against military and civilian targets was a clear warning that more brutal attacks would follow. Israel had suffered those types of attacks before, and no one in the West knew what to do about them. At home many began to state we should just leave the region entirely.

Historical Note: During 1945 the Japanese used kamikazes to destroy our naval shipping. Their desperate attacks caught everyone by surprise, because to a western mind suicidal attacks are wrong. Even by the end of the war there still was no surefire way to stop a determined pilot from crashing his plane into a ship except for a direct hit by a large cannon. Our Naval losses were so extreme, that when the atomic bomb became operational it was quickly and correctly decided to use it to end the war. That decision prevented the planned invasions of Japan itself, and the extreme losses to both sides that would have followed.

Around the USMC command it was obvious that the airport area by its very nature was open and exposed to terrorist attacks. The recovery effort from the Embassy blast and collapse went on, as victims were dug out and removed in a grueling procedure that would be repeated many times hence. (Including 9/11/01)

On the 17th Pres. Reagan gave a press conference on normalizing relations between Israel and Lebanon. Our efforts were meant to bring peace and in that we had succeeded. We helped the Lebanese reorganize their internal security and safely take over. His statement was true, but also identified our efforts as helping the Gemayel government. Even though the stability created benifitted Muslim civilians, the Fundamentalists and terrorists saw it as anti-Muslim.

Battalion Landing Team BLT 1/8 rotated in during May 1983. They reported directly to the 6th Fleet, but as with the other units in Lebanon they were part of the work being done by the State Dept. the MNF, and the DOD. (Pres. Reagan was as Commander in Chief responsible for their operations.)

BLT 1/8 operations continued with training and peace/humanitarian patrols. As with the other units they were not permitted any armored vehicles or helicopter units. Their break-in period was fairly quiet, but most of the USMC personnel became wary. They knew they were being watched. By early May quick hit and run attacks by Islamic terrorists were becoming commonplace. On June 8 RPG's were fired at one of their observation posts. Sensing the danger the Marines of 1/8 began improving their forward positions.

Then in July USMC units began taking artillery and rocket fire, something a small civil rebel force would not have. As was learned in Vietnam, artillery shells make audible sounds as they cut through the air, but rockets do not. This enemy was using Russian made 122mm rockets, the same as was used against us in Vietnam.

Numerous casualties were incurred, but still no armor, artillery or air support was sent in.

In mid-August and the "intentional" shelling around the airport commenced. The Lebanese Islamic faction called the Druse were using these attacks as a way to force the Gemayel government to give them a larger place at the political table. Numerous government ministers were kidnapped when they dared to enter the Druze-Syrian controlled areas to insist the Syrians remove their heavy artillery from *their country*.

Tragically the LAF was unable to force their way into the area and destroy those cannon themselves. That Druze artillery was a serious threat to the Christian held areas, and was "unneeded in the now peaceful country". But Druze leader Walid Jumblatt knew that things were going to change soon. Those cannon were his and he intended to use them. There would be no peace.

Foreign Affairs

In Europe the run of Socialist political victories now included Sweden and Spain. (For the Spanish leftists their victory was a settling of scores for their loss in the 1938 Civil War.)

Around this time Russian leader Brezhnev died in Moscow and KGB chief Yuri Andropov officially replaced him. It was unusual for a new Russian leader to be picked so quickly, but the Politburo wasted no time. Unlike Stalin's sudden death, the Soviet leaders knew Brezhnev was dying and did not want to have a period of instability. Not with Reagan in the White House.

In response to Reagan's quid-pro-quo medium range missile buildup in Europe Andropov offered a drawdown of Soviet missiles from almost 600 down to 160. That offer was rejected by NATO, as the member nations rightly insisted that all of the Soviet weapons be withdrawn. *Peace in Europe had been maintained for 35 years without having medium range nuclear missiles emplaced.* It was Russia that decided to up the ante and it was up to Russia to ease the tensions by removing them. They refused.

On June 8, 1983 Pres. Reagan addressed the English Parliament, the first time any U.S. President had ever done so. His speech was upbeat and offensive minded. *He celebrated the virtues of our open-minded democracies, and predicted the coming collapse of Communism.* He made a strong attack on the Soviet Union and their aggressive imperialism, and urged the world's citizens to "leave Marxism-Leninism behind. He also praised the

British effort in the Falklands not as a war to claim a pile of rocks, but as a cause against aggression. The same one all of us were now waging across the globe.

Reagan told all, "Karl Marx had said that a revolutionary crisis would occur when the demands of the economic order conflicted with those of the political order. Marx had expected that those crisis's would destroy the capitalist world, but ironically his expected crisis was now happening in the Soviet Union. By denying human freedoms and dignity to its own people, Communism was crumbling from within.

Their economy is the one failing, not the capitalist ones. They are destined for the ash heap of history". *(88)

The president expressed optimism that there would be a long-term triumph of democracy. He praised the Solidarity movement in Poland for standing up to their Communist rulers, and the recent elections in El Salvador as they fended off a growing communist insurgency. We must crusade on the behalf of freedom. His speech was perfect.

By late summer Pres. Reagan had increased U.S. military involvement in the volatile and strategic Latin America despite the Democrats in Congress. *"Our support for freedom fighters is a form of self-defense, "* just like NATO. (89)

However the Democrats were against all of the President's initiatives, as were the leftists leaders in Mexico, Venezuela, Columbia and Panama. Their so-called Contadora Group wanted Cuba and the U.S. to leave the region in peace. Inanely the liberals of Hollywood and the Hamptons actually endorsed Nicaragua's Ortega as if he was a good thing. In reality he was just another Communist despot that was killing his country and its citizens. But you would never know that from the parties and the press.

Implausibly the Democratic controlled House sent a letter to Ortega praising his efforts to bring "democracy to Nicaragua"! Democratic Senators Harkins and John Kerry flew to Managua to meet with Ortega, and they returned boasting that he was a "misunderstood reformer" not a Marxist. *Those same Democrats then voted down all humanitarian aid for the Contras.* A week later Ortega flew to Moscow to meet with the Soviets to discuss his upgraded arms needs.

During July Libya's Col. Muammar al-Qaddafi sent his forces into northern Chad. As always the ruse was to assist "rebels striving for freedom", but this was just another invasion by a megalomaniac. Reagan had grown to like the Chadian leader, Hiss`ane Habr`e. We had supported him during his exile in the Sudan, and Reagan was determined to support him against Qaddafi. Twenty five million in aid was approved. Mitterrand however was reluctant to help even though Chad had been one of their old colonies. (Habre` was not liked by the French, which likely explains why Reagan liked him.)

As the French hesitated to commit any assistance, Libyan armor and troops poured across the border intent on reaching the southern part of the country. That section known as the Aouzou strip was believed to rich with uranium and oil. Pres. Reagan sent an aide to Paris with stacks of recent satellite photos on what the Libyans were doing. Habre's militia forces were actually fighting well, using Toyota pickup trucks mounted with machine guns or anti-tank rockets as fast moving strike forces.

(Similar to the WII Rat Patrol units used in N. Africa. This improvised tactic would become a common operation with guerilla and insurgent forces in the desert regions and is still in use today.) Unsure of what to do the Libyans slowed their advance.

But Habre`s troops needed help from a modern military force in order to defeat the Libyans and their Soviet supplied weapons and tanks. In mid-August France finally decided to intervene, and were aided secretly by the CIA. Libya's Khadafy was accused by Pres. Habr`e of using the patented and brutal Soviet style attacks against their small border towns. Hundreds had been killed and Habr`e called it genocide. Col. Khadafy (aka Qaddafi) naturally denied any involvement, but the insertion of the French ground forces stopped most of the Libyan attacks.

Back in Beirut the factional hostilities continued to grow as a Christian church was desecrated with a poster of the Ayatollah Khomeini. Over the past days the Israeli IDF was slowly pulling units out of their former checkpoints in East Beirut and turning them over to the Lebanese Armed Forces, LAF. That force was a religiously mixed one with more than half of the members being Muslim. Hidden among them were dozens of traitors and spies.

In late August the Marines were finally allowed to fire back at the ever present enemy snipers. On August 28, two Marines were killed and fourteen wounded as the fighting in the city escalated. Brazen Islamic gunman roamed freely as the unreasonable Rules of Engagement placed upon the MNF allowed the enemy to move around without fear.

On the 30th an unhappy America learned of the deadly two day battle inside Beirut. Administration spokesmen wrongly downplayed the fighting. Soon after a new war erupted as car bombs and snipers became a daily routine in the terror war that was being waged for control of Beirut's streets. Agitated Muslims staged a dangerous protest near the replacement U.S. Embassy, and a rescue column had to run a gauntlet of artillery fire to get to them. More casualties ensued.

As had been common in Vietnam, the civilians would know that trouble was coming and leave their fields or disappear from the streets and markets. USMC outposts had limited ammo and could only fire at know enemy fighters. They received little fire support from their parent units of the Fleet, but they did get some help from the LAF. A week of moderate fighting ended suddenly. It was a pattern that would be repeated often as heavy Islamic attacks began on Sunday (Christian Sabbath) and diminished as each day went by.

Although the airport was not subjected to the heavy small arms fire as had the outposts, they were an easy target for indirect fire from rockets, mortars and artillery. On September 4 they were hit with air-bursts of artillery and volleys of rocket and mortar fire. That was followed by heavy machine gun fire that swept across the area. An LAF counterattack into the hills was thwarted and seemed to bring in even more Druse and Syrian artillery fire.

By this point there were over 600 large guns located in that enemy sector. But as per the State Dept. directives, the commands could not use ships cannon, aircraft or USMC artillery. Marine counter-fire consisted of only company issued 60 & 81mm mortar fire. This latest battle lasted a day and a half as more casualties came in.

(According to the battle reports the refusals to use our heavy weapons came from Washington. They did not want it to seem that we were a hostile participant in this War, even though we were.)

On the 6th a new fight began with more enemy rockets and more USMC losses. Finally in mid-September U.S. navy ships shelled the Syrian held areas that everyone knew contained most of the enemy fire. French commander Legionnaire General Francis Coullin complained bitterly that his political masters refused to allow them to join up with the Americans to make a stronger force. (In Unity there is Strength.)

Soon after the Lebanese Christian sector at Souq-al-Gharb was attacked repeatedly by Syrian backed terrorists. No matter what the politicos thought or wanted, the MNF was no longer on a peacekeeping mission. Col. Geraghty USMC sent repeated alerts through the chain of command warning of the dangers and requesting his armor, artillery and helicopters.

And to make things even worse, the Israelis were pulling away from Beirut. That was prompting the enemy forces to become even more aggressive. Pres. Reagan publicly wanted the IDF to leave, but privately he asked them to stay on. They could not.

On September 1, 1983 the Soviet Union shot down Korean Airlines KAL Flight 007 killing all 269 passengers and crew. The Soviets denied any involvement in the destruction of the airliner for over a week while Pres. Reagan accused the Russians of outright murder. *Sec. Schultz had an intelligence tape played in which the voices of the Russian pilots and their commanders were clearly heard tracking the plane for over two hours, and then ordering the firing of a missile that destroyed the airliner.*

Soviet Commanders had sent fighters up to intercept the jet. One of the fighter pilots reported in that the aircraft seemed to be an off-course commercial airliner and was altering course away from their base. He was ordered to shoot the aircraft down anyway.

The Soviets had ruthlessly waited until the jetliner was almost clear of their airspace before shooting them down, expecting the wreckage would disappear into the sea and be considered a crash. Throughout all of that time they never attempted to contact the jet by radio or visually to warn them away.

Presented with this evidence the Russians had to admit they did it. This civilian aircraft had passed over the Kamchatka and Sakhalin Peninsulas, the same area FDR returned to Stalin to get his help against Japan. (Help they never gave.) To try to placate the intensely negative press the Soviets claimed the plane was spying on their military bases. (An RC-135 recon plane had flown near there over an hour earlier. They had completed the mission and left long before the KAL flight arrived.)

Soviet explanations and public relations attempts failed and the aging communists realized they had made a serious mistake. Andropov accused Reagan of developing an "outrageous militant psychosis". The liberals of the world tried to use this tragedy to insist that this was why we needed arms control, and more talks with the Soviets. Sec. Schultz did meet with Gromyko in Madrid, but the accusations continued.

(In his memoirs Gromyko stated that Schultz was the toughest American he had dealt with in his thirty years. After the collapse of Soviet Communism transcripts of that night showed that two of the Far Eastern Defense commanders felt the aircraft was an off-course civilian aircraft. *Defense Minister Ustinov overruled them and ordered the attack.)*

Middle East

On September 23, 1983 Gulf Air Flight 771 from Pakistan to the UAE (United Arab Emirates) was destroyed by a bomb in the luggage compartment killing 112. *A passenger had checked a bag at the gate, but never boarded the aircraft.* Abu Nidal and his terrorists were the ones responsible. They were demanding extortion money from the Gulf oil states, and this was their warning to all. Kuwait and the UAE paid the money.

Iran again outlawed its Communist party. The Tudeh party was founded in 1945 during the Soviet occupation of Northern Iran. Though they had followed the Ayatollah's policies, the anti-Soviet fervor from the brutal Soviet war across the border in Afghanistan was now backfiring.

U.S. intelligence began picking up disturbing radio signals to and from Lebanon pushing for more attacks against the MNF. (What was done with that information? Was it passed on to the USMC Commanders in country?)

The new war in Lebanon continued with 6,000 or more artillery and mortar rounds being fired by each side. The only way to stop the heavy shelling was to attack the Syrian positions and obliterate them. USMC commanders wondered what was the purpose of our staying around as "peacekeepers"? We were just stationary targets for the enemy. However higher officials did not want the mission to end and be seen as running away. All realized that there was no hope for peace in Lebanon, not with Syria and Iran actively aiding the Druse faction.

On September 16 Druse artillery again fell around the replacement U.S. Embassy and the ambassador's residence. That finally got a response, and the navy fired dozens of rounds into the Druse artillery positions. A Lebanese Air Force unit also attacked that area destroying tanks and more of the cannon. U.S. Naval gunfire was called in on the 18th, and approval was finally given for U.S. naval air strikes. In spite of this increasing fighting, higher officials including the USMC wrongly downplayed it.

On the 19th an additional 340 rounds of naval cannon fire went in against the Druse positions, and numerous naval aircraft flew support missions. Sec. Def. Weinberger was against this escalation but was overruled by Sec. Schultz. He felt our forces needed the fire support if they were to remain on station. Unconcerned with casualties, the Moslem forces stepped up their fire and sent in local ground attacks.

The previously unscathed Italian and French forces now became targets and their casualties increased. French warplanes retaliated by bombing hostile targets in the Syrian sector. Despite their high losses the Druze and PLA forces (the ones who had snuck back) were quickly resupplied and reinforced with Soviet made T-55 tanks.

On September 23 news reports revealed that the battleship *New Jersey*, one of four that were being modernized under the Reagan naval buildup was seen sailing in the Mediterranean. She arrived off of Beirut on the 25th. The next day a cease-fire was suddenly enacted.

On the Sept. 26 up-to-the-minute transmissions from Iran were again picked up by intelligence units. Iran was ordering more attacks against the USMC positions. (89A)

Sniping and occasional ground attacks continued. On October 10 a new presence was noted in the Muslim positions, hard bitten professional soldiers who wore Russian battledress uniforms. They looked Arabic, and it was assumed they were Syrian front-line troops. Then another Islamic group showed up wearing white headbands with red Arabic letters. These were assumed to be the Iranian fighters that had been based at the training camp at Baalbek. Local civilians began leaving the area in increasing numbers and speed.

A few days later on October 16, 1983 IDF units were operating near a Lebanese Shia procession that was in observance of Ashura, a Shia Muslim ceremony. Near the village of Nabatiyah an IDF patrol tried to pass by them and a battle broke out. It resulted in a renewed fervor in the Shia population, and constant fighting with any Israeli's in reach. Martyrdom is a canon of the Shia faith, and was being used here as a weapon against everything not Shia. (Iraq's Saddam Hussein always kept a lid on the Ashura observances to maintain control of their Shia population.)

Fallout from the Shia hostility resulted in intense fighting all around the MNF positions. Operational reviews were needed as was some truth from the senior officials. The National Security Council met on October 18, 1983 to discuss Sec. Weinberger's proposal that our people leave Lebanon. For Weinberger our unclear objectives in Lebanon were only placing our people at risk.

Even with our limited intelligence gathering, warnings of renewed fighting and of probable terrorist actions came in. Again the Sec-Def was overruled and the Marine mission continued. For the USMC units ashore it was clear that they were targets in a sad tale of power and hatred. A car bombing near the Kuwaiti Embassy almost killed the USMC commander on the 19th.

On October 23, 1983 two large truck bombings were made on the MNF on direct orders from Tehran.

Despite the clear and present dangers roadway barriers were never erected around our major facilities to prevent a repeat of the prior Embassy attack. Using the same method as they had at the U.S. Embassy, two Hezbollah truck bombs demolished the Marine barracks at the Beirut Airport and a French Marine barracks in the southern suburbs. (An Iranian photographer had setup his camera on a hill overlooking the airport so he could take photos of the attack.) In total 241 USMC died, along with 58 French marines.

Although the battleship *New Jersey* shell an area known to have Hezbollah fighters, Iran itself wrongly went untouched. Sec-Def Weinberger was against any retaliatory strikes. This inaction was a terrible mistake for it convinced the Islamists that America was still weak and could be attacked without fear.

(*Both Iran and Syria were quickly implicated in the bombings. Instead of a direct strike at them, Pres. Reagan decided to give more help to Iraq to hurt them indirectly.*)

To facilitate commerce at the airport the only barriers around the USMC barracks were some barbed wire and a chain link fence. Both were easily breached by the bomb truck, a yellow Mercedes. Those trucks were common sights at the airport, and on that Sunday morning it crashed through the wires and drove right into the building. The guards had not been locked and loaded, and could not fire at any potential attacker.

This bomb was around 12,000 lbs of high explosives wrapped in canisters of flammable gases. It was believed to be the largest non-nuclear blast in history at that time. **As was common with Islamic terrorists they had done their homework.** The driver drove the truck into the center of the atrium of the heavy weight building used as the USMC barracks and CP. The massive blast lifted the building off of its supports and when it fell back down it crushed itself.

Untold dozens had been killed in the blasts directly, others from their terrible wounds. Many more were buried and crushed inside the wrecked building. Rescue operations commenced within minutes but could not keep pace with the demand because of a lack of heavy equipment and operators.

The French Marines suffered from the same type of attack. French, Italian and British troops joined the effort and Israel offered the use of their fine trauma centers, but it was refused for political reasons. Some of those who died might have been saved as the Israeli medical facilities were only twenty flight minutes away.

Muslim snipers continually fired at the rescuers, and security posts had to be reestablished to stop any follow on ground attacks. News crews became irate that they could not enter the security zone while Lebanese civilians and LAF troops did enter and most helped out. (As is common in all tragedies, looters and thieves took advantage of the disaster.)

Eventually the news people did get into the area and many acted like swine taking gruesome photos while laughing and talking. Numerous times the media people had to be threatened to show respect for the USMC victims. Back in the states the news media was intrusive and their sanctimonious efforts at getting "stories" from family members resulted in the military restricting their access.

Pres. Reagan took a lot of flak for the losses and for our even being there. His response was that it was imperative that America maintain its credibility by staying involved in world affairs. His ideals were warranted, but the senior commanders and State Dept. officials did not take the steps needed to protect the base or the personnel. After so many months of being in the same place security should have been upgraded weekly. Especially after the Embassy was truck bombed.

At Camp Lejeune, North Carolina home of the USMC 2d Division, BLT 2/6 was ordered to prepare for movement. Their headquarters company and a few units were flown into Beirut by 1800 hrs on the 24th. As the flights came in enemy tracer fire was directed at them and became a common sight. BLT 2/6 command, staff and company members were re-designated as the new HQ company of BLT 1/8. Their assignment was to restart the battered unit and continue their original mission.

(The 24th MAU was scheduled to be relieved by the 22d MAU in early November, but the 22d was re-directed to Grenada instead. Surviving members of the 24th were told their relief was postponed indefinitely. When the Grenada operation ended the 22d went to Lebanon and the 24th was sent home.)

After that devastating bombing the Marines on the line dispensed with the idiotic Rules of Engagement that had been instituted. Many an Islamic fighter bought the farm during those last weeks thinking that they could not be touched.

On November 7 a one-hundred member enemy assault force moved towards the USMC positions. LAF soldiers and tank fire aided in the total destruction of those attackers. The Muslims used the bombings and local fighting to setup dozens of well prepared bunkers close by. Sheets of enemy fire and dozens of RPGs struck the security outposts. Not until dawn did the firing finally end. Hundreds of additional Muslim attackers lay dead.

Grenada

On October 25, 1983 (two days after the bombings in Lebanon), U.S. troops suddenly swarmed over the small Caribbean island of Grenada. Cuban proxy troops had been operating in the country for years, since the 1979 "Grenadian Revolution". As shown before Marxist Maurice Bishop had overthrown the government of Eric Gairy and quickly made overtures to Russia and N. Korea. Before the coup Cuban subversives had been active on the island for years. With Bishop in power almost 1,000 more Cubans arrived to train the Grenadian police and army. Their plan was to create a 10,000 man force that would control the island and then export their efforts to other countries. Military agreements were quickly made with Cuba, the USSR and N. Korea.

During early 1983 "advisory construction units" began building a large, modern airport with an extra long runway. U.S. intelligence agencies concluded that the extension was not needed for commercial flights, but would be the perfect size for Soviet military supply aircraft, bombers and as a potential Cuban military base. (That same work was being done in Nicaragua, which was why we knew what was coming.)

Then on October 13, 1983 Maurice Bishop was arrested by the Cuban military commander under directions from Bishop's number two man Bernard Coard. Several more Grenadian leaders were also arrested. After days of turmoil Bishop was freed by some of his supporters. His retinue marched to the downtown center of St. George the capitol. But Coard's supporters were even more left-wing than Bishop, and his forces recaptured the freed prisoners executing Bishop and several others.

A twenty-four hour shoot to kill curfew was ordered by the revolutionaries. A female CIA agent provided some on-site intelligence, but the situation was unclear. Word of this situation got out and the nearby nations of Jamaica, St. Vincent, St. Lucia, Dominica and Barbados urged something be done. Senior Administration officials decided to act rather than take a chance on another hostage situation. Contingency planning started on how to evacuate the 1,000 plus U.S. students who were attending the medical school and tourists on the island.

Operation Urgent Fury was ordered conducted. The U.S. ground force component consisted of light infantry from Army Rangers, the 82 Airborne Division, Navy SEALS and two companies of Marines. They faced over two thousand Grenadian and Cuban soldiers, the majority of whom were also light infantry. Because of the surprise and rapid assault by our forces most of the active fighting ended within two days. Some of it was intense and required the support of USAF AC-130 gunships which used nearby Barbados as their ground support base. The mopping up of the Communist die-hards took about two additional weeks. Canadian and New Zealand troops arrived as peacekeepers.

Even though some improvements had been made in our military since Pres. Reagan took over the overall performance in Grenada was not good. Losses occurred which should have been prevented, command and control was poor, and the rushed operational plan had needless problems. (Navy Seals were dropped off too far from shore and three of them drowned. Helicopters were wrongly sent unescorted on daylight missions and shot down by communist heavy machine guns, while others crashed over the crowded airspace etc.)

As always the U.S. media and the Democrats expressed outrage over our military response. The NY Times compared our actions with that of the Soviet invasion of Afghanistan. *However the NY Times did not protest the Russian invasion.*

Despite the media hysterics the people of Grenada and the U.S. medical students and tourists were quite pleased with the outcome. Polls in the U.S. showed that the vast majority of Americans supported the move to oust a Marxist-Leninist government. This was the first U.S. action in our hemisphere since the Dominican operation in 1965.

(One of the unreported problems of this operation was that Grenada was still part of the British Commonwealth. Reagan never even spoke to Thatcher about the island's issues or the pending U.S. military action.)

Pres. Reagan gave many reasons for our actions, such as the protection of 1,000 American medical students and tourists, active calls for help from Grenada and the nearby islands, and the construction of that military capable airstrip by Russian and Cuban troops. While not stated directly, a message was being sent to the other leftist leaders that Reagan would not tolerate another Marxist state in the region. *Cuba's Castro was extremely upset by our actions, and by the lack of response from Moscow.*

After the fighting ended our Intelligence units worked their way through the island and uncovered hundreds of documents that were quite revealing.

Grenada's New Jewel Politburo *had happily reported that in just four short years they had bankrupted the once viable nation. Grenada could no longer pay their debts. Economic collapse was soon to come, and with that event they (Communists) would have complete control over everything and everyone on the island.*

They also requested that their comrades in Nicaragua and Cuba show them how to keep two sets of records in order to trick the capitalist banks into making new loans to them. Another set of papers thanked California Democrat Ron Dellums and his staff for their correspondence with Castro and Bishop over the past months. *(Dellums and staff wanted them to succeed in their takeover of the peaceful Island nation.)*

In the written minutes of one staff meeting were notations explaining that the new Granadian airport would be used by Cuban and Soviet military forces to complete the takeover of the entire region". *(90)

That plan was over, and after this operation the Sandinistas suddenly wanted to have better relations with America. They also pursued negotiations with their neighbors, as the fighting slowed down. Libya also reduced their hostility.

Lebanon

On November 18 the dispirited 24th MAU was relieved from Beirut and sent home. They had done a fine job in trying to keep the peace. The 22d MAU took their place as reinforced bunkers and bombproof trenches were built. As always, too little too late.

By this point Syria and the U.S. were embroiled in an undeclared war with advanced Russian made SA-5 missile units firing at U.S. Navy jets flying CAP (Combat Air Patrol). After the bombing the IDF destroyed an Iranian training camp in Baalbek. French aircraft destroyed a similar Iranian camp a few days later. The Soviets had recently brought in their best SAM system. On December 4 a U.S. strike against Syrian positions in the Shouf area resulted in the loss of two navy jets and Lt. Robert Goodman being captured.

Meanwhile Druse artillery continually fired upon the 22d MAU killing eight more marines. That last strike finally resulted in the *New* Jersey firing her main guns into the Shouf killing multiple dozens of the aggressive enemy. Arab extremists and Syria's Assad threatened more attacks as revenge. Enemy artillery fire continued into the new year, but now it was being returned with relish. Around that time the LAF began to fold up as their Muslim soldiers deserted to go home or to fight with the Druse.

In the U.N., a Soviet veto stopped any chance of having U.N. peacekeeping troops sent to Lebanon. Because of the Soviets the devastation and the killing were allowed to go on, but to them that was not a bad thing.

Israel sustained some of their operations, but was unsure of what to do next. *Despite their battlefield success against the PLO, Lebanon was collapsing because the Muslim leaders and hostile nations wanted it so.* Only an extensive Western occupation force plus attacks into Syrian held areas could turn the tide and promote freedom and safety for Lebanon. Tragically no nation wanted to be part of either of those requirements.

Superpower Tensions

Though they did not respond militarily, the Russians had indeed taken notice of recent events. It furthered their suspicion that Reagan was looking to start a serious war. Over a year earlier KGB chief Andropov had initiated a worldwide in-depth search for any evidence an American attack was coming. Called *Operation Ryan*, the KGB ordered all of their agents and assets to look under every rock for clues. Russia's GRU, Soviet Military Intelligence was also instructed to analyze everything they knew. (Double agent Oleg Gordievsky, London KGB head of station, reported in that there was a real fear of Reagan in Moscow.

At this same time NATO was set to conduct a pre-announced war-game code-named *Able Archer*. It was set to go off on schedule from November 2 to November 11, even though we had just gone through the terrorist bombings in Lebanon and the Grenada operation. *Moscow actually expected a large scale U.S. attack was going to occur, because that was how they planned to make their first strike against the West, under the cover of an exercise.* (It was also how the Egyptians covered their surprise attack on Israel in the Yom Kipper War in 1973.)

During those tense days the Russians convinced themselves that patterns on our NATO installations had changed and an attack could come. They even sent a Victor class submarine into the waters off of the Carolinas to take note of any major military naval traffic near Norfolk, NC. (That base was created for our operations in WWI, and would be the natural collection point if we were again sending units to Europe.)

Their sub had been picked up by our underwater **SOSUS-underwater sensors,** and a U.S. frigate and an attack sub stayed close by watching them as they watched us. On October 31 the Russian sub snagged the frigate's towed sonar line tearing it away. Happy with their successful theft they tried to sail away, but the line became entangled in the sub's propeller. That forced the Russians to surface to free their propeller and the American frigate rushed close by and took the classified sonar cable back.

And to ratchet up the Russian anxiety a little higher, during early November the first of the U.S. nuclear cruise missiles were being offloaded at NATO bases.

As was commonplace massive anti-war protests were sweeping through Europe to denounce the missile deployments. Again the leftist media would only showcase the dissent and not the real reason for the deployments. Those demonstrations were not able to sway P.M. Thatcher or Pres. Reagan on this issue. On November 22 the West German Bundestag approved the Kohl government's choice and the missiles began arriving the following day.

Though our intelligence was incomplete enough information had gotten out to convince many of our principals that a war with Russia was becoming probable. (Ironic that both sides saw the same scenario looking at the evidence through different prisms.) That situation was one of the reasons why the Pershing's and cruise missiles were now so valuable. They were easily moved and hard to stop. Western leaders hoped those weapons could be the trump card to preventing a Russian first strike / war.

What was unknown by any of the Western powers was that the KGB and its cousins had over 500 agents active inside Western Europe! One of the most important of those spies was an agent named Topaz. For five years E. Germany's Reiner Rupp had worked his way up the NATO hierarchy and was able to gather a large amount of intelligence. NC 161 was a document that was so secret it could only be read in a locked cell. It compiled everything NATO thought it knew about the Soviets. (Naturally a lot of it was wrong.) Rupp was not only able to read this top-secret report, he was able to photograph it and get it out to his masters.

His spying and reporting on NATO were so detailed that the Soviets would have won WWIII in Europe had they attacked the West at that time. Those "secret locations" for the U.S. Pershing's and cruise missiles had been uncovered by him. All of those sites were targeted to be taken out in the initial Soviet attacks.

So extreme and well designed were the Soviet war plans that in the event of WWIII Russia had many of their smaller submarines fitted with 20 mega-ton warheads. Once a war had begun those subs were to be emplaced near our coastal cities. **Their war-plans called for the subs to detonate their nuclear warheads underwater. Tests had showed that localized tsunamis would be formed from the blasts destroying all of our coastal cities.** And nuclear debris from the blasts would ensure those ports would be unusable for decades.

(Yet people believe the Cold War was our irrational thought.)

At that time Soviet alert satellites were of poor quality and outdated. Their planning and intelligence units were outmoded and too ideological. They constantly misread information (like Able Danger), into thinking that events and communications were more than they actually were.

With all of the listed factors now converging the Soviets had illogically convinced themselves that the U.S. and Reagan were slowly building up to begin a nuclear war. Warsaw pact units went on alert. **Then the Soviet military actually went into high alert and were within minutes of launching hundreds of nuclear weapons at us. But no one in the West knew it!**

A few months earlier another near miss had occurred. A Soviet alert satellite had sounded a missile launch coming from America five times within a few minutes. It's sensors had actually picked up the reflection of sunlight off of nearby clouds, but the poor programming used in their outdated system recorded the event as five separate missile launches from the U.S. (Similar to our issues a few years earlier.)

Site commander Lt Col. Petrov refused to believe that such an unusual attack was occurring and he did not hit the panic button. Twenty minutes later the sun had set and the satellite sensors reset showing that there were no launches. **Only his level-headed thinking prevented a panicked Russian nuclear launch, and a follow on retaliatory launch by us.** However the Soviet high command dismissed him from service, for "not acting on the launches the satellites picked up".

It was months before the West learned of those extreme close calls (and potential nuclear attacks) from the double agent Gordievsky. Once alerted the major political and military figures in England and America were shocked to think that the Soviets had reacted so insanely to the very publicized war-game, and a mistaken sensor. They were also unhappy that none of our intelligence services or units had picked up that the Soviets were about to attack us twice. **Those incidents were, and still are proof that a missile defense shield is a good idea.**

During December 1983 Soviet General Nikolai Ogarkov made a public statement claiming that Reagan's America wanted to launch a first strike and start a nuclear war. Acting out of their irrational fear the Soviets sent some of their Delta missile submarines back into the Atlantic to operate near our shores. They joined up with the normal Yankee class submarines that were always there to form submarine packs.

With the reports from those earlier near-misses were joined with these latest Russian submarine deployments, a dangerous picture formed. Sec. State George Schultz realized that our side needed to calm the situation down and quickly. He spoke with various Soviet diplomats to try to reduce the tensions and to resume arms reductions talks.

On January 16, 1984 Pres. Reagan gave a speech to get arms reductions to the point were there were no more nuclear weapons. It was his first foray into the peace process with the Soviets, and it did calm them down. Reagan felt that with the rebuilding of our military underway and his SDI program causing everyone fits it was time to re-test the waters on negotiations. *But now we would negotiate from a position of increasing military strength.*

America

As the New Year of 1984 came in the U.S. inflation rate had fallen back to the low levels of 1972. This was quite an accomplishment considering how high it had been just two years ago, (18%). Our economy continued to grow as the economic despair of the Carter years vanished.

In the political realm the U.S. Commission on Civil Rights decided to stop the use of quotas to hire and promote black applicants. Back in the mid-1970s quotas had become the norm to settle racial discrimination lawsuits. But as time moved on the use of quotas had fallen from normal to last resort to ended. Pres. Reagan appointed this review board and they were following his directions to end the practice. Many Democrats, Civil Rights leaders, the media and minorities called the decision a setback for racial causes, but quotas for one group actually means discrimination for the other groups.

(In 1995 the Supreme Court would finally make a ruling on quotas. They stated that they were unconstitutional unless the government could show a compelling reason to enact one. If so the quota must be limited in scope and in duration.)

The Civil Rights Division was created in the 1957 Civil Rights Act that the Republicans had pushed through the Congress, and President Eisenhower had signed.

(Again it was the Republicans who had pushed for and passed Civil Rights, not the Democrats who opposed this needed law.)

Over the years that Commission had been politicized by the following Democratic administrations who used them as a con to control the civil rights program. "Their Commission began reforming our social structure to meet the Democrats power lusting objectives". Those efforts were made to help the Democrats at the ballot box, not to right any wrongs and give equality to all.

[I feel that the voters should decide this issue, not bureaucrats or some liberal judge appointed by a liberal politico. If our citizens vote on and insist on using quotas then it must be enacted and used equally throughout the nation in **all jobs and titles.** Those quotas should be based on the population percentage of the whole country, based on the latest census. If Blacks make up 14% of the population, then 14% of all positions should be set aside for Black job holders. If Hispanics make up 20% of the population then they would have 20% of the positions in question, etc, etc. In that way each "racial group" would be represented according to their population percentage and no group would be advanced over another. Every ten years the quotas would be changed based on the latest census. If not enough qualified people of a certain race can be found, the ones holding the job would be considered "temporary" and would be replaced as soon as a qualified racially acceptable person was hired. *This program should also encompass all scholarship programs and admissions policies into public schools and colleges.* Again the idea is to be equal and fair.]

In the never ending battle by some Americans against Christianity and the social principles that this country was founded on the Supreme Court heard a case over Christmas nativity scenes. **In their March 1984 ruling the court stated that it was legal for cities to show Nativity scenes during the Christmas season.**

Undeterred by the Supreme Court, the anti-religious crowd filed more and more legal challenges against religious displays. They would continue the filings until a different court with a liberal judge ruled against our religious freedoms. And the liberals always plotted on stacking our judicial system and the Supreme Court with enough leftists to revoke parts of the Constitution. (It is far worse today, and again the voters should decide that issue.)

Foreign Policy Issues

Turkey the southern most partner in NATO underwent a coup. Their civilian leadership was deposed and the military took over. Asst. Sec Def. Richard Perle was sent over to get a feel of what was happening. Turkey was the last country in the Western defensive arc for the Persian Gulf region. If they became neutral or turned pro-Soviet the West could be in for a big problem. Perle's trip appeared successful as a roadmap for the return of civilian rule was being organized.

But on the down side the Turks were returning to being a religious (Islamic) country. The increasing actions and propaganda from the Islamists was undoing decades of secular pro-western progress in the nation.

Iran continued with their terrorist acts by striking numerous targets in Kuwait. The U.S. and French embassies, Kuwait airport, their main oil terminal, an electrical generating plant and a building housing U.S. dependents were all struck within 90 minutes on December 12, 1983. Fortunately not all of the bombs exploded. The ones that did caused extensive damage. One bomb targeted the U.S. Embassy murdering four and wounding twenty. Again the administration did not strike back, but continued aiding Iraq. Peaceful Kuwait soon became a police state with dozens of Islamists arrested.

The next day Kuwaiti Air Flight 221 was hijacked and the passengers and crew tortured to show the Kuwaiti's what could soon happen to them. With Iran threatening additional attacks the previously captured bombers somehow "escaped" from prison.

Muslim extremists had taken over most of Lebanon. Westerners were routinely being kidnapped and held for ransom to gain the release of captured terrorists and to get ransom money. Because of the perpetual instability in the country the Administration decided not to risk any more of our people than necessary, and all civilian staffs were reduced to a minimum.

Pres. Reagan announced on February 8, 1984 that the 22d MAU would soon pull out of Lebanon and remain aboard their ships off the coast. Italy and France did the same. The Administration could see the futility, and heard the Congressional disapproval that our efforts. Unless a large military occupation was made, something no one wanted, Lebanon was doomed.

Maybe we should have reacted more strongly against the Syrian military positions, especially in the days after the Embassy bombing. That would have been a warranted retaliation, and if strong enough maybe it would have convinced the Syrians to leave the Lebanese alone. Perhaps then the peace everyone sought could have been attained.

As the last Marines left our navy ships fired parting salvos into the Shouf. Despite the MNF exit, Israeli military missions were still going on as was the factional fighting inside Beirut itself. Lebanon was in dire straits, and their Cabinet stepped down to protest the direction the country had gone.

(The United Nations should have come together and partitioned the country into two separate religious nations, Christian and Islamic. Then the West could have supported and protected the Christian nation, and the Muslim nations could do the same for the other part. That should have ended the religious fighting, and any Christians who were terrorized in the other Muslim nations could have moved there to escape persecution.)

General Secretary Andropov died of kidney disease on February 9, 1984. He was quickly replaced by Konstantin Chernenko, yet another old, hard line communist. Vice President Bush went to Moscow and offered a summit between the leaders of Russia and America. They refused, unless Reagan ended the SDI program. During the past months the Soviets were still safeguarding their missile submarines by keeping them in home waters. Dozens of Soviet surface ships and aircraft scoured the Barents sea in an effort to keep the snooping NATO submarines away. The Soviets still expected an attack even though negotiations were being held for arms reduction.

As the fighting between Iran and Iraq worsened the U.S. and Britain sent warships to the Persian Gulf to insure that the vital oil tankers were not attacked. Though Saddam was viewed with suspicion, Fundamentalist Iran was clearly the bigger threat to worldwide interests. Iranian forces were crossing into Iraq and threatening to take Basra. In order for us to help them Iraq had been taken off of the list of terrorist sponsors. Soon after our intelligence units tracked the war zone and provided real time information to the Iraqi's, which stopped the Iranian advance.

Saddam again threatened to shut off France's oil if they did not provide him with his most recent purchases. He wanted the Super Etendard jets which could carry their advanced Exocet anti-ship missile. It had proven quite effective in the Falklands War sinking a few British ships. Within weeks of the deliveries Iranian tankers were being picked off.

Many in the administration questioned the merits of helping Saddam, and many discussions highlighted the Soviet issue. If Russia became Saddam's mentor, Iran would be surrounded by Soviet client states. If the Soviets dropped Iraq and helped Iran then Iran would probably defeat Iraq and take everything. No matter which way it went, Western interests would suffer. It was felt that with France and America helping Saddam we could potentially keep the status quo and hurt Iran for their terrorist acts. *In 1984 the world was still seen as Soviet vs Western interests.*

On April 16, 1984 Greek authorities arrested a Jordanian national named **Fuad Hussein Shara** at the Athens airport. Intelligence had linked him to many previous terror attacks. During their investigation the Greeks picked up a British woman named Diane Codling a business partner of Shara. *Inside her suitcase was a barometric bomb that had failed to detonate on a flight logged in from Athens to Tel Aviv.* She had also flown from London to Athens with that same bag, but the bomb had not been detected anywhere! During the interrogations it became clear that Codling never realized that she was an unwitting suicide bomber placed on those flights. (The Islamic terrorists had observed that female passengers got less scrutiny than males, and much less if they were European.) *Incredulously Shara was later released by the Greeks.*

On April 20 a large bomb exploded in the baggage area at Heathrow airport in London. Over two dozen were wounded, though no group took credit. It was believed that another barometric bomb that had not gone off in the air, had detonated during the baggage handling.

Western intelligence then learned of another suitcase-bomb plot. On May 7, 1984 one **Jamil Khalid** with a United Arab Emirates passport brought a dark brown suitcase into Eastern Europe with a final stopover in W. Berlin. After leaving the airport he entered the city as investigators tried to locate him. On June 25 authorities raided an apartment in the U.S. sector and found two suitcase bombs. **Yussef Hassan** and **Abdel Darwish**, both were members of the PLO's May 15 terrorist group, and both were arrested. But they were only deported by the Germans, and Khalid somehow escaped.

A few months later an Iraqi Colonel Hawari who ran operations against Syria made contact with the recently leaderless and now bankrupt members of May 15. After convincing them of his credentials they began working for the Iraqi's under Hawari's title. (Saddam Hussein used the group to strike at Syrian targets.) Hawari made sure to clear his new operations with Arafat, who was still angry at being forced out of Lebanon. That kept the peace and the PLO handled all "legal issues".

Sec State Schultz had warned the president that we were losing the war of ideas in Central America because of the extensive outside Communist support.

CIA Director Casey went there to get a first hand appraisal of our efforts. One of his other (aggressive) schemes involved using sea-mines in the Nicaraguan ports of Corinto and El Bluff to slow enemy supplies. The sea-mines worked, damaging numerous ships, but one of them was a Russian ship. The Contras could not do that type of operation, the CIA did. When the Congress found out about those events they were livid and voted to end all aid to the Contras. They insisted it was "illegal for the U.S. to overthrow a standing government", and definitely illegal if any of our people were involved with those mines. Democratic legislators went to work to stop all of Pres. Reagan's effort in Central America.

On January 23, 1984 FMLN terrorists bombed a commuter airline in El Salvador murdering one and injuring five others. On February 28 those terrorists bombed two trains murdering another eighteen innocents and wounding twenty-one more.

Despite the continued violence, during March 1984 elections were held in El Salvador for the first time since 1977. Areas that were controlled by the leftist guerrillas were difficult places to try to vote as the people had to face roadblocks, rifle fire and other intimidating obstacles. But the people voted, for the centrist candidate Salvador Duarte, and not the leftists.

That April the Reagan Administration again sent emergency military aid to El Salvador without Congressional approval. His action again infuriated the Democrats. By this point CIA's Casey had become a pariah to the Democrats, and he was forced to apologize if he wanted any hope of saving the Contras. Even so they limited our support to just $24 million dollars for the year. The Congressional animosity continued throughout 1984.

To try to makeup some of the lost Contra revenue the NSC diverted some $10-15 million to them, and organized outside help to make up the rest. That included having the Saudi's kick in $1 million per month. Israel, private citizens and conservative foundations were all discussed as sources of outside funds for the Contras. Legal experts were brought in and they determined that as long as U.S. taxpayer funding was not used, this was not illegal.

As resolute as the Administration was to support the people of Central America and enable them to stay free, the Congress was equally single-minded to see them fall to Communism. On October 10, 1984 the Democrat's in Congress passed the third Boland Amendment. This one not only cut off all U.S. funding, but the Administration was prohibited from soliciting funds from other countries!!

Despite that latest Boland amendment Casey still wanted to pursue the third-party funding idea as a way to continue to hurt the Soviets. He correctly noted that many nations supported our anti-Soviet/Cuban efforts in Africa, SE Asia and Afghanistan. (And it was not an issue to the Democrats.) In fact the Saudis, Moroccans, Zaire, France and S. Africa were all involved in thwarting the Soviet Communists in Angola. And Australia, Singapore, Thailand and Malaysia were helping the Cambodians.

Casey felt this new law was illegal as well as illogical.

Why were the Democrats in Congress discouraging efforts at freedom in our own back yard? And why was it wrong for other anti-communist nations such as Israel and Taiwan to help us out?

With that Congressional vote in place, Sec. State Schultz was looking ahead to a Central American disaster. How would we cope with the problems that will certainly spill over into Honduras, El Salvador and Costa Rico. How do we keep the spirit of hope alive in countries that are being abandoned because of an order by the Democrats in Congress??

Libya's Khadafy had also been busy during 1984. On March 16 he attacked a broadcasting facility near Khartoum, Sudan. Then he tried to talk Nigeria into taking a $2 billion loan if they would help him fight in Chad. He dangled another loan to get Ethiopia to help. During April the Libyans instigated violent confrontations in London, and in July his commandos operating out of a container ship planted sea-mines in the Red Sea. Nineteen ships were damaged trying to trade with the Sudan. (Since they would not help him fight Chad, Qaddafi decided to fight them too.)

In September Khadafy admitted that his nation had also sent arms and troops to aid the Sandinistas. (Once again proof that Nicaragua was not engaged in a "civil war".)

In a separate agreement with France, Libya agreed they would leave Chad in the next month. Soon after the French troops pulled out. **Khadafy then sent more troops in.** Inside France there were serious divisions over what to do, and if Khadafy was as bad as the Americans claimed. French ministers and businesses wanted to keep selling the Libyans anything they wanted to keep them in their sphere and make money. But Libya was a sponsor of terrorism and a danger to all. What would happen in the long view if they succeeded and took over Chad?

Pres. Reagan went to China in late April to sign additional trade and cultural pacts. America would help them build nuclear reactors to make electricity and develop a major coal mine. The idea was to continue having the Chinese engage in worldwide commerce as a way of moderating their Communist ideals. *In touring a free market near Xian, Reagan stated "that free enterprise was clearly working even in communist China. This was a testament to how freedom could achieve success".*

His visit encouraged those few dissidents inside China who were trying to promote political freedom.

With the coming end of the British occupation of Hong Kong, officials of the two nations signed agreements for its peaceful return back to China's control in 1997. Communist China stated that the territory would preserve its special status as a free enterprise area for an additional *50 years*. This agreement suited China's long term plans as Hong Kong allowed them access to lucrative western commercial and financial contacts.

Peking made a similar offer to Taiwan to speed up the reclamation of that island nation. But the people who lived there had fled the communists in 1949. They had prospered in their freedom during the past decades, and wanted no part of rejoining China. Tensions flared anew.

The Administration saw a chance to make the Soviets pay heavily for Korea and Vietnam. Our early efforts in Afghanistan had accomplished what was asked, to help the rebels and hurt the Russians. But by mid-1984 even the Congress wanted to do more, though they still wanted Nicaragua to fall.(?) CIA Director Casey felt that with more support we could drive the Soviets out.

Over the past two years Texas Democratic Congressman Charlie Wilson had convinced many of the principals that our support could win the war in Afghanistan. Wilson had been a major force in promoting and helping the Afghans, and he was able to get them $250 million in aid for 1984. That was more than the previous five years combined! (China also stepped up their support as a way to hurt our common enemy.)

Pres. Reagan then changed the purpose of our Afghan aid. We were not trying to hurt the Soviets, now we were trying to beat them. As quickly as possible the Administration began sending additional military aid to the Afghans. Surprised by this windfall, (the Saudis matched it), President Zia decided to go for broke and he opened the floodgates. By late 1984 supply caravans of trucks moving from Pakistan to the Afghan border were easily observable by satellite. Even Western journalists were reporting openly on our aid and the war. (Zia was poking the Russian bear, expecting that Reagan would keep him safe, as Soviet strikes into Pakistan increased.)

Reagan imposed an embargo on all Russian goods and deregulated our falling oil prices to reduce the income that the Soviets had been getting for their oil sales, costing them even more. Casey went back to Pakistan and up to the border camps. While there he was given a demonstration of Chinese mine clearing equipment that could clear small lanes through the Soviet minefields. Civilian and combat casualties were rising from those terrible weapons, and better equipment was needed. The Chinese equipment worked fine and we created our own version.

Unknown to most, Casey was also secretly increasing the numbers and types of rebel raids into the Soviet Union.

Outside of Pakistan's-ISI reach lay the northern tribal areas of Afghanistan. Commanding many of those rebels was one **Ahmed Shah Massoud**. He operated on his own timetable, and with his own blueprint right against the southern edge of the Soviet Union. His forces routinely crossed the border to strike at the enemy.

By 1982 he had bested the Russians six times, and was known as the Lion of the Panjshir. In the spring of 1984 his spies learned the Soviets were going to devastate the region with aerial bombings and air dropped mines. Massoud successfully evacuated over forty thousand Panjshiris from their valley and got them into hiding.

In their effort to crush the rebels and their civilian supporters, the Soviets sent in thousands of their Spetznaz special forces. Dozens of their flying tanks called Mi-24D Hind attack helicopters came in. (Seeing the effectiveness of our attack helicopters in Vietnam the Soviets naturally copied our idea, but made theirs larger, more heavily armored and armed.) The presence of those flying tanks and airborne troops began to turn the battlefield advantage back to the Soviets. But fortunately a new U.S. weapon had been developed for the infantry, the Stinger anti-aircraft missile.

Iran began attacking the ships of countries who were backing Iraq. On May 16, 1984 three oil tankers belonging to Kuwait and the Saudi's were set afire by Iranian bombers. On the 19th Iraqi jets sunk a Panamanian cargo ship that was bound for Iran.

On the 28th the U.S. sent 400 of our new Stinger antiaircraft missiles to the Saudi's. The Saudi military was a small force and not equipped to handle the many military problems they faced. If Iran could shut down the Gulf shipping it could result in an economic collapse worldwide. It was hoped those Stingers would convince the Iranian aircraft to stay away.

(It is interesting to note that the liberal-pacifists who routinely chant no war for oil would find themselves starving in the cold and the dark if we did not act. What would they say then?)

In response to the recent attacks the Arab League demanded that the belligerents stop bombing neutral merchant shipping in the Gulf. For the most part Iraq had only been attacking ships at or near Iran's Kharg Island oil complex, while the Iranians were attacking shipping all over. The League declared that Iran was now the aggressor in the war. (Syria and Libya tried to prevent the vote and public condemnation of their ally Iran.)

Inside Iran the Ayatollahs had finally been able to complete the swing of the country over to their side by using murder, intimidation and the propaganda value of the Iraq war. Attacks and protests had stopped, and public showings of thousands of Iranian women dressed in traditional garb were seen marching through the streets armed with AK-47 assault rifles. Pictures of those who had been sacrificed in the war were also on display. Like the ploy Stalin used in 1941, the Ayatollahs used the war to direct the people's anger to a different enemy.

To help their struggling war effort all of the former military pilots who were still alive (and in prison) were given a choice, fight for Iran or you and your families would be executed.

To insure the pilots did not fly away once they were airborne, their families were held hostage.

On the 40th anniversary of D-Day President Reagan and the leaders of the industrial democracies headed to Europe to commemorate the sacrifices of those who had fought so that the world's people could live under freedom, not tyranny. This speech was one of Reagan's best and convinced many of the righteous struggles that we were engaged in.

And in a further statement of cooperation French officers allowed us to observe a revolutionary communications advancement they had made. *It was called RITA, and it enabled the user to make phone calls from anywhere by using the electronic infrastructure already in place.* Callers were not tethered to a land-line, and the Pentagon was stunned by the concept, which was put to good use in the first Gulf War. (This was actually the creation of the cell phone industry.)

In return for that favor we outfitted the French with our new AWACS aircraft. A 707 commercial jetliner had been retrofitted to carry a dome radar and advanced communications equipment. That orbiting aircraft would be able to manage the increasingly sophisticated electronic and aerial battlefield from a position a hundred or so miles away from the action. Their radar was so powerful they could pickup enemy aircraft hundreds of miles out and vector our interceptors to them without our jets turning their radars on. In that way our jets could slip in "electronically quiet" and therefore unnoticed. Those aircraft again revolutionized the aerial battlefield.

As the next U.S. presidential election cycle neared Walter Mondale, a protégé` of New Dealer Herbert Humphrey, and Carters former vice president was picked as the Democratic nominee. For the Republicans President Reagan was again chosen. Reagan promised to continue the American Dream with opportunities for all. The economy which had slumped until 1983 was rushing back. Interest rates had fallen, employment was increasing monthly, and our military was getting stronger. The malaise that had shrouded the nation had been lifted and all of us could feel the return of the American Dream.

The Soviets could also see that America had renewed. They realized that their walking out of the INF and START negotiations had backfired. It allowed Reagan and America to take actions they did not anticipate.

In the Philippine capitol of Manila, 900,000 protestors marched against the rule of Ferdinand Marcos in August 1984. This poor nation had been beset by growing hatred for that autonomist ruler who took power in the 1950s. The Philippines were given independence by the U.S. just after WWII, and had been a staunch ally. Clark Air Force base and Subic Bay Naval Base were vital to our Pacific military strategy, and stability was needed as it looked like the corrupt reign of Marcos was doomed.

With no warning on Sept. 20, 1984 the new American Embassy in East Beirut was blown up in another suicide car bombing. Iran and Hezbollah agents again used a suicide car bomb murdering twenty four with dozens wounded. This new Embassy had been relocated to the Christian side of Beirut in the hopes of avoiding any further terror attacks, but once again our security efforts failed. Islamists renewed their calls to drive the U.S. out of Lebanon.

After the bombing U.S. Intelligence uncovered a mockup of our new embassy at Iran's Revolutionary Guards barracks in Baalbek, Lebanon. It was clear that Iran was behind the attack, but again the Administration did not retaliate. Hezbollah's leader Imad Mugniyah was the leading terrorist targeting Americans, and a huge role model for Osama bin Laden.

In El Salvador leftist rebel attacks were defeated at Suchitoto, while a July attack by the leftists killed over twenty-five police officials.

Nicaragua's Contras received over $10 million in aid from private sources, and the governments of Israel, Argentina, Guatemala, Venezuela and Taiwan. The Contras were raising almost $1.5 million per month in their fight against the Communist Sandinistas.

(Since Pres. Reagan and his people were unable to get aid from the Democratic controlled Congress, his friends and contributors worked out their own way to save Central America despite them.)

Upset by the Congressional stupidity, Reagan had told Robert McFarlane his National Security Advisor to find a way to save those people. *The NSC was not "legally included" in the language of the Democrat inspired restrictions, so that entity began searching for new income sources.* Knowing they could not break the new law, McFarlane and his cohorts eventually found an unlikely source to raise money, Israel.

Indira Gandhi, India's four time Prime Minister was assassinated on October 31, 1984 by two of her security detail who were identified as Sikhs. Indira would be remembered as having helped her fledgling nation find its place in the world. But current religious tensions within the nation were rising towards civil war.

Most people do not know this, but during the years 1951-1985 India had received over $12 Billion in U.S. aid. That amount was more than what we gave to Europe in the Marshall Plan! Thanks to our aid, India was able to triple their annual food production even as their population doubled. But as always in the arena of world politics, our help was not returned with good relations.

In Poland a revered priest was found tortured and murdered after he was picked up by State Security Police. Solidarity leader Lech Walesa appealed for calm in the hope that some good can come from yet another despicable example of the communist rule. After the previously arrested Solidarity leaders had been released from prison they began using video and audio tapes to secretly communicate. Their movement was growing, but they knew they had to work under the radar if they wanted to stay alive and free. State Security agents were everywhere, and arrests were common.

America

At the Republican National Convention U.N. Ambassador Jeanne Kilpatrick's outstanding speech highlighted how well Pres. Reagan had been able to stem the advancing Soviets. (The media derided her speech but the truth was hard to ignore.)

During the 1970s Communism had won or made considerable progress in S. Vietnam, Laos, Cambodia, S. Yemen, Angola, Aden, Mozambique, Ethiopia, Somalia, Afghanistan, Congo, the Seychelles, Nicaragua and Grenada. Since Reagan's election in November 1980 the Communists had gone no further. They had been defeated in Grenada and were being challenged in Africa, Afghanistan and Central America. He was on the right course.

Democratic Nominee Mondale stated that Reagan's support for the Contras had "strengthened our opponents and undermined our moral authority".(?) (91) He and his party could offer no solutions to the world's problems, problems they had created. The party picked Geraldine Ferraro as his running mate in a thinly veiled attempt to woo the female vote. All of the anti-American liberals and media were against Reagan "the Cowboy".

Back in 1970 only 17% of the career bureaucrats in the Federal Government were Republican. That number had not improved during the past fourteen years. Even in the Supreme Court there was a hidden enemy. *Of the thirty-three clerks employed by the court, only six had voted for Reagan.*

To further help their candidate Mondale, the major media organizations went so far as to lie as they reported pre-election polls showing that Mondale was running close to Reagan. But on November 6, 1984 the truth came out as Pres. Ronald Reagan again won by a landslide. He and V.P. Bush lay claim to 49 states, only Mondale's home state stayed with the Democrats. Reagan again captured 59% of the popular votes cast and promised to continue his work on restoring our military and economy, saying "You ain't seen nothing yet."

One distressing reality needs to be presented. As popular as Pres. Reagan was, the core of liberals / Democrats did not vote for him no matter how well he and the country was doing. That polarized group made up almost 40% of our nations voters. Those numbers would increase as their propaganda being taught in schools and colleges twisted the minds of the next generation. In addition, the perks and handouts given out by the Democrats would also "sway" the populace to their side. Just look at how treacherous Obamacare and the Obama cell phone programs are. Designed not to help, but to buy the votes of the simple minded who don't see the big picture. Those factors make it extremely difficult for a Republican to win as they must hold onto their normal base and convince the independents (15%) to vote them in. (As the Democrats expand their rule, our freedoms are being taken away as the Deep State seeks to control most of our lives.)

A study on crime in America found that it cost $40,000 per inmate to keep them in jail for a year. Earlier "studies" did not list the educational, medical or dental costs as inmate costs. This burgeoning liberal society with its ridiculous rules is slowly taking over our nation. Within those "requirements" it was (and still is) creating a terrible burden on the citizen-taxpayer. There are rules for extended education, and ridiculous far reaching health benefits to inmates which include sex changes, advanced medical treatments etc. What is worse, is that America does not spend that much money per year on our young students! And the money that is spent on education is wasted because there is no discipline among the young, their families or in the schools. The wealthy send their children to "private schools", far removed from the dysfunctional public school systems. Their young get the best of everything, while the children of the middle and poorer families struggle to get ahead but can never catch up to the anointed ones.

And as these social facts were being revealed, the U.S. was suffering through a terrible increase in crime as illegal drugs were taking over the nation's cities and towns. In the 1950s marijuana use was making inroads, during the 1960s heroin use shot up, cocaine was the drug of the mid-70s and into the 80s, turning some cities such as Miami into drug empires. Hundreds of buildings were built there in an effort to hide the vast fortunes created by those drugs. During the previous decades organized crime had run the drug trade, but with the rise of cocaine, drug cartels in Latin America were organized. No place was immune from these magnified dangers, or the financial burdens. And it promised to get worse with the coming of the latest peril, Crack cocaine.

A society that produces street predators and white collar criminals will have to build more jails. A society that produces drug addicts will need treatment centers and more jails. And the society that looses its youth will not long survive.

The Democrats want to "solve all issues" by spending tax money inside a federal program that they control. Every issue needs a government program, financed with tax dollars and overseen by ever more bureaucrats. The easier and less expensive solution would be producing stable, educated children, and eliminating the drug dealers. But that would require discipline in the homes, a religious /moral upbringing, personal standards, and a population that was determined to see that through. That is not what the Democrats are producing or wanting.

Iran-Hezbollah

By 1985 Iran was in bad shape in their war with Iraq as they used up their supply of U.S. made weapons and spare parts. They needed our arms embargo upon them lifted. Inside the Administration that issue was a serious one as Iran was an enemy. But helping them with some arms would help us in two ways. Iranian terrorists were holding seven Americans hostage in Lebanon, and if they wanted some spare parts those people had to be released. Second, any money raised from those sales could be redirected to the Contras to get around the recent Congressional ban. A plan was hatched to solve both issues.

In December 1984 Hezbollah terrorists forced a Kuwaiti plane to land in Tehran. There they murdered two American civilians.

On February 23, 1985 another bombing occurred in Paris. One person was murdered and eighteen wounded as Hezbollah struck again.

Paris suffered yet another bombing when Hezbollah attacked the Rivoli cinema wounding eighteen.

On March 8, 1985 a car bomb in Beirut was used to try to kill radical Shia cleric Sayyid Hussein. The cleric was not at home but eighty of his followers were killed with over 200 wounded.

At home numerous complaints from the Congress accused Pres. Reagan of causing that bombing. A 1976 directive signed by Pres. Ford banned any political assassinations by the United States, fallout from the Diem and Allende disasters. (William Casey the stricken CIA director stated on his death bed that he had ordered the attack on Hussein as retaliation upon Hezbollah for their attacks upon our people in Lebanon and Kuwait.)

Foreign Affairs

In Columbia FARC leftist rebels murdered fifteen peasants on February 23, 1985 in a classic case of Communist intimidation. (Soon after Congress restored "humanitarian aid only". With non-stop bad news coming from Central America, they decided they did not want to be blamed if all of those countries fell to Communism.)

Long time Albanian ruler Hodja died in early 1985. Born to wealthy Muslim parents, he was active in the partisan fight against Hitler and Mussolini. After the war he renounced God and turned to Stalin and Communism. During his rule which began in 1946, Albania had became a strict Communist state and was one of the nations helping the Greek communists in their 1946 "civil war". His loss was yet another blow to the communist system that was kept going only on the will of those old guard rulers.

In the Soviet Union Premier Chernenko also suddenly died on March 12, 1985. This was the third time in 2 1/2 years that the Soviet leader had died, and again the Politburo quickly stepped in. This time they named Mikhail Gorbachev as their new Premier. Gorbachev was just 54, and the youngest member of the Politburo. He pledged to take Russia into major arms reductions.

Because of the prevailing Cold War mindset, the word on him was that he was clever but modern. He would repackage the same old Soviet rhetoric and make it sound good. After the state funeral V.P. George Bush and Sec. State Schultz met with Gorbachev privately for 1 1/2 hours. They came away impressed, but were also wary. (You don't rise to power in the Soviet Union as a nice guy.) Gorbachev told them there never were any madmen inside the Soviet leadership, and there are none now. (He conveniently forgot about Stalin.)

U.S. policy makers realized that with all of the old guard Communists gone, real progress towards peace was possible. Sec. Schultz informed Gorbachev that Pres. Reagan wanted to be personally engaged with him, and Gorbachev readily agreed.

Days later Pres. Reagan proposed that the two leaders meet soon to discuss the proposals of arms reduction. Talks were still going on between our nations, but little progress was being made. *(As before the Soviets insisted that SDI had to end before anything else could proceed. Sec. Schultz and Russia's Gromyko were both tough negotiators.)*

Gorbachev was fortunate in that he had "grown up" within the Soviet system. Unlike the former old guard leaders, he was educated, and knew that changes had to be made to save them from collapse. (Like China.) While in public he appeared benign, in the dark he was hard and tough. He was a true Communist believer, and attempted to complete Andropov's reforms by attacking corruption and inefficiency one step at a time.

But Gorbachev also decided to escalate their wars in Afghanistan, Angola and Nicaragua in an effort to win them. He was rolling the dice. They greatly increased their aid, and became more aggressive in their tactics. Angola received $1.5 Billion in additional military assistance, Nicaragua picked up a $600 million line of credit, and Vietnam was given a $Billion in economic aid. Gorbachev also directed the KGB to increase their terrorist bombing campaign in Pakistan, part of their augmented Afghan effort. (Everyone knew where the fighters, weapons and aid came from.)

In Angola, Soviet forces joined up with the 40,000 Cubans who were still there as they strove to push Joseph Savimbi's anti-Communists out of the country. Total Soviet aid to the MPLA was in the $Billions, and battlefield losses to Savimbi's forces were serious. S. Africa was forced to send their forces back in to prevent the communist takeover.

Those latest Communist offensives were so intensive and threatening, the U.S. Congress was forced to end their 1975

Clark Amendment which had prohibited America from aiding or getting involved in Angola.

(On August 8, 1985 the ban was officially ended by Congress.)

On November 12, a week before the Super-Power summit in Geneva, Pres. Reagan approved sending lethal covert assistance to help the Angolan forces of Savimbi. *Included in their aid were Stinger anti-aircraft missiles and TOW anti-armor missiles.*

The free ride in Angola was over.

In Nicaragua, Soviet efforts were also drastically increased in supplies, men and in command. Their effort was so blatant that even the Democrats in Congress took notice. Again the Soviets had reasoned that since the U.S. Congress had stopped all funding to the Contras, they must not care about the country. So the Russians jumped in with both feet. But the top Democrats suddenly woke up, and many changed their opinion of the Boland amendments.

On June 19, 1985 El Salvador suffer twelve killed to leftist rebels who struck a nightclub.

But those distant battlefields were not the only areas being restructured by Russia. The Soviets under Gorbachev continued their strategic improvements by deploying the SS-25 mobile ICBM, they flight tested a rail version of that ICBM, made improvements to their standard ICBM the SS-24, began development of a new class of ballistic missile submarine with better missiles, developed a new air defense fighter the MiG-29, began flying a new strategic bomber, made advances to their munitions, launched their fourth aircraft carrier, and tested two new attack submarines! (Many of "their new designs" had been stolen from the U.S. by their spies.)

Military upgrades were not the only thing on their agenda. The KGB and other hardliners were keeping the tension high on the U.S too. On March 24, 1985 a Soviet border guard in Berlin shot and severely wounded a U.S. Army major named Nicholson. The Soviet guard force refused to render any aid, and Nicholson bled to death on the street. The Administration and NATO were furious, and many wanted to end all negotiations and trade. Sec. Schultz angrily protested to Dobrinin, but also insisted that the negotiations had to continue. (The Soviets grudgingly issued no shoot orders to their people in Berlin.)

Then it came to light about a Soviet effort to target our servicemen and women across W. Germany. Sources behind the

Iron Curtain spoke up (after the above incident), that the shooting was just the tip of the iceberg. Soviet agents had been assigned the mission of finding "dead-drop sites" inside buildings or in areas that U.S. personnel and their dependents were likely to congregate. **Those sites would not be used to hide micro-film, but explosives! The KGB had arranged for their bombs to mimic the ones used by terrorists, so they would be blamed.**

When the CIA checked into those claims **they found fourteen bombs** at various locations. *(92) It was believed that the targeting and placements had been done during 1983, when the Soviet campaign to stop NATO's-INF deployments was in full swing and "innocuous demonstrators" were all over the place. Again some in the Administration were prepared to cut the Soviets off from everything as this incident just proved how deceptive and ruthless they were. In June the number of Soviet diplomats in the U.S. was reduced as was the number of Russians working at our embassy.

In early April 1985 a coup ousted the pro-western leader Gaafar Nimeiry in the Sudan. Taking over was Gen. Abdel el-Dahab. This former military leader continually resisted calls from neighboring Libya to join in the Arab efforts of perpetual war with Israel. Instead el-Dahab insisted that the Sudan would remain pro-West in its foreign policies, and he wanted to reduce the Islamic control over everyday lives. He vowed that democracy would return to the nation.

But Sudan was beset with serious problems, one of which was Libya's Momar Quaddafi. Though Sudan has a relatively small border area with Libya, it has a large one with Chad. And Chad was still in Quaddafi's sights. Destabilizing the Sudan would help his overall efforts. *What no one realized was that the undercutting inside Sudan was creting the conditions for an Islamic Extremist takeover.*

On April 9 another female suicide car bomber struck an Israeli patrol killing two.

On April 12, 1985 Islamic Jihad set off a bomb in the El Descanso Restaurant in Madrid. They tried to target U.S. service personnel, and eighteen people were murdered with eighty three wounded. The bomb collapsed the three story building on the patrons.

Israel picked up intelligence that a large attack was coming in by sea, and positioned naval forces around the eastern Mediterranean. Late on the night of April 21 a small freighter moved towards their coast. It was intercepted, and after firing on an Israeli ship it was shot up and sank. Eight survivors were picked up and interrogated. They were what was left of a twenty-eight member Palestinian commando unit that had been tasked with striking Tel Aviv with AK-47 assault rifles, grenades, RPGs and explosives. They had trained for this mission since May 1984, and left their Algerian base on April 12. They were under the control of Abu Jihad the long time terrorist commander of Fatah's (PLO) military. Soon after three more Israeli's were murdered in Cyprus. Israel used air attacks against the PLO center in Tunis. (Abu Jihad was killed two years later.)

Arafat was putting on a public relations effort, trying to distance the PLO from terrorism in public. In private the PLO had numerous offshoots that were nothing but terrorists such as their Black September group, the Popular Front for the Liberation of Palestine PFLP, the Palestine Liberation Front PLF, Fatah's Special Operations Group, the May 15 Movement and Force 17.

June 14, 1985 TWA Flight 847 from Cairo to San Diego was hijacked by **Imad Mugniyah** and his Hezbollah and Islamic Jihad terrorists. U.S. Navy diver Robert Stetham was identified, murdered and callously thrown off of the plane. The rest of the hostages were held at gunpoint until 700 Shia terrorist/convicts were released.

One of the hijackers was a man named **Ali Hammadi**. He would be arrested at the airport in Frankfurt, Germany in 1987 for trying to smuggle in **liquid explosives concealed as toiletries**!

June 19 Frankfurt, Germany was struck by a bomb at their airport. Terrorists from Abu Nidal murdered three and wounded 74. Fortunately a second bomb was found and diffused.

July 1 Madrid became the next target for Abu Nidal as bombings and grenade attacks murdered one and wounding twenty-nine.

July 22, 1985 Islamic Jihad set off two bombs in Copenhagen. Fortunately only one civilian was killed with twenty six wounded. One bomb caused heavy damage at a Synagogue and the other damaged a U.S. run Northwest Orient Airlines building. Several other unexploded bombs were found around the city and disarmed.

Spies

As shown earlier Carter and the Democrats had savaged the CIA and FBI in the late 70s. *There was a **99 percent drop** in FBI domestic security cases as the agents were only allowed to perform* *limited counter-espionage, and only on foreign suspects.* At that time there were **over 1900** Soviet and East Bloc officials freely moving around our country. Fallout from those foolish restrictions would result in a feast of spying. For America 1985 would soon be known as the **Year of the Spy**.

As shown in *Fatal Flaws Books 1&2* throughout the past sixty years we had had dozens of citizens who spied and / or supported Russia. But what was alarming now were the numbers of Americans who thought nothing of selling out any secrets they could. And most of these citizens were not recruited to be traitors, they were walk-ins. Those traitors included military servicemen as well as civilian employees who would simply drop by an enemy embassy or annex and walk in the front door. For the FBI agents who were watching the Soviet embassies this traffic was getting out of hand.

But with those Congressional restrictions in place, few of those people were being followed or identified. That allowed years of unfettered sellout and stolen secrets.

On October 2, 1984 Richard Miller, an FBI agent was arrested for espionage, their first one ever. The next month Kael Koecher a CIA contract agent was arrested for working for Czech Intelligence.

Soon after Naval Intelligence received a disturbing notice from the FBI. They had interviewed a Barbara Walker who had recently called in. She insisted that her husband, a retired navy chief petty officer named John Walker was a spy, and had been for over 20 years.

Inside NIS offices the senior investigators realized that this was the source of all of the "prior luck" that the Soviets had had these past years. Once alerted to his spying, Walker was followed by Federal Agents as he attempted to pass additional sensitive information to a Russian national. He was arrested, and by June 1985 it was learned that his son John Walker Jr, his uncle Arthur Walker and a friend Jerry Whitworth were also involved.

This spy ring had given the KGB our naval encryption cards which enabled the Russians to access all information that was sent out to the fleets. Walker had also given the Soviets tracking information on our ships and submarines. He even taught the Soviets what they needed to do to make their submarines quieter. So quiet, that their latest submarines the *Akula's* were as silent as ours. His information had also alerted the Soviets to the locations of our SOSUS sensors on the ocean floor!

For a few bags of money those traitors had done incredible damage to our nation. Their work was as detrimental to America's security as the vast Communist spying in America during WWII.

Retired KGB senior agent Oleg Kalugin and our own Naval leaders would later state that had a war begun, the Soviets could have delivered a fatal pre-emptive strike upon our submarine force. In all likelihood they would have won the war. Yuri Andropov called Walker and his ring their number one spy of all time!

Soon after another spy named Ronald Pelton was uncovered. Pelton had worked in a sensitive NSA communications department for over a decade. Having issues at work, he left the agency in 1979 and was quickly in financial trouble. Pelton simply walked into the Soviet Embassy in Washington D.C. (like Walker had), and offered his classified information for a price.

From memory Pelton gave away many incredibly sensitive secrets on our communications and eavesdropping capabilities. Numerous spy missions were also compromised, and some foreign nationals were found out and executed.

One of the most vital secrets he gave out was on *Operation Ivy Bells*. A special submarine had been outfitted to secretly slip into Soviet coastal areas in the Pacific and place taps on their undersea communications equipment. The Soviets felt their submerged cables were untouchable, so they had low level encryption. For years the taps picked up all types of communications regarding submarine movements, operations, supply issues, personnel, training and even personal communications. That incredible feat was what gave us warning of the next generation of Soviet missile subs that could carry larger missiles with a 4,200 mile range.

Since the 1950s Murmansk was their main submarine base for the Atlantic Ocean operations. (During WWII that was the main point of our convoys that supplied Russia.) A new tap had been placed in the Barents Sea near Murmansk in 1979. In 1981 a new tap was also been placed on their cables in the Pacific. *Warned by Pelton's information, both taps were "discovered within days and the lines went dead".* (Because the new taps were actively searched for by Soviet naval units and then quickly found, it was obvious a spy had tipped them off that they were there.)

Pelton also revealed a lot about our espionage efforts in Russia such as placing fake tree stumps with antennas near Soviet bases to pickup any communication signals given off. He even told them about NSA satellite capabilities. Alerted to our efforts the Soviets changed all of their codes, signal types and swept the areas around their facilities to end all signal capture. That meant that we were back in the dark, which could have proven deadly in a war.

(All of these events were part of the big intelligence picture of the past few years. When joined with the changes to Soviet military operations, it convinced many in the Administration that the Soviets were going to start a war.)

In June one of our most valuable Soviet agents was exposed and arrested. Adolf Tolkachev had provided us with detailed information of Soviet aerospace and missile weapons. He was suddenly picked up and executed, and embassy officer Paul Stombagh was expelled from Russia.

Then Oleg Gordievsky the (previously mentioned) KGB section chief in London was recalled. Usually when that happened a spot in Siberia or a pistol was waiting for them. Gordievsky was interrogated by the KGB and awaiting his fate when the British hatched a plan to get him back from Moscow. Under the KGB watchdogs, Gordievsky went for a jog on July 19 and disappeared. (In September the Brits announced his defection.)

It was obvious someone was burning our Russian sources.

On July 11 young CIA officer Sharon Scranage was arrested for providing intelligence to her boyfriend, a Ghanaian government employee

A short time later the FBI arrested former CIA officer Edward Howard for selling secrets to the Soviets. Howard never should have had the clearances he did since it was known he drank and used drugs. A polygraph just before he was to go to Moscow on assignment alerted the CIA that he was unfit, and he was fired. Inanely the polygraph was done **after** he had learned all about CIA operations in Moscow! Howard realized he was being watched by the FBI and eluded the surveillance escaping to Moscow! It was believed that Howard had burned Tolkachev and Gordievsky.

It turned out the arrests of Howard and Pelton were possible because of a "defecting KGB agent". *Vitally Yurchenko* had "*voluntarily come in*", during August at our Rome station. While he was being debriefed he provided some information / clues on Russian counter-intelligence operations. He told the interviewers that an American had called him in 1980 at his office in the Soviet Embassy in Washington D.C. From that information the FBI went through old surveillance tapes and found the one with the mystery caller. They played the tape for the NSA, and Pelton was recognized. Yurchenko also told them that the Walker spy ring had been the crown jewel of the KGB. (Since they had been arrested that conversation was part of his ruse.)

Three months later Yurchenko suddenly left his safe house in America and secretly returned to Moscow. It was felt Yurchenko would face certain death, but in actuality Yurchenko was sent to the U.S. to burn Pelton and Howard. They had little useful intelligence left, and there was a vital new source to protect, *Aldrich Ames.*

Ames was also giving the Soviets the names of our agents inside Russia, as well as some of the CIA's most vital secrets. One of those concerned a sophisticated tap that had been placed on communications cables in Moscow. Instead of shutting down that line as they had done with the Walker information, they kept them active but transmitted false information. *Yurchenko did his job to perfection and Ames was able to continue his treason until 1994.*

Historical Note: For Communist Russia, information was always the key to success. Back in WWI the large Russian Armies won victory after victory over the Austrians. But they were repeatedly and soundly defeated by smaller German forces in Prussia. Russian commanders had discounted the fact that their radio transmissions were not secure. The technology adept Germans intercepted their battlefield transmissions and defended against them accordingly. *Fallout from the increasing Russian losses was the Bolshevik revolution and the birth of Communism.*

Then on November 21, 1985 Jonathan Pollard a naval intelligence analyst at NIS was caught spying for Israel. During his 18 month spy career Pollard and his wife had passed thousands of classified documents to his handlers.

The next day a Larry Wu Chin, another CIA analyst and translator was arrested for passing secrets to China. A recent defector had named him, and revealed that Chin's spying included vast amounts of material on U.S. scientific, strategic and military capabilities. *(All primary targets of Chinese spies today.)* Chin's spying had gone undetected since the Korean War! Over the decades he became quite well off, (a clear warning sign), and upon his capture he regretted nothing. After being convicted on all counts Chin "killed himself" in his cell.

West Germany was also beset with a spy ring in which five senior officials in Bonn were arrested as Communist spies. U.S. officials were sent over to try to assess the damage done to

NATO. However the main spy in the ring, the earlier mentioned Reiner Rupp had escaped detection again.

(One simple solution to reduce the non-stop spying was a system designed by 3M Company. Under their program any classified document would have a security label attached to it. Anyone who tried to copy the document would trigger a security system which would lock the photocopier cover in place and trigger an alarm. Anyone who tried to remove the security label would visibly damage the document alerting others that something illegal had been done. Our Intelligence and Military Services felt the program too expensive and ineffectual, and it was never implemented.)

Amid all of those noted spying cases yet another one was moving on unseen. FBI agent Robert Hanssen was on the surface a conservative and anti-communist agent. Yet in 1979 he decided to deliver a package to a Soviet trade mission that was a front for the GRU. (Soviet military intelligence.) In the package was the name of an FBI mole inside the GRU. The agent was quickly caught and imprisoned.

For two more years Hanssen sold secrets until he was caught by his wife. He stopped for a while, but in 1985 he began spying for the KGB. His position in the FBI's counter-intelligence section and his high security clearance gave him unfettered access to reams of information. Both he and Ames revealed the identities of three Soviet double agents. Two were executed.

Using his government training and knowledge he was successful for years, and we never learned the true source. Though he was obviously troubled in his personnel life, (a clear warning sign), his superiors paid no attention to his personal problems. Not until 1986 would some actual Soviet spies be unmasked.

A 1985 report from the Senate Select Intelligence Committee listed 800 Soviet citizens operating inside the U.S who were assigned to the U.N.. When followed most reported to one of their embassies each day. When you add in trade missions and embassy staffs, the FBI claimed there were **1,200-1,400 Soviet officials here**. The Soviet Foreign service managed all of those assets, and insured U.N. policies benefitted the USSR.

In addition to those large numbers the Soviets also controlled over 200 East Bloc staff who also worked at the United Nations. That gave the Soviets a tremendous edge in moving and using spies around the country. We simply could not keep up.

(That does not include sleeper agents or illegal's who are secreted into the country.)

Former U.N. official Arkady Shevchenko who defected to the West told his handlers to watch for any "Soviet official" who freely spends money, for they are KGB. Their agents have unlimited funds to use to spy and recruit American dupes.

Another incredibly aggravating point, U.S. taxpayers fund most of the U.N. operations. That taxpayer money is then spent by the East Bloc nations to spy on us. And cash-strapped Russia gets kickbacks from their U.N. employees, to the tune of $20 million per year. (They skim 20% off the top.)

Gennady Zakharov was a Soviet scientist working for the U.N. He was picked up on August 23, 1986 since he did not have diplomatic immunity. (Finally a Russian spy was caught.) The Soviets retaliated days later and arrested Nicholas Daniloff who worked for *US News and World Report*. The Soviets must have wanted Zakharov back real bad as a quick trade was made for Daniloff.

With all of this drama unfolding Pres. Reagan ordered 25 KGB officers out of our country by name. The Soviets again retaliated by ordering five Americans to leave their country. Reagan countered by expelling five, and then another fifty Soviets out of the U.S. The Soviets then expelled five more Americans, and ordered all 270 Russian workers out of our embassy. (Cooks, maids etc) In October 1986 the expulsions ended and both sides calmed down. (At least we got rid of some of their spies.)

But new troubles soon arose. Yurchenko had mentioned a program of Soviet tracking of our agents in Russia. When analysts looked back at the records they remembered a strange powder that had been found on agents clothing. Samples had been taken as far back as 1976. It was identified in 1982 as nitrophenyl pentadiene, but not until 1984 was it learned the chemical was toxic and mutagenic. *During 1985 - 86 additional samples were found on our embassy personnel. Gorbachev may have been their new leader, but the Soviets had not changed their ways.*

At that point in time some 4.3 million of our citizens held security clearances. About 1.4 million worked for defense contractors at 14,000 "secured facilities". That included over 1,400 Soviet émigrés whose security investigation was impossible because they had come from behind the Iron Curtain. It turned out that dozens of trading companies were owned by front companies run by our enemies.

In addition to the above agents and officials who had been caught spying, numerous civilians and enlisted military personnel were being investigated monthly. For a full listing of this insanity read *Merchants of Treason* by Allen & Polmar.

Russia and America

New Russian leader Gorbachev was fairly candid about the growing problems inside Russia. He decried the abuse of alcohol, and tried to promote a stronger nation. Vodka production was cut and the drinking age raised from 18 to 21. In addition to their decreasing health, the communist superpower was also suffering from a low birth rate. At their present pace the nation would become a country of elderly and incapacitated citizens by 2020.

(Europe was and still is facing the same problem. If not for the immigrants from Africa and the Middle East their societies would not have enough workers to function.)

Gorbachev reported to the Politburo that the Soviet Union had again failed to meet their five year economic goals. This was their second five year failure in a row, and he openly discussed their many serious economic problems.

Since 1970 the Soviets have had to import foods from the West, a condition that was astonishing, and dangerous for them. (Prior to WWI and the tragic takeover by the terror-minded Bolsheviks, Czarist Russia had been one of the main exporter of foods to the world.) Gorbachev admitted that their socialization of the farms was not working. But he was not yet prepared to follow China's farm liberalization despite the fact that it was working.

(Gorbachev had been the Commissar of Agriculture from 1979-82, and those farm failures had happened on his watch. Luckily for him when Brezhnev died Andropov took over. He was Gorbachev's patron and protector. Had Brezhnev lived a few more weeks hearings were to be held on their farming failures.)

Soviet industry was also poorly managed and falling behind most of the smaller nations. Gorbachev announced new programs and efforts to eliminate corruption. He may not have known it, but time was running out for the Soviets. And despite his efforts, by 1987 nothing had changed in the Commissar controlled nation.

Through the spring and summer of 1985 Gorbachev proposed a few arms-control issues. As always the proposals favored the Soviets and most felt he was singing the same old song. He also discussed regional issues such as Africa and Afghanistan.

Any talks are better than none, so the administration continued the negotiations.

Then on July 3 long-time Foreign Minister Andrei Gromyko was replaced by Eduard Shevardnadze, the Commissar of Georgia, and a neophyte in foreign policy. *This was a major signal that the old guard Communists were out.* Real negotiations were possible, and a summit was announced for November in Geneva so Gorbachev and Reagan could meet in person. Schultz met with Shevardnadze for the first time July 30-August 1, 1985. Though no real headway was made on any issue, the U.S. team could see that this new Russian attitude was different.

By late 1985 the U.S. was considered a debtor nation. America now owed more to other countries from imports, services and investments, than the rest of the world owed to us. Not since 1914 had this been so. (World War I had drained the economies of the world and we became the great supplier of credit, goods and arms.)

In contrast to that disturbing news, Reagan's SDI research and development was beginning to bear fruit. The first part of his nationwide space defense system using high orbiting vehicles was successfully tested. An anti-satellite missile (ASAT) was launched from an F-15 fighter and impacted a satellite moving at 17,000 miles per hour. Upset by those events the Soviets warned that the tests could cause an arms race in space.

What most people do not know, was that the arms race in space had already begun back in the 1968. That was when the Soviets tested their first anti-satellite weapon! Their initial version was fitted to an SS-9 booster rocket and launched into space on a similar trajectory as the targeted satellite. It was planned that after a few passes around the globe guided by radar their hunter-killer satellite would close the distance and explode destroying the target satellite with shrapnel.

By 1971 the Soviets had launched seven of those versions.

As shown earlier a moratorium was negotiated by Pres. Nixon in 1972 to stop any further ASAT development. The treaty was signed by both nations. **But in 1976 with America in decline the Soviets resumed their R&D and advanced a lot.**

(Having satellites close-up to one another is the heart of most space missions. That capability was called "docking", and was originally tested with our Gemini space missions. That perfected ability is what enabled the lunar Landing capsule to dock with the Apollo capsule after the moon landings, the US-Soyuz 1976 joint space mission, the space shuttle flights to pickup to repair or refuel damaged satellites, and the rockets that deliver payloads and personnel to the international space station.)

In 1982, **(before SDI was even discussed),** the Soviets launched their Cosmos 1379 model satellite which was guided by the more advanced optical-infrared system. Those Soviet hunter-killer satellites could reach altitudes of 1,400 miles. That meant all of our photo-recon, ocean recon, weather units and the space shuttle were within reach of their weapons. **By 1985 they had dozens of those units in space ready to strike.**

But those were not their only space based weapons.

Back in the 1960s it had been learned that high altitude nuclear explosions produced electromagnetic pulses that generated high amperage pulses which destroy electrical circuits. They also create wide bands of high energy protons and electrons in the upper atmosphere and in orbit, similar to the Van Allen Belt. That side affect brought down a British Ariel satellite when it passed through one of our atmospheric tests in the Pacific in 1962.

Using that knowledge, Soviet atomic space weapons were designed to pulse our satellites into junk. To "harden the satellite circuits" from pulses, expensive semiconductors made from gallium arsenide were needed.

We also discovered that our satellites needed protection from being blinded by Soviet lasers. That effort involved closing openings or "buttoning up", moving to a new orbit or releasing decoys to confuse a Soviet attack.

The Soviets had thousands of scientists and engineers working on their ABM and anti-satellite weapons systems. Most of it had not stopped even after the ABM treaty had been signed back in 1972.

When Pres. Reagan decided America needed SDI, the Soviets had **12,000 SAM launchers**, (surface to air missile), based around their country. Many were high altitude missiles designed to attack our satellites and any incoming missiles. They also had 10,000 radar stations and 1,200 high altitude interceptors on standby to further protect them from any U.S. missile attacks.

That was why so many Soviet military officials wanted to destroy us sooner rather than later. They were immune to our nuclear counter-attacks.

In addition to their hunter-killer satellites, the Soviets were heavily invested in using "electronic counter-measures" to jam, disable, disorient and simply shut down Western satellites. That method was the most economical, essentially instantaneous, and had no range limit. Scientists call this type of interference "spoofing". Defense analysts felt the Soviets excelled at creating that type of electronic interference. It was also believed the Soviets could soon expand their ASAT systems by using ground based lasers as well as anti-satellite missiles. (Like the missile we just tested.)

As it was the Soviets had sixty-four ABM (anti-ballistic-missiles) based just around Moscow. It was certain dozens more were secretly located around the country. That same weapon system could be reprogrammed to target any of our satellites that came within their range.

By the end of 1984 the U.S. was increasingly dependent on dozens of satellites for command, control, communications and intelligence functions. In July 1984 the Soviet naval ammunition depot at Severomorsk suffered a series of massive explosions. Our satellite imaging allowed us to learn that they had lost a considerable number of naval missiles that carried conventional and nuclear warheads. Without having spies inside Russia, satellites were our only means of learning anything. It was vital that we defend those recon assets as well as our own shores from the growing threat of Soviet spaced based weapons.

(In our time our reliance on satellite systems has become total. Should an enemy take out our expensive and hard to replace systems America would be forced to surrender or face total destruction.)

Just weeks after our successful ASAT missile test the Soviets suddenly expressed a desire to reduce strategic arms by 50%, if the U.S. put an end to the SDI program. Pres. Reagan did not comment on their proposal, as a 50% reduction in arms was meaningless. At that time the Soviets had over 40,000 nuclear weapons! But their desire to talk again gave evidence that negotiating from a position of strength is the only way to deal with Communists or dictators.

The only people opposed to our SDI program were the Russians and our liberals, especially the ones in the media. Hysterics and false reporting were a common theme in their effort to reduce our defenses. Multiple times the Democrats in Congress tried to end the program. **Senator John Kerry attempted to freeze SDI spending in 1985, in effect the program would have died.** (Again why would the Democrats fight so hard to stop a defensive system designed to keep us safe??)

Prior to the upcoming Geneva Summit Pres. Reagan was given a crash course on Soviet duplicity and negotiation techniques. CIA's Robert Gates updated the president on all of Russia's social and economic issues. One of their weakest links concerned unanticipated defense costs. The Soviets needed to end SDI, and success in their proxy wars to end that drain.

They were already looking to 1989 and a new U.S. president. They would try to hold out any givebacks until Reagan left office. CIA doubted if Gorbachev's reforms could work in restarting their economy. Our efforts however were working, and Pres. Reagan was prepared to meet his rival in Geneva.

Afghanistan

As mentioned earlier the one Afghan leader who was constantly besting the Soviets was **Ahmed Shah Massoud**. Ahmed was a student of previous guerrilla wars and realized, unlike the unschooled academics and politicians who occupy the worlds microphones, *that war and politics were intertwined.* He and his Tajik tribal forces occupied the northern areas and used mobile forces to strike at the Russians. In nine major battles his forces had won every fight. The CIA had been sticking to the original Pakistani-ISI rules and not crossing (to far) into Afghanistan to operate and meet with the rebels. Luckily the British and French did cross over, and they had made frequent contact with Massoud and were helping his efforts.

By early 1985 we too began getting aid directly to him. What was never reported at that time was that our satellites would pick up Soviet tank units when they neared Massoud's area. That intel was passed along and his forces would ambush the tanks using anti-tank mines. No matter which route the Soviets took, the mines were already waiting for them. Once a few vehicles became damaged and the column stuck in place Massoud's fighters would close in and attack from all sides. The one-sided battle would end before Russian reinforcements or air cover would arrive.

But then came the commitment of Soviet Airborne units and the Hind gunships. Highly motivated airborne and Spetznaz units were sent into rebel valleys and strongholds. Then the heavily armed and armored Russian helicopters were able to run down the escaping *Mujahedeen* with impunity.

In addition to those changes in tactics the Soviets air dropped millions of small mines to terrorize the civilians and drive them out of the country. (Soviet mines were even found in dolls and toys.) Hard fought battles occurred in the Konar and Panjshir valleys, Paktia province and at the city of Herat. Training of the Mujahedeen was improved by using Special Forces and SEAL teams to create a true rebel army. We even taught them in explosives work, and by 1986 their effective cross border raids were a common tactic.

Around that time the CIA learned of the varying nationalities amongst the rebels. It was believed that during the war some 300,000 Islamic fighters had entered Afghanistan from every Islamic country. **Roughly 35,000 were Islamic Extremists,** and most of them fought within their own **Muj groups**. One of the main Muj leaders was the previously mentioned **Abdul Rasul Sayyaf.** *Unintentionally our Cold-War effort to hurt the Soviets was also creating our next enemy.*

Few of those separate groups got along, so it appeared that after the war ended Afghanistan would remain a basket case of tribal alliances. Robert Gates the Chief of the CIA Intelligence Unit wrote; "No one should have any illusions about these people coming together after the fighting ends." *(93)

But no one expected Afghanistan to become a terrorist haven either.

Pakistan's military intelligence the ISS was still running most of the U.S. directed military and humanitarian aid. A large amount of the covert funds that were sent to the region came from Saudi Arabian Intelligence, the GID. The work by the above forces and help from Islamic banks and charitable organizations had turned the rag-tag Afghans of 1980 into a solid militia force.

The ISI (and William Casey) targeted Soviet officers, and the best place was their garrisons in and around Kabul. Car, pen and utensil bombs were being used regularly to increase their casualties. And while those attacks succeeded, it furthered the already viciousness of the Soviet retaliations.

Throughout the early war the Soviets had not attacked the known rebel sanctuaries in Pakistan. But as shown before that changed in early 1985. By mid-year Soviet intercept teams would plot a supply convoy moving inside Pakistan near the border and send their HIND attack helicopters in behind them. Then they would spring an ambush using Spetsnaz troops and the gunships. Those tactics also helped to turn the tide back to the Soviets.

To counter this fatal weakness it was decided by the Administration to send the new hand-held anti-aircraft *Stinger* missiles to Pakistan. Recently developed, the Stinger missile had an infrared homing head and good speed. It was simple to use and the small warhead was perfect for bringing down low flying aircraft. Also sent over were crew served weapons and British wire-guided anti-armor missiles. To carry those heavier weapons and supplies around the harsh terrain of Afghanistan, thousands of Chinese mules were imported.

What helped the Administration make that weapons decision was the battlefield input from the previous approval of sending Stinger missiles to Angola. **After a minimal time period Savimbi's forces had incredible kill-ratios.** So high that many in Washington refused to believe it. Video evidence came back showing it was true. Because of those new weapons, Savimbi's solid troops, who were greatly bolstered by the S. Africans, actually stopped the 1985 summer Soviet-Cuban offensive in Angola! Without air-cover the Communists were fighting as light ingantry, cutoff in the dense jungles. (As we had in Vietnam.)

During September 1986 the first batch of the U.S. made Stinger missiles finally made it to the Afghan war zone with a trained rebel team. **In its first use, three out of the four missiles fired took out Soviet gunships and their crews.** After seeing video of that attack the Congress upped the money supply for Afghanistan to $470 million! Abdul Haq and Ahmed Massoud were able to get additional funding, and Massoud finally received his secure communications equipment.

(However no Stingers went to him, on orders from the ISI. Pakistan did not want Massoud getting too strong, for their secret post-war plans did not include him.)

Additional Stinger teams crossed the border and the use of those missiles increased causing serious losses. **In that first year of use over 270 Soviet aircraft had been shot down!** (One damaged Hind gunship was eventually captured by the rebels. The CIA secretly dismantled it and had it shipped to Langley where it was dissected and counter-weapons designed.)

With the loss of their trump card the aggressive Soviet air-mobile attacks were blunted, and they became the hunted. Even medical evacuations became impossible. By mid-1987 the *Mujahedeen* were actually winning. They could routinely ambush Soviet supply and armored columns, and even attack their bases without fear of the helicopter units. To try counter that effort the Soviets began using MiG-25 fighter-bombers dropping cluster munitions and chemical weapons. But the Russians soon learned that even those jets could be hit if they flew into a valley.

(Although the Stinger operation was successful many in the U.S. feared Soviet counter-attacks upon Pakistan. And many also worried that without proper controls terrorists could get their hands on some of those weapons and create havoc on commercial airlines. To forestall that issue the CIA kept an accounting of the missiles and tried to maintain a list. But in that back-channel war environment it was not completely accurate.)

Chief of Saudi Intelligence Prince Turki-al Faisal and his chief of staff Ahmed Badeeb were the principal agents who oversaw the distribution of the CIA-Saudi money in Afghanistan. Their trips to Islamabad were filled with briefings, payouts, and strategy sessions, updated with the latest U.S. satellite photos. To protect the weapons and supply investments, rebel staging areas and supply depots had been created using caves hidden in constricted valleys. Soviet units could not penetrate them without undo cost.

Badeeb had been a teacher years earlier, and one of his students in Jeddah was that rich Saudi, **Osama bin Laden**. Bin Laden had become a self-appointed financier, builder and supply depot for the Mujahedeen, and a peripheral agent of the Saudis. His construction units built roads, hospitals, crude housing and supply areas.

Some of those projects were intended for his "personal army", and his first camp opened in 1986. He moved his family to Islamabad amid the growing influx of Brotherhood and Wahhabi Muslims. *Moving in those high and secret circles gave bin Laden unprecedented access to funds and contacts. All kinds of contacts.*

The Pacific

By 1986 China was realizing their economic turnaround.

Back in 1978 Deng had listed four sectors that absolutely had to be modernized, Agriculture, Industry, Science and their Military. A major benefit from their economic improvements meant the Communists had a lot of extra income since they owned everything. As expected they began modernizing their military, (possibly a reaction to their defeat in 1979 to Vietnam.)

Their navy acquired new destroyers and frigates for blue water operations. Coastal units were updated with hovercraft and fast attack boats. Their submarine force of conventional boats was increased to 107 subs by 1985. Their tanks were given laser range finders while their air force began employing all weather aircraft. Chairman Mao had kept their nuclear forces small and of medium range, while the Deng leadership was testing ICBMs with 7,000 mile ranges. (So they could reach us.)

China also began launching satellites into space, and worked on but had trouble with MIRV technology. *This rapid growth in*

China's military forced the cash strapped Soviets to keep 50 divisions and hundreds of aircraft east of the Ural Mountains in two separate commands. Though the tensions had thawed from their border battles in the 1960s, there was still a deep suspicion between them.

(That issue was one of the reasons why Nixon opened the door to Red China in 1972, and why the Soviets were so suspicious of our efforts. Brezhnev even "warned Nixon" at their meeting in Moscow, (a few months after he returned from Beijing), that in ten years all would fear China. Nixon would later write that in 1972 most of the people on the streets of Beijing walked. In 1982 most Chinese rode bicycles. By 1993 huge traffic jams filled their streets. Asia's giant had awakened, and by 1987 was the third most powerful military just in sheer numbers.)

Former Pres. Nixon wrote in 1993;

"The three major powers in Asia, Russia, China and Japan are not natural enemies, but they are not natural friends either". *(94)

America is able to act as a buffer not because those powers like us, but because they respect us. We are not viewed by any of them as an aggressor seeking territory. World leaders who can decipher the "tea leaves" need to understand that in a short while Asia will be a major player in world commerce, and world tensions. *(95)

Upset at the continuing dissent in the Philippines the Reagan Administration warned longtime Philippine Pres. Ferdinand Marcos that he must make reforms or face a potential civil war. To assist him in getting elected, Marcos had lied when he said he had been a freedom fighter against the Japanese in WWII. (Politician-scam artists are the same everywhere.)

Initially he showed promise as an administrator, but corruption soon took over. Marcos was a staunch anti-communist ally that America needed in the far reaches of the Pacific, so his problems were ignored. During his 20+ year rule the U.S. did not interfere in Filipino politics, though our large military presence in the islands had impacts, some good some not.

His nation had been vital to our effort in SE Asia, but in 1972 he had declared martial law. Since that time Marcos had become a despot in a nation that had been reborn as a democracy in 1946 after being a U.S. protectorate. Like most autocratic rulers, Marcos and his government were unyielding to the needs of his people. It was always hoped that democracy would take hold, but the hardships and protests continued.

During August 1983 opposition leader Benigno Aquino had been killed as he stepped off of a plane in Manila. (He and his wife had been in exile in the U.S.) His murder sparked much protests among the population. As always Communist insurgents had been active there and were finding willing listeners. Unwilling to face another Communist insurrection, the Reagan Administration was trying to prevent one by convincing Marcos to move on.

Corazon Aquino took over the opposition party for her murdered husband, and faced Marcos in the following election. Marcos claimed victory, but all were convinced of voter fraud. Large scale protests began, and in late January 1986 Pres. Reagan asked Marcos to resign in order to save the nation. Marcos fled the Philippines in February taking residence in Hawaii until his death. After he departed investigations uncovered massive theft by Marcos and his cronies.

Mrs. Aquino served as president until 1992, enacting major reforms and reviving the economy and democracy. Unfortunately she was incapable of understanding the entrenched corruption she had inherited and tried to end, nor the Communist insurgents that were always ready to fight. **And everyone missed the Islamic Extremists that were infiltrating into the nation and region.**

More Islamic Terrorism

On Oct. 7, 1985 Italian cruise ship the ***Achille Lauro*** was hijacked by Palestinians terrorists of the PLF while cruising off of Egypt. A 69 year old disabled Jewish American named Leon Klinghoffer was murdered by the terrorists and thrown overboard. Those terrorists had wanted to dock the ship at Tartus, Syria to disembark all of the U.S. and Israeli passengers as hostages, but diplomatic pressures on Syria stopped that plan. Realizing that their operation had failed Arafat sent his aide Abu Abbas to end it before it became a public relations disaster.

While the talking was ongoing Pres. Reagan sent units of the 6th Fleet to intercept the vessel. *It was not docking in Syria no matter what the terrorists wanted.* Seal Team Six and Delta Force Units flew from the U.S. with the intent on using the British Air Base on Cyprus as their forward operating base. Most Western countries including the U.S. use a rule of thumb, once hostages are killed negotiations are out. Israel assisted in keeping track of the ship while the Special Operations teams planned their attack.

Just before the planned rescue mission was to commence the terrorists returned the ship to Port Said, Egypt and the PLF terrorists conveniently escaped into the waiting crowd. The next day the four shooters and Abu Abbas flew off in an Egyptian jet trying to get back to Tunisia. However their aircraft was intercepted by U.S. carrier jets and forced to land in Sicily. Seal Team 7 was waiting.

Without warning the Italian Government of Bettini Craxi cowardly refused to turn them over. In fact Abbas was put on a Yugoslav airline and flown to Belgrade and sanctuary! Italy also refused to extradite the other four from the plane or any of their accomplices (10) to the U.S. for trial. They were tried in Italy where the terrorists were convicted but served minimal time in prison. Craxi did not want to anger the Muslim world.

During the investigations it was learned that Abbas had handpicked this team, and their weapons had been stockpiled in Genoa, Italy by their accomplices. They had trained for a year and done two trial runs over the past months. They knew the ship would not deviate from their normal tourist route. Their planning showed the intensity and dedication that all Islamic terrorists were willing to go through to strike. (They should show so much dedication to helping their people prosper.)

Days after the attack Arafat told the Budapest media that Abbas was a loyal leader and would not be abandoned. Abu Abbas was in fact the PLF leader, and like many in the PLO he was disenchanted with the "diplomatic efforts" of Arafat. He demanded constant attacks. *When Syria took over in Lebanon and the PLO was forced out, Abbas joined sides with Iraq in opposing the Syrians.* Even though they had hard feelings Abbas visited Arafat in Tunisia just after the Israeli bombing of their headquarters at Hammam el-Shat. Two days after that visit came the attack on the *Achille Lauro*. (In a May 1986 interview broadcast on NBC News, Abbas called Pres. Reagan enemy number one, and admitted that his people had made the attack.)

November 23, 1985 Egypt Air Flight 648 flying from Athens to Cairo was hijacked by Islamic terrorists from Abu Nidal's group. Sixty were killed and thirty eight wounded when Egyptian commandos tried to storm the jetliner in Malta.

November 27, 1985 Italian authorities arrested one Omar Sadat Abdel at a cousin's home in Verona, Italy. In the basement were twenty kilos of explosives and numerous weapons and ammunition. Abdel was using a Jordanian passport and had just returned from Yugoslavia after meeting with Abu Abbas. Even though the Italians had helped him, Abbas was organizing a new attack there.

December 27, 1985 Islamic terrorists linked to Libya and their main terrorist Abu Nidal attacked the airports in Rome and Vienna. In those attacks nineteen were murdered and over one hundred thirty were wounded. Those attacks caused most of the Western nations to increase their internal security. (But not here.)

One of the shooters in Rome survived and was interrogated. *He revealed that his team was with Abu Nidal and that they had trained at a Syrian military facility in the Bekaa Valley in Lebanon. Syrian intelligence had provided some of them with passports and operational information.*

Libya did the same for the other terrorists, and they also provided the weapons for the Rome attack by sending them to Italy in their "diplomatic pouch". Apparently Craxi's cowardly approach did not work in keeping the Islamic terrorists at bay.

Public outrage over the attacks resulted in Syria's Assad telling Nidal it was time for him to leave, (temporarily). The last thing Assad wanted was for American or NATO air attacks hitting his country. (Because of our earlier help in his war with Iran, Saddam had expelled Abu Nidal in 1983. He then took up residence in Syria with his PFLP cohorts, determined to strike at American targets every time he could.)

Nidal's main Syrian camp was located at Duma near Damascus, while the camp near Chibban specialized in suicide attacks. Abbas made sure to leave publicly, but his terrorist camps stayed open. With Assad's blessing Abu Nidal quickly and publicly relocated to Libya, while Syria maintained ties through training and intelligence sharing.

Around this time U.S. Intelligence (helped by Israel) had figured out the locations of Nidal's camps and base areas in Syria. Pres. Reagan and CIA's Casey wanted to get Nidal and were trying to decide if they should bomb the camps or try to capture him to stand trial. *Like all of the terrorist leaders he never stayed in one place long enough to fix his location.* Trying to capture him was almost impossible, and that was why Craxi's appeasement was so hard to take.

In Washington it was felt that a main source of the terrorist attacks of the past year was Libya and Nidal. In early 1986 Libya's Khadafy welcomed him and his terrorists. They even setup training camps so Nidal and company could train new terrorists. *(Some of those camps were built by a French company under the guise of making agricultural centers.)*

There were at least twenty terrorist training camps in Libya in the mid-80s. Camp 1 was near Jar Dinah, and was where Sandinista terrorist Patrick Arguello and his accomplice Leila Khaled of the PFLP trained for their attempted hijacking of an El Al jetliner. That camp trained in explosives, shoulder fired rockets and hijackings. **Camp 2** at the Gialo Oasis trained Africans and various Islamists, **Camp 4** was used by the IRA, **Camp 6** was used only for Egyptian and Sudanese terrorists. And the list went on and on. In addition to the training centers, Libya offered rewards for any killings and attacks as a way to promote terrorism at any time.

(Besides arming and training many of the Islamic terrorists, Libya was also the country arming the Irish Republican Army, IRA. Their explosives and weapons attacks the past decades had caused hundreds of civilian and military casualties which included a devastating bombing in Dublin. Ironically that vicious attack greatly eroded the support for the IRA, and it eventually ended in their demise.)

Pres. Reagan was quite upset at the death of a twelve year old girl who was murdered at Rome's airport. The Administration had been calling on the world (especially France) to cut Libya off from all trade. By late January 1986 Pres. Reagan publicly accused Libya and Col. Khadafy of supporting international terrorism. All Libyan assets were frozen and all commercial ties were ended. U.S. citizens were told to leave the country.

A large naval task force was sent to the area to began conducting practice operations. We had had enough of the recurring terrorist attacks. Unlike Iran, Libya was easily accessible from the Mediterranean. Pres. Reagan directed the NSC planners to strike at the first opportunity.

(Some of the problems with striking Iran was the restricted access in the Gulf and potential Soviet actions. Since Syria was a major client state of the Russians they too were out as no one could be sure what the Soviets would do. And Sec-Def Weinberger still adamantly opposed any direct actions against them.)

Targeting studies on Libya began and France was asked for information. France's Mitterrand became upset with our planned actions and attitude, but he also realized that Reagan would not back down. Always bizarre, France had harbored Islamic terrorists before including the previously mentioned **Imad Mugniyah** who had murdered our Ambassador William Buckley in Lebanon, bombed our Embassy and barracks in Beirut and hijacked the jetliner murdering navy diver Robert Stetham.

Despite the restrictions from France, the NSC sent a draft to Reagan on invading Libya from Egypt, while other forces came in from the sea. Many in the CIA and State Dept. objected to the plan as too much "Normandy" for those terrorist acts. There were a dozen negatives that could pop up, and it was felt limited air strikes were more suited.

Then on March 24, 1986 Libya provided the impetus for retaliation when their jets and SAM sites fired on our navy jets flying in the Gulf of Sidra. In short order multiple Libyan patrol ships were sunk and the offending SAM and radar site destroyed.

A week later Libyan gunboats tried to intercept a U.S. destroyer sailing offshore. That attack was beaten off killing 35 more Libyans and sinking two more of their boats. For the administration this was some payback for Nidal's terror attacks, but it was not enough to dissuade this terrorist enemy. Qaddafi spread the word that he was at war with America, and terrorists should start striking everywhere. Intelligence came in that a series of terrorist attacks was going to happen.

At the CIA a new office was formed, the CTC- Counter-Terrorism Center. This center formed on February 1, 1986, run by Paul bremmer, and was directed to end the bureaucratic nonsense that was hindering much of the CIA-anti-terrorist operations. For Pres. Reagan a functioning CIA was necessary to protect our citizens and country. If it was used properly that agency would be extremely important to stop a terrorist attack.

The CTC took over an open area on the 6th floor at Langley. Agent Robert Baer recalled it was a burst of energy as those first dozens of people assigned strove for excellence. *Sub-units keyed on each known terrorist group.*

Among the major questions that came up was the legality of deciding if terrorism was a law enforcement issue or a national security issue? Should the suspects be captured or killed when found? **After much discussion it was decided that terrorism was a concern to both fields. Terrorists should be captured when possible, but killed if necessary.**

Representatives from the State Department were added to the normal analysts and operations people in this unified and well organized effort to oppose the foreign terrorists of Abu Nidal, Hezbollah, Libya and the other PLO and Islamic groups that were killing innocents. Of all of those groups, secretive Hezbollah was the hardest to learn about. Our recon satellites routinely scrutinized and photographed known terrorist training camps.

On February 3, 1986 a bombing at a Paris shopping center wounded eight. That bomb was also traced back to Iran's Hezbollah.

On the 4th another Hezbollah bombing wounded four more at a Paris book store.

Then on March 17 a very dangerous Hezbollah bombing occurred on a high-speed commuter train heading to Paris. Nine more were wounded. Senior officials were convinced this insidious poison would make its way here.

The CTC was directed to stop them.

America and Russia

In November 1985 Pres. Reagan and Sec. Gorbachev met in Geneva to try to work out a compromise on arms reductions. As always both sides were adamant about keeping their major programs. Russia was way ahead in sheer numbers of weapons and wanted it to remain that way. They again demanded SDI be scrapped. But that was the one program Reagan would not end. Since no breakthrough occurred the media foolishly became upset that Reagan "did not give in". (The same stupidity they show with Pres. Trump and his hard negotiations with everyone.)

During mid-January 1986 Gorbachev wrote a letter expressing his desire to eliminate all nuclear weapons by the year 2000. Their first reduction would be taking the medium range missiles out of Eastern Europe. But that could only happen if SDI was ended. (Only basic scientific research on SDI would be allowed by the U.S., research the Soviets planned on stealing.)

Our arms negotiators were surprised as this was almost the exact proposal Reagan had submitted back in 1981. But back then Reagan included removing the Russian medium range missiles in Asia as well. With this new Soviet offer there was no doubt we finally had the Russians over a barrel. *And that barrel was SDI.*

It was learned that Gorbachev was going to make this proposal publicly to try to catch the Administration off guard. The Soviets hoped the Western media would take their side and force Reagan to accept this "generous offer". But surprisingly even the Germans refused it because it did not address the cruise-missile threat that was keyed upon them. They would still be within range of the missiles based in Russia. From Asia our allies also complained loudly that they must not be forgotten.

Many discussions were held over the next weeks and in late February 1986 the Administration announced a no go on that proposal. **It was restated that the zero-option was the only proposal the West was interested in.**

At this point leaks (from long serving leftists inside the State Dept and among the offices of the arms negotiators) were causing serious problems in trying to negotiate. Our ideas and proposals were leaked to the Soviets by those traitors / Communist supporters as a way to force the acceptance of Soviet proposals and undercut and weaken the U.S. position.

Latin America

As shown often the Caribbean and Latin America were always on this Administration's watch list. Fed up with the leftist-repressive and corrupt regime of Haiti's Jean-Claude Duvalier, Pres. Reagan directed his staff to work with Haiti's military to "dislodge him". On February 7, 1986 they succeeded and Duvalier fled to France. As was common in that poor country, attempts to unite under democracy would soon fail.

Historical Note; Haiti was the second nation in this hemisphere to win their independence with a slave revolt over France in 1802. The nation thrived until 1915, when Democrat Woodrow Wilson forcibly occupied the country with an austere, segregationist rule, which stayed in place until 1934. It spawned a hatred for the U.S government, and Democracy fell away.

On November 6, 1985 thirty-five M-19 Columbian leftist rebels stormed the Columbian Palace of Justice firing at anyone they saw. Shooting their way to the fourth floor they had taken over 300 hostages. Columbian soldiers rescued some 200 civilians, and then they assaulted the 4th floor. Sadly over 100 civilians and soldiers died in the fighting, and the Palace suffered heavy damage. It was well known that those rebels were being supplied from Nicaragua.

On March 17, 1986 another large scale rebel ambush killed eight and wounded over a dozen more. Angry over these latest attacks Pres. Reagan warned the Democratic run Congress that it was vital that $100 million in aid be approved for the Nicaraguan Contras. Since Daniel Ortega and his Communists had taken over they had built a powerful army by Central American standards. Fortunately Ortega was unsure on what he wanted to accomplish next, and they slowly drifted into economic collapse.

Unlike the failed U.S. response to Cuba, Reagan wanted to defeat the Sandinistas before they could successfully export this poison. **On March 20, 1986 the Democratic controlled House again voted down his request.** At this same time the Soviets, (as mentioned before), announced a $600 million credit line to the Sandinistas. *(96)

On the 25th Reagan changed tactics and ordered emergency aid for the Honduran Army which was also fighting Communists. The Senate reluctantly passed Reagan's aid package on the 28th. (Some of that aid then went to the Contras.) Columbian rebels continued their murderous attacks throughout the summer.

As shown earlier, faced with the Democrats' continued refusal to fund the anti-Marxists in Central America and the Boland amendments, members of Reagan's staff had come up with a way to get around them. Private donations had been collected and funneled to the Contras, and that new idea was started.

Israel would sell arms to the Iranians, and a portion of that money would be added to the kitty for the Contras. The effort was kept as secretive as possible as weapon sales went forward with Israel as the broker. Three American hostages were released, and $12 million found its way to the Contras. But when a Lebanese paper intentionally printed the storyline the President's image and honor became tarnished. Two of his staff resigned and the angry Democrats launched the Tower Commission to try to bring Reagan down over this Iran-Contra affair. (Similar to Watergate it was the lower staffers who were involved. Unlike Nixon they were dismissed.)

Terror Attacks and Libya

On April 2, 1986 TWA Flight 840 LA to Athens was bombed and severely damaged. An Islamic woman had boarded the flight at Rome and placed a bomb under a seat which killed four Americans when they were sucked out of the plane, one was an infant. Nine other passengers were wounded. To save the jetliner the pilot made a successful emergency landing. The Islamic terrorists claimed that bombing was for the U.S. Navy's battle with Libya in the Gulf of Sidra.

On April 5, 1986 a West Berlin disco catering to our servicemen and women was bombed killing three and wounding two hundred thirty. That bomb had been placed under a table by Abu Nidal's terrorists. Intelligence agencies had picked up messages from Libya which pinpointed the source of those latest attacks. By the 8th the evidence from the investigation became crystal clear, the attacks had originated from Libya. Their embassy in East Berlin had provided the bombers with the operational intelligence for the attack. That was the last straw.

(The terrorists who were caught admitted that the Syrian embassy in East Berlin had provided them with the explosives. Additional attacks were also being planned to strike at U.S. citizens in the Sudan, W. Germany, Turkey, Syria, Spain and in Africa. This was the same blueprint bin Laden would use against us in the 1990s.)

During the repetitive Hezbollah attacks against us in Lebanon the Administration did not strike back directly as many had wanted. After the harsh rhetoric from Pres. Reagan concerning Russia it was wrong that there had been so little response to those Islamic attacks. This time the Administration decided to strongly react.

Retaliatory attacks against Libya were organized and it was hoped we could get to Khadafy himself. Over the next few days attempts were made to garner support from our European allies, but only England stepped up to help. On April 15 nighttime air raids were conducted on Libya targeting military installations and Khadafy's residences in Benghazi and Tripoli. Pres. Reagan went on television to explain to the public that intelligence had shown a direct link to Libya and the many recent terrorist attacks. "Today we have done what we had to do. If necessary we shall do it again."

Over all our air attacks were not as good as they could have been, but they did cause major damage to the Libyan air force, navy and intelligence headquarters. Qaddafi had just left one of the residences when it was blown up. For a while he stayed under the radar, as our allies decided to join in on some sanctions.

France and Spain had both refused to allow any U.S. over-flights over their soil. Their intransience forced the USAF jets taking off from England to fly a much longer route over the Atlantic and then into the Mediterranean, some 2,400 miles. Pilot fatigue could have been an issue during the missions.

France was as always a contradiction. Paris Police had recently stopped a suicide van-bombing against our Embassy. That time we were lucky, but until the source of the problem was stopped the attacks against us would continue just as Israel was living through. Undeterred by the lack of French support the Administration began aiding anti-Khadafy elements within Libya.

If we could end him it would be a solid warning to the other terrorist sponsors. Libya expelled many European companies and citizens from its shores, but they were suffering from the economic sanctions. Khadafy's ruthless secret police insured his hold on Libya and its oil wealth. His terrorism was unrelenting.

Syria was still continuing their visible support of terrorism and the PLO. And hiding in the shadows, Kuwait and the Saudi's were actually the main financial backers of the PLO!

On April 17, 1986 **Nizar Hindawi**, *(an Adu Nidal follower) tricked his pregnant girlfriend into bringing a suitcase bomb (semtex) onto an El Al flight leaving London.* Fortunately the bomb was discovered. Again the young women knew nothing about it. To avoid arrest Hindawi hid out in the Syrian embassy in London.

During the investigation it was learned that Hindawi had trained in Nidal's terrorist camp at Duma near Damascus. (The recent Berlin bombers had trained there too.) After his training he was sent to London accompanied by his Syrian handler an Air Force major. Hindawi was told to befriend a local girl with the intent of using her to bring the bomb on board an aircraft. Because of this callous event, Britain imposed sanctions on Syria. Unfortunately the rest of liberal Europe took little interest. And Socialist Greece actually aided Syria, which for the anti-Israel and anti-U.S. Prime Minister Papandreou was a normal action. *Months later Greece sold or gave away twenty of their blank passports to Islamic terrorists!*

Iran

Across the deserts the resupplied Iran was again pushing Iraq back. Over 300,000 Iranians took control of the Fao peninsula which closed off Iraq from the Persian Gulf. France was still sending in planeloads of ammo and weapons to Iraq, but the Iranians were dug in and could not be blasted out.

In addition to our intelligence updates, Reagan had instituted a tougher diplomatic policy to try to isolate the Iranians. Nations were warned not to do any business with Iran or face American sanctions themselves. That effort was successful and the price for any type of weapons or supplies purchased by Iran skyrocketed. Iran retaliated by mining and attacking all oil tankers in the Gulf with their fast attack boats.

The Soviets then offered to send in the Red Navy as a way to "thwart the Iranians and protect Iraq". To prevent that scenario

U.S. and British naval ships organized convoys to protect the shipping. Again our people were protecting the interests of other nations who would not or could not do so.

Nuclear Crisis at Three Mile Island and Chernobyl

Back on February 21, 1979 then Chairman of the KGB Yuri Andropov wrote a secret memorandum to the USSR Committee for State Security. *KGB had learned about design deviations and flaws that could lead to mishaps and accidents at many of their vital nuclear facilities.* Andropov warned that the Directorate for Nuclear power was not devoting proper attention to that possibility.

Just one month after his warning, on March 28 a partial meltdown occurred at the Three Mile Island (TMI) nuclear plant in Pennsylvania, USA. That facility had only been open for a year when a cooling valve failed leading to the partial meltdown. Dangerous radioactive gases poured from the reactor as equipment failures, poor training and poor decisions almost caused a severe atomic disaster.

In the case of TMI the pumps supplying the coolant water stopped working which allowed the reactor to overheat and melt. (Similar to your car, if you lose the water pump or radiator, the engine overheats. I was still at Oswego College north of Syracuse. Our science department recorded radiation levels at three times their normal rate, even though we were 300 miles north of Three Mile Island.) *Cleanup at TMI took 14 years, and the damaged reactor was entombed in concrete.*

Historical Note: Admiral Hyman Rickover had spurred the U.S. Navy into the atomic age in the 1950s as he championed water cooled nuclear reactors. Soon after the navy converted to that power source Pres. Eisenhower promoted a plan to use atomic reactors to make civilian commercial electricity. All of those reactors used the Rickover design of being water cooled. In the 20 years since the first reactor went on line, dozens had been built with many new ones in the works. *Until Three Mile Island.*

On April 26, 1986 a terrible nuclear failure occurred at the Chernobyl Nuclear Plant in the Ukraine, USSR. The total meltdown and resulting steam-hydrogen gas explosion released a hundred times more radiation than the atomic blasts that struck Japan in 1945. As always the Soviets worked hard to keep the disaster a secret, but satellite images and the increasing radiation fallout in the Baltic and Scandinavian nations were proof that a nuclear event had happened. Soviet leaders reluctantly released information about the explosion, **six days after it had occurred**. Because of their delayed notification millions of people were put at risk as a highly radioactive cloud moved from the site all across the region for ten days.

Unlike the more stringent safety requirements at nuclear plants in the West, Soviet systems were regarded as primitive and dangerous. At Chernobyl a serious design flaw existed, (one of the ones Andropov had warned about in 1979), and caused the crisis along with the poorly trained staff. Coupled with the Three Mile Island accident in Pennsylvania, the Chernobyl explosion would spell the end of nuclear reactors as a trusted energy source. (Dozens of nuclear projects were cancelled and the one just built on Long Island could not be used for years. Even when it opened it could only run at partial power.)

In the Ukraine 130,000 people were hurriedly evacuated that week, and another 250,000 that month. One fifth of the population in Belarus had to be relocated, and two million acres of farmland was abandoned. Western satellites monitored the extensive radiological disaster from space, (which is how we knew), but no one from the West was allowed on the ground. Imagine the horrible results if a nuclear attack happens somewhere.

On May 14, 1986 Gorbachev finally spoke publicly about the explosion. He reluctantly admitted that mistakes were made at the reactor during "the tests" they had been running. The Soviets refused to give any information on the amount of radiation released or on the casualties incurred. It was believed that thirty-one had died in the blast and another 50 firefighters and workers died soon after. It was expected that over 100,000 would die from various cancers caused by the radiation. (Witnesses spoke of a yellow rain that fell from the skies a day after the explosion.)

Ironically at the Argonne Nuclear testing Facility in Idaho engineers had just made an extraordinary successful test of a self-regulating reactor. That new reactor type used liquid sodium as the coolant instead of water. Sodium has a super high boiling point, over 1,000 degrees, and it cooled the reactor far better than water ever could. What made that reactor so revolutionary was the fact that if you lost the coolant, the reactor shut itself down without any damage. **This was the safe nuclear energy source that everyone was looking for.** But after the two nuclear disasters listed above the industry was a pariah, and worldwide protests demanded all nuclear power be shut down.

(One of the most ignored hazards to nuclear energy was actually the nuclear waste. Spent fuel rods and other nuclear wastes were highly radioactive, and no one knew what to do with them. Most of it was kept on the site of the plants in special containers, but they are still radioactive and an incredible hazard to the nation. When I went to college at Oswego, NY 1975-79 the nearby nuclear power station had to keep their spent fuel on site as there was no place to ship it. That same threatening issue is still present, even at our nuclear weapons plants. Hundreds of tons of nuclear waste are just lying around.)

New York

In NYC Ed Koch had won a third term as mayor. Within weeks many of his political backers and allies were being indicted in multiple corruption scandals.The list of arrested officials was mind numbing, and gave proof to the call for term limits as a way to try to control graft in politics. Koch had come into office during the City's darkest days. His administration had continued the normal Democratic programs and he was slowly able to get the budget under control with Federal help and a strict fiscal controller.

By giving away tax grants and other perks to the developers the city was able to keep the construction industry alive which increased tax revenues and provided a big economic stimulus. But as Koch's reign continued the typical politics and favoritism so prevalent in NY and especially among the Democrats created a culture of corruption. (For more information on those events in NYC the reader should lookup, *City for Sale*.)

As shown earlier the biggest push for the city's tax revenue was the stock market revival under Pres. Reagan's economic plan. Financial companies were hiring by the hundreds, and the yuppies (young urban professionals) appeared. Flush with good paying jobs developers began buying up vacant lots, vacant buildings and undervalued properties. Those baby-boomers desired the city life and a needed real estate revival took over. Those of us in the FDNY saw a large decrease in fires and arson as life returned to some of the destroyed neighborhoods. In my case Alphabet City on the Lower East Side.

Even with the boom times Crime was still out of control, and the usual excuses were in place demanding more police, more funding etc. At that time NYC had over 40,000 police, a higher number than many countries have in their army. That new wave drug called crack appeared. This was a highly addictive form of cocaine and turned our streets into killing fields as gangs fought for sales areas. Not until conservative Republican Rudy Giuliani was elected in 1993 would the violent crime situation be turned around. But by then multiple thousands had needlessly died.

(In 1992 the murder rate in NYC hit 2,275 for the year. We in the FDNY faced this drug scourge on a daily basis. In two weeks we had seven homicides near my Times Square Firehouse, Engine-54 & Ladder-4.)

Foreign Affairs

During heated debates in June 1986 the House reluctantly approved Pres. Reagan's aid package for the Contras. Reagan had worked hard to convince the few Democrats who were needed to join in his effort to topple the Sandinistas. On July 11, 1986 Pres. Reagan, who never gave up on his commitment to the Contras placed the approved U.S. aid under CIA jurisdiction. His multi-year fight against Communism in Latin America was finally in full swing. *The Communists would have to fight to stay in power, and that would prevent them from fomenting revolution nearby.*

NATO finally agreed to follow Pres. Reagan's plan to renew production of chemical weapons, the first time since 1969. His idea was not to become murderous animals like Saddam Hussein, but to convince the Soviets that NATO could strike them back with any weapon system the Soviets might try to use. Pres. Nixon had signed an agreement with the Soviets to end the production and use of those horrible weapons back in 1973. But again the Soviets had lied, continuing the production and stockpiling of their chemical weapons, thousands of them.

During the past decade the East Bloc had been positioning growing numbers of their ever more lethal chemical weapons systems within first strike range of the unprepared cities of Western European. *Their plan was simple, blackmail the Europeans into giving up or face certain death.*

As the leader of the free world and NATO, Pres. Reagan's foreign policy was directed to match or exceed the Soviet WMD (Weapons of Mass Destruction), threats anywhere possible. In that way all hoped the Communists would stop their increasingly menacing actions. As before the peaceniks and liberals of Europe had been loathe to accepting any of America's ideas or weapon systems. But they were curiously silent when the Soviets placed their weapons within range of Europe's cities and people.

At that same time numerous arrests of French business leaders were occurring as they were still (illegally) selling advanced equipment to the Soviets. But France was not alone in that duplicitous action as Japan, Norway and others were also guilty of chasing profits. *Japan and Norway sold the Soviets computerized milling machines to produce submarine propellers that were as quiet as ours.* And naturally with the large sums changing hands corruption was close by.

Our Democratic run Congress cut the funding for SDI from $5.3 Billion down to $3 Billion. They also voted down any funding to be used for deploying SDI weapons. Since Reagan had stood firm on that issue these past years, the Democrats in Congress were doing the Soviets work for them.

Sec-Def Weinberger had warned the Democrats that the program had to be funded to stay viable, and Reagan refused to bow to the Soviets and cancel the SDI program. At times the two leaders had resorted to shouting matches. But the president was convinced that his SDI program was the only true way to end the reliance on MAD and nuclear weapons.

Throughout the summer of 1986 Gorbachev and Reagan exchanged additional proposals giving and taking things off the arms control table. They decided to meet again for more concrete discussions. Once more leaked reports of their letters and proposals caused lobbying groups into fits as they fought to present their solutions or to protect certain constituents.

Reykjavik, Iceland was the scene of the next super-power summit. On October 10-11, 1986 the leaders returned to the negotiations to try again. Rather than having a set conference, the two men decided to meet with just translators and Foreign Secretaries and hash things out. Nearby staff meetings also continued, as Paul Nitze and his group were fighting with the Russians on other disarmament issues.

Both leaders agreed they could cut the numbers of ballistic missiles to roughly 1,600, and warheads down to 6,000 within five years. Then they agreed to eliminate all nuclear weapons.

(Their staffs arguing in the back rooms refused any such thoughts, as would our allies. Communist conventional forces were overwhelmingly larger than NATO's, and no one in Europe wanted to find out if our few tanks were better than their thousands.)

Thinking he had Reagan in a trap Gorbachev again insisted that SDI be eliminated or confined to the research labs. Reagan still refused, and he then told the Russians that when we complete SDI we will give you a copy. Gorbachev refused his offer. They went around one more time and progress was made on some minor arms reductions when Pres. Reagan got annoyed with the gaming and told Schultz this meeting is over, lets go. For Reagan, SDI was America's salvation.

Naturally the leftist media became hysterical and claimed the meeting (and Reagan) was a failure. *But those leaders had come close to eliminating those terrible weapons.* And any dialogue was better than no dialogue as it gave both sides a chance at communicating. For Gorbachev he had gain played his hand and came up short. We now knew how badly the Soviets needed SDI ended. They would agree to give up all of their offensive nuclear weapons to get it. Our side knew they would negotiate again. *(97)

Back in May the Soviets had removed Babrak Karmal from power in Afghanistan and replaced him with one Mohammed Najibullah. But this change of rulers could not stop the rebels.

On November 13 the Soviet Politburo met in secret at the behest of Gorbachev. *Marshal Sergei Akhromeyev informed the gathered principals that despite deploying over 50,000 of their Afghan troops along the border with Pakistan, the enemy pack mule supply system continued to bring in weapons and supplies.* And no matter how many Afghan rebels they killed, there were always another batch sneaking in to continue the fight.

Gorbachev was embittered that over a million of their troops had fought in Afghanistan, and yet despite the horrendous costs they had borne nothing was accomplished. (Just like we felt with Vietnam.) He directed the Politburo to set a timeline of one year or at most two to organize a neutral government and allow them (Russia) to exit the country. Their economy was in serious jeopardy, and this war was a large drain on it.

A few weeks later Gorbachev privately warned Najibullah that he had just 18-24 months to solidify his position in power.

That was all the time the Soviet military had left.

Months later Gorbachev asked his government to give their people a greater voice in picking their leaders. Unlike the old-guard Bolsheviks, Gorbachev was more understanding of the changing world. He was also increasingly frustrated that the U.S. did not believe in their attempts at ending the Afghan war. (Maybe the fact that the Soviets lied to us about everything for the past fifty years had something to do with it.)

Though Reagan did not know of any of this, his Administration's efforts were doing just what he and they had hoped, stressing the Soviet economy and forcing them to stop their aggression.

Because of our efforts in helping and arming the Afghan rebels, the Soviets did not roll over the country and crush them into submission. They had a serious multi-year war on their hands. By 1987 Russia was unable to continue the fight.

This same scenario had been occurring in Africa and Central America too! Carter and the 1970s Democrats had handed both regions to the Communists.

But Reagan fought them, and now both groups were losing. That is the primary difference between the pacifist/liberals in the Democratic party, and the realists in the Republican party.

(Had Carter won in 1980 it is doubtful if this dire economic situation in Russia would even exist. It is also possible that the Europeans would have given up to the Soviets. *Instead of collapsing, the Soviets would have won everything.*)

Islamic World

Pakistan was again flaring into turmoil as opposition leader Benazir Bhutto was jailed on August 14th. The 33 year old was the daughter of former P.M. Bhutto who had been overthrown in the 1977 coup led by Gen. Mohammad Zia ul-Haq. (The senior Bhutto was later executed as a way to keep him from causing Zia any more problems.)

During the rallies for Benazir chants of Death to America rang out even though the U.S. had been aiding Pakistan and the Mujahedeen. Bhutto would be freed on September 8.

Pakistan like so much of the Middle East had been created by the British Colonial Office. Five of their provinces were drawn up solely to suit British interests, not to create a unified nation. It was held together because of its army and having harsh rulers. But with the recent influx of terrorists and criminal castoffs flooding their lands, it was becoming harder to maintain control.

On September 5, 1986 Pan Am Flight 73 enroute to NYC was hijacked in Karachi, Pakistan. Islamic terrorists directed by Abu Nidal were planning on shooting only the Americans on the plane. During the 16 hour standoff Pakistani troops struck and the terrorists opened fire in the cabin murdering twenty and wounding one hundred twenty civilians.

On September 6 Abu Nidal's group struck again murdering twenty two Jewish worshipers and wounding six others at an Istanbul Synagogue. The two shooters slipped into the building and bolted the door closed. (Some suspected the shooting was done to prevent a meeting of Egypt's Mubarak and Israel's Peres.) In retaliation Israel bombed the PLO HQ in Tunis on October 1, 1986. Sixty terrorists were killed and the HQ was destroyed.

Paris was struck on September 8 by Hezbollah when a bomb exploded at the Paris City Hall post office. Two were murdered and twenty eight others wounded.

On the 12th another Hezbollah bombing in a Paris supermarket wounded fifty-four.

On the 14th another Hezbollah bomb exploded in a Paris café killing two policemen.

On the 15th another Hezbollah bomb killed one and wounded fifty at a Paris Police station.

On the 17th yet another Hezbollah bombing was made by tossing one out of a car on a Paris street. This attack murdered seven and wounded sixty more. *French authorities finally begin a crackdown on Islamic suspects.*

On December 25, 1986 Iraqi Air Flight 163 was hijacked by four Islamic Jihad terrorists. A grenade went off while in the air forcing an emergency landing. Then a second grenade was used crashing the aircraft. Sixty three were murdered with 100 wounded.

Libya was setting up more terror attacks, and the NSC worked on making a second large attack on them. And France finally admitted that Libya's Khadafy was a problem.

During the late summer Libyan forces were again bombing French and Chadian defensive positions and advancing back into Chad. France's Defense Minister Andre` Giraud quietly asked for U.S. aid, and the Reagan Administration provided intelligence and transportation. Updated weapons were also sent over, and two MiG-23 fighter-bombers were shot down by Chadian gunners using our Redeye missiles. Upset at the increasing pace of hostilities Giraud wanted French fighter jets to intercept all the Libyan flights. Pacifist Jacques Chirac (who had been reelected) was against any direct confrontations, and wanted all French forces pulled back.

With U.S. help Chad's President Hiss`ene Habre` directed a bold 1986 attack on the rear of a Libyan air base shutting it down. Using camels the Chadian units had moved unseen through the southern deserts coming into the rear of the Libyan base. Their assault used the new Milan anti-tank missiles which destroyed the Libyan jets at the airfield, plus numerous armored vehicles. That fight stopped all forward movement of Khadafy's thieves, and hundreds of their troops were captured. One of them was the commander, Col. Khalifa Haftar. Upset over this defeat, Khadafy abandoned all of those men in Chadian prisons.

Strangely Chirac was upset over the battle, and threatened to stop all aid if Habre` did so again. Days later a French antiaircraft unit shot down another Libyan bomber that was threatening Chad's capitol of N'Djamena. *Radio intercepts from the local Libyan forces revealed that two Soviet Advisors had been on that bomber.* That intelligence and the dozens of files from the captured airfield proved what Pres. Reagan had been saying all along, the Soviets had been using Libya to get into N. Africa.

Habre`s people also delivered captured Russian SA-13 SAM's to U.S. and French officials. They were the most advanced in the Soviet arsenal and were an intelligence windfall.

Even so, France continued to aid the Soviets with vital machinery and technology transfers. In late November Mitterrand met with Gorbachev and set the table for later accords in which French taxpayers gave Russia a 12 billion franc credit line and opened the French Space Center to Russian scientists! This was a appalling bloodless victory for the KGB.

Soviet Military Doctrine stated, **"That mastery of Space will be vital in the next major war".** *(98)

William Casey then hatched a plan. With Habre's help, we would turn the Libian prisoners into a rebel force to overthrow Khadafy. CIA agents approached Col. Haftar with their plan and he agreed, it was time to end Khadafy.

(Tragically Habre was overthrown in 1990, resulting in years of intense secrecy over that plot. The plan came to fruition in 2011 with the Arab Spring as Haftar's forces were reunited and resupplied. He led the rebel forces that overthrew Khadafy!)

Reagan's America Changes Everything

In the U.S. the midterm elections of November 1986 had the Democrats winning a solid majority in the Senate and gaining even more in the House. Since they controlled the legislative branch they decided not to work with the soon to be ending Reagan Administration.

As mentioned before a scandal had erupted as information came out that the U.S. was indirectly selling arms to Iran and giving the money to the Contras. Unlike Nixon, Pres. Reagan went on the radio and admitted that some mistakes were made in the affair but he refused to admit that the entire episode was a mistake. Such is the twisted world of Foreign Policy that we were arming the enemy of our allies and ourselves in order to help our Central American neighbors fight off Communism. **(But again that was because the Democrats in Congress had refused to.)**

With control of the Congress the Democrats held numerous hearings on Iran-Contra, and they were determined to hurt the administartion. (Perhaps Reagan should have taken his appeal to help the Contras to the public forum instead of sneaking aid to the Contras.)

During the hearings CIA Director William Casey took ill. Sadly He died in May 1987, and never knew that his solid work the past years would succeed in bringing the collapse of the Soviet Union. (He was a key figure in the Contra issue.) During his last days, three Pakistani-ISI teams crossed the Amu Darya River into Soviet Asia and attacked an airfield, a factory and a convoy. The Democrats grew very angry over those latest missions, and so did the Russians.

By this point in time Pres. Reagan had amended relations with Israel and formed a joint defense arrangement so each nation could train with the other. He had also made aggreements and was stockpiling munitions and supplies in Egypt, Oman and Bahrain. It was becoming common to see joint U.S. military maneuvers in many of the nations in the region, and a U.S. naval squadron was operating permanently in the Persian Gulf. (His forward thinking in the Persian Gulf region would prove vital in just a few years.)

On February 28, 1987 Gorbachev unexpectedly announced that arms control was no longer tied to SDI. Pres. Reagan spoke about his offer on March 6, (a respite from Iran-Contra), and announced that Sec of State Schultz would go to Moscow for another state visit. Soviet Premier Gorbachev proposed a missile free Europe, and at each meeting Gorbachev continued to argue with Sec. Schultz over Reagan's hardline stance.

As always the pacifists were all aglow over this Russian offer, but Schultz refused to accept the proposal until he had consulted with our allies. Western military analysts were worried that this Russian move was just another trick to protect their overwhelming superiority in conventional forces. They felt that once we pulled our latest weapons out of Europe the Russians might just attack. (This nervousness was prompted by the fact that during the past weeks our navy had been chasing Soviet Victor III submarines away from our East Coast.)

Then in May 1987 an unexpected decision was reached in Moscow. *It was announced that a new military doctrine would be emplaced,* **protecting the Soviet homeland.** Western analysts were unsure of what that actually meant, but for the Communists it was game changing. Gorbachev presented to the leaders of the Warsaw Pact that their goal was to prevent war.

They would not start any conflict unless attacked, they placed no new territorial claims, and would not use nuclear weapons unless attacked.

Unknown to the West, Gorbachev also told those leaders that the Soviet Union would not intervene militarily in Eastern Europe. This was the beginning of the end.

At a following conference in June 1987 Gorbachev finally admitted that the Soviet economy was in bad shape and that they must make major changes. He advocated discontinuing all of their price subsidies and central economic controls. Similar to the successful moves implemented in China, small businesses were to be encouraged to operate, and the Soviet transportation systems must be improved. (It was still common for foods to rot on the farms because there was no way to get them to the markets or storage facilities.)

This latest proposal was compelling in that Gorbachev appeared to be making real reforms to help his country and its people. His efforts at openness were exposing the lies and propaganda of Communism.

Gorbachev forgot that the only way the Communists could stay in power was to have absolute authoritarian control over everything. He wanted to bring his people away from the past, but he did not have the vision to see the near future.

As CIA's Robert Gates would aptly state; *That was his glory and his tragedy.* *(99)   Momentous changes were about to occur.

Pope John Paul II was scheduled to make his third trip to his Polish homeland in June 1987. Prior to his visit he had met with President Reagan and his wife Nancy in Rome. They spoke of their shared beliefs in the unity of mankind, freedom and human rights.

This Pope had been instrumental in providing hope and spiritual guidance throughout the world, but especially those trapped behind the Iron Curtain. He was the most beloved Pope in memory. Poland's Gen. Jaruleski was confident that his strict policing policies had ended Solidarity and their drive for freedoms, so he finally allowed the Papal Visit to come in.

The ruling Communists decided to make it hard for him to see any of their citizens. Much to their surprise the Pope's visit was finding large and adoring audiences. Repeated attempts to interfere and threaten the masses were made. But John Paul's impassioned speech at the birthplace of Solidarity rejuvenated the Polish people and the national mood was reborn. *All across the country the slogan and logo of Solidarity was seen and repeated.*

At the same time President Reagan met with Gorbachev in Berlin for another conference on arms control. While they were there large groups of people were gathered at the Berlin Wall, the single most visible monument to the Cold War.

(The wall had been built in 1961 to keep the prisoners of Communism from escaping to the West.)

On June 12, 1987 Reagan again stunned all with his passionate speech for freedom, and his request for Russia to show their commitment to that freedom. Pres. Reagan stated, **"If you seek liberalization come to this gate, Open this gate Mr. Gorbachev, Mr. Gorbachev tear down this wall."** *(100)

Unkown to the Soviet intelligence services, this speech was heard throughout their empire, even in the Gulags. All across the continent those imprisoned by Communism realized they were not forgotten by the fortunate citizens of the West. A new emotion began sweeping Europe, and the Communists were dumbfounded.

Then in July Premier Gorbachev agreed to a global ban on superpower intermediate and short range nuclear missiles.

On July 29 Reagan agreed to his proposal stunning all. Weeks later in Geneva the Soviets changed some of the wording to insist that Germany have no missiles too. The Germans quickly disagreed since all of the disarmament talks had been about Soviet and American missiles. No mention had been made to remove any of the Warsaw Pact missiles, so no mention would be made to remove theirs.

During September Sec. State Schultz again met with Soviet Foreign Minister Shevardnadze. At their meetings Afghanistan naturally came up and the Russian bluntly told his counterpart that the Soviets had made the decision to leave Afghanistan within a year. *He asked Schultz to help them stop the spread of Islamic Fundamentalism.* Being that Russia had Islamic republics along their southern rim, they were already seeing and fighting this growing entity. They wanted the U.S. to reduce the arms and aid to the rebels, and stop Pakistan's ISI from assisting the spread of this dangerous political following.

(One of the unintended consequences of the Soviet invasion was the call to arms by the Islamic world. *Afghanistan became a rallying cry for the Fundamentalists, and it enabled them to train, equip and organize an Islamic army.)*

Acting CIA Director Robert Gates met with his KGB counterpart Vladimir Kryuchkov on December 4, 1987 in Washington DC for an unprecedented face to face. Unknown to Gates, the KGB was still getting intelligence from Aldrich Ames. At their meeting Gates was told there were still over 100,000 Soviet troops fighting hard in Afghanistan. Kryuchkov asked for U.S. help in getting them out by stopping our aid.

CIA had received recent updates on the war effort, and all were upbeat since the introduction of the Stinger missiles. The Muj forces had defeated all of the Soviet tactics. Soviet troops were being bested constantly, their losses in men and equipment were significant, and morale was gone.

(CIA believed the Soviets were incurring costs of over $20 billion annually to support their client states and proxy wars. Cuba alone needed $5-7 Billion a year to stay afloat.)

Diplomatic debates over Soviet desires to leave Afghanistan raged back and forth. The Chinese never believed it for they had a saying about Soviet intentions, "What the Bear has eaten, it never spits out". *(101)

Kryuchkov also warned Gates that the U.S. needs to fear not just a Shia Islamic Fundamentalist Government based in Iran, but a Sunni one too. They could setup soon in any of a dozen nations that were now at risk. (He was so right.)

With arms talks progressing Party Secretary Gorbachev visited the U.S. on December 7-10, 1987. Many American political and military leaders spoke with him, and polite conversations occurred on all manner of subjects. Despite our many differences and non-stop complaints from our liberals, diplomacy had continued between the superpowers.

On December 10, 1987 Pres. Reagan and Premier Gorbachev signed the first treaty to cut the size of the nuclear arsenals from both countries. Within three years the Soviets and U.S would eliminate their respective (1752, 859) medium range missile stockpiles. Those weapons had been at the heart of the East-West tensions for the past decade. Reagan repeatedly joked "Doveryai no proveryai", Trust but verify. Gorbachev agreed.

Conservatives were wary that the West would never be certain of Russian compliance, as they had lied on every previous treaty they had signed. Communists do not have a prying free press to watch over the politicos or their military, and Russia is a big country with plenty of places to hide things.

At this point in time we used recon aircraft like the KC-135, U-2 and SR-71, and low earth orbiting satellites, medium altitude ones from 1,000-10,000 miles high, ocean recon satellites and geo-synchronous units based 22,300 miles high to try to keep watch. But watching was not always knowing as human spies were extremely hard to come by behind the Iron Curtain, or in the Muslim world. And the Communists were masters at camouflage and treachery.

It was clear even to Pres. Reagan's biggest critics that his hard attitude with regard to combating and negotiating with the Communists, his refusal to trade away SDI, and our deploying medium missiles to Europe had accomplished exactly what he and everyone else had always desired, nuclear disarmament, peace and safety in Europe.

Prior to Reagan's policies (and Mitterrand's speech in 1983), all of the West's efforts to negotiate with the Russians were attempted while they were increasing their missile deployments, proxy wars and conventional forces buildup. All of those efforts made them stronger, and the West's attempts at arms reductions were met with impunity. But after Reagan and Europe's leaders stood firm and completed our missile deployments Soviet intransience ended, and they wanted to talk. Each time they met with the West they insisted missile reductions could only occur with the end of SDI. **Each time Reagan refused.**

This INF treaty restored the peaceful status quo that had existed before 1977. Though this treaty only cut 10% of the total number of nuclear weapons, it was a fine starting point for the two superpowers to work from.

(So many talking heads and inept politicos in this world delude themselves into demanding and expecting a "perfect or complete fix" at every meeting or for every law that is enacted. *It is much more important to make progress on a problem, and then expand on it as results come in.* A perfect example of this strategy would be using the many ideas to improve the flawed Social Security system to keep it viable for the next generation that will need it.)

Their three day summit ended with some further agreements for reducing the strategic arsenals of both nations, and all Soviet demands for eliminating SDI had been shelved.

Later in a private meeting Gorbachev spoke with Pres. Reagan and VP Bush in a direct effort to reduce U.S. aid to the Afghan rebels. Gorbachev gave a promise that their troops would leave Afghanistan soon. Reagan refused to commit at that time, and Bush was non-committal, though Bush did state that the U.S. was not looking to impose a pro-American government on the country.

In actuality we had no real policy in place for Afghanistan other than to hurt the Soviets. During the past year the CIA had warned repeatedly that once the war ended the country was going to be a terrible mess economically and politically. Sadly no political direction was ever devised by our leaders.

(In all likelihood no direction from us would have been possible. Pakistan, Iran and Saudi Arabia all had their own ideas for the future of the destroyed country, and Democracy was not it.)

In contrast to the happy faces in America, France's Mitterrand and Chirac were not overly pleased with this INF treaty. Once we had actually placed our missiles Europe had enjoyed five years of no Soviet saber rattling. With those American weapons soon to be gone, the always present Soviet conventional forces were still an overwhelming entity. Both leaders feared the Soviets would again get aggressive despite this limited drawdown. And with the higher number of pacifists in Europe in 1987, this time they might have enough political sway to simply give up and surrender.

Of the 52,000 tanks in the Soviet inventory, 28,000 were stationed to attack NATO. They also had 27,000 meters of bridging equipment stationed there, along with 10,000 fixed and 4,000 mobile SAM launchers, 1,200 fighters with 2,800 in reserve. Not mentioned were the very high numbers of troops and artillery, or the immpressive numbers of Warsaw Pact forces.

Mitterrand went to Moscow a short while later and again met with Gorbachev. France agreed to give the Russians a $2 Billion dollar credit to finance numerous civil projects. Even though the Cold War was still in effect, it appeared to some that the French were hedging their bets. *(The Soviets were still giving aid to their proxies, so basically France was bailing them out.)*

Gorbachev had become the darling of the western media with his warm smile and quick handshakes. On the way to the White House he stopped his motorcade to greet some of the crowd. To observers it appeared as if he were an American politician instead of the head of an enemy nation dedicated and equipped to destroying us. He went back to the Politburo with concrete proof that his policies of Glasnost, (openness), had worked to reduce the Soviet-U.S. dangers.

Inside the Soviet Union a deep rot was striking them from within. Over the past decade they had reached parity with the U.S. in many of their weapons designs and capabilities, thanks to their spies. But at this point the Soviets could not afford to build and maintain them. By late 1986 their submarine force was reaching U.S. standards for quietness, and they knew where our submarines and INF missiles were thanks to those traitors.

Many of the disagreeing Soviet principals felt that with the intelligence their spies had given them, they could (and should) have fought and won a nuclear war by striking us and Europe first!

Fortunately for the world Gorbachev had become the leader of the Soviets and not some die-hard Communist. With no warning Gorbachev next announced unilateral cutbacks to their military to the tune of 500,000 men! He also stated that some armored units would be recalled from Eastern Europe and disbanded. Our intelligence and military leaders were in awe. (This is what Gorbachev meant with his proposal to just protecting the Soviet homeland.)

Always looking at the big picture, Gorbachev and the Politburo decided that they would make leadership changes in Kazakhstan. Dinmukhamed Kunayev was the leader there and a member of the Soviet Politburo. Gorbachev secured his retirement on December 16, 1987. Instead of selecting another member of the ruling Kazakh tribe, Gorbachev chose a minority Chuvash member named Gennady Kolbin. Violent rioting quickly broke out involving thousands of protestors and police. Dozens were killed on both sides. One thing this episode brought out was the growing tribal hostilities and the deep resentment inside those captive republics of the Soviet Union. (Just llike Yugoslavia.)

Gorbachev's glasnost policy (openness), had allowed that episode to be publicized, and that convinced all of their captive citizens that they could protest. Long dormant nationalism began to stir. *(102)

This successful Washington Super-Power conference gave Pres. Reagan some relief from the "Iran-contra" scandal that the Democrats had been pressing these past months. Despite the voluminous negative reporting by the major media and the hysterics by the Democrats, this issue meant nothing to the American people. They liked Reagan and all of his policy efforts. His popularity only fell from 80% to 75%!

Back in the early 1980s Pres. Reagan tried to resurrect some of the FBI's domestic operations to prevent any homegrown terrorism. But he was repeatedly stopped by the Democrats because it might hurt their voting blocs. *Their politically motivated refusal would come back to haunt us a thousand fold on September 11, 2001.*

In an effort to end the fighting in Central America Pres. Oscar Sanchez of Costa Rica, the only Democratic nation in the region, forced upon his fellow rulers a peace process. (Columbia had recently suffered three more violent attacks.) On August 7, 1987 at a conference in Guatemala, Pres. Sanchez was able to convince the at times bizarre Ortega that he had to accept some democracy or he would be taken out by the U.S. Ortega reluctantly concurred, but then he went to Libya to celebrate 20 years of Qaddafi's rule. Joining that dangerous circus were Arafat and the PLO, and Syria's Assad, both sponsors of terrorism. (And as shown earlier both had assisted Ortega's takeover in Nicaragua.)

Politics

Trying to find something to run on the Democrats were already vying for position for the upcoming 1988 presidential race. Gary Hart, Jesse Jackson and Mario Cuomo were the front runners in the party. Hart like so many in the Democratic Party was caught having affairs and soon dropped out. Jackson did not have a large enough following and would drop out, while Cuomo was rightly besieged with complaints of corruption and fiscal improprieties.

During his twelve years as New York State Governor 1983-94 he had and would continue to secretly sell off all of the State's assets using 30 year bonds. (They will all come due by 2023.) Cuomo needed those illegal, secretive sales to raise revenue to fund his out of control social programs without having to "raise taxes". (The same scam LBJ used in 1966-7.) Those "sales" had limited legislative oversight, and over the past years gave Cuomo and his administration Billions which they wasted on more liberal nonsense. By acquiring revenue that way he sneakily hid the truth of the state's current financial problems, and condemned the state's fiscal future.

(In 1991 Cuomo's next scam was selling Attica State prison to the Urban Development Corporation. The UDC was created in 1968 to help low income people afford housing, not steal $200 million dollars in the sale of a prison built and paid for decades ago. **But here is the insane part of this scam. Over the 30 year life of this one bond NYS taxpayers will shell out another $690 million dollars to pay for it.** To hide his crimes, after his 1994 defeat to Republican George Pataki, Cuomo had all of the state's records during his twelve years in power shredded!

(NYC budget director Alair Townsend called the Cuomo actions a criminal art form.) *(103)

Planning ahead for the next election the Democratic run Congress passed a bill "granting amnesty to millions of illegal immigrants". Their move was politically motivated in an effort to placate the minority voting blocks and to enable those "new citizens to participate in the coming presidential elections". (No one plays dirty politics better than the Democrats, and they pull the same scam every four years.)

Islamic Issues

Sheikh Abdullah Azzam the radical cleric from the Muslim Brotherhood had played a big part in the war against the Soviets in Afghanistan, and against the moderates inside Egypt.

Hamas was another offshoot of the Muslim Brotherhood and formed in 1987. It was greatly influenced by Azzam, and was used as a balance force against the PLO and Yassir Arafat by operating in Gaza. Eventually Hamas took over Gaza under **Ahmad Yassin** and morphed into a terrorist movement that attacked Israel constantly.

They were also quite successful at infiltrating into America and setting up fake charities and training centers. **Abu Marsook** ran their **"Islamic Association for Palestine", (IAP),** and established chapters in Indiana, Arizona, Illinois and California. They were not alone. Over the past years Azzam was spreading his influence inside America. His unyielding work had inspired multiple thousands of jihadists. By 1987 his **"Alkifah** network of charity centers" was being used to support Jihadist efforts in Bosnia, Afghanistan, the Philippines, Egypt, Algeria and elsewhere.

In NYC an FBI informant reported that weapons had been seen inside the Al-Farook Mosque on Atlantic Avenue in Brooklyn. *FBI agents applied for a wiretap to investigate the report but were denied by a judge because "there was no evidence of a criminal conspiracy".* (That ruling was predicated on the Democratic restrictions they had passed earlier, and refused to alter when Pres. Reagan wanted them changed to reflect this new threat.)

In actuality the Alkifah Refugee Center based at the Al-Farook Mosque was a center for counterfeiting tens of thousands of U.S. dollars, shipping arms and explosives to Hamas, and falsifying passports to enable like minded jihadists to enter the U.S. But without being able to investigate them no one could ever know if a criminal conspiracy was occurring!

During 1988 the first *Conference of Jihad* was being held at that Brooklyn Alkifah Center. In a speech that was videotaped, Azzam told his two hundred plus audience to carry out Jihad everywhere, even in America! Fight the infidels any place you can.

Through Azzam's efforts and the financial support of **Osama bin Laden** this network of Islamic "charity centers" and Mosques was spreading across the globe. Alkifah centers were now open in Great Britain, Norway the U.S., Germany, France and Sweden. And they were reaching an audience of over 50,000 each month. *(This was a separate effort from the Saudi-Wahhabist sect, and the dire problems that Egypt's Mubarak had warned about in 1979.)*

Azzam's Alkifah center in Tucson, Arizona was where one **Wadi al-Haj** was an active member. Haj was well placed and effective in the terrorist network. When future terrorists Ramzi Yousef and Ahmed Ajaj entered the U.S. in 1992, they were listed as workers at the Al-Bunyan Islamic Center in Tucson to help them get into the U.S. That is how efficient their organization had became in just the past few years.

(A rival cleric at the Masjid Center preached about tolerence and anti-terrorism. That cleric, Rashid Khalifa was murdered, and Haj was a suspect.)

A similar conference for *MAYA, (Muslim Arab Youth Association)* was held in Oklahoma City in December 1988. Azzam expanded on his Jihadist theme stating that Afghanistan was the training ground for their Jihadist effort.

It was time for Islam to rule the world.

But Azzam was growing unhappy with bin Laden's "wasteful efforts" in building terrorist camps in Afghanistan. He wanted all of the Islamic charity and aid that was raised to help the Muslims suffering in Afghanistan and other war ravaged nations worldwide.

And he wanted all of that money to be funneled through *his Alkifah centers*. He did not realize that bin Laden had other plans, and that he was not included.

Inside America Islamic extremist activity was increasing all across the country. By 1989 the University of South Florida in Tampa had transformed from its small origin into a beacon of higher learning. **They were also a center of an Anti-American jihadist movement.**

On 130 Street in Tampa a sign was erected memorializing one Izz al-Din al Qassam. He died in Palestine in 1935 fighting the "British and Zionists". To the Palestinians he is a revered martyr, and Palestinian Islamic Jihad (PIJ) follows the belief that Israel and America are a plot against Islam. Both must die.

Qassam's house in Tampa was used as a Mosque and run by professor **Sami al-Arian**. Al-Arian was the leader of another Islamic program, the ICP, (Islamic Concern Project.) As always he claimed the ICP aims were "charitable, social and dedicated to advancing multiculturalism".

In actuality he used it to propagandize their Jihad.

Though the school did not promote that issue, being a professor gave al-Arian his legal cover story and pulpit which he used on his own time. ICP produced dozens of articles promoting the Jihadist cause. As time went by ICP brought in Islamic terrorist leaders from all over the globe to give lectures inside America. It included the previously mentioned **Sheikh Omar Rahman,** the wanted fugitive of the EIJ (Egyptian Islamic Jihad). ICP also raised funds for Jihadist charities and formed tax exempt foundations to shield them from scrutiny. (More on this story to follow.)

Since the mid-1980s the Iranians had been attacking Kuwaiti oil tankers with aircraft and gunboats. As the losses and attacks mounted the Kuwaiti government asked Pres. Reagan to reflag their ships under the stars and stripes. U.S. warships would then escort the tankers all the way through the gulf. Convoys were also used to protect the tankers and shipping losses decreased.

Then in late 1986 Iraqi jets launched a French made *Exocet* anti-ship missile that severely damaged the *USS Stark* which was operating in the Persian Gulf. Thirty seven U.S. sailors were killed in the "accidental attack". At that time there were no signs of hostilities between Iraq and the U.S., but the event could have been staged for intelligence purposes or as retaliation for Iran-Contra. With the prior tilting of U.S. policy towards Iraq, Pres. Reagan had hoped to keep in check the growing danger of Iran to the region. (Aid to the Afghans was also thought to help control Iran.)

As shown before the fanatics in Iran had resorted to using suicidal teenagers to overwhelm Iraqi forward positions in mass attacks. In early 1986 it appeared as if the southern Iraqi city of Basra might be taken. But our intelligence help and French made artillery had a major impact on the ground war. Iran slowly began losing ground. In April 1988 the Iraqi's routed the exhausted Iranian ground forces by an extensive use of chemical weapons and an effective armored assault. With the Fao Peninsula cleared the Iraqi's began chasing the Iranians across the open ground.

On April 5, 1988 Kuwait Airlines Flight 422 a 747 jumbo jet from Bangkok, Thailand to Kuwait City was hijacked by **Imad Mughniyah** and his well trained IJO (Islamic Jihad Organization) terrorists. They kept the hostages for sixteen days flying between three continents in an effort to release seventeen members of the Da'wa Shia group who were held in a Kuwaiti prison. Those terrorists had been arrested for their parts in the terrorist bombings on the U.S. and French embassies in Lebanon in 1983. (However the Kuwaitis insisted they could not be tried in America.)

The hijacked flight first landed in Iran where fifty-five hostages were released. Three of the remaining males were found to be members of the Kuwaiti Royal Family, and threats and counter threats came and went over a few days. The plane next flew to Cyprus to be refueled. After more than a week of discussions the terrorists began beating passengers with threats of conducting a slow massacre of the hostages.

And they threatened to purposely fly the jetliner into the Royal Palace in Kuwait. (A huge missed warning sign).

The flight next went to Algeria were a few more hostages were released. At the end of day sixteen the terrorists were allowed to leave the country and the hostages were released.

Statements from the passengers showed that Iran had aided the terrorists by providing additional arms and explosives to fight off any potential commando raids.

After their "escape" Mughniyah was sent to the front lines in Lebanon leading a few ambushes against the Israelis. He could not adjust to the new slower pace of terrorist operations, or to Iran's updated long range plan. Similar to Trotsky and the Russian Revolution, Mughniyah was now too radical, and no longer useful to the bigger picture of an Iranian caliphate. The Iranians marginalized him and he faded from use ending up in Saudi Arabia. They too refused to turn him over to us!

(In 2008 he was finally killed.)

Over the past months numerous naval clashes had occurred between the Iranian and U.S. Navies in the Persian Gulf. One attack had multiple Iranian patrol craft charging at the U.S. cruiser *Vincennes*. Using their main gun the *Vincennes* sank three of the Iranian ships. Then in July 1988 the ship's officers thought they were being targeted by an Iranian air attack. They fired an anti-air missile which tragically brought down a civilian airliner. All aboard were killed.

Without warning the eight year Iraqi-Iranian war came to a sudden end in August 1988. Iran had been bled white, they were steadily losing ground, and lately it seemed that America might intervene and join in. Thus far between 1-2 million "Iranian troops" had died. Iran's rulers decided to end the fighting to "protect their Islamic revolution". (Had we joined the fight with air attacks Iran would have collapsed quickly to the advancing Iraqi troops.)

Khomeini told his followers the ceasefire with Iraq was like drinking a bitter cup of poison. Many of "his people" probably wanted him to take a drink. *From 1979 to 1986 the U.N. reported that over 10,000 known executions had been carried out by the Iranian Islamic Fundamentalists.* During the latter half of 1988 at least 1,000 more citizens were slaughtered, and that included women and clergymen. Families were made to pay for the bullets used to execute their loved ones.

Dozens of thousands of Iranians had been imprisoned, and all who were suffered brutal tortures at the hands of the Iranian Extremists. (Everyone was a suspect.) With this sudden peace in place, Iran's clerics were able to concentrate on and end all of the remaining internal threats to their rule. That peace also enabled them to continue aiding all of the terrorists and hostile groups operating in Europe and the Middle East.

In addition to their Hezbollah chapters in Lebanon, the Iranians had infiltrated terrorist cells into most of the countries of the Middle East and even Brazil and Uruguay! Iran's extremists pumped out non-stop anti-American propaganda and gave conferences and training to hundreds of terrorists who were now loose across the globe.

To counter U.S. economic sanctions Iran had used middle-men and fake companies to sell its oil. (Some of it even went to the

U.S.) *And similar to Iraq, extremist Iran worked diligently during the war to procure modern weapons and to make their own Chemical, Biological and Nuclear arms. They have never stopped.*

One of the least mentioned horror stories from the Iranian revolution was the careless disregard the Ayatollah and the clerics had for any of Iran's citizens. During the height of the war Khomeini had ordered hundreds of thousands of plastic keys from Taiwan. Those keys were given to children aged 12-17. They were told those were the keys to open the gates of paradise.

Those same children, over 450,000, were sent to the front lines to become human minesweepers! With the innocence of youth they raced into the Iraqi minefields detonating them with their bodies. Then the real Iranian troops would advance over their destroyed bodies. Not all of those children were killed outright, and many suffered grievously before finally dying uncared for in the fields. A few survivors were left maimed in horrible fashion.

All of this was the ghastly result of Jimmy Carter's inane feeling that Khomeini would be more open to human rights than the Shah. In actuality Khomeini and his successor Ayatollah Khamenei were so brutal they made the infamous list joining Hitler, Stalin, Mao, and Pol Pot for pure evil.

This sudden change in war fortunes made Iraq seem to be the victor, and it appeared that we were now friends. But Iraq was simply the enemy of our enemy, and our aid was directed to that end and then stopped. By the end of the war Saddam's military was five times larger than in had been back in 1980. Thanks to our help he had done well the past two years.

As soon as the fighting ended in August 1988, Saddam again used his chemical weapons on the troublesome Iraqi Kurds murdering thousands in the village of Halabja. His Mirage fighters used agricultural sprayers to disperse the clouds of death. Despite the genocide, business went on as usual.

More Terrorism

On November 29, 1987 Korean Air Flight 858 was blown up by N. Korean agents to protest the policies of South Korea. All 115 aboard were murdered.

On July 11, 1988 the Greek cruise ship *City of Poros* was stormed by three PLO gunmen who murdered nine and wounded ninety-eight. The gunmen fled from the ship using a speedboat.

They had also placed a large car-bomb at the ship pier, but it exploded after the ship had left the port causing few casualties. Those terrorists were again run by Libya and PLO's Abu Nidal. His aggressive group Black September was devoted to the Palestinian cause, was responsible for shooting Israel's ambassador Argov in 1982, and approximately 200 other attacks worldwide. That including the 1986 attack on the Pan Am jumbo jet in Karachi, Pakistan that killed and wounded more than one hundred. (Nidal was one of the senior members of the PLO, and ironically his father was a good friend of Chaim Weizmann, Israel's first president and a founder of the Haganah, the Jewish underground army. When he was young Nidal even went to Weizmann's home.)

August 17, 1988 Pakistan's President Mohammad Zia was killed in an unexplained aircraft crash. *With him was the capable and effective U.S. Ambassador Arnold Raphael and General Akhtar the father of the Afghan jihad.* America had many competent Soviet specialists, but few who knew and understood the Middle East as well as Raphael. He would be missed. A forensics team was sent over but could find no clear evidence of sabotage. The U.S. made C-130 went into the ground shortly after takeoff with the propellers turning.

(One possibility that was not explored was that one of the pilots dove the plane into the ground on purpose. This method was mentioned by the Iranians for Flight 422, would be used off of Nantucket in 1997, attempted in Paris in 1998, and successfully done on September 11, 2001.)

Pres. Zia had been vital to the effort to supply the Mujahedeen, and his continued support helped drive out the Soviets. But those years of effort also unleashed a torrent of criminal activity and undesirables within the border provinces of Pakistan. His death could also have been the result of a parting retaliatory action by the Soviets, political rivals within Pakistan, Islamic terrorists who disliked his connections to the West, or his overall plan for Afghanistan.

Another possibility was that the death of Gen. Akhtar was what was desired. He certainly was a potential rival for Afghan power. In any event their absence would create chaos and a power vacuum that would be exploited all too soon.

According to the in-depth work *Inside The PLO,* days after the downing of the Iranian airliner by the *USS Vincennes* **Ahmed Jibril** leader of the PFLP was in contact with the Iranian

Revolutionary Guards in Baalbek, Lebanon. At that time the Bekaa valley was the terrorist capitol of the world, and over one thousand Iranians controlled this small city. All of the earlier attacks against the Americans had originated from this stronghold.

(Syria controlled everything outside of Baalbek.)

Jibril and the PFLP were offering the Iranians a similar target, a U.S. 747, but only for a hefty price. Word got back to Tehran and more meetings were held there. The Iranians agreed on the PFLP price of four million dollars. What the PFLP team did not realize was they had been tracked while in Iran and again when they made their way to W. Germany.

Mossad alerted the Germans to the pending threat and they stormed two PLO safe-houses. Inside were two completed barometric bombs set for 31,000 feet along with piles of weapons and eleven pounds of semtex. *Thirteen conspirators were arrested, but once again all but two were released by the weak willed Europeans.* What the West Germans missed when they foolishly released those plotters was that there was another safehouse in Frankfurt. Inside were other weapons and another barometric bomb. The released plotters quickly went underground and/or returned to Syria and Lebanon. That took the heat off of the ones who had been missed.

The PLO were experts in using and forming plastic explosives to look like cute doll faces and even marzipan candies. Regional authorities had quietly intercepted such shipments all across the Mediterranean. But the PLO kept making and sending them out, knowing that over time some would get through.

It was believed that two Muslim women were tricked into bringing a bomb onto **Pan Am Flight 103**. This method had been tried before, as far back as 1972 on an El Al flight. Another possibility was that a drug mule snuck the bomb aboard thinking it was illegal drugs. In any case a barometric bomb went off as planned on December 29, 1988 destroying the airliner and murdering over 270 people.   (More to follow.)

The two PFLP terrorists who had overseen the plot left Germany and flew to Libya and Algeria. Two days later a message was intercepted between the Iranian embassy in Beirut and Iran's Interior Ministry. *Tehran sent congratulations and approved the final payment to the PFLP.*

Jabril often spoke of how much support his group (the PFLP) received from others, especially the Libyans and Syria. Many times Libyans fought with Jabril's group and vice-versa. In one attack on Israel they used E. German made hang gliders, and were taught how to fly them by E. German agents.

Reagans Last Months in Office

The year of 1988 was heralding major changes behind the Iron Curtain. Poland was continuing to rebel with demands for freedom using strikes and protests. And now Lithuania was joining them. Their freedom movement was called **Sajuda**, named for the concert pianist who inspired their masses with his non-violent protests. As with Poland, the Christian faith of the Lithuanians was a large part of their strength. As before the Communists were confused on what to do.

In Angola our aid had enabled the UNITA forces to take the fight to the enemy. In early January 1988 the Cuban-Angolan Communists tried to trap UNITA forces inside Cuito Cuanavale. Unable to force a win the communists tried a siege. During those tense months negotiations led by the U.S. had continued in trying to end the war. In early May an agreement was finally reached, the the Cubans would leave Angola, and the S. Africans would exit their base areas in Namibia. *(A big part of that peace plan was the planned cutbacks in supplies by the Soviets.)*

On December 22, 1988 a peace treaty was signed by Sec. Schultz and Shevardnadze. All Soviet-Cuban support was ended to the MPLA, and we ended our support to UNITA. For thirteen years the Communists had tried to takeover that land. After spending Billions and losing over a hundred thousand lives they again came away with nothing.

(Once again it was the Democrats who had abandoned Angola back in 1975, while Reagan and the Republicans helped them to stay free. If Carter had helped them back then perhaps all of those casualties could have been avoided.)

Back on September 30, 1987 our lethal assistance program to the Contras was ended, fallout from Iran-Contra. On February 28, 1988 all CIA paramilitary assistance was also ended. America could no longer help the Contras regain their country.

The Reagan Administration principals were downcast as the Democrats had pulled us out just as the Contras were close to winning. Cutoff from all outside help the Contras were forced to sign a cease-fire with the Communists of Nicaragua on March 23,

1988. This agreement allowed them amnesty, mutual recognition and a chance to return to the country as citizens.

But over the next weeks the circumstances for the former Contras declined steadily, as the Sandinistas intensified their efforts to find and root out anyone connected to them. Once again the "peace treaty" was meaningless. The U.S. embassy was closed, and all personnel kicked out.

The only good point in this situation was that the Soviets had ended their military and economic support. By the end of the year the Sandinistas were faced with a serious issue. If they continued doing what they were doing everything would collapse as they had no outside props. They decided to have an "election", as that could help them receive some economic relief from America and the Western banks. They were certain they would win.

The cycle of Presidential candidates slowly began to wind down as the Democrats eventually picked Michael Dukakis the liberal governor of Massachusetts. At his acceptance speech he declared that competence was more important than ideology. He miscalculated. The American people understood that a poor ideology (liberalism), was not what they wanted no matter how competent a candidate thought he was. Throughout the campaign Dukakis often demonstrated the common theme of "blame America first" school of thought. By this point in time many liberals had deluded themselves into believing that the two political systems of democracy and communism were converging.

The Republicans wisely stayed with V.P. George Bush. He had a long career of private industry and government service, and was well versed to be the next president. Unlike many unqualified candidates who aspire to the office, Bush had served in numerous federal governmental capacities over his lifetime and understood the position. He promised to be a president for education, and wanted a kinder America.

In an effort to help their candidate the major media as was their norm were biased in their efforts. Dan Rather attempted to confront Bush in a television interview and it ended up helping the Vice President. During the second televised debate Dukakis tried to appear nice but tough. He could not pull it off, just like an ad that had him sitting in an Abrams tank. One of the negative issues that came up against him was a prison furlough program that resulted in more crime. Dukakis supposedly had an early 18 point lead when the Bush team highlighted that prisoner program.

When the votes were cast in November 1988 the proven liberal was soundly defeated by the voters. George H. Bush won with 53.4% of the vote, took 40 states and 426 electoral votes. (But once again the Democrats voted as a bloc.)

In the Congress it had taken a lot of work, but a minor Welfare reform bill finally passed in late 1988. The author was the hard working and intelligent Sen. Moynihan from NY. Though this bill did not have everything he wanted, he accepted it as a watered-down version of the changes he had tried to enact with Pres. Nixon in 1973/74.

Back then Moynihan's plan would have revolutionized the 1965 Welfare system by providing assistance not just to the unemployed, but to workers who made little (minimum wage) from their labors. *Many of those citizens were quitting their jobs because the Democrats Welfare program actually gave them more money!* (That factor is still true today. Had they been given some federal assistance those citizens could have kept working and their struggle would have been lessened by the assistance from the government.)

Historical Note: Moynihan's 1973 Welfare restructuring plan would have *required* those on public assistance to go out and get a job. The Democrats 1965 Welfare program did not have any such rule because they wanted them to sit around and do nothing.

Many in the media liked Moynihan's 1973 plan. Pres. Ford had taken over in 1974, and he was able to get the Moynihan bill through the House, but not the Senate. All of those Senate Liberals and a even few conservatives voted against it for their own arrogant ideals.

(Once the bill moved into the Congress the Democrats cut it apart. They could not allow a Republican President to do what they had failed to do when their Great Society plan was pushed through. Many of the welfare bureaucrats also fought the plan because they would lose power over the large amounts of money they controlled, and for some their cushy jobs.) Moynihan is one of the few Democrats would have been a good president had he run. Ideology and the party did not control him.

Ronald Reagan had served two full terms as our president and left the office with grace and dignity. (A feature that few Democrats have shown.) Reagan had come into office to a nation mired in a deep economic, military and spiritual decline. His faith in god and our country, and his unwavering can-do attitude brought us incredible prosperity, renewed our military, our morale, and he setup and ran a successful plan to stopping Soviet Communism. His hard attitude had produced major reductions in nuclear weapons, and that made the world safer for us all.

There are not enough positive things that can be said as thanks for what he gave all of us. *Without him the Soviets may well have won the Cold War, and America would have collapsed.* No one can say what would have been the end game if that had happened. Would we have survived, or been enslaved?

The only thing that history knows is what did happen, we would win the Cold War, freeing over 500 million people!

Section Four

The Bush Years   Freedom and Strength

As mentioned above on December 21, 1988 Pan Am Flight 103 from Frankfurt to Detroit was blown up over Lockerbie, Scotland. More than 270 were killed, which included some innocents in the village. Intense investigations were conducted lasting months as all of the aircraft parts and debris were collected and reassembled. That proved a bomb had been used.

According to the video documentary on Flight 103, this flight had picked up unaccompanied luggage in London, and it was believed that was how the suitcase bomb made it on board. *Forensics traced the bomb back to Libyan agents.*

(During the lead-up to the 1999 trials some people believed, and we have already discussed here how the PFLP terrorist group had actually been hired by Iran to avenge the loss of their airliner to the U.S. Navy.)

Two alerts had been picked up forewarning an attack was coming. The first was the prior arrest of the Islamic terrorist cell in Germany making those advanced barometric bombs called Bombeat. (Those bombs fit perfectly into regular luggage.) During those arrests two of their bombs were recovered, but one or possibly two were not.

The second warning came in on December 5, 1988. An Islamic male called the U.S. embassy in Helsinki and stated that a flight from Frankfurt would be bombed. *The U.S. Government issued alerts to all air carriers, and they replied that they would be diligent.* At that time the airlines were allowed to use "self-regulated" security, and even charged an extra $5 to "comply with the terrorist alerts". But in reality they did next to nothing. Despite the evidence pointing to the probable conspirators, no action was taken over this brutal attack.

President elect Bush and his transition staff had (again) met with Gorbachev to discuss the changing world picture. Gorbachev's reductions in Soviet military forces were promising, but not game changing. Bush and his staff did not want to get sucked into making sweeping policy changes until a clear picture emerged. But American and Western liberals were already claiming the end of the Cold War, and that we should disarm.

The Europeans were pleased, especially Germany. Even Margret Thatcher was quite happy with Gorbachev thus far. What few of those dupes understood was that Gorbachev was having increasing problems within the Politburo over his reforms. No one was sure if he would last.

One event that helped cement the growing ties between the U.S. and this new Russia was the devastating earthquake in Armenia in late 1988. George Bush's son Jeb and his grandson George P. Bush went to the beleaguered region to deliver food and medicines. Over 50,000 had died with a million left homeless. The tearful effort by the American aid workers actually made quite an impression on the callous Soviets. (Our humanitarian aid had never been witnessed first hand by them before.)

Unlike most of our presidents, George Bush had met with (our enemy) Gorbachev many times before he took over. They had already created a personal relationship that was bridging the Cold War mentality. George H. Bush had served under three presidents, Nixon, Ford and Reagan. He stated that Reagan was his best teacher, using a few firm principals to guide his policies and actions. Out of all of the people serving as president, this one had a rock solid foundation to work from and guide his policies.

After Bush took over Henry Kissinger was used as a backchannel contact with the Russian leader. In early 1989 Gorbachev warned Kissinger that he was trying to change a difficult, entrenched system that did not understand what was happening to it. He was being challenged from within, and needed a "few peaceful years" to complete his plan. Kissinger assured him that we had no plans to foment trouble for the Russian leader. (Unlike what would have happened if the roles were reversed. America is not and never has aspired to be a colonial power.)

As was done during Pres. Reagan's eight years foreign affairs was a vital part of our national security, and close attention was rightfully given to it by all hands.

Following the standard procedures for Republican presidents, **every morning George Bush was given the National Security briefing inside the oval office. That briefing was given by the CIA and outlined the latest developments around the globe.** Emphasis was on any issues that would affect our safety and security. All of the key administration principals would be there which included, Pres. Bush, Vice-President Dan Quayle, Chief of staff John Sununu, National Security Advisor Brent Scowcroft, Robert Gates NSA deputy, and William Webster at CIA. Both Scowcroft and Webster were solid long serving administrators. (Webster had run the FBI for six years until he was transferred to the CIA in 1987.)

One of the most important early topics for the incoming Administration was aid to Afghanistan. By 1987 our aid effort was under the scrutiny from Congress and various committees. Many were rightfully becoming concerned with the lack of oversight. The original effort had been managed by just a few agents and supervisors, and personal contact had run the operation. But all of those people had moved on and everything now had changed.

With the Soviets pulling out tensions were growing between the rival Afghan groups for political control. And Zia's vision for Afghanistan had died with him.

Ed McWilliams was a special envoy sent to Islamabad to begin a fact finding mission to see how things were going as the Soviets exited. For weeks he traveled into Afghanistan speaking with local leaders such as Abdul Haq and Yahya Massoud. Most of their complaints were the same, Pakistan's ISI, the Muslim Brotherhood and officers of the Saudi GID were actively pushing to have Gulbuddin Hekmatyar take over the country.

All of those groups were eliminating local leaders and intellectuals in the Afghan resistance. Anyone who could challenge Hekmatyar.

Meanwhile seventy percent of the Afghans in the refugee camps wanted the return of King Zahir Shah to power. McWilliams also learned that the ISI was only distributing food and finances to those who supported their choice for ruler. He was appalled at how quickly all of our goodwill and hundreds of millions in U.S. aid were being hijacked by a ruthless cabal of anti-American Islamists and ISI officers! His report was quite negative, and was disputed by many at State and in the CIA. That is one of the great weaknesses in any government, the bureacracy can work behind the scenes against the leaders wishes.

By early 1989 Iraqi oil production was increasing as French and Russian companies were finding additional supplies. Infused with extra cash Iraq courted and convinced the French to build a huge aerospace venture in Iraq. It was worth over $6 billion to France. Weapons and tool companies across Europe went to Baghdad to showcase their wares, and only the U.S. stayed away from the arms bazaar. The western media ignored this event, and most missed the significance. Saddam intended to build his own strategic weapons, and join the second rank of powers. *And this would include ballistic missiles that the French helped design.* (Unlike Reagan, Pres. Bush allowed some U.S. companies to do business in Iraq.)

To the south the Saudi's were maneuvering too. Reports had been coming in during late 1988 that the Saudi's were bringing in Chinese medium range missiles. Photo-recon was conducted and sure enough a large base had been secretly constructed in the middle of their desert. *Captured in the images were Chinese support troops and the new missiles being setup.* It appeared that the Saudi's were conducting their own missile crisis as those weapons would reach Israel.

(All eyes had been focused elsewhere and no one had picked this up on this strategic problem. The only lead was a signal from a test launch. The CIA had failed in their primary mission.) Sec. State Schultz quietly asked the Saudi's not to continue with their work. They reluctantly agreed, because now that the cat was out of the bag it was a sure bet Israeli jets would be arriving.

Throughout the CIA's turbulent history they had been unsuccessful on many strategic issues. They did not pick up on the North Korean attack into S. Korea, they did not believe the Chinese would join in the Korean War, they did not warn of France's imminent defeat in Vietnam in 1954, or of the actions of Nasser in 1956 which led to the battle over the Suez Canal. They had no one operating inside Russia to keep tabs and they secretly produced Sputnik in 1957. Then came Cuba's fall, Castro being a Communist was missed, as was the following Missile Crisis in Cuba. There had been no insight into N. Vietnam's war plans, capabilities or operations. Those Communists fought hard and well, and their TET offensive was another complete surprise to our leaders. (But not to the recon troops in the field.)

The CIA did warn of the 1972 and 1975 invasions by N. Vietnam, but were caught short with the 1967 and 1973 Mid-East wars. After Carter gutted the agency there was little intelligence warning about the growing movement of Islamic Fundamentalists or revolutionary Iran. Russia's invasion of Afghanistan was also missed until just before it came off, and the near first strike nuclear attack by the Soviets in 1983 was also missed.

As a result of those types of intelligence failures, the U.S. government was constantly reacting to the changing and many times dangerous strategic issues, instead of working to prevent

them. In many cases our reactive, last ditch actions were wrong. It takes a long time to work people into dangerous areas to gather intelligence. The Europeans and Israel are adept at those types of missions because they always had to be.

History clearly shows how the Europeans warred routinely. For them *There Were Tigers All Around,* and it made them proactive. Back in the day when the "Sun Never set on the British Empire", their Foreign Service was instrumental in "nipping problems in the bud". However America was always safe behind her ocean moats. There was never a need for well directed diplomacy, intelligence, subterfuge or duplicity.

As a result of that lack of worldly experience, America would fail at most of its foreign policy attempts. *And once America tried to lead there was the constant nuclear threat from the Soviets. The Cold War had a major affect on all of our policy actions and thinking, it was always them or us.*

But in the world of 1988-89 it seemed that things were finally quieting down along the superpower front. Inside the CIA and NSC, concerns were growing over what would happen in Afghanistan. Most felt the Najibullah regime would collapse or try to make deals with the local warlords to stay in power. **If he fell, the CIA expected an Islamic Fundamentalist regime would take over.** They did not think it would be pro-West or U.S. despite all of our years of help. And no one knew what to do about a second Islamic Extremist movement controlling a nation.

In the Soviet Union their economic problems were getting worse. Years of central control had caused their currency to become almost worthless. The only useful products they had for sale were their reserves of oil and natural gas, and weapons. But with the lower demand for oils, drastic reductions in prices had occurred and they were not earning what they needed to stay afloat. Gorbachev had publicly announced his massive cutback in Soviet troop levels stationed in Eastern Europe, not to lower tensions, but because they could not afford to keep them. (This is a problem the U.S. and the West has also faced.)

Over 500,000 troops and their equipment were being recalled and deactivated. Fallout from that announcement began quickly as all of the countries that had languished behind the Iron-Curtain (and Soviet tanks) for so long saw a chance for freedom.

And in keeping with his cost savings measures Gorbachev officially announced the end of Soviet combat in and the occupation of Afghanistan. The Afghan war was not popular in

Russia, just like Vietnam was unpopular in America. Russian losses were believed to be well over 25,000, but that information was closely guarded in Moscow. And returning soldiers were prohibited from speaking about their tours in the war torn land as the gulags were always open for business.

During the years of 1985-89, the U.S. under Pres. Reagan and then Bush had supplied over $3 Billion in arms and aid to help the Afghans. This relatively small financial price had been justified by tying up and bleeding the Soviet Forces. Diplomats had met many times in Geneva to work out an Afghan peace treaty, and their Geneva Agreement called for a rapid Soviet withdrawal. But the constant attacks by rebels forced the Soviet forces to use the slow and steady pullout that we had had to endure in Vietnam.

The rebels were encouraged not to slaughter the retreating Soviets as they had done to the British a century earlier. And as the Soviet pullout started a Soviet SU-25 was shot down almost intact. The CIA negotiated with the ISI to purchase the jet, and days later the pilot too! *Luckily for him we turned him over to the Soviet embassy, instead of the ISI handing him off to the Afghan women.*

During February 1989 the last of the Soviet troops exited Afghanistan. Their puppet regime led by Mohammed Najibullah would remain in power, but even the Politburo knew his time was limited. Afghanistan was never a true country, it was a collection of tribal areas that no one was able to unite and rule.

Andrei Sakharov the former imprisoned dissident scientist spoke to the Soviet Congress of People's Deputies and purposefully told them; "The War in Afghanistan was a criminal adventure killing over a million Afghans. It was a blatant attempt to destroy an entire people, and was a terrible sin that lies upon us." *(104) His speech and attitude was direct and truthful, something not seen in Russia since 1919.

Not long after a major attack occurred in Pakistan. A massive explosion happened at the major supply base used by the Pakistani's and CIA to equip the Mujahedeen. The large amount of arms and supplies at the base burned and detonated for hours. Was it retaliation or a last ditch effort to help Najibullah?

With Gen. Zia gone most of the Pakistani leaders had changed too. Pakistan elected Benazir Bhutto as Prime Minister, (with help from the army), their first democratically elected leader in more than a decade. America supported her and she reciprocated. Being a women trying to govern a Muslim nation she had many detractors. That included some of the senior army officers who had sent her father to the gallows a decade ago. She correctly distrusted the ISI and their chief Mamid Gul. U.S. Ambassador Robert Oakley warned all of his staff to tread lightly and shore up Bhutto as best we could.

Her first foreign policy problem occurred in March 1989. The ISI attempted to take Jalalabad, Afghanistan and install their own "rebel leader" as a first step to taking over the country. Gul's promise of a quick victory turned into a bloodbath killing thousands of Afghans. Complaints flooded through our embassy and the CIA over our part in it, which was untrue. We had worked with the ISI the past years, but not there. Administration principals were unable to agree on how or what to do. To aid Najibullah the Soviets flew in tons of additional weapons, ammunition and food.

China

President Bush went to China during February 1989 and met privately with the Chinese leader Deng Xiaoping. Deng had become a Communist in France during the 1920s, as did so many others, (Ho Chi Minh, Kim il sung). He was another survivor of the long March through China in 1933, and rose through the ranks becoming a vice-chairmen. He was purged during the insanity of the Cultural Revolution, and Zhou en-Lai reinstated him in 1973. With the deaths of Mao and Zhou, power grabs disrupted the Chinese government until Deng took over in 1978. It was he who pushed for reforms and modernization. Deng also instituted the one-child policy to try to control their exploding population, and stressed individual responsibility to enable them to advance.

The earlier economic reforms he had enacted were not only improving China's economy, but as shown earlier pro-democracy movements had begun appearing back in 1986. To encourage this political reform Pres. Reagan had continued loosening our trade policies with China. Now that he was President, George Bush stayed with our rapprochement with this visit.

China was basking in their newfound economic opportunities, and their young students were naturally the most vocal in wanting matching political reforms. But Deng had not approved those, only economic reforms. Many of the Chinese hard-liners and old guard Communists were still upset at what he had done thus far by straying from "pure Maoist-socialism".

Because of their previous meetings Deng and Bush had a good working relationship. They had first met in 1975 when Deng was sitting two seats from Mao, (quite a comeback from prison), and again in the Reagan years as Vice President. During the 1981 visit Deng gave a luncheon for the Americans and they discussed the growing problem of Vietnam. (This was after China had been beaten by them.) Bush said to Deng that America had tried to alert everyone in the 1950s and all through the second Vietnam war what the communists under Ho Chi Minh were like. Deng was unhappy with the slight, and replied that had China and America not been estranged things would have been far different there.

(And had Truman not lost China things most certainly would have been different, there would have been no Communists in China, Vietnam or N. Korea!)

As world diplomacy dictates, our previous history at arms was ignored to continue moving ahead. During this present meeting Deng gave another (semi-slanted) history lesson as a way of highlighting China's strategic concerns.

"For 150 years China had to endure the terrible burden of the European colonials as they set about trying to invade and control our land. Then we (the Communists) fought for control of our country for over twenty years as the West backed Chiang. China also had to endure many territorial issues with Czarist Russia, and then the Communist controlled Soviet Union. In 1931 the Japanese invaded and we fought them for over a decade losing millions more. The destruction they wrought was incalculable, and *then came Yalta.*

At that conference you Americans (FDR) conspired with the Soviets to steal our territory, as Chiang was not even invited to the meetings. (That was true. *Fatal Flaws Book 1,* FDR sold out the world to Stalin and his Communist empire.)

As a result of that secret deal Russia gained over 3 million square kilometers of Outer Mongolia, and would have kept Manchuria had we, (the Chinese communists) not won the war with Chiang and returned to that land.

(Deng again conveniently ignored the fact that they were supplied by the Russians, and had Chiang and the Nationalists won they would have returned to Manchuria. Ironically Manchuria was where the Nationalists lost a major battle to the Communists who had been greatly aided by Stalin's support, and Truman's numerous mistakes. See *Fatal Flaws Book 2.*)

After we took over in 1949 Stalin helped us economically, but Khrushchev did not. We have been divided from Russia since. In 1963 wefought them twice, and are faced with new Soviet backed enemies all around us in India, Vietnam, Afghanistan and N. Korea. Presently our economic revival is being challenged from within (hard-liners), and is having a hard time. Many of our young want immediate political reform, but that is not possible "as chaos will result" and the economic reforms will be disrupted.

That was a quiet warning to Pres. Bush not to get too aggressive in seeking social and political freedom for China. *Deng also mentioned that China was looking to recover all of the territories that they formally had, Hong Kong, Macao, Taiwan and the Diaoyutai Islands from Japan.*

This was a warning that China was not forgetting or forgiving anything. Deng hoped Gorbachev would succeed in reigning in the Soviet hardliners so progress could come to their land, and he considered Bush a friend. Our countries had worked together to drive the Soviets out of Afghanistan, and he wanted America to continue to work with China as the world was being transformed. The president cooperated and reiterated that America and China should be friendly towards each other. Deng retired later that year.

The FBI

In a secret ceremony held at the FBI headquarters director William Sessions awarded the Presidential Medal of Freedom to 84 year old Morris Childs. (This great honor was actually kept secret until 1996, after Childs had died, along with the Soviet Union.) The reason for this secrecy was that Morris Childs was an executive in the CPUSA, Communist Party USA. He also worked for the FBI.

During the late 1950s Childs had successfully infiltrated into the higher councils of the Soviet Union during his twenty plus years undercover. One of his major intelligence coups was reporting that the Soviets had not been directly involved in JFK's murder. Despite all of the traitors and spies that had betrayed us, Childs was never discovered. Only a few at the FBI knew his true identity, and all references to him hinted that a bug had been planted in the Kremlin.

Sadly this was a last hurrah for the FBI's intelligence unit. Years of liberal Congressional oversights and multiple laws restricting their parameters had shut down their clandestine abilities. And the next enemy was at our gates, Islamic Extremists. As shown before Pres. Reagan tried to resurrect the FBI's intelligence gathering by making anti-terrorism a priority. But opposition by the Democrats continued to undercut their abilities.

.

1989, The Year Everything Changed

Vice President Bush had visited Poland in 1987 and his appearance legitimized and invigorated the struggling reform movement. After meeting with General Wojciech Jaruzelski, *Bush met with the leaders of Solidarity inside the U.S. Embassy.* He promised them every support we could give. Now as President he was asked to return to Poland.

During the spring of 1989 Poland was taking a courageous lead in making reforms and trying to escape Moscow's grip. Hungary was not far behind, and in early May they began dismantling the border fences with Austria.

On June 4, 1989 Poland held elections for their National Assembly. At that time 65% of the seats were reserved for the Communist candidates, but Solidarity won all of them! In their Senate, Solidarity candidates took 99 out of 100 seats. This was a dangerous event as their people were ending Communist control of their government. This new Assembly would vote for their next president on July 6, three days before Pres. Bush was to visit. *Some wondered if Poland would still be there.*

Czechoslovakia was also experiencing a reawakening as they canonized their patron religious figure Saint Agnes. Protests began springing up and the Communists moved quickly to stop them using water canons and tear gas. Again the Soviets stayed out of the issue.

Gorbachev even visited the Pope in Rome to counsel patience. But the die was cast as Soviet control in Eastern Europe was collapsing. *Gorbachev was allowing Communism in E. Europe to fall so he could try to save it in the Soviet Union. It was a fatal miscalculation.*

Then China returned to the front page.

Hu Yaobang was another reformer and the expected successor to Deng. But in the early spring Hu was ousted by the Chinese hard-liners. He suddenly "died" on April 15, 1989, and was replaced by "moderate" Zhao Ziyang. Student protestors mourned Hu's unexpected death and marched to Tiananmen Square in Beijing, a central and important intersection in the capitol. Close by were the Great Hall, the Forbidden City and the residences of China's most senior officials. Student leaders presented a list of demands to their rulers desiring more freedoms, less corruption and general improvements. Local police attempted to breakup the demonstrations with the usual beatings and arrests, and Deng publicly condemned them.

On May 4, the anniversary of China's original democratic protests (in 1919), a much larger protest formed up. Tens of thousands filled the square. Zhao gave a conciliatory speech which seemed to calm the protestors and many left. But news crews from the Western media started arriving to cover the upcoming state visit by Russia's Gorbachev. They learned of the student protests, though none were expecting what would soon happen.

Gorbachev's much anticipated visit was the first by a Russian leader since 1959, when Khrushchev tried to end their antagonism. Khrushchev's trip failed, and afterwards the Soviets even considered a nuclear strike to reign in the defiant and increasingly dangerous Chinese. *Over the years the Russians had placed a third of their conventional and nuclear forces on the common border expecting a war.* (There were numerous border battles.)

With the increasing presence of western news coverage students returned to the area with some beginning a hunger strike. Others converged into Tiananmen Square to show solidarity with Gorbachev and his democratic reforms. Their masses became so great they prevented the visiting dignitaries from being able to enter the Great Hall. *Deng and the Chinese Politburo saw the crowds and demonstrations as an insult and a threatening presence to their rule.* (Just what Deng had warned about back in February.)

After Gorbachev left for Shanghai the Chinese hard-liners dug in their heels and sent in some troops and vehicles to evict the protesting students and workers. Zhao wanted the party to meet some of the student demands, while the now angry Deng and the always harsh hard-liners refused any such action.

Premier Li Peng argued with the student demonstrators in a televised meeting. The next day Li announced martial law as larger numbers of troops arrived. In reaction to that move thousands of residents blocked access to the square and the protests grew and became more vocal.

The initial assignment of (Peoples Liberation Army) PLA troops were from the local area and they refused to take harsh actions even after a replica of the Statue of Liberty was erected in the square. They were soon replaced with mechanized troops from outside the province. Events began to calm down in late May, but then the crowds again returned.

On June 2, 1989 the shooting finally began and hundreds were killed in the one-sided fighting. (Many more would die behind closed doors.) After two days of conflict the square was cleared. Only the famous incident with a civilian challenging the tanks remained to be seen by the world media. **Soon after all liberal-minded writers, editors and teachers were fired from their positions and replaced with old school Communists.**

China's version of the gulag filled quickly as thousands more were arrested. (More than twenty five years have gone by, and hundreds of those protestors are still in prison!)

Throughout those two months of turmoil the protestors had stayed informed from the television coverage, radio programs, from the *Voice of America,* and by using walki-talkies. One of the quiet fallouts from that student rebellion was a rule requiring all students to spend one year on a collective farm or an industrial plant to see what hard work really is.

Soviet news programs covered the turmoil, but made no public statements on the state's response. People behind the Iron Curtain saw that even in China their citizens wanted freedom.

Americans were taken aback at the violence, and our news coverage was negative. The Bush Administration carefully said little in public. China was slowly modernizing and Bush did not want a return to the prior hostilities. A secret delegation was sent over to try to smooth things out, but made no progress. As always China was extremely sensitive to any negative press or talk. They denied anyone had died at Tiananmen Square, and refused to discuss the matter after those initial meetings.

On June 24 moderate Zhao was removed as General Secretary and replaced with hard-liner Jiang Zemin. China's political attitude hardened as the months went by. They could see the weakening of Communism in the Soviet Union and Eastern Europe. China's Communist rulers were not going to give freedom any chance to stripping their power.

But calls and demands for freedom were not just in Beijing. Tibet was also growing restless as their thirty-eight year imprisonment by China was boiling over. As shown in *Fatal Flaws Book 2*, Tibet had been savagely invaded by China in 1950. Since that time well over a million Tibetans had died under Communist Chinese rule. It was estimated that half a million more had been forced out of the country.

As of 1989 the remaining population was only around two million souls. Despite the Communist efforts, Tibetans were still proclaiming their loyalty to the exiled Dali Lama. During the past two years increasing protests and riots had broken out and hundreds more had been killed in the latest violence with China. Their story was barely covered by the mainstream media, and again the Administration wrongly decided not to pursue the issue.

Gorbachev returned to Moscow from his China visit and decided to expose the failures of their Communist party in an attempt to get his reforms enacted. If he could get rid of the last of the old guard, the newer members like him could take over. (Back in June 1988 he blamed the country's ills on the corruption of the old guard.)

From May 25-June 9, 1989 the first Congress of the People's Deputies met in Moscow and Gorbachev insisted the proceedings be televised so the people could see their progress. Behind the Iron Curtain the people were spellbound as complaints were being aired towards the KGB, Gorbachev and the Communist Party. In July Siberian coal miners went on strike demanding better pay and working conditions. *And no one was shot.*

Gorbachev did not realize it, but he had opened Pandora's Box. Without fear, these people were going to revolt.

It was quickly seen that his attempts at reform had all failed. His anti-alcohol program cost the Soviets tax money as stills and bootleggers filled the gap. Despite their efforts, they were unable to modernize their industries to increase production or quality. And Russia lagged far behind in computer science. His efforts to modernize actually caused even more disruptions in their economy. Life in the USSR was getting worse, if that was possible.

To gain some good relations and capitol, Gorbachev was parading through Europe promising an end to hostilities. He wanted to create his version of a "common European home", and the excited Europeans were clamoring for an end to NATO and all nuclear weapons.

Dangerously and surprisingly, Gorbachev also announced the end of the Brezhnev Doctrine which gave the Soviets the right to promote Marxism, and the right to invade any ally who strayed from it. (Germany 1953, Czechoslovakia 1968, Afghanistan 1979)

He also hinted that he would not intervene in the ongoing political reforms in Poland and Hungary. However the neighboring communist states were strongly criticizing those reforms for all were afraid. Who could say what was going to happen next.

In short order political challenges sprang up in the Baltic States of Estonia, Latvia and Lithuania. All three countries had won their freedom from Czarist Russia in 1919, but were then stolen by Stalin in 1939 with his pact with Hitler. *The WWII allies never agreed to that theft, but FDR never addressed that situation or the Russian invasions of Poland and Finland either.*

After the war ended Stalin insisted on keeping control of the Baltic nations and vast sections of Finland and Poland. But in 1989 stirrings of freedom began anew. In a moving symbol of courage, Millions of those oppressed people lined their roads holding hands as a sign of their Solidarity and determination for freedom.

Estonia was the first in declaring their sovereignty, followed by Lithuania. Nationalists began fomenting hostile dissent. In Moscow the Central Committee denounced those moves and warned that the Baltic states were not to be accorded the same freedoms as Eastern Europe. Gorbachev warned them of dire consequences if they pushed for outright secession.

The Bush team was in a vice. Western conservatives had never accepted the previous failures at the end of WWII, but had been pushed into it because of FDR and his "agreements at Tehran and Yalta". And Truman refused to back-track from any of FDR's agreements. Now those conservatives saw a chance to right a lot of wrongs, and they pushed for action. But Bush and Thatcher knew that the West had to move slowly as Gorbachev was walking a tightrope with his reforms. Those Communist officials and bureaucrats saw him as an enemy, and in Russia that could be fatal.

Even with those increasing political tensions in Eastern Europe Pres. Bush was still going on his scheduled trip during the month of July. Poland was (as usual for a Communist nation), an economic failure. They had large deficits, mounting inflation, sinking productivity and poor public morale. The Poles asked for $10 Billion in U.S. aid, a sum not possible in the deficit running U.S. government. If an aid package was to be offered it would have to involve the Western Europeans too.

On July 10, 1989 Pres. Bush landed in Warsaw, Poland, the second visit by a U.S. president. *(Pres. Nixon's trip there in 1972 had been met with huge adoring crowds which irritated the Soviet leaders.)* Poland was still part of the Warsaw Pact, and those visits were a risk if some communist decided to attack.

When VP Bush spoke with Gen. Jaruzelski back in 1987 he could see the Polish leader was in turmoil between his love of country and his fear of the Soviets. Now in 1989 the general was in a more open mood, and their conversations were more relaxed. But Jaruzelski was reluctant to run in the upcoming Polish election out of fear of losing. (As had every other communist leader once the people had a vote.) Pres. Bush explained that at this juncture he needed to run to ensure the political transition would be smooth. A coalition government could work, but it must move slowly and be non-threatening. Having him run would be "part of the process".

In a toast those leaders agreed that though Poland was still divided, the Poles themselves would see it all worked out. It had been decided by the State Dept. to give just one speech in Poland and one in Hungary so as to not overly incite the people.

Pres. Bushspoke to the assembled crowd that Poland was where the Cold War had begun, and it is also where the Polish people could end the division of Europe. It was Poland's time of destiny, and America would stand with them as they rediscovered a new land of their own making. *(105) The crowds cheered loudly.

On June 16, 250,000 Hungarians attended the reburial of Imre` Nagy, their Prime Minister who was executed / murdered in the 1956 Hungarian uprising. Those people were also growing restless for freedom. The Bush team landed in Hungary on July 11, deep behind the Iron Curtain. George Bush had been the first U.S. Vice-president to visit Hungary, and he would become the first U.S. president to do so. While giving his speech in Budapest a sudden rainstorm drenched all. In a show of great politeness the president gave his coat to an elderly Hungarian woman. That simple act and his small upbeat speech electrified the large crowd.

Pres. Bush moved into the mass of people shaking their hands and greeting them not as communists or enemies, but as people. He was overwhelmed at their support and empathy. Though there was no Solidarity movement or political party to directly challenge the Communists in Hungary, everyone could feel that radical political change was coming.

Even though the war with Iraq had ended Iran's economy was still in shambles and their army was shredded. They were no longer the military threat they had been.

In June 1989 the Ayatollah Khomeini died and was replaced by "moderate cleric" Hashemi Rafsanjani. Iran desperately needed foreign capitol to restart the nation, but few wanted anything to do with them. And billions of Iranian funds were still frozen in the U.S. from the embassy attack. (Why weren't they confiscated??)

Attacks against commercial shipping in the Gulf had ended and the U.S. Navy stopped their escort duties. Bahrain had become a small base area for our navy, and with the Soviets out of Afghanistan the vital Gulf region seemed to be stabilized.

Sadly fighting still raged in Lebanon, Afghanistan, Sudan, Ethiopia, Angola, Mozambique and Sri Lanka. In Lebanon and the Sudan the wars were religious in nature, Islamic versus Christian minorities. In Ethiopia, Angola and Mozambique the wars were Marxists versus western backed, and in Sri Lanka it was ethnic and political.

Afghanistan was still at war. Hekmatyar's forces helped by the ISI ambushed a Massoud unit killing over two dozen of his most senior officers on July 9, 1989. Attempts had been made to broker a peace between the rival factions, but the Arab support of Hekmatyar was too invested in his rule. Through him the Fundamentalists saw an Islamic state and empire, and those views were becoming more and more extreme.

Radicals like Ayman al-Zawahiri wanted all of the pro-western rulers such as Egypt's Mubarak, Pakistan's Bhutto and the King of Jordan put down. (Some of them also included Saddam Hussein and Assad in Syria as they had strayed from true Islam.)

Cleric Abdullah Azzam was still influential in Peshawar, and his spirituality stressed patience to gradually build an Islamic state one convert at a time. He continued to resist the radicals desires to strike out all over the region as Afghanistan needed help to rebuild. His compassion was not welcomed.

And Gorbachev's words did not match with Soviet ambitions. Though they had pulled out of Afghanistan they were still aiding the Communist regime they left behind, and were still active in Angola and Namibia.

In addition the Soviets had just sent a shipment of MIG-29 jets to Cuba. Those types of aircraft were banned under the 1962 agreement because they were nuclear capable. The Soviets shipped them anyway. (To test Bush??)

Despite that superpower duel a Central American peace plan was signed by the leaders of all of those nations. As before they hoped that with their efforts the fighting would finally end and all of the disputed borders be respected.

During November 1989 communist rebels tried one more attack in El Salvador hoping to spark a national uprising. It failed and the Salvadoran army responded harshly.

(A Nicaraguan supply plane had crashed in El Salvador. It was carrying Soviet ground-air missiles and other crew served

weapons for the Communist rebels. Again highlighting that this was not just a civil or regional war.)

As shown earlier, Nicaragua's internal fighting ended in mid-1988 and the Sandinistas agreed to hold free elections. Ortega and all of leftist America was confident of his Communist victory at the polls. Our media was now so far to the left, their polls showed Ortega would win handily, and that the Reagan and Bush administrations were wrong for ever doubting that the Sandinistas were Nicaragua's future.

But in their February 1990 election Ortega was crushed by Violetta Chamorro 55-41%! Her triumph spelled the end of Communism in Nicaragua, and this pattern was occurring all over the World!

With democracy taking over Nicaragua, the astonished liberals folded up their tents and sulked away. Media coverage ended, and they lost all interest in the region. Once again dozens of senior Democrats were proven wrong, and that list included John Kerry, Charles Schumer, Jimmy Carter and Chris Dodd.

(Jimmy Carter had insinuated himself into the election process. He was completely confident that *with his help, his friend Ortega* would win handily and the "obstructionist Reagan-Bush mindset" would fail hard. As usual with Carter, an election nightmare unfolded and Ortega was voted out.)

Back in Poland, General Jaruzelski who had been the leader in the crackdown in 1980 was pushing for and approved private enterprise for small businesses. Jaruzelski's government was willing to share Parliamentary power with Solidarity the trade union turned political party, but they had underestimated the extent of political unrest. As shown before, on June 4, 1989 Poland held elections as promised, and the Communists had been routed. (The same day the Chinese crushed the demonstrators at Tiananmen Square.)

The people of Poland had spoken out for freedom and they were going to end communist rule in that country. *The Polish Communists restored to the Catholic Church all of the property that had been seized by the party decades before.* They also allowed Catholic schools to reopen.

On August 16, 1989 Lech Walesa announced that he would form a new cabinet under his direction. Polish Communists refused to participate in that new government, but Gorbachev phoned party leader Rakowski and convinced him to join in. It was better to be inside working against them, than be outside doing nothing.

The world anxiously waited for the Soviet Bear to react and strike, but nothing happened. To alleviate Soviet strategic concerns Walesa stated that Poland would remain in the Warsaw Pact. *This non-action from the Soviets was a clear signal to the rest of Eastern Europe that their freedom was at hand.*

Back in November 1988 Hungary had announced a plan to legalize non-communist political parties. Ruled by Janos Ka`dar since the 1956 uprising, Hungary was the most liberalized of the nations in Eastern Europe. (Ka`dar had turned on Nagy resulting in his execution, then he changed speeds and allowed reforms to come in at his direction.)

Throughout 1989 the Hungarians worked to reform their constitution. Premier Miklos Nemeth was the driving force. On September 18, 1989 they agreed on a multi-party system for a parliamentary democracy. On October 7 the Hungarian Communist party voted to dissolve itself and became the Socialist party. Few rejoined that veiled effort, and their march to change quickly turned into a race.

Hungary would renounce Communism, the second country in just seven weeks! The people welcomed their freedom, and then opened their borders with Austria. Ka`dar was forced from office in late 1989 and later died in oblivion. (And as shown before Nagy was reburied in a formal ceremony as a hero of Hungarian freedom.)

In an impressive show of confidence and of thanks, Poland and Hungary asked that America's Peace Corps send volunteers to help them rebuild their economies.

By the late summer of 1989 East Germany also began having demonstrations. E. Germany had been turned into a solid Communist entity by Stalinesque clone Erich Honecker. Throughout his reign he refused to enact any type of reforms, and thousands of people went to prisons and were killed trying to protest or escape. But with the missing fences on the Austria/Hungarian border thousands of East Germans who had been imprisoned behind the Berlin Wall "voted with their feet" and began a growing exodus into Hungary. From there those refugees could escape across the open border into Western Europe or show up at Embassies requesting asylum. Hungary ignored this exodus in the name of freedom. However E. Germany accused Hungary of fomenting unrest.

In just one day 10,000 E. Germans crossed into Austria!

Honecker decided to allow those initial "traitors" to leave, (as Castro had in 1980), but each day more and more citizens exited. Facing the same crisis as they had in 1961, on October 3, 1989 the E. Germans tried to close their borders by using troops. This time Honecker did not use violence, though veiled threats were made.

As the unrest spread massive demonstrations began. Not since 1953 had that happened. Back then Soviet troops crushed their rebellion. Gorbachev was visiting on October 6, and all of this turmoil proved quite embarrassing for him. He was met with large demonstrations as he presided over the fall of their empire.

Gorbachev told Honecker there would be no Soviet troops this time. Fearing their collapse Honecker ordered the use of force in Leipzig to breakup a demonstration of 70,000. Local leaders refused to comply. A week later another demonstration began, this time 150,000 took part. Again there was no use of force.

On October 18 the regime of Eric Honecker fell.

He and his colleagues were arrested and a replacement regime installed. Still the protests continued, reaching 500,000 at one rally on October 31. In the West the leaders of the free world grew anxious. W. Germany's Helmut Kohl was convinced escaping Communist refugees would cause a crisis in Europe. He feared the total collapse of the GDR, as everyone felt that would surely result in a Soviet military response.

On November 7 the entire government in the GDR resigned. Not until November 10 was a new government formed. By then the country was in open revolution. E. Germans approached the Berlin Wall without fear of death. And large crowds of West Berliners went to their side of the despised Berlin Wall and began attacking it. News crews filmed the events.

On November 10 the E. German border guards gave in to the masses and opened the gates. Western news crews rushed to cover the momentous event as West Berliners joined those from the east in crowds of jubilation. Their freedom was at hand.

Just two years before President Reagan had asked Gorbachev to tear down that unbreakable barrier. It had been the worldwide icon of communist tyranny for almost three decades. No one could approach this barrier to freedom and live. **Yet with no warning it was being torn down right before our eyes.**

Free to "travel", the East Germans happily crossed into the West. For many their decades of imprisonment stayed in their minds, and the majority returned "home" for the workweek. But as the weeks went by more and more E. Germans were seeing and realizing the vast disparities between their worlds. Over 350,000 decided to remain in the West.

In Washington the mood was somber, as no one knew if Soviet tanks would appear. Pres. Bush gave a muted talk on the fall of the Wall, but was careful not to gloat. And he made sure everyone in his Administration understood that vital point.

There was still much work to be done to secure this peace.

Predictably the amateurish press and Democrats wanted Bush to crow and dance over this event, but he remained low key. None realized that Gorbachev was in danger. The Soviet Politburo was warning that any attempt at German reunification meant war. The statesman that he was, George Bush wrote and called Gorbachev pledging cooperation and restraint.

(It is tragically ironic that those same liberal groups had all fiercely fought and ridiculed every anti-Communist initiative and action that Presidents Reagan and Bush had made in the past decade. Yet it was those very actions and policies that were causing the Berlin Wall to fall.)

The interim E. German government promised free elections in 1990. Their brutal and effective secret police (the Stasi) was disbanded, and all political prisoners were released. When George Bush had been the director of the CIA, *the Stasi were among the worst offenders for training terrorists and in destabilizing weak governments.*

Their spies were among the most ruthless and aggressive, and were used by the Soviets to do the dirty work. So invasive were the E. German secret police that they had multiple thousands of glass jars containing fabric scraps of citizens under watch. With those fabrics and scents tracking dogs could hunt for any who tried to defect. They even built false building fronts similar to Hollywood movie sets to give the appearance that the buildings facing W. Berlin were as prosperous as the West's. Nothing was overlooked to maintain the Communist lies, and their control over the country.

Historical Note: Because of Adolph Hitler and the Nazi's, Germany had been a pariah at the end of WWII. Hitler had fought the war not just to control Europe but to control the entire world. Had it not been for a few vital mistakes, (see *Fatal Flaws Book 1*), he may well have succeeded. Hitler also fought the war to win a racial and genocidal victory as all undesirables were to be eliminated. He would rid the world of Jews, Poles, Slavs and any other race he felt to be subhuman.

Upon their defeat the first thing the Allies did was to abolish Prussia, the state that had produced such a warlike country. Germany itself was dismembered and ruled by the allied nations. Stalin refused to acknowledge France as an ally, and he denied them a place in Germany. (The U.S. and Britain split a section off from their sectors and gave it to France.)

By the end of 1945 Germany's military, economy and country were all destroyed. *Armed allied troops and tanks were everywhere, and the only things Germany had to look forward to was infinite subjugation and punishment.*

Yet despite those post-war trials their people and what would become the nation of West Germany shouldered the mostly benign years of Western allied occupation under the leadership of Conrad Adenauer. (The section ruled by the Soviets was brutalized.)

W. Germany slowly regained their sovereignty and rejoined the community of nations. They became the linchpin of the allied anti-Communist containment effort in Europe, as was showcased by the Berlin blockades. Their economy improved and then blossomed as they became a world economic power. All the while their western benefactors had refused to give in to the aggressive Soviet demands to sign a peace treaty that required permanent separation of the German nation.

Despite the risk of war with Communist Russia and the Eastern bloc states, reunification of Germany would only occur when the West approved it.

Weeks after the Berlin Wall came down W. Germany's Hemut Kohl was exuberant. The world was fundamentally changing, and he wrote of the influx of educated citizens flooding their shore. Their smiling faces were suddenly free from fear and suspicions, and there had not been any hostile reaction from the Soviet Union.

He warmly told President Bush; **"Without the United States and your incredible support, without your nation standing firm and protecting the free world these past decades, this day would not have been possible."** *(106)

(Ask yourself dear reader, has any nation, ant empire, any group of nations ever done and risked so much for others throughout the timelines of History?)

Bulgaria had been the Soviets most obedient ally for almost forty five years. Their land had not been invaded by Soviet troops in WWII, and they always had close cultural ties. Todor Zhivkov had been Bulgaria's president and party chairman since 1954. There were no opposition groups or dissidents of any type, so

Zhivkov never expected any of the nearby protests to reach him. His main detractor was Foreign Minister Petar Mladenov a post-war Communist who felt it was time for a change.

October 1989 saw a large pro-democracy march in Sofia, and Zhivkov's instant reaction was to use force. Mladenov then accused Zhivkov of ruining their economy, and that he had forced the deportation of thousands of ethnic Turks. As the other East Block nations began to crack apart, Zhivkov's enemies decided to act. Their military joined in with Mladenov as he secured Moscow's blessing.

On November 10, 1989, (the day the Berlin Wall came down) the Bulgarian politburo met and deposed Zhivkov. Mladenov attempted to repeal the anti-everything laws against the Turks and Muslims in general, but was surprised when violent protests spring up. No one among the ethnic Bulgarians wanted the Turks or other Muslims around. The Bulgarians had attained political change in the hopes of having democracy, and they did not want the Muslims to be part of their nation. Being neighbors to that other world the Bulgarians were giving a sign of what would soon come to our world.

Islamic populations do not meld with the indigenous populations or other religions. They want to supplant them.

Czechoslovakia underwent their "revolution". They had tried this before in 1968 but had been brutally repressed. Their citizens were cautious and unauthorized protests were quickly broken up.

Back in January 1989 protest leader Vaclav Havel was arrested and imprisoned. He had became a beacon and a symbol. Months later their citizen protests slowly grew in size. After weeks of watching the GDR fall apart, and of watching thousands upon thousands of E. Germans escaping with no reprisal, the Czechs knew the end was in sight.

Alexander Dubcek their imprisoned leader from 1968 appeared on Soviet television in an interview on November 3, 1989. His words further inflamed the dissidents, and then the GDR opened the gates to their common border.

On November 24, 1989 after a week of demonstrations by hundreds of thousands of people, the Czech Communist Party, run by hard-liner Milos Jakes, was forced to accept the "resignation" of Jakes. Pres. Gustav Husak who had ruled with an iron-hand since the 1968 uprising was the next one ousted as were all of his followers. Over forty years had passed since the Czechs had had a non-Communist government.

Friday November 24 Alexander Dubcek, their leader for change back in 1968, reappeared with Victor Havel. *Forced into a solitary exile for twenty one years, Dubcek returned as a gaunt 67 year old to a hero's welcome in Prague's Wenceslas Square.* Weakened by his imprisonment, Dubcek still wore the same sly smile he had in 1968. Though much of his life had been stolen by the Communist oppressors, he must have been immeasurably happy at the finish. **And those of us who watched all of this on television were mesmerized.**

Romania was the next nation that fell under the spell of freedom, but battles had to be fought. That land had been ruled by Nicolae Ceausescu, Europe's "close cousin" to Pol Pot. Ceausescu had refused to allow any Soviet troops to remain in his country or to allow any Warsaw Pact military maneuvers inside his borders. Marching to his own drum the Romanians did not take part in the invasion of Czechoslovakia in 1968, preferring to threaten their own people.

His rule was so severe that there were no opposition entities or leaders. The *Securite*, Romaina's secret police tolerated no dissent or deviation from the Communist manifesto. This was highlighted in 1987 when hungry coal miners protested for food near the city of Brasov were killed. No one expected a repeat protest in 1989, and the Commissars were shocked when it happened.

Unhappy with Gorbachev's *perestroika*, the Romanian Communists resisted the changing tide. As late as November 17 their "secret police" stormed every demonstration with severe brutality. But this time there was no Khrushchev or Brezhnev to send in tanks. As freedom was occurring in Czechoslovakia, a brief but bloody Civil War began in Romania on December 16.

A protest in Timisoara Square over the expulsion of a pastor was crushed with extreme violence. Protestors were mowed down with tank and automatic weapons fire. Even the wounded were hunted down and murdered in the hospitals. In all several thousand Romanians were murdered by the state security forces. Ceausescu returned from a trip to Iran to deal with the crisis personally.

But the end of his rule was achieved when the army finally turned against him. *He was quickly tried for his many brutal crimes against his people and executed on Christmas Day.* His body was left lying in the snow. Despite the decades of terror and the abuse of millions of their people, Nicolae Ceausescu was surprisingly the only Communist ruler to be killed.

On December 10, 1948 the United Nations General Assembly had approved a Universal Declaration of Human Rights. This was one of the most important achievements from the failed peace of WWII, and our Congress mandated the State Department keep detailed records on human rights for every nation. Since 1974 that UN mandated issue, and the 1975 Helsinki Accords sought for and signed by Pres. Ford continued the push for worldwide human rights. *Since its passage, those Accords prevented the Communists from being able to crush their fledgling political opposition.*

After forty plus years of brutal Communist repression an incredible transformation had just occurred in most of the countries dominated by the Soviet Union. (The CIA had a big hand in making that happen by smuggling in western books, flyers, magazines, radio and television news.)

For those of us who had lived through those decades of fear, and who understood those momentous events for what they were, it appeared that we had finally achieved, **Peace in Our Time.**

(Not everyone was happy with the collapse of Marxism. Inane American liberals were beside themselves worrying that the loss of the "safety net of Communism" would result in social and economic upheavals in the freed lands. Media clips were so one sided it was scary.)

The collapse of Communism in E. Europe also had a serious affect on the Chinese. They had smugly been proud of their actions at Tiananmen Square. But now they realized that the world was changing. *They resolved to not allow any flexibility or moderation in their rule. It was far too dangerous.*

By the end of 1989 tremendous changes were also being made in the Soviet Union. Gorbachev knew they were needed, and in February 1990 he declared that the Soviet Communist Party must abandon its monopoly on power. On February 7 the Central Committee voted to make it so. The formation of the Soviet Congress of Deputies allowed dissidents to enter the political arena and hold office. That included former gulag resident Physicist Andrei Sakharov and Boris Yeltsin who had been ousted from the Central Committee the year before. Even though the communists held the majority of seats, this was a major triumph for freedom. Their governing sessions were broadcast to the public so they could watch the political process unfold.

Russia had essentially changed, and demonstrations began occurring in the open as the Communist Soviet Union, the last of the Colonial Empires began to unravel.

Historical Note: When the Bolsheviks conquered all of their adjacent areas in the early 1920s the Communists had tried to control 104 different nationalities. Most of that was done with terror and a heavy use of force. During Stalin's reign of terror he routinely deported hundreds of thousands of people from their homes to different areas of the empire in an attempt to break them. The first to suffer that fate had been the Tartars.

After WWII ended Stalin attempted to create a buffer of Communist states around Russia. Fear and force had maintained that control. But with their economic collapse imminent, Gorbachev allowed those other nations to leave the Soviet orbit, and all subsidies ended. Russia was bankrupt.

The CIA predicted in May 1990 that a dangerous situation was coming, and any major event could bring chaos. By mid-summer strikes, ethnic problems and their declining living conditions were coming to a head in Russia. The Administration grew worried.

With this failure of Marxism-Leninism now apparent, it was also apparent that it had occurred because Capitalism-Democracy had made it so. The West's overwhelming technological superiority was able to provide a rich and relatively content way of life to their citizens. Something the Communists could never do.

Also visible to even the hardest Communist was the incredible transformations within the destroyed WWII enemies of Germany and Japan. In just forty years two nations that had been devestated in the war were becoming the leading capitalist economic powers on their continents. In contrast Soviet Russia's advancements had peaked in the late 1960s, their economy peaked in the mid-70s, and they gradually became an economic basket case. Even their propagandized citizens knew it.

A deep social and emotional sadness appeared, for they realized it had all been a terrible lie. Gorbachev was aware of their many problems, but it is not clear if he knew how bad things really were until he took over. He had hoped to turn things around by the year 2000. It is doubtful if he would have had a chance to do so through their centralized economic system with its endemic corruption and bureaucracy.

Vast sections of the Soviet economy were centralized. Much of it was run by Party Leaders who turned industries and farms into fiefdoms. As a result tons of money and resources were diverted to become pet projects, wasted, stolen out of greed or misused for favors. So much was lost from the nation's production, their required quotas were consistently missed.

As stated before it was common to see thousands of acres of needed crops left rotting in the fields because no one cared enough to harvest them. Their farmers had to meet quotas too, and once they did why bother to harvest any more. You could not sell it, and they had nothing worth bartering for. And even though the Soviets had vast energy reserves their people suffered terribly from fuel shortages during the cold winter months. That too affected production, morale and economic output.

Gorbachev was looking for help from the West to reform his nation. Privately Margaret Thatcher warned that we must not make any defense cuts yet, and that we had to help Gorbachev stay in power and succeed. **All of the past weeks of relative calm were due to our quiet approach and his control of Russia.**

As shown before, in addition to leaving Afghanistan without achieving any of their strategic goals, Gorbachev was forced to cut back on their foreign aid to save money. *That decision convinced the Vietnamese it was time to leave Cambodia, and the Cubans packed up and left their proxy wars in Angola and Ethiopia.* **Without the Soviets bankrolling those wars, our world was becoming peaceful.**

Bush and Gorbachev secretly met at Malta for a few days. Their vital meetings were held onboard naval ships so no one could hear or report on them. Gorbachev lectured Pres. Bush that the world watches as America passes judgment over an issue, and then takes action on it. Yet who controls you? Pres. Bush tried to explain the checks and balances of our democracy, which was an alien notion to the communists.

Gorbachev felt that Nicaragua would fall on their own, and that the U.S. should not intercede there or in Panama. Possibly he was afraid that any unrestrained U.S. military actions would result in his ouster by an increasingly hostile Politburo who could see their own demise coming. *Pres. Bush told him not to worry, we would let world events play out on their own.*

Even in Latin America the rise for freedom came through. After sixteen years of brutal military dictatorship, free elections were being held in Chile. On December 14, 1989 Patricio Aylwin a Christian Democrat handily defeated the presidential candidate that their former ruler Gen. Pinochet had given his blessing to.

Brazil was next, for on December 17, 1989 they had their first presidential election in twenty eight years. Centrist Fernando de

Mello defeated the leftist candidate and took the reigns of power from their militarily led Congress.

Argentina and Uruguay held their second elections, while Paraguay's long time ruler was finally thrown out of office.

But even with all of that good news there was still much work to be done. Cuba was a land of sad extremes as Castro refused to allow any of Gorbachev's reforms. Their people suffered, and with the political changes in the Soviet Union, Cuba was about to suffer more economic problems. Most of their subsidies were ended.

(By 1992 there was no soap, detergents, cooking oils or any of the normal consumer goods to be found. Meats, fish and poultry were strictly rationed, as most store shelves were empty. Fuels also became scarce and power outages common.)

N. Korea was still trapped behind a comprehensive system of depravation and rigid control. Starvation was a key tool used to keep the masses in check. And your station in life was determined by ones loyalty to the Kim's. Their original ruler Kim Il Sung was still alive and very much in control of N. Korea. Most of the nation's assets were used to provide for the Kim's and their security forces. Dissent was not tolerated and millions had died.

That is the legacy of Communism everywhere. But you will not learn of those inconvenient truths from the leftist media.

More Terrorism and Violence

As the terror attacks into Israel continued, tit for tat violence ensued. It was estimated by the State Dept. that the Palestinians had taken 20,000 casualties in the past year alone. And during 1989 Palestinian extremists began assassinating anyone suspected of collaborating with the Israelis.

On Jan 8, 1989 the Medellin Drug Cartel continued their regional violence by storming a government office in Simmacota murdering twelve. They targeted any officials within sight, jurists, police and reporters.

On January 29 leftists in Honduras assassinated the head of the Honduran military and his driver.

On February 23 leftists in Argentina murdered 13 and wounded fifty-three.

February 28 unknown Islamists firebombed a Bronx newspaper for printing an article supporting Salman Rushdie and his book *The Satanic Verses*. (They claimed it was anti-Islam.)

March 3, 1989 the Medellin Cartel struck political enemies murdering one man and wounding another in Bogota.

April 3, twenty seven were murdered in Cordoba, Columbia

May 24 leftists in Bolivia murder two missionaries.

May 30 another leftist attack in Columbia used a bomb to murder four and wounded thirty-seven.

July 5 six more political rivals were murdered in another Columbian bombing.

July 6 a Palestinian from PIJ hijacked a bus near Tel-Aviv and drove it off of a cliff murdering sixteen and injuring twenty-seven.

During July 1989 **the JTTF** (Joint Terrorism Task Force) in NYC was alerted that a group of Palestinians who frequented the Al-Kifah Refugee Services Center in Brooklyn might be planning to set off bombs in Atlantic City casinos.

FBI agents began a surveillance of the center. On weekdays they followed the head cleric **Mustafa Shalabi,** and on the weekends they followed one **El-Sayeed Nosair** and his group of hostiles. Nosair's group would go out to Calverton on Long Island and practice small arms training at a shooting range. It was an open secret that the Mosques in America were sponsoring training for the volunteers who had been going to Afghanistan.

But with that war ended why was the training still going on? After a month of watching them the bombing issue was deemed closed and the surveillance stopped.

On August 29, 1989 a traffic stop in Connecticut found a suspicious vehicle near another shooting range. Found inside were six Middle Eastern men, and an arsenal of weapons and extra license plates. Further investigation showed that "the men were being trained to fight in Afghanistan", but the extra license plates belonged to **El-Sayeed Nosair.**

Wrongly this unusual discovery was not pursued. In a year Nosair would be on the front pages. Of the other men in the vehicle no formal record was kept. (Nosair's normal associates consisted of a **Mahmoud Abouhalima**, **Mohammed Salameh**, and **Bilall Alkaisi**. All names that would soon reappear.)

That same summer a biological attack was conducted in California. Nature-activists unleashed the med-fly, which destroyed millions of dollars of crops.

France's UTA Flight 772 flying from the Congo to Paris was blown up by a bomb over the Sahara on September 19, 1989. Libyan agents were again involved as they coldheartedly murdered all 170 on board protesting France's support for Chad.

A cargo of olives had been intercepted heading for the United States. Inside the unsealed cans were tiny C-4 pellets disguised as olives in shape and color! Seeing this devious plot investigators felt certain that additional shipments had slipped past.

During November Spanish Police seized the *Cedar*, a commercial cargo ship bound for Europe. **Hidden inside its cargo hold was over 1000, pounds of C-4.** This cache was inside sealed tin cans along with 258 micro-second timers. All of it had been smuggled aboard by Hezbollah in a well organized plot.

Throughout the past two months Columbia had been the scene of constant terrorist attacks (8). On November 27, 1989 Avianca Flight 203 was bombed by Pablo Escobar and the Medellin Drug cartel. His reason was to kill a political rival, but he also murdered 110 innocents.

On December 6, 1989 Bogota, Columbia was rocked by a huge truck bomb that destroyed a dozen buildings. Again the Medellin cartel was involved as they ruthlessly murdered seventy and wounded over six hundred.

Fallout from these callous acts was that the Bush Administration began to crack down on the cartels and drugs coming from South and Central America.

Mikhail Gorbachev was leaving NYC in a motorcade on December 8, 1989 when a Pepsi can was tossed at his car. A nearby policeman grabbed the thrower, but wrongly did not arrest him. The suspect was **Sayeed Nosair**, and it was not just a pepsi can he had thrown. It was a home-made grenade given to him by **Mustafa Shalabi**. The IED did not detonate, and was dismissingly tossed away as trash.

(Years later an informant talked about that "simple incident", and what was supposed to have happened. *The Islamists were certain that with Gorbachev killed in NYC, a nuclear war would break out between America and Russia.* Once the superpowers had killed each other off the Islamists would strike out taking over the entire Middle East and Europe.)

Islamic World

As shown before after the Soviets invaded Afghanistan in December 1979 the nearby Arab nations began supporting the rebel war. Similar to Castro in 1980, many Muslim countries opened their jails and gave their criminals a one -way ticket to Afghanistan via Pakistan. It was expected that most would die fighting the Soviets.

A young Saudi named **Osama Bin Laden** was a devote of their Wahhabi sect, which preached strict adherence to Islam. He was 22 when the Soviets invaded Afghanistan, and like so many was outraged that they had done so. His role model was the hostile cleric **Abdullah Azzam,** the fiery Palestinian speaker who traveled to the Afghan war zone to preach and inspire the young Muslims. He promoted Jihad and martyrdom, promising the young fighters that great rewards awaited them in heaven. (*His videos were even found in Oklahoma City at an Islamic Conference years later.*)

Like many Bin Laden had joined the banned Islamic group the *Muslim Brotherhood,* and took up their call for Jihad. He traveled often between Saudi Arabia and Pakistan to contribute to the war effort. As a son from a wealthy family his initial work (promoted by Azzam), had been at construction projects, raising money and smuggling in arms and supplies. *Osama Bin Laden* was soon one of the main intermediaries in the war, and his multi-year effort enabled him to make hundreds of contacts among the legitimate rebels and the jihadists that had flooded into the region.

By 1985 bin Laden moved his four wives and his children to Pakistan to stay near the war. He used family assets to construct fortifications, infrastructure, caves and tunnels. During 1986 he met and worked with EIJ, (Egyptian Islamic Jihad) radical leader **Dr. Ayman al-Zawahiri,** who had been involved in the murder of Pres. Sadat.

Zawahiri had treated hundreds of wounded Arabs from the fighting, and was certain that all of these trials were a prelude to the eventual defeat of **America!** He convinced bin Laden that they had to use these young fighters to free Islam from the infidels and their influence. Bin Laden established a well organized center of operations, and a group of like minded zealots began to form.

This was the creation of al-Qaeda, the base.

During their war years bin Laden and Azzam met a few more times to discuss their joint efforts. As time went by the increasingly militant bin Laden thought Azzam was "too moderate" for this new time. This is hard to understand as Azzam was still preaching that there was no sense stopping after they had defeated the Soviets. To Azzam the Middle East was full of corrupt secular rulers who had abandoned their true faith.

Those extremists believed that since the end of the Ottoman Empire in 1919, the Islamic World had known nothing but defeat, subjugation and misery. All at the hands of the Western world. Their recent victory over the Soviets was the first time in modern history that an Islamic army had bested a non-Islamic one. For them the Soviets were not just non-believers, they were atheists, and that was why they had lost.

And as the months went by all could see the Soviet Empire was crumbling. *To Azzam that was a sign, that Islam was to take over.* Their renewed armies would soon do the same to decadent America. On November 24, 1989 Azzam placed his two sons into his car to travel for Friday prayers. **But when he turned the key the car exploded killing all.**

Bin Laden was never proven to have been behind the attack, but he was the main beneficiary. He was now in control of all of the jihadist elements and finances in Afghanistan. His vision of the coming conflict with America would be the one they followed.

(Reagan aide Dana Rohrabacher had traveled into Afghanistan and Pakistan many times in the 80s as we supplied weapons and material. Though he never met bin Laden in person, he traveled through bin Laden camps. His guides warned him not to speak English as bin Laden would kill any American he came across.)

In late 1989 a new ambassador arrived in Pakistan, Peter Tomsen. He reprised the trip agent McWilliams had made the year before, meeting with dozens of Afghan leaders which included Yahiya and Ahmed Massoud, and Abdul Haq. Most of those Afghan leaders had turned against the CIA and the U.S. since our policies still favored Pakistan, and by default the ISI candidate.

They had warned McWilliams that the Pakistani's were bringing Islamic radicals to power instead of Afghan exiles. Pakistan was not interested in helping Afghanistan, but in creating some type of extremist entity they controlled.

As shown before Soviet Foreign Minister Shevardnadze had also warned Sec State Schultz in 1988 about the Islamic Fundamentalists. (Reagan's former Sec-Def Casper Weinberger had admitted that we knew we were unintentionally helping Islamic Fundamentalists in the 1980s. But like Churchill had said in 1942, "If Hitler had invaded Hell I would have made favorable references to the Devil.") *(107)

A new plan had to be created, and Tomsen reported back to Washington. But since the KGB had destroyed that large supply base in Pakistan the rebels were having a hard time in finishing off the remaining Communists. They needed more help, but the Bush Administration was following Gorbachev's request and turning to other concerns. With the Soviets gone, Afghanistan went on the back burner. And then Panama and Kuwait needed help.

With the Soviets gone Bin Laden had also left Afghanistan. He returned to Saudi Arabia, was heartily welcomed back and given a desk job in the family construction business. He found that type of work no longer satisfied his desires, he needed and wanted to do more. Rebels in Yemen were again causing problems for the Saudi Royals, and bin Laden approached a man he had known in Afghanistan, *Prince Turki al-Faisal* the head of Saudi Intelligence. Bin Laden offered him his "Arab army" to fight a Jihad in Yemen, and remove the rebels and the godless Communists who backed them. Prince Turki wisely refused the offer, unsure of how it would end.

Iran was no longer burdened by the costs of the Iraq War, so they used their peace dividend sponsoring terrorism and buying electromagnetic isotope separators from China. They were secretly installed in the city of Karaj, west of Tehran. The purpose of that equipment was to make nuclear weapons.

China's Precision Machining Company also sold the Iranians a three axis turntable, which could be converted into grinding explosive lenses for nuclear triggers. And Pakistan's A.Q. Khan sold them nuclear bomb research while Gen. Aslam Berg opened discussions on trading Pakistani nuclear know-how for Iranian oil. *Saddam was not the only one in the Gulf who wanted a nuclear bomb.*

Panama

The extreme violence in Latin America was getting a lot of attention. President Bush's next foreign policy problem centered in Panama with their drug smuggling dictator Gen. Manuel Noriega. Back in the late 1960s Noriega had been recruited as an asset of the CIA and he provided intelligence on the region. He also aided the DEA in their antidrug work giving dates and suspected places of smuggling. As the years went by Noriega moved up the ladder of Panamanian politics and became a high ranking official.

The effort to transfer ownership of the Canal to Panama continued with Carter's duplicitous treaty. Changing ownership and control of the Canal was run through a Canal Authority that was put in place to oversee the smooth transition.

In 1981 Panama's former ruler socialist Gen. Omar Torrijos died in a suspicious plane crash. (Torrijos had overthrown the elected democratic civilian government back in 1969, and he was never considered friendly to the U.S.) His death was seen as a possible good thing because Noriega was thought to be an anti-Communist.

Over the years Gen. Noriega's position was continually helped along by the U.S. and in 1983 he took over in Panama. But instead of installing a democratic government as was desired, Noriega became just another harsh dictator. Unknown to the U.S. agencies that dealt with him, Noriega was also an agent for Cuban intelligence. (It was thought they were behind the Torrijos plane crash to get Noriega in power.)

It also turned out that Noriega's previous work with the DEA had enabled him to eliminate all rivals in the Panamanian drug trade. By 1985 he had become a greedy and corrupt drug figure who was stealing millions from the national treasury.

His main political rival was one Hugo Spataforo. He was found murdered and stuffed into a U.S. mail bag. Pres. Reagan's team tried to turn him around in 1987 but Noriega was too far gone. All U.S. support was ended. In 1988 Noriega was officially charged in U.S. courts with drug smuggling and sanctions were applied.

During that time the national elections in Panama were won by one Guillermo Endara. Noriega annulled the election. When the Bush presidency commenced in January 1989 they tried to work things out with Noriega but his hard line stance was turning violent. Harassment and attacks against U.S. civilians and military personnel became commonplace. Secretive and democratic radio host Kurt Muse was finally found and arrested with help from Cuban agents. (Muse, a U.S. citizen was imprisoned and tortured.)

Free speech was being shut down and it appeared the country was being turned into a left-wing entity with help from Castro. Our sanctions did not wake Noriega up, in fact just the opposite occurred. Noriega's became belligerent and entered into a partnership with the Columbian drug cartels. With that alliance came a terror campaign against any American. Gangs harassed everyone, and Cartel terrorists constructed several car bombs using the Soviet made Lada station wagons. Those cars would be loaded with a 200 kilogram charge similar to the ones used in Bogota, by the Medellin and Cali cartels.

Panamanian Army officers finally approached the CIA about backing a coup attempt, but the lawyer ridden and bureaucratically choked off agency balked. There were too many fears that the CIA would become embroiled in a controversy if Noriega was killed or if they failed to notify some sub-committee. A local coup had tried in October, but was beaten off and the conspirators tortured and killed.

Because of their strategic position between two oceans and two continents, Panama had a potentially bright economic future. They had a growing International banking and finance industry, seaborne commerce was increasing, and the Canal was their crown jewel. Panama city was dotted with hi-rise structures indicative of their growing prosperity. *No one living there should have been poor, but the unending corruption was stealing the nation's wealth.*

As per the Carter treaty in the year 2000 all U.S. military and civilian presence would end. It was vital that the nation's leadership be run by law abiding and democratic citizens, otherwise a worldwide asset would come to ruin which would affect everyone. But since Noriega was considered a criminal and his followers an organized criminal enterprise, the safety of the Canal, the nation and thousands of Americans who lived and worked there were in jeopardy. Noriega's thugs had told members of the Canal Authority that they would be captured with their families and used as ransom if Noriega was ever arrested.

For some reason on December 15, 1989 Noriega's rubber-stamped legislature named him as their head of state and declared that Panama was at war with America. (Eastern Europe was shedding their Communist rulers at this time.)

The next day a U.S. Army officer was murdered by Noriega's men and the wife of another serviceman was accosted and he was beaten unconscious. Noriega and his henchmen had turned into a sadistic group of torturers and anyone could be grabbed right off the street.

Since the CIA wanted no part of trying "a coup or other type of dangerous plot", no other options were available to the Administration except a complicated military intervention. This incursion would have to be well-planned and carried out using all branches of service. To reduce the numbers of potential hostages, as many U.S. dependents as possible were flown out before the operation could commence.

During the early hours on December 20, 1989 operation Just Cause began. That first night twenty seven different targets had to be secured to have any chance of success. Planning for this difficult operation had started months before. Military staff spent months trying to organize things, but even so SNAFU (situation normal, all fouled up) still showed up.

Most of the initial work was done by Special Operations members, plus Rangers. They and regular Army and Marine Units had been secreted in under the veil of training exercises.

In addition to the ground units six **F-117 Stealth fighter-bombers** had been sent in to take out selected targets. Also included in this large operation were airborne command posts, over 140 USAF cargo planes, aerial tankers, F-15 fighters, search and rescue helicopters, dozens of Blackhawk and Huey transport helicopters, Apache attack helicopters, AC 130 gunships and other aircraft.

Facing this force was the Panamanian Defense Force, PDF which consisted of weak to good units depending on their training and commanders. The PDF was armed with Soviet weapon systems that had come in from Cuba, such as the dangerous ZPU-4 anti-aircraft vehicles, shoulder fired SAM-7 & SAM-14 anti-air missiles, AK-47 assault rifles and Russian machine guns. Cuban advisors had been operating in Panama for some time overseeing training programs on those weapon systems and battlefield techniques. (As was learned in Grenada and Afghanistan, many of those Soviet weapons systems were quite effective.)

Key Panamanian military installations and large forces would be fixed in place and surrender requests issued. Hopefully the Panamanians would lay down their arms in the face of this intensive operation. Otherwise casualties could be high. Despite all of our planning and efforts to achieve surprise, PDF units became aware that something was coming. Normal PDF patrols, listening posts, radio detection units and a fishing trawler had picked up the incoming air units miles from their objectives.

Seal Team four was given the mission of sneaking into the city's harbor and securing Paitilla Airport. Just as they made it ashore the battle at the Comandancia, (Noriega's command center) began. They were halfway to their objective when on site PDF units realized what was afoot and took to their positions. Because of our restrictive rules of engagement the PDF troops fired first and seven Seals were hit in the initial volley.

As had happened in Iran and Grenada, the Military Bureaucracy insisted that the mission had to be a joint mission. The Seal's were dependent on an air force gunship for fire support, but the communications were down. The lightly equipped Seal team was being shot up and unable to call for help.

A few miles away F-117 stealth fighters came in unnoticed to drop smart bombs in the parade ground at the Rio Hato Military Base. That base held Noriega's best troops. The purpose of bombing the parade ground was to limit casualties to the sleeping troops, and to show them what was coming if they did not surrender. All ordinance landed exactly as planned, but it did not deter the PDF troops who raced to their fighting positions.

Next in were the AC-130 Spectre gunship and two Apache attack helicopters firing canons and mini-guns into hardened PDF defensive positions and armored cars. Once again snafu appeared as the Apache's could not complete the mission. Fortunately the gunship knocked out the last ZPU just as the planes transporting the Rangers flew into position. They exited from their planes to parachute 500 feet to reach ground. Despite the gunship support the Rangers were also fired upon by the PDF ground troops before they even exited the aircraft. Numerous men were wounded and injured from the low-altitude drop onto everything imaginable.

Torrijos-Tocuman Airfield was the next target. Again Rangers dropped in from 500 feet to begin securing the airfield. And again despite the prep-fires from helicopters and a gunship the PDF was waiting and firing at them. Most landed safely and took up their positions.

Nearby Noriega was in his residence with his personal guard. Blasted awake by small arms and explosions, two of the guards hustled Noriega into a land cruiser and they sped off down some back alleys. Close by a small convoy of U.S. APCs attempted to break into the heavily defended Comandancia, but they too took many casualties.

A Delta Force team rescued Kurt Muse from his cell, but then their helicopter was shot down wounding three more men and a small AH-6 scout/attack helicopter was also shot down wounding both pilots. As usual nothing was going to plan.

To prevent Noriega's men from sabotaging the Canal itself platoon elements were sent to secure locks, power plants and access roads. Fortunately all missions there were successful. But sealing off the city of Colon was a different matter. It was filled with a battalion of PDF troops and hundreds of Noriega loyalists. Firefights quickly began as the reinforced U.S. troops gained fire superiority. Colon was eventually closed off.

Three nearby bridges had to be secured and the USMC contingent was successful and on schedule. All that night and into the morning incoming units from the 82nd Airborne were parachuted or helicoptered into areas to secure their objectives. Most were heavily defended incurring more casualties. There were two more days of limited combat, as the country was secured. But despite our efforts hundreds of Panamanians had died.

Noriega could not escape and sought asylum inside the Vatican Embassy. U.S. units surrounded the Embassy and waited the dictator out. On January 12, 1990 Noriega finally gave up and was arrested. A trial was held, he was convicted and sentenced to forty years in jail on numerous crimes.

Overall this military operation went off far better than the one in Grenada, but still there were problems to be worked out. Civilian casualties were too high as some fighting occurred in residential areas. Our paratroops dropped into areas that were well guarded resulting in dozens of U.S. casualties. Twenty three U.S. troops died with 330 seriously wounded or injured. Overall coordination and teamwork were much improved, and the ultra-secretive F-117 Stealth fighter saw its first action and performed well. (Stealth was a relative term. The aircraft had a small radar signature so it was hard to find at night. In the daytime it could have been shot down.)

As units moved through the country they uncovered large caches of secretive arms that filled entire buildings! The larger weapons were still packed in crates marked "Surveying Tools or Drilling Equipment". *Uncovered were 51,386 weapons plus over 600 tons of ammunition and explosives!*

All of those assault rifles, light and heavy machine guns, mortars, recoilless rifles and light artillery were of Soviet-bloc origin. Almost all were still packed in protective grease which meant they were not being used locally.

It appeared that Noriega was working with the Cartels and Cuba to start a regional war to bring down all of the local governments. They had planned on creating a huge Cartel run-entity across Central America.

One of our best pacification efforts involved paying civilians to bring in arms and ammunition. Thousands of weapons were exchanged for cash in a no question policy. (Almost 9,000 weapons were turned in.) That helped diffuse any potential guerrilla action, though it did not stop the widespread looting, or the PDF ignited arson fire that destroyed blocks of the El Chorrillo barrio.

Also uncovered were millions in bundled cash that was inside Noriega's many compounds. Again testament to his position in illegal drug trafficking and in looting the national treasury.

At the Marriot hotel numerous news reporters had been staying inside. They had been unable to roam the streets to get stories because of the violence, and told their networks they were being "held hostage" by the PDF. Network executives angrily demanded the White House rescue their employees which was done that first night by a unit of the 82nd. Numerous PDF troops were killed as the 82d troops made their way through the streets to the Marriot, but no PDF troops were found near or inside the structure. *It turned out no one was being held hostage.*

With the fighting ended Military Civil Affairs officers went to work to help organize the incoming President Guillermo Endara government. It was vital that the Panamanians get back on their own feet. On the 22d a new national police force was being formed, the Fuerza Publica. They would replace the PDF, and new recruits were soon sworn in with Vice-President Guillermo Ford watching. (In the spring election that Noriega had annulled Ford was arrested and beaten weekly.)

Diehard Noriega or Cartel men raked the ceremony with rifle fire and mortars. The offenders were all killed as the liberal news outlets complained even more. By this point almost 300 reporters had shown up with all of them wanting VIP treatment. As they had done since Vietnam, the leftist media overhyped any negative stories and downplayed any solid ones. CBS news ran with a story of a mass grave with 4,000 dead, while Ramsey Clark one of the traitors from Vietnam charged a vast conspiracy and cover up had occurred. **All of those claims were reviewed and proven false.**

U.S. Southern Command stated there had been 314 PDF KIA and 202 civilians killed. All remains were turned over to Panamanian authorities. One down side that did occur involved our military efforts at the Sandinista and Cuban embassies. Both had been surrounded during the operation to prevent Noriega from getting in. But on the 29th some of our soldiers entered the buildings which was against diplomatic protocols. Even though the troops uncovered a cache of RPGs and other weapons the move was illegal and was stopped. Soon after our forces returned home.

Europe

On the worldwide front the demise of the Cold War had an instant and dizzying impact. Soviet scientists, students and artists became instant celebrities in the West. Military and civilian specialists visited each other's countries and businessmen barnstormed into Russia looking for commercial deals. Even retired CIA and KGB operators met for lunch to rehash old cases. Emigration became a normal event as thousands left the former communist world. But fear was still there.

Talk of German reunification continually surfaced, and few wanted that to happen. Certainly not Poland, France, England nor Russia. Even in America many were shaking at the thought. All of the above countries had paid a terrible price for the German wars, and France had been invaded by them three times in 1870, 1914 and 1940. How could a united Germany ever again be trusted? Would a reunited Germany press for the return of lands ceded to Poland when Stalin stole eastern Poland?

With the end of economic support from Russia the East Germans began to ask for financial aid from W. Germany. Kohl agreed to provide some help, but the E. Germans would have to undertake deep political and economic reforms. They initially refused, but by December 1989 the former East German government was gone and a coalition was in power. They agreed to the reforms, as the arrests of former Communist officials began. Citizen unrest was growing, with civilians storming governmental offices to keep the destruction of records and evidence from occurring. Even some Soviet military installations were struck alarming the Soviets who gave orders to protect themselves.

P.M. Thatcher again pressed for everyone to slow down. There was too much change happening too fast. Talks on German reunification had to wait, there was plenty of time. She warned we have won the battle of ideas, but NATO and the Warsaw Pact should stay intact as a way to provide stability.

If we undermined things any further, we may miss the chance for democracy in Russia. Our hopes rest on Gorbachev staying in power. Throughout December 1989 meetings were held on the future of Europe.

And with all of the above happening sectional fighting broke out between Christian Armenia and Muslim Azerbaijan killing hundreds. Soviet troops had to be used to keep the peace.

Historical Note: Most of the world has forgotten, if they ever knew, that the commonplace 20th century genocides began around **1902, with the Islamic oppression of the Christians living in the Ottoman Empire in Turkey, Syria and Armenia.**

A pause in those horrors occurred in 1908, but the murders resumed within a year. President Taft angrily sent naval forces into the region to protest the Turkish-Ottoman actions, but due to our substantial trade with them, (starting in the 1890s), no further measures were taken.

During those years charitable American missionaries had spread throughout the region, and with them came western inspired hospitals, schools and colleges. On the surface relations between the religions seemed to return tto normal. Amongst the growing trade of goods, Oil which was prevalent in the region was becoming a valued resource and multiple drilling projects began. Cultural exchanges were also common, but then in 1914 WWI began and everything changed.

President Wilson and his administration tried in vain to keep the Turks neutral to avoid them suffering a crushing defeat. But the Ottomans were ruled by the arrogant Pasha clan, and they actively joined up with the Kaiser and Germany, becoming enemies to the Western Allied forces. Spoken English was banned in their empire, and all French and British citizens were expelled.

Not long after the Turkish rulers declared a holy war against all Christians. Wilson's Administration was implored for help as thousands of Americans were imperiled. U.S. Naval forces returned, and a call advising all Americans to leave the Middle East was given. (The Middle East was a recent title given to the region by the British in 1902.)

Upset by the U.S. show of force Djemal Pasha the military governor of the province of Syria openly warned that any actions by a western power would result in Christian massacres. Diplomatic complaints and accusations grew worse as the worldwide situation collapsed into a brutal War. Not wanting to alienate everybody, the Turks made up with the Americans and we sent Red Cross units to Turkey to care for their sick and wounded!

But even with our help massacres of Christians renewed with a fury as hundreds of Armenians were hanged in the streets of Erzerum. Soon after thousands of Christian men and boys were conscripted into labor battalions to build fortifications for the Ottomans.

The Pasha family had wanted to increase their empire, and they attempted to fight the Czar's forces in the Caucuses. The Ottoman's were poorly led and badly beaten losing an army. As the Ottoman forces retreated back to their territory, they took out their frustrations by using genocide upon the Armenians. (They tried to claim the Armenians were helping the Russians.)

Talaat Pasha informed the Armenian patriarchs to leave the region, as Muslim fanaticism became easy to mobilize.

They wantonly murdered and plundered with the goal of exterminating all traces of that "hated religion and civilization". *(108) In September 1915 Talaat wrote, "An end must be put to their (Christians) existence, with no regard to age or gender." *(109)

Witnesses attested to trainloads of Armenians being shipped off from all areas of the empire, even from Aleppo, Syria. They existed in worse conditions than cattle had to endure. *Hundreds of Armenians had horseshoes nailed to their feet and were forced to endure agonizing marches into the deserts. Turkish soldiers would herd entire villages into freezing rivers, incinerated them inside their churches or marched them into the deserts to die of thirst.*

It is believed that over 800,000 had been murdered by the summer of 1915! Countless thousands had been forced to convert to Islam. The inventions of telegraphs and telephones allowed communication of those atrocities to get out. The Western Allies deplored the killings and vowed retaliation.

To save as many innocents as possible American missionaries formed an underground railroad similar to the one used to free the southern slaves in America. Adhoc hospitals cared for their starving and sick as best as they could, and they shuttled thousands of Christian Armenians into Russian held areas.

Pres. Wilson made a terrible choice when he decided not to get engaged over those crimes. He feared that America could be dragged into the war, and of prompting even worse massacres. Wilson's ambassador to Turkey was Henry Morgenthau, a Jewish immigrant from Germany who excelled inside America's freedoms. Unhappy with his posting to Ottoman Turkey, Morgenthau would later state he had misjudged the Christian missionaries and their work.

"They were the advance agents of civilization, and they were the American spirit at its best." *(110)

Morgenthau reported back to Washington D.C. in detailed fashion on the murders, rape and genocide the Turks were inflicting upon the Christians in the region. He lamented that he was a Jew, representing the greatest Christian nation in the world, working in the capitol of the Mohammedan nation which was clearly in its death throes. He warned Talaat that America would never forget these massacres. You are defying all ideas of justice.

The Muslim interior minister cared not, only to cash in the American life insurance policies that so many Armenians had owned! *(111)

This genocide continued into 1916 reaching the barbarity of the Spanish Inquisition. To fight this horrible brutality Morgenthau and his allies raised millions in aid. He kept the NY Times appraised of conditions in the region so they could get the word out, and worked to get thousands of those Christian refugees resettled in America. (In just two decades his people would be the next ones to suffer from this evil.)

Germany used unrestricted submarine warfare in 1915 sinking multiple U.S. cargo ships and the liner *Lusitania*. Wilson had campaigned for reelection in 1916 on the premise he had kept us out of the war, but after the *Laconia* was sunk in February 1917 he asked Congress for a Declaration of War against Germany.

Wilson wrongly insisted that we not fight the Ottoman's. His strange reasoning eluded everyone in America, and in Europe. And even though Austria-Hungary was added to our war list, the Turks and the Middle East were never threatened by America! Though his lack of action had some missionary reasoning, Wilson was totally wrong for ignoring them.

As would happen to so many others who showed some empathy or nobility, his deeds seriously diminished our standing in the region. **It also prevented any American influence in the peace treaty that might have changed the future policies which affect us today!** *(112)

Henry Morgenthau had returned to the region in late June 1917 to try to convince the Ottoman's to make a separate peace with the Allied powers before it was too late. But the mission failed thanks to that British subterfuge. They did not want us meddling in their Middle East!

When the war ended in November 1918, France and Great Britain alone lay claim to the Ottoman Empire. Wilson's unilateral neutrality lost him any place at the Middle East peace table. It was the Colonial governors of France and England, and their decisions that would create the "new map" of the region.

And secret negotiations in London insured that the British alone liberated the area of Palestine, to create a Jewish homeland.

Wilson's 14 points proposal had offered self-determination for all, and was greeted with smiles around the world. But his words were not backed up by a force of arms or aggressive diplomacy. Thus we were left on the sidelines. *Colonial governors would make the decisions in the occupied lands and created the future enmity of the Muslim people!*

Islamic World

Pakistan continued with their plan to install Hekmatyar and his radical forces as the rulers in Afghanistan. *CIA informants* reported that the Saudi citizen Osama bin Laden was providing millions in secret support for this plan.

On March 7, 1990 the conspirators attempted a coup in Kabul. Defecting Afghan air units dropped bombs onto the Palace buildings and grounds while defecting armored units tried to open a corridor for Hekmatyar's forces to flow through. Surprisingly the coup failed.

This Bin Laden was also providing money to bribe legislators to vote Bhutto out of office in Pakistan. Having a women run a Muslim country was an anathema to the Islamists, and if she was ousted an Islamic radical could possibly take over. Bhutto had made many enemies over the past months by replacing numerous high level Pakistani principals in her effort to function and to stay in power.

The State Dept. reached out to the Saudi's that it was time to reign in those radicals. What we wanted was a group of the best *Afghan Commanders* to rule as a united assemblage called a shura. As always the Saudi's agreed verbally, but they continued to support their side.

Unknown to the American diplomats, the Saudi's secretly increased their support to the ISI. They needed to speed up the takeover of Afghanistan before the Americans grew interested and tried to intervene.

(U.S. contributions to the Afghans had ended completely. Our aid to Pakistan was also ending since they continued with their secretive efforts to get nuclear weapons. And Pakistan was still trying to start a guerilla war with India over Kashmir.)

In Iraq Saddam Hussein had stopped calling for the violent liberation of Palestine, and had mended fences with Egypt. During the end of 1989 he joined with Egypt, N. Yemen and Jordan to form the Arab Cooperation Council. Our State Dept. and many others felt that Saddam had been changed by the war. But in reality he was playing for time. In Saddam's warped mind the West and the rest of the Arab nations actually owed him for fighting Iran and keeping them at bay. Iraq had spent multiple billions during the eight year war and more re-arming. He expected some payback.

France had given him extensions on repaying his massive debts, and provided Iraq with sophisticated side looking surveillance cameras that were mounted on a squadron of Iraqi jets. Those planes were based in Jordan, and were flying recon missions along the Jordanian-Israeli border, improving Iraqi targeting intelligence up to 50 miles inside Israel. Few understood that that information would soon be put to use, or knew that Saddam expected his warheads to be nuclear.

In Jordan the first anniversary meeting of the Arab Cooperation Council met in Amman in early 1990. King Hussein proudly met his guests and gave them the grand tour. Pres. Mubarak and Saddam Hussein actually seemed to get along, but at a dinner speech Saddam showed his true intentions.

He had analyzed the changing world and how it would impact the Middle East, and gave a vitriolic attack against the United States. With the decline of the Soviet Union, America would become the main power in the region and would use this power to the detriment of the Arab world. As proof of his claims Saddam highlighted the increased Jewish immigration into Israel from the former Soviet bloc, and the continued presence of U.S. warships in the Persian Gulf. America's aim was to dominate our region and control our oil. We must reactivate our "oil weapon" against the West. Pres. Mubarak was stunned and left the council early.

This meeting showed all that the old and violent Saddam was still around. Coupled with his unending re-arming, the leaders in the region knew that trouble was brewing. Since the end of the Iran War, Iraq had purchased billions in discounted weapons from the dying Soviet bloc. The list included Scud short range ballistic missiles capable of carrying chemical and biological weapons, T-72 and T-62 tanks, hundreds of armored vehicles, artillery of all calibers and the latest MIG-29 fighters. His teams were feverishly working on a "super-gun," and were still trying to acquire nuclear weapons. (Some of which could be fired from that super-gun.)

Saddam demanded that the other Arab nations give him $30 billion as payment for his army's protecting them from the Iranians. (Iraq owed about $100 billion.) No one in the West heeded those warnings, believing that Saddam was just posturing to deflect the increasing worldwide criticism over his treatment of the Kurds. (Saddam had continued to use poison gas attacks to end their quest for freedom. Over 5,000 men, women and children died in one attack.)

Iran was militarily broken after the end of the war with Iraq. They had used up all of the spare parts to maintain the U.S. weapons the Shah had bought, and that included whatever they picked up from Israel. Since we did not replace their equipment the major of those weapons finally became useless.

Iran then went to Russia and China to procure new arms, **and the materials to make Chemical, Biological and Nuclear weapons.** They desperately wanted to acquire updated missiles and aircraft. Cash starved *Russia signed a deal to build a new "civilian nuclear reactor"*. That would provide Iran with their nuclear needs for a bomb. With the war ended, Iranian aid to Hezbollah increased as did their terror attacks against Israel.

The Soviet Union

In February 1990 new political upheavals occurred in the Soviet Union. Elections were held for city councils and parliaments in Russia, Belarus and Ukraine. Large demonstrations were occurring, and Gorbachev challenged the Communist Party to allow multi-party runoffs and economic reforms.

For the past year and a half the Baltic States had been making their intentions known for freedom. Back in the summer of 1989 their "communist parties" were calling for independence, the same as was happening throughout Eastern Europe, the Caucuses, the Ukraine and even Belarus.

During December 1989 the Lithuanian Supreme Soviet decided that the political monopoly of the Communist party should be ended. On March 11, 1990 the Lithuanian Parliament declared itself independent of the Soviet Union. Once again the world waited for a Russian attack. Gorbachev warned the Lithuanians not to leave the union. Military actions were threatened, and Soviet aircraft flew low over their cities as a show of force. Their aircraft also dropped leaflets warning the Lithuanians they had to remain part of the Soviet Union.

Sec. Baker and Soviet Foreign Minister Shevardnadze met to discuss the fragile situation as some fighting did occur. The Bush Administration was under increasing pressure to recognize the Lithuanians from the imprudent media and Democrats in Congress. (A resolution in March requiring us to recognize them missed passage by just a dozen votes.)

Weeks later the other Baltic States of Estonia and Latvia also declared their freedom. Minor clashes occurred with the local Soviet troops, but no serious action was taken at that time because Gorbachev and the Soviet forces were preoccupied with the growing problems to their south. Azerbaijan was fighting with Iran, and Moldavia wanted to be reunified with Rumania as large protests were going on. Armenia also wanted their independence, and was also fighting with Azerbaijan. (Soviet troops had to fight their way into Baku earning much hatred from the Azeri's.)

Despite the millions of Baltic citizens deported and enslaved by Stalin, despite the hundreds of thousands of "replacement Soviet citizens" brought in, despite Stalin's renewed efforts during the Soviets second attempt at racial genocide in the 1930s, the Baltic states remained in their hearts as sovereign states and peoples.

During April 1990 meetings were held to try to find a peaceful solution. But the hostile Soviets were thinking of implementing a complete embargo on oil and natural gas deliveries, resources the Baltic States were completely dependent upon. (And the exact issue Pres. Reagan had warned about in 1984)

France warned everyone that though we are all in spirit with the Baltic people, there was no possibility of sending in troops to insure their freedom.

Historical Note: Though FDR was always touted as a great leader during WWII, he made multiple poorly thought out concessions to the Communists in Russia.

FDR did not condemn or cutoff ties to the Russians when they supported the Socialist revolutionaries in Spain in 1936. Stalin had sent vast supplies of modern arms, and hundreds of Russian advisors to help the Spanish socialists win. At any given point there were 600-800 Russians advising and fighting in the "Spainish Civil War". Hundreds of Russians died and were wounded, ironically fighting the Germans who were helping Gen. Franco's fascist forces.

This effort was Stalin's first step to turning Europe. He felt a Socialist Spain would be beholden to him, and would be his base of operations infiltrating into western Europe.

Stalin then joined forces with Nazi Germany in August 1939, and annexed the Baltic states of Estonia, Latvia and Lithuania. Those takeovers were never recognized by most of the countries of the West, legally or diplomatically, and all three maintained their national legations in the U.S. (FDR said and did nothing.)

Weeks later Russia cowardly invaded Poland from the east after the Poles were committed to repelling the Nazi invasion from their western borders. *That invasion sparked the call for war in Europe.* (FDR did nothing.)

Then in November 1939 the Russians coldly invaded neutral, non-threatening Finland. The Finns put up a tough defense stopping the Russian armies for months, but they had to surrender after Stalin bombed their cities and his reinforced armies renewed their attacks. (FDR did nothing.)

Throughout those events FDR said and did nothing over those egregious actions. He supported Stalin throughout the war, and at gave huge concessions to him the peace talks at Tehran and Yalta. FDR's failures greatly assisted Stalin, and led to the Cold War, and all of the fighting and suffering since.

As expected, on April 20, 1990 the fuels were cutoff to Lithuania, and Soviet naval forces began blockading their ports. More discussions were held in Washington with many in the Congress now pulling their heads out of their butts as they realized there was little we could do short of war. France and Germany felt the fighting could break out at any time, and warned Lithuanian leader Landsbergis that he had to suspend their push for independence. *He retorted that his country was the victim of another "Munich".*

(Even with the Russian hostilities, Estonia and Latvia both were declaring their independence hoping help would come.)

On May 1, 1990 the U.S. Senate decided to withhold all trade benefits to Moscow until the embargo against Lithuania was ended. The Soviet Military then demanded that Gorbachev and Shevardnadze make no more concessions to the West that would endanger their security. *The CIA was warning that Gorbachev was rapidly losing control of the Soviet Union. Social upheaval and ethnic conflicts could intensify.*

July 1990 was another historic month in Europe. After months of negotiations the economic and monetary union of the two Germany's took place. East Germany ceased to exist, and was rejoined to West Germany. German leaders Kohl and Genscher flew to Moscow to discuss their reunification talks. West Germany would accept all financial obligations for the former East, and extend a $3 billion credit to the Soviets.

Neither Gorbachev nor anyone else in the Politburo liked the idea of a reunited Germany, and they greatly disliked that Germany would remain a part of NATO. It was decided that allied and German troop levels would be reduced to pose no threat to the USSR, and no NATO forces would move past the points they were already at. In that way former E. Germany would be considered unthreatening and act as a buffer. (No one in the West ever harbored any thoughts to invading Russia. Too many had tried and failed.)

In the Soviet Union the eighth congress of the Communist Party convened. They were fighting for survival as Gorbachev fought against the hard-liners, and eventually won reelection as General Secretary. He pledged to continue their moderating policies. Lithuania was forced to end their quest for independence, and the Soviet blockade on them stopped.

(In yet another obvious display of their leftist ideology *Time* magazine declared Gorbachev as their man of the decade. Somehow Pres. Reagan's vast accomplishments of reviving our moribund economy, rebuilding our military, restoring vitality to our alliances, and checking every Communist attempt at expansion since 1980, ending Soviet Communism and freeing 500 million people was overlooked. For our leftist media it was proper to lavish praise at a man who could still strike us with nuclear weapons at any moment.)

America

As shown earlier the FBI had been warned about one of their agents, Robert Hansen. Their higher ups had brushed off all of the prior alerts and they even ignored the notice from Hansen's brother-in-law who was an agent based in Chicago. Months later they were notified by Hansen's sister that there was large amounts of cash in their house. FBI agent Wauck investigated the call in 1990 and found that Hansen was spending large amounts of cash, hard to do on an agent's salary but easy to do for a spy. *Wauck warned his superiors that Hansen could be spying for the Russians, but incredulously he too was ignored!*

Not long after Hansen was caught hacking into the computers of his supervisors. Yet again he was not investigated.

In NYC another unexplained terrorist attack had occurred. **Sayeed Nosair** was mingling with the patrons at Uncle Charley's gay bar during April. What none realized was that Nosair was moving around deciding where to plant a home-made explosive. A six inch pipe was filled with M-80s and the fuse was lit. Over a dozen patrons were hit with glass shards and shrapnel, though all of the injuries were minor. The significance of the act was missed and Nosair escaped again.

(*Nosair had been facing deportation for overstaying his original visa. To stay here he married a Karen Sweeny, an American convert to Islam.*)

Middle East

Throughout the year of 1990 Saddam Hussein had continued attacking his own people in an effort to maintain his rule. On April 2, 1990 Saddam made an announcement that their scientists had perfected an advanced binary chemical weapon. He proudly proclaimed that this type of weapon had never been built in the third world before. (Iraq had used chemical weapons often in the war with Iran from 1984 - 87, but those had been the same simple type used in WWI.)

He claimed "We will make the fire eat up half of Israel if it tries to do anything against Iraq." This time the world took notice. The U.S. State Dept. downplayed the episode, but in March alert customs officials had stopped an Iraqi attempt to smuggle special electrical switches out of England. *Those switches could be used for atomic weapons.* Soon after they stopped an effort to procure the parts needed to build a super-gun that could fire projectiles over a hundred miles.

During the past two years Israel was being renewed with the influx of 25,000+ new immigrants who had escaped from Eastern Europe and Russia. Israel had been employing tough measures to secure the West Bank and Gaza as attacks from Hamas, the PLO and Hezbollah were a constant source of dangers.

The PLO had heartily agreed with Saddam's violent rhetoric. Quietly most of the despotic leaders in the Arab world applauded Iraq and Saddam. Only Egypt's Mubarak tried to calm the situation down.

The Arab League held a special meeting that May in Baghdad. At their "harmonious meeting" Saddam again turned the discussions to his need for finances and his problems with the Arab Gulf States to his south. (Kuwait, the UAE and the Saudis.) Those other nations were selling more oil than the treaties allowed which was costing Iraq money.

OPEC derived its market strength on the discipline of its members. Each country was given a quota of oil to sell based on their reserves. In that way they could regulate the supply and keep the price high. But conservation and new supplies outside of OPEC had collapsed the price in the early 80s, so every sale was important. Saddam also complained that all of the loans that had been made to Iraq during the Iran war should be forgiven as his country had done all of the fighting.

The other Arab leaders realized that Saddam was again a threat, but no one wanted to face up to the potential menace. Saddam was also sending arms into Lebanon to arm the Christian Militias, a direct threat to Syria, his backstabbing neighbor.

Another issue the West missed was that Syria was pulling most of their forces out from Lebanon. Hezbollah had bested them in the war for hearts and minds, and it was they who were leading the fight against Israel. Hezbollah's constant violence had turned Lebanon into a no-go part of the world. Westerners would not set foot in the country, and few Arabs would either.

During July 1990 a secret meeting was held in Damascus between Syria and Iran. Their tense discussions displayed the reality that Syria was second to Iran in Lebanon. In prior years the Syrians could have gotten help from the Soviets to fend off the Iranian ambitions, but no longer. *The world had Fundamentally Changed.*

Soon after a delegation of U.S. Senators met with Saddam Hussein in the city of Mosul to discuss relations and to increase trade with Iraq. Congress had thoughts of applying sanctions on Iraq for using chemical weapons, while the Administration wanted to use commercial trade as a means of leverage. If sanctions were applied then America would have nothing it could use to moderate Saddam. As much as everyone was distrustful of Iraq, it was still seen as a block against Iran.

For the past two months Saddam had been posturing and threatening the nation of Kuwait. On July 17 he let his anger out in the open by airing his grievances against Kuwait and the United Arab Emirates. "Saddam again stated the loss of revenue from low oil prices, and of how those countries were stabbing Iraq in the back with a poisoned dagger.

Iraq had sacrificed the flower of its youth to protect those houses of wealth. *If they continue to hurt us we will have no choice but to take action to set things right."* Saddam ordered two armored divisions to the border and mobilized two others.

Kuwait's Emir, Sheik Jaber al-Sabah was mortified and called for an emergency session of their elected parliament. He mobilized their small military and went to speak with the Saudi's, Kuwait's traditional ally and the strongest member of the Gulf Cooperation Council. The UAE followed suit, as Iraq had brazenly attacked their offshore rigs during the Iran War.

In theory this league was to work to help each other, but even now the Kuwait's were given a cold welcome. The reason was oil.

Everyone including the Saudi's were upset over the current low oil prices. Kuwait was ignoring their listed quotas. Most felt that all Saddam wanted was some loan forgiveness and access to the Kuwaiti offshore islands of Warba and Bubiyan. Those islands would give Saddam a desired deep water port, and if Kuwait would give in the problem would be solved. (Similar to the appeasement France and Britain tried on Hitler in the 1930s.)

Our Ambassador in Kuwait, Nathaniel Howell met with the Kuwaitis and reported in that they were truly worried. They felt this was not a matter of oil, but of control. Twice before Iraq had tried to take over Kuwait, and both times had been stopped.

(As shown before Kuwait was given full independence in 1961 when the British ended their colonial effort. Baghdad immediately tried to reclaim the country. Threatened with an invasion the Kuwaiti's asked for and received military help from England. *Iraq was stopped that time, but they never renounced their claim.* Kuwait was admitted into the U.N. that year.)

On July 24th U.S. intelligence warned the Saudi government that Iraq had stationed over 30,000 troops near the Kuwaiti border. Still the Saudi's did not believe that Saddam would act. U.S. satellites and our intelligence agencies continued monitoring the Iraqis, but saw no logistical buildup. Their conclusion was there would be no fighting.

The next day at the OPEC conference and at private meetings Pres. Mubarak of Egypt offered to act as a mediator to stop any potential hostilities. He first went to Iraq to talk with Saddam and then went to Kuwait. After their meetings Mubarak told the press that Saddam had no intention of invading, (though his main worry was that the U.S. might overreact.)

U.S. Ambassador to Iraq, April Glaspie met with and warned Tariq Aziz and Saddam not to attempt to invade for the U.S. would not tolerate it. But she also said that America had no opinion on the Arab-Arab border disputes.

What she did not know was that Jimmy Carter and his State Dept. had made quiet assurances to Saddam back in 1980. America would not object to Iraq reclaiming Kuwait, as a potential tradeoff helping us against Iran.

Not understanding the ebb and flow of U.S. politics, to Saddam the Carter assurances meant he could do as he pleased whenever he was ready to. After Carter was defeated the Reagan Administration policies and the war with Iran prevented him from acting on Carter's words. Since his war with Iran had accomplished nothing, he now wanted his backup prize.

Saddam contemptuously reminded Glaspie of the U.S. backstabbing effort in the Iran-contra episode, and of how he had fought for America's interests against Iran. He told her America's press insults me and Kuwait's oil thievery is ruining our economy. *"Had we not stopped the Iranians you could not have without using nuclear weapons. Yours is a society that could not lose 10,000 dead in one battle."* *(113) (True)

Saddam like most of the world's totalitarian rulers was able to convince and double-talk that he meant no harm. *"We promise no action until we have met with the Kuwaiti's."* The Ambassador reported that "good news" back to the State Dept. As usual with American diplomats, no one understood what Saddam meant when he said; *"When we meet with the Kuwaiti's"*. *(114)

Back in Washington D.C. National Warning Officer Charlie Allen dissented from the standing viewpoint of the State Dept and CIA. He saw that the Iraqi's were operating under a condition of *EMCON*, there was no radio or electronic communication traffic. He was certain an attack was coming, and had been warning of it for weeks. His bosses dismissed him as an alarmist and he was almost fired. (A week after Iraq invaded he was given a decoration and everything was kept quiet.)

In addition to Allen's warnings additional spy satellites had been shifted to that area, instead of having to cover Russia. They too had picked up Iraq's initial mobilization and movement of units. In the past days Saddam continued moving more units in. By August 1 Iraq had over 100,000 troops plus 300 tanks near the Kuwaiti border. Recent photos showed the supply/logistic units had arrived.

Seeing those changes the CIA changed their outlook and warned that an attack was coming. Pres. Bush was alerted an attack could happen at any time.

To the other Western leaders the meetings between the U.S. Ambassador, and the regional heads of states with Saddam, and the productive OPEC meetings in Geneva was welcomed news. Iraq had stated the "negotiated fix" was accepted, and that OPEC would set up committees to regulate oil production. The world was still enjoying the peace benefit from the collapse of Communism in Europe, and no one wanted anything to break the positive world outlook. Among the Western powers diplomatic talk was centering on peace dividends, and of bringing the troops home for good. *Most of them felt that the Kuwaiti's would just have to buy their way out of this problem.*

Iraq had a large war machine staffed with an army of a million men, the largest air force in the Middle East, over 5,000 armored vehicles, medium range ballistic missiles and an array of chemical weapons that Saddam had already used. *Saddam's military force was battle tested, though not overly proficient.*

Iraq's border force was getting stronger and more militant as the days slipped by. And Saddam was being helped with satellite imagery provided by France. *Updated overhead views of Kuwait and Saudi Arabia showed there were no military preparations by either nation.*

During the early hours of August 2, 1990, Saddam Hussein sent numerous divisions across the undefended Kuwaiti border in a multi-pronged invasion.

Kuwait would be conquered in just six hours. The world was taken aback by Iraq's assault as passenger jets were still landing in the airport when the Iraqi troops attacked. Saddam was certain that no one could or would do anything about it,

For There are Tigers in This World, (2)

And They are Always Watching.

One citizen group in Britain angrily felt that their government had secreted a commando team on board a passenger jet flying to Iraq. Their aircraft landed just as the Iraqis were invading. All of the civilians were captured and imprisoned awaiting execution, while the young men suspected by the civilian passengers of being commandos disappeared as soon as the jet landed.

Fortunately for the free world George Bush had won the presidential election in 1988. This former aircraft carrier torpedo-bomber pilot who had fought in the Pacific in WWII knew full well the lessons of history. He was not an appeaser or a weak president. Action had to be taken.

In deference to Vietnam Pres. Bush was going to get the world to help us. He contacted our UN ambassador to get the wheels moving, and he reached out to the Russians to included them in the process. Sec. State Baker was in Russia meeting with Shevardnadze. They issued a joint message against the Iraqi's.

It was also quite helpful that British P.M. Margret Thatcher was visiting the President in the U.S. when word got out of the invasion. Eight years earlier she had been surprised by the Argentine invasion of the Falklands. She had reacted decisively and strongly then, and advised Pres. Bush that he too had to act resolutely. Both knew that this invasion could not be allowed, but at the time no one was sure of what to do.

In France Mitterrand who had been a supporter of Iraq was informed of the invasion and of the U.S. efforts in the United Nations. Mitterrand agreed, Iraq had to leave Kuwait.

Historical Note: Looking back at our history America always seems to be divided on foreign policy. Prior to 1898 our national leaders had mostly followed George Washington's farewell address and remained an isolationist nation. The Monroe Doctrine was created in the 1820s to warn the Europeans to stay away from the Americas. That policy had kept the peace in our region for decades, though in 1889 there was actually a call to fight Germany over their conquests in Samoa. But the issue was ended quietly.

Then in 1891 another close call drew up with Chile over their treatment of U.S. sailors. In 1895 a fight with Great Britain almost arose over a territorial dispute they had with Venezuela. Soon after that near miss we supported Cuba's 1895 claim and rebellion to get their independence from Spain.

Most of our leaders wanted to stay isolationist, and did not want a war with Spain. But in 1896 Republican William McKinley trounced Democrat Bryon for the presidency. McKinley was one of those who wanted Spain to exit the region, and give Cuba their independence. *(At that point America had twice the industrial might of the number two nation, Great Britain.)*

By 1898 Secretary of the Navy Teddy Roosevelt, (like many), wanted us to fight Spain and support the Cubans. He directed the battleship *USS Maine* to show the flag in Havana, Cuba. He was supported in this aggressive policy by many elected leaders such as Senator Henry Cabot Lodge. Then came the explosion of the *USS Maine* in Havana Harbor which sunk the ship and caused dozens of casualties. (Recent forensic examinations of the blast laid the blame on a coal dust explosion in one of the storage bunkers.)

A call to war rose up led by McKinley, Roosevelt and publisher Randolph Hearst. America's navy quickly defeated the Spanish naval forces in two separate battles, and we bested the Spanish army in Cuba with U.S. and rebel Cuban ground troops. The other European powers were not happy with America butting in to free Cuba, as this action could now be repeated anywhere on the globe and threaten one of their colonies. But they could not reverse it either, not without a war.

Victory in that small war showed the world that this former colony was becoming a world power. In the peace treaty America took possession of Cuba, Puerto Rico, Guam and the Philippines.

Our leaders then stunned the Europeans when we granted Cuba a measure of independence, instead of acting like they would have and keeping them as a colony.

Just two weeks after the end of the war a German fleet showed up in the Philippines demanding land and base rights. Much debate was raised in the halls of power on if we should hold onto those former Spanish colonies too. It was felt that it would be safer for those people if we gave them some independence, but held onto them for now as territories, to keep the parasitic Europeans out. Our goals may have wanted to be altruistic, but at that time all lived in a world of competing, self-motivated empires.

(The statement "The Sun never sets on the British Empire" was true, because England actually had colonies all across the globe and the sun always shone on one of them.)

Two years later President Teddy Roosevelt became the first voice for national political change. Roosevelt was following on Pres. McKinley's stance of an aggressive foreign policy. (McKinley had sent troops to fight in China to suppress the 1899 Boxer Rebellion in which Chinese rebels wanted all round eyed foreigners out of their country, including us. That was part of the lecture Premier Deng gave to Pres. Bush the year before.)

In his first address to Congress, Teddy stated that peace was only possible if nations defended themselves and had a just regard for the rights of others. *America would not seek to secure any territory at the expense of any of our neighbors, nor we would we seek any exclusive commercial arrangements.* Freedom and Open Trade were the cardinal precepts of the American design. (But Teddy soon forced Colombia into giving up the Panama area to make the trans-ocean Canal.) *(115)

A year later Roosevelt backed the claim of the Europeans who were still owed a debt by Venezuela, but America was outraged when the Europeans attacked Venezuela. (The attack had actually been approved by the World Court at the Hague.)

Soon after Roosevelt again turned away the Germans when they tried to lay claim to a port in Santo Domingo for a debt they owed. Those actions were too close to home, and work was starting on the Panama Canal. Once the Canal was completed America became obsessed with the region. Such a strategic asset had to be protected as any potential enemy could exploit a problematic regime and build a hostile military base. *(We would end up "intervening in the region" almost twenty times!)*

In 1917 Woodrow Wilson committed America to fight in Europe in WWI. His claim was that we had to make the world safe for Democracy, (Ours). After the war ended Wilson wanted the Old World to change their controlling, colonizing policies with his League of Nations. He wanted that World body to settle all international affairs to avoid war. Strokes soon left him incapacitated, and the nation with no leader.

But America's Congressional leaders were not willing to give away our reigns of power any more than the Europeans did. The League became a reality, but never had any real control or power. And America never joined it. The heavy losses we had suffered in those few months of fighting and the poor peace that followed convinced many of our leaders that America must avoid foreign affairs.

For the next decade America was involved in various world treaties to limit naval buildups, and joined the list of nations worried about the Russian Bolsheviks as they conquered every nation around them. *None of the post-War Republican presidents would recognize the (terrorist regime) of the Bolsheviks, and that included Herbert Hoover who had saved millions of Russians from starvation with his humanitarian missions.*

Pres. Hoover tried to get the world to react to Japan's invasion of Manchuria, but none wanted a new war.

FDR came into office during the Great Depression and tried many policies to end the economic collapse. *He may have wanted to steer clear of the wars springing up, but he slowly led America into them. And despite his many socialists-economic programs, it was WWII that ended the Great Depression.*

FDR made many foreign policy mistakes during the war, and Harry Truman who replaced him made many after the war ended. Truman switched from his previous neutral policy positions because his mistakes during 1945-48 forced him too.

It was his grievous errors that lost China and led us into war in Korea and Vietnam.

Eisenhower ended the Korean War in 1953, and kept us out of Vietnam. But then the Democrats stole the 1960 election and JFK greatly expanded our commitment there. LBJ jumped into the conflict in 1965. Nixon ended the Vietnam War in 1972, and kept Russia out of the 1973 Mideast War. He made great strides in international relations, and Pres. Ford continued the trend.

But the Congress and Jimmy Carter resolved to end all of our foreign policy missions. Soviet Communism advanced unchecked across the globe, until Ronald Reagan confronted them and they collapsed.

Now in 1990 the Bush Administration was facing an invasion of a peaceful neutral nation by yet another violent dictator. As the leader of the Free World he had to decide on what to do. His actions or non-actions would affect the entire world.

In a schooled world *Decision Making* is based on information, some open source and some secretive. Each individual and nation works in an organized fashion upon that knowledge in ways that can be common or unique. But ultimately the decision making falls to a select group of people who are in the position to make and enact them.

Intelligence is centered on two factors, the gathering of information / intelligence, and the analysis of it. Between the two it is far easier to collect information than it is to decipher it. In a free society like ours gathering intelligence is a piece of cake. In a totalitarian state like Russia or Iraq it is quite difficult unless you have been able to get agents and assets inside. There were no American agents or assets in Iraq in 1990. And despite the multi-year efforts by President Ronald Reagan and George Bush the CIA was still not fulfilling its mission of intelligence collecting.

Analysis of any information / intelligence you uncover is done by citizens, and in a national setting it is usually controlled by a bureaucracy. Everyone's personal decision making is predicated on their life experience, strengths and weaknesses. In a bureaucracy that decision making is also affected by who is in charge of that unit and what is their background? Who else is allowed access to the information and what are their pedigrees? Do they have an intelligent and analytical mind to sift through the data or are they just a desk rider or political bureaucrat with their own political agenda, or a drone waiting for a pension?

It is not uncommon to be overwhelmed with the amount of raw data that is being picked up. Trying to decide what is important and what is noise also affects the analysis of the information.

Those *Intelligence Issues* affect all nations, such as happened to America and Russia in 1941, Korea in 1950 and Israel in 1973. Intelligence failures were a pivotal factor that hurt all of them. For Korea, Russia and Israel it was almost fatal. All misread the war signals until it was too late to prepare. Russia was saved by American aid, the enormity of their land and Hitler's mistakes. Korea was saved by luck and American armed forces. For Israel, the Syrians fought poorly in 1973. Had they been better led Israel would have been defeated. At Pearl Harbor America was hurt by the Japanese attack, but we were aided by the vastness of the Pacific theatre, the vital war in China, and Japanese mistakes.

In this current case of Iraq's invasion, most of the signals were misread until it was too late. Kuwait was quickly conquered. Now the main question was would the world unite to save them?

Historical Note: The embittered Arab world of the 1920's had been promised much by Britain and France for helping to defeat Germany and their Ottoman allies in WWI. But after the war ended nothing was done by the Europeans to benefit the Arabs, and in fact they sought to control them.

As shown before the boundaries of the nations in the region had been re-created by the French and British to suit their colonial needs. Their selfish effort and their colonial mindset had created the movement of Islamic Fundamentalism. Combined with the growing feeling of Arab Nationalism, a mounting hatred of the West grew.

A decade later Adolph Hitler was looked upon as cult figure in the Arab world. His defiance and initial defeating of the colonial masters France and Britain gave renewed hope to the Arabs for the freedom they sought. Hitler's hatred and murder of the Jews was also allied with their own feelings. The Baa`th Party was formed in Iraq and Syria during the hostile late 1920s, and mirrored Hitler's Nazi movement. But after another savage bloodletting, Germany was again defeated. Arab hopes were also ended.

After WWII the United Nations was formed and all members who joined agreed to the decision making from that world body. The area of Palestine was partitioned, and after some hard fighting the state of Israel was created. Israel thrived while the Arab world stagnated. If not for their oil, those nations would have been ignored completely by the rest of the world.

Oil sheiks used their commodity to make their controlled (until 1972) profits, but they did not use their oil wealth to help their nations. While they enriched themselves, the majority of their citizens lived in abject poverty. Only the Shah of Iran gave back to his citizens.

Over the next decades more Mid-East wars followed and the Palestinians who left Israel were never granted a homeland by their Arab brothers. Religious hostilities grew and became worse, and so did most of the leadership inside the Arab world. Nasser was the one bright spark, but he squandered his years in power by fighting with Israel. Throughout the decades turmoil and hatred ruled.

Now in 1990 Saddam Hussein was again invading. He was a vicious tyrant, and his enemies had died by the hundreds, often brutally. All who dwelled in the halls of Iraq's government feared him. (Saddam would have done quite well in the Kremlin of old.)

With no free press or courts of law to contain him, he was free to do as he wanted. (As is the case with all dictators.) With the world fearful of Iranian Islamic Fundamentalism he had enjoyed even more leeway in his actions. Many in his world supported him over Iran's zealots. Saddam Hussein was portrayed (by some) as the one Arab leader who could shed all the remaining fabric of colonialism, and bring about a true Arab Nation.

Grasping at straws the Palestinians claimed he was the re-born Saladin, the Muslim commander who chased the Christians from Jerusalem. But Saddam was no Saladin in deeds or creed, he was an evil man who coveted power. *He had spent vast sums on weaponry and his military. Since he had failed to conquer Iran, he decided to take Kuwait.*

At the United Nations the Security Council met and demanded Iraq withdraw. This rapid and unyielding diplomatic action occurred only because of the breakup of the Soviet Union and its Communist allies in Eastern Europe. This was similar to what had happened with the U.N. actions over Korea in 1950. The Soviets were boycotting the U.N. over the refusal to admit Communist China, and they missed the vote on Korea. That mistake allowed the U.N. to authorize the members nations to fight the invading N. Korean Communists who were backed by Stalin.

Had it not been for the incredible changes in political fortunes of 1989, the Communist bloc countries would never have agreed to the 1990 U.N. referendum on Iraq.

They would also have prevented any U.N. approved actions or sanctions. Over the past decades it was the Soviet Union and its Communist allies, (along with France) who had armed, trained and equipped Iraq's military. In all likelihood the pre-1990 Soviets would have stepped up their military aid, and sent additional advisors and weapons shipments to their client state to allow him to continue his invasion. That would have meant that if Bush and Thatcher wanted Saddam to leave Kuwait, our countries would have had to do so on their own, and at the world's peril. But with this **New World Order,** even the fledgling Russian Federation was against the Iraqi invasion.

Within hours Saddam's strong forces controlled all of Kuwait's government buildings, the international airport, the central bank and the Emir's palace. Their Emir, Sheik Jaber wisely escaped south to Saudi Arabia while his younger brother was cornered and gunned down. To try to confuse the Western world Saddam claimed that the Kuwaiti people had risen up against their rulers and that his forces would leave as soon as a new government had been installed. Days later Saddam annexed all of Kuwait stating it had actually been part of Iraq before the British had changed their maps. Kuwait would now be their 19th province.

President Bush took the appropriate initial steps of freezing all of Iraq's and Kuwait's assets that were in the U.S. He next banned any importation of Iraqi oil, and economic sanctions were emplaced. He stressed the importance that all of the member nations of the U.N. must agree to support any and all sanctions against Iraq.

Wisely Bush evaded all questions about using force. At that time there were 3,800 Americans in Kuwait with 130 at the Embassy. There were also 500 civilians and 42 embassy staff in Baghdad. Thus far there were no reports of harm to any of them, and almost every nation was in the same boat. But with Saddam in charge things could change very quickly.

Many of the European nations had become pacifist and totally against any kind of war. Most of their populations had been willing to sell their souls to Soviet ideology and weapons rather than accept Pres. Reagan's proposals to strengthen their ramparts. (The Cold War was won in spite of their conciliatory attitude towards Russia.)

Now in August of 1990 they reacted just like the appeasers of the 1930s, they wanted peace at any cost. To them this aberration in the desert was just a passing shower. Diplomacy would cause Saddam to back off or not. Unthinkingly they did not care what happened in those empty deserts.

National Security advisor Scowcroft was upset that so many in Europe were willing to let the issue settle into a *fait accompli*. If it was them they would be screaming for help.

Pres. Bush traveled to Aspen, Colorado and met with Margret Thatcher and the British ambassador. Thatcher warned all that Saddam would not stop with just Kuwait. If the West did not intercede Saddam would eventually continue southward. The world needed to apply pressure, and the Saudis had to be a part of the effort. Britain still had close ties to Kuwait, the Emirates and Oman. In fact there were many British Officers serving in the region on liaison and training missions. (And those Commandos.)

Recognizing the regional and strategic dangers P.M. Thatcher was adamant that Iraq must be expelled from Kuwait, and she gave all of England's support to the effort. Most of the European nations refused to join in any global effort, and the weak reaction from the rest of the NATO nations caused much negative press and chatter over in England.

Thatcher stated; "It is sad that at this critical time Europe has not fully measured up to expectations." *(116)

In America many legislators wanted to end NATO and let the Europeans protect themselves.

After a day of weakness France's Mitterrand decided to send their aircraft carrier the *Clemenceau* as a show of force, and in case they were needed to protect their citizens. But unknown to him, his Defense Minister Chev`enement who was a die hard Socialist and pacifist ordered the removal of their jet fighters and bombers. He replaced them with trucks and light helicopters.

He also directed the French military officers not to engage in combat with Iraqi units, and to not cooperate with U.S. demands for intelligence on French weapons. His overriding concern was that if the French weapons were compromised in that way and easily defeated, they would never be able to sell them again.

(When Mitterrand learned of his duplicity he was outraged and reversed all of his rulings. Chev`enement later resigned when the French provided the coalition with intelligence on their weapons from launch codes to jamming signals.)

Pres. Mubarak of Egypt was also outraged over the Iraqi invasion. Just days before Saddam had promised him that all of his moves were just saber rattling. Mubarak asked Pres. Bush to give the Arab leaders two days to try to sort things out on their own. Even Syria's Assad was worried, for a stronger Iraq would mean eventual trouble for Syria. Both stated they would join a defensive coalition if it came to that.

President Turgot Ozal of Turkey wanted action by NATO to hurt Saddam. He was correct when he stated we must not allow a repeat of the mistakes that led to WWII.

Days earlier Pres. Ozal had met with an Iraqi emissary who tried to get Turkey's support for the invasion. The Iraqi brazenly told Ozal that they had no intention of leaving Kuwait, and that the West was bluffing a response. Pres. Ozal was convinced that the UAE and the Saudi's were next if the West did not act soon. He called Pres. Bush with his warning.

(Pres. Ozal had made aggressive changes to his nation during the mid-80s by lifting trade restrictions, liberalizing policies, and integrating Turkey economically with Europe and America. *His policies were working as income and production nearly doubled by 1993.* Tragically he died later that year.

His replacements turned ever so slowly to the Fundamentalists for their future, and in our time of 2019 they have taken over! Turkey could soon be a major enemy.)

After easily overrunning Kuwait, Saddam made an appalling military mistake similar in scope to some of the errors Hitler and Japan had made in WWII.

Saddam stopped his forces at the Saudi border. He should have sent them southward immediately to take control of Saudi Arabia's oil wells and terminals.

By limiting his conquest to Kuwait he denied his forces and himself any strategic leverage that they might have been able to exert on the world stage. And because of that failure Pres. Bush was given the time he needed to create and build a coalition against him.

(Imagine what would have been had Iraq overrun the weak Saudi military and then rigged all of the Saudis' wells, pumps and distribution system to explode on command. Like the criminal that he actually was, Saddam could have used the Saudi oil industry as a hostage and kept the world at bay. *And the longer he could delay any military action against him, the stronger his overall strategic position would have been. He would have controlled all of the oil.*)

On his return to Washington Pres. Bush was adamant that Iraq had to leave Kuwait. Analysts showed the Iraqi's were quickly consolidating their hold into a permanent position. They would now control the second and third largest oil reserves in the Gulf. Saddam could dominate OPEC, and set any price he wanted.

And flush with Kuwaiti bank accounts, Saddam could double his military capabilities and use Arab mercenaries as a hostile army. Who could say what country would be next.

At that time there was still no consensus as to forcing him out of Kuwait. Sec. Defense Cheney and Chairman of the JCS Gen. Colin Powell updated all of the Administration principals with our present military picture. We were resource poor, but a carrier battle group was headed to the Persian Gulf. Saudi Ambassador Prince Bandar was asked to come to the White House for an update. He was not receptive to having any Western troops in his country, even to stop Saddam.

Later that day at Camp David the President met with all of his team and advisors. Their feedback and frank discussions on Iraq answered all of his initial questions. Gen. Powell outlined a military option in which we sent troops to protect the Saudis and prepared them to move into Kuwait. He warned the venture would be expensive and required calling up the reserves. An extensive operation in the Persian Gulf would prevent us from responding to a second crisis.

Gen. Norman Schwarzkopf had become the commander of Central-Command (Cent-Com), because Powell had picked him over the normal rotation which would have been a Navy Admiral. Schwarzkopf gave the assessment of Iraq's military stating that they have large conventional forces but poor command and control. Their air force cannot stand up to ours, and if we can get our planes in fairly quickly, about 400 in a week, that would prevent them from running amok.

Both Powell and Schwarzkopf lamented on the poor leadership from the JCS during Vietnam. They were determined to prevent those mistakes this time. That meant giving their true opinions even if the Administration principals did not want them. *(Politicians hate getting contrary advise. In Vietnam LBJ and his principals refused to hear the battle-wise opinions from the JCS. They did what they wanted, and turned Vietnam into a quagmire.)*

The President hoped that the sanctions and diplomacy could end the crisis. During those first days he had spent considerable time talking to the leaders (29) of the world, many he had known for years. From those informative sessions Bush grew hopeful that peace could be maintained. But there could be no compromise or acceptance of a "Hussein led puppet government in Kuwait. This invasion could not be accepted". When asked by the media what we could do Bush replied; "Just wait, watch and learn."

One of the most important decisions Pres. Bush reached that first weekend was to send Sec- Def. Cheney to Saudi Arabia to speak to King Fahd. (Bush had two long conversations with the Saudi King prior to Sec Def Cheney's arrival.) Unlike Turkey, the Saudi's were militarily weak and terrified they were next.

Three days after the invasion Secretary of Defense Dick Cheney, Cent-Comm commander Gen. Norman Schwarzkopf and some staff arrived in Riyadh to speak with the Royal Family. At the meeting Cheney and Schwarzkopf presented to the Saudi King the updated satellite photos of Iraq's forces which showed the Iraqis had consolidated their total control over Kuwait.

Saddam was still sending thousands of additional troops and equipment over the border. The latest satellite shots showed that hundreds of Iraqi tanks were now poised on the Kuwait-Saudi border. Saddam's tanks were only a day's drive away.

They presented the case that Saddam might attack the Saudi's regardless of whether they helped out the coalition or not. At that time the Saudi defense force, in an effort to be unthreatening, still had not left their bases. If Saddam wanted to take the kingdom there was nothing to stop him.

One unstated issue that was important to Pres. Bush was our need to protect our regional embassies and the thousands of Americans working in the Gulf. *Since all of the Gulf states had weak militaries it was possible Saddam would soon have thousands of additional U.S. and Western hostages.*

America had no dedicated land bases in the Persian Gulf region, which meant we had no ground and limited air power. (Our Carriers could sail anyplace they wanted and strike anyone we wanted. But for sustained operations you need land bases.) Saudi permission was an absolute necessity for the use of their nation as a huge forward operating base. Without such an agreement there was no reasonable way to force Saddam out of Kuwait. (Similar to what England was for Normandy in 1944-45, what Japan was for Korea in 1950-53, and what the Philippines were in Vietnam.)

The small military force the Gulf Cooperation Council maintained, and the 100,000 man security force the Saudi's had could not hope to slug it out with Saddam's well equipped forces. They were up against a wall and they knew it.

If Saddam had been smarter, he would have walked right over them. Baghdad was already sending notice that the closing of their Saudi based oil pipeline would be an act of war. Publicly Saddam was saying he was not interested in Saudi Arabia, but then he had said the same thing about Kuwait. (Hitler too always said just this last country and then we are done.)

The Saudi's had a small native population and were required to import workers to do almost everything in the nation. As custodians of Mecca and Medina, the two most sacred sites in the Islamic world, the Saudi's did not want *non-believers* in their country. Their foreign policy was cautious, and they did not hesitate to buy off potential threats. They had invested heavily in Saddam and Iraq during the Iranian war, and that may have been what kept him at bay after taking Kuwait.

The Royal family debated the issue of having foreign soldiers in their country, but it was the King who had to decide the outcome. Discussions and disagreements were made and heard. **The King determined that day that if the Americans would defend his country, he would do what was needed for the overall effort.**

He agreed to allow outside forces to enter and save his kingdom, but insisted that Muslim nations had to come in too so it would not look like a western colonial power had moved in. Morocco and Egypt were two of those on his list. It was also desired that no public announcement would be made until our units were in country. (No point riling up the Islamists.)

The Cheney team then split up and made additional stops in Egypt, UAE, Bahrain and Abu Dhabi. Each meeting was a success, as the U.S. forces would be welcomed, and all would pitch in. Meanwhile the U.N. Security Council had voted 13-0 to pass Resolution 661 which imposed multiple sanctions on Iraq. Thatcher was with Bush in the Rose Garden when they gave a joint statement on the crisis.

Saddam picked that moment to have the U.S. counsel Joseph Wilson come to him for an hour of angry contact. Saddam stated that they would never leave Kuwait. We will not be inactive during this war, and America will lose the Middle East. Cagily Saddam offered Egypt, Jordan and Yemen multiple billions in free money if they backed him instead of the U.S. (At that time Kuwait had $500 billion in various banks that Saddam now controlled.)

As shown earlier Osama bin Laden had returned to his native Saudi Arabia. He had expanded his family's and his personnel wealth with his business ventures. But Osama openly sided with the virulent strain of Islamic Fundamentalism, and was soon causing political problems in his own country.

He also continued supplying the terrorist camps, (6) that he had created in Pakistan. He had wanted to use his fighters to start a new jihad in S. Yemen to chase their Marxists out. Prince Turaki had refused his offer. But working from his base in Jeddah, bin Laden opened up the fight there without permission. The Yemeni government quickly rounded up some of his fighters and demanded the Royals reign him in. (Which they did.)

With this new threat from Iraq, bin Laden went to the Saudi Royal Family to again offer his and his army's services. They could avoid having American of other Western infidels on their land if the Royals would let him run the war with battalions of Islamic martyrs. Bin Laden sought out Prince Sultan the Saudi Minister of Defense and presented a ten page battle plan. He would use his family's construction business assets to build new fortifications along the borders, and he would supply an Islamic army from the Afghan war to defend the kingdom. All the Saudi rulers had to do was keep the hated Americans out.

Prince Sultan told him no. There were no caves in their deserts, no natural defenses between Kuwait and their people, and no place for anyone to hide from the 4,000 Iraqi tanks sitting close by. *Bin Laden was very unhappy with that response, but he was astounded to learn that American infidels were to be allowed in. He pledged to fight that affront.*

(Prince Turaki had worked with bin Laden in Afghanistan for years. He reported that this bin Laden was far different than the one who had been fighting the Soviets.)

And despite all of the years of Saudi aid, Afghan leaders Sayyaf and Hekmatyar also denounced the Royal Family for letting infidels in. Turaki sent his aide Ahmed Badeeb to Pakistan to silence them, but they cursed him in public too.

Thus far two U.S. carrier battle groups were headed to the Gulf with the ever present Marine Amphibious Units. About a regiment of troops, weapons and vehicles. That was the extent of the ground forces we could offer at that time.

On August 9, 1990 the White House announced that with Saudi Arabia in imminent danger additional U.S. forces would be sent to help.

Since their creation in 1983, CENTCOM had been war-gaming for just this eventuality. They had a basic battle plan already on paper, and within hours of the presidents message the previously alerted 82d Airborne Division was loaded onto transport aircraft and sent on its way. Two standby Marine Brigades also flew directly to Saudi Arabia to be joined up with their pre-positioned ships sailing in from Diego Garcia. They would join up with the Amphibious units sailing in with the fleet forming an understrength division. (Pres. Reagan's buildup was in action.)

The U.S. Air Force initially sent two squadrons of F-15 fighters and a recon unit that flew the RC135. That aircraft could pickup all types of electronic signals. England lead by the indomitable Margret Thatcher promised to send two squadrons of Tornado and Jaguar jets to help with more to follow by sea. **Operation Desert Shield was starting to come together.**

Now it was Saddam who began to worry. When he spoke with Ambassador Glaspie weeks earlier there was no mention that America would respond like this. His timetable for exerting control over Arabia was in trouble, his economy was being cutoff from exports or imports, and even his brother Arab nations were joining the cause against him. Pres. Mubarak of Egypt had worked for a decade to mend fences with the other nations of the Arab world.

(Egypt was outcast for Pres. Sadat's peace with Israel.) Yet even he was joining forces with the Americans.

Led by Pres. Mubarak, 12 of the 20 members of the Arab League joined the allied coalition. They demanded Iraq exit Kuwait and the legitimate government be returned to power. Contributing military forces to the cause were Egypt, Syria, Lebanon, Mauritania, Morocco, Sudan, Somalia and Djibouti. Three Arab League members voted no to the resolutions, Iraq, Libya and the PLO. Jordan, the Sudan and Mauritania expressed reservations about the effort, but agreed with the sanctions, while Algeria and Yemen abstained.

Out of all of the member states of the Arab League, Jordan had the most to fear. They had a long and porous border with Iraq, harbored large numbers of pro-Iraqi Palestinian refugees, and received 95% of their oil from them. Almost 45% of Iraq's oil sales went through Jordan to the port of Aqaba on the Red Sea. In joining this coalition King Hussein knew he was playing with fire, but Pres. Bush worked hard to keep him safe and on the team.

Unknown to most of the world, Algeria was undergoing their own Islamic insurgency. The Islamic Salvation Front, ISF was getting stronger every year, and in 1990 had won numerous parliamentary seats. When they were denied controlling political power they routinely murdered dozens of soldiers, government officials and police.

The Bush administration was unsure on how to react to this right-wing Islamic issue. We had backed the Islamists when fighting the Soviets, but this war was different. *They were not fighting Communists, but a pro-western government.* An extensive policy review was needed to see who and how we should support. For the time being the Administration backed the Algerian Army's takeover and suppression of the Islamists.

A short while later the Algerian president was assassinated and a terrible civil war began. During the next years tens of thousands were killed in this hidden struggle between the Algerian people and the Fundamentalists who were trying to impose an Islamic state. **That was the first battle in that new war.**

(During November 1991 Algerian Islamists marked the second anniversary of the death of Abdullah Azzam the Fundamentalist cleric who had been "taken out". They captured and cut off the heads of numerous Algerian soldiers.)

Inside the Persian Gulf an international naval flotilla was almost in place. They would blockade Iraq as soon as the legal questions had been settled. Bush wanted the U.S. ships to begin the blockade on the 16th but that earned the ire of many of the coalition states for "jumping the gun". (The Saudis however wanted to use force quickly to wipe out Saddam's forces in Kuwait. More than likely they wanted a quick get in and get out scenario to avoid any internal issues.)

Gen. Colin Powell and Gen. Schwarzkopf had both served two tours in Vietnam and were can-do type people. Their overriding concern was that U.S. troops would wrongly be committed piecemeal to this situation, in inadequate numbers and with no clear purpose. That was the way Vietnam had been fought, and they were completely against that useless and dangerous scenario.

Powell followed a simple attitude, I'll do whatever the President asks of me, but he insisted that he be given **all of the forces he deemed necessary to complete the mission.**

Both men had served in the Infantry, and both told the president that to hold the line against the Iraqi armored forces would require several divisions of troops including our own armored forces. He also warned the President that *pushing* the Iraqi military out of Kuwait would be difficult. That would entail a large commitment in time, troops, supplies and money. Unlike Lyndon Johnson and his inane people, George Bush listened.

After Ronald Reagan was elected in November 1980 the military highlighted how weak we were in the Persian Gulf. At that time there was no unified command arrangement or battle-plan to be found, just the RDF concept from Carter.

CENTCOM, or Central Command was officially created in 1983, and given responsibility for all of the Middle East. They had been allocated (on paper) seven USAF fighter wings, two bomber squadrons, five Army Divisions, a Marine Regiment, three USN Carrier Battle groups, a Surface Action Group and five Maritime patrol squadrons. The small U.S. installations in the region were enhanced during the Reagan years, including the previously mentioned pre-positioned supplies. (Over $500 million had been spent to build a secret airfield in SE Egypt.)

Pre-positioned heavy weapons systems were being kept on seven large transport ships at the British base of Diego Garcia in the Indian Ocean. As already seen, this equipment would be sailed in to join up to the Marine Units that were flown in. As planned the operation was an extensive Navy directed fight as we had no real land bases in the region. (Just like the battles in the Central Pacific in WWII.) Marine and Navy fliers would handle most of the air-war in the Persian Gulf region, unlike the pre-positioned Army and Air Force equipment in Europe that was setup for the NATO fight against the Soviets.

As the war in Afghanistan dragged on it became apparent that the Soviets were not going to be able to invade Iran. And Iran was tired up fighting Iraq. With time to spare the Reagan Administration's naval buildup progressed and two more supply ship flotillas were added which tripled the combat capability of the maritime pre-positioned squadrons.

Planners realized that the older Marine M-60 tanks, (Army cast-offs), were going to have trouble stopping the Soviet T-72 and new T-80 tanks. The Army's new M-1 *Abrams* tanks would have to get into the fight. Armored units required a large baggage train of other vehicles and support troops to complete the total mission package. All of it would have to ship either from Germany or the U.S. That massive transport need was a potentially tough undertaking even in this "modern age". All of the vehicles and equipment would have to get to a port and be loaded aboard the transport ships. Then sail to the war zone without being sunk by the dozens of Soviet subs that could be after them, unloaded near or at a port facility, and then driven to the battles.

By the 1980's the Soviets had a large and dangerous submarine force capable of sinking our ships with multiple advanced weapon systems. Planners knew that we would probably lose ships in the month long trip, and that would hurt our ground combat capability. That was why it would be safer if they were already in the area. (Using overland routes into the Middle East the Soviets were not so endangered.)

To speed up the unloading effort eight large roll-on roll-off ships were built. Capable of carrying an entire Army Brigade, this type of ship eliminated the need for port cranes and handling that was required to unload from a regular supply ship. Vehicles and equipment were driven onto and into the ship, and then driven onto a shallow shore when and where they were needed. Those eight ships were kept empty and in U.S. ports awaiting the call to arms. Now that time had come.

(Few people realize or even think about how extensive the logistic problems are to get a large military force onto a foreign battlefield.)

Back in Washington, Gen. Schwarzkopf updated the principals as to the capabilities and limitations that his Command had war-gamed. At home the public was not happy to hear the possible clarion call to save some wealthy oil Sheiks who had been milking us for the past twenty years. Some in the Congress began arguing against getting involved, and the left-wing media began to sound the doom and gloom that we were headed for another fall.

At that time exports of oil accounted for 90% of Iraq's foreign trade. With no chance to sell any, and with all of their overseas assets frozen by the U.N. sanctions, it was hoped that Saddam might just wake up and give up.

Iraq had only two ways of getting their oil out of the country, overland pipelines through Saudi Arabia, Turkey and Jordan, and the waters of the Persian Gulf. The Navy would shut the oil-tanker traffic, and Jordan had already closed off its oil pipeline. Turkey and the Saudi's were earning a lot of money from their pipelines, with the export poor Turks getting $400 million per year. That was not something they could easily give up. But Turkey was a solid NATO member and as such Pres. Ozal agreed to go along with the U.N. sanctions.

The Saudi's were actually a harder sell because of their "stature" as the largest oil producer. They would be needed to pump more of their oil to make up for the loss of Iraqi and Kuwait's oil on the worlds markets. In reality it was a no-brainer, for the Saudi's stood to make a lot of extra money with the additional oil they would sell. And the price of that oil had gone up since the Iraqi invasion. Protected by our forces, they agreed to shut the Iraqi pipeline.

The worst surprise for Saddam was the Russian reaction. Gorbachev was anxious now that the reality of Communism had shown its true self by destroying the Russian economy. He greatly needed western capital and business to shore up his ailing nation. In that frame of mind Russia agreed with the West, and approved all five of the U.N. resolutions that demanded Iraq withdraw from Kuwait and their government be restored. Whatever "friendship" Iraq had had with Russia, it was subservient to Russia's interests. But then that is always the reality.

During the past month the Iraqi invaders had stolen over 50,000 Kuwaiti vehicles, stripped thousands of residences of everything of value, looted vast stores of food, and seized millions in gold from the Kuwaiti central bank. Also taken was the artwork, computers, airplanes, streetlights and anything else of value that had been within the nation's borders.

Saddam knew full well what had happened to America during the Vietnam War and throughout the 1970's. He felt that the U.S. Government and people would not have the stomach for this fight. He was certain that a negotiated settlement would come about, and at the least Iraq would keep some part of Kuwait. Unknown to him the NSA was using the RC135s to monitor all of his communications between Baghdad and the Iraqi Embassy at the United Nations. Saddam repeatedly stated he was confident they would win against us.

To counter this pending coalition Saddam made a statement on August 12 that linked his action to the Palestinian cause. Iraq would pull out of Kuwait if Israel left the territories they occupied, and Syria withdrew their occupying army from Lebanon. The announcement was cynical and clever. Palestinians everywhere rejoiced over the news as did many Arab people. Miraculously the effort did not get traction, and Pres. Bush was able to keep the balance between the various political groups.

On the 15th Saddam made his second gambit by sending a letter to Iran's Pres. Rafsanjani vowing to give back the captured territories and release all of the Iranian captives. In an instant Saddam was throwing away all of the gains from his eight year war in the hope that Iran would send aid across their common border. Iran accepted the offer, but then gave nothing in return.

With the decrease in tensions with Iran, Iraq was able to shift some divisions from the Iranian border over to Kuwait, but his giveaway actually forced Saddam to hold onto Kuwait. The captured Iranian area had provided fine access to the Gulf, but now that the access was gone. Saddam later admitted to the Soviet envoy that now he had to keep control of Kuwait. (Similar to Hitler, Saddam did not know what he was doing.)

President Bush was the complete opposite. In just two weeks an extensive coalition had been organized and defensive units sent over. Saddam was a criminal who was to be humiliated and forced to exit Kuwait. The process could be enacted by war or sanctions, but that was up to Saddam. Everyone knew to gather the forces needed to fight a war would take months, and during that time of buildup Pres. Bush enacted a four part strategy.

First America's profile was to be kept to a minimum. Even though we were the force behind everything, all efforts and actions would be under the United Nations name. *Second, as many countries as possible* had to become part of the effort to join with U.S. and British forces. By making the coalition a truly multinational force, Bush could counter Saddam's claims that this was just American or Western imperialism.

Third, the financial needs of the coalition had to be borne by all. Europe was getting 42% of their oil from the Gulf, while Japan was importing 67%. America was only getting 24% of our oil from the Gulf. Thus those other nations had a greater stake in this effort than we did, and they had to help defray the costs. **(Japan and Germany did not want to help at all, and had to be forced to!)** Meanwhile the Saudi's donated much of the extra revenue they were getting to the cause. By the time the air war was underway the coalition had collected $51 billion dollars.

And the fourth part of his strategy was to keep an anti-Saddam solidarity among the Arab nations. The Arab League was split in its vote against the invasion since most of the Middle Eastern nations were ruled by dictators. And even if they went along with the U.N. sanctions their people might not. It was vital to make this a worldwide effort so dissent would be reduced. Again the Administration worked long and hard to that end.

On August 15 the 7th Marine Expeditionary Brigade was ashore and joined with their equipment. The 7th had 123 M-60 tanks, some artillery and 124 tactical aircraft. Though this force was small it was potent, and they moved northward to join-up with the RDF troops. (Most of the initial RDF units flew directly from the U.S. to Saudi Arabia, a huge undertaking in its own.)

More USAF squadrons had also arrived and were distributed to the region's base areas. Saddam had missed any chance to make an easy grab. As additional U.S. forces landed in Arabia, Saddam tightened his grip on Kuwait.

The fear that Iraq would strike our lightly armed troops disapated, but a new problem arose, *Saddam began taking hostages.* On the 19th the Iraqi's announced they were detaining all foreign nationals until "this aggression against Iraq was contained." (Detention of foreigners had already been happening since few civilians had been permitted to leave.)

All "prisoners" were kept near potential targets to prevent them from being bombed. Saddam demanded that all nations close their Kuwaiti embassies and relocate their staffs to Baghdad. In that way Saddam insured he held onto the diplomats too.

Iraq's invasion had trapped about 3,000 U.S. citizens and the same number of British citizens in Kuwait. Around 2,500 more were in Iraq, and over 200,000 Indian workers had also been caught. No one was saying it out loud but the world had a major civilian hostage problem that had to be rectified. Saddam even went on television stroking a small British boy's head. The sight sent chills throughout the globe. But it would be months before anyone could actually do anything to stop him.

On August 22 Saddam ordered all embassies in Kuwait closed or they would be closed forcibly. The U.S. and eight others refused to close theirs, and they reinforced for a siege. (Non essential personnel were somehow evacuated.)

On the 24th the Soviets agreed with U.N. Resolution 665 to use force to seal the naval blockade on Iraq.

Back in the states an Air Force think tank was formed with a Col. Wharton in charge. *His group developed a multi-part battle plan that used the Air assets to strike and remove the Top of Iraq's military chain and work down to the level of the ground forces.* Those attacks would take time, but they would strike Iraq with large forces daily, and not stop until they were "deemed successful" by the military commanders in theatre.

Gen. Schwarzkopf liked the idea of a large, devastating Air War, as it was the exact opposite of the inanity LBJ and Sec. McNamara had forced on the military in Vietnam. However the Navy did not like the plan out of fear of Saddam's missile weapons The Persian Gulf was small and constricted, and their newer missiles could be deadly as was found on the USS Stark in 1987. (As in WWII, the navy wanted a quick in and a quick out.

Communism Falls

Gorbachev and the Soviet diplomats tried a few tricks to help out Iraq. One entailed resurrecting a U.N. committee which might take control of the warships enforcing the blockade. Naturally the British and U.S. commanders wanted no part of that.

Another Soviet initiative to help Saddam would have allowed him to keep the Rumalia oil fields and two islands at the head of the Gulf. Iraq would then exit from Kuwait. That offer was declined by the coalition, and by September Gorbachev and his ministers were so preoccupied with their own problems that Pres. Bush was able to have a free hand over Kuwait.

Both leaders met to discuss options and Bush impressed upon Gorbachev that Saddam must not profit from this invasion. He invited the Soviet leader to send forces to the Gulf, but Gorbachev declined which was surprising. There were over 5,000 Soviets interred inside Iraq. Most had been technical specialists for Iraq's weapons.

Within their old sphere the Soviets were having serious issues. One "domestic action" involved the violent stopping of protests in the Baltic States. With the media concentration on Iraq the aggressive Russian military action in the Baltic's was not publicized. *Their actions were more brutal than their 1968 repression of Czechoslovakia, but not as bloody as the 1956 invasion in Hungary.* (Since those states have direct access to the Baltic Sea, they were considered vital for Soviet control of that waterway. Due to our actions and needs in the Gulf, Pres. Bush did not press the issue.)

Historical Note: After taking over Russia in 1917 the Bolshevik's led by Lenin renounced Russia's old empire. But as soon as they had achieved full control of the country, the Bolsheviks began to re-form their own empire by force of arms. Ukraine fell first, followed by Belarus. However the Bolshevik effort in the Baltic's and Poland were unsuccessful despite Gen. Tukhachevsky's leadership. (As shown earlier, not until 1939 were the failures to take Poland and the Baltic states "rectified" by Stalin.)

But Bolshevik conquests were achieved upon the rest of their neighbors. In the southern area of the Caucuses stood Armenia, Azerbaijan, Georgia, Kazakhstan, Moldova, Tadzhikistan and Uzbekistan. Most of those populations were Islamic with the exception of Armenia and Moldova. None of those nations were treated well by the anti-religious communists.

(*And in more tragic irony, the Orthodox Russians under the Czar's rule had worked to protect the Christians who lived under the Islamic Ottoman rule. That was one reason for the Russians siding against the Kaiser and his Ottoman allies in WWI!*)

By re-conquering those lands the Communists were approaching the extent of the Czar's Russian empire. (Their original empire was the third largest, behind Great Britain and the Mongols.)

After Lenin died in 1924 Stalin eventually took over and implemented his harsh "population engineering program". Millions of people were uprooted and relocated from every country in an effort to change the population makeup. Despite his brutal efforts he could never turn any of those former nations into a true part of the Soviet Union, and they never forgot who they were.

In March 1990 the people in Belarus and the Ukraine voted to end their Communist parties. The Baltic states followed suit, as did Moldova and Uzbekistan in June. As the entity of the Soviet Union further dissolved the formation of the Russian Federation was enacted and Boris Yeltsin was elected as their first President.

This placed Yeltsin on an equal footing with Premier Gorbachev who was ruling a fatally wounded empire.

Russia declared their sovereignty on June 12, 1990. That fall Gorbachev attempted to present a new union out of the old Soviet one, but none of the freed republics wanted any part of it. *With their collapse soon to come, Foreign Minister Shevardnadze resigned on December 20, 1990.*

One of Gorbachev's last major foreign policy moves was renewing commercial ties with Germany. They had greatly helped each other before WWII, and needed each other once again. As the Soviets ran out of money entire industries collapsed causing massive unemployment. The most affected sectors were in the military-industrial sector and weapons research. Many of those unemployed scientists and researchers went to work in the Middle East, and many were making weapons for Iran.

Freed from the stifling Russian control, nationalism soared in all of those captive countries. A religious resurgence was also blossoming throughout the former USSR, but it was most acute in the Islamic states.

Sunni Islamic Radicalism in Afghanistan was still being supported by Osama bin Laden and his followers, plus Pakistan and the Saudis. Those extremists viewed this "western inspired war" against Iraq, as an new affront to Islam.

Their jaded outlook was soon to translate into major attacks.

Even Yugoslavia's Communist Party voted to give up its monopoly on power. They declared the country a multi-ethnic democracy! In the province of Slovenia a center-right coalition was formed and voted for independence. Croatia also voted for freedom, while in Serbia the Communists maintained a hold on power. Always a tense area, more violence would soon begin.

To their north Lech Walesa became the first democratically elected President of Poland. Though the event heralded a dramatic change in political direction, the die-hard communists were still a presence in the nation.

In south Asia the nation known as Myanmar, (formally Burma) had their first free election in thirty years. Their people wanted to end the military's rule, and said so at the ballot box. But the Generals refused to enact the vote.

All around the globe America's efforts at promoting democracy were finally coming to fruition. Now America wass trying to save an Islamic nation from a brutal dictator.

The Persian Gulf

The international coalition arriving in Saudi Arabia slowly took shape. Though most of the NATO countries did not send ground troops many sent small air or naval units. Germany and Japan sent only money, while Saddam's hostile Arab neighbors Egypt and Syria sent armored units.

France's Mitterrand gave a hasty speech in late September stating that the al-Sabah family did not have to return to Kuwait for peace to be reached. He also spoke of a need for an international conference to meet and work out the problems for the region. He was basically agreeing to the Iraqi invasion of Kuwait and the ouster of the ruling family. And what was worse he was agreeing with Saddam about "linking" Kuwait to the Palestinians. The anti-Israel media jumped on the bandwagon, but again the idea failed to take.

During October Gen. Schwarzkopf had to present his proposed attack plan to the White House and sent some of his staff. No one on the NSC staff approved of the plan of simply invading Kuwait and trying to drive the Iraqis out. All of the NSC but especially Cheney and Brent Scowcroft were appalled. There was no imagination, no generalship. Scowcroft recommended attacking from the western desert, but was told that the present coalition did not have enough ground forces or fuel tankers to enact that option. *(Which was why it was not presented.)*

Soon after Sec-Def Cheney visited the Soviet Union. In an unprecedented event he was allowed into the Soviet Military Command Center and openly discussed many topics with his counterparts. One of the most important was the type of weaponry the Soviets had provided Saddam. Particular emphasis was directed to any "weapons no one knew about". With this changing of the times the Soviet principals assured Cheney that all Saddam had of their arms were conventional weapons.

By November 1990 the siege on Iraq had been in effect for three months. Iraq's money supply was dwindling and it could not be replaced by oil sales. Prices inside the country were rising and foods were becoming rationed. Saddam however was content to see his people starve. He was a dictator who had long ago extinguished all opposition and critics.

The principals in the Coalition knew that it could take up to a year for the sanctions to work. Iraq had their own oil reserves to supply energy needs, enough food for a year, and plenty of ammunition and spare parts. A year was a long time to keep large, expensive military forces committed to the area. And even if the sanctions did work, a large peacekeeping force would have to be maintained indefinitely. *As time went by the atrocities against the people in Kuwait continued unchecked.* Kuwait needed their country liberated now.

Inside the Arab nations their populations began to complain about going against a brother Arab. And the idea of infidels, especially western women defending the holy sites began to cause some to see the coalition effort as a new Crusade. All during this time the talking heads and pundits were proclaiming doom and gloom over Pres. Bush's efforts. And the Soviets were still playing both sides of the crisis, one day saying one thing and the next a complete opposite. It was hard to tell if this coalition could stay intact for a year.

Sec. of State Baker went to see all of the heads of state from the coalition, while the Saudi's worked with Schwarzkopf on a suitable command arrangement for the various forces if a war did begin. Egypt's Pres. Mubarak was solidly on the side of the coalition, and Pres. Ozal of Turkey stated that the U.S. could fly from Turkish air bases. The Chinese were not pleased with the thought of a war, but let it be known that they would not use their U.N. veto to stop it.

Historical Note: The U.N. Charter was altered when Pres. Nixon renewed ties to Red China. The expulsion of the Nationalist Chinese from the U.N. meant that Two Communist Powers sat on the Security Council. Both had veto power to stop any U.N. action they disliked. But on Iraq both voted for expulsion. At that time China was still militarily weak. Their massive buildup would begin later that year and has continued unabated to this day.

Despite the naysayers, the mid-tem elections in America were over with only small changes to the makeup in the Congress. Americans were not completely happy with events in the Gulf, but had not expressed their anger at the ballot box. *Pres. Bush had an approval rating of over 70%.*

By this point we had been able to emplace 230,000 troops with 800 tanks and hundreds of aircraft in the continued effort to enact *Desert Shield*. In addition we had supplied $Billions in arms and supplies to the regional nations and the coalition partners. For now the coalition had to sit still and wait for the sanctions to work.

New York City - Islamaic Terrorists

Over the past decades New York City became an extremely violent place. Another murder had occurred on November 5, 1990. This one was different from the **2,000** other murders that occurred each year, in that the victim was Meir Kahane head of the Jewish Defense League. His killer was an Egyptian national who also shot an elderly bystander as he tried to escape the midtown Marriot Hotel. This murderer turned out to be, **Sayyid Nosair**.

He and his friend **Bilall Alkaisi** had been waiting in the back of the ballroom for Kahane to finish his talk. After the shooting Sayyid escaped out of the back of the building, and Alkaisi exited from the front. Nosair expected to see his getaway driver **Mahmoud Abouhalima** waiting for him in his nearby car, but security had chased him away minutes before. Nosair then jumped into a cab and were caught in traffic.

Carlos Acosta a U.S. Postal Police Officer had seen the attempted escape and intervened. He shot Nosair critically wounding him just as Nosair fired and wounded Acosta. Ironically Nosair was saved at Bellevue Hospital, while a few beds away Kahane died.

Meanwhile Alkaisi had jumped into Nosair's car and escaped with a lookout named **Mohammed Salameh**.

Investigating detectives found an address for Nosair in Jersey City, NJ and they went there after midnight. Upon knocking the door opened and there was Abouhalima and Salameh. Both admitted they knew Nosair, and both had been at the shooting. They were brought back to NYC for questioning.

The detectives on this case already knew this was not just a lone gunman, Nosair obviously had help. They learned that Abouhalima had provided the weapons, but one **Wadi el-Haj** from Tucson had given them to him.

But at the NYPD HQ Chief detective Borelli stupidly refused any thought that this was a conspiracy. He ordered the detective in charge of the case to release the other two suspects!

Borelli then announced to the media that Nosair was a "lone gunman", with no ties to known terrorists or the Middle East. The case was considered "closed", just the way the NYPD brass and so many "others" like it.

This inane decision crippled the investigation, and allowed those terrorists to act again. (It was learned that Bilall Alkaisi had been an instructor at one of bin Laden's Afghan terrorist camps!)

Detective Norris of the JTTF knew that Borelli's NYPD public relations pitch was nonsense. It took them a while but they had tracked down Nosair's real address in Cliffside Park, NJ. Members of the JTTF carried out 16 boxes of evidence.

Found among his possession were bomb making instructions and photographs of NYC landmarks such as the World Trade Center, Statue of Liberty, Rockefeller Center and Times Square! All of the photos had Arabic writing on them that no one understood. There were also classified training manuals from the U.S. Army's Special Warfare School at Fort Bragg, North Carolina, and copies of teletypes routed to the Sec. of the Army and the Joint Chiefs of Staff! Detectives wondered how and why someone like Nosair had those classified manuals and messages in his possession. *(Was an investigation ever done to find out ??)*

Fort Bragg, North Carolina was the U.S. Army base that former Egyptian sargent **Ali Mohamed** had been assigned to when he became a U.S. soldier. Some of the markings on those files were actually in Ali's handwriting, though at that time that fact also slipped by since no one was looking at him. One of the manuals was titled the Manchester Manual, our how to instructions to resist interrogations. (More on this complicated story to follow.)

It also turned out that Mahmoud Abouhalima had followed the standard illegal script for getting into and staying in the U.S. *He used a six-month tourist visa to get in, then over-stayed his visa knowing there was almost no chance at getting caught.*

In 1986 the Democrats passed an amnesty to all illegal immigrants, and he was free to stay here and carry on his terrorist missions.

During the Nosair investigation the JTTF detectives, (who were outside of NYPD command), took away a total of 47 boxes of personal papers and cassette tapes. Most of the wording and speeches were in Arabic, and the evidence was filed away to be deciphered at some future time. On those cassette tapes were multiple jihadist recordings from various Islamic clerics.

Notably some of them were from **Sheikh Omar Abdul Rahman**. On one message Nosair was heard telling Rahman that "we have organized an encampment and are concentrating here".

(But to the NYPD Chief Borelli there was no conspiracy!)

Upon deeper investigation it was learned that this Sheikh Rahman had entered the U.S. in May 1990 claiming persecution, and he wanted asylum. But he began his hostile preaching's soon after he arrived. **In actuality he was a wanted fugitive from Egypt, and never should have been allowed into the U.S.**

Once he came in, the aforementioned cleric Mustapha Shalabi invited him to the al-Farooq Mosque to lecture. Rahman was a true jihadist who wanted a religious war to occur everywhere, but especially inside America.

Police and FBI agents found a "hit list" of Jewish Leaders and U.S. politicians who supported Israel. There were notes describing pending attacks on the "enemies of Islam". Those "pending attacks" would occur at **popular tourist sites** and in their **tall buildings** that they are proud of and in which their leaders gather. **(Somehow no one understood these implications!??)**

That alarming language in those notes and on those tapes was often heard and repeated at the *Alkifah Refuge Center* housed in the *Al-Farooq Mosque* on Atlantic Avenue in Brooklyn. As shown before a well orchestrated Islamic propaganda program had been promoted by the eliminated Palestinian cleric **Abdullah Azzam**. Among Azzam's followers in Egypt were **Mohammed al-Salameh, Mahmud Abouhalima** and **Mustapha Shalabi**.

Shalabi had been brought to the U.S. in early 1989 to begin indoctrinating our youth starting in Brooklyn. It was time to start the next phase of their war against the West and he would run Azzam's refugee center on Atlantic Ave in downtown Brooklyn.

One of Azzam and Shalabi's converts was **Sayyid Nossair,** the murderer of **Kahane.** Soon after Azzam was blown up, and Shalabi's loyalty was only to him. All of their funding was now under his control, and he was determined to follow Azzam's guidelines. *He too suffered an "untimely death" on February 26, 1991, and conveniently replaced by Sheikh Omar Abdul Rahman.*

Kahane's shooting and all of this gangster-style intrigue was exactly what JTTF agents had alerted everyone about years earlier when they issued their warnings regarding the new Islamic radicals they saw. *They dug out their surveillance photos taken at the Calverton rifle range, and there was Nosair.*

On the third day after the shooting the FBI took possession of the original 16 boxes of evidence. Days later they insisted that they had returned them over to the Manhattan District Attorney's office, when DA Morgenthau demanded it come back. *Somewhere along the way the evidence went into a "dark place".* Tragically large amount of information picked up from the arrest of Nosair was never examined in full detail due to the lack of Arabic translators, and the "misplacing" of those other boxes. Everything had been collected and noted, and then buried in the files.

Not until the bombing of the World Trade Center in 1993 was the vast amont gone over properly!

Detective Norris of the JTTF was certain that had his office had control of all of that material they would have had it translated prior to Nosair's trial. Then the additional evidence would have proved his feelings were correct, this was a treacherous iceberg they had just found.

At this time NYC was in the heights of our "crack-war". Every day there were 6-9 murders, most by criminals, Columbian drug cartels and street dealers.

The annual murder rate was over 2000 per year.

(At my Times Square firehouse on W 48 & 8 Avenue we had seven murders around us in just two weeks. Ladder Co-3 where I had worked until my promotion to Lieutenant had just had a shootout right next door. Not until **Republican Rudy Giuliani** became mayor in January 1994 would this insanity be stopped. When he left office in 2002 the murder rate had dropped precipitously to just 300 annually. Thousands of minority lives were saved, and NYC was re-born as Companies moved back, hirings soared, construction boomed and the good times returned.)

Desert Shield

Britain's Thatcher was pressing for air strikes without waiting for some additional provocation from Saddam, while Pres. Bush wanted to work within the U.N. framework. The Democratic run Congress insisted that Bush had to work with them before committing to any type of military action.

At another meeting with Gen. Powell the president was alerted that air power alone could not force Saddam out, only ground forces could do that. (An unassailable premise that TR Farhenbach spoke about with his great work *This Kind of War*.)

The original ground offensive was centered on an attack into Kuwait and pushing the Iraqi's out. No one liked that idea because it went into the strength of the Iraqi defenses. *Options were few because of the location of the battle area and the limited forces present.* After their first plan was rejected, Generals Schwarzkopf and Powell presented a solid case for increasing their forces so it would give them the chance at other attack options.

On November 14, Sec. Cheney announced the call up of 125,000 reservists. It was also announced that VII Corps was being redeployed from NATO to the Gulf. (This was the first time we had pulled units from Europe since NATO was formed.) Additional forces from the U.S. and Britain would also have to be sent over. Congressional liberals were in an uproar over this reinforcement, claiming that Bush had waited until after the election to prepare for a larger war.

Recent intelligence had shown that Iraq had added almost 100,000 more troops to Kuwait, but there was another reason for decision to add the additional troops now. *A time stamp had been approved among the coalition principles, they wanted to act by mid- January 1991.*

Sending those additional forces would take that exact amount of time to get to Saudi Arabia and organized for battle. The original Desert Shield force would be augmented with another 1,000 heavy tanks. This was the force Cent-Com needed to enact their revised plan for *Desert Storm.* Saddam should have recognized that those additional deployments were proof that war was coming. But he refused to see that reality.

On November 16, 1990 Pres. Bush traveled to Europe to see the results of the "Velvet Revolution". The president stopped first in Prague, Czechoslovakia. He met with their president Victor Havel, the man who had recently been beaten and imprisoned. Alexander Dubcek was also there, the leader of their 1968 Spring protests. Czechoslovakia was struggling with the economic problems of the time, but everyone was in full agreement that resisting Iraqi aggression was the price for liberty.

The crowd in Wenceslas Square topped 750,000 exuberant people, people who were now free thanks to the unyielding support from the United States. Those crowds energized Bush and convinced him that we had to fight for the Kuwaitis. After stops in Germany and France he and his wife Barbara flew to Saudi Arabia and had Thanksgiving dinner with the troops. Seeing all of their young faces brought the first couple back to their own trials during WWII. After that dinner the president met with multiple Arab leaders while Sec. State Baker did the same.

(Former president Carter actually wrote to the U.N. and every head of state stating that no resolution for war should be issued. He urged all to support the Arab League and the Palestinians, and abandon Kuwait. True to his character, he still could not admit that this latest crisis was one of the fallouts from his unfathomable failures.)

During the trials in Kuwait the Taif Agreement was passed by the U.N. to try to end the Lebanese Civil War. Israel was not doing well in their operations in southern Lebanon so nothing was improving. Backed by the U.S., this agreement gave Syria a free hand in Lebanon as the only way to end the suffering.

This Agreement was thanks for Syria sending their forces to help the coalition drive out Saddam Hussein. Bolstered with this support Assad informed the Iranian Revolutionary Guard units it was time to leave their stronghold in Baalbek.

Iran wisely decided that Hezbollah should end their terrorist tactics, and turn to "nation building" as a way to curry favor. They could still attack the Israelis, and they would build up their defenses and weapon systems to become a match for the IDF if they ever returned. Both Iranian groups would watch the Syrians to see if they could manage the new Lebanese government they were trying to form. Hezbollah released many of the hostages they had taken which included Terry Anderson and Terry Waite.

(It was also quite possible the Iranians were unsure if America was only going to attack Iraq. For them it was better to play nice for a while and see how things turned out. They may also have expected that the U.S. would crush Iraq and kill Saddam, enabling Iran to take them over.)

Final preparations for Desert Storm were being worked on as USAF Gen. Larry Henry formed a planning group that was dedicated to destroying Iraq's integrated air defense system. Northrop Corp. suggested using older navy drones as decoys which would trick the Iraqi's into firing at them. Their idea was sound and the operation was setup and organized within 30 days. (Many U.S. companies gave help like that.)

On November 29 the U.N. passed their 12th resolution, # 678 which authorized war. Iraq had until January 15, 1991 to get out of Kuwait.

Iraq's U.N. representative voiced his alarm over the potential war as did many in America. Due to Saddam's prior use of chemical weapons, casualty estimates from the Pentagon suggested over 10,000. Dissenters preferred that we wait for the sanctions to cripple Iraq rather than risk our people to save Kuwait and their oil. But what none of them understood or understand even today was that loss of the world's oil supply meant loss of the world's economy. Every day Kuwait was occupied the country was being ravaged as were their helpless citizens. And if the coalition fell apart Saddam could have stayed in place for years.

In the U.S. Congress the Democrats opened televised hearings in late November to try to stop any potential war. Many of them wanted us to use sanctions even if it took up to two years. The hearings became politically charged and a soapbox drama unfolded. Every speaker and official who testified had a different idea and agenda. Robert McNamara the deceitful, manipulative Sec-Defense that got us into and ruined our efforts in Vietnam predicted over 30,000 casualties. Robert Novak and others from the defeatist media gave 20,000 as their casualty figures, while pacifist George McGovern proclaimed the war was not worth taking 50,000 dead. Many claimed the cause was lost before a shot was fired, and the administration clueless, Bush was destroying his party. As with Vietnam those complainers and their doom and gloom reports were simply emboldening Saddam and his minions.

With so much negativity and divisiveness in America, Saddam felt there was no real war potential, so why give in.

Henry Kissinger then gave testimony that shut down many of their claims. He warned the Congress that sanctions might work, but by the time you decide they did not work it would be too late for a military resolution to this crisis. It is wise to proceed as we have, but a final decision will have to be made soon. This coalition is politically fragile and expensive to maintain. If you withdraw the military forces before the issue is decided then Saddam and the tyrants win. What will be the outcome for that failure.

Amnesty International sent out an 88 page report of the human rights violations occurring inside Kuwait. Few of the liberals cared to read it, or to present the findings at the hearings.

Sec. Baker was scheduled to go to Baghdad to see Saddam but the ever intransient leader made excuses to avoid it. On December 6th Saddam suddenly released all of his Western hostages. Possibly he thought the gesture would stop the West from attacking.

During the next few weeks the world was on a roller coaster of diplomatic missions and talks. And during that time the coalition buildup was being completed. Mission targeting and planning was in overdrive. At a briefing for the White House military planners had organized a thirty day air war to degrade Iraq's forces. Losses were expected to be high, about 150 aircraft. Cent-Com was still working on their ground attack plans and wanted more time, which again caused friction between Powell and Schwarzkopf.

After the Christmas recess ended the legislators began returning to Washington. More calls went out to wait on the sanctions, and the leftists demanded a resolution that Bush had to ask the Congress before firing a shot. Democratic senator Barbara Boxer again used 15,000 dead as her casualty number, while Ted

Kennedy repeatedly declared the president was destroying himself and his party. Senator Kerry urged the Senate to stop any action as long as things get no worse in Kuwait.

Sec. Baker went to the Congress urging them to authorize the U.S. action in Iraq as time was not on our side. A vote was convened (which is justifiably required), which would allow the president to commit our forces to fight a war in Kuwait if needed. Reluctantly the resolution passed on January 12, 1991, *in the House 250-183, and barely in the Senate 52-47.* Ten of the Democratic Senators voted yes to the resolution. Had they not done so the U.S. could not legally have fought. (What would have been the outcome??)

At Gen. Schwarzkopf's command center his planners had been busy digesting tons of last minute intelligence and organizing their battle plan. Cent-Com even used the Library of Congress to access old surveys and maps of Iraq. Unknown to the outside world Special Forces teams had secretly gone into the vast deserts to check on the accuracy of those maps and reports. They determined that an armored force could cross the empty deserts in the Kuwait-Iraq region.

This U.S. led coalition was equipped with the most modern military force the world had ever seen. *Pres. Reagan's rebuilding of our military was about to shine.*

Across the border Saddam had over 5,000 tanks, 6,000 armored vehicles and 5,000 artillery pieces. His air force flew 600 Soviet and French made fighters and bombers, and had 160 attack helicopters. Since the humiliating 1981 Israeli strike on his Osirak nuclear reactor Saddam had lavished spending on French and Soviet state of the art anti-air systems. They were comprised of radar directed missiles and guns.

To help carry the battle to the coalition rear areas he had hundreds of the older Soviet medium range SCUD missiles. Although inaccurate, if he sent them aloft carrying chemical weapons the missiles could be strategically deadly. Wisely Saddam had supplies hidden all over the region. **(And with the thoughtless help provided by purchases from European companies he had made a large number of chemical weapons.)**

To counter Saddam's strengths the U.S. and Coalition planners had crafted a perfect war plan. They would blind the enemy and whittle him down using the superior allied air forces. (This was based on Col. Wharton's original plan, though he was not there.

After an incident with senior USAF General Horner he was sent home.)

Only when the Senior Coalition Commanders felt the time was right would they unleash the massive ground forces that had been built up. Gen. Powell had asked Pres. Bush that we not engage in battle until we had the overwhelming force needed **to win quickly**. Military views were only adhered to concerning the fighting, (*Cheney and others were insistent that any political or strategic thought were part of their duties.*)

When Cent-Com's first attack plan was refused for lack of "imagination", Cheney wanted to know why. Alerted to equipment shortcomings, Cheney moved quickly to fix the problem. His generals got everything they asked for and came up with a good attack plan.

Schwarzkopf did not want the terrible individual soldier rotation that had been used in WWII, Korea and Vietnam. He wanted to enact if needed, a rotation of entire units every 6-8 months. That would ensure cohesion and morale among the units. Sec-Def Cheney decided there would be no rotations period. Units would stay in place for the duration of the operation.

Over the proceeding months the Israelis had urged acting quickly for to delay would enable Saddam to better prepare his Soviet based defenses. Egypt and the Saudi's were worried that the longer the delay the more trouble would brew in their lands. But Pres. Bush was able to ally any fears and keep the members focused. In reality everyone had to wait for the buildup and planning to be completed before anything could be done.

Historical Note: During WWII the U.S. had to train and equip the military forces that would fight, and then ship them to the war zones. That was why the U.S. Army did not get into the war in the Atlantic Theater until November 1942 in N. Africa, and in the Pacific as a supporting force for the Marines on Guadalcanal, and on New Guinea supporting the Australians.

In 1990 we had outstanding Army and Marine ground forces ready to go, but did not have enough shipping to move all of them at once. The Arabian ports were not equipped to unload the heavy mechanized forces that did arrive, and the Saudi's had no railroad. After the difficult unloading from the ships, all of the supplies and equipment had to be driven to the staging areas by large vehicle carriers. More time was needed for those operations to be completed, and everything was being done at a slow pace.

Again this point underscores why Saddam should have raced southward to take Saudi Arabia too. Had he captured and/or destroyed the ports at Jubail and Dammam there would have been no way for the coalition to disembark their equipment from the ships at those ports.

(That was the same scenario that would have happened at Pusan, S. Korea that first night the North Koreans invaded in 1950. Luckily the South Koreans intercepted the North Korean ships and the 1000 N. Korean commandos, saving Pusan and their nation.)

With the arrival of the many allied units the coalition had to prepare housing and support bases for the troops. Similar to Vietnam, a massive logistical effort was needed and it would take time to be organized and made operational. One of the most underreported Achilles heels for the coalition was water. *All of it had to be made by building desalination plants and then transporting the water out to the units. If that capability had been destroyed the war could not have been fought.*

In the early days of August the first units sent in were the Marines in theater and the airlifted airborne brigades of the RDF Rapid Deployment Forces. As the effort became better organized the mechanized units went and then the armored units. Once the entire 1st Mar Division, the RDF Rapid Deployment Force which consisted of the 82 and 101 Airborne Divisions, the 24th Mechanized Division and the British 1st Armored Division were ashore there was no chance that Saddam could have moved south at all.

As Gen. Schwarzkopf and his team observed the additional units coming in their movements could be synchronized with the overall battle plan that was being developed. Once this massive Allied force was in theater the question no longer lingered on **if** the Allies could push Saddam out of Kuwait. Now thoughts turned to how to do it without playing to Iraq's strengths.

With his reinforced coalition ground force came alternative attack possibilities. And that factor highlights another reason why it is so vital to stay militarily strong, it gives you more options. After their first plan had been rebuffed Schwarzkopf's team came up with a solid ground attack plan (copied from Scowcroft). It was based on what Saddam had planned and expected us to do. As Sun Tzu had explained centuries ago, "All warfare is based on deception". *(117)

Team Schwarzkopf would use the ever present Marine Amphibious units as a diversionary force. The specter of an amphibious landing (as used in WWII & Korea) along the long Kuwaiti shore caused Saddam to emplace multiple divisions and hundreds of weapons at or along the coastline. That reduced the firepower and units that could oppose any overland attacking forces. This deception was enhanced by using aerial attacks and naval shore bombardment to "prepare the beach areas for the invasion." The media was allowed to film and report on the drills.

Pres. Reagan had re-activated and improved all four of the Iowa class battleships during his naval buildup. Those massive ships had been upgraded with better munitions for their main 16 inch cannon, harpoon anti-ship missiles and tomahawk cruise missiles. The tomahawks could carry nuclear or conventional warheads and travel almost a thousand miles with almost pinpoint accuracy. Attack submarines were also in the lineup, and they too could launch those missiles. The Iraqi's dug in along the shoreline were in for some rough weeks.

Just south of Kuwait's border sat a dozen strong coalition units waiting for their chance to charge across the Iraqi wire. It appeared to all who were watching that the coalition was going to hit the Iraqi's from two sides, east from the sea, and south from Saudi Arabia. Thus the two known and shown coalition forces had **fixed** the enemy along the Kuwaiti shoreline and the Kuwaiti / Saudi border. And that was where Iraq's forces prepared their defenses and setup their units.

But with those latest reinforcements now ashore and in place, the final part of the upgraded coalition battle-plan could be enacted. *Cent-Com began secretly sending units westward into the trackless desert. No one outside the main command center knew they were going out there, and no one but Cent-Com knew why.*

At this point the coalition was preparing to conduct the first step in their war plan, the aerial onslaught. America alone had moved almost 1500 aircraft to the Gulf. All told the coalition had almost 2,000 planes. USAF Gen. Charles Horner and his team had worked tirelessly to craft an up to date targeting list. All aspects of the aerial attack had been checked and re-checked to try to match the aircraft and its weapons to the mission.

And unlike Vietnam there would be none of that "graduated response" nonsense. If war did happen the intense aerial attacks would be crippling.

A four part aerial campaign had been planned.

Phase one would strike every strategic target in Iraq which included communications and command targets, fixed scud missile sites, airfields and aircraft.

Phase two was targeted upon Iraqi crew served weapons inside Kuwait. The third phase was against the Iraqi Army itself, and the last phase was to be direct ground support for our attacking units.

On January 13, U.N. Secretary General Javier Perez went to see Saddam for one last try at peace. Saddam kept him waiting for hours and then gave him a litany of propaganda. Perez returned empty handed and dejected. Sec. Baker returned to Geneva for more talks, but the last-ditch political maneuvering there proved futile.

During those last days Saddam gave speeches to the Islamic faithful and promised to bleed the enemy in the "mother of all battles". Saddam and his planners were preparing to fight the coalition in the same way they had fought the Iranians in their last war. It was a fatal mistake for Schwarzkopf and his team were out to avenge the ghosts of Vietnam.

Gen. Powell had been asked by the nervous media how we were going to cope with the "massive Iraqi Army". He stated; "First we are going to cut it off, and then we are going to kill it."

Desert Storm

At 2 am Iraq time January 17, 1991 the Air War phase began.

(I was on duty in Engine Co 54 in Times Square. We saw the news tickers (idiotically) stating that flights of military aircraft were taking off all over the Gulf region. Media in Iraq soon reported on explosions they could hear and see. We prayed for those over there, and then a violent manhole explosion and fire occurred sending the passerby's scurrying out of Times Square.)

Iraq followed the Soviet air defense system which used early warning ground intercept radar sites. A line of them had been placed along the southern borders of Iraq to pickup any aircraft trying to enter their airspace from Saudi Arabia. With all of the strategic targets that needed to be taken out the planners had run out of attack aircraft for those border radars. That first night of aerial missions depended on taking them out.

To fix this major problem a bright spark among the planners suggested using the Army's *Apache* attack helicopters and the USAF A-10 *Warthogs*. Both aircraft were designed for use against enemy armored vehicles and both had effective cannon and missiles. The A-10 was an older design dedicated to stopping a Soviet armored invasion of Europe. This jet had dual controls and was solidly built around a deadly 30mm cannon. Flying at medium speeds the jet powered plane would drop down and shoot missiles or fire the cannon at the weak areas of the vehicles. (That idea for those planes came from the operations of German WWII super-ace Hans Rudel who knocked out hundreds of Russian tanks.)

The *Apaches* were the mid-1980s replacements for the *Cobra attack helicopters* that had proved so effective in Vietnam. (The Cobras are still in service in the Marine Corps.) *Apaches* use advanced optics to scout for enemy units and shoot the fire and forget *Hellfire* anti-tank missiles. They also have an effective 20mm cannon for close in firing. After some worried discussions they were given the radar missions along the border.

To help them navigate in the trackless desert it was decided to have two MH-53 Pave Low Special Operations helicopters lead the way. They used state of the art computerized navigation and flew just 100 feet off the ground to approach the targeted radars. Behind each MH-53 flew four Apaches. The two flights were separated by 25 empty miles of desert.

Units had practiced this attack for a week in the Saudi desert. Cent-Com insisted that the targeted radars be struck at exactly the same time to give the impression that a power outage occurred. All hands performed perfectly as the unseen Apaches unleashed numerous Hellfire missiles which knocked out everything at the sites. While the radar attacks were occurring the A-10s took out the nearby support units and anti-air defenses. The road ahead was now open.

As planned EF-111 electronic jamming aircraft followed those first flights in creating more electronic confusion for the Iraqi air command. Right behind them were the F-117 Stealth fighter-bombers, en-route to Baghdad. Minutes later hundreds of coalition aircraft crossed the border unseen.

High in the sky this aerial onslaught was being watched, directed and advised by the AWACS command aircraft. Those large converted passenger jets carried a massive radar dome that enabled them to monitor and manage the airspace from above. (Also used but not publicized were the RC135s and even U-2 spy planes to provide on site video-photo intelligence.)

The F-117 Stealth fighters used advanced computers to control flight functions, and angled frames and composite materials to virtually eliminate their radar signature. They had been used in the Panama fight the year before, but had not gone up against anything like Iraq's massive anti-air defense. Iraqi radar operators in the field caught slight glimmers of light on their screens but could not maintain the contact. Seconds later they could hear the whine of the passing jet engines and then nothing. Minutes later the F-117s reached their targets and dropped their laser and video guided bombs to score perfect strikes in downtown Baghdad. One of the first targets was the Iraqi Air Defense center.

Iraq's gunners could not get any targeting information on those flying ghosts so they just pointed their guns up and fired away. In addition to the unseen F-117's attacks, Navy tomahawk missiles had been fired from the battleships *Wisconsin* and *Missouri*, and from a submarine As programmed they flew across the water and landscape to strike their predetermined targets almost to perfection. Knocked out that first night were the Iraqi command and control centers, phone exchanges, the Presidential palace, the Defense ministry, government buildings, Scud missile sites, chemical weapons depots and additional radar sites.

A CNN news team had stayed in Baghdad and provided video of the night sky. Iraqi gunners fired thousands of shells skyward, but hit nothing. While touring the city the next day one reporter remarked, "It was as if the allies had practiced microsurgery on Baghdad". The targeted structures were wrecked, while the buildings next door were untouched.

(Briefings for the media showed footage of the numerous pinpoint strikes that occurred in buildings, bridges, airfields etc. This was the same type of attacks Nixon had used on Hanoi in 1972. But back then those reporters cared less about the successful missions and cursed his efforts. In 1991 they were amazed.)

Consistent with the forced policy that was used in Korea (after the battles at the Chosin Reservoir), and following the same structure used in Vietnam, all of the Marine Air assets were controlled by a Joint Forces Air Officer. Marine *F-18's* flew against targets in Kuwait and southern Iraq while the *Harriers* stayed near the coast harassing and attacking anything they could. Their work was integrated into the air effort as a whole.

Air Command released those planes back to USMC control in time for the ground war. Close in air support is a mainstay of the USMC operations, and as shown in *Fatal Flaws Book 1* was begun by the USMC units during the 1920s-30s in the "Banana wars in Latin America. (German military attaches in those countries watched with awe at the concept, and created their own programs for use in Spain and WWII, where Hans Rudel was king.)

After that first round of air attacks, at 0400 hrs Navy drones were unleashed giving off a radar signature of a large bomber force inbound. Because they had lost their main integrated radar units in the first bombing runs, the Iraqis turned on their local radar units for the missile batteries and anti-air cannon. What the Iraqis did not know was that behind the drones they were firing at were dozens of (Vietnam era) F-4 Phantom jets that carried HARM missiles. Those weapons were designed to find and target radar beacons. Once locked onto the signal the missiles would still hit even if the unit was turned off. Within minutes most of those individual radar units were also destroyed.

It did not take long for the Iraqi operators to realize that if they wanted to live they had to shut the radar units down and keep them off. Without their radar to direct their multi-gun or anti-air missile batteries, all of the enemy fire was undirected and haphazard. The highly touted Soviet designed anti-air system failed their owners, and that increased the effectiveness of the regular allied air strikes that were starting to fall onto their runways, transport systems and other strategic targets. Within hours Iraqi command and control and much of their air force was knocked out.

President Bush addressed the nation at 9pm EST. It was the largest audience ever with 79% of the televisions in America tuned in. He simply stated that the U.N. directed effort to free Kuwait had begun. We would continue our work until Saddam leaves the country. A nervous nation prayed for peace and for our people.

Around 10pm Sec-Def Cheney called Bush from the Pentagon. The first reports on the air attacks were in, 56 navy planes had attacked and all had come back. Some 200 plus air force planes had also gone out, and so far there were no losses. Everyone was stunned. By dawn it was learned that only one plane did not come back, a navy F18 with Lt. Scott Speicher.

As the first day of attacks continued the reports and BDA, (bomb damage assessment) were quite encouraging. Coalition planners had felt that our air losses could be as high as 25% that first night. They were astounded when every F-117 came back from their missions over Baghdad. Overall the first night of the air war was a smashing success. Nearly seven hundred aircraft had flown and only one had been lost. With little fanfare Iraq's military was blinded and their communications shut off.

(The one air group that would suffer the worst losses was among the RAF units that were sent to destroy enemy airfields. Their tactics dictated flying low to deliver their weapons and that placed them within reach of the intensive enemy ground fire. After losing quite a few aircraft that first week it was decided to change the guidelines.)

Saddam began firing his *Scud* missiles into Israel and Saudi Arabia. Rumors were rampant with some claiming chemical weapons had been used. The high explosive warheads from the five missiles that reached their targets destroyed many buildings but caused no deaths. The Israeli leaders had anticipated the event.

Saddam was hoping to enrage the Israelis prompting them to attack which would end the coalition. Sec. Baker was hard at work keeping the Israelis at bay, while Gorbachev was again trying to save Saddam to placate the hardliners in Russia. Pres. Bush refused that last-ditch request.

The Scud missiles that were fired into Saudi Arabia were shot down by a new weapon system called the *Patriot* missile, one of the offshoots from Reagan's SDI. That unit would track the incoming weapon and then launch its own missiles when the intercept was acceptable. *That first night the Patriot was 100% effective.* To help the Israeli's defend themselves, and to keep them out of the war, Pres. Bush sent numerous *Patriot* batteries to Israel.

Sec-Def Cheney then instituted the only political orders to the battlefield commanders, they had to destroy the remaining *Scuds*. Schwarzkopf did not understand the political needs and was reluctant to interfere with their well laid out air plan, but Cheney angrily insisted. That meant transferring many aircraft from their primary duties of degrading Iraq's military might to performing roving *Scud* patrol. Numerous Special Forces teams were also committed to this arduous duty. *With that commitment the Israeli's stayed out of the war.*

The talking heads who claimed to know so much were certain that Israel would strike back from the Scud attacks and wreck the coalition. But as usual they were wrong. Israeli P.M. Peres accepted the U.S. aid and stayed out of the fight.

(Israel had preplanned to attack Iraq through Jordan's airspace if they needed to. If the Jordanians refused them overflight rights the Israeli's were also prepared to destroy Jordan's air assets too. That would have caused huge political problems for the coalition, possibly ending it, just what Saddam wanted. Had Saddam used chemical warheads in his *Scud missiles* Israel would probably have attacked them no matter what Bush had said.)

To prevent any WMD use, Sec. Baker had met with the Iraqi Foreign Minister a few days before the war began. **He warned the Iraqis that if weapons of mass destruction, WMD's were used** during the fighting, America would invade Iraq and hang Saddam and his supporters as war criminals in the center of Baghdad.

The Scud threat was the only major allied intelligence mistake of the war. Planners had felt that Iraq only had 48 of the obsolete missiles, when in fact they had over 200. It was also felt they only had a few of the fixed launchers, so once they were destroyed the missile threat should have been ended. But no one knew that the industrious Iraqi's had fabricated dozens of mobile launchers. Thus they could hide them and fire away whenever they wanted.

After some successes in the first few days of Scud hunting the air crews had a hard time finding and attacking the remaining missiles. The Iraqi's had learned the same thing the Germans, the Koreans, the Chinese and the North Vietnamese forces had. When fighting America, stay out of the light.

After the war ended it was also learned that W. German Jurgen Geitler who worked in their Foreign Ministry in Bonn was stealing hundreds of classified documents on Iraq. *In that paperwork were detailed intelligence accounts on Iraqi Scud Missile locations and numbers. Geitler gave the stolen Intel to the Iraqi Embassy!* That information was used by the Iraqi's to help them hide the Scuds from view. Geitler was later convicted of espionage but the pacifist German courts gave him only four years in jail. *(118)

(The worst casualties the U.S. suffered during the war was from one of the last *Scuds* fired that killed 28 soldiers in their barracks in Dhahran. *Geitler should have been tried here for the loss of those soldiers and given life in jail, or better yet, hung.*)

On the 20th Saddam had the few captured allied airmen paraded on TV. Their battered faces betrayed the harsh treatment they were enduring. Saddam then ordered all foreign journalists to leave the country except Peter Arnett and CNN. The Iraqis used CNN to film locations they wanted seen, and liberal CNN complied. To the Administration and non-liberals it was transparent that the left leaning media was happy in their role of trying to prove the war was wrong. Arnett was especially hyper-critical of all things being done. (He was disgraced years later for false reporting.)

During the first week of the air war Iraq's pilots tried to fly up and engage the coalition planes. They lost nineteen jets in uneven battles to the coalition flyers. To shut down the Iraqi plane threat Gen. Horner ordered that all of their aircraft hangers and shelters must be attacked. If this threat was eliminated Iraq could not make any long range attacks on Israel or Saudi Arabia unless they used their Scud missiles.

Coalition aircraft were using the latest designs of "smart bombs" that could be directed to their targets using global positioning technology, by following laser beams into the targets, or by using video directed weapons. The Military gave the impression that the weapons were 90% accurate, but the dust and clouds reduced the effectiveness down to 40%. Still they were very effective.

After a few days of those crippling airfield attacks many Iraqi pilots flew off to escape into Iran. Some were shot down, but by the third week over 130 Iraqi planes had made it to safety in Iran. This became a new problem in that Iran was still an enemy. Had they made a deal with Saddam to use those jets to attack the ships in the Gulf? Due to the animosity between them , and a fear of our strikes, no attacks came from Iran. And they refused to give the planes back after the war ended. By remaining neutral Iran made hundreds of millions from the higher oil prices.

(Again it was also possible that Iran was nervous over our intentions and did not want to provoke a battle with so much U.S. air and naval power just a few miles away. They would have been devastated in two weeks.)

As the days went on the coalition was able to send almost 3,000 flights per 24 hours over Iraq and Kuwait. With the destruction of the strategic threats completed more sorties were employed against Iraq's artillery units and supply points.

Later the old workhorse the B-52 began flying from Diego Garcia and Britain to drop their 30 tons of bombs on the Republican Guard units. Those six armored Divisions were the best trained and equipped divisions in Saddam's army, and it was desired to weaken them before the ground war began.

Recon flights by U-2s brought back great shots of Iraqi defenses and positioning, and the photos were used to schedule the next rounds of attacks. The RC-135 used a side scanning radar that could pick up ground targets 150 miles away. They also located supply and weapons convoys as they moved, and could generate that information in real time to the aerial managers who would redirect nearby air-strikes onto them. Iraq's forces were being worn down, and there was nothing they could do to stop it.

After almost two weeks of being battered Saddam realized that his military and country were being systematically destroyed. He needed to fight back, and on the night of January 29 Iraqi armored forces attacked southward taking the northern Saudi town of Khafji. (The town had been wisely evacuated and was only lightly defended by recon units.)

This attack was a well planned offensive using three Iraqi armored divisions. Their mission was to humiliate the Saudi front line units at Khafji, trick the coalition into starting the ground war early, and bleed the Americans. Saddam hoped that seeing U.S. dead on TV would make America give up.

But the Iraqi's underestimated this new U.S. military. Their mobile air defenses were no match for the coalition air units, especially the U.S. ones. As Iraq's armored vehicles and supply columns advanced they were struck at will causing heavy casualties.

For political reasons the task of retaking the town was given to Saudi and Qatari soldiers with help from some Marines and their attack helicopters. After two days of fighting (mostly by the Marines), the Iraqis had been pushed out losing dozens of vehicles, hundreds of casualties and over 500 prisoners.

Almost all of the Iraqi reinforcements had been intercepted miles from the town by coalition air units, and decimated as they tried to advance. One Iraqi commander stated that the coalition air power had done more damage to his units in thirty minutes than Iran had done in eight years. Word got back to Saddam that their assessments of these Americans were wrong.

The media had wanted the battle to be long and bloody so they could say we told you so, but the Iraqi troops were overwhelmed and over-rated. (Although had it not been for the USMC ground units holding the line the Iraqis could have ended up in Riyadh.)

Saddam portrayed the battle as a great victory as did his supporters in the Arab countries. But his desire to lure Schwarzkopf into prematurely launching the ground campaign was again wrong. Schwarzkopf called the fight, "about as significant as a mosquito on an elephants butt."

After the battle Cent-Com planners realized that the majority of the Iraqi military was second rate. But Schwarzkopf wrongly did not adjust his overall plan to reflect that information. He stayed with the original systematic attack plan and timeline.

The Khafji battle ended on the 16th day of the air war. By that time much of Iraq's war and chemical weapons facilities had been destroyed, most of their bridges were down and the flow of supplies to the Iraqi forward units was down to a trickle. In the northern Gulf more than 40 Iraqi patrol boats and warships had been sunk. Due to the attacks on Iraqi electrical plants the electricity was knocked out as was Iraq's oil refining.

(The U.S. used special munitions that would cause short circuits stopping the electricity without destroying the structures. In that way the country could quickly rebuild after the war ended.)

The coalition began dropping leaflets onto the entrenched Iraqi's promising humane treatment if they surrendered. Then bad weather moved in which caused heavy cloud cover over Kuwait. That prevented the attrition that Schwarzkopf had demanded, and he would not initiate the ground war until those Iraqi units had been beaten down. Schwarzkopf was still nervous about potential casualties, and he and Powell got into another heated argument over when to begin. Schwarzkopf wanted to wait another month.

In total the Coalition air attacks went on for five weeks, and used various attack techniques to take out about 200 Iraqi tanks each day. Due to the safety factor that Cent-Com demanded only attacks that were known to have destroyed something were removed from the enemy's tally. Cent-Com did not want inflated attack reports that might end up having been wrong resulting in greater losses to the ground forces. Thus some sites were attacked multiple times even though the weapon or vehicles were out of action.

None of the U.S. commanders attempted to keep a "body count" of Iraq's troop losses. Those Vietnam vets were totally against that practice then and now. And the intelligence people could never really be sure how much attrition an enemy unit had suffered because most of the Iraqis hid in bunkers and tunnels. That factor also resulted in multiple attacks against units that were already eroded. *All of those factors helped to mask the weakened condition that was now the Iraqi army.*

Around this time the commander of the Marine Air Wing Gen. Moore began weaning Marine air units from the Coalition Air Commander. About fifteen days before the ground war began all of the USMC air units were back under their control. Marine Air began sending fifty plane "gorilla strikes" of F-18 *Hornets* and A-6 *Intruders* to initially erode the enemy AAA units in Kuwait. Meanwhile artillery and rocket units were targeted by Marine *Harrier*-jump jets that could fly low to the ground.

The Iraqi's had a 300mm rocket that when fired left a crater 12' across and 3' deep. To trick the Iraqi's into firing them company sized raids would go up to the Kuwaiti border with an artillery battery. Those units would fire a few salvos at the Iraqi positions and then scoot away. When the Iraqi gunners fired back their position would be noted and the orbiting "gorilla strike" would pounce upon them. After a while the front line Iraqi units stopped firing at all.

In mid-February Iraq produced an offer that seemed to accept U.N. resolution 600. But deeper into the statement was the linkage over the Palestinian cause, the erasure of Iraq's debts, and that all of the "aggressors" had to take their forces and leave the Gulf. Pres. Bush quickly rejected the proposal and called it a cruel hoax.

In Moscow the hard liners were upset that Gorbachev had given America a free reign in the Gulf. On February 18 Iraq's Foreign Minister Aziz went to Moscow to work on a separate peace proposal. His nonsensical plan eliminated the Palestinian linkage aspect, but wanted the end of sanctions when 2/3 of Iraq's forces had left Kuwait. Again Bush replied that the Soviet plan fell well short of what was required to make peace.

Privately U.S. officials were upset at this latest Soviet effort. They feared that a last minute plan would allow Saddam a way out. Iraq had been raping and pillaging Kuwait for months, and the country was in shambles. On January 23 the Iraqis had deliberately unleashed a huge oil spill into the waters of the Gulf. The ecological damage was unprecedented as 120,000 barrels per day were spilling into the sea. A plan was hatched using smart weapons to destroy the nearby pumping station which stopped the oil flow. But the loose oil was still causing terrible environmental harm. The Administration wanted to hurt Saddam for this viciousness.

A day later a new Iraqi peace plan was unveiled which gave some more ground but still saved Saddam and his army. To take back the peace effort from the Soviets, Bush and his team prepared a statement telling Saddam what he had to do to avoid the ground war. "Kuwait City would have to be evacuated within 48 hrs and the rest of the country within a week.

Saddam's answer was to begin setting Kuwait's oil wells on fire. Powell and Schwarzkopf had another argument because of that potential peace plan. For Powell it was time to attack before the Iraqis could exit unscathed.

Unknown to most people Marine recon teams and Special Forces teams were already across the border taking prisoners and marking paths through the minefields. Iraq's forces had constructed a solid line of anti-tank ditches and high berms. Artillery concentrations, fire pits and barbed wire added to their overall border defense. To an average military the fortifications were imposing, but our engineering units had begun figuring ways across those barriers.

(The Saudi's had constructed their own defensive sand berms along their border with Kuwait to prevent Iraqis from moving south. Those were quietly breeched by the Marines a week earlier in preparation for the ground war.)

A few miles back from the Iraqi ditches and sand berms sat hundreds of front line bunkers and strong-points. Those positions held 20+ divisions of conscripted troops and their older tanks. They were to be the first units to engage the coalition troops who crossed the border.

Miles behind them were several armored and mechanized divisions that were to counter-attack any coalition forces that made it across the first defenses. And further to the north sat five of the Republican Guard divisions. Those tank heavy units were supposed to counterattack any coalition units that reached them. But all of those Iraqi forces had been subjected to air attacks for weeks. Some had lost 50% of their force.

At a meeting with the NSC Gen. Powell told the president that most Iraqi units had been reduced by at least 40%. Many in the military would rather we let Saddam walk out than fight because those senior officers greatly feared the Iraqi chemical munitions causing piles of U.S. dead. Cent-Com expected we would be taking heavy casualties and ordered 10,000 coffins.

As shown before, to insure the Iraqis faced south some of the coalition units would attack from the Saudi-Kuwaiti area. Two Marine divisions would be in the vanguard of that cross border attack, and they were reinforced by the US Army's Tiger Brigade, (Abrams tanks). Along with those U.S. units were two divisions of forces from the Arab nations. At the same time the Marine Amphibious units would fake a landing from their ships. To further the deception the battleships continued to pound the coastline with their 16" guns and the media was allowed to watch and comment on the amphibious practice sessions and discuss the coming "invasion of Kuwait".

All the while Ten Allied divisions were sneaking out to the west. With no air force or recon elements Saddam was blind to this massive relocation.

This was the main part of our striking force. Their mission should the ground war be needed would be to strike northward into the empty desert. At predetermined intervals units would break off and attack eastward into the western flank of the Iraqi formations that were inside Kuwait. It was expected that those Iraqi units would be facing southward to defend against "the expected main attack". They would be surprised and collapse when struck from their rear / western flank. (Schwarzkopf had 60 days of supplies relocated there just in case his forces did run into resistance.)

Those ten divisions were split into two separate corps.

The VII Corps contained the 1st Cav Division, the 1st and 3d Armored Divisions, the 1st Div mechanized, 2nd Armored Cav Regiment, the 11th Aviation brigade and the attached British Armored Division. That force had over 1500 tanks, Bradley scout/attack vehicles, plus hundreds of other vehicles, attack and scout helicopters. This was the hammer that was going to smash Saddam's forces.

The XVIII Corps contained the 82nd and 101st Airborne, 24th Div Mechanized, the 12th & 18th Aviation Brigades, 3d Armored Cav Regiment, France's 6th Light Armored Division and a division of Saudi and Pakistani troops. The Arab forces were to guard the far west flank from any Iraqi forces operating in the western desert, and were assisted by the French forces (25,000), which had some modern tanks. The U.S units assigned to XVIII Corps were tasked to race northward to seal the Euphrates River valley from any Iraqi counterattacks or resupply from Iraq itself.

They could also advance into Iraq if needed.

This American Army that was about to go into combat was smaller in numbers than the peak in Vietnam. But this army was better trained, equipped and led at the company and battalion level than any force we ever had. Saddam's forces were about to find that out the hard way.

Over the last few days the air campaign had been concentrating on the enemy along the Kuwait border. The final phase of softening up was ending. During a nighttime rain storm on the 22/23 a battalion of Marines crossed the Kuwaiti border and advanced undetected for 12 miles. They dug in alongside the Iraqi sand berms and discovered large gaps in the enemy defenses thanks to the work of the air crews. Their advance teams prepared breeching charges to get through the local minefields / obstacles as they waited for G-Day.

At noon the deadline passed, and President Bush gave the go-ahead for Sunday February 24, 1991.

(Powell and Schwarzkopf again fought over the start date. Originally Schwarzkopf had said the 21st, then he changed it to the 24th, and then he wanted the 26th. Powell warned him they had to go now as the Russians were trying a last ditch save. Pres. Bush made the call to attack.)

At 4am on Sunday the 24th the French forces and a brigade of the 82nd began moving towards As Salman, a place in the far western desert that contained an airfield and a crossroad. Their trip was about 95 miles from where they started and the allies would face about 10,000 Iraqi's. The town and airfield was taken with the loss of two French soldiers with 25 wounded.

At dawn the 101st sent 2,000 helicopter troops northward to setup an advance base called Cobra, some 50 miles inside Iraq. After they had secured the site, heavy lift helicopters brought in artillery, ammo and fuel tanks. With that forward operating base (FOB) established the rest of the division would be on its way and operate from inside Iraq.

In the eastern sector just south of Kuwait the two Marine divisions also attacked at first light. Massive barrages of artillery and MLRS rockets blasted the forward Iraqi positions. Their shellfire masked the berm breeching operations by the advance teams, and the sounds of the initial attacking forces. Each Division proceeded northeast on its own axis and rolled over the first line of Iraqi's. Most of those conscripted Iraqi troops surrendered quickly.

At the second sand berm defensive line the enemy put up more of a fight. With help from Marine Air and some Army Apache helicopters those defenses were also quickly broken. **At this point the Marines were already 20 plus miles into Kuwait!**

Using the low storm clouds and the incredible smoke condition from the hundreds of burning oil wells, some of the Iraqi armor units were actually able to get in close to the marine units. In some cases Marine *Cobras* had to air-taxi down the roadways because the visibility 100 feet off the ground was so bad. Despite some close calls USMC CG Walt Boomer reported great progress and light casualties.

By the end of that first day, (the 24th), they had advanced halfway to Kuwait City and captured over 16,000 Iraqis! (Supporting Joint Arab forces which were on each side of the Marine units. They advanced next to them forming a solid coalition line inside Kuwait. Most of the prisoners were handed off to them due to the language issue.)

Back at Cent-Com Gen. Schwarzkopf realized that with the speed of the Marine advance he faced a big problem. Their planning had expected the USMC advance units to be moving slowly because of enemy fire and casualties. VII Corps was not supposed to start out until Tuesday the 26th.

They needed to move out now, but when he called them he found they were not ready to go! With the Marine advance as fast as it was they could be outflanked from their left. And the enemy forces in that area had T-72 tanks.

As was usual the Marine divisions had few tanks, and almost all were the old M-60's from the Vietnam era that the Army had ditched when the M-1 Abrams came on line. That was why the Army's Tiger Brigade had been loaned to the USMC, to give them some modern armor punch. But even they would not be enough to withstand a strong Iraqi counterattack from their west.

Faced with this unexpected problem Schwarzkopf ordered the rest of coalition units to attack at once. (He and his senior commanders should have realized from the battle for Kafji that the Iraqi units in Kuwait were not first rate and the ground war timeline could need to be adjusted. VII Corps should have been ready to move as needed.)

Gen. Luck in command of XVIII Corps had already anticipated that move from the radio reports of his units and from the Marines. Many of his units were on the move by the afternoon on the 24th! By that evening most of XVIII Corps had crossed the Iraqi border and were headed north for the Iraqi city of An Nasiriyah which sat astride Highway 8, deep inside Iraq.

Their sequenced movements were well rehearsed and by Monday night (the 25th) the 101st had leapfrogged another 60 miles to setup a second FOB (Forward Operating Base Gold). This base was located near Highway 8, the Iraq-Kuwait highway.

XVIII units were setup as so; far out to the West were the Arab forces and the French Division. To their north-east was the 82 Airborne minus the Brigade assigned to work with the French, then the entire 101st, and lastly the 24th Mechanized Division.

The entire western area of Iraq was closed off from Kuwait.

VII Corps however was caught unprepared for the advancing of the schedule. Their units did not cross the border until late on the 25th! As they advanced through the never ending desert a large train of supply vehicles followed. The greatest fear for some of the commanders was if Iraqi forces had somehow moved west from Kuwait and happened upon the helpless fuel and supply trucks. Because of that nervousness those senior commanders would constantly order halts in order to scout the area around them.

That infuriated the forward most Company and Battalion commanders who knew that nothing was in their way. (They had just moved past those areas and would have fought the Iraqis if they had been there.)

Schwarzkopf had been unhappy with the choice of Gen. Franks to head VII Corps as he was not an aggressive commander. The incessant safety delays coming from VII Corps HQ made him even more upset. Schwarzkopf's deputy was Gen. Yeosock, and he too was not up for the tasks at hand having just had surgery. Yeosock was supposed to be running the ground war in the western area so Schwarzkopf could stay at the main HQ in Riyadh. But Yeosock stayed at the Army's HQ which was also in Riyadh! Both commanders were 300 miles from the front!

That lack of command presence hurt the effort to get things moving. (Schwarzkopf never flew up to see Franks in person. It was hard to be critical when you had no first hand experience of the situation. And if Cent-Com was not happy with a general's drive a Commander has the right to relieve them.)

Unlike WWII, there were no senior armored commanders like Patton or Abrams present on the front line to monitor the situation and keep the aggressive pace going. Those needless delays actually allowed the Iraqi unit commanders a chance to fight back, and for many others to escape. Even with the advance in the timeline the slow pace at VII Corps meant that their units could not make their right turn to attack eastward until early Tuesday morning the 26th.

The unit on the right flank of that massive force was the British 1st Armored Division. They would be the first to turn, and guard the left flank of the Marine Divisions as they chewed up any Iraqi units in their sector. Britain was using their version of the M-1 tank called the Challenger. It was another first rate tank that was more than a match for the Iraqi armor.

To help the British cross over the border and the high sand berms the U.S. 1st Infantry Div was attached to them. Their well trained engineers bulldozed gaps in the tall berms, dropped bundles of pipes into the anti-tank ditches on the other side and then covered everything up with sand. In all 16 breeches were cut so those units could proceed in fast paced battalion sized groups.

Within hours of crossing the border over 1,700 prisoners (of conscripted border troops) were taken. Around 11pm on Monday February 25 the advancing Brits had overrun another battalion capturing the commander. A few hours later in the early morning hours of the 26th, they ran into the Iraqi 12 Armored Div. right where they had been expected. After crushing them the British began their turn eastward and continued on.

Inside Kuwait the Marines and Joint Arab Forces had continued to advance and were closing in on Kuwait's airport. The Iraqi second defensive line units were putting up a much better defense, and sent in many local counterattacks.

During the second night, (the 25th), a tough battle occurred when Iraqi T-62 tanks launched a counter-attack from the smoky Burquan oilfield. This battle actually became the largest tank battle in USMC history. Again the low cloud cover and smoke hampered any fixed wing air support, and *Cobras* were forced to swoop in under the clouds to try to help the troops on the ground. But with the poor visibility their actions were limited.

At one point the 1st Mar Div had two CP's, (Command Posts) that were taking direct enemy fire right through their tents at knee height. (The last time that had occurred was at the Chosin Reservoir campaign in Korea 1950.)

Gen. Myatt's forward CP was struck at a place called the Emir's farm near a blazing oil field. All the CP staff had for protection was their LAV's, (Light Armored Vehicles) which only had a small 25mm cannon. Luckily the Cobra's arrived just in time and the enemy attacks were defeated with Iraqi prisoners again being measured in the thousands. The POW situation was now causing problems because of the sheer volume.

On late Monday (the 25th) Saddam issued another nonsensical order instructing his army to pull back to the positions they had been at on Aug 1. In that way he felt Iraq would be in "compliance" with UN Resolution 660 and the war should end. That was the scenario Pres Bush feared most, a Saddam scam that would try to save his army.

In reality though this order was impossible to implement for Iraq had no command or control, and they would be trying to vacate a large battle area under direct fire from every weapon the allies had. (It was also possible Saddam might have lingered on the past two days hoping that the Soviets would come to his aid and force a ceasefire. But by that point in time the Soviet Union had numerous problems of their own.)

Pres. Bush spoke on how the latest Iraqi broadcast was an outrage. The Iraqi's were not "withdrawing" they were being forced out of Kuwait in what was appearing to be a rout. All Saddam was trying to do was to stay in power. His potential peace proposals were not exacting enough, and so our forces would continue on.

At the U.N. there was little pressure to invoke a ceasefire, especially with the advances being made. Updates showed good progress and light casualties.

Gen. Powell sent over another update that the Iraqi's were clearly withdrawing. And Kuwaiti resistance operating inside their country was reporting that advance USMC units were already entering Kuwait City! It had been planned that the Saudi and Egyptian units should enter the city first, for political reasons, but our forces were faster.

After two non-stop days of driving and fighting off small enemy units, the 24th Mech Division of XVIII Corps reached the Euphrates River. They overran the Iraqi airfields at Talil and Jalibah and shot up over a dozen enemy MiGs that were sitting in unseen shelters. Outside of Talil airfield the Iraqi forces put up a considerable defense, but they could not defeat the newer weapons and motivated troops we had.

It soon became apparent that the Iraqi commanders did not know that U.S. forces had already closed Highway 8 behind them. One of the Iraqi units had loaded a few of their T-72 tanks onto transport trucks for the "drive back to Baghdad". Their transport column drove right into the defenses that the 24th Div had just established along the highway, and were blown apart. That was when they learned they were cutoff and panic set in.

When the British made their right turn the remaining VII Corps units continued northward. Each unit was to turn eastward one at a time at a designated time and place. In that way a solid front of attacking armored forces would trap and engage any Iraqi units in that sector. The U.S. 3d Armored was the next unit in the coalition line. Their mission involved destroying the *Tawakalna* Republican Guard Division which was equipped with T-72 tanks.

Late on Tuesday February 26 scouts from the U.S. 3d Armored finally found the Iraqi tank units in their sector. As was planned scout helicopters would fly 10 miles ahead of the tank columns to give the commanders time to adjust to the coming battles.

U.S. made rocket launchers called MLRS would send a volley of 18 missiles into the first sections of the Iraqi armor. Each missile contained dozens of small bomblets that strike the vehicles on the roofs, the least protected part of a vehicle. Numerous vehicles were destroyed as well as high losses to the exposed infantry and artillery in that area.

Next to pounce were the A-10 *Warthogs* firing hellfire anti-tank missiles and their 30mm anti-armor cannon. When they had finished their attacks the on station *Apache* helicopters struck. And after that maelstrom was completed the Iraqi's then had to face the *Bradley's* and *Abrams* tanks racing in at them. Once the U.S. armor became entwined with the Iraqi's the calls for air attacks had to end. Then it was tank to tank fighting. (The 3d Armored was the most tank heavy division in the U.S. Army. They had been staged with NATO in Europe to fight the Russians.)

In two separate engagements 2nd Armored Cavalry units had crashed into and through the extended battleline that the Iraqi commanders had tried to reorganize. That night the *Tawakalna Division* was destroyed, and it was learned that the T-72 tanks had a fatal design flaw. Their ammunition was stored in the turret for ease of use. It was a common sight to see the turret blown off the tank after they were struck by a U.S. anti-tank round.

The most feared weapon the Iraqi's had was their heavy Soviet made artillery. But the speed of the American attacks boggled the enemy's responses. Time after time the Iraqi's shelled areas long after the U.S. forces had speed on. And American units had portable radar teams with them. They could plot the locations of the Iraqi artillery positions from the shells they had fired and within a few minutes American counter-battery fire or aerial bombs were falling on top of that Iraqi artillery force. Not long after the Iraqi troops refused to fire their artillery at all.

All of VII Corps had finished their march north, and all had turned eastward. Next to be attacked was the *Medina* Republican Guard Division. Again the hapless Iraqi's were being systematically destroyed by coordinated tank cannon fire, artillery, helicopters and jets. On Wednesday morning (the 27th) the Republican Guard division, the *Hammurabi* tried to put up a fight. But it too was hit by artillery and air attacks before they could organize any defense against the quick paced American Blitzkrieg.

One reporter from the Washington Post described the incredible scene below him as a fast-paced steel wedge that was 60 miles wide and 120 miles deep!

Then the "fog of war" made itself known and command mistakes caused the U.S. units to stop moving. For nine hours the attacks were stopped. Because of that unwarranted command failure much of the *Hammurabi Division* was able to escape.

(When the war ended it was believed that one third of the Republican Guard tanks escaped. One causative agent was the initial delay in executing the forward movement of VII Corps. The other issues were the command failures, and the weather had turned cloudy preventing most fixed wing flights. No one had planned for that, so there were few all-weather aircraft assigned to support the ground forces. With no one watching the back door in northern Kuwait many of the Iraqis managed to sneak out.)

To the east the next big fight for the Marines was at the Kuwait City airport. Using all weapons available the 1st Mar Div knocked out another 320 Iraqi tanks, including 70 of the previously feared T-72s. The Marines then split up with the 1st Div staying in Kuwait City while the 2nd Div went north with the Army's Tiger Brigade to try to trap the Iraqi's inside Kuwait at Mutla Ridge. With the USMC advance being so quick, and he Iraqi's having no command or control, none of their pre-planned counterattacks could be executed in time. That factor actually saved a Republican Guard division for instead of attacking they withdrew.

The 1st Marine Div. and the Joint Arab Forces liberated Kuwait City along with British and U.S. Special Forces teams. For months Saddam's minions had thoroughly destroyed the city during their occupation. Now they raced to escape towards Basra.

A massive convoy of stolen vehicles moved north with two divisions of Iraqi forces. Their "column" was 25 miles long, and was attacked first by the Tiger Brigade with their M-1 tanks. Word of the escaping enemy column quickly spread and air attacks began arriving using cluster bombs, missiles and cannon fire. Hundreds of burned and broken vehicles and thousands of dead Iraqis littered the highway.

Liberal pundits decried the fight as the "highway of death" and heaped scorn on our forces for the savagery. Too bad none of them had been trapped with the Kuwaiti's during the long months of occupation. Their outlook was sure to have been different. (The scene of destruction looked similar to the Nazi escape attempt from the Falaise pocket in France in August 1944.)

On Wednesday Gen Schwarzkopf gave a televised talk describing the fight so far and the successes. The great "left hook" had worked and the coalition was presently attacking at will. More than 3,000 enemy tanks had been destroyed or captured.

Schwarzkopf glossed over much of the details, such as the fact that many of the Republican Guards were escaping with their heavy weapons.

His briefing prompted the administration, (led by Powell), to push for a quick ceasefire to avoid any more criticism by the media that we were "piling on". Discussions in the White House mirrored those among the coalition, it was time to stop. When Powell was asked he gave no dissent and called Schwarzkopf for his opinion. The Cent-Com commander was not happy and wanted to consult with the field commanders. Not all of their objectives had been reached, and many Iraqi units had and were still escaping. But at 6pm EST Schwarzkopf agreed to end the fighting at midnight. The land portion of the battle had lasted just 100 hours.

Pres. Bush and his advisors made a mistake allowing the pacifist viewpoint to affect the battlefield. They should have consulted with Schwarzkopf directly to see what he thought about if, or when they should impose a cease-fire.

That night at 9 pm the president addressed the nation and told all that Kuwait was liberated and that Iraq's army was defeated. Our military objectives have been met, The Coalition was the victor, and the war was over.

(One overlooked episode after the ceasefire was a large armored fight near the Rumalia oil field west of Basra. The battle began around 0100 on Thursday (the 28th) along Highway 8 when U.S. troops from the 24th Mech Div were in a firefight with a busload of Iraqis. Mortar and artillery fire was exchanged with other Iraqi units during the hour long battle. Then at 0800 another skirmish setoff a larger battle and 340 additional Iraqi armored vehicles were destroyed including thirty more T-72 tanks. *Any ceasefire should have been emplaced around noon Iraq time, so our forces had some daylight to work with.*)

During their invasion and occupation Saddam's forces had routinely tortured, raped and murdered thousands of Kuwaiti's. Their bodies were left to rot in the sun. Weeks after the August 2 invasion Iraqi security people began rounding up young Kuwaiti men and callously executing them.

Next came the arrests and ransoms of hundreds of random citizens. Once the bribe was paid the victim was brought home and then shot in front of the family. Their bodies had to remain on the steps for the neighbors to view.

The third phase of the Iraqi terror was the ghastly torture of hundreds of citizens. They suffered multiple fractures, tearing out of their eyes and severe burns, while women were repeatedly raped and then mutilated.

Even the animals in the Kuwaiti Zoo died terrible deaths.

The Iraqi's stole everything of value from every source found. They even destroyed one of the oldest known copies of the Koran. The fine medical library from the teaching hospital at Mubarak al Kabir was stolen in its entirety. The library at the main University was looted every day for a month until the building was empty. What they could not steal the Iraqi's destroyed. They burned every hotel, store, bank and even the car dealerships!

Saddam's occupiers lived like animals dumping trash and human wastes everywhere they moved. Almost 100,000 Kuwait's became refugees roaming the empty desert. As a result of the devastation, Kuwait had to expel almost 500,000 Palestinians who ironically lost everything they had worked for. (Thanks Saddam.) None of the whining liberals ever mentioned any of those "inconvenient truths" either.

Unlike Vietnam, Schwarzkopf did not allow the media unfettered access into the war zone. Reporters were confined and controlled so that their negativity would not affect the troops or the home front.

Kuwait'i citizens came out from their hiding places waving flags and banners thanking the United States. America's armed forces had won an impressive victory and shed the black veil that Vietnam and LBJ had covered them with. All of the allies in the coalition had helped greatly during the past seven months and would continue their largess over the next few.

But all of them understood that it was America's might that had won the day and kept the nations of the Middle East free.

The coalition lost only 90 killed in direct combat, and most of those lost were Americans. (U.S. losses were 79 killed, 212 wounded and 45 MIAs.)

After the victory was declared a new problem appeared. Gen. Schwarzkopf had been told that the Iraqi town of Safwan had been captured and he planned to hold the armistice there. When it was found to be untrue U.S. forces were told to take the town. When the units arrived they found five battalions of Iraqi armor there, and they refused to leave. Tensions remained high for hours until reinforcements began arriving and a flight of A-10s thundered past. Reluctantly the Iraqis left.

None of the Coalition principals had given a thought to the ceasefire. They gave no instructions or advice to Schwarzkopf, and when he went to the negotiating table there were no senior civilians from the Administration or the U.N. present to give him any advice or instructions!

Being apolitical, (which is hard to understand for a senior general), Schwarzkopf did not bring any advisors with him to help him in the negotiations. As a result of those oversights the subject of Iraq flying helicopters was allowed even though it included attack helicopters. Schwarzkopf was asked a second time about the attack helicopters and he still allowed them to be flown.

(After it was completed the Administration decided not to "undercut" Schwarzkopf's peace agreement. When the Shiite rebellions started in southern Iraq, Saddam's armed helicopters machine-gunned them at will. That mistake was remembered by the surviving Shiites, and was one reason why none trusted us when we returned in 2003.)

Another serious mistake was the assurances that all U.S. troops would leave Iraq as soon as possible. While it was desired for our people to come home, that "troop factor" should have been used to get further political leverage against Saddam. Because of that oversight the best B-choice that we could get was to setup a safe area in southern Iraq that the Iraqi military could not venture.

Margret Thatcher had stated that since we were sitting on the Rumalia oil field the coalition should use that as leverage to recoup all of the costs of the war and the massive environmental cleanup. That trump card was also missed.

When the question of the POWs came up the Iraqi's guaranteed the release of all forty-one coalition captives and 2100 Kuwaitis. It had been thought that over 3,000 Kuwaitis had been taken prisoner. That discrepancy was also allowed to fade away. (Over 600 Kuwaiti's disappeared, as has happened in every war.)

Another unwarranted failure involved Iraq's in-house weapons production. Iraq was allowed to begin production and rearm immediately, and it included missiles with ranges under 150 kilometers! The peace treaty signed in a tent on March 3, 1991 was full of holes. We would be back.

Since Gen. Schwarzkopf had only been concerned with the ceasefire as it related to the coalition forces no controls had been placed on how Saddam would react to the uprisings in Iraq. Allied troops were soon inundated with lines of bloody refugees. Shiite militia even went to the U.S. troops begging for help and arms, but were denied aid at the bequest of the administration which wanted to remain neutral. (Large arms caches were being blown up right in front of the rebels.)

Thousands of Shia refugees used demonstrations for the Western reporters to press their case for help. Still the administration remained silent. In addition to the regular arms caches being uncovered and blown up, numerous caches containing chemical weapons were also being found and destroyed. Iraqi hospitals were full of casualties from the chemical munitions inside Iraq. (It was possible that exposure to some of those weapons/fallout contributed to the Gulf War Syndrome many of our service members suffered from after they returned.)

Politically some in the Administration were worried about the Shiites taking over Iraq, and then aligning with Iran. That would present an entirely new and more dangerous entity than Saddam, and was possibly the reason we gave them no aid. (Such a Shia entity would then control 35% of the world's oil supply, the Stait of Hormuz and easy access to the rest of the oil in the region.)

Iran had been secretly arming and organizing the Iraqi Shia militias to rise up. They did not think we would have let Saddam live, and the Iranians expected a quick takeover. The wiley Saddam fooled everyone.

During the war the United States had employed 50-year old battleships, 40-year old B-52 strategic bombers, 25-year old Vietnam era F-4 *Phantoms*, and F-111 *Raven* and *Aardvark* bombers up to the latest stealth fighters and smart weapons. All of those weapons and systems were created with the genius and talent of the West's scientists, engineers and builders.

But it was Ronald Reagan who had rebuilt America's military. Without his election to office, his surviving that asassination attempt, his will and the foresight of his military planners, this incredible victory could not have been obtained with the minimal loss of life that it was.

The Stealth fighter project actually begun back in 1974. Theories had to be tested and engineered, and then mockups designed and built. But the plane needed faster and stronger computers to allow it to fly, and that created a time lag for the computer industry to catch up. Composite materials also had to be created and fitted with radar absorbing materials. Test flights of the first prototypes were not done until 1982.

Additional time and training were required for the pilots to become proficient with this complex weapon system. Not until 1988 was the F-117A stealth fighters operational and housed in active groups and squadrons. As stated before their capabilities were initially tested in the fight in Panama, but no one could be sure that the stealth program would actually fool a highly developed enemy's anti-aircraft system. Not until that first night in January over Baghdad.

Out of almost 1300 sorties flown by the F-117A over Iraq not one plane was even scratched by Iraqi anti-aircraft fire. Those amazing planes were able to go right into the dragon's den, successfully drop their bombs with pinpoint accuracy, and escape unimpeded.

Coalition air units flew 110,000 missions, dropped 88,000 tons of munitions, though only 6,500 tons consisted of smart bombs. Most of the work was done with the basic gravity bombs. During Desert Storm sixty-three U.S. aircraft were lost along with twelve coalition Tornados. But the sacrifice of those brave pilots allowed the ground war to be waged at a much lower cost. That is the true way for airpower to be used.

It is important to again highlight that the well led coalition air campaign did not make Saddam surrender. As always it was the presence of U.S. and coalition ground troops, and the manual destruction of his army that made him give up. Guesses placed Iraqi losses at over 100,000, but no one kept count. Iraq lost over 3,000 tanks, 1,400 armored vehicles, 2,200 artillery pieces and most of their air force. (*But between 1/3 to 1/2 of the Republican Guard units escaped intact.*)

With the war quickly over, and the potential disasterous economic damage contained, the U.S. and world economy flourished during the 1990's. That would not have been the case if Saddam had taken Saudi Arabia too.

Aftermath

With the fighting ended it was revealed that Kuwait had lost more than its possessions. As stated before Saddam had opened the taps for the oil holding tanks to allow oil to free-flow into the waters of the Gulf. Knowing he was losing Saddam had his minions savagely blowup all of the Kuwaiti oil wells **(almost 700), and their refineries. It was guessed that every day five million barrels of oil were burning,** releasing tons of pollution into the air. Pres. Bush had warned Saddam that he would be held accountable if he destroyed Kuwait's oil fields, but he was afraid to press the case because it would have meant renewed fighting and our having to occupy the country.

Black, heavy, toxic smoke from the oil fires covered the region in a dense sulphur smell. As the intense smoke condition joined with rain it became a tar like substance that covered the Kuwaiti desert. Oil well firefighters began arriving six days after the ceasefire. No one could have envisioned the sights and sounds as hundreds of roaring oil well fires. They sounded like jet engines as they burned unconstrained. There was no sunshine, just perpetual darkness. Many of the workers thought this is what the end of the world would look like. It was initially felt the effort to extinguish all of those fires could take five to ten years!

(Again this is what Saddam could have done to the Saudi oil wells had he been smarter and attacked them too.)

Before and during each oil well operation explosive demolition teams had to scour the area searching for Iraqi mines, (hundreds of thousands), unexploded ordnance from both sides, and improvised explosives that had been laid at the last moment by the fleeing Iraqis. Those had to be defused, disarmed or blown in place.

It took months for the engineers and work crews to create the roads and infrastructure needed to actually get to the oil well fires. Because of the heavy coating of oil across the area a special clay was needed to create roadways. That clay would not absorb the oil and would thus become a stable roadbed. But it had to be brought in by the boatload and then trucked into position!

Vast quantities of water would be needed to cool each fire. Heat levels were so intense the heavy equipment would melt if the water was not used. Holding ponds had to be constructed near each well to hold the water. Pipes that had been used to move oil to the docks were converted to carry sea water back to the holding ponds. High pressure firepumps had to be brought in, setup and used to pump the water from the ponds to the firehoses and water cannon. **Again all of those logistic issues had to be dealt with before any firefighting could even start.**

Forty countries contributed firefighting teams to the effort. Initially there were less than 100 of these specialists worldwide. But by the end of the firefighting there were over 1,000 well trained specialists.

Each country brought their own tricks to the fight. Texans used dynamite to blast the flames from the raw oil. That split-second separation combined with the cooling operations would extinguish the fire. The Hungarian team used an old T-34 Russian tank body to move two Mig-21 engines into position near the fire. With the engines running at full blast, it forced the fire and oil to separate putting out the fire. Improvising was the word of the day as no two fires were alike.

Once a fire was out the old well-caps were cut free, a new collar attached and then a new cap installed. With the oil well flow contained the terrible pollution was stopped and the fire-crews moved on to the next one.

It took six months to extinguish the Kuwaiti oil fires and cap the wells. The environmental cleanup took years!

Saddam hoped to make himself into a major Arab leader, but all he did was kill multiple thousands, and wreck his country and Kuwait. *Again this was a perfect example of how dangerous totalitarian rule is to the world, and how vital Democracy is in keeping the peace.*

The Arab World was partly to blame for this war. Saddam's "victory" over Iran was hailed, and Arab leaders turned a blind eye when Saddam dropped cyanide and other chemical gases on his Kurdish people. Before the invasion of Kuwait he had hung a British journalist, threatened to burn all of Israel, and bragged about how lethal his chemical arsenal was. No Arab nation rebuked or threatened him, instead he was cheered and allowed to continue his depravity.

Saddam Hussein and his failed invasion of Kuwait were simply a victim of bad timing. Had he invaded a few years earlier, or if his benefactors the Communist Soviet Union had not fallen apart, they would never had just stood aside and allowed America and the West to act. They would have blocked the vote in the U.N. Security Council stopping that political avenue. And if even if they agreed with the UN, we would not have been able to pull VII Corps, the hundreds of aircraft plus crews and staff, nor the naval forces out of Europe to fight in the Middle East.

Our coalition partners would not have dared to either. If we had fought the Iraqis on our own, more than likely the Soviets would have joined in. Most of the Arab countries were also dependent upon the old Soviet Union. Had the Soviets still existed, those countries would probably have backed Iraq and not the West.

But with the fall of Communism and the Soviet Union, America was the only world power left. And we decided to fight this aggression before it got worse.

It is also noteworthy to bring up that George H.W. Bush won the 1988 election instead of the democratic candidate. It is highly doubtful that a weaker /liberal president would have grasped what Saddam was doing, and what he was capable of doing next. Also a weaker leader may have fought the war in drips and drabs instead of sending the onslaught that Iraq had to face and lost to. If he fought at all.

As the leader of the free world Pres. Bush had to convince over a dozen other world leaders, the skeptical Democratic ruled Congress and the American public just what was at stake. (Something Dukakis would never have been able to do with his non-existent foreign policy background.) The fact that Pres. Bush and his team were so successful in the face of such domestic and international odds speaks volumes on their capabilities.

If nothing else hopefully this historic episode will convince the American people how vital it is to vote for the person and his capabilities, not sound bites and artificial appearance. The American people must trust their instincts and not the slanted lies and propaganda that the major media constantly push.

(Look at the past forty years of Democrats, Carter, Mondale, Dukakis, Clinton, Obama, and Clinton. None of those people could measure up to any of the Republicans they faced in words or deeds. And examine how good the Trump team is doing versus the eight years of failure and deceit from Obama and his pack of liars.)

For America the Gulf War victory must not be allowed to create the impression that all such wars will be so "easy". It is highly doubtful that the world stage will unify the way it had during that time frame. Would America and its Allies again have convenient and safe base areas and port facilities close by? Would other nations bankroll the war as had been done in the Gulf?

And it is extremely doubtful that the next enemy would allow us five months time to buildup our forces and five weeks of uninterrupted aerial assault before the ground war began? There are many reasons to fear the next major war.

With the war ended the Arab nations began pushing for everyone to leave Arabia. Part of that worry was based on Saddam's propaganda efforts that the Americans would never leave. They needn't have worried for when the fighting was over the U.S. brought its massive force home. Once again our leaders showed the magnanimity of the United States of America.

No other nation that has ever inhabited this blue planet has ever conquered an enemy by force, and then walked away from the spoils. Yet America has done so after every foreign war since 1900.

America and America alone has fought for other people's freedoms and asked nothing in return, except a place to bury our fallen. America's sons and daughters had just saved the economies of the world's nations, thus saving those nations too. The limited minds of the worlds liberals looked upon the war as "just a fight for oil". But like WWII, Korea and Vietnam, The Gulf War had to be fought and it had to be won. *No one could have predicted what would have happened had Saddam been allowed to conquer the other nations of the Persian Gulf.*

If nothing had been done over Kuwait, why would Saddam have stopped? Saddam was actually perplexed as to why the Americans let him survive, and he basked in his "triumph".

Iraq had faced the most powerful force any Arab nation had ever fought, and he was still in alive and in power.

In the Arab world that was quite a victory.** (119)

After the war ended a peace conference was conducted in Madrid. With the Cold War winding down a real chance at world peace was being created, and it was hoped that the next dictator would thing twice before trying something like that.

Pres. Bush and his principals thought that with the terrible defeat he had suffered Saddam would be overthrown from within. The Administration supported the rebellious Kurds in the north and Shia in the south at Najaf and Basra, but with words only. Both groups were ruthlessly attacked by the rapidly rebuilt Republican Guard units and their attack helicopters.

The Administration then compounded those errors by not attacking those Iraqi units while they savaged their civilian populations. We still had air and naval forces in the Gulf, and could have defended both of those civilian groups. *And again no Arab nation stepped up to stop those assaults either.*

Saddam's aggressiveness prompted us to establish no-fly zones, and our pilots flew 34,000 sorties each year to patrol Iraq and keep him in check. In addition we had to keep troops in the area to insure the Iraqi civilians could return to their homes.

There had never been a mandate for or thought of invading and occupying Iraq, unless he used WMD's. We had no directive to do so from the U.N. or from our Allies either. It was doubtful that our Arab partners would have stood idly by if we had taken it upon ourselves to just invade Iraq. Naturally long-term questions came up; If we had taken over Iraq or if we go back and take over what would have been the cost in lives and treasure? Who would have been placed in charge of the country? How long would we have had to stay? No one could answer any of those issues, so we left the region as per the status quo.

Sadly as had happened to Winston Churchill in 1945, President Bush would not win re-election despite what he had done for the world. (All of us would pay dearly for that outcome.)

To the convoluted minds of dictators that election event clearly showed the weakness and stupidity of the Democracies. Being voted out is unthinkable. They have no interest in Democracy, their people or any rule of law. Only Power is coveted by those rulers.

A special commission was proposed to operate under the U.N. and evaluate Iraq's numerous WMD programs, UNSCOM. Prior to the war the Israeli's had reported that Saddam was close to getting nuclear weapons. *The ever-arrogant bureaucrats within the CIA insisted the Israelis were wrong.* (Israel dropped the matter rather than reveal their sources.)

It was discovered after the ceasefire that hundreds of Iraqi WMD weapons were still live, and that many nuclear and biological targets had not been hit at all. Inspectors then found an Iraqi report detailing their extensive nuclear program.

Of their twenty operational nuclear sites, only two had been known about and bombed. The rest had escaped the war unscathed!! Reports sent to Washington showed vast nuclear campuses on the scale of the Manhattan Project from WWII! Despite all of the $ Billions spent on our intelligence services, this massive nuclear program was unknown. Iraq's nuclear director was one Dr. Hamza. Like many former Nazi's after WWII, he would escape to the U.S. with help from the CIA.

In April 1991 UNSCOM was in country and sending out inspection teams. All of the Iraqi WMD weapons would be required to be disclosed in full detail by Saddam and destroyed. But the U.N. had no Army, and no ability to coerce the wily and dangerous Saddam into cooperating.

Incredibly his secret WMD programs were being reactivated. Saddam and his minions were able to delay access to, hide their programs and even use those dangerous weapons to crush the rebellions inside Iraq. Saddam refused to work with UNSCOM, to protect his WMD programs. Their monetary value might only be worth $2-3 billion, while his actions actually prevented him from selling oil worth potentially $20 billion. But that was the importance Saddam placed on those weapons, for they kept him in power.

Using Jordanian front companies the Iraqi's quickly went around the U.N. weapons sanctions. His intelligence forces were active all over the globe finding new supplies and they would plan an important assassination as payback for their defeat.

As the months went by Saddam's continued intransience was causing many to regret not taking him out, and many began to call for his head. Sec of State Baker wrongly convinced the President to negotiate a settlement and cancel the renewed bombings he was planning. Saddam stayed in power which mandated the U.S. keep large forces in the area for regional safety and protection. Envoys shuttled around securing permanent basing rights and agreements. (And that may have hurt him at the polls.)

However the Saudi King was not unhappy that we stayed, knowing he was safe behind our military. As thanks the Saudi's purchased large quantities of U.S. weapons. But each commercial-military agreement that was concluded meant that more U.S. military and civilians were required to stay on as advisors and technicians. *All of that increased our footprint and visibility, and that continued stoking the furor of the Islamic Fundamentalists.*

Another unstated fallout from the war was the loss of credibility that Yassir Arafat and the PLO suffered by backing the wrong side. They were also wrong about the U.S. and coalition intentions. And with Iraq's defeat the PLO lost another sponsor, and funding fell off. Iraq was the only Arab force that could have fought the Western powers. With Iraq's defeat a new rebellion began inside the PLO.

During this time frame (1987-93) the First Intifada was occurring, the Palestinian uprising over the control of the West Bank and Gaza. Arafat knew he had to act to stay in power, and he duplicated Anwar Sadat's path to make peace with Israel. Envoys and meetings were held across the region with Norway's help.

In an effort to defeat the intifada, Israel captured and expelled 415 senior members of Hamas. Israel hoped that with their leadership exiled, Hamas would fall apart. But Hezbollah saw opportunity, and met those exiles in Lebanon with food and clothing. They insured that the exiles would have whatever they needed to get on with their struggle. Iran was going to teach those Palestinians discipline, and earn new allies in their long view endeavor.

For Iran the Gulf War was a school like no other. They saw with their own eyes just how formidable America and its weapons were. They knew there was no way they could ever defeat us in a toe-toe fight. That was why they had insisted on such tight security over their terrorist operations in Lebanon during the 1980s. The intelligence and communications security the Revolutionary Guards and Islamic Jihad used in Lebanon became the norm for Iran's military, and their expanding WMD programs.

And duplicated by all of the terrorist groups that followed.

As the Soviet Union dissolved tons of weapons were being sold at rock bottom prices. Using front companies, the Iranians purchased everything they could. No one was minding the Russian store, and vast arsenals of up to date weapons slipped out unseen. Iran rearmed, and by the mid-90s if America came calling the

Iranians would fight as the Viet Cong did, disguised as civilians and armed to the teeth.

Fresh with new allies the CIA station in Riyadh came up with a good plan to aiding the Afghan rebels who were still fighting the Russian backed Communists. They rounded up the tons of munitions and hundreds of serviceable Soviet bloc weapons abandoned by the Iraqis in Kuwait. Saudi GID transported those weapons and ammo to Pakistan and the ISI would distribute them to the Afghans for use against the remaining Marxists.

(But that was a terrible plan, for we had no way of knowing where those weapons went! The CIA should have just sent them to Massoud's forces.)

Despite the previous hostility of Hekmatyar and Sayyaf (during the Gulf War) the Saudis continued to fund them as it fit their master plan..

CIA reports from Afghanistan persisted with their warnings on the increasing radicalization of the fighters there. They were also cautioning that many of those young radicals were a threat to all of the more modern regimes in the region.

Saudi Prince Turki agreed on that issue, but claimed the Saudis were watching what was going on. Internally the Saudi Royals were also worried. It was well known that the Royals were not as Islamic as the radicals, spending time in Western resorts across the globe and behaving like the despised westerners. Protests began to grow, and at their intelligence meetings **Bin Laden's** name repeatedly came up.

Islamic Extremists in America

Back in America the 1989 death of the cleric Azzam went unnoticed, but had resulted in a power struggle inside his empire. The Brooklyn Islamic Center was at the heart of that turf war, and Mustafa Shalabi eventually lost. In late February 1991 his body was found, five days after he had disappeared. He was shot in the head and suffered multiple stab wounds. Investigators came to believe that Bilall Alkaisi and Mohammed Salameh were the assassins of Shalabi, but it could not be proven.

The main issue many of the Islamists had with Azzam and Shalabi concerned the money that was piling up. The true clerics wanted it spent in Afghanistan to help them rebuild, while the aggressive jihadists like bin Laden and Rahman wanted to fund new wars. And we were their target.

The previously mentioned **Wadi al-Haj,** the Fundamentalist living in Tucson was supposed to take over for Shalabi. He had "conveniently shown up in NYC the day Shalabi disappeared". *Haj was another Islamic terrorist who stayed in the U.S. because he married an American in 1985.*

As mentioned before, he had been a suspect in an Islamic hit in Tucson, and his name was known by federal investigators. But his services were being requested by Osama bin Laden, and he was suddenly told to relocate. After a few days of making dozens of phone calls to other U.S. based terrorists, (which included Sayeed Nosair), Haj quietly left the U.S. for Afghanistan.

The Brooklyn Alkifah Refugee Center and the Al-Farook Mosque would be run by the radical Egyptian Cleric **Sheikh Omar Abdul- Rahman**. He was a frequent speaker at the Al Salam Mosque in Jersey City, New Jersey too. Rahman was a fervent believer in radical Islam, and in spreading Islam by force.

Many times during the 1980s he had traveled to Pakistan to speak with the Mujahedeen. Like Azzam, Rahman's initial propaganda efforts worked to inspire the masses who were fighting the infidel Soviets. By 1989 that work was completed and it was time they turned their actions on America. With Shalabi out of the picture Rahman and his associates took over all of the NYC area Alkifah Refugee Centers and Mosques. **From that point on they were training jihadists for the coming war with America.**

Months after the Kahane shooting JTTF agents had been placing more of the faces in their photos to names. One that stood out was Richard Smith, an American born Black militant who had a penchant for guns. Since he was seen with the Islamic suspects it was obvious there was a connection, a potentially dangerous one. They followed Smith around for a week as he purchased a lot of ammunition for assault rifles. On another day he took the agents into Bedford-Stuyvesant to the Al-Taqwa Mosque.

An informant there warned them that Smith was not only arming the Arabs in Brooklyn he was teaching them urban guerilla tactics. (But with no crime, they could go no further.)

By the spring of 1991 another group calling themselves the Forty Thieves had pulled off multiple armed robberies shooting police and bystanders. During July 1991 one of their leaders, a man named Marcus Robinson was arrested in Chester, Pennsylvania. JTTF agents asked him what was going on.

He calmly told them he was a soldier in the growing Islamic Jihad movement taking root around the world.

Soon after the agents paid a routine visit to Mahmoud Abouhalima. He wasn't home, but the janitor told them it was about time they showed up. Mahmoud had bomb making materials in his apartment, and the janitor gave them a single blasting cap capable of setting off a large bomb. Agents needed a search warrant to go any further, and by the time they returned Mahmoud had removed the evidence. (No one stayed to watch??)

Meanwhile Nosair had become a celebrity among the Islamists. His friends and followers visited him often in jail and money rolled in to fund his defense. That wealthy Saudi named Osama Bin Laden had contributed $20,000. Nosair's murder trial began in November 1991 and became a carnival type atmosphere as Smith's Black militants provided "security for his lawyers".

Leftist activist and lawyer William Kunstler defended Nosair during his court case in November - December 1991. Despite the clear evidence of guilt, Kunstler was able to beat the murder charge and have it reduced to a weapons and shooting charge. Nosair would only face a few years in prison, and he continued with his own radical preaching's on the inside.

This inane verdict again proved to the Islamists that America was a foolish place ripe for the taking. It would not be the last time Islamic terrorists would use our legal system against us.

The Philippines

Mount Pinatubo was an active volcano in NW Luzon in the Philippines. On June 15, 1991 the large and dangerous volcano erupted with a massive roar, and became the second largest eruption on this planet in the past one hundred years. Local officials had worried over this possibility from various signs, and had already evacuated close by villages. However to the east was the large and vital USAF base at Clark Field. Clouds of toxic gases and tons of ash began descending on the region forcing us to abandon the base. As the event continued even Subic Bay Naval Base in Manila had to be evacuated, and both bases suffered serious damages.

For the Filipinos the new government formed after Ferdinand Marcos was chased out was becoming a mixed blessing. Governing is difficult as each special interest group tries to push their agenda. One group insisted that the Americans leave and never return. This eruption helped their wish, and during 1992 it was made into law as the U.S. bases were closed. For the Filipinos this was supposed to be a great event, but before the celebrations died down their "sword of Damocles" began to arise, China. With no military power left in the region this area became ripe for picking, for there are no such things as a power vacuum.

With the collapse of Communism in Europe and Russia, only China remained as a dominate Communist entity. (Though N. Korea was becoming more dangerous each year.) China's reborn economy was growing at 10% per year. That growth was opening up all kinds of renewal, especially in their military. Many economists believed they could eventually take over as the world's largest economy. It was hoped that as they prospered the Chinese people will no longer believe in the State, they would believe in themselves. But after Tianamen Square, there were no more protests for freedom.

The End of the Soviet Union

As shown before the previously mentioned Soviet crackdown in the Baltic's was a major reason for the growing discord between Gorbachev and Boris Yeltsin who was leading the charge for further change in Russia. Russia was the largest and most populated of the old republics. Eighty percent of their residents could trace their lineage to that country. Russians also constituted a large minority in Ukraine, Georgia and the Baltic's, as they had been sent there to colonize them. Yeltsin wanted freedom for Russia, which meant ending all ties with the other nations.

Gorbachev wanted to replace the Soviet Union with a new state of associated republics. However six of them, Latvia, Lithuania, Estonia, Moldavia, Georgia and Armenia wanted no part of the Soviet sphere. In effect if they left that would be the end of the Soviet Union.

By March 1991 the rush to freedom was causing collapse of their union. Coal miners were striking, foods were becoming scarce as farmers were hording whatever they could, and the Communist party was threatening action. Violence could be unleashed at any time.

At the White House the Bush team pondered the state of the world's health. Progress in Russia must proceed slowly to avoid a complete collapse. Their military was becoming more vocal, unpredictable and dangerous. Sec. Baker had gone to Moscow on March 17 to discuss the various issues, and by late April a measure of stability returned when most of the principals agreed to work together. The agreement was called the Nine plus one process, which provided for a new constitution, nation-wide elections, a voluntary economic union and permission for those republics who wished it to leave.

Returning from a military exchange program in Moscow, Gen. Powell reported on the deep dissatisfaction in the upper reaches of the Soviet military. *They openly detested the turncoat republics and the reformers.* All of their senior officers had been indoctrinated into hating the West. They prepared all of their lives to fighting and destroying the West, and yet now we were turning into their only friend. And what was worse, the Soviets desperately needed our aid to stay afloat. There were plenty of new tanks and jets around, but not one new bus ran on the city streets.

Around this time a top Soviet scientist defected.

He was a deputy director of a vast secret program to research and build biological weapons. Their program employed over 30,000 scientists at forty locations!

Pres. Nixon had signed a treaty with the Soviets in 1973 to outlaw and eliminate those lethal weapons, and we had ended ours. But as always the Communists did just the opposite. When Sec. State Baker confronted his Russian Federation colleagues over this egregious lie they claimed that we had lied about destroying our programs, (even though we did destroy them.)

The Administration was uncertain where to go next. If we continued to help them we could eliminate many of those weapons programs. If we reacted harshly the Russian military may take over leading to what? And black marketers could begin selling their weapons to who knows.

Hard liners in Russia saw a chance to stop the destruction of their world. On August 20, 1991 they attempted a takeover. The Bush Administration refused to acknowledge any entity except the one the people had voted on. Yeltsin remained defiant and refused to give in. News coverage showed the Russian Parliament under armed siege. Fighting was expected at any moment.

This was the worst case scenario that Thatcher and Bush had worried about the past two years. Who would control the nuclear weapons in such a tense environment?

For some reason the coup plotters had failed to shut down all communications inside Moscow, and Yeltsin was seen as still in charge. A few days later the coup was ended, which sealed the fate of the Soviet Union and Michel Gorbachev. The Communist Party was banned, as Yeltsin and his followers seized all of the levers of power. (Banking-Finance, utilities, etc)

Watching all of the above unfold the disgruntled Soviet states declared their total independence.

From Moscow, Yeltsin and his new Foreign Minister Andrei Kozyrev led the exodus from the Soviet Union, and by the end of 1991 it had collapsed. Both leaders assumed that democracy would eventually be achieved and their separated Russia would become a part of the "West". Sadly that was not done due to challenges from within and from inaction from the Western nations, especially America.

(Former President Richard Nixon had met with Boris Yeltsin and felt that he was someone we should help to succeed. *"Russia's people and nation needed to be treated not as a defeated enemy, but as an ally who helped us defeat Communism. Russia did not lose the Cold War, the Communists did."* *(120)

His advice to Pres. Bush was to jump in with financial and political support. **Nixon warned him "The Cold War is only half over. Communism has been defeated, but Russian freedom is not yet won".** *(121)

Bush did not take to Nixon's advice as quickly as Pres. Reagan had, but a month later a comprehensive aid package was drafted. Tragically Gerorge Bush did not win the 1992 election. His replacement had no knowledge of or any ideas on foreign affairs, and our aid package was not implemented properly or in time to help Yeltsin and Kozyrev succeed.

As they had done to every possible western backed leader from Diem onward, the left-wing media harped and criticized on everything they disagreed with in Russia.

(Kozyrev later admitted that Pres. Reagan had been correct, the Soviet Union was an "Evil Empire. Years later many of the former principals of the USSR would come forward and agree that it was Reagan's policies, especially SDI that prompted their collapse. They simply could not keep up.)

Despite the liberal propaganda, Russia's Communists took advantage of the chaos from WWI and took power from the interim Kerensky government by force of arms. The Bolsheviks then stopped fighting the Germans, which caused serious problems for the allied powers. After the war the Bolsheviks tried to re-conquer most of their neighbors, and they maintained their atrocious rule by using force of arms. Those nations who had escaped would be swallowed up by Stalin during WWII.

Eastern Europe would be liberated from Nazi control by Russian forces, which is the same as having been conquered by them. Communist governments were installed in all of them.

To maintain their rule the Russians sent troops and tanks upon the restive civilian populations in 1953, 1955, 1961, 1968 and 1979.

"Michel Gorbachev was the first Soviet ruler who refused to send in the troops and the tanks to keep control.
And that was why he was the last Soviet ruler." *(122)

Nations that had been claimed and conquered by the Soviets after WWI demanded and finally won their freedom. The Baltic States, Georgia and Azerbaijan voted for independence. The rest remained as republics in the Russian Federation, for now. Most of those countries would become independent within a year, including the Ukraine.

Russia's military would remain in place, to control the nuclear weapons and exert overall protection of the Federation.

However in the Intelligence World fear quickly replaced the euphoria as the principals realized that *"no one was watching the Soviet military store."* Who was really in control of the thousands of nuclear weapons that dotted the former Soviet Union?

Already disgruntled military officers and officials were selling advanced Soviet weapons in the open arms markets for top dollar. In the past month over 700,000 additional officers and men were cut from the Soviet army alone. More were being dismissed from the navy and air forces. Who could guess at what was going on behind the scenes. And those sales were happening all over the world.

Iran bought three of the latest Kilo class Russian subs in mid-1992. All were of advanced designs capable of closing off the Strait of Hormuz, one of the most strategic geographical features on the planet. Over 15% of world trade uses that narrow waterway, and those subs could also shut down the Red Sea.

The Bush Administration was of mixed views on whether to proceed cautiously or aggressively. Robert Gates suggested establishing embassies in each new republic, and instituting humanitarian assistance. (The Europeans were doing that already.)

Pres. Bush favored going slow and cautious so as to not alarm any hard-liners in Russia. He wanted the *SALT* talks to be renewed as a sign of peaceful intent. (It had not been ratified after the Soviet invasion of Afghanistan.) Eventually they were, and SALT II was signed in the last days of the Bush administration but not ratified by the Senate until December 1995.

In the end Party Secretary Michael Gorbachev lost control of everything, and was replaced by Russia's Boris Yeltsin.

On Christmas Day 1991 the Soviet flag was lowered from the Kremlin for the last time.

The Cold War was officially over.

But the next war was just getting started.

Historical Note: Few people realize or understand the intensity of the Soviet Communist effort to takeover the world. As shown before it started with their neighboring nations after WWI. Stalin next insisted Russia join in the Spanish Civil War, 1936-1939 in the hopes of a Communist victory and base area. Then came their unprovoked invasions of Poland and Finland in 1939, the 1948 Berlin Blockade, the Korean War 1950-1953, Indochina, the Eastern Europe uprisings in 1953 & 1956, the Berlin Wall in 1961, their efforts in Cuba, the second Vietnam War 1961-1975, the 1967 Mideast War, the 1968 invasion of Czechoslovakia, the 1973 Mideast War, their proxy wars in Africa 1975-1987, the Soviet invasion of Afghanistan 1979-1989, and countless battles waged in the shadows.

During their aggressive and subversive efforts, 239,000 Soviet troops and "other personnel" had died fighting to take over. They lost more men and women trying to take our freedoms, than we suffered in fighting for them.

At various times we were in direct combat with them, in Korea and Vietnam. That information was kept secret from the American people for fear they would demand we fight Russia.

And the Soviets kept their high losses a secret from their people to prevent any potential revolts. **That is the reality and the treachery of the Soviet Union and the Communists.** (123)

The Islamic World

As the battles in Afghanistan continued the collapsing Soviets ended their suppport. Ahmed Massoud and his forces were moving from the northern areas towards Kabul while Hekmatyar was doing the same from the south. CIA was advising the Administration it would better for us if Massoud won the war.

But on January 1, 1992 the legal authority to conduct operations in Afghanistan was ended. We could not and would no longer "interfere in Afghanistan". *(124)

With our exit the radicals had a free hand.

After the collapse of the Soviet Union, Ed McWilliams found himself assigned to the inaugural U.S. embassy in Dushanbe, Tajikistan. The predominately Muslim nation was being remade as a new republic. Reports quickly surfaced that Najibullah's days ruling Afghanistan were numbered. Massoud's Tajik alliance with Abdul Rashid Dostum and his Uzbek militia (40,000 strong) was pushing the military balance away from the Marxists.

Najibullah echoed his former Soviet masters when he warned that Afghanistan would turn into a nest of radicals and terrorists if his rule ended. But there was no one in the world who wanted a Marxist ruler.

After the coalition forces had finished combat operations in the Gulf War the arduous task of tearing down of base camps and the re-loading of thousands of tons of weapons, ammunition supplies and equipment had to take place. Much of that massive amount of gear was re-embarked on ships and sent back to where it came. A fair amount however was left for the Saudi's and Kuwaiti's to build back their forces and to keep in country in case we had to come back. (Which we did in 1994.)

Small contingents of U.S. personnel stayed on in the region to monitor Saddam, establish and patrol safety zones and help to train the Saudi forces on their new weapon purchases. Base agreements were signed with Bahrain, Kuwait, Qatar and Oman.

However the Muslim extremists found that even this "protective policy" was an affront to them. They loudly complained and rebelled that infidels were still in the sacred lands.

One of the most vocal was Osama bin Laden. He remained an outspoken opponent in allowing any non-believers to stay. The Saudi rulers did not permit his complaints to go on indefinitely, and Bin Laden was finally placed under house arrest.

During April 1991 he "escaped", and took with him $250 million. Initially he returned to Afghanistan, but felt threatened by the Saudi agents still working in that country. He decided to move on to the Sudan. Things had changed, the Islamists ruled now.

Libya's subversions had finally ended the pro-western government in the Sudan. **The National Islamic Front,** an Islamic Fundamentalist regime had taken over in a bloodless coup a year earlier. Their religious motivated coup was similar to the one that had occurred in Iran, but the NIF used a Sunni version of Fundamentalism for theirs.

They were run by **Hassan al-Turabi**. Considered a scholar, the western educated and well spoken Turabi preached a virulent form of hatred that welcomed hundreds of like minded believers and potential terrorists. They accepted all displaced Arabs, especially those with money.

Unknown by most of the world, the NIF also conducted a genocidal purge of non-Muslim Sudanese who lived in southern Sudan. Only Muslims would be allowed to live there.

Treated like royalty, bin Laden was soon sipping tea at a convention of international terrorists and supporters. They hailed from Spain, France, Italy, Argentina, Mexico, Canada, Kenya and the U.S.. Representatives from Hezbollah, Hamas, Fatah, the Egyptian Islamic Jihad EIJ, Yasser Arafat and the PLO were all present. Ideas and contacts were spread and made, with all types of terrorist skills represented.

Bin Laden brought in hundreds of his old cohorts and Arab war veterans, and began to expand his rebellious movement called *al Qaeda*. Surrounded by so many like minded Islamists he quickly increased the number of his followers. Tired of his moniker of being a "moving bank", bin Laden was determined to rid the Arabian soil of infidels. He would do that by killing Americans.

As Khomeini and Azzam had said, America was the last power standing in the way of worldwide Islamic dominance. To the Islamists that fact was self-evident by the U.S. led coalition efforts to control and constrain Saddam's Iraq. They believed it had nothing to do with the helping the people of Kuwait.

While they were together those terrorist principals decided to form a plan to establish a pure Islamic Caliphate across the region. **They would remake the glory of a Muslim Empire, and everyone in it would live under strict Islamic guidelines. And they would be the ones in control.**

Historical Note: At its peak the original Islamic Caliphate had extended from the Pyrenees to the Philippines, as far south as Zanzibar and as far north as Grozny and Vienna". (125) They had outstripped Rome as the greatest empire in land mass, but had been fatally hurt during the Battle at Lepanto in 1571.

As time moved on technological advances in Europe created new empires, and the Ottomans were displaced by the Dutch, Spanish, Portuguese, English, French and Russians. WWI saw the final collapse of the Ottoman Empire, and the carving up of the last of their lands by the French and British.

Politically the Islamic world was a region of separate states, most ruled by tribal leaders, or in the case of the Ottoman lands the Europeans. *In effect the Ottoman Empire was decolonized.*

This was the same as they had done taking over from the Romans, (and what just happened to the Soviet Union.) After WWII, Islamic influence was further undercut by America's economic empire, western actions, and the Cold War.

Now in 1992 Turabi's goal was to unite all of the Shia and Sunni jihadists in a cooperative anti-American coalition. It would be the best of all worlds as they joined together.

During the end of 1991 and into early 1992 discussions were held between Iranian extremists and al Qaeda personnel. An informal agreement was reached to support one another in operations against Israel and the U.S.!

Soon after al Qaeda terrorists traveled to Iran and Lebanon for training in explosives, security and intelligence gathering. Bin Laden was particularly interested in how to use large truck bombs against U.S. targets. They saw in Lebanon how a few mass-casualty attacks could drive the Americans away. That was the empowerment of terrorism, brutality. These new terrorists were battle-tested and students of guerilla warfare. Many were self-educated, all were confident they would win.

They had observed that the PLO's futile decades of struggle had not worked. They felt Hezbollah tactics were better. *A few, large, violent attacks were superior at provoking fear than a large number of small attacks.* Determined believers using explosives could control a superpower. And they had both in abundance.

To help his hosts in the Sudan, bin Laden setup a construction company, an investment company, built a new airport, a leather factory, housing, terrorist training camps and he established control of the region's commodities. A local weapons industry was also created, and it included trying to make and purchase WMD's.

Four of the largest terrorist camps were at al-Khalafiyya twenty five miles north of Khartoum. The Akhil al-Awliya camp was on the Blue Nile south of Khartoum, Al Mirat was north of Umm, and al-Mazari northwest of Khartoum. Those camps catered to all nationalities. *Three thousand Revolutionary Guards from Iran went there for additional training.*

Sudan provided diplomatic cover to the terrorists in training, and they used their "diplomatic pouch" to transport weapons and explosives into the targeted countries. Although Iran sponsored more terrorists than the Sudan, the ones in the Sudan were more focused on what they wanted to achieve.

For bin Laden trips to Afghanistan were no longer pleasing as the local warlords were fighting among themselves. There was no longer a jihad to unite behind.

But in the Philippines, he was finding fresh and fertile ground as Muslims in the southern part of the nation were battling against the Christians in the north. It was the Christians who ruled there, so that was a perfect place to destroy, as had been done in Lebanon.

Bin Laden sent key lieutenants there to establish new al Qaeda cells. It included **Muhammad Jamal Khalifa, Ramzi Yousef, and Khalid Sheik Muhammad**. With world shaping events happening everywhere, there was a chance to make inroads without being noticed.

To the north the old Soviet Union was gone and their southern republics were of mostly Islamic populations. More opportunities to create strict Islamic states were there, beginning with Chechnya. Bin Laden sent fighters, arms and aid to fellow Saudi **Ibn Khatab, who was the actual leader of the Chechen revolt.**

So supplied, the Chechen operations became well organized and they began making headway against the Russian military. Russia knew this revolt was being caused by Wahhabist (Saudi jihadists) outsiders, and bin Laden was considered a Saudi agent. The fighting grew intense at times, as did the terrorism.

In Bosnia the al Qaeda effort was a showcase of organization. Fighters, logistic people, and money men showed up in force and setup charities, front companies and a banking network. They formed their own brigade of jihadist fighters called **the Muj**, who excelled at torture, mutilation and murder. Many of their ranks would reappear as enemies to America.

During June 1992 the Bush administration officially acknowledged the issue of Islamic Fundamentalism.

In the Meridian address the State Department stated that America wants and supports free elections in every nation. But we are suspicious of elements that would use the democratic process as a way to come to power, only to destroy that very process to control and dominate the people. (Clear references to what had happened in Iran and what was still ongoing in Algeria. And here.)

That review made a point of stating that Islam itself is not looked upon as an "ism", something that is hostile to freedom. (Politically correct or just unknowing?)

The State Dept. wrongly reported that they did not see a coordinated effort to impose Islamic Fundamentalism upon the region! *(Even though numerous warnings had come from Russia, the CIA, Jordan, Egypt, Tunisia, Morocco and Algeria!)*

Again the Administration did not address nor did they come up with a plan to fight Islamic terrorism or the many terrorist groups that were in existence.

We had closed our embassy and stopped all operations inside Afghanistan which included any effort at trying to moderate the divided nation. Abdul Haq warned that Afghanistan would become fifty or more separate kingdoms as the tribal influence of that ancient land could not be undone. That is what Afghanistan is, and will always be. But he was wrong.

Pakistan's ISI had found and was promoting a new ruler. One that would help them and their plans.

There were mistakes that occurred during the Afghan War and in our rushed exit. CIA was dependent upon the Pakistani's in supplying and aiding the Afghans. The few ties we did have were abandoned as we rushed for the exit. When the terrorists took over the country in the mid- 1990s the CIA had no agents in place to watch and learn or try to act against them.

As was recognized in the 1980s, when America merged with the powers of the Middle East to fight the Soviets, an army of Arabs was sent in without anyone considering who or what they were. Many of those volunteers were misfits and outcasts from their own countries. A percentage had ties to existing terrorist groups like the Muslim Brotherhood or its offshoot Egyptian Islamic Jihad. Some of those "volunteers" were recruited, trained and equipped with help by Osama bin Laden and others who were extremists. With the Soviet pullout the dissolution of that rebel force resulted in large numbers of trained and effective fighters who were suddenly unemployed. They began branching out into new and existing terrorist organizations.

Al Qaeda would be formed from those outcasts.

No thought was given to helping Afghanistan rebuild and recover. The country was basically left to its own fate as U.S. budget considerations and indifference took over. After the Afghans defeated the Soviet puppet regime they turned on each other. Civil war and chaos reigned, promoted by Pakistan and the Saudis. Following the murder of Pres. Zia, Pakistani Intelligence ISI allowed and promoted a new religious faction to form and operate in Afghanistan, *the* **Taliban.**

The Taliban used restrictive Islamic law, (Wahhabi sect), to bring order. They were assisted by the well armed war veterans and al Qaeda terrorists that were unemployed and available by the thousands. And in that time many of the moderate Afghan leaders were being eliminated as a way assist the Taliban. *Only in the Northern tribal areas were the warlords able to stay in power.*

Pakistan's ISI leader General Akhtar Khan saw that the Bush Administration wanted to bring moderates to power. The one idea that gained favor was to bring was to bring back their exiled King Zahir Shah.

Khan was totally opposed to "the American's bright idea", and worked to prevent it from happening. That was one reason why many suspected that General Zia and the others were "taken out" in that plane crash.

As Pakistan continued their quest for nuclear weapons the U.S. cut off aid in an attempt to stop them. Politically unstable and threatened with a possible takeover by extremists, Pakistan was also at risk. With some money, some willing fighters and effective weapons, changes could be made. They had defeated one superpower, what could they accomplish next?

Computers

In the U.S. a revolutionary technological transformation was slowly expanding into every facet of life. Computers had been around since WWII, and as time went by they improved in functions and in size. Researchers in the 1960s noted a strange condition existed in which the computers could communicate with each other. That function was called the Internet, and started in the early 1960s among the research world. By the 1970s supercomputers had became the norm and that communication occurrence began to grow from researchers into a broader use community by 1981.

Pres. Reagan's tax and economic programs had spurred a massive amount of R&D in the industrial world. Computer technologies were in the top of that list. By the mid-80s small businesses began using computers as part of their daily work.

As costs and size decreased computers began appearing for home use. By 1991 companies like Microsoft, Cisco and Apple were expanding the use of computers into homes and classrooms, and their use exploded across the world. That early Internet, at the time called the World Wide Web, was one of the growing offshoots of this computer dominated world. It was becoming available across the globe to normal consumers, thanks to the increasing use of commercial satellites for communications.

One of the most earth changing, yet unforeseen fallouts of the Internet, was the acceptance and use of English, and the promotion of western culture worldwide.

That factor was causing fits in the Islamic Fundamentalist world. Their control of the masses was being compromised, and so were their youth. Most of the repressive regimes in the region began closing off their societies to keep the hated western influence out.

Somalia

As stated before in the 1970s the Soviets had turned on the Somalis and were ordered out of the country. Fighting broke out between Somalia and Ethiopia, and their former Soviet advisors were soon on the Ethiopian side divulging everything they knew about the Somalis. Over 20,000 Cuban troops also joined the fighting which was being won by the communists .

Reza Pahlavi the Shah of Iran had tried to get the Carter Administration to help them in 1977, but Carter refused. The Shah stepped in and provided it himself, until he was betrayed and his rule was ended.

After the Soviets invaded Afghanistan the Carter Administration wokeup and began giving the Somalis aid. But Carter refused to provide aid to the Ethiopian rebels even after the Soviets turned on them too. That failure was a turning point as the Soviets stepped up their activity and the violence in the region got worse.

During Pres. Reagan's two terms our aid programs were increased as the Reagan team sought to *confront the Soviets* at every place possible. Like so many autocratic rulers, Somalia's Sid Barre made sure that most of the profits and aid went into his pockets and those of his supporters.

After a decade of fighting with Ethiopia, after being cutoff from their former patron the Russians, and then beset with inter-tribal conflicts, Somalia of the 1990s was a basket case of problems. Years of U.S. diplomacy and aid were unable to change that reality, and news shots of starving Somalis became a common sight.

By late 1991 Barre's ruling clan was no longer able to hold onto power and a civil war erupted. No one rival group was strong enough to establish itself so the misery and the death continued and became worse. U.N. relief workers tried to create a food / aid supply line, but they were constantly beset by hostile gunmen. At times gunmen would storm their vehicles taking the scarce food supplies by force. Mass starvation was on the horizon.

By the fall of 1992 the situation was so dire that Pres. Bush sent in the Marines. Their first unit in country was the MAU, Marine Amphibious Unit. As in Beirut a decade earlier, this reinforced battalion had its own armor, artillery and air support on the ships of the task force. But unlike Beirut, this force was allowed to use their armor and air support to enforce the peace. After a few battles the Somali warlords realized that it was best if they stayed away from the Marines. They would wait for better circumstances.

The U.N. humanitarian mission began making inroads and the situation stabilized. In foreign affairs the Bush Administration was second to none. But as a politician he was a poor choice.

Yugoslavia

As shown before, the collapse of Communism began in Communist Yugoslavia too. The Socialist Federal Republic of Yugoslavia, SFRY was comprised of separate republics that had been forced together under Tito's iron hand. After Tito died his replacements could not hold on. Decades of Communist central control over the economy caused further issues as new political entities sprang up. Most were nationalistic, and the different ethnic groups again had problems Serbian and Croatians' began to emigrate, and they began to fight over territory and ethnic makeup.

Inside the old boundaries of Croatia the native Croats wanted independence while the Serbian citizens living there wanted to remain within Serb dominated Yugoslavia. Croatian militias and police units were poorly equipped, but they began fighting with the well equipped Yugoslavian Army to attain their freedom. The European Community wanted those separate republics to become free as ethnic cantons, and even promoted their actions. (Breaking them up made them weaker politically and militarily.)

During December 1991 the Europeans recognized the new nations of Slovenia and Croatia. Bosnia-Herzegovina was invited to join in. The Slovenes managed their internal transition rather peacefully as they were mostly a homogenous province, but they still had to fight with the Serb dominated SFRY to win their freedom.

In Croatia the Serb population had been kept safe under Tito's hard rule, but with the fight for independence gaining steam violence ensued. Fighters from Serbia crossed the disputed border to join the Yugoslavian army units. The fighting intensified. During January 1992 a ceasefire was arranged and the battle-lines became static as U.N. peacekeepers arrived. Croatian President Franco Tudjman met with Serbian Pres. Slobodan Milosevic to discuss partionining areas of Bosnia and Herzegovina to create Croatia's new borders.

Bosnia and Herzegovina were of mixed populations with the three major entities being native Bosnian Muslims, (Bosniaks), Croats, and Serbians. As was normal under Communism all religions fared poorly and Islam was no exception. But during the 1960s some religious freedoms had been allowed in Yugoslavia. By 1971 Islam was the majority religion in Bosnia, and autonomous regions of Muslim Serbs were declaring their alliance to the SFRY. Bosnia began to fragment as Belgrade sent weapons to their Serb allies.

By August 1991 Serbian leaders boycotted Bosnian Parliamentary sessions. In October the Serbs organized their own National Assembly in Banja Luka, and a new war loomed.

Croatia was already fighting the SFRY when on March 3, 1992 Bosnia also voted for independence. Their Serbian population boycotted the elections and threatened civil war. The U.S. and Europeans recognized the new country of Bosnia in a hope of avoiding war. But soon after Yugoslavian forces attacked with the intent to drive the Bosniak populations out of the eastern regions. America and the U.N refused to get involved, and by summer of 1992 the Serbs controlled 2/3 of Bosnia.

Ethnic cleansing begun in the Balkans.

Serbians began flying aircraft into Bosnian territory attacking population centers. To stop the atrocities the Bush administration reluctantly supported a U.N. directed no fly zone. Our State Dept. began flying in food supplies to prevent starvation. It was projected that up to 150,000 *Bosnian Muslims* could die during the cold winter that was soon to come. (Most of the world officials were reluctant to become engaged in the region because it has always been so volatile.)

Islamic Terrorists

As shown earlier the Islamic cleric **Omar Abdel Rahman** was a long-time member of the extremist group, *Egyptian Islamic Jihad*. After the arrests from Sadat's murder four of the attackers had been executed. That caused large, violent protests among the radicals, and Rahman was arrested when rioters killed 100 Egyptian police officials in Asyut.

Years later a follow-on crackdown on fundamentalists he was jailed again. *Rahman escaped, and in 1990 went to the American Embassy in the Sudan where he obtained a visa despite being on a terrorist watch list!* As shown before he appeared at the Alkifah Islamic Refugee Center in Brooklyn, NY and took over when the previously mentioned cleric Shalabi "was conveniently murdered".

During his career Omar Rahman spoke at many Islamic centers including those in Peshawar, Pakistan. His students were numerous and they were committed to the jihadist cause. By 1992 he was indoctrinating hundreds of young Muslims in the NYC region, and his sermons called for action against the enemy of Islam, America.

In the mid-80s an Egyptian soldier named **Ali Mohamed** had caught the attention of our intelligence people. *He emigrated to the U.S. and married an American he met on a flight from Egypt.* As mentioned earlier, Ali soon enlisted in the U.S. Army impressing all. He began working in our Special Forces based at Fort Bragg, trained our people and gave lectures about Islam and the Arab culture. By the late 80s he was a common figure in the intelligence community and at times even worked for the FBI.

In reality though he was a double agent working with the Islamic Fundamentalists, and reporting back on what he learned inside the U.S. It was he who had provided the classified manuals and documents to Sayeed Nosair.

Ali had fought the Israelis back in 1973, and converted to the Muslim Brotherhood and EIJ soon after. Sheik Omar Rahman was his spiritual mentor, and Ali was often at Mosques listening to his calls for jihad. (Four of the Sadat assassins had come from Ali's old army unit, though he was in the U.S. at the time of Sadat's murder.) Ali next fought against the Soviets in Afghanistan, and was in contact with the Islamic radicals based there.

After joining our military in 1986 he made contact with Islamist radivals based in New Jersey. That was where Ali met **Sayeed Nosair** and one **Khalid Ibrahim**.

Khalid Ibrahim was active in the Office of Afghan Services for the Mujahedeen, aka Alkifah. That was the group that recruited volunteers to go and fight the Soviets.

Alkifah had their main office in Peshawar, Pakistan and three dozen others scattered across America and Europe! The primary ones in America were in Brooklyn, Jersey City and Tucson, and run by the Palestinian cleric Abdullah Azzam. But when Osama bin Laden "replaced the murdered Azzam", all of those Alkifah offices were converted to al Qaeda fronts. (Mustafa Shalabi was in the way, so he too was removed.)

Ali Mohamed next joined with al-Qaeda, and gave training sessions to their followers in New Jersey on guerrilla warfare. In Connecticut the training centered on weapons, and was given during the weekends. Among his first students were Nosair, Ibrahim and Abouhalima. *(Again that was where that traffic stop occurred, and possibly he was one of those in the car.)*

Ali left the U.S. military in November 1989 moving to Santa Clara, California. His new line of work was smuggling illegal aliens and suspected terrorists into the U.S. Vancouver, Canada was his primary route in.

During that time Ali provided "information" to the FBI on other illegal activities, which diverted their attention away from him, and gave him a de-facto shield that he was a good guy. But he traveled often to Afghanistan and Pakistan where he moved up in the circles of the militant Islamists which included bin Laden. There he oversaw the buildup of al Qaeda training centers which included bin Laden's main one in Khost.

During 1991 Ali organized and supervised bin Laden's move to the Sudan along with 2,000 Afghan war veterans. *Out of all of the militants that were a part of the Islamic War on the West, Ali Mohammed was one of the most important.* And his work against us was just starting.

Emad Salem had come into the U.S. a little while before Ali Mohamed. He too worked with the FBI giving tips whenever he could on the KGB and Russian Mafia. He eventually came to the attention of the JTTF. They tried to get him into the suspected Alkifah -Jihadist group. A few weeks after Nosair's murder acquittal, Salem was traveling to Detroit with Sheikh Rahman. It had been decided by the terrorists that Salem could atone for his prior Islamic failures by assassinating Pres. Mubarak when he came for a visit. He needed to train and pray for guidance.

Time went by and Salem began hearing reports of a plot to set twelve bombs at Jewish sites in NYC. Salem and one **Ali el-Shinawy** visited Nosair in Attica prison for more information on that attack. Their targets would be Temples, banks and Jewish Centers. El-Shinawy told Salem they needed to pick up hand guns and detonators from another plotter called "Dr. Rashid. *Salem was able to pass this information to the FBI.*

Bill Clinton

The next round of presidential candidates jumped onto the media stage, and a long list of Democrats again showed up. After a year of campaigning Bill Clinton the former Governor from Arkansas was in the lead. *By this point the major media was completely indoctrinated with the liberal mindset and viewpoint.* Unlike many candidates, Clinton was given a free ride over his many transgressions, including abusing women and refusing to release his scholastic and medical records. As they had done with Adalai Stevenson in 1952, the leftists claimed that Clinton was a scholar. But there was no proof as he refused to release his collegiate records. That was the first chance to have gotten him out of the race. (Obama would follow the same script in 2008, but he also refussed to release a real birt certificate.)

Despite his many character faults, his lack of accomplishments, no military or foreign policy experience, his Draft Dodging during the Vietnam War, his admitted use of marijuana and a list of questionable dealings and affairs, Clinton was picked and backed by all of the liberal groups.

There were many reports of affairs/groping/abuse of women, from women who had worked for or knew Clinton. (Paula Jones, Kathleen Wiley, Juanita Broderick, and a women who recently worked for the Clinton's, Gennifer Flowers.) But even NOW, the National Organization of Women ignored those obvious transgressions and backed this serial adulterer to the max. That is what the Democrats do, they stick together when power is at stake.

Historical Note; One of the most feared sexual episodes among the dozens that have occurred by Democrats was a liaison concerning one Ellen Rometsch. *She was one of JFK's many mistresses, and it was uncovered that she was actually an East German spy!* Robert Kennedy the U.S. Attorney General secreted her out of the country with help from FBI Director J. Edgar

Hoover, to ensure this career ending affair was never discovered by our citizens. *When word did leak out, RFK threatened (again) numerous journalists with "severe repercussions" if they ever wrote about the issue.* Robert also illegally contacted the Senate Oversight Committee and "convinced them to let the matter drop".

There is no law the Democrats will not beak, especially when fixing our elections. (Trumans 1934 Senate race, LBJ in 1948, the 1960 presidential election that put the Kennedys into power, etc.)

An audit into Clinton's years in Arkansas showed many potential criminal / financial problems. He had claimed he was the poorest Governor in the country with a $35,000 per year salary, but the audit showed he was given almost **$750,000** per year in other monies that were not recorded as income! All of his "personal living expenses" which included, food, travel, security, shelter, entertainment, utilities, housekeeping, administration etc, were paid from Arkansas State Funds. Yet none were claimed as income which constituted tax fraud. The IRS did not audit him. *(VP Spiro Agnew had to resign in 1974 for failing to claim $35,000.)*

Other problems for Clinton surfaced over the *Whitewater land scam*. His wife Hillary Clinton had been one of the partners in that crooked land deal. Hillary was also involved with long time friend Jim McDougal's dubious ventures, including Madison Guaranty which was a corrupt savings and loan institution he ran.

Castle Grande was another scam where near worthless land was sold at inflated prices to buyers who used government backed loans from **Madison Guaranty.** Most of the loans were defaulted on, and the U.S. taxpayers were stuck with the bailout of millions of dollars! Despite having an Ivy league education she claimed she only did low level work on the projects and never knew they were scams. **The Inspector General of the FDIC looked at many of the documents that Hillary prepared and believed that they had been made to deceive the Federal Bank examiners.**

Even so none of those potential fatal scandals were investigated by the major media, and any that were being highlighted did not receive much airtime. In that way the media "helped" their candidate move on.

The Clinton's had a vast network on their side, the *deep state of the Liberal Left*. This destructive group has dominated the Democratic party and the mainstream media for decades, and have abandoned any previous notions of individual responsibility.

(During the JFK and LBJ years 1961-1968 having mistresses in and around the White House plus other affairs on the outside was a common and accepted practice. Everyone knew about it, but no one brought it up, no one complained and no negatives issues arose. *None of the Republican presidents ever treated their wives so callously, nor would they have been allowed to by the media.*

Those same years saw numerous "Watergate type episodes of spying on potential enemies" by the Democrats. **The most illegal wiretaps ever put in place in this country occurred during those eight years.** *In 1963 alone RFK placed over 250 wiretaps, and it included some on Dr. Martin Luther King who the Democrats claimed they supported!)*

For the Left, there is nothing that cannot be overlooked. It is always someone else's fault, parents, capitalism, racism etc. Their advancement of this lack of moral clarity has resulted in the loss of personal discipline, morals, family structure and belief in the individual. Replacing those virtues were abortion on demand, unwed pregnancies, a massive rise in single parent families, teen pregnancies, pornography disguised as art, political correctness and sensitivity training on bizarre social scams such as the homosexual lifestyle that our children are forced to endure in grade school. And a desire that the government should control all aspects of your life. With a compliant media and thousands of followers covering his tracks, the Clinton's were free of any serious examination into their affairs.

President Ronald Reagan had correctly believed that there were three liberal entities hard at work to hinder our freedoms and destroy America. Those entities were, **Special interest groups, the liberal Media and liberal Democrats.** * (126)

Abraham Lincoln once said of right and wrong,

"It is the eternal worldwide struggle between two opposing principals." *(127)

But for the liberal left there is no right or wrong. Just a pursuit of their agenda no matter how far it strays from the ideals that founded this nation. To further their goal they have split the nation into voting blocs in order to separate us from each other. They spout the (PC) politically correct slogan that diversity is our strength, when in reality, **in Unity there is Strength. Diversity is what splits us apart and weakens us.**

Long ago the leftists infiltrated our nations colleges and universities propagandizing the young minds that America and our founding principals were bad. By the early 1990s they had taken over most of the local school boards too. With that mission almost completed they could control the thoughts of our young through adolescence and into adulthood creating an army of autobots that believed the Democrats party line and their propaganda hook, line and sinker. Our true History is no longer taught.

Even our amendment that gives us Freedom of Religion has been prostituted by the liberal left into their outlook of freedom from religion. In that devious way they were re-creating our society so that it has no religion, no morals and no societal compass. Their endgame began with a reckless Supreme Court ruling in 1963 that banned (based on their lawsuit), "coercive prayer" in public schools.

John Adams our second president warned,

"Our Constitution was made only for a religious and moral people. It is wholly inadequate for the government of any other. *(128)

And that dear readers is why our country is falling. Liberals believe in nothing, especially in America.

In 1992 they were promoting a poster child of their lies and scams. With all of their people on board, and help from a dupe named Ross Perot, they got him into the White House.

Terrorist Threats

Despite the peace and progress in 1992 there were still enemies that wanted to destroy us. For the remaining Communists it is the "state that matters". For the Islamic Extremists it is Islam. Both groups wish for their beliefs to be the only worldwide political force, (just like the liberals in America).

By 1992 Islam controlled one sixth of our planet's population. They are reproducing three times faster than any other social / political or religious group. Only two countries can compete with them in pure numbers in that regard, India and China.

China will be adversely affected by their one child policy by 2030, while all of Europe, Japan and Russia will be similarly affected by their low birth rates. Every population requires 2.3 births per couple to enable the populace to replace themselves. Any number less than that will result in a population decrease and eventual societal collapse as aging takes its toll.

Poor and educated Muslims have been spreading across the globe settling in every nation except China and Japan. (Neither country allows immigration, though China is fighting with Muslim extremists coming in from Mongolia.)

However most Muslims do not assimilate into the host country. **They do not want to, and it is forbidden by Sharia Law!** *For the extremists in their mists the world must unite under Islam, and the non believers will be eliminated.* One way or another.

(By 2016 many towns in America are now Islamic, and Mohammed is the most popular name in London.)

After Anwar Sadat was murdered Pres. Mubarak imposed strict controls on Islamic Fundamentalist speech to prevent any more Omar Rahman's from arising. Though he was successful there, the Leftists in the West have never agreed to that restriction. Hostile voices are free to speak out, and as every year goes by more and more Muslims are coming into the nations of the West. Many were sent as spies /Manchurian candidates to destroy those host countries. Some entered as terrorists, while others preach hatred daily. But all were protected by our liberal laws and foolish liberal citizens.

None of the principals in the Democratic Party pay any heed to those truths. It was Jimmy Carter who opened the gates to the Islamic Revolution by abandoning the Shah of Iran. Fallout from that Revolution included the Afghan War, Pres. Sadat's murder, the collapse of Lebanon, dozens of terrorists attacks, the Gulf War and the recent genocide in the Balkans.

Inside the complacent West serious danger was just an idea away from happening.

Well known and and exemplary Italian journalist Oriana Fallaci, (she had been a partisan fighter in WWII), interviewed the Ayatollah Khomeini back in March 1979.

Her time with that radical cleric convinced her that the Islamic Extremists sought to destroy all Western societies. She wrote; "The art of invading, conquering and subjugation is the only art at which the sons of Allah have excelled. Islamism is the new Nazi-Fascism. There is no reasoning or compromise with them, no hypo-critical tolerance.

The simplistic minds who do not understand this reality are feeding the suicide of the Western world." *(129) Excerpts of her interview ran in the NY Times in October 1979.

While our political campaigning had been in full swing radicalized Islamic students and young Muslim males continued to meet at the *Alkifah Refugee Center* in Brooklyn. Many breathed a hatred for the West, but especially America. They intently listened to the sermons from Omar Rahman who was unrelenting in his calls for action against the source of every conspiracy against Islam, America.

The way to their victory was a war of attrition against the great Satan. Five or six commando type operations would frighten the great power and they would then run from international affairs in their quest to be left alone. **America is weak in character and would run like a coward.**

This coming war against the U.S. was actually a secondary result of the collapse of Soviet Communism. Prior to that event the Islamic world had two opponents that vied for their attention. The West was hated for interfering in the Muslim world, while the Communists were their main weapon supplier and supporter. However the Communists were feared for their aggressiveness and secular rule. Since the state was all important the Communists tried hard to reduce Islam's hold of daily life. Millions had died.

Historical Note: Had the Soviets not been confronted and contained by the West after WWII, *(starting in Iran ironically), they could have taken over the entire Middle East.* If that had happened they may have been able to end all Islamic religious fervor back in the 1940-50s with their usual harsh tactics.

Over the past decades the Islamists rebelled and skirmished over Soviet controls, but they reacted violently and pulled together when the Soviets invaded Afghanistan. To the Islamists this was an attack upon Islam by an infidel, and it had to be crushed. With Russia defeated by their fighters, only America stood in the way of a renewed Islamic Empire.

Islam has from the start been a religion that was promoted by the sword. It glorifies jihad, sacrifice and conquest. For almost a thousand years from the time the Moors first landed in Spain to the Turkish siege of Vienna, Islam has been a constant threat to the Western-Christian world. The Crusades were fought to regain control of the Holy land from the Muslims, and that hostility continued for centuries afterward.

It was the advent of the industrial age, which produced stronger nations and advanced militaries in Europe. That prevented any additional Islamic conquests in Europe.

A long period of quite was created between the formerly hostile worlds, but it was never a true peace. The Ottoman Empire was a great Islamic entity, but it slowly retracted as the centuries went on. What was left of it was broken up after their defeat in WWI. Artificial national boundaries were created by the colonial rule of France and Great Britain. That was what had inspired the

Islamic Fundamentalists, and gave impetus to the growth of the *Muslim Brotherhood.* After the past seventy years of defeat and humiliation, the Islamists planned a comeback.

And now they had an army to do it.

Sayyid Nosair was a member of that army, and of the newest Islamic terrorist group which their leader **Osama bin Laden** called *al Qaeda.* During his 1991/92 trial some of Nosair's legal bills had been paid by bin Laden. Evidence found inside Sayyid's apartment linked him to a group called the **Afghan Services Bureau**, Azzam's creation. As shown earlier because of the FBI's lack of translators vital files taken from his apartment were just sitting in boxes untouched.

After his conviction and imprisonment in Attica in the summer of 1992, Sayyid began preaching and planning more attacks against America. His supporters went to the prison to hear his plans. As mentioned before, one of those men was **Emad Salem** who was a part time FBI informant. After weeks of preparation for their anti-Jewish attacks, Salem was taken to meet the secretive Dr. Rashid. They met at *Abu Bakr*, another Mosque in Brooklyn. Rashid told Salem that he could get them ready made pipe bombs at $1,000 each. Salem reported all to his FBI handlers who then insisted he had to wear a wire to make the case legally sound. Salem wisely refused, and was foolishly fired. Luckily the Jewish plot was slow to develop. This was **Incident # 1** in the **Islamic Extremist War against America.**

(I am creating a list of terrorist incidents from this point because this was the first organized, deliberate attack against America / the West by these Islamic Extremists.

Following Incidents consist of plots, actual attacks, attempted attacks, arrests and the acquiring of vital intelligence / information that should have prompted some action by the U.S. government. Most of the attacks in Israel I did not list because they were a separate enemy. When you read this extensive list you will be stunned at how much you did not know or never even heard about. And the Clinton administration worked hard keeping these attacks /plots secretive by downplaying all of them.)

Wrongly the FBI agents in the JTTF, Joint Terrorism Task Force did not disseminate all of the information they had learned on this plot throughout the Federal Legal and Intelligence System. Most of those suspected bombers were not U.S. citizens, they were foreign nationals plotting terrorist attacks inside the U.S. This was exactly the kind of attack Pres. Reagan's **Counter-Terrorism Center (CTC)** was designed to oversee and deal with. *Yet they were never updated.*

Mohammed Salameh, Nidal Ayyad and **Bilall Alkaisi** had raised $8,500 to begin a chemical factory to make a large explosive. Alkaisi was forced from the group for lack of commitment, which created the need to find a new explosive expert. *Mohammed Salameh made over $4,000 in calls to Baghdad looking to get help with their terrorist plans.*

From his communications abroad two experienced terrorists were dispatched. On September 1, 1992 two non-descript Muslim men, **Ramzi Yousef** and **Ahmed Ajaj** landed at JFK airport in NYC. At first all appeared normal.

Yousef had lived in Kuwait with his Pakistani father, and while living there they were treated as "guest workers" by the oil sheiks. As a teenager they moved back to Pakistan where the father embraced Islamic Fundamentalism as did the son. Yousef grew up and went to college in Wales, and fell in with a local chapter of the Muslim Brotherhood. In the late 1980s he went to Afghanistan to become a jihadist. *He lived and trained in bin Laden's terrorist camps where he excelled at bomb making.*

Ajaj had actually come into the U.S. the year before seeking "political asylum". *He then secretly left the U.S. in April 1992 under a false identity and passport.* He returned to the main al Qaeda terrorist camp at Khaldan in Afghanistan. (The CIA had previously listed that location as a terrorist training center.)

It was at that camp that Ajaj had met Yousef. They trained with other terrorists and practiced with various explosives. But their specialty was ammonium-nitrate truck bombs, the kind used by Hezbollah. **They were among the first al-Qaeda terrorists to be cross-trained by Hezbollah, part of the agreement reached in the Sudan!**

With his previous change of identity Ajaj was able to journey to known and suspected terrorist strongholds without leaving any paper trail that he had ever been there. According to our immigration records, "he" was still in the NYC area. A perfect cover and alibi.

(This episode is exactly the reason why all people who enter this country must be photographed and fingerprinted into a scanner with a database. Whenever anyone comes in or goes out of the U.S. the hand / photo scanner records everyone. In that way no fake identities can be used, and it would be easier to catch known and potential terrorists as they moved around.)

With this current flight into JFK airport both men assumed there were no issues that would interfere with their mission. But Ajaj was detained because Immigration agents found his notes and videos on bomb making! He also had three fake passports, plus other false documents on him. Investigating further it was revealed that he had traveled from Houston to Pakistan to the UAE and back to Pakistan recently. How and why would a "pizza deliveryman" travel like that? He was charged with passport fraud and arrested.

Yousef was also detained, but quickly claimed he wanted "asylum" from Saddam's Iraq. Mindlessly he was released pending a hearing. Naturally Yousef did not return for that hearing and he "disappeared" inside our shores. (As happens over **60%** of the time.) **Incident # 2**

After Yousef left the airport he took a cab to the Mosque in the East Village in Manhattan. There he met up with **Mahmoud Abouhalima**. Abouhalima had also fought the Soviets in Afghanistan, and been an assistant to the recently murdered Cleric Shalabi. Abouhalima had just returned from Germany using a permanent alien status as a farm worker. He was presently working as a NYC cab driver, and as shown before had been a suspect in the Meir Kahane shooting from 1990 as the getaway driver. (He hid out in Germany for a while.)

Abouhalima took Yousef to Brooklyn and **Ibrahim el-Gabrowny's** home. They contacted **Mohammed Salameh**, and Yousef was taken to Salameh's apartment in Jersey City, New Jersey. There he met **Musab Yasin**, and his brother **Abdul Yasin**. *Both had also recently come in from Baghdad.*

Also joining the group was **Nidal Ayyad** a naturalized citizen from Kuwait had a degree in chemical engineering from Rutgers. This was the cell that would make the first major terrorist attack inside America. (Quite a well organized and tangled web is it not?)

After his arrest and conviction Ajaj was serving a minor six month sentence for having bomb making literature. *(??)* The court was petitioned by his co-conspirators, and unbelievably they released his "personal property" to a friend!! **All of his notes, books and videos for creating the explosives went back to the group.** Telephone records also showed that this group had called Ajaj in prison multiple times, yet no investigation of those callers was ever done. (Why was that type of information allowed to be released??)

To insure his anonymity, Yousef then claimed to have lost his passport, and pretended to be one Abdul Basit. No search of that name or passport was made, and he was issued a temporary one. *Yousef was directed to report to a hearing, and again disappeared.*

Their cell continued to plot secure that no paper trail could come back to haunt them. By using multiple aliases Yousef could avoid arrest and deportation since he was now a "new person". And when it was time to escape he could slip out unnoticed because no one was looking for that identity.

(Illegal entries by immigrants were a continuing problem at our airports, but especially at JFK. *During the late 1980s, almost 20,000 illegal's per year entered through JFK claiming they "lost their papers".* Our system then rewarded those people by giving them a temporary green card and a summons to appear at an immigration hearing which they never show up at. No one knew who or where any of those illegal's were! It is far worse today.)

After having fired Salem the JTTF was floundering in the dark. In an effort to rattle their cage, the FBI summoned a few of those suspected conspirators to come in for questioning and fingerprinting. None of them cooperated with the authorities, and all were quickly released.

A month or so later CNN reporter Steven Emerson was in Oklahoma City covering a boring storyline at the Convention Center. He decided to drift through the lunch time crowds and found himself at an Islamic meeting of the *Muslim Arab Youth Association, MAYA.* He was denied entry at first because he was a non-Muslim, but eventually found a patron who took him inside.

During his hours at the event he was horrified to hear speaker upon speaker preaching violence upon the West and Jews. **Even Khalid Misha'al the head of Hamas was there speaking.**

All of their literature and even the coloring books promoted jihad and hatred. Emerson called a friend in the FBI who told him no one there knew anything about that subject. *He was also told that as a result of the mid-70s Congressional laws and oversight the FBI could no longer investigate any suspicious or hateful rhetoric, only criminal activity.*

Around this same time the JTTF investigation of the Black Muslims returned to life. Phone requests had been coming in for rope and weapons training with AK-47 assault rifles. And calls from the suspects to Sheikh Rahman and Sayeed Nosair seemed to be implying things were progressing on the Jewish Plot or something worse, urban warfare. (Unfortunately the NYPD had to pull back most of their resources from covering terrorism.)

On December 19, 1992 Mahmoud Abouhalima called Salem. He did not return the call nor did he contact the FBI to report in. (Still fired) Yousef and his cell had almost finished getting the parts they needed for their bomb. What they now needed were detonators, and they had called Salem.

They made additional calls to the Black Muslims to see what munitions they had. They used what was left of their original $8,500 to purchase more chemicals, a car, and rent a storage shed at the Space Station Storage in Jersey City. It was there they would construct the actual bomb.

(From later interrogations the Jewish Plot was still desired by the original plotters. Yousef changed things. He picked the World Trade Center as the target, for its symbolism and ease of access.)

Election 1992

As the U.S. presidential campaign progressed Bill Clinton ran as a "New Democrat" who promised welfare reform, the end of racial quotas, an effective energy policy and federal stimulus for infrastructure. He claimed that there isn't a government program for every problem and that people must show more responsibility. He promised Change. (Just like Carter and Obama.) On paper he seemed to be a fresh idea, but in reality Clinton was just another shabby Democrat created in the same light as Tammany Hall.

He had never worked in the private sector, never accomplished anything and never risked anything. The Clintons did not even own a home so they knew nothing of the struggles by average Americans. Yet as always their "I feel your pain" sentiment was believed by so many who are easily deceived.

Senior Democratic Senator and Medal of Honor recipient Bob Kerry called Bill Clinton "an unusually good liar".

Jesse Jackson put Clinton's character issues another way, "I can maybe work with him, since I know who he is and what he is. *There is nothing he won't do, he is immune to shame"!*** This was the candidate the Democrats put forward. (130)

Pres. George Bush on the other hand had accomplished many great things during his first term. The Soviet Afghan War had ended with the Soviet pullout in mid-February 1989. Communism the great lie and global threat had been ended in Eastern Europe and Russia. **Never in the history of mankind had so many people (over 500 million) been freed from oppression so quickly, with so little loss of life.**

Germany which had been separated since 1945 was slowly being reunited as a nation and people. All across Europe the newly freed "east-bloc" nations were brimming with hope.

In the Middle East the Persian Gulf War had ended quickly with little losses to the coalition. Kuwait had been freed, though Saddam Hussein was still in power in Iraq. At present the immediate threats to that region were ended.

And Pres. Bush had recently signed a nuclear reduction treaty with Gorbachev reducing those terrible weapons by another 5,000!

As shown before, during December 1991 Gorbachev was ousted from power in Russia. Bush could have gloated and made a big show of the fact the Cold War was won in the most part by America and the Republican efforts, *but he did not.* Always a quiet person Pres. Bush made a televised speech thanking Gorbachev for all of his work in guiding the Soviet Union during the past six years. The world was fortunate, that the total failure of Socialism had been revealed.   *(131)

It was now being replaced by Capitalism and Democracy.

Historical Note: America had pulled back from the world after WWI. New aggressive leaders strove to take over in the broken post-war world. WWII was the result. After that war ended Truman pulled us out of the spotlight and decimated our military colossus. Communism stepped into the breech. Their quest for power forced us into the Cold War, and the fighting that went with it. All of our efforts during the Cold War, the Truman Doctrine, the Marshall Plan, the formation of the CIA, NATO and SEATO, and the wars in Korea and Vietnam were done to try to contain and prevent the Communists from expanding any further.

That was the key to their survival.

Every country the Communists took over was plundered of wealth and resources enabling their great lie to continue. Only twice did the Soviets became directly aggressive, the 1962 Cuban Missile Crisis and in the Yom Kipper War in 1973. JFK made a secret deal that ended the Cuban Crisis, (he created), while Nixon threatened the Soviets with war if they sent their forces into the

Middle East War. Knowing they did not have the strength to win, and that Nixon would fight, the Soviets backed off.

But during the period of 1975-81 the Soviets were allowed to expand into the Third World because the Democrats gave up the fight. Had Carter stayed in office, the Communists may well have turned Western Europe, and they would have won in Afghanistan and possibly invaded Iran. They also would have taken all of Central America, most of Africa and some of South America. Awash with those new assets, the Soviets would not have collapsed economically/politically as they did.

Fortunately for the world Ronald Reagan came into office in 1981, and he stood in their way. All of his efforts were fought over by the Democrats, but he won that war too.

During the forty plus years of the Cold War we had lost over 130,000 of our sons and daughters trying to Contain the Reds. It was a small price compared to losing the Cold War.

(In 1815 the Europeans fought the brutal battle of Waterloo. They defeated Naploean, but lost 50,000 men in a single day. Lord Wellington the victor would aptly state; *"The only thing worse than winning a battle, was losing one."*) * (132)

Pres. Bush and the Republicans had enjoyed a high rating from the public throughout 1991. But Bush had wrongly voted to increase taxes in his first term despite having stated he would not. (The Democrats ran the Congress and tricked him into voting for a tax increase for the wealthy that was a part of the "clean air act".) As a result of that preventable mistake Bush lost a lot of conservative support *in their short-sighted foolishness.*

In October 1991 a severe storm had destroyed the Bush home in Kennebunkport, Maine which tied them up for weeks. The leftist media turned that against him. Then during the height of the campaign his Chief of Staff resigned, and Pat Buchanan a strict conservative imprudently campaigned against him. Buchanan's negative comments and stringent ideas hurt the senior Bush in the polls further eroding his conservative support.

Economic indicators had reported that the small recession we had been in had ended during the summer of 1992, but the liberal media did not report on that in their continuous effort to help the Clinton campaign.

And then yet another unneeded political mistake occurred due in part to the premature death of senior advisor Lee Atwater. The small recession caused many people to hurt financially as they waited for their jobs to call them back. Pres. Bush refused to extended the unemployment benefits to those still out of work. As a conservative minded man Bush like Pres. Hoover wanted the economy and markets to take care of all things. But those people needed some additional help and he should have extended their benefits, especially in an election year.

Candidate Clinton issued a string of complaints that garnered much undeserved press, such as the genocide in the Balkans where he blamed Pres. Bush for not taking action. He also complained that our air power should be used to help the U.N. peacekeepers. *But Clinton had been adamant against us fighting in Kuwait.*

With the end of the Cold War, candidate Clinton wanted America to pull back from world leadership, and let others pick up the need. As history has clearly shown, his feelings were totally wrong. *"To have a strong domestic policy a nation absolutely must have a strong foreign policy."* That is how every strong nation and empire was formed, and that was how it was maintained. *(133)

Former Pres. Nixon succinctly stated; **"The Cold War divided the world, but the end of it did not unite the world". There was much work that needed to be done, and only America could provide that leadership.** *(134)

Between those two candidates, only George Bush was a true leader who could make peace happen. Yet as was typical of this generation of Democrats, (Carter, Mondale, Dukakis, Clinton), they understood nothing of how the world actually worked. *Power is Power, and someone will always be the leader no matter how small the group or nation is.*

Andre Malraux, a French writer, philosopher, WWII Résistance fighter and Government Minister under Charles de Gaulle spoke with Pres. Nixon in 1972 on the paradox of America. He stated, **"The United States was the first nation in world history to become a world power without trying too".** *(135) Nixon agreed, telling him we are essentially an isolationist nation who become involved in world affairs only because we had to. *After WWII there was no one else who could lead and provide the security to keep Democracy safe.*

Clinton's deceptive election campaign strategy was similar to the one used by JFK in 1960, attack the better candidate with lies and half-truths. Like so many of us Bush did not know how to sell himself or his many accomplishments, and his campaign was lackluster and he seemed out of sorts.

And to add to the 1992 election mix wealthy businessman Ross Perot opened a foolish and illusory 3d party candidacy to challenge

Pres. Bush. Driven by some personnel hatred, or a secretive effort to hurt the Republicans, Perot who was a friend of the Clintons refused to back out of the race despite the clear fact that he could not win. His campaign promised to "cleanup Washington and bring it back to reality".

But in reality all he did was to take away the independent voters that are so vital for post-depression Republican candidates. (Perot would repeat his intrusive efforts in 1996 with the same outcome.) This third party vote dilution had happened before, most notably in 1912 and again in 1968.

Back in 1912 Teddy Roosevelt and his Bull Moose party took 27.4 % of the vote, more than the Republican incumbent Taft received at 23.3%. **As a result of that vote split Democrat Woodrow Wilson won the presidency with just 41.8% of the vote.**

In 1968 Democrat Herbert Humphrey got only 42.7% of the vote, Nixon and Agnew won with only 43.4 % of the popular vote, while George Wallace's racially charged third party effort received 13.5%. Some of Wallace's votes came from the conservatives Nixon wanted, while most of Wallace's votes came from the southern Democrats Humphrey needed. Many of them were conservative minded too, and they did not like Humphrey or his liberal plans. Had Wallace not run most of them would have supported Nixon. (Despite the close popular vote tallies Nixon would probably have won since he had 301 electoral votes.)

Additional help for Clinton came in the way the debates were laid out. TV producer Harry Thomason was a longtime Clinton pal and coached him on what was going on and what to do to look good. A practice stage was laid out in a grid so Clinton would know where to stand. Perot's chair was made inches larger so he would look like a kid, and the cameras were arranged to help Clinton at all times.

As a final effort to insure the defeat of George Bush, Lawrence Walsh the special prosecutor who was still looking into Iran-Contra decided to indict Reagan's Sec-Def Casper Weinberger just before election day. He also illegally hinted that Bush may have been involved, even though he was not.

(A post election study showed the Washington press corps voted 89% for the Democrats. That number was up twenty points from Eisenhower's 1952 election. It is far worse today. Arrogantly the media still refers to themselves as "mainstream".)

When the November 1992 election results were counted Clinton got just 42%, Bush took 39.5% and Perot took a strong third place with 18.5% of the votes.

Thanks to Ross Perot, Bill Clinton "was elected".

America and the World would pay dearly for that terrible election result. At this point in time it was vital that the presidential election be filled by a true leader, not a scam artist.

A dangerous menace had been formed and was spreading throughout the world, organized Islamic Extremists. Their first strikes had already happened, and more were soon upon us.

And once again TR Farenbach's words ring true;

That There are Tigers in This World, *(2)*

And They Are Always Watching.

The Islamic War against the West is Unleashed

Without warning on December 29, 1992 bin Laden's terrorists launched their first major attack against the West. They targeted European and American tourists and military personnel who stayed at two popular hotels in Aden, Yemen.

The Hi-rise hotels the Goldmore and the Aden were at opposite ends of the city's harbor. Both catered to their western guests with alcohol, rock music and even Christmas lights. Women were dressed up and acted in a manner that would infuriate an Islamic Fundamentalist. At that time the hotels also housed one hundred U.S. Marines assigned to a refueling/transport squadron.

They were there in support of the USMC humanitarian mission still ongoing in Mogadishu, Somalia.

Just after 9 PM an alert guard spotted two suspicious men near a vehicle in front of the *Aden Hotel*. He confronted them, and with their attack in danger one terrorist detonated his bomb rigged suitcase. The explosion wounded the guard and the three terrorists. All were arrested, and numerous additional bombs were found in their vehicle and defused.

The wounded terrorists admitted who they were, and that they had trained in camps in Afghanistan that were funded by that wealthy Saudi, Osama bin Laden. Yemeni authorities went into high gear to find their co-conspirators but were too late.

Over at the *Goldmore Hotel* those terrorists were able to place a bomb on the forth floor. It exploded killing and wounding over a dozen guests and staff. Searches found an additional twenty five bombs, mines and other weapons placed throughout the hotel. *It was meant to be a night of death.* Word of this episode went out to the world's intelligence agencies.

The CIA station chief in Yemen informed the CTC that Yemeni intelligence people suspected a terrorist leader named Osama bin Laden was involved. He was already well known in the Arab world.   **Incident # 3**

Iraq

After the Gulf War ended the United Nations Special Commission UNSCOM was formed to investigate. Though many weapons and munitions had been destroyed during and after the war, Saddam was not releasing all of his secrets. And the one secret that was causing sleepless nights was Iraq's nuclear program. As shown before, Israel had warned the U.S. that Iraq was close to a bomb, but no one believed them.

Then U.N. inspection team uncovered an enormous nuclear facility which had been unknown to the CIA or anyone else. It had not been bombed during the war, and the R&D uncovered at that site showed much progress in atomic bomb making.

A follow on report stated that the Iraqi nuclear records were being hidden in the Agriculture Ministry. An intelligence raid was conducted to recover the damning papers. But while the inspectors were inside searching the floors Iraqi forces surrounded the building. Frantic messages went out as the inspectors tried to hold on to their find while a bombing mission was organized to protect them. During the standoff they were able to get information out via a CNN broadcast/interview. Officials were stunned to realize how far along the Iraq's had been, Israel had been right.

(If Iraq had not lost their nuclear reactor to that Israeli airstrike in 1981, nuclear weapons would probably been used in the Middle East. What would have been the worlds fate?)

By January 1992 Saddam and his minions had repaired and reactivated over two hundred production lines dedicated to Iraqi armaments and "civilian needs". In that way Saddam could claim the plants were needed for civilian use.

With incentives available Saddam's agents worked the globe picking up what he needed to continue his search for weaponry and WMD's. Once again Europe was open for business, and Saddam's people only faced risk if they fell within reach of U.S. customs.

Many times the parts and supplies were sold to front companies in Jordan and then trucked into Iraq. By late 1992 his remaining French built Mirage fighters were patched up and flying "training missions" along the no fly zones in defiance of the ceasefire rules.

Saddam continued to harass and delay the UNSCOM inspectors at every possible chance. And he refused to allow inspections inside certain plants that were suspected of producing components for WMD's.

Pres. Bush's last official act in office was on January 17, 1993. He decided to send a volley of cruise missiles into Iraq. Many of the suspect plants were destroyed by the strikes, and France which had done a lot to rebuild them condemned the attacks as "going beyond the U.N. scope".

(One of the targets on that last day was Saddam Hussein. He was hosting a conference for Islamic Fundamentalists at the Al Rashid Hotel in Baghdad. Saddam's luck held out again.)

Most people don't know this, but the al-Rabiya complex that was struck on January 17 was actually making parts for uranium enrichment. Unfortunately the strike was only partially successful and within weeks the resilient Iraqi's renewed manufacturing the parts needed for uranium enrichment.

And they did so despite four visits from the UNSCOM inspectors and two from the IAEA.

One Iraqi trick was to put vital equipment inside long haul trucks and drive away as the UN inspectors were detained at the main entrance. IAEA senior inspector Ekeus was relentless in pursuing all WMD leads, while his fellow Swede Hans Blix was pressing the agency to stop the inspections and get back to business as usual. Blix's own team found **603** dual use machine tools that had survived the Gulf War, and could be used making WMD's. Yet he reported all was well.

(*In June 1993 a French freighter was caught trying to bring chemicals needed for uranium enrichment into the Jordanian port of Aqaba.* The ship was turned away and the affair hushed up, but the French renewed their requests to end the Iraqi embargos.) More problems would soon surface.

Section Five

The Clinton Years   Appeasement and Subversion

Weeks of arrests, investigations and harsh interrogations of those picked up by Yemeni intelligence in the December 29 terrorist attacks in Aden were completed.

The trail was definitely traced back to Osama Bin Laden. Yemini Intel had learned that all of the terrorists from the attacks had trained in bin Laden's Afghanistan terrorist camps. A search of one of their apartments uncovered large amounts of money and twenty-one additional explosive devices. Also found were TNT, timers, detonators and documents written in code.

Once deciphered, everything led back to bin Laden.

Armed with that solid proof the Yemeni Minister of the Interior contacted Interpol for help in tracking down him down. They knew full well that more attacks would come. All of the terrorists and suspects caught in the bombing and the investigations were tried, convicted and imprisoned.   **Incident # 4**

The Clinton Administration was updated on all of that intelligence. Even though they knew those attacks targeted hundreds U.S. military personnel and Western tourists, the Administration did not get involved or pursue the known attacker. Instead, Pres. Clinton ended the use of Aden, Yemen. All military personnel were directed to use other places as stopovers.

Though their attacks had failed to inflict the heavy casualties they had wanted, bin Laden had won the day "as the Americans left with their tail between their legs".

(Four of those convicted terrorists would later "escape", and eight years later one of them was picked up after the September 2000 attack on the *USS Cole*.)

Bill Clinton and his incoming administration were the typical collection of liberal ideologists and political appointees. Most had no experience in anything except liberal causes and governmental jobs. Many were retreads from the failed Carter Administration.

Clinton was so unqualified for the presidency that his acceptance speech contained just 140 words on Foreign Affairs.

His wife Hillary brought several of her Rose Law Firm pals into Washington to run the Justice Department.

That would ensure the Clintons were protected from any troublesome legal investigations.

As stated earlier the Clintons had never even owned a private house as they had always lived in government supplied housing. He was the exact type of person that Pres. Reagan warned about when he stated that "Government is the problem".

His liberal administration held the Military and Intelligence Agencies in low regard, and had a deep distrust of both. None of those principals except Al Gore and James Woolsey had ever served in or worked alongside any of our military or defense agencies. Vice-President Al Gore had reluctantly joined the Army in the late 60s because of his father's insistence. He was in Vietnam in a Public Relations Unit for just five months. Gore had special protection as a Senator's son and never was in danger. But he wrote often to his Senator-father stating how much he was against the war and America's foreign policies.

National Security Advisor Tony Lake and the CIA Director James Woolsey had both been serious protestors of the Vietnam War, but Woolsey had served in and left the army as a captain. None of the administration principals (except Woolsey) had ever known fear, privation or looked upon Communism as the enemy of mankind, so none of them believed we were ever in danger. And terrorism was way down on the new Administration's list of concerns. Now they were the " leaders of America"

Just four days after Clinton was sworn in **Mir Amal Kansi** walked along Route 123 in Virginia and shot four motorists who were entering the CIA facility with an AK-47 assault rifle. Three of his victims died. **Incident # 5**

The young Pakistani escaped by simply flying out of our country. Neither the CIA nor FBI learned anything about the shooter or what his motives were.

Later that month the terrorist cell led by Ramzi Yousef moved into the Jersey City building that was set back from the street. They began the actual construction of their large truck bomb. Yousef had contacted Ajaj's lawyer and had him pass a message to

Ajaj who was still in an immigration lockup that things were progressing.

Inside the Brooklyn Islamic center the blind cleric Omar Rahman was predicting in his sermons that great carnage would occur in the coming weeks. Speaking in Arabic, only those fluent would understand. *Hundreds of innocent attendees knew what was coming, and not one of them called in a warning!*

Agents in the JTTF had been following the suspects of the Jewish Plot and the recent arms supplies. On a farm near Harrisburg, Pennsylvania the suspects attended a full blown training camp with martial arts areas, sniper firing and rappelling. Since the war in Afghanistan was long over what were those people doing?

Agents began running license plates from the vehicles. Abdel Rahman's aide was present, **Abdo Haggag**. Also present was one **Siddig Ibrahim Siddig** a Sudanese translator, and the always present Mohammed Abouhalima. Just as the agents were close to tying both plots together their supervisors objected to them "spending a weekend in Harrisburg". **They were told to come back and not follow anyone.**

Palestinian terrorist **Eyyad Ismoil** arrived in the U.S. on February 21, 1993 to help out. All of the explosive charges were soon completed and the last parts set nearby. The plotters had scouted out all of the routes to the **WTC, World Trade Center,** and the B-2 parking level.

On Tuesday February 23 Salameh rented a yellow Ryder Truck in Jersey City. On the 25th Salameh took delivery of three tanks of compressed hydrogen gas which were to be used as an accelerant for the explosion. The truck contained 1,500 pounds of ammonium nitrate, three tanks of hydrogen, four cylinders of nitroglycerin, blasting caps and the fuses.

To create a cover for himself Salameh claimed the truck was stolen. He listed an incorrect license plate on the police report so their truck would not be stopped the next day. To avoid the New Jersey Police who might look for the "stolen truck", Yousef and his partner Eyyad drove the truck into Brooklyn to spend the night.

The next morning they drove the vehicle into lower Manhattan and entered the B-2 parking level of the World Trade Center complex under the Vista Hotel. They parked next to a large support column on the southern wall of Tower 1, the North Tower. **They thought their bomb would destroy that column and cause**

a total collapse of the North Tower into the South Tower killing everyone at the complex. With the fuses set both exited the truck and left in the escape car with the others. **Incident # 6**

At 1218 on February 26, 1993 their truck bomb detonated.

Historical Note: The initial idea for the WTC complex had begun in 1955, but not until January 1960 did the idea begin to coalesce. Lower Manhattan was old and showing its age as the Port services in the area were dilapidated, vacant and out of date. With the exception of the Wall Street area, most of the major businesses had left for Midtown with their wider streets and newer buildings.

Nelson and David Rockefeller desired a Trade Center to rejuvenate the area, which was home to their main office building, the Chase Manhattan Bank. As NYS Governor, Nelson wielded considerable influence as he pulled the Port Authority into promoting the plan.

At that time the Port Authority of New York (and later New Jersey) was in charge of all port services and commerce. They wanted this new commercial complex on the East River side of downtown, south of the Brooklyn Bridge. Complaints from the New Jersey officials changed the location of the complex to the Hudson River side of Manhattan. (At least the NJ officials could see the damn thing.)

To sweeten the deal for New Jersey, the Port Authority agreed to take over some of their outdated commuter train lines. Once rebuilt those rail lines would be called PATH, and they became a big success. (Their main terminal was in Hoboken across the river from lower Manhattan.)

Merchants in the "proposed area" known as radio row began protesting the "theft" of their buildings in a dubious ruling called *Eminent Domain.* That rule was centered on a municipality taking over a site for the "common good". To help the deal pass by the "political powers" it was also proposed that the large amount of excavated land from the new construction would be placed alongside lower West Street to create a new section of Manhattan. That area would be called Battery Park City, and this "extra project" would produce $ millions in new fees, taxes, jobs and secondary commerce. It was a win-win for the big money players, and the WTC plan passed the court challenges in March 1966.

Radio Row and the old piers in the area were quickly demolished, ecavation began and the streets were altered to create a separate 16 acre site. Architect Minoru Yamasaki had won the day as his firm was picked by the Port Authority to design the new complex. He was inspired by the architecture of the Doge's Palace in Venice as well as other structures that used arches and vertical columns in the facade. After numerous test models his final plan for the WTC consisted of two 95 story towers surrounded by four smaller buildings. It was the Port officials who decided to go for the title of the highest buildings, and they pushed the structures to 110 stories.

Well heeled lawyer Lawrence Wien argued against the complex for many reasons, such as fires or explosions. But his most Cassandra like thought centered on one fear, that an airliner could crash into the buildings. *(136A)

(On February 20, 1981 an Aerolinas Boeing 707 almost did, pulling up with just seconds to spare.)

To build those massive towers in the unusual style the Port Authority decided on using newer construction techniques and materials. One of the primary innovations was the use of the "kangaroo cranes" Australia had pioneered. Those cranes were built inside the structure and raised themselves up on jacks as the building grew. (Their first use in America was on the National Cathedral in Washington D.C.)

Structurally the World Trade Center Towers did not follow the normal steel grid based construction similar to the Empire State Building and that style of design. Those older buildings were built in what we in the FDNY called "heavyweight" design. They used a "steel cage" with dozens of heavy I-beams set throughout the structure in an interconnected grid to be mutually supporting and sturdy. *All of the structural steel was then covered with masonry or stone to protect it from fire.* The floors were made of high aggregate concrete and were 8-10 inches thick. Public wall areas were also thick, usually hollow tile or block. Fires were easily contained, and with the structural elements well protected, there was never any threat of partial or full collapse. (A perfect example of that sturdiness was the 1947 crash of a B-25 into the Empire State Building. Only two floors had strcutural damge.)

Instead of that safe, heavy style, Yamasaki's towers would use **59 exterior steel columns** *on each face of the building spaced 40 inches apart.* That narrow spacing would create a sense of safety for the occupants high up in the towers, and provide rigidity. To build those "walls", forty to fifty foot sections were assembled on the ground with steel crosspieces near the top and bottom known as spandrels. Cranes raised each pre-assembled steel section and placed it on top of the section below. Welds and rivet joints joined the sections together. The exterior steel was only clad with a protective and decorative cover of stainless steel and aluminum. Windows completed the exterior facade.

Hidden from the street view was a center core area which housed the interior columns, (app 50), and all utilities, stairs and elevators. **There were no cross-member I-beams or other structural columns in the floor areas. That would have taken up valuable floor space so they were eliminated.**

Instead the only "cross members" would consist of lightweight metal trusses that would span the space from the center columns to the exterior ones. Spot-welded in place on small steel ledges, they would "tie" the center steel columns to the exterior steel columns.

A thin corrugated sheet metal deck was laid upon those light weight floor trusses and used to form the base of the floors. About 4-6 inches of light concrete was poured onto the deck to make each floor slab. All interior walls were made of Drywall, (sheetrock) in varying thicknesses, and that included the stairway / elevator enclosures! There were no masonry or other fire-proof enclosures around any of the steel, just some sprayed on cement-based coating on the trusses and decking.

To cap the top of the towers a multistory steel grid called a Hat Truss was constructed. That lattice like feature supported the roof, but also interlocked all four sides of the building and the core area from the top with welds and rivet joints.

This new construction system resulted in a lightweight building which reduced the normal steel requirements in a building of that size by 30%. But in being lightweight and cheaper there were two major flaws. Lightweight buildings are greatly affected by wind loads because of their lack of mass. Test models swayed a lot in wind tunnel tests, and test subjects placed in a mock tower and subjected to that swaying all became sickened.

To control the swaying *the Port Authority had to install 11,000 visoelastic dampers at key points to act as shock absorbers.*

The second construction issue was a Fatal Flaw.

Built in this lightweight fashion the buildings could not withstand an uncontrolled high temperature fire. Without a dense thermal barrier around the structural steel such as masonry, they were easy prey for high heat degradation. The floor systems were so cheap and weak as to be almost no barrier in preventing vertical fire spread in that type of fire. There were no fire sprinklers, so any small fire could advance into a high temperature fire. High heat will weaken all steel, and in time that steel will fail.

Those buildings were in great danger in a fire.

Built around the two main Towers were three smaller 8 story office buildings, WTC 4, 5, 6, and a 37 story hotel called WTC 3. By 1984 Pres. Reagan's tax initiatives had rebounded the national economy and NYC was becoming a boom town. After years of having empty offices, the WTC complex was fully occupied.

With the need for more office space, in 1986 the 47 story WTC building 7 was built across the street from the original complex on the north side of Vesey Street. That location was the only site "still available", and WTC-7 was constructed over a Con-Ed transformer substation. To enable this smaller tower to be built over that substation an unusual truss system had to be designed. *The construction of WTC-7 was accomplished with few problems, but if anything were to happen to that truss that tower would collapse.* **(Another Fatal Flaw.)**

Across West Street from the WTC complex was the collected fill from the original WTC excavation and construction. That fill sat unused from 1967, and was routinely compacted and refilled. In the early 1980s construction began on the southern part of that site, and Battery Park City began building. Initially only residential buildings were built. (I should have bought one of those condos.)

A marina and shopping followed, and by 1990 the multi-building office complex called the **World Financial Center,** (WFC) went up on the northern end of that land. Those buildings sat right across West Street from the WTC complex. Mirroring the mid level buildings like WTC -7, the WFC buildings stayed under 50 stories. Two pedestrian walkways were constructed over West Street so the two financial complexes could be joined and provided safe non-street access.

During the normal 1993 work day the World Trade Center complex held over 50,000 people. Many tourists would go up to the top of the South Tower (Tower 2), to the observation decks to look out at the striking views. On most days there were numerous school classes present, and during those visits two hundred children or more could be present.

(My wife Jeannemarie had started working as a tour guide for the Port Authority in 1984. They escorted people to the top of the South Tower observation deck and roof. She later transferred into the payroll unit and worked in Tower 1, (North Tower) on the 70th floor. I visited her at work dozens of times over the years, and watched all of the construction of the adjoining buildings. She had recently left the Port Authority to have our family. At this time I was a Lt. in Engine Co. 54 in Times Square. I was off that day on a swap, and would go to the bombing on the night shift.)

The enormous explosion from the truck-bomb completely destroyed five levels in the parking and service areas of the complex. The blast created a crater almost 200 feet across and 5 stories deep, killing six and injuring dozens. Electrical power was knocked out stopping all elevators and ventilation equipment. Nearby the PATH train station was damaged as a 200 foot section of the ceiling collapsed injuring more people.

The explosion also caused the ignition of hundreds of vehicles in the parking levels with their fuels, oils, tires and plastic interiors. As the fire progressed tons of building and office materials in those lower levels also ignited. The underground fires burned unabated for over ten minutes, causing a dense black smoke condition that traveled vertically via the dozens of elevator shafts and stairways. Within minutes the toxic smoke had risen 50 stories high, and after twenty minutes the smoke reached the highest floors.

(This same life threatening issue had occurred in 1975 when an arsonist caused a large fire on the lower floors 7-13 of Tower 2. Luckily the fire was low enough that the FDNY could knock it down with large caliber water streams from the exterior. Had that not been the case the WTC would have been the site of a "Towering Inferno". Unlike the movie, it was probable the building would have collapsed.)

First arriving units were confronted with dozens of casualties and a dark smoke condition exiting from the parking garage area. Additional alarms were called in as the units realized hundreds of people were trapped in elevators, and dozens of thousands were caught in darkened and smoke filled offices, stairs and corridors. Hose teams bravely advanced into the heat and darkness of destroyed rooms, hallways and stairways trying to find the source of the fires. Debris was everywhere causing confusion and difficulty in moving around. Ladder and Rescue units rescued and removed the injured and those trying to escape. Over 1,000 civilians were injured as well as 88 firefighters.

This day would become the shining example of the FDNY's capabilities, when everyone in the complex was saved except for the six souls (and an unborn baby) who were caught in and died in the blast.

Despite being perpetually under-funded, FDNY *Officers and Firefighters* would improvise, adapt, and overcome the numerous problems that they faced saving and evacuating all, and extinguishing the fires in just four hours.

Minutes into the firefight FDNY and Police radio reports were stating the place seemed to have been blown up. Members of the JTTF who were based at the nearby 26 Federal Plaza had felt the shaking from the blast and heard the steady stream of fire apparatus going past their building. Their office radios were soon reporting the need for dozens of ambulances and the PD bomb squad. JTTF members realized what had happened and they responded to the complex.

Because of the inanity of the NYC Mayors and high ranking city bureaucrats (mostly Democrats), the FDNY's well planned helicopter roof rescue plan was not enacted. That inexcusable failure forced the firefighters to walk up 110 stories in both towers! It took three hours to climb to the top and as they moved the firefighters ventilated where they could and evacuated and saved those who were trapped, *for hours*

(Due to a series of Hi-rise arson fires in lower Manhattan office buildings the FDNY had developed a helicopter-roof access rescue plan in 1984. The Koch and Dinkins administrations **refused to fund it,** telling the FDNY to work with the PD and borrow their smaller observation helicopters. Coordination between those two agencies was always bad. *Police commanders and their rank and file refused to take any orders from the FDNY, even though the Mayor's own directive stated that the FD was the lead agency.* **Thus our helicopter rescue plan was never used, not in 1993, nor in 2001!**)

By that afternoon Democrat NY Governor Mario Cuomo called the White House and told Pres. Clinton it was suspected that a bomb had caused the extensive damage in the WTC. Earlier the FBI had already determined that fact, and they had already informed Clinton that the WTC was bombed. They codenamed the event "Tradebom"

Even after this second call listing this as a bombing, Bill Clinton was still "unconvinced". He had his secretary put out a cautious line that the NY authorities suspected a bomb had detonated. (If he admitted that a bomb had been used it would mean that terrorists had struck, and he would have to act.)

Bill Clinton was a typical 60s liberal, lawyer-politician, bureaucrat and schemer. He had never taken a strong stance on or in anything, nor had he been in any type of emergency situation in his life. A massive, deadly foreign terrorist bombing, the first of this kind inside America, could have caused him huge political problems. So he refused to acknowledge that fact or take any action. Even on the following Saturday there was no sense of crisis in the White House.

Perhaps if the terrorists had succeeded in destroying the Towers, or had the casualty toll had been higher, maybe then Clinton might have reacted.

(In his outstanding book, *Losing Bin Laden*, Richard Miniter hits the point in showing how Clinton **refused to see the reality** or the evidence of this extensive terrorist plot to topple the World Trade Center and kill 50,000 innocents.)

That night tour I worked in Engine Co 54 and was assigned to the Trade Center blast as a relief unit. The day tour had just come back from the bombing and it was hard to believe what they were saying. Looking at the incredible devastation as we moved around we thought that this would be the worst devastation we would see in the FDNY. We were wrong.

Once the fires were extinguished and the rescues and removals completed the task of draining millions of gallons of raw sewage and water from the lowest levels of the complex commenced. The explosion had destroyed multiple water and sewer lines, and all of that liquid drained from the two-110 story towers filling the lowest levels. After the liquids were removed the forensics people could get down into the crater and sift through the evidence.

As they had at Lockerbie, Scotland, the FBI was able to put the pieces together and determine what vehicle had housed the bomb! Incredibly a single piece of the truck had been found in the debris pile and it had a secret serial number. After another day of investigation that number enabled them to trace the truck part to Ryder Trucks.

During his weekly radio address Clinton weakly spoke of how the full measure of Federal Law enforcement resources would be brought to bear to catch these cowardly perpetrators.

He disingenuously stated that the victims families were in their prayers and that **"the tragedy"** struck fear into the hearts of those inside the complex. "Just this morning I spoke with FBI Director Sessions who assured me that they were working with Treasury, NYPD and the FDNY to find out who was involved and why this happened. Americans should know we are doing everything to keep them safe". Again Clinton did not call the bombing an attack, nor did he call it terrorism. Those victims did not die in a fall, they had been murdered by terrorists.

In that same address Clinton stated and formulated his disastrous policy of looking at Islamic terrorism as just a criminal matter. Clinton did not have the CIA or INS involved in trying to prevent this from ever happening again, and military action was totally out of the question. Clinton called in the lawyers, not the Marines. Thus the terrorists had no need to fear from an armed reprisal.

Historical Note: President Jefferson was the first of our leaders to face a foreign problem, attacks on American ships in 1802. He reacted by sending the U.S. Navy and Marines to take out the Barbary Pirates operating out of northern Africa. His prudent actions protected all of the shipping in the Mediterranean and coastal N. Africa for decades.

By classifying the WTC bombing as just a civil criminal matter, meant that by law no details of the bombing would get to Langley and the CTC. All of the evidence, investigations and lab tests were locked away in the FBI's NYC office at Federal Plaza. Vital information would be kept secret for years so as to keep the evidence from being "tainted". CIA Director James Woolsey knew it was critical that Clinton's policy be changed.

As shown before the State Dept, the FBI and CIA had each detailed officers into this unit to make sure that vital terrorist-linked information like this would be shared and worked on together. Thus the CTC was the perfect vehicle for a detailed multi-national investigation of an act such as the bombing at the World Trade Center. And they had a secret "Presidential Finding" written into their operations by Pres. Reagan.

It specifically allowed covert operations to arrest or destroy dangerous terrorists if needed.

Information that should have been collated at the CTC would have shown that Ramzi Yousef had called bin Laden from New York just before the attack. He stayed in bin Laden owned safe-houses in Pakistan before and after the attack. Not until the trials of the WTC bombers ended in 1996 would the CIA get the full file.

James Woolsey privately fumed at the stupidity of Bill Clinton.

Having served in many presidential administrations, (he had previously been an Ambassador, arms control negotiator and Asst. Sec. Navy), he could see that Clinton was totally disinterested in foreign affairs. He also realized Clinton had no abilities or capacity to understanding strategic issues or strategy.

Clinton never should have become president.

And even though he was appointed to the CIA by this president, James Woolsey still had not gotten an appointment to actually see him! After this deadly attack they had much to go over. But Clinton refused to ever meet with Woolsey and be briefed directly.

Every president since FDR opened their day with a security briefing. Since 1948 when Truman created the CIA, that daily briefing was done by the Director or an Asst Director of the CIA. **But not with Bill Clinton.**

By not having any face-face security or intelligence meetings, lawyer Clinton could always claim "he didn't know."

Despite Clinton's directive that this was a criminal case, Woolsey had the CTC pursue their own limited investigation.

A few days later Bill Clinton was in New Jersey at a "jobs event". Even though he was just minutes away from this massive terrorist attack, **Clinton never went to see for himself how close we came to losing 50,000 innocent people.** It was not a worry to this self-absorbed governmental lawyer. His indifferent attitude and poor leadership set the stage for his later failures to stop global terrorism from growing and repeatedly attacking us.

Minority Leader Newt Gingrich had warned the new president to be cautious in cutting the defense and intelligence budgets as there were still a real requirement for both. Just look at how no one had predicted that Iraq would invade Kuwait. Clinton was unmoved and continued with his planned and substantial cuts to the Dept of Defense.

Then on February 28 another serious domestic issue popped up in **Waco, Texas**. ATF agents, (Alcohol Tobacco and Firearms) launched an unprecedented military style raid on the Mount Carmel compound of one David Koresh and his religious followers. Claiming they were trying to serve a warrant, the agents became embroiled in an intense gun battle losing four of their agents to six of the citizens. The unneeded raid was arrogantly called "Showtime" by the ATF agents, in a thinly veiled effort to "highlight their abilities". But it backfired causing numerous casualties and resulted in a tense multi-week standoff.

After the World Trade Center Bombing Yousef and Ismoil had been taken to JFK airport and flew out with no trouble. Ismoil went on to Jordan and tried to hide out there, while Yousef went on to Pakistan. A few days later Abouhalima flew to the Sudan.

Their confederates who had stayed behind would eventually be caught because Salameh tried to get his deposit money back from the rental truck to buy his plane ticket to Pakistan. To the major terrorists the capture of the others meant little, as they were considered sacrificial lambs in the struggle. (A foolish waste of men.)

That incredible lead from the rental truck part was eventually traced back to Jersey City. Truck office staff told the investigators the truck had been rented to one Mohammed Salameh. They also mentioned that the renter had been calling every day trying to get his deposit money back from the "stolen truck".

Mohammed Salameh had already been on the FBI's and NYPD radar, as they knew about the growing network of Islamic extremists that were living in the tri-state area. As shown before many of those radicals had been training with weapons at known gun ranges in Connecticut, (the previous traffic stop), and in Pennsylvania. *Salameh was one of those men.*

Investigators traced the address Salameh had used for the truck rental to 57 Prospect Park Southwest in Brooklyn, Apt 4C. They were surprised, because it was the same address as Ibrahim el-Gabrowny, Sayeed Nosair's cousin. (He was the suspect who had told the informant Salem about their pending Jewish Plot.)

JTTF investigators then realized that they had been on the trail of a treacherous ring of terrorists when their supervisors foolishly pulled them off of the case a month ago!

A search warrant for el-Gabrowny's apartment was enacted and he fought with the detectives. In his pocket were five Nicaraguan passports with false names and photos of Sayeed Nosair and his family. Apparently a secondary plot was being organized to spring Nosair from jail. El-Gabrowny was arrested.

To arrest Salameh with no fuss the agents devised a plan to lure him back to the truck office to get his deposit money. On Thursday March 4, 1993 Salameh fell for the trap and was picked up. In his wallet was a business card for Nidal Ayyad.

A search of Salameh's "legal residence" at 34 Kensington Avenue in Jersey City lead to Abdul Yassin. He cooperated, and led them to 40 Pampro Avenue the site of the actual bomb making. Yassin was thanked for his help, and wrongly released. (He then fled the country.)

As shown earlier bureaucratic restrictions emplaced during the Carter years had prevented the FBI from investigating those men until a crime was actually committed. (You would have thought those stupid rules would have been discarded after the bombing, but with Clinton and the Democrats running our government they were kept in place.) But as the evidence mounted more leads led to the arrest of Nidal Ayyad on March 10. That uncovered even more names and false passports.

Also found were additional explosives. It was soon learned that Nidal Ayyad had been the one running around trying to buy the urea-based fertilizers needed for their bomb.

After his escape from the U.S., Mahmoud Abouhalima traveled to Saudi Arabia and then to Egypt to hide out. His movements and location was uncovered, and the FBI requested the Egyptians pick him up which they quickly did. He was taken to a secure facility and "questioned". When the Egyptians had finished with this terrorist they called the FBI and dumped Mahmoud into the sand outside of a small airfield. (He was quite happy to be taken into U.S. custody.)

During the plane ride back to America he asked if they had caught up to Ramzi Yousef. Agents realized that Yousef had been the one running the show. Within two weeks four of the WTC bombers had been arrested. A month later Mohammed Abouhalima was picked up for helping his brother escape. Abdul Yassin was still at large after his errant release.

If the reader remembers Salameh and Mahmoud Abouhalima had been picked up after the Kahane shooting. They had been released because the NYPD Chief Detective did not want to have a "conspiracy" with that shooting.

Those two had also been under surveillance by the JTTF for the Jewish Plot, and the weapons plot. But as shown before those agents had been told to stop the investigation by their supervisor.

With the past weeks of effort paying off the FBI realized that this was not just a random attack. These bombers hailed from four different Middle Eastern countries, and had ties to Sheik Omar Rahman and Sayyid Nosair the killer of Rabbi Meir Kahane. Two interconnected groups were involved, those in the Jewish Plot and the Black Muslims in the Weapons Plot. All of them were also linked to the Alkifah Refugee Center in Brooklyn which was run by Sheik Rahman, but funded and affiliated by a guy called **Osama bin Laden.** Most of these suspects were similarly traced to a Jersey City mosque called the *Masjid al-Salaam*. It too was run by Rahman but funded by sources from the Middle East.

This was a well supported terrorist network that stretched from Brooklyn, Queens and N. Jersey, into the Middle East. A textbook conspiracy.   Incident # 7

Once the JTTF investigators in NYC joined forces, they realized that one team had been after the Arab suspects, while another team had been investigating the Black Muslims who were actually helping the Arab plotters.

This was exactly why the CTC had been founded, to oversee, control and keep everyone in the loop concerning terrorism.

(And this was why the local and "separate units" did not know what the other one was doing. The JTTF was a good idea, but they should have been required to at least report to or been assigned to work through the CTC.)

Because they were not in the loop, the JTTF agents did not know of the connections of these bombers to the attacks in Aden two months earlier. However the CTC would have put them together because they did know about Aden. But Bill Clinton dliberatly kept the CIA out of the investigation with his claim of a civilian criminal case.

As shown before Bin Laden had been named in the terrorist attacks in Aden by Yemeni authorities. Now his name had come up at the WTC bombing. He needed to be found.

Around this same time frame the CIA passed on some information Egyptian Intelligence had learned from an informant in NYC. A terrorist cell affiliated with the blind cleric Rahman **(who we still had not deported),** was planning on assassinating Pres. Mubarak during his U.S trip in May. They also stated that the cell was being trained by Black Muslims here, one of whom was referred to the doctor. *(A clear reference to Dr. Rashid, and more evidence of a vast and dangerous conspiracy.)* **Incident # 8**

The JTTF decided to approach **Abdo Mohammed Haggag**, the blind cleric's aide. They had learned that he was on the outs with the cleric and felt he could be convinced to help. *They had also been told to find and re-sign Emad Salem.* (That order was from the same bureaucrats who had fired him months before because they did not think his intelligence was worth $500.00 a month.)

On March 20, 1993 agents approached Haggag with their offer, but he refused on religious grounds, (working with Americans). *What those agents did not know, was that Haggag was the one who had tipped off the Egyptians in the first place!*

(Haggag was yet another terrorist who had married an American in order to stay here.)

Surveillance on the Black Muslims then revealed some new and disturbing leads. One of their members, **Yaya Abu Ubaidah** was in Vienna picking up cash for their operations. That money came from a charity called the Third World Relief Agency, the Islamists European counter-part to the Afghan Services Group based in Brooklyn. **Investigations uncovered that this group was also backed by that same Saudi, Osama bin Laden.** Over the past few months Yaya had come into the U.S. with over $100,000. It was obvious something else was being planned. **Incident # 9**

From the WTC arrests and investigations the FBI knew that the main bomber was Ramzi Yousef. His fingerprints had been found at the bomb factory. Then they learned he had come in using an Iraqi passport. His nickname was Rashid the Iraqi. They then realized that Yousef had entered the U.S. with the earlier arrested Ajaj, but had somehow escaped our shores after the WTC bombing.

They also discovered that Ramzi had called that bin Laden guy from New York right after the bombing.

Yousef was now on the FBI's most wanted list. There were also references to Yousef's uncle who went by various names, one of which was **Khalid Sheik Muhammad**, (KSM). It was unclear how he fit in to this plot, but the FBI wanted to talk with him too. Another suspect, the wrongly released Abdul Yasin, had escaped back to Baghdad and was now employed by the Iraqi government.

(One of the classified parts of the WTC bombing that few know about was that a Hydrogen Cyanide gas mixture had been added to the WTC bomb. The terrorists hoped hundreds would die from the poisonous cloud, but it had burned up in the intense fire. *That poison was a staple of Iraqi gas attacks.)*

Safe on the other side of the world Ramzi Yousef sent a letter to the NY Times explaining their actions and reasons for the WTC attack. Claiming that he and those like him were a battalion in their Islamic Liberation Army. *They had hundreds of suicide bombers ready to strike civilian and military targets inside and outside of the United States.* Any casualties that occurred were the result of your government's policies. America must stop all economic, political and military support for Israel, leave the Middle East and stay out of our region. If you did not more attacks would follow. A draft of this letter was found on one of the computers of the WTC bombers.

(After his schooling in Great Britain Yousef had actually been doing fine in a solid job in Kuwait. Then Saddam and his army had shown up. Forced to flee like everyone else, he ended up back in Pakistan broke and homeless. He joined up with the extremists and trained in bin Laden's camps. Yousef had wanted to kill over 200,000 people in the World Trade Center attack, with help from the cyanide.)

A poorly researched CIA paper circulated on April 2, 1993. It described bin Laden as a person who advanced Islamic causes and was known to circulate among the Afghan terrorist training camps. (That report should have highlighted the previous attacks in Aden, and the WTC, but for some reason it did not.)

A basic NSC report (from the White House), on April 20 admitted that hundreds of Islamic militants had passed through the Afghan terrorist camps during the past twelve months. Another clear warning sign of pending trouble, and proff that the Administration knew terrorism was about to get worse.

That fall the CIA was asking their worldwide stations to assess the vulnerability of bin Laden's network, and listed bin Laden as a target for further intelligence collection.

Waco, Texas

The siege at the Branch Davidian compound ended in a savage attack and fire that killed most of the civilian members inside. Federal agents had made little progress in getting the members to come out despite using Psychological warfare and harassment for days on end. Many of their tactics were reprehensible, and the ATF illegally used Army armored vehicles and helicopters.

Attn. Gen. Janet Reno had approved their plan to attack the civilians using tear gas as the first weapon, and then the armored vehicles would crash through the buildings.

On April 19, 1993 the federal action degenerated into a melee. Around noon fires broke out in the main building and quickly consumed the compound and the inhabitants. Much deserved negativity followed, but incredulously no one was held accountable. Reno took the blame but was not fired because Clinton needed her to shield him.

(In a disturbing video on NewsMax an examination of the film shows the gas used to fill the buildings was flammable, and a factor in the fireball. Also multiple civilians were seen being gunned down while trying to escape the flames. At the hearings those obvious truths were denied by officials.)

Corruption in the Administration Begins

In China their Hexi Machinery and Chemical plant was still having problems with the booster rockets they were trying to build. **They were actually building intercontinental ballistic missiles,** and needed help from the West, specifically America. At that time it was not possible for our companies to sell advanced machinery and knowhow like that to China.

But in January 1993 Bill Clinton took office.

He placed former DNC chairman Ron Brown in charge at the Commerce Department. *With a litany of other "friends" at the helms of the various federal agencies, the Clinton Administration began changing the procedures for granting export licenses to China.*

Key to their effort was changing the sales oversight from the Pentagon (serious scrutiny), to the Commerce Department (no scrutiny). Soon after the first contract went to Motorola to help China with "satellite launches".

Then another Chinese company appeared and wanted to make "commercial aircraft." That would require help from McDonnell Douglas, and it too was approved. In short order advanced machine tools and metal shaping machines were officially permitted for sale and sent to China.

That never should have occurred, for those same machines were used to manufacture the parts for our B-1 bomber and our new peacekeeping missile. China's National Aero-Technology Import and Export Corporation "gave promises to use those machines only for civilian purposes."

This marked the beginning of the sellout of America by Bill Clinton and his cronies as they made tons of money, endangering all of us.

More Terrorism

All four WTC bombing suspects were found guilty. **Shockingly one hundred eighteen others were listed as potential but unindicted co-conspirators. And it included Iraq.** This was not some minor criminal plot, this was a vast worldwide conspiracy! Yet Clinton had no reaction. **Incident # 10**

Emad Salem had returned and reported to the JTTF that a tall Sudanese man who worked for Sheik Rahman as a translator had talked to him in the *Abu Bakr Mosque* in Brooklyn. This Sudanese asked Salem if he would join his plot to blowup some buildings. Rahman had told this stranger that he (Salem) was a good explosives man.

This Sudanese man's name was **Siddig Ali-Siddig,** *the second man in the car with Haggag when the JTTF agents had tailed them going to Rahman's home from Pennsylvania!*

Upon checking deeper into those names, the FBI finally discovered that Egypt had made repeated requests to have Omar Rahman extradited for terrorism. **However INS and the State Dept. "rejected their request", because Rahman had claimed he was being persecuted and needed asylum.**

(Yet another outdated policy that must be ended.)

Investigators knew that this "persecuted individual Sheikh Omar Rahman" had been the one who was promoting the attack on Egypt's Pres. Mubarak when he was to visit. And now he was planning something else. **Still he was allowed to stay**.

After rejoining the anti-terrorist effort Emad had agreed to be wired. He taped the conversations of Siddig Ali as they discussed the plan on murdering Mubarak. He learned that Sudanese officials in their U.N. embassy were providing vital information to Siddig on how to pierce Mubarak's motorcade as they moved from JFK airport to the Waldorf Astoria in Manhattan.

They knew which car Mubarak would be in, and the exact route they would take. Siddig bragged that their information came from the Sudanese Ambassador. Emad Salem was able to warn his FBI contacts and Mubarak's trip was " suddenly cancelled".

Rahman was also organizing another bombing attack. This one would be a devastating blow to avenge his convicted students. **Rahman wanted simultaneous bombings of NYC landmarks, plus the destruction of the U.N. building, 26 Federal Plaza, the George Washington Bridge and the Holland and Lincoln Tunnels.**

If successful those bombings would devastate the NYC region economically as well as cause untold numbers of casualties. Emad Salem was as shaken as the JTTF agents were when he informed them of this latest plot. Agents decided to look again at the boxes of evidence taken from Sayeed Nosair's arrest.

They remembered that his notebook contained clues that this landmark attack was already being planned. Clues they had missed back in 1990. In addition to the notes there were tapes of Sheikh

Rahman speaking from Peshawar, Pakistan, but referencing "camps inside America". Radical followers could be found in Europe as well. This was an extensive international terrorist plot.

Salem stayed with this pack of conspirators through May and into June. Siddig-Ali told him safe-houses were lined up in the Sudan for them to hide out in after their attacks, but they would need one in NYC to work in. Through the JTTF, Salem "found one" in Queens, equipped with video and audio surveillance.

It was learned that many of these latest Jihadist trainees had been at the paramilitary training site in Pennsylvania. Strategy sessions at their new safe-house determined they would need to kill the guards at 26 Federal Plaza to access the underground parking garage. An Uzi sub-machine gun was acquired for that purpose. The Black Muslims reappeared to offer logistical and tactical support, especially in getting C-4 and hand grenades.

On May 21 el-Gabrowny brought Siddig-Ali and Salem to Attica prison to speak with Nosair. He was pleased with their progress but suggested they also kidnap Richard Nixon and Henry Kissinger since it was they who had turned Anwar Sadat and saved Israel back in 1973. Siddig-Ali added some local politicians to their hit list, including Senator D'Amato a supporter of Israel.

Rahman was hard to get on tape as he was always evasive. He felt the U.N. was a legitimate target, but bombing them would not help their cause in that they had already become pro-Islam and were viewed as a symbol of peace. The Federal building should be struck, but Rahman counseled patience.

"The one who killed Kennedy had trained for three years." *(Was he referencing John or Bobby's murder?)*

As the Landmarks / Day of Terror Plot continued JTTF agents followed the suspects as far as Philadelphia in their quest to acquire the large volume of explosives, timers and fertilizer they would need. In Mount Vernon a **Mohammed Saleh,** a gas station owner and Hamas member supplied the fuels they needed for the bombs. *(It turns out that Mohammed Saleh and Siddig Ali had also married American dupes to stay in this country.)*

By this point the agents had seen enough, and Salem also warned them they had to act soon. On June 24, 1993 agents raided the terrorist safe-house in Queens capturing five of the plotters which included Siddig-Ali. In other raids more suspects were arrested bringing the total to thirteen. It included Sheikh Rahman, Sayeed Nosair, el-Gabrowny and the Black Muslims.

Thanks to the quiet bravery of Emad Salem thousands of innocents in and around the NYC area were saved from a brutal death. Incident # 11

Salem's recordings and the tapes from the safe house were instrumental in locking the defendants to the conspiracy. Nine of the suspects were convicted which included Rahman and Sayeed Nosair. (Visitor logs and phone logs linked Nosair to this plan and the defendants.) Also heard were conversations about Ramzi Yousef, Mohammed Salameh and the rest of the WTC bombers. *It was learned that one **Ahmed Saleh**, was another Hamas member who had worked in the Sudan to train terrorist recruits.* He too was picked up.

As had happened in the investigation of the WTC bombing, numerous unindicted individuals were uncovered. Two of those were **Siraj El-din Yousif**, a Sudanese diplomatic operative, and the well known **Siddig Ali**, the Sudanese translator for Rahman. Both of the above men were saved by their diplomatic cover, but expelled for their part in the incident.

(Siddig was heard on tape bragging on how Sudan's U.N. office would provide covers to getting the bomb vehicle into the U.N. parking garage next to the main building.)

Also named was that missing suspect from Arizona, **Wadi el-Haj**. Searches for him continued to come up empty, until he was located in Nairobi, Kenya. How and why he was there?

Another alarming clue was that a USF, University of South Florida professor named **Sami Al-Arian** had made a series of calls to Siraj Yousif around the time of their plan. He too was being investigated. (More on these stories to follow.)

As he had done at the WTC bombing, Clinton and his principals dismissed the significance of this latest terrorist attempt. They treated this as if it were a simple criminal case. The pipe-bombs of the 1960's moronic radicals were civilian cases. These well planned and substantial assaults needed to be treated **as acts of war.** This was the second major Islamic terrorist attack / attempt inside our nation in just four months!

Had it succeeded the NYC region would have been crippled with multiple thousands murdered. Again Bill Clinton showed no concern, and again the CTC officials were kept out of the loop.

The Middle East

Back in Iraq UNSCOM leader Hans Blix continued to go against his colleagues by claiming that all was well and it was time to end their inspections. Most of his colleagues were totally against him, and Rolf Ekeus spoke in Washington on March 24, 1993 stating that Saddam was intent on restoring his military-industrial base. To thwart the U.N. sanctions Saddam had declared all of his outstanding foreign debt null and void. That freed up billions in assets, and with his black market oil sales he was flush with cash. His rearming continued.

During April 1993 Kuwaiti Intelligence agents uncovered a plot by Iraqi intelligence to kill former Pres. Bush when he arrived in the Middle East for a trip.

Sixteen people were involved in a sophisticated SUV- bomb scheme that was supposed to kill everyone within a 400 yard radius. (Similar to the bombing against Bashir Gemayal in Lebanon in 1983.) An alert policeman had discovered the bomb because of a traffic accident.

Reports of this plot were not uncovered by the CIA or FBI, it was learned from a British newspaper. (For some reason the Kuwait's were trying to cover up the incident.)

Two separate but parallel investigations were conducted, one criminal and one concerned with intelligence. By early June 1993 the reports were completed and Iraq was known to be involved. After weeks of discussions and further "investigating", Pres. Clinton finally allowed an attack on Iraq set for June 26, 1993.

However he authorized only a limited cruise missile strike that could only target Iraq's Intelligence service building. The other potential targets were not to be struck.

To prevent any "unnecessary casualties", the tomahawk cruise missiles were fired after midnight when the building was mostly empty. Saddam and his followers were amused by the pathetic effort. Clinton's weak response was also observed by bin Laden and the terrorists of the world. They had nothing to fear.

As a die-hard liberal Clinton had absolutely no idea how things worked in the real world. And he was totally in the dark on strategic issues, military matters or on how the cruise missiles actually functioned. He complained to the NSC staff that they did not have TV cameras on the missiles so he could watch the strike happen. He was also upset that we could not communicate with the missiles once they were fired. (??)

Clinton called CNN to see if they could give him some information about the missile strike. (The NSC staff were not informed of his call, and were stunned that he would be that dumb.) CNN called a cameraman's cousin who lived in Baghdad near the Intelligence building. That relative told them the building was blown up, and they reported back to Clinton. He then went on TV and told the world what we had done.

(Obama did the same idiotic thing in 2012. He told the world that Seal Team 6 took out bin Laden. A month later their helicopter was shot down killing over 20 of those priceless warriors.)

Islamist violence was still raging in Algeria, Tunisia and Egypt. Fundamentalist insurgencies were spawned by the return of thousands of Afghan war veterans. Bombings, massacres and assassinations were becoming common place. Clinton's State Dept. and the NSC were unsure on what to do. Of those countries only Egypt was considered an ally, even though Algeria and Tunisia were secular and increasingly pro-Western in their views.

The CIA supervisors in all three countries sent detailed warnings about the growing movement of Islamic extremism. CIA principals felt we had to do everything possible to help Mubarak, (unlike Carter abandoning the Shah.)

With the fall of Communism it was desired to expand democracy to as many countries as possible. But Clinton was not prepared to "push that ideal into the Islamic world". **Instead the Administration tried to reach out to the "less violent Islamic leaders to make deals". All of their dismal attempts were quickly rejected.**

Afghanistan was falling into chaos as was predicted. CIA sent repeated warnings on the terrible state of affairs, but again Bill Clinton showed no interest or concern. Warren Christopher at State echoed his sentiment, and his department offered no solutions. Those new Democrats wanted nothing to do with the foreign policy issues from Reagan and Bush.

They also cut all funding for AID, the Agency for International Development. Afghanistan was completely on its own.

With Iran becoming ever more of a danger from arms purchases from Russia, the UAE, United Arab Emirates wanted American arms. Sales grew to over $10 billion. The Europeans became upset that they were missing out on the sales, but our proven weapons were sought after.

One reason for the increasing concern by the UAE was a series of nighttime landings by Iran's Revolutionary Guards. All of their insurgents were caught after some local fighting, but it highlighted how porous the shores of the UAE (and everyone else) actually were. Like most of the wealthy nations in the region, their military was rated as poor. Their rulers hoped that having the best weapon systems in place it would give them an edge for when the Iranians returned.

At the many Mid-East regional weapons shows local intelligence had learned that the Iranians would bring in "large quantities of weapons and ammo". However the majority of those munitions were not intended for displays, but to be sold and smuggled to their militants hiding out in the host country.

And to top the list of suspicious activities, U.S. satellites had taken photos of a new missile plant near Isfahn, Iran. *That plant was assembling North Korea's latest Nodong medium range missiles.* Intelligence agencies knew those variants could reach Israel, Turkey and the U.S. bases in Saudi Arabia. It was a certainty that some of the missiles they were building were being kept in Iran in secret. *The CIA was now active in trying to locate and acquire any loose nuclear weapons and material that was hemorrhaging from the old Soviet Union.*

The oil rich republics along the Caspian Sea opened for business to Western markets and corporations. Business was booming, and as far as this administration was concerned they had stepped into a golden age. Since money runs the world of Clinton, his State Dept. pushed a $600 million chemical deal with Iran through the Conoco company. Not until that "arrangement" hit the headlines did Clinton step in and "impose a trade embargo" on Iran ending the dangerous deal.

(France then jumped in hoping to reap some of the available commerce. Mitterrand's years in office were satirized in a book, *Mitterrand and the Forty Thieves*. His replacement Chirac set the stage for the next Gulf War.)

Ali Mohamed

In June 1993 an Islamic terror suspect was arrested in Vancouver. **Ali Marsouk** was an Egyptian national who had ties to EJI, Egyptian Islamic Jihad. Marsouk had tried to enter the U.S. with fraudulent papers but was caught. To protect this valuable asset, **Ali Mohamed** was sent in to help. Mohamed tried to ally the Canadians of their fears and called on his friends in the FBI. With that help Marsouk was simply deported by Canada instead of everyone investigating him further. **Incident # 12**

Alerted to this incident FBI agent John Zindt decided to interview Ali Mohamed. When Ali was asked about another name that kept popping up, he redirected the FBI away. The name in question was that Saudi national **Osama bin Laden.** According to Ali, this Osama was not a terrorist, just someone who disliked the Saudi Royals. But he did say that bin Laden wanted to drive all of the Americans off of the Saudi peninsula, and was creating an army to topple the monarchy.

Suspicious of Ali, Agent Zindt contacted the DOD about his interview. *But this information never made it to the CTC, JTTF or the FBI higher ups.* (Again this was why the CTC should have been involved.) The NSA was brought in to further the investigation, but those interviews remained classified, even now! The connections between Ali and bin Laden were not discovered.
Incident # 13

Unknown to U.S. authorities, Ali Mohamed had twice secreted EIJ leader **Ayman al-Zawahiri** into the U.S. Zawahiri made visits to the West Coast for intelligence gathering, fund raising and face-face meetings with others involved in the anti-America plots taking shape. Omar Rahman was probably one of his stops as they had been in the EIJ and Egyptian prison together.

Clinton Politics

In keeping with his amateurish thinking about foreign affairs Bill Clinton then made a decision that directly threatened the entire nation. **He cancelled the SDI initiative that had been started by Pres. Reagan.** Despite the naysayers and the Democrats, the research and development of that program had resulted in the ground based Patriot Defensive missile system that had worked so well in the Gulf War. Other programs were being developed, but "Clinton felt that with the end of the Soviet Union, America was no longer in danger." (Obama would do the same thing when he took over in 2009.)

Like so many other myopic leftists, Clinton felt that the U.S. had to abide by the 1972 ABM treaty we had signed with the Soviet Union, *even though they had already broken it, and the Soviet Union no longer existed!*

As shown before our intelligence agencies had noted a massive civil defense system of underground shelters, residences and industrial bases being built across Russia. One site in the Ural Mountains was larger than the city of Washington D.C.!

In addition to that threatening fact the previous work on their ABM system had produced an extensive capability of approximately 10,000 defensive missiles. Many of them have a nuclear warhead that will detonate in high altitude destroying incoming warheads /missiles. Why were the Russians still spending billions on this system when they were desperate for income? If America had wanted to attack them, there had been plenty of opportunities. But Clinton said and did nothing over that alarming issue, **instead he disarmed us.**

(Restraints that we unilaterally and foolishly followed from that broken 1972 treaty had prevented the Patriot anti-missile system from working better by tracking incoming missiles by satellite. That ABM treaty was no longer valid or applicable, but our safety certainly was and still is. That is the primary function of any government, to protect the people. *And Russia was not our only enemy armed with missiles. Still Clinton cared not.*)

One of the many lies that the Democrats and their friends in the media continued to claim was that the ongoing Federal Budget Deficit was due to the tax cuts enacted by former Pres. Reagan. It is true he did cut taxes as the top rate plummeted from 70% down to 28% between 1981-1986. But his tight fiscal policies ended the astronomical inflation we had suffered through during Carter's term.

The severe recession we had been in since 1978 had increased our poverty rate from 12-15%. But once we came out of it in 1983, all of the naysayers and complainers were proven wrong, again. The poverty rate fell to under 10%. From Reagan's two terms and Bush's follow-up term came incredible growth in the U.S. economy, which helped all classes and races.

During those twelve years of Republican presidents there were 93 consecutive months of growth, and 19 million new jobs had been created! America enjoyed surging exports and huge declines in inflation and interest rates. The Dow Jones Industrial Average of Stocks grew from 800, to over 3,000. And U.S. global exports grew from $219 Billion to over $420 Billion (by 1999.)

Those same Democrats had condemned our rising trade deficits, and the rise of Japan Inc, insisting that Reagan impose Socialistic restrictions on imports, and use tax funds to "save industries" that could not compete. He refused, and the economy improved and restructured as the market required, resulting in the sustained growth we had.

That growth **actually doubled Federal revenues.** Exceptional economic times were here, but the Federal deficits not only existed, they continued to grow despite this vast influx of additional tax money.

Those deficits were the result of the Democratic led Congress refusal to cut Federal spending as Pres. Reagan had asked them to do back in 1981!

(That was the same problem that Pres. Nixon had faced and tried to address back in 1973, and it continues unabated today. The Democrats also took away the right of Presidential Impoundment in 1973, which was the only chance a president had to stop wasteful spending.)

Those Democrats had a thousand reasons not to cut the wasteful Federal spending under Reagan and Bush, which had grown into a deficit of over a one and a half Trillion dollars by 1993! But now that a Democrat was in office, they suddenly needed "to save money"!

For Clinton that target was the Dept. of Defense. He slashed military spending, the SDI program, and the defense R&D that had actually won the Cold War. (A war the Democrats created.)

One of the main problems in cutting spending is the way additional amendments are added to a desired law. When a law is passed everything that was added in is passed too. Even if the add-on is wasteful nonsense. In that way "pork barrel spending" goes on unchallenged and mostly unnoticed by the public. Only the watchdog groups really look at the page heavy and lawyer written laws. And that allows the thefts of our tax revenue to continue.

In mid-1993 Clinton and the left refused to accept the successful economic realities of the past 12 years. They insisted on having higher taxes for the "rich", and instituted a "sin-tax" on the purchase of yachts, private jets and other enticements of the "wealthy". Their action quickly resulted in a large decline in those "sin-purchases". That resulted in the layoffs of over **100,000 workers** who had been employed in industries that catered to those items! (But the Democrats are for the little guy.)

Their "sin-tax" actually increased the national debt due to the increase in unemployment benefits being paid out from their layoffs, and less tax revenue coming in from the sales of those "sinful items and lost payroll taxes!

After their first months in power Hillary Clinton planned and pushed for a massive and un-requested health care reform bill. If enacted the new law would crush small businesses under the required paperwork and the costs of their new coverage. *Elizabeth McCaughey* a sharp New York Assemblywomen researched and published a line by line critique of the Hillary health plan.

Her extensive work showed how destructive and expensive the plan would actually be. *Prior to her solitary research effort no one in the media or in our Democrat led government would do an in-depth assessment..*

The Administration continued to push this ridiculous plan along in the hopes it could be passed before more opposition could be mounted. Their plan would attempt to control one-seventh of the national economy. Fortunately for America enough lawmakers became aware of how bad the potential legislation was and it failed to pass. The Clinton's and the Democrats were crushed and embittered.

(In 2010 the Democrats pulled the same deceitful scam, but that time it got through. *House Speaker Pelosi sanctimoniously stated, "We had to pass the Health Care Law to know what was in it"!!* Everything that was in their Health Care scam was bad, and everything Obama said about it was a lie. Costs are going through the roof, and millions lost their *former plans and doctors.* Obamacare exists only because of **massive taxpayer subsidies** that are secretly paid to the Insurance companies to keep (bribe) them in the program.)

Before and after taking power another scam was being planned by this White House. Hillary Clinton placed extreme pressure on the staff to fire the seven long term employees at the White House Travel Office. This non-partisan group, which was now called Ultrair was run by a Billy Dale. His team had worked for 32 years with each of the sitting Presidents and staffs arranging charter flights and travel amenities for the press corps. At that time the seven personnel "worked for the government", but handled no government funds. All costs were paid by the media outlets when they were billed for the travel.

Before Bill Clinton was even inaugurated an article had appeared in an Arkansas business publication which revealed the Clinton's plan for the takeover of the Travel Office. World Wide Travel from Little Rock "expected to pick up the contract" based on their ties to Clinton confidant David Watkins.

To "grease the wheels" for their scam, Clinton aide Jeff Elder stated in December 1992, (before they were even in the White House), that there were "serious problems in the White House Travel Office" and he would not be surprised if some of the staff were fired.

To assist the Clinton's in their "takeover", White House counsel Vincent Foster was involved. He had an assistant named William Kennedy who had also worked with Hillary at the Rose Law Firm. He called in the FBI and the IRS to probe "improprieties" at the offices of Ultrair. There was no way they could know of any "such issues" so quickly, and this event clearly showed an abuse of power.

FBI agent Dennis Sculimbrene complained of these obvious White House machinations to his supervisor, warning that Clinton aides were trying to find an excuse to fire Ultrair. Nothing was done over his report, and on May 19, 1993 the entire staff of Ultrair was summarily fired and replaced with "Clinton people".

A Weekly Standard article on this affair showed that one Darnell Martens had proposed this exact scenario on January 29. He and a friend, Hollywood producer Harry Thomason would become "general aviation advisors" to the Clinton White House. In that role they would be able to "review all non-military government aircraft to determine financial and operational appropriateness." (??)

(*The intent of this memo clearly shows prior forethought into the takeover of the travel office by the Clintons and their friends, long before any investigations had even been done.*)

Their scam backfired quickly, and even the Democratic mouthpiece the Washington Post was suggesting foul play. The media people knew and worked with Dale and his staff for years, and quickly saw that the storyline was a fake. White House efforts to "massage" the story also failed as the Clinton's actively misled the press. *FBI agents were illegally summoned to special meetings to get them onboard with "the official storyline".*

To further cover their tracks the IRS was sent in to do audits in the middle of the year. Normally they only audit a tax return you have filed, but not in this case. And since Ultrair was a new company formed in late 1992, they had not even filed one yet!

More unwanted questions arose, and then it came out that Foster's assistant William Kennedy had threatened the FBI to get to work on this issue or he would bring in the IRS.

(To save themselves the Clintons would eventually use Kennedy as the fall guy and he resigned in November 1994.)

After the Travel Office firings and fallout hit the headlines Clinton hid out on Air Force One to escape the criticisms. While in LA Clinton treated himself to a $200-dollar haircut. Hollywood's coiffeur came onto Air Force One while they were sitting on the tarmac with the engines running. Because of that factor other commercial planes could not land and were forced to circle the airport until Air Force One departed. More harsh and deserved criticism followed.

Unable to take the heat Bill Clinton decided to "re-hire" five of the UltrAir workers who were clearly innocent of anything. This too backfired as the White House had originally claimed that the "evidence of impropriety and mismanagement were so great the entire staff had to go." More complaints rose up as George Stephanopoulos the press secretary tried to claim "they had never been fired", just placed on leave. In the end the Clinton's scamming cost the U.S. taxpayers another $250,000 in legal fees.

Congress tried to pass an additional $500,000 to cover the legal costs for those innocent employees, but Clinton refused to sign it sanctimoiously claiming "his staff was harassed through all of this!" The Senate overrode his veto with Senator Orin Hatch yelling about Clinton's hypocrisy.

None of the UltrAir workers ever returned to their original jobs. The White House Travel Office became a shambles under the Clinton people, who tried to bill reporters $87,000 for flights! The corrupt Justice Department's prosecution of Billy Dale was as petty as it was ridiculous. Dale was cleared of all charges. And Clinton refused to apologize for ruining this man's life.

It became apparent in the past weeks that Janet Reno was not appointed to be the nations Attn. General. She was placed there to watch out for and serve the Clinton's amid all of their affairs, legal, illegal and immoral. Soon after she took over at Justice "she " fired all ninety three of the U.S. attorneys. Hand picked replacements (Democrats) were installed, again to shield the Clintons and their affairs. Clinton associate Paula Casey was installed in the U.S. Attorney's office in Little Rock. From there she could control all of the previous investigations into the Clintons.

Then on July 20, 1993 White House Counsel **Vince Foster**, a long time friend and business partner to the Clinton's, was reportedly found dead in his car in Fort Marcy Park. Paramedics who were on scene stated that he was pale with no exterior signs of injury when found. There was no blood in the vehicle nor on the pistol that was found.

Bill Clinton was notified of the discovery and instructed his Dept of Justice appointee Janet Reno to have the Parks Department investigate the event!!

Never in history has a President picked who would investigate a civilian death. And no one this close to the President was ever found dead in a park under such mysterious circumstances before. The Parks Dept. obviously was ill-equipped for an investigation of this type, and their initial report was that the death was a suicide by a single gunshot in the mouth. **However they made this public claim before an autopsy was even done!**

The *80 year old pistol* found at the scene was reportedly found in Foster's hand alongside his hip. If he had shot himself in the car by sticking the pistol in his mouth the weapon would have fallen on the floor or on the seat.

When Foster's autopsy was completed it revealed that there were no powder burns on or around his mouth, in his mouth or anywhere on his body. That showed that his gunshot wound was fired from a distance, something a suicide could not do.

The pistol that was found was very old, rebuilt from used parts and had no paper trail. It fit the description of a "drop gun", something used in a crime that can't be traced. Foster's wife stated she had never seen the pistol before.

Parks Police claimed that Foster's thumb had an imprint from the trigger and that was the basis for their suicide ruling. But Dr. Vincent Di Maio a leading forensic examiner stated that that claim was impossible. A trigger would not have been able to leave an imprint from just one use.

In the background of the case it turns out that Foster was coming under investigation along with Hillary Clinton and Jim McDougal in the previously mentioned Whitewater / Madison Guaranty Scandal which involved a phony land deal in Arkansas. Taxpayers lost $63 million dollars in that land swindle that bilked thousands of investors. The resulting bank failure had to be covered by the FDIC, aka the taxpayers.

It also came out that a short time after Foster was found "dead in his car", the Clinton's went into Foster's office in the White House and removed multiple files concerning the many pending investigations. (That was illegal, tampering with evidence.)

In a column written by Robert Novack, he wrote there was clear linkage between many of the recent Clinton scandals and Foster's death. A *Weekly Standard* article explained that a full investigation into the Travel-gate affair was needed in order to understand the events leading up to Foster's death, and why the White House was in such a panic that night.

But the incident fell away because the Democrats running the Congress and the major media did not pursue it.

Leading Congressional Democrats fought all attempts at investigating those scandals, but glaring inconsistencies begged for investigation.

(1) As the investigation into Travel-gate deepened Vince Foster had purchased a special, highly sophisticated alarm system for his home.

(2) During July Foster had met with James Hamilton a noted criminal attorney. On the weekend of the July 17-18 the Fosters drove to the shore for a quiet time. Instead a longtime Clinton pal and partner was there waiting for them. Their talks were not recorded.

(3) On Monday July 19 (the day before Foster's death) Clinton inexplicably fired FBI Director William Sessions. The questionable timing of the act worked to compromise the investigation of Foster's death which conveniently occurred the next day.

(4) On the day of his death Vince Foster met with old Arkansas friend Marsha Scott, and later with Pres. Clinton. "Strangely" neither one could recall what they spoke with Foster about.

(5) Foster left the White House at 1PM. *Autopsy results placed his time of death around 2:30-4pm.* Between 5:30-6pm the White House secretary placed a call to Arkansas Governor Jim Tucker. She told on-duty State Trooper Roger Perry that Foster went out to his car in the parking lot and shot himself.

That call was made before Fosters body had even been found!

(6) Paramedic George Gonzalez was the first to see Fosters body. He stated that Foster was not in the car but in the park. Foster was laid out neatly with his arms straight down at his sides. There was little blood and the pistol was in his hand. Experienced homicide detectives all stated the scene was staged.

(7) Strangely the Park Police lost or destroyed all of their forensic reports and photos of the crime scene, so no one could recreate or go over anything. And blond and light brown hairs were found on Foster's clothing, but no investigation of them was ever made.

(8) The lead investigator from the Parks Dept. had never handled a murder before. And the Park Police never test fired the suspect pistol to even see if it could fire, or to see if it could be matched by ballistics to the fatal bullet!

In addition to the Travel Office Scandal and Foster's death, over 900 FBI files on private citizens were found illegally in the White House! All of the files were about people who were considered "enemies of the Clintons". (This scandal was called Filegate.) The Clinton White House again concocted multiple reasons why those files were there. Each story was proven false, and became sound reasons for legal action against the Clinton's.

Soon after the senior FBI agent in the White House was forced to retire. He had witnessed and complained about their illegal actions, and was forced out. This too was another serious charge against the Clintons, but again the media and the obstructionist Democrats allowed it to fade away.

These are just a few of the inconsistencies and scandals our country would have to endure with this "New Democrat" in power. (For a deeper look into the Foster killing and other scandals read *Making Waves* by Reagan, *The Death of Outrage* by Bennett, *High Crimes and Misdemeanors* by Ingram, *Bitter Legacy* by Ruddy & Limbacher, *Guilty* by Coulter or *Absolute Power* by Limbaugh.)

The important point to be learned was that this newly inaugurated president was up to his eyeballs in constant scandals and potential criminal activity.

Multiple Arkansas business partners and friends were being indicted with fraud, conspiracy, theft etc. That included the McDougal's, Arkansas Governor Jim Tucker, and Webb Hubbell who Clinton had installed high up in the Justice Dept. to keep an eye on things. There were many others yet to come.

Weeks later a special prosecutor was finally installed. But by that time numerous records had been destroyed and some witnesses had fled or "died". Hubbell was about to assist prosecutors when $700,000 suddenly showed up in his legal aid fund. He decided to sit in jail for refusing to testify.

Despite all of these past weeks of scandals the major media refused to dig into anything as they had with Watergate or Iran-Contra. Had those ideologues done the job the press is supposed to, be the conscious of the republic, a failure and or criminal would have been removed from the Presidency.

Their refusal to investigate the many Clinton scandals is actually one of the worst failures in American History. Because of them Bill Clinton was able to get into and stay in office. More terrible travesties would befall the nation and the world.

French philosopher Alexis de Tocqueville had stated over a century ago, *"America is great because it is good. When the people cease to be good, America will no longer be great."* *(136)

Political appointee Louis Freeh replaced the fired Sessions at the FBI. *It was "decided to reorganize" the FBI's top posts under Clinton's new political correctness guidelines of diversity over performance.* Cronies and PC people were appointed to high positions on October 13, 1993. None were qualified for those senior positions, but were brought in to act as hatchet men and politicize the agency. Freeh abolished the position of deputy director for investigations, and forty seven section chiefs. All of those efforts worked to weaken the security of our nation and contributed to the attacks on 9/11. (Despite the prior terrorist attacks, the FBI did not institute a basic training course for terrorism analysis.)

More Islamic Issues

FBI officials in San Francisco were becoming suspicious of **Ali Mohamed**. Some of his reports were proving to be inaccurate, and he was traveling to terrorist areas way too often. Some felt he might even be working for that shadowy figure bin Laden. *However senior officials in the FBI dismissed the San Francisco office concerns.* Ali was allowed to continue his travels, and his next destination was Mogadishu, Somalia. Joining him there was **Abu Hafs**, bin Laden's military commander.

Pakistan conducted one of their rare crackdowns on radicals. Four hundred and eighty had been rounded up and sent to prison. Bin Laden organized a fund to get them released, (bribes) and flew them to Khartoum, Sudan. There they became soldiers in his burgeoning radical army. His holdings in the Sudan were increasing, and he was becoming a commanding figure in the desperate land.

In the fall of 1993 the Administration faced foreign policy problems in Algeria and Egypt. *Similar to earlier failed Democratic diplomatic efforts, (Truman-China), Clinton wanted the Algerians to have a dialogue with their adversary Islamic Fundamentalists.* As was forewarned, talking did not accomplish anything with those extremists and Algeria fell into civil war.

By this point it was clear that the Fundamentalists were spreading their reach throughout the Middle East. One analyst at the CIA who knew them from the Reagan's years stated that the movement was almost unstoppable. Islamist governments would spread unless they were harshly defeated in serious fighting. Since that endgame was not being planned for, the West would have to adjust their policies to deal with them.

Egypt became the next dilemma. As shown before this was the original home of the Muslim Brotherhood, and the violent EIJ. They were threatening Pres. Mubarak who had become a good ally to the U.S. As was happening in Algeria, those terrorists were murdering public officials, police, military officers and even intellectuals and writers. **Anyone who stood for anything other than Fundamentalism was targeted.** Those were the same "scored earth" tactics used by the Communists, the Fascists and the Iranian extremists as they forced their way into power.

CIA issued another warning which appeared in the London Times. "Islamic Fundamentalist terrorists would continue to make gains across Egypt leading to its collapse". *(137)

Director James Woolsey became increasingly worried and offered whatever assistance they could to prevent another Iran. U.S. special forces trained an Egyptian variant that made multiple raids upon the terrorists. But as had happened in Iran and Nicaragua under Carter, the Clinton State Dept. was unhappy with the methods used to maintain Mubarak's control. **They ended our assistance**!

Mubarak however refused to letup his efforts. Algeria's civil war convinced him the Islamists meant nothing but death. Egypt had been mortified when Carter backed the Ayatollah. And ever since he had taken over for the murdered Sadat, Mubarak complained often about how the West and the U.S. failed to take action against the Islamic right. As far back as 1986 he had called for an International conference on terrorism, knowing it was spreading into a worldwide entity.

Pres. Mubarak warned all that the Islamists had already established multiple bases inside the West. He even listed known locations in Geneva, London, Germany and New York-New Jersey! But his warning was ignored by the Administration. **Incident # 14**

And he was infuriated that the U.S. still would not give him **Sheik Omar Rahman**. Had Egypt been able to work on him as they had with Abouhalima, they may have broken up some of the terrorist rings such as the one that struck the WTC back in February, or the day of terror plot.

Clinton's Sec. State Warren Christopher, (a Carter retread), met with Mubarak and asked him how to deal with the Islamists. Mubarak angrily pounded the table and yelled crush them. Mubarak could not fathom how the U.S. continued to urge cooperation with this viscious enemy. **He ridiculed all who wanted "dialogue", for being the fools that they were.**

(This Administration's inanity mirrored Chiang Kai-shek's issues with Pres. Truman in 1945-46. Truman insisted that Chiang sit down and negotiate with the Chinese Communists. Because of Truman's interference, Chiang and the Nationalists lost their Civil War, leading to new wars in Vietnam and Korea.)

As far as the Clinton State Dept. was concerned crushing terrorists may be justified, but not the Muslim Brotherhood. They ran schools, clinics, mosques and charities, and were considered by State as a semi-political party. That antiquated feeling may have been true 20 years earlier, but not in 1993.

Woolsey and many in the CIA knew the terrorists were hiding within the benign facades of Islamic charities and schools. **But a year into this administration, he still could not get a face to face meeting with Clinton to discuss the dangers!**

In the halls of diplomacy the Oslo Accords were being worked out. Israel's PM Yitzhak Rabin and Yassir Arafat of the PLO signed an agreement in which Israel would slowly withdraw their forces and residents from Gaza and parts of the West Bank. In return the PLO would stop their violence and terrorism. The vacated areas would be governed by representatives from the PLO as elected officials. Again the hope was that democratic ideals would bring peace.

But the Fundamentalists did not want peace, they wanted an Islamic state across the region. Hamas would take over for the weakened PLO and terrorism quickly returned to Gaza. (In mid-1994 Jordan joined in the peace talks. Yitzhak Rabin was assassinated for his efforts on November 4, 1995.)

Trials for the WTC bombers began in August 1993. Because of Bill Clinton's inane ruling, this case was treated as a civilian criminal case and the suspects were able to ask for extensive information to bolster their "legal defense." **They were given access to the World Trade Center engineering studies and structural plans.** Their defense was based on a fake claim that they were simply trying to make a political statement, not to destroy the buildings. *If they wanted to destroy the buildings they would have "acted differently"*. Ajaj, Abouhalima, Salameh, and Ayyad were all convicted in March 1994. (Yousef and Ahmed Yassin were still at large. More on this soon.)

But the main point was still missed by the media and Clinton. They had tried to murder 50,000 people with that bomb.

Somalia

During the many months that the Marines had been keeping the peace in Somalia *with Operation Restore Hope,* hundreds of Soviet bloc weapons had been confiscated. Few Somali's dared to challenge the enforced rules and calm was restored, food and supplies were given to those in need. By the late spring of 1993 the USMC mission in Somalia was ending as they were to rotate home. *(Had the Marines been able to use the same aggressive methods in Lebanon during the early 1980s things might have worked out differently there.)*

Clinton and his team of lawyers looked at the Somali situation in purely political terms. That the ongoing situation was a potential liability for him, as "any good press" had already been garnered by former President Bush. Somalia was nothing but a potential problem. Similar to Truman and Korea in 1949, Clinton passed off the Somalia peace-keeping mission to the United Nations.

The Marines would be replaced by U.N. peacekeeping troops. However U.N. Sec-General Boutros Ghali cagily insisted that if the U.N. took over America must keep 1,000 combat troops on station in order to have some teeth in the U.N. troop mix.

That decision resulted in U.S. Army troops being sent over with the State Dept. placed in charge of running the U.S. part of the mission. Unlike the USMC time in country, the U.N. commanders refused to send out patrols to disarm the militias, or to keep them off balance. And they had restrictive rules of engagement which prevented any proactive operations.

For a short while the peace seemed to hold until a June 1993 ambush resulted in 24 Pakistani troops being slaughtered. Somali warlords had dug-up their hidden arms caches and sent a large group of women and children towards some Pakistani troops. *Hidden among the innocents were heavily armed rebels.* The fight was over quickly since the Pakistani's never expected the attack. Killed in the gunfire were some of the women and children, which the liberal western media quickly and wrongly blamed on the U.N. Fallout from the attack was the demand to arrest warlord **Farah Aideed**. That effort would involve using more U.S. troops which were hurriedly sent over.

Four bombing missions were made on suspected Aideed compounds but he survived each attempt. As the weeks went by additional ambush type attacks occurred before the U.N. forces recognized that the rebels / terrorists were using women and children as human shields in their attacks. (Same as every other bunch of swine.) And similar to the Viet Cong/NVA operations in the Vietnam TET offensive, the well armed militias and terrorists had quietly infiltrated back into the cities and towns.

During those dangerous weeks the Somali militias were joined by some of bin Laden's terrorist forces from the Sudan. Among them were **Abu Hafs and Ali Mohamed.** Both had snuck in and were watching the U.N. and U.S. operations. They returned to the Sudan and informed bin Laden it was certain they could succeed against the U.S. troops.

Muhammad Atef, who was al Qaeda's training director and at that time bin Laden's successor, had also been sent into the country to train the Somalis and plan their attacks against the Americans. He too returned with good news, the Somalis were ready. When Atef was sent back to Somalia, Ali Mohamed was his assistant. They reported back on their progress. It was time.

The Clinton Administration had committed a company of the 10th Mountain Division, some Army Rangers and some Delta Force troops to try to stop the criminal warlords. Those units were comprised of lightly armed infantry troops. Mirroring Lebanon in the early 80s, they were not allowed to have any armored vehicles nor attack helicopter support. (The Marines had both, and used them keeping the militias in check.)

By late summer 1993 the city of Mogadishu had become an armed asylum and Somalia was returning into a lawless land run by the warlords. It was folly to think that a small contingent of light troops could stop what was happening. Bin Laden sent in another team of al Qaeda bomb makers and guerrilla specialists along with additional weapons and supplies.

This latest terrorist team was led by **Mohammed Makawi**, a former Egyptian army officer, and a cohort of Ayman al Zawahiri's and Egyptian Islamic Jihad. One of Makawi's special skills was in the use of the Soviet made RPG. Like all Soviet military equipment the RPG was designed for easy use by a peasant army. It had a shaped charge warhead that was powered by a gas reaction that exited out of the rear. This warhead was powerful enough to take out tanks, but in Mogadishu it was to be used on the American helicopters. They knew a Fatal Flaw.

During the past weeks American Radio intercept teams could hear the recently upgraded militia mortar teams giving and receiving instructions and directions in Arabic. *Somali's don't speak Arabic,* **but bin Laden's men did.** Bin Laden's mortar trainer was **Abu al-Banshiri,** and he recommended they attack the U.S. barracks areas directly. Kill them in their beds.

During the past weeks low level attacks had killed several U.S. troops and wounded more than a dozen with no major reaction from anyone. Included in those attacks were IED's,-improvised explosive devices. Our improperly equipped troops were driving around this war zone in trucks and humvee's, the Army's multi-purpose vehicle. Neither vehicle was armored, and the enemy was quick to learn that they were susceptible to those explosives.

On August 8th four servicemen were killed by a roadside bomb.

On the 23d six more troops were wounded by another bomb.

Pres. Clinton and his people did not react to those attacks. Similar to LBJ and his failed Vietnam policies, the Clinton administration believed that those attacks and attempts must be met with carefully measured responses. (His missile strike in Iraq.) He and his team felt that they could "control and plan" graduated and calibrated attacks against an enemy that had no concern for loss of life, theirs, innocent civilians or ours. Administration principals did not stay on top of the Somali effort, they passed the responsibility over to their deputies who knew even less.

Despite the prior requests, no armored vehicles or attack helicopters were sent over. One retaliatory attack was made by a USAF AC 130 gunship which destroyed one of Aideed's arms warehouses. After that mission the Somali weapon caches were dispersed, and Aideed went into hiding. Complaints by liberals over the powerful gunship and its use resulted in its being recalled by the administration.

An additional request for firepower by the U.S. commander Gen. Thomas Montgomery was made on September 14. Again he asked for armored vehicles and attack helicopters and passed it up the chain of command. Gen. Powell chairman of the JCS scaled back some of his list, but approved most of it.

However Sec. of Def. Les Aspin vetoed that latest request on September 23. It was felt the presence of armored units would be a "signal of escalation".

At this point the U.N. had 18,000 troops from thirty two nations involved in Somalia. They were under the command of a Turkish General, and communications were hard as the troops spoke differing languages which included some English. Many of those troops were Islamic, and their loyalty was questionable. Payoffs to the warlords were made and seen as some of the peacekeepers wanted no part in the turmoil. That further disrupted the U.N. team effort and the trust that was absolutely needed in such a dangerous place.

On September 25th a U.S. Black Hawk helicopter was shot down during a militia ambush when the attackers fired an RPG into the belly and tail rotor. The fuel tanks blew-up and the helicopter crashed amid a raging fire. (This attack was the work of bin Laden's terrorists.) The two pilots survived the explosion and crash but were trapped within a small enclave. They held out against militia attacks for over an hour and were finally rescued by a United Arab Emirate – APC, (armored personnel carrier) on a United Nations patrol. (The wounded pilots survived but the three crewmen died.)

Again there was no reaction from the Administration.

On October 3d and 4th, mortar and small arms attacks were made on the U.S. troops causing more casualties. The White House was facing increasing criticisms over the lack of progress and the growing casualties. Instead of helping the peacekeepers, the Administration pressured the commanders to act.

In June a CIA team had been sent to Somalia to try to recruit informants. Their efforts were limited and restricted, and by the fall they had found a little over twenty individuals. Most of their information was not actionable or was considered "unhelpful". Five snatch and grab missions were attempted and all used the same technique of using helicopters to swoop in and grab the suspects. *The key to their safety was operating at night.* But because of pressure from the administration another similar mission was ordered for October 18th.

However this time it was to be a daylight raid conducted in downtown Mogadishu. Word of this raid got out, and the militia members organized their counter-attacks. As they had done before, the U.S. troops flew into the city and quickly captured some suspects. This time a road convoy had been organized to come in to pickup the suspects and our troops. But within minutes of the raid dozens of smoky fires were set in the narrow streets to hinder visibility, and armed roadblocks were setup at key intersections to trap the truck-humvee convoy. Additional fighters were sent onto rooftops and into doorways. Enemy fire was intense as the U.S. casualties increased.

Then two Black Hawk helicopters were shot down using the same RPG technique. In the first crash the pilots died while five others were injured. Having rehearsed this scenario (because of the previous shoot-down), a rescue plan was implemented with a Ranger squad going on foot to the crash site and a fifteen man team dropping in to insure security. Heavy fighting continued as the Somali militia attempted to storm the crash site. Hundreds of attackers were shot, but they kept coming. (Similar to Korea, the follow on attackers picked up the weapons from those killed and wounded and continued the attack.)

At the second crash site four members had survived and alerted the circling command helicopters. Two Delta snipers volunteered to stabilize the site as there was no rescue force available for this crash. Initial Somali attacks were low level, but soon after the attacks became better organized and grew into waves. One pilot was captured while the other five troops were shot and butchered with machetes. Their bodies were dragged through the streets and filmed.

Street fighting became intense everywhere and the lightly armed U.S. force was fragmented into smaller groups. Each was surrounded by hundreds of enemy fighters. As the convoy continued driving through the streets trying to make rescue and recoveries, their vehicles were riddled with gunfire, killing and wounding more of the U.S. soldiers. Air support consisted of only light helicopters and sniper / machine guns attacks.

All of the attack helicopters and USAF gunship units had been removed from Somalia as being too powerful for a peace mission.

Unable to force any escapes the lightly armed units were trapped inside the city and spent a long night fighting off repeated attacks. *They were removed the next morning by Pakistani and Malaysian armored units.* After a day of heavy combat, 18 U.S. troops had been killed with over two dozen wounded. Most of the captured suspects had also been shot.

At this same time a serious situation had also occurred inside Russia. Hardline Communists were storming the television stations and the Russian Parliament in an effort to stage a coup against the fledgling Democracy. CNN was broadcasting live from Moscow on that situation when a filmed report from Somalia was put on the air highlighting that disaster. Images showing our dead soldiers being dragged through the streets brought much negativity.

Clinton was livid that we weren't killing enough of "those dogs". When they kill us they should be killed in greater numbers. *(138) (Strange feelings for someone who showed no concern for the 50,000 people almost murdered at the Trade Center in NYC.)

Clinton and his administration were harshly criticized. Outrage over the CNN video grew as the administration was unable to explain away the irrational weapons and safety restrictions. Sec-Def Aspin was used as the scapegoat and fired. Unlike Pres.

Reagan and Beruit, Clinton blamed the Pentagon, the U.N., the press and his staff for not "keeping him informed".

(Just like Kennedy did in Cuba.)

After two days of heated meetings, "it was decided" that Clinton would announce the U.S. contingent would leave Somalia no later than March 31. In that way the Administration deluded themselves that it would not look like a pullout or a retreat. Clinton's spin doctors were hard at work trying to sell the storyline.

A week after the disaster 1,700 reinforcements arrived in Somalia with armored vehicles and helicopter gunships. When the troops went back out into the city they were accompanied by an array of armor and air support. In addition to that obvious strength, U.S. sniper teams were used to take out any Somali's who were observed carrying weapons.

There were no more major attacks while the U.S troops operated in that fashion. Calm was restored and the UN relief effort renewed. Yet even with those positive signs Clinton insisted our forces leave the country. It was obvious he did not care a bit about those desperate Somalis. (Racism?)

In September 1995 a Senate Committee placed the blame for the heavy losses in Somalia on the Administration's absurd political considerations which were put ahead of the security of the troops on station. (Just like Beruit.)

Jihadists

Investigative journalist Steve Emerson continued his low level examination of Islamic Jihadists operating inside America. During December 1993 he attended a five day Islamic conference in Detroit. *Speakers were present from Hamas, the Muslim Brotherhood, the Palestinian Islamic Jihad and other violent terrorist groups.* An FBI agent gave a talk on civics and laws on weapons thinking this was a meeting of a local civic group.

Emerson went to Washington and met with FBI officials to ask them what their agent was doing, and if the agency knew what was going on there. Again he was told that since the Congressional legal changes were implemented under Carter, the FBI could not act or investigate until a crime was actually in progress! "Religious and civic groups" were especially off limits.

Bin Laden's constant criticism of the House of Saud resulted in his citizenship being revoked and all of his remaining assets being confiscated. It is illegal to criticize the Saudi regime or any of their policies. The Saudis claim it is an act of terrorism and anti-Islam. Any who dare to speak out are imprisoned and punished under Sharia Law. Bin Laden responded to their actions by building camps and safehouses on the northern border of Yemen. With new fighters based so close to his old homeland he hoped to destabilize the Saudi rulers and bring them down.

Fresh from their success in Somalia, Ali Mohamed was sent on his next mission during December 1993. He was to work with their cell based in Nairobi, Kenya. Al Qaeda terrorists were already in place, and needed Ali to scout the U.S. embassies in the region to determine if any attacks were possible.

The leader of that cell was **Wadi al-Haj**, *the same one from the Alkifah refugee centers in Tucson and Brooklyn.*

As shown earlier Haj had left Brooklyn to become bin Laden's assistant. After working in the Sudan for a few months he was relocated from Khartoum to Nairobi to bring together the al Qaeda cell forming there. Haj was another naturalized American citizen who could travel freely on his U.S. passport. In Nairobi he ran an "Islamic charity" which provided the funding for their cell. State of the art photo/video equipment from China and Germany was used during the scouting operations, and cell members used a makeshift laboratory to develop their photo-recon pictures.

To oversee all of this growing activity bin Laden sent his "military aide", **Abu Ubaidah al Banshiri**, and an on site manager **Khaled al-Fawwaz**. Fawwaz had originally gone to Nairobi in late 1992 to begin the process of sneaking al Qaeda people into Somalia as aid workers. Coming in from Kenya they did not attract as much scrutiny as they would have coming in from the Sudan. Their plan worked perfectly as was seen in Mogadishu.

Computer experts used software to make models of and examine the building construction of their targeted buildings. It was vital that their bombing plans be done perfectly this time, as they had failed at the World Trade Center. Senior terrorists worked with al-Haj and everything was progressing on schedule. By January 1994 the first reports of Ali's targeting recons had reached bin Laden. He and his military council which included Ali Mohamed, Banshiri and Mohammed Atef, (AKA Abu al-Masri), agreed that the U.S. embassy in Nairobi was an easy target.

To support the training of those al Qaeda cell members, they were sent to Lebanon to train in the Hezbollah camps.

They would again copy Hezbollah designs for making truck bombs, the same as was used at the WTC.

Around this time one **Jamal al-Fadl** was sent in search of uranium. His initial contact was an Abu Dijana who directed him to find one Moqadem al-Mobruk, a Sudanese official.

Mobruk arranged a meeting with Banshiri and explained that the price for the uranium was $1.5 million. Fadl next had to go to the al Qaeda financier Abu al-Suri to get the money. After weeks of effort and great cost al Qaeda ended up purchasing simple red mercury. Fortunately for the world they had been duped.

On March 1, 1994 jihadist **Rashid Baz** who was "working as a NYC livery driver" shot at a van of Jewish rabbinical students on the Brooklyn Bridge murdering one and wounding three others. This attack was again ignored by the federal authorities, and treated as just a civilian anti-Jewish attack. **Incident # 15**

(In light of all of the recent terrorist attacks this should have been investigated fully. Where was Baz he from? How did he get here and who were his contacts?)

Bill Clinton

Thus far everything Clinton had tried during 1993 and into 1994 had been a failure. He didn't even know how to return a salute to his military guard. His first two picks for attorney general were both shot down due to scandals, and Hillary-care had been stopped by an avalanche of negative feedback when it was found to be a scam. Clinton's only initiative his first week in office was to end the ban on gay's in the military. That too was met with howls of protests and was changed to don't ask don't tell.

Clinton's 1993 tax increase was rammed through the Democrat controlled Congress as VP Al Gore cast the deciding vote. *Senator Moynihan (Democrat) called this disaster the largest tax increase in the history of public finance.*

The Clinton-Gore Tax increase hijacked another $115 Billion in personal taxes, $31 Billion in fuel taxes, $25 Billion in Social Security Taxes and $29 Billion in Medicare Taxes from our paychecks. This was the second Democratic tax increase in four years. (The other was the one the Democrats tricked Bush into signing.)

Those tax increases basically undid the tax relief of Pres. Reagan. Once more the typical household (that pays taxes) saw their tax total rise to 34% of their income. Thus the working citizen labors for four months just to pay taxes!

(Again, the Democrats are for the little guy.)

The murder of White House Counsel Vince Foster, the firings of the White House travel staff, and the FBI files found in the Clinton's possession brought more unwanted questions. Their non-stop damage control efforts weakened his administration. A Special Prosecutor had finally been appointed to look into Whitewater and other serious issues, and even Sen. Moynihan stated the move was necessary.

But the prosecutor was having problems getting answers and documents from the obstructionist Clintons and their friends. They delayed and prevented any cooperation, and Janet Reno made sure she stayed out of the way.

During her tenure in Dade County, Florida, Miami became a mecca for drug dealers, money launderers and corruption. DOJ number two Philip Heyman resigned in mid-1994 because of the way Reno was "running things". And strange coincidences were clearly evident among the Clintons and their people.

Between January 1988 and January 1991 eleven suspicious deaths had occurred among Clinton workers, supporters or security staff. Since 1992 when his campaign kicked off, eighteen additional people who had worked with, had business dealings with, or who were investigating the Clintons had also been killed.

Those issues screamed for criminal investigations. But again the press and the DOJ stayed away from the stories.

And more issues came up when incoming intelligence reports stated that Islamic terrorists had been involved in the fight against us in Somalia. The CIA was unable to provide any "legally direct intelligence" to validate the reports, so lawyer Bill Clinton refused to believe any of the information. **Incident # 16**

During March 1994 Clinton did what he had said he would and he ended the successful peace mission in Somalia. His action abandoned those poor, teeming masses to a terrible fate. Without the strength of our forces being present the U.N. mission was ended completely and the chaos quickly returned. The civilians were helpless pawns of the warlords. And Clinton who complained so loud about Bosnia, did not care at all. (Racism?)

In the Sudan bin Laden was exultant.

Twice in twelve months his small forces had chased America from a Muslim country. Both times it took just a single night of battle. He called Somalia his greatest battle, as Allah had granted them a victory. Pres. Clinton was seen by those terrorists as a pathetic and weak official, and America as a feeble giant. There was no reason for the Fundamentalist Muslim world to dread the U.S. any more. America was far less fearsome than the old Soviet Union. For bin Laden there were many more Americans to kill in nearby Saudi Arabia. Plans were made.

In the Balkans the civil fighting continued. Yet now that he was in charge, Clinton had done nothing. Bosnia's static fighting of 1992/93 was changing into a slow, steady push as the Serbs tried to drive the Bosnian Croats and Bosniaks out. Mass killings were becoming commonplace, and by January 1994 the Serbs controlled 70% of the country.

On February 5, 1994 mortar attacks were made on a crowded marketplace in Sarajevo, the capitol of Bosnia. The heinous attack killed 43 civilians and wounded 75 more. With the U.N. peacekeepers needing help, **NATO decided to intervene.**

Their initial mission was to prevent Serbian aircraft from flying over U.N. restricted airspace. But on August 28, 1994 Sarajevo was again struck in another mortar attack killing 68 and wounding 144. The Administration was again silent, but **NATO decided to use air strikes on the Bosnian Serb forces.** (Someone had to do something.) All of the above added to Clinton's woes as it revealed how little he and his team understood foreign or military matters.

Terrorist Attacks and Threats

A plot to blowup the Israeli Embassy in Bangkok was unintentionally foiled. A truck had been hijacked and a bomb installed in it. On March 11, 1994 while en-route to the embassy the vehicle was involved in a crash and the nervous driver fled. It was believed that Ramzi Yousef had been behind the attempt. **Incident # 17**

In April 1994 a theatre was bombed just outside of Amman, Jordan. Again authorities there quickly linked the bombing to bin Laden's terrorists. **Mohammed Jamal Khalifa** was implicated in the bombing with ten others. **Incident # 18**

Jamal was one of the ones bin Laden had sent to the Philippines with Ramzi Yousef to start their al-Qaeda network. Khalifa was a known brother in law to bin Laden, and the Jordanians felt they had enough evidence to claim Khalifa had financed the attack. A warrant was put out for his arrest, he fled and Jordanian courts convicted him in his absence and sentenced him to death.

Yet on December 1, 1994 he somehow arrived in the U.S.! Two weeks went by before the screwup was caught and he was arrested here. The Justice Department wanted to keep him because he was traveling under a false visa and was sought for questioning over recent terrorist attacks in the Philippines. **Incident # 19**

But both INS and the State Dept. agreed that Jamal would go back to Jordan for his crimes. Inanely he was flown out before he could be interrogated over the Philippines attacks!

Though the other ten terrorists in Jordan were convicted and sentenced, Khalifa "somehow won an acquittal". He secretly returned to the Philippines!

(The Jordanians did not hold him after his trial ended. Had we been able to arrest him again, who knows what would have been learned. *Another What If.)*

On June 27-28, 1994 the Matsumoto terrorist incidents in Nagano, Japan occurred. Terrorists released **Sarin gas** at numerous sites causing eight deaths and two hundred sickened by the toxic clouds. This case was not aggressively pursued at that time, but it was actually a practice run for the pending subway attacks in Tokyo. **Incident # 20**

On July 18, 1994 a van filled with explosives detonated and destroyed an Israeli social center in Buenos Aires killing 85 and wounding over 250. Argentina had the 6th largest Jewish population in the world, and Hezbollah sent **Ibrahim Beinac** to drive the van. Iran was quickly implicated but the world and the administration stayed quiet. **Incident # 21**

July 19, 1994 Alas Chiricanas Flight 901 was destroyed by a bomb murdering twenty-one. That flight routinely carried many Jewish passengers, and was presumed as an attack by Islamists on an easy target as their security was lax. **Incident # 22**

July 26, 1994 a car bomb in London struck the Israeli embassy. That attack was a protest to the continuing peace negotiations between Jordan and Israel. Five Palestinians were arrested as their bomb wounded twenty civilians. **Incident # 23**

In August three hooded N. African terrorists murdered two Spanish tourists at a Marrakesh hotel. During the investigation it was found the terrorists had trained in Afghanistan terrorist camps. **Incident # 24**

A month later the CIA station in Riyadh reported that American targets were being scrutinized with hostile intent by Iranian agents and their allies. Director Woolsey visited the kingdom in December, 1994 to go over the threats and discuss joint plans for monitoring and disrupting any attacks. It was clear that Iranian and other regional terrorists were operating inside Saudi Arabia. *But as would become commonplace the Saudi's did not follow through.* **Incident # 25**

For the past year Florida Congressman Bill McCollum tried unsuccessfully to get the Administration to wakeup to the Islamic Terrorist threat that Bin Laden and global Islamic terrorism presented. He repeatedly wrote to Clinton, his National Security Advisor Tony Lake and CIA Director James Woolsey to focus their efforts on global terrorism.

McCollum was the founder and chairman of the House Task Force on Terrorism and Unconventional Warfare. He had been active in helping the Afghans during their war with the Soviets, and had made many contacts in that region. McCollum had a staff member named Yossef Bodansky who spoke Farsi and Arabic. During the Afghan war Bodansky had been able to mingle with the locals and learned much about the growing movement of the Islamists. From local newspapers, magazines and broadcasts Bodansky became the one source who truly understood what was happening in the Islamic world.

McCollum and Bodansky had learned from meetings with former mujahedeen that this wealthy Saudi named Osama bin Laden wanted to impose an Iranian style Islamic republic in their lands. They also learned that Bin Laden's forces were connected to dozens of murders and bombings in Afghanistan, Pakistan and Yemen. And he was committed to killing Americans.

Their sources warned the numerous training camps bin Laden had constructed and ran were graduating scores of new terrorists every six months. They were convinced that it would not be long before we were attacked again. He could not convince Bill Clinton or his Administration of the pending threats. **Incident # 26**

(Bodansky would write two books on the growing terrorist threats, both before 1997. His work included an authoritative biography on Osama Bin Laden.) **Incident # 27**

Then a Newsweek interview with Bin Laden came out. He affirmed that the killing of Americans was justified. Again there was no reaction from the administration. **Incident # 28**

Bin Laden's name was appearing in raw intelligence reports with increasing frequency from the Middle East to Bosnia and the Philippines. At that time many in the CIA still referred to him as a rich kid who was playing terrorist. But Richard Clarke, Tony Lake and other Administration officials asked the CIA to find out about him and his organization. (What happened to the previous files from Yemen, the WTC or the Day of Terror??)

The FBI was told by Attorney General Janet Reno to cooperate with the NSC staff and share all relevant data on any terrorist criminal investigations. According to Richard Clarke, lawyers within the FBI tied up the intelligence releases in a sea of red tape! **(139)

Despite the unending information that was coming in on terrorism Clinton showed no interest to this growing threat. In fact, Clinton directed the FBI to spend vast resources on anti-abortion bombings, "right wing Militias" and "issues here" instead of looking into the worldwide threat of Islamic terrorists.

Foreign Affairs

Chechnya was a former Soviet province, and had been demanding autonomy like so many other states. As shown earlier the Russians refused to grant it claiming it was a part of the original Russia. They had been fighting Islamic separatists and militants for over a year, and terrorist attacks were increasing in frequency and violence. By 1994 a civil war started.

Many of bin Laden's terrorist cohorts were now training, operating and assisting in Chechnya and in the Balkans. Russia again asked the U.S. for assistance in combating this threat, but this administration did not see any of those issues as a risk. Instead Clinton was upset "at the human rights violations" occurring in Chechnya, and did not believe the Russian claims that most of the atrocities were from the Wahhabi jihadists. **Incident # 29**

In Bosnia the United Nations sent in more peacekeepers to try to stop the genocide. After numerous warnings the U.N. forces shot down Bosnian-Serbian planes that were operating over the no-fly zone. Peace for Bosnia was obtained at the Dayton Accords.

Neighboring Croatia launched two large offensives to force the Serbs out of their country. They succeeded, and even advanced into Serbia itself. Slovenia and Croatia were the two most developed republics in Yugoslavia. Their quests for freedom and the civil fighting the past four years were bankrupting the Yugoslavian economy. The wars had to end soon.

Throughout 1994 France was working hard to get the U.N. sanctions lifted in Iraq. It was time to get the Iraqi oil flowing. One trick that had been used by the Ba'thists was the "need to flush the old oil out of the pipelines lest they corrode" scam. Roughly 12 million barrels went to the distributors with each system flush, and Iraq netted about $70 million each time. France had won large contracts to help rebuild Iraq and they lobbied the U.N. hard to get the work started. They had also been promised vast rights in the production of a new oil field. But to get the oil out the sanctions had to go. A lot of the equipment France would bring in was dual use, which was causing worries in the U.N.

Only the Saudi's helped us in our effort to control Iraq. Any country that did business with Iraq lost out in Saudi Arabia. (France lost some big contracts.) Ironically Saddam shot himself in the foot when he again became belligerent towards Kuwait in October 1994. The forces he moved along their border appeared as if they might launch another attack. Sec-Def. William Perry rushed reinforcements into Kuwait, the southern no-fly zone was expanded and a no-drive zone also instituted.

UNSCOM chairman Rolf Ekeus and his people were still trying to evaluate over half a million fresh pages of documents on Iraq's WMD programs. This latest find was uncovered on a chicken farm owned by Saddam's son in law **Hussein Kamil.** (He defected to Jordan in July.)

Kamil informed UNSCOM that Iraq had weaponized their bio-weapons before the Gulf War! Though the weapons had been destroyed, Kamil claimed the WMD stocks and equipment had not. (France had been a great help to Iraq's WMD programs, and acted against Israel since 1968 to be seen as an alternative to the United States. France also helped the likes of Iran and the PLO. Even though France had suffered numerous terrorist attacks, they continued to try to buy off the Islamists.)

During this same time frame the Clinton Administration gleefully announced "progress" in their talks with the ever hostile North Korea. With the fall of the Soviets, N. Korea had been seriously hurt economically. They needed help from the West to avert collapse and Kim il Sung devised a plan. They had been trying for years to acquire the technology to build a nuclear bomb. In 1994 they let it slip that they were removing spent fuel from their Yongbyon reactor, a potential strategic issue since that fuel could be used to make weapons grade nuclear material. Threats to the region would be endless if the North succeeded.

The Administration desperately wanted the N. Koreans to turn in their spent fuel rods to the U.N. and allow inspectors to visit. N. Korea refused, and the situation became tense. Former president Carter traveled to N. Korea to act as an uninvited "go-between". From his unsanctioned visit he, Clinton and the N. Koreans eventually "struck a one sided treaty" that became the norm for this poorly performing Administration.

North Korea would get 500,000 tons of oil from America each year, plus $4 Billion in aid from America, Japan and S. Korea to help them construct two more "peaceful" nuclear reactors. They would get 10 years to dismantle their weapons program and 5 years to turn over their current stockpile! In return North Korea "promised not to use the *new reactors* to make atomic bombs and to accept IAEA inspections"!

There were no stated penalties for non-compliance.

For Clinton and his illogical administration, just the illusion of success was good enough. With this "deal" the Communists had conceded nothing, picked up tons of aid and money, continued using their existing facility at Kumchangni, *and kept their massive chemical weapon stockpile armed and ready.*

CIA Asia specialist Kent Harrington reported back on the incredible difficulty in negotiating with the duplicitous Communists. (That issue should not have been a surprise for that is always their way. FDR's failures with Stalin, Truman and Marshall's failures over China, the two year negotiation marathon trying to end the Korean War, then came JFK and LBJ's failuers over SE Asia, Nixon's trials with them, and the many failed treaties with Russia.)

The leftist media proclaimed this deal was a great thing for the world, and that the conservatives were wrong about being worried over N. Korean intentions. To insure the Republicans in the Senate did not obstruct his "goals", **Clinton illegaly stated the negotiations were structured as "a framework", not an actual treaty**. Treaties must be ratified by the U.S. Senate, and there was no chance that would happen with this disaster. (Obama used the same scam in 2014-16 with his idiotic "Iran deal". Even though it failed to pass, he gave Iran $150 Billion days before he left!!)

Ranking Republican Senator Robert Dole sarcastically remarked that it was always easy to "get a treaty" when you give enough away to the other side.

Columnist Charles Krauthammer (another former Democrat,) sardonically wrote of how the Clinton State Dept. led by Warren Christopher mixed cravenness and cynicism to claim their capitulation to N. Korea was "Good News" for the world.

Madeline Albright, (quite a play on words), was Clinton's Ambassador to the United Nations. She was another longtime liberal who understood nothing of Communists or tyrannical despots as evidence by her unwavering support for this foolhardy "deal". (She had been an advisor to Walter Mondale during his lost effort in 1984, and joined the usual Democratic chorus obstructing and downplaying everything Pres. Reagan tried to do.)

Albright was also a huge proponent of *Assertive Multilateralism. (??)* To the world's liberals, and especially those in the U.S., **America should not be the leader of the free world, the United Nations should be**.

Her assistant Karl Inderfurth was a major believer and practicing member of that premise. He also believed that all U.S. intelligence /information must be shared with the U.N. Our intelligence people were stunned that anyone would want to do that, share our most secret knowledge and entrust our safety to unelected people from other nations.

(Winston Churchill had spoken on that very subject many times, and felt it was ludicrous for any nation to give up their own power to someone else's discretion.)

To get this "deal", Carter, Clinton and everyone else ignored that N. Korea is an enemy nation, and has the worst record in the world of human rights violations. Between 1.5-3 million have died in the past decade just from starvation! Another terrible famine was ongoing, resulting in cannibalism. It would last four years and kill unknown millions. Those who survived suffered severe and lifelong afflictions, and this savage kill off was not the first time it had happened.

During the Communist rule of Kim Il-sung all national assets were used for their military and party faithful first. (His son Kim Jung Il continued that practice.) Live lobsters were flown in for them every day, even though the people starved. And N. Korea maintained a well-fed 1.2 million man army, always on first-strike alert. Over the past decades numerous secret tunnels had been uncovered going from N. Korea into the South, as a way to strike unseen. Their plan throughout those years was to launch another surprise invasion, and win.

After having sold out his country and the world with this moronic deal, Carter was given a Nobel Peace Prize by the left leaning Nobel committee. For some strange reason the Noble people never gave one to President Reagan for his work in freeing over 500 million people from Communism, or for ending the 40 years of wars and nuclear threats from the Soviets.

No sooner was the ink dry on this "deal" that the North Koreans renewed work on their atomic bombs. IAEA Director Hans Blix reported that their inspections were being closed down, and the N. Koreans were acting very suspicious. He believed they already had enough plutonium for at least one atomic bomb. A showdown became a major issue by the fall of 1994, but as would become his normal pattern, Clinton refused to act preferring to appease the hard core ruler. (The media downplayed the issue to protect him and the upcoming election.)

Japan was asked to assist the U.S. forces if war became a serious possibility, but once again the Japanese decided they did not want to. *They had been forced to buy their way out of the Gulf War, and wanted to do the same now.*

This time their intransience was not accepted by our military. Had a war started it was possible our alliance would have ended. Even though they had just suffered a severe recession, and their post WWII constitution prevented them from "initiating military action", they could "legally fight for their defense". They needed to increase their defense budgets and help us police the world's trouble spots, especially the one in their backyard.

(That same issue is true for NATO. In 1961 JFK argued with the Europeans to step up their defense budgets to help shoulder the burden, and Nixon and Reagan did the same. In 2018 Pres Trump also warned them that the free ride was over.)

In a National Intelligence Estimate (NIE) completed in early 1995 the CIA warned North Korea was not complying with any parts of the "Framework". *(140) Clinton did nothing.

But the inanity of this administration continued.

During 1994 Secretary of Energy Hazel O'Leary "decided to open up" U.S. nuclear laboratories to all "foreign students".

Her actions were in keeping with Clinton's ineffective and dangerous foreign and domestic security policies. **Our nuclear labs were now allowing potential enemy agents and terrorists into the buildings. Security concerns were ended by her, and all background checks and assessments were stopped!** (Who gave her permission to do this?)

According to those "new Democrats", the Cold War was over and all of the world's people were our now our friends. Hundreds of "Middle Eastern students" were allowed to work and learn at our most sensitive installations!

O'Leary also declassified tons of our most secret nuclear files claiming an "openness initiative"! She even cut the security force at the Rocky Flats nuclear complex by 40%. Edward McCallum the head of security butted heads with the ignorant O'Leary on many occasions, but was repeatedly ignored. The private security contractor made a lot of profit during her tenure, and O'Leary ended up on their board of directors making a nice salary when she "left the government". More to follow.

To cut "costs", Bill Clinton decided to close our nuclear research facility at Argonne in Idaho. For the past four decades that facility was were we tested all types of nuclear science, especially nuclear reactors. After the Three Mile Island and Chernobyl disasters nuclear energy was no longer a wanted or trusted energy source. **But as shown before in April 1986 a revolutionary reactor had been put on line at Argonne.** It used liquid metals as the coolant, and upon any leak the reactor automatically shut itself down. Those liquid metals had a much higher boiling point, 1600 degrees, than water, 212 degrees, and would not overheat as water cooled reactors did. That remarkable new system had been running and tested repeatedly without incident since 1986.

This was the safe, non-polluting energy source the world needed to eliminate fossil fuels. **But Clinton had all of it shut down anyway.**

In the mid-term elections of November 1994 the Republicans made history by winning a majority of seats in the House and Senate. *Not since the 1946 election had the Republicans had full control of the Congress.* This stunning reversal was fallout from the many Clinton scandals and the administration's general incompetence. Political commentators tried to put a smile on the election by stating it was not what the Republicans offered as the failures of Clinton and the Democrats that led to their defeat.

Led by Newt Gingrich the party promised a balanced budget and welfare reform in their "Contract with America". Clinton had run on a platform of welfare reform, but he repeatedly refused to do it. (Not until 1996 did the Republicans force his hand.)

In NYC Deputy Mayor John Dyson stated that it was important to put all Welfare recipients to work. *The NYC plan was modeled on the successful one Gov. Thompson in Wisconsin used called Workfare.* Instead of just giving the poor money, getting those people job experience and tutoring might well get them on the road to success. Dyson spoke of the city plan as increasing our current workforce from 210,000 workers to 1,300,000 workers. Imagine what we could accomplish with that large pool of manpower. He referred to the current Welfare plan as "goofy", paying the poor not to work, and getting poor young women to make illegitimate babies to get extra money. That last policy basically condemned both mother and child to a life of poverty.

Single mothers fall into three main categories; Widows- 6.5%, Divorced- 37.8%, and Single girls/women having children- 41.3%. More than half of those single mothers live below the poverty line, which means their children do too. *By 1996 70% of young people in juvenile detention centers were from single mother homes. Even the liberal bastion the Village Voice quoted those brutal statistics in their articles on poverty.*

In the three decades since LBJ and the Democrats passed their Welfare programs, they have cost the taxpayers **$5.4 Trillion dollars.** They also destroyed the lives of millions as llegitimate births shot up **over 500%,** divorce went up **250%,** violent crime exploded **by 600%,** and fatherless families went from 17% to 90% in the major cities. Those problems struck the minorities and the poorest citizens the hardest. Not since Prohibition has a federal program done such damage to our nation.

More Islamic Terrorists

Ali Mohamed had returned to the U.S. and was again grilled over his movements in East Africa. Once more he cleared of any wrong doing, and sent to NYC to observe the trials for the Day of Terror bombers. Rahman and his cohorts were defended by liberal activist Ramsey Clark (Vietnam War traitor.) Again all were convicted of conspiracy and attempted murder.

While in NYC Ali received a list of potential suspects, (almost one hundred), whose names had come up during the investigations.

Bin Laden was again on that list, yet Ali claimed that none of the names were noteworthy.   **Incident # 30**

Steve Emerson's investigative work the past two years resulted in a PBS television special called "***Jihad in America***", and was broadcast on November 21, 1994. One of the most notable statements came from one Mohammed al-Asi of the Islamic Education Center in Potomac, Maryland. He answered a question from Emerson; *"I don't think there is a war here, a war front here in the United States at this point. I think if the whole scenario continues the way it has inevitably the United States is going to be reaching a war front. But not right now".* *(141)

Islamic groups complained and protested before the show even aired. Even though the documentary stated multiple times that the militant Islamists were a small portion of the population, the protests continued in an effort to shut down the show. Emerson was labeled a crusader and a racist. The show and his articles won awards for his informative and detailed work traveling to the Middle East and speaking to so many subjects.   **Incident # 31** The Administration was again silent.

(All of our enemies, Nazi's, Communists and Liberals have used this same tactic. They libel and slander any opponent in an effort to discredit them and stop their message. Just look at how the leftists at Berkley University acted in 2017 to shut down Ann Coulter's talk. And since Donald Trump won the presidency this illegal activity is happening all over our country.)

During the investigation of the World Trade Center bombing Ramzi Yousef's fingerprints had been found at the Islamists bomb factory in New Jersey. His capture a top priority, and Richard Clarke was assigned the task. Clarke had been a lower level staffer on the NSC whose work under Pres. Reagan had confirmed how to defeat the Soviets. But with this promotion he was actually being used as a feint for Clinton. If this effort failed no one would know about it. If it succeeded the president got the credit.

As before, neither the CIA nor the CTC was allowed in the loop to find this terrorist. The bombing of the WTC was still listed as a civilian crime!

After his unsuccessful bombing at the WTC, Ramzi Yousef hid out for a while in Pakistan. He decided that Benazir Bhutto, who was again running for Pakistan's Prime Minister, should be killed. Yousef and his friend **Abdul Hakim Murad** tried two abortive attempts against Bhutto, but failed. Yousef then became involved in the previously discussed plot against the Israeli embassy in Bangkok. That too failed. But he did not give up on terrorism.

He worked on making a homemade liquid explosive from simple chemicals. And even with the million dollar bounty on his head Ramzi eluded American intelligence for over a year. He returned to Manila, the capitol of the Philippines on the direction of bin Laden, to assist the growing Islamic terrorist group which Yousef had helped setup two years earlier.

Back then he had been recruited by the previously mentioned **Mohammed Jamal Khalifa**, *(the terrorist who was arrested and acquitted in Jordan.)* Along with his uncle **Khalid Sheik Mohammed,** they had trained the Islamic terrorists on the Philippine island of Jolo. This new terrorist group would be called **Abu Sayef**, in memory of one of the main Islamists killed in the Afghan war.

As was their policy, those terrorists were partially funded by a phony Islamic charity that was being run by Khalifa. They also specialized in kidnapping civilians and demanding large ransoms. (Except for any U.S. missionaries who were caught. Those were beheaded.)

Abu Sayef was run by a **Abdul Rajak Janjalani** who had fought the Russians and spent years in Peshawar raising funds for his own empire. He was close to Jamal Khalifa, and had been traveling to the Philippines since the mid-80s getting things organized. His front was as an officer for the IIRO, "International Islamic Relief Organization." Those NGO's "Non-Governmental Organizations", provided cover jobs and papers for all of the terrorists that entered, and allowed them safe means to move money, supplies and equipment.

During the summer of 1994 Ramzi Yousef also spent time in Malaysia on the island of Basilan giving sophisticated explosive training to the Abu Sayef members encamped there. Bin Laden was certain this Islamic guerilla army could succeed, and **Wali Kahn Amin Shah** who was another close associate of bin Laden joined the effort to get Abu Sayef up and running.

Yousef's intense hatred for America had motivated him to work on his next large scale attacks. Bill Clinton was scheduled to visit the Philippines on November 12, 1994 and they hoped to have a nice phosgene gas surprise for him. Unfortunately the tight security that protected the president prevented them from getting close enough to try and the plan was scraped.

Yousef had created his home-made liquid nitro-glycerin, while he was hiding out in Pakistan. His efforts landed him in the hospital twice for suffering strange burns to his hands, but he was not investigated. **His idea was to bring his home-made liquid explosives onto jet airliners.** If they could mix the secreted components together while flying, they could blow up passenger jets. *(As highlighted earlier, this feat had been done before in 1987, see page 243.)*

To try out his creation he and fellow terrorist Wali Khan mixed and placed a small amount of the nitro-glycerin under a seat in the Greenbelt Theatre in Manila. Shah set a wristwatch timer and they quietly left. Their bomb detonated as planned wounding eleven. Yousef was pleased his creation worked, but this attack alerted the Filipino's that dangerous terrorists were operating in their country. **Incident # 32**

On December 11, 1994 **Philippines Airlines Flight 434** from Cebu to Tokyo was severely damaged by his liquid bomb. Yousef had boarded the plane with the components separated as **toiletries in a carry-on bag**. Once on board he sat through half of the first leg of the flight, then went to the bathroom to mix the components. He mated the bomb to the batteries and wires he had hidden in his hollowed out shoe. A cascio watch was used as the timer. When he returned from the bathroom he changed seats claiming that something bothered him at the other one. He set the timer, placed the bomb under his new seat and exited the plane at their first scheduled stop.

Flight 434 made a normal stop to pickup passengers, and no one noticed Yousef's bag under the now empty seat. The aircraft took off and a short while later his liquid bomb exploded with one man killed and ten wounded. After forty harrowing minutes the pilots landed the severely damaged plane on Okinawa.

When Yousef changed seats he thought his new position was over the main fuel tank. He was off by two rows. Because of that small error the plane did not blowup and disintegrate as he expected.

Forensics people were able to examine the blast area, debris, evidence and the casualties. From the damage to the deceased they were able to ascertain that the bomb had been under his seat. Forensics also uncovered the remains of the timer and residue of the home made explosive. It was the same as the theater. This was not a quick, random attack. This was a dedicated and well thought out plot. Filipino authorities went on high alert.   **Incident # 33**

Knowing that his formula could be brought past security checkpoints as simple "water bottles and toiletries", and that it was easily mixed while onboard, Yousef planned his big attack. Khalid Sheikh Mohammed, (KSM) took over the operation, and during the rest of 1994 he chose and supervised the terrorists for the coming assault.

They had already brought in Wali Khan Shah, an Afghan who had trained in the al Qaeda camps and was another trusted member. Shah had previously opened a front business in Malaya to fund their terrorist activities. Two other terrorists were brought in for security and as assistants, and Muslim women were used to open bank accounts and launder the money.

KSM had twice brought a U.S trained Kuwaiti airline pilot and friend of Yousef named **Hakim Murad** to Pakistan. There they spoke about pilot training and aircraft operations. More plans were discussed, and KSM saw a huge opportunity.

But this al Qaeda cell was going to place Yousef's liquid nitroglycerin bombs on eleven U.S. bound flights flying over the Pacific Ocean in a 24 hour period. Cell members would mix the explosives onboard and set the timers to detonate while over the sea. Their bombs would be hidden inside the life jacket pouch.

Then the terrorists would exit the aircraft at the last possible stop. If everything went as planned all of the targeted planes would blowup, breakup and sink into the vast Pacific. **In that way no evidence would be found and they would be able to continue the carnage for months!** In addition to the financial costs of the lost aircraft, those terrorists expected air travel to be suspended worldwide causing great damage to the world's economy. (This is what the attack on Pan Am Flight 103 was supposed to do, but it exploded over Scotland and the FBI unraveled the plot.)

This cell would also assassinate the Pope during his upcoming papal visit. One of their first ideas on that part of the plot called for Murad to crash a small plane into the Pope's vehicle. However that idea was ended when they learned all aircraft would be banned from the city. Their next thought was to use a simple suicide bomber, that they could easily do. This was a well planned, extensive plot and it had a good chance of success.

It was codenamed Bojinka. (Serbian-Croatian for loud bang.)

On December 24, 1994 **Air France Flight 8969** was hijacked by four Algerians who murdered three of the passengers.

Their plan was to fly the aircraft over Paris and either crash or blowup the jetliner into the Eiffel Tower to kill as

many innocents as possible. Incredible fortune intervened as Commandos stormed the aircraft and killed the terrorists while it was refueling in Marseille. **Incident # 34**

Investigations revealed these men had trained in Afghanistan and were members of al Qaeda! Once again since the attack had failed the significance of this effort did not make an impact on anyone, especially Clinton and his Administration.

What everyone needed to ask was what if it succeeded?? How did they hijack this aircraft? What needs to be done to prevent this from ever happening again?

Back in Manila Ramzi Yousef rented unit 603 in a building just down the street from the Papal Embassy. Locals grew suspicious of the secretive residents and the constant chemical smells emanating from their apartment. But no one called the police. Each terrorist was ticketed for which flight they were to plant a bomb, and everything was ready to suicide bomb the Pope on January 11.

January 6, 1995 was the last day of preparing the various chemicals, *when the terrorists had a fire in their apartment.* Because of the toxic smoke they were forced out of the unit leaving all of their notes and personal effects behind. Authorities responded to the fire, and Yousef sent Murad back to try to get his laptop and papers. An alert police officer spotted some of the cell, and Wali Khan Shah and Hakim Murad were arrested. Murad called Yousef to warn him their effort was ended and to get out. Yousef eventually escaped back to Pakistan with his uncle KSM, and Wali Shah who had wrongly been released.

Murad tried to spin various stories protesting his innocence, even trying bribery. But what the Manila police found in the apartment was overwhelming evidence of a large pending terrorist attack. Included in the evidence cache were Manila street maps, explosives, hazardous and toxic chemicals, pipe bombs, textbooks, documents, false passports, papal clothing and accessories. Evidence taken away from the apartment filled three police vans.

Forensic testing matched the chemical signature of their home-made explosive to the bomb used at the Greenbelt Theatre and to the explosion on Flight 434.

The Filipinos knew they had just made a huge arrest.

It took days for the Filipinos to catalog everything from the apartment, and they found Yousef's laptop. Philippine police computer expert Rafael Garcia cracked the extensive coded files and they were fully analyzed by *January 8, 1995.* His laptop had contained four discs of information outlining the entire **Bojinka**

Plot, their future plans, and the planned escape routes of the terrorists into Pakistan and Qatar.

On the discs were the targeted flight schedules and tickets, detonation times for the bombs, names of associates, contact lists, phone numbers, records of their dealings with a London trading Corp., a meat market in Malaysia, **the Islamic center in Tucson, Arizona,** an Abu Dhabi bank and statements on what they were going to accomplish.

One document they uncovered revealed that *the International Relations and Information Center,* an NGO in the Philippines, was actually a front company for *al Qaeda.* Its leader was the well known, **Mohammed Jamal Khalifa.**

Also found within the computer files were long term plans to use chemical weapons and poisons against the people of the Philippines, the plan to kill the Pope, the abandoned plot to kill Clinton, and another scheme to kill the Pres. of the Philippines Fidel Ramos. Incidents # (35-39)

Authorities discovered how far along the terrorists were in their upcoming attack on the Pope. His vehicle was scheduled to drive right past this building, and a papal cassock and bomb vest were found ready for use. One of those terrorists was supposed to impersonate a catholic cleric and get close enough to the procession to suicide bomb the Pope and kill as many Christian leaders as possible.

Hours after this scheme was revealed, Anti-Terrorism "Czar" Richard Clarke was in his White House office. He learned of this plot from the Philippine Authorities, **and Clarke ordered the U.S. Airlines to ground their Pacific based planes until all of the bombs could be located.** He was told that bureaucratically only the Sec. of Transportation could do that. After much legal debate it was decided that since his office represented the President he could thus order the grounding of the aircraft.

<u>His order</u> was again sent out grounding those aircraft not airborne and causing the ones already airborne to turn back. Nothing was found on any of the Pacific bound 747s because the attacks were scheduled for the next day.

A directive was given that from that date no perfumes or toiletries could be carried on board! (It would be years before the same precautions were administered here. *WHY?)*

An FBI team arrived in Manila the next day but found themselves at odds with the CIA team on site. Both agencies wanted Yousef, though the CIA was ineffective in helping find him. For the FBI this case needed to be investigated as a crime scene with concerns over evidence, witnesses and their testimony. CIA wanted no part of any court case or testifying, they just wanted to learn what was going on.

Since Yousef had already been indicted in NYC for the WTC attack the FBI had legal jurisdiction and took the lead. Because of the 1970s Democratic rules and Bill Clinton insisting these were civilian cases, not until 1996 did the two agencies start working together. The FBI was allowed to see some of the CIA terrorist database, but were stunned at how unprepared and ineffective the CIA was. Their NYC- JTTF team knew more than the CIA.

(Again this was fallout from the 1970s as hundreds of agents were fired and few young people would take the job. Attrition also set in as the rest of the old hands retired over the politicalization Clinton had done to the CIA. And the people hired since the late 1970s were always worried over their careers and running afoul of some Congressional panel.)

Murad was taken to a special facility in Manila and "interrogated" for days. His questioning was harsh (deservedly), and he revealed all as he talked about their work, their many successes to date and that they were glad to target America.

He plainly stated to the Philippine investigators that they often spoke of hijacking airliners to use as flying missiles to attack American targets like the CIA, the World Trade Center, the Pentagon or the White House!

Murad explained that he had first discussed this airliner hijacking plan with Yousef in Quetta, Pakistan in October 1994. **Their ideas also included crashing a plane into a U.S. Nuclear Power Station to unleash a nuclear catastrophe.** Another potential plot had him flying an explosive laden commercial plane into the CIA headquarters in Langley Virginia. Murad had trained at flight schools in New York, Texas, California and North Carolina. He was extradited back to U.S. on April 12, 1995, and his testimony would be used to convict Yousef. **Incident # 40**

Philippine investigators wrote up a special report on their airliner attack plan. There was no question about Murad's authenticity or his determination to execute this suicidal air attack. At that time there was no idea on how to sneak a large bomb or explosive aboard, so the large airliner was to be the actual weapon.

With Murad in custody agents continued the Bojinka investigations. On January 11 Philippine Police found Wali Khan. He had bribed his way out of custody that first day but was tracked down and rearrested in Malaysia. Khan was also extradited back to the U.S. He had in his possession four passports from four different countries. A clear warning on their sophistication and capabilities. Yousef however had made it back to Pakistan.

All of the Bojinka computer files had been deciphered and distributed. When the FBI counter-terrorist team returned from the Philippines they personally briefed the NSC which included Richard Clarke.

On January 23, 1995 Clinton signed executive order 12947 imposing sanctions on twelve terrorist groups. (How scary.) Clinton and his top officials claimed that no one in the Administration knew of Murad's interrogations, those potential terrorist plots or their implications. But this intelligence bonanza was obviously passed on. No actions (except those "sanctions"), were taken by Clinton or any of the principals to prevent the hijacking attacks Murad spoke of. **Incident # 41**

Though Yousef was safely hiding out, he had no close associates left to help him. His last contact was one **Istiaque Parker,** who had previously backed out from Yousef's plan to bomb two flights going from Bangkok to London. They met up at bin Laden's hotel in Islamabad, the *Pearl Guest House.* There Yousef described his plan to kidnap and ransom the Philippine ambassador to use as a trade for Hakim Murad.

Parker again became afraid and contacted the U.S. Embassy on February 3, 1995. FBI agents insisted Parker knock on Yousef's room door to insure he was in. He would then leave and the Pakistanis and FBI would enter and arrest him.

Ramzi Yousef was captured in Islamabad on February 7, 1995.

Khalid Sheik Mohammed was sleeping in the next room, but was missed because no knew he was there. KSM hid out for a while and then fled to the Sudan. He was still wanted for questioning over the WTC bombing, and he had given money to the legal defense of Salameh in NYC over that bombing. Now with the **Bojinka Plot** exposed, KSM was on everyone's radar.

A week after Yousef's arrest two U.S. Embassy personnel were murdered in Islamabad in retaliation. (Clinton did nothing.) While flying in a helicopter over NYC an agent told the handcuffed Yousef to look over and see that the WTC towers were still there. Yousef confidently told them not for long. When asked by FBI agents why they were after us instead of Israel, Yousef replied that they were difficult to attack. "When you cannot strike your enemy, you strike their friends."

Around this time the CIA finally conducted an actual briefing at the White House. They described bin Laden's operations in Khartoum, Sudan as the "Ford Foundation of Sunni Islamic Terrorism". *(142)

Numerous nationalities were being trained there, as well as planning for future terrorist operations. Osama bin Laden readily financed all of the terrorist activities. They also reported that CIA agents in the area had been threatened and followed, and a plot to ambush the embassy had recently been broken up. Numerous hardcore terrorists lived among bin Laden's followers, and all of them wanted to attack America.   **Incident # 42**

After the **Bojinka Plot** was unraveled and the information was discussed in the White House, the only thing Clarke was able to convince Clinton to do was to stop the fundraising by front groups that were operating in the U.S. *One of those groups was the Holy Land Foundation in Texas.* Agents were planning to enter and seize their records when FBI Director Freeh and Treasury Sec Rubin objected. According to Clarke, Freeh did not want to alienate the Arabs, while Rubin felt the issue would be challenged in court. Even some Republican lawmakers objected to the infringement on "banking secrecy".   **Incident # 43**

Other advisors in the White House sphere also tried to make changes to our anti-terror protocols. Political guru Dick Morris met with Clinton and some staff on March 16, 1995 to push for changes to getting drivers licenses for immigrants. **Morris's idea was to make the expiration date on the immigrant's license the same as the one on their visa.** In that way all of the individual's legal paperwork would match.

It was well known that half of the illegal aliens in our country deliberately overstayed their visas. INS was poorly managed and could not handle the vast number of cases (150,000 per year) that popped up. But if they had a referral come in from a State DMV office alerting them of an expired visa, the INS would be reminded and have an address to go to and pick up the person. In addition to that help if local police made a traffic stop they could see the person was an immigrant who had an expired visa -license. They could then hold onto the individual until INS arrived.

Led by liberal press secretary George Stephanopoulos, Clinton refused to the enact the idea for fear of hurting any

voting blocs. Morris pushed the idea again on April 5 and was again shot down. For those leftist Democrats and liberals, Morris's idea was a "terrible scam using big brother" to police the immigrants instead of just having the overworked and understaffed U.S. Border Patrol and INS try to keep up.

Other politicos who were against the idea complained that the INS courts were so backlogged they can't process the ones they already have. *Having more suspects in the system would just be a major scandal affecting the voters!* **Incident # 44**

(For Morris those incidents still haunt him. **Three of the 9/11 hijackers were picked up on traffic stops before the September attacks.** Mohammed Atta was stopped in Miami during January 2001, Nawaf Alhazmi in Oklahoma City in May 2001 and Ziad Jarrah on interstate 95 on September 9, 2001. *Atta and Jarrah were two of the terrorist pilots, Flight 11 and Flight 93 respectively.*)

During March 1995 French Counterterrorism judge Jean-Louis Brugui`ere personally provided to the U.S. a report detailing bin Laden's nest of terrorists operating out of Afghanistan and his support network from inside Pakistan. In the report were names, descriptions of foreign cells, rosters, photos of safehouses, recruitment officers, welcome centers in Islamabad and Peshawar, and cell offices in N. America, Europe and Asia. As would become commonplace, the Clinton White House showed no interest. **That report is "still classified".** (142A) **Incident# 45**

On March 20th 1995 a Japanese terrorist group unleashed deadly Sarin Gas inside the crowded Tokyo subway. Ten were killed and over a thousand were injured. The group had five members dropping gas canisters in the subway cars while five others served as lookouts. This attack was a clear warning to the civilized world that these maniacal criminals were determined to wreak havoc. **Incident # 46**

After receiving the intelligence on this attack Clarke and those in his sphere were dismayed to learn how unprotected America was. When the U.S. had signed the 1973 treaty banning bio-weapons we had destroyed all of ours. Our vaccination programs to stop enemy bio-weapons had also fallen away to nothing because Russia was supposed to have eliminated their programs.

In the buildup for the first Gulf War we had virtually no stocks of vaccines in event of a bio-attack by Iraq. As shown earlier after the Soviet Union collapsed we learned they still had a large, active bio-weapon program! We had no answer to those threats then or now.

Clarke then learned that our Army had no chemical-biological detection vehicles either. America was an easy and unprepared target for these non-nuclear WMDs. He also learned that all of our old Civil Defense plans and supplies stockpiled due to the Cold War had been allowed to fade away to impotency or been tossed out. *Even the U.S. Government's emergency bunker in the Appalachian mountains had been closed down by the Clinton Administration because the "Cold War was over".*

Historical Note: Since 1973 the Soviets had greatly expanded their bio-weapons programs producing ghastly weapons using the Ebola and Marburg viruses. Russian scientists and technicians also perfected shells, bombs and other munitions to carry, Anthrax, Botulism, Smallpox and the Black Death. In the years following that treaty, cordial Soviet leaders were negotiating multiple civilian treaties with the U.S. on trade, farm supplies and technology. *And all the while they were keeping this heinous and illegal secret to themselves, ready to exterminate us at a moments notice.*

That March Belgian investigators arrested some Algerian terrorist suspects and uncovered a terrorist training manual on how to make a detonator using a wristwatch as the timer. (The Bojinka Plot timers.) Their manual was dedicated to bin Laden and their cause. **Incident # 47**

In April 1995 Filipino guerillas swearing loyalty to Rasul Sayyaf sacked the Mindanao island town of Ipil. Those Islamic terrorists murdered sixty three, wounded dozens more, took over fifty hostages and robbed four banks. **Incident # 48** (This was their first major attack.)

On June 26, 1995 a group of EIJ (Egyptian Islamic Jihad) terrorists using Sudanese passports attempted to assassinate Egyptian President Hosni Mubarak in Ethiopia. **Incident # 49**

In August **Eyyad Ismoil** the last bomber from the World Trade Center bombing was finally located and arrested in Jordan. Both Yousef and Eyyad were tried and convicted in criminal court. But as shown earlier in keeping with Clinton's foolish claim that this was just a criminal case the defendant's lawyers were given the World Trade Center blueprints, architectural drawings, schematics and all of the engineering studies that were used to build the Towers. Both were convicted and imprisoned for life.

More Clinton Politics

In early 1995 McDonnell Douglas Corp was reporting that some of the previously mentioned advanced machine tools they had sold to China had been diverted to Chinese military plants that made missiles and military aircraft. This was a clear violation of the sales agreement. *However Clinton's Commerce Department waited six months before they began investigating.*

In addition to that security breech a lot of research and work by Motorola Corp was paired with China's Great Wall Industry Corporation. The benign sounding company wanted help with eleven launches of their Iridium satellites for communications. As part of the agreement, a *smart dispenser* was developed to launch several satellites from a single launch!

That same technology was a vital component of the MIRV for nuclear weapons, and never should have been allowed near Communist China! Numerous mid-level Commerce Dept. staff wanted to suspend their licensing and export privileges. *But Commerce Dept. principals stopped any and all penalties even though this had vastly improved their weapons capabilities.* For this administration cash was king, even if what they were doing was illegal and dangerous to our security.

By the end of 1995 nothing had been done to stop the terrorists or their money laundering system, though a few more sanctions were emplaced upon Iran. FBI's Neil Herman was looking over the evidence collected from the Kahane murder, the bombing of the WTC, the Day of Terror Plot and the Bojinka Plot.

With the complete file from Yousef's laptop, he too realized that all of it was part of an international conspiracy. Yousef was able to fly around the world staying in safe houses and enjoying a support network that kept him supplied and functioning. We needed to start preparing, however Bill Clinton had such disdain for the U.S. Military and Intelligence organizations that he still had never met with the head of the CIA!

As stated before James Woolsey was picked for the CIA Director by Bill Clinton. *But he was never able to see him in person which is the normal, logical system.* For months Woolsey went to the White House to give the normal morning briefing, but was kept waiting in an outer room to no avail. Treated like a pariah, Woolsey stopped going. Low level CIA officers would be sent to the White House each day with a sealed intelligence briefing. A junior White House staffer would take it and bring it into the oval office. After a while the staffer would return the file to the CIA officers and see them out.

No one was ever able to see or discuss those briefings with Clinton directly! Clinton was able to evade having to act on anything, but more importantly, this provided Clinton with a "legal excuse / alibi" that he did not know about this or that, because he had not been briefed!

Clinton had a White House team formed under his "counter-terrorism czar" Richard Clarke. In that way the scheming lawyer could keep his hands clean from any actions or problems, and tie up any issues within a bureaucracy that he controlled.

In March 1995 the NSA picked up a communication from Iran that claimed the CIA was about to assassinate Saddam Hussein. Tony Lake the National Security Advisor was furious and ran to see Clinton. Instead of calling Director Woolsey to find out what was going on first hand, lawyer Clinton directed Lake to call in the FBI and begin a criminal investigation.

Not until April 1996 was the "case closed", the agency cleared and the incident found to be a ruse by the Iranians! (Probably a revenge move for the previously stated additional sanctions placed upon them.) But that nonsense tied up the intelligence principals for a year, and Clinton then used this ruse as a way to fire Woolsey.

With the continuing cutbacks to the CIA budget, declining morale within the agency, and a solid economy, that further eroded the CIA's ability to keep tabs on the world. The continued scarcity of terrorist- language translators was extreme as *less than 10% of the intelligence being picked up electronically was being deciphered.* During the Cold War there was a furious rush to get translators, and most of the intelligence could be processed in a timely fashion. But in this new war, one that Clinton and the Congress paid no heed, we were starting off deaf, dumb and blind.

Woolsey had recognized that problem early on and wanted new funding for hiring translators. But Clinton and Democratic Senator DeConcini repeatedly ignored his requests. Both Democrats had been slighted unintentionally by Woolsey a year earlier, so they refused any of his efforts to strengthen our national security. (They sure showed him.)   **Incident # 50**

And the Aldrich Ames CIA spying scandal did not help things. Ames had started in the CIA in 1962 and worked at many locations in various titles. In 1981 he recruited a Columbian woman named Maria, and in 1985 they married. (A major warning sign.) Soon after he began selling classified information to the Soviets. Within a year ten CIA agents spying in Russia were caught. (That type of success is impossible without the help of a mole inside the U.S.)

*Ames's information was deemed so critical the Soviets sent a fake defector to the U.S. in 1985, a*s shown earlier. Even after the Soviet Union broke up Ames was still selling our information. (The infuriating thing about the whole issue was that Ames was a heavy drinker who was obviously living beyond his means. Yet the CIA did not discover his treason until 1994. By then he had revealed all of our secret sources inside Russia and was responsible for the death of many agents.)

Soon after that episode came out NJ Democratic Senator Torricelli triggered more Congressional hearings that forced the CIA to end their program of using "shady informants and spies". Organized Crime was ended because of the ability to use a bad guy to catch bigger bad ones. Why was this such an issue for the Democrats versus the CIA?

As a result of their stupidity another round of retirements occurred, and the anti-terror Operations Unit became paralyzed. Case officers did not want to even try to find informants because there were to many hurdles that had to be jumped. Our intelligence gathering dropped. *(After Clinton and his liberals took office they expanded on their inane anti-CIA policies.* The CIA's Rome Station posted a sign, "Big Ops Big Problems, Small Ops Small Problems, No Ops No Problems".)   (143A)

An example of this bureaucratic quicksand involved former agent Robert Baer. In 1992 he was posted to Tajikistan which was between Russia and Afghanistan. Once Clinton took office in 1993 every proposal he submitted for intelligence operations was shot down by the new Clinton era CIA-lawyers / bureacrats. All the while they tried to push a sexual harassment team on his unit. (They were in the middle of nowhere.)

Baer would state that every agent was told if one of your informants does something illegal you are to blame. As a result of those restrictions no one in the field did anything. In one of his operations Baer was coordinating with anti-Iraqi forces when he was accused of plotting to kill Saddam Hussein. (The case stated above.) He and the CIA were both cleared, but he had had enough of the brainless Clinton administration politics and retired in 1997.

Oklahoma City Bombing

As shown before in February 1993 there was a series of mindless confrontations between Federal authorities and a religious group known as the Branch Davidians. Federal officers had numerous opportunities to arrest the leader David Koresh when he was outside the compound. Instead they tried to storm the Waco, Texas center to search for weapons. Four ATF officers and six Davidians wee killed in a gun battle. A siege was enacted and on April 19, 1993 Federal agents stormed the compound using armored vehicles. During the gunfire and a follow on fast moving blaze, 86 residents were killed including many children.

In senseless retaliation for that 1993 Waco fiasco, the Murrah Federal Building in Oklahoma City was blown up with a truck bomb on April 19, 1995.

The Murrah Building held numerous federal offices, and murdered in that brutal attack were 168 workers and 19 children present at a day care. Over 500 others were wounded. Initially the attack seemed the patented work of Islamic terrorists as the truck bomb was similar to the ones they use.

(Oklahoma City was also the place were Steve Emerson had seen Islamic terrorists at a convention there two years earlier.)

An intensive investigation began and the first bomber was officially caught two days later on the 21st. A Timothy McVeigh had been arrested ninety minutes after the bombing while driving a car with no license plates. While he was held in a local lockup, a piece of the bomb truck was recovered and yielded a serial number. The bomb truck was identified, traced back to the rental shop, and there was McVeigh on video taking the keys.

McVeigh was a former soldier, one of Gen. Schwarzkopf's bodyguards in the Gulf War. He told his lawyers that he had been at Waco during the fatal siege and observed federal agents firing incendiary rounds into the buildings. He claimed that was what started those fires, and this bombing was payback for a corrupt and murderous government.

McVeigh's partner and former Army buddy Terry Nichols was also picked up as were two others. Those suspects also claimed that this bombing was in reprisal for the unprovoked Federal attack and mass murder at Waco which was covered up by the Clinton Administration.

Unlike the previous bombings from known Islamic terrorists, Clinton and his Administration quickly labeled this attack as a terror bombing! They also claimed it was the work of "white supremacists" and the FBI was told to follow that scenario. Unlike his pathetic reactions to the murderous bombing at the World Trade Center, the Day of Terror plot or the other attacks, Clinton demanded the death penalty.

However all may not have been as it appeared in Oklahoma.

There was an unknown dark-skinned male with McVeigh at the truck office, and that man was Arabic looking. That vital issue was not reported to the public.

At that rental trucking company the workers who were interviewed all stated that the renter of the truck was definitely McVeigh. But the unidentified man who was with him was Arabic looking. There was no reason for them to lie, but no mention of that suspect was ever made. The Administration pursued the white supremacist angle only, and no further investigations were made on the Arab suspect (s). But there was more.

Multiple eye witnesses stated that two Middle Eastern looking men were the ones who had actually parked the truck in front of the building and then quickly exited.

Many stated that the pair escaped in a pickup truck at high speed. One woman insisted that she observed an olive skinned male with short dark hair exit the passenger side of the truck and go to the rear cargo area. He appeared to do something, and the explosion occurred soon after.

She was so certain of her sighting an FBI sketch was made of the suspect, though with the blast so large he never could have escaped on foot.

At the site a total of eight separated left legs had been found. Seven were analyzed and returned to the victims of the blast. But the eighth leg was "unidentified" as no unclaimed victims existed. **No DNA analysis was ever done on the leg to determine nationality.** That important piece of forensic evidence was ignored and obscured.

Investigators learned that McVeigh's accomplice Terry Nichols had gone to the Philippines numerous times in the months before the attack. While he was roaming around, Philippine intelligence saw him meet with members of **Abu Sayyaf,** the Islamic terrorist organization organized by bin Laden.

According to the Filipino's, the people Nichols met with were bomb makers! Yet even after hearing those reports FBI superiors stopped looking at the potential Islamic terrorist ties on the second day. Agents were told to concentrate on the "White supremacy" angle only. (New laws were quickly passed targeting "white supremacist/survivor groups". People the Democrats hate.)

During the trial McVeigh's lawyer Stephen Jones argued that it was impossible for his clients to have constructed such a large and complex explosive with no prior experience.

Another inconvenient fact that was never examined at the trial was that, **No Forensic Bomb Residue was ever found on McVeigh, his skin, knife, clothing, car or inside his residence. His fingerprints were not found on any surface either!**

And to make this trumped up tale even worse, after the trial and verdict, McVeigh's defense lawyers learned that our Government had kept hidden an additional 100 boxes of evidence from the defense and the public!

What was in those boxes that no one was allowed to see??

A short while after that attack the Philippine Government began a new and harsh crackdown on Abu Sayef. One of those captured confessed under their "harsh measures", that an American had met with their people the year before. That Islamic suspect also discussed in depth the recently disrupted but still classified **Bojinka Plot**. With the security procedures that al-Qaeda used he could only have known about Bojinka if he had been a part of that cell. And he could only have known about Nichols if he had been near him when he was trained!

(What became of those interviews??)

In his book *Against All Enemies,* former anti-terror czar Richard Clarke brings up even more issues.

It was a known fact that both Khalid Sheik Muhammad and Ramzi Yousef had operated in Cebu setting up their al Qaeda spinoff Abu Sayef. **Nichols was in Cebu at the same time.** Yousef was the bomb maker from the 1993 WTC attack, and the main terrorist in the Bojinka Plot. Those facts screamed for a profound investigation. **But it was not done.**

Investigating into Nichols past uncovered that all of his prior attempts at bomb making had failed. **But after his trip to the Philippines it worked.** Nichol's wife had stayed on in the Philippines after he returned to the U.S. Even after her return to the U.S., Nichols still made frequent phone calls to Cebu. Who was he talking too?? **Incident # 51**

The final "coincidence", was that several al Qaeda terrorists had attended the Islamic conference that had been held in

Oklahoma City two years earlier. That was the same conference Steve Emerson had accidently been at. Had McVeigh or Nichols been in contact with those terrorists then? As shown before, because of the 1970s Democrat mandated restrictions on the FBI, no surveillance was ever conducted there. Since no one was ever photoed or video-taped, no one would ever know what was going on at that or other Islamic conferences.

Despite all of these serious questions, no further investigations were made by the FBI, CIA, NSA or the Administration. For them it was the same failed mindset as the NYPD used at the Son of Sam serial killings, the Kahane murder, and Clinton used at the 1993 WTC Bombing; No conspiracy, Case Closed.

As a result of the Oklahoma City attack all Federal buildings were directed to place barriers to prevent potential bombers from getting close enough to the buildings to inflict major damage. This had been done in NYC years earlier with many "important targets".

Additional security improvements were directed by the **Marshals Report**, which had been tasked with investigating other vulnerabilities. What is inexcusable was that those same safety recommendations were not mandated for all of our facilities in the hostile third world, and known terrorist havens.

Former FBI agent Bob Blitzer was an assistant section chief in the CTC, Counter-Terrorism Center Middle East Section. From the investigations he made of the 1993 WTC bombing, and the foiled attempt to bomb multiple targets in NYC the summer of 1993, Blitzer stated that a significant amount of vital information had been uncovered but went ignored. Most of the evidence pointed to mosques in the NYC area. Except for one guy, all of the terrorists from the summer of 1993 terror plot came from the mosques controlled by Sheik Rahman and his terrorist associates. Some had fought in Afghanistan, and most were well trained. Countries like Pakistan, the Philippines, Malaysia and other predominately Muslim countries were constantly mentioned. At the time of the 1993 interrogations no one realized the depth of the problem. *But the picture became much clearer now.*

Blitzer also stated that the interrogations of Murad in the Philippines on the 1995 Bojinka Plot were shared with the U.S. law enforcement and the intelligence communities.

Reviews from those files produced detailed classified reports by the CIA and FBI. One was titled, *"Ramzi Yousef; A New Generation of Sunni Islamic Terrorist"*. That report was from the

FBI, and it mirrored earlier works on the worldwide aspects of these terrorists. Unlike the Iranian's, those Sunni extremists had no common homeland, just a common purpose to attack the non-Islamists and America. (143)

That FBI report also stated that the *Saudi International Islamic Relief Organization* and the *Muslim World League* were important resources for those terrorists. (A later audit showed that by 2000 at least $3 million had gone from the Saudi's to bin Laden, and another $60 million went to the Taliban.)

That same report warned of the vulnerability of America to Islamic terrorist attacks. **The authors specifically mentioned Murad's plan to hijack an airliner to use as a flying missile!**

The CIA report went even further, warning that our national symbols such as the Capitol, White House and Wall Street area were clearly at risk targets. "We assess that our Civil Aviation will be a prominent target by foreign terrorists." *(144) Yet nothing was done by Bill Clinton.   **Incident # (52)**

Around that time FBI Director Freeh tried to get Clinton to change the legal rules to make it easier to get search warrants to investigate cases of terrorism, ***Clinton again refused.***

Freeh also tried to at least get increased surveillance of potential terrorists. ***Again Clinton refused.***

Journalist Steve Emerson's research group was amassing tons of information with over 6,000 hours of video and audio-tape recordings on Islamic extremism. Their electronic library was full of information on terrorists, supporters and front groups as they subscribed to over one hundred radical periodicals a month as well as obtaining documents from sources, conventions and gatherings. (All sources the CIA and FBI were forbidden to access and monitor!)

Emerson was also getting death threats. Federal officials would offer only limited help, and never gave him a federal pistol permit. Instead they gave him a collapsible mirror so he could look for bombs placed under his car!

He and his group of interns and journalists began working harder to unravel the Islamist veil in this country. They went over mountains of unexplored evidence and information from the 1993 WTC bombing. It was obvious even to those civilians that an International Terrorist Network existed, and they were going to try to prove it.

Emerson had a friend who translated Arabic files and documents, while they also went over the thousands of telephone calls made to the Middle East by the <u>dozens of unindicted suspects</u>. His group divided the phone calls up by country, and using Arabic speakers they began making cold calls to the listed phone numbers. Most of the calls went unanswered or they hung up upon hearing a voice speaking English. But on one call they ended up speaking to one of Sheikh Omar Rahman's sons. Another call put them in touch with the PIJ (Palestinian Islamic Jihad) spiritual leader.

One day a call came in to them from Brooklyn. The caller was a member of the Republican Brotherhood, a group that was opposed to Hassan al-Turabi's Fundamentalist regime in the Sudan. This caller stated he had uncovered boxes of documents that were the property of the (well known) Alkifah Refugee Center at the A-Farooq Mosque on Atlantic Avenue in Brooklyn. This was the center that had been the headquarters for Sheik Omar Rahman and the terrorists from both of the 1993 attacks. **Emerson contacted the FBI over this treasure trove of information, but was told as per the DOJ rules the FBI could not touch it.**

(Why wasn't this evidence seized from the previous arrests??!)

Emerson's group decided they would try to do some spy work. They had their Sudanese friend go into the building to identify and steal the important documents and smuggle them out to their car. They then raced to Manhattan to photocopy everything and return it to their guy who covertly replaced them. They did this successfully for three nights!

Inside those thousands of pages were financial records, false passports, address books and vast quantities of information that proved the Refugee Center was involved in the world-wide jihadist movement. Tragically they did not get all of the information that was there, and the FBI never tried to. When Emerson's group tried to pass on their windfall they were told it was not legally obtained and therefore of no value!! **Incident # 53**

Declassifying the Venona Project

One of the understated benefits to our new "friendship" with the former Soviet Union was the opening of secret Soviet Archives. Inside their files were tales of espionage, secret war plans, double dealings and hints that the world had escaped destruction by just a hair more than a few times.

Also revealed within those files were the extensive number and identities of Soviet spies operating inside the U.S.

In the flurry of openness the U.S. Army decided to declassified their super-secret WWII **Venona Project** on July 11, 1995.

(With a strong push from Sen. Moynihan of NY.)

Inside those files were decoded transcripts of Soviet cables that had been picked up and translated during the war. *So secretive was this effort, that FDR was not told of the program because everyone knew he would have shut it down!* FDR had refused to believe the many previous reports of Soviet spies operating inside the U.S., and despite being warned by Churchill about Russia, FDR had benevolent feelings for the USSR and Stalin.

As shown in *Fatal Flaws Book 1 & 2*, the original Soviet defector had been one Whittaker Chambers. When he left the Communists in the late 1930s he stated he was leaving the winning side to join up with those on the losing side, the side of freedom. His story listed dozens of spies and gave specific warnings about the Hiss brothers. FDR totally discounted his story and the other reports on Russian spies in America. *Two of FDR's top aides were Soviet spies, Alger Hiss and Harry Hopkins.*

As shown before Hiss had stolen secret documents and hidden them away, and Chambers had proof. In 1948 Congressman Richard Nixon was involved in recovering those documents which sealed Hiss's fate. During the "agonizing trial" of Alger Hiss in 1950, Chambers sarcastically stated; Innocence seldom utters outraged shrieks, but the guilty sure do. This trial was unbearable to America's elitist liberals, how dare anyone judge them, and they vowed revenge.

Due to the continued obstructions by the Democrats and the Truman Administration, few of those post-war Communist spies were ever caught, prosecuted or even fired from their government jobs. And during that time the liberals in the media and academia were outraged over any attempts to do so.

Truman and the Democrats closed the HUAC (House Un-American Committee) hearings in 1949, when they re-claimed the Congress. That prompted Senator Joe McCarthy to bring his own complaints about those same Communists to television news crews in 1950-52. The liberals and media destroyed McCarthy over a two year period, and he died soon after. Anytime any liberal wants to bring out false hysterics, they invoke "McCarthyism".

But with this release of the Venona files, Senator Joseph McCarthy, the much maligned, and lone anti-Communist voice in the early 1950s was proven correct. Many of those he had called out were Communist spies, and over **300** had been active inside the U.S. Some worked in sensitive positions, **and that included Hiss and Hopkins.** FDR and Truman had been played, and the world suffered dearly for their failures.

Little mention was ever made of that treasure trove of truth from the major media. To those on the left it "no longer mattered", for the Cold War was over. But the truth of what had happened, and the necessary visibility of the guilty and the traitors is incredibly important.

It highlights how those on the left worked in the shadows trying to bring down our country. Had they been successful, and they came close, in all probability the entire world would have turned Communist. Throughout the Cold War only America stood in the way of a Communist world. (Even today the liberals are still trying to destroy this country as many of them still want us to become Socialist, even though it failed everywhere it was implemented!)

Iraq

In NYC the U.N. Security Council passed resolution 986. Misnamed as the oil for food program, the resolution was supposed to strictly monitor Iraqi oil sales. They were earning billions each year and Iraq was supposed to use the money to rebuild their infrastructure such as water treatment plants, electrical grids and to provide foods and medicine for their people. Thirty percent was to be kept by the U.N. to pay the various legal claims from their invasion of Kuwait.

Saddam insisted that all monies be transferred in and out of the Banque Nationale de Paris, (BNP). In that way Saddam hoped his friends the French would allow him some leeway in using the funds. But this time France did not look the other way, and quickly $13 billion in assets were on hold. Unable to access that money the Ba'thists decided to increase their purchase of dual use equipment to restore their WMD programs. Saddam used front companies in the UAE, Jordan and Egypt to get what he wanted.

Each cooperating Western government was supposed to monitor any sales from their country to Iraq. Most did not as any sale was a good one. Once a sales approval was given by the host country the vendor would submit a license to the U.N. 661 committee for their approval. Out of all of those doing business in Iraq, Britain rejected the most requests because Saddam was still denying U.N. inspectors access to areas they wanted to search.

France however blocked none, and France was again selling billions in arms to Iraq.

Communist China also jumped into the cash flow sending millions of servings of "adult milk" to Iraq from their main weapons company, NORINCO. China also sold Iraq advanced fiber-optic communications cables and communications equipment. Germany and Russia were also selling weapons by the boatload, and within a year the oil for food program was a joke. Saddam had rearmed.

Islamic Trouble

Thousands of Afghan war-veterans had gone south to Kashmir to help the Pakistani's in their border war with India. Others went north to Bosnia or Chechnya to help the Muslims fight those wars. Still others went to Somalia to fight the American attempts to bring peace. Most however returned to their Middle East homes and incited trouble there. As shown earlier Algeria, Tunisia and Egypt were the most at risk for extremist takeovers.

Egypt had given birth to the Muslim Brotherhood but had grown weary of their negative influence and trouble making. while Algeria had a socialist regime that was looked upon by the Fundamentalists as treasonous. During 1992 the Algerians outlawed the Islamist group FIS in an effort to be rid of them, while neighboring Tunisia's progressive democratic government headed by Pres. Zinedine ben Ali knew he was a target for assassination by those same militants. Their trials had continued over the past years with Algerians fighting a civil war.

In June 1995 Egyptian Pres. Mubarak flew to Ethiopia for a meeting of the Organization of African Unity. Aware that numerous terrorists were operating out of the Sudan, Egypt's intelligence service recommended that Mubarak use an armored limousine and place snipers on nearby rooftops. (Similar to the U.S presidential motorcade.)

EIJ terrorists were indeed waiting for him in Addis Abba, and they tried to block the streets so they could fire at and bomb his limousine and motorcade. Mubarak barely survived. This attack was one of many that had occurred, and several Egyptian officials had already been murdered and their foreign embassies bombed.

Even so the Clinton Administration and State Dept. were still naively insisting on having a dialogue with the "Islamic moderates". *Mubarak angrily scolded the State Dept., "Who are the moderates? No one has ever pointed them out to me".* (145)*

He continued berating the Clinton officials on how the Carter Administration had conducted secret talks with the Ayatollah and his fanatics before they seized power. **That appeasement changed everything for the worse.**

The Clinton Administration was simply following in the same fatally flawed footprints of FDR and his Soviet ideals, Truman and his loss of China, LBJ's entire Vietnam inanity and Carter's failures. Clinton's staff on the NSC actually felt those Extremist changes to the Middle East were "inevitable", and they wanted to "manage the transition with minimal cost".

For Clinton and company sitting safe and ignorant in Washington, the current rulers in the region needed to "broaden their social base" by integrating the Islamists into the political field. Administration principals and staffs continued to maintain discreet two-faced dialogues with Algerian and Egyptian Islamists, just as Carter had done with the Ayatollah. Wisely neither Algeria or Egypt thought much of the Clinton, or his Administration's thoughts or ideals.

Mubarak would launch an all out assault on the Muslim Brotherhood arresting hundreds and closing down their institutions. *Their power and control fell off.* The unhappy Clinton Administration wrongly predicted that his "hard move" would quickly backfire.

Following that attempted assassination episode, Egypt and other nations in the region tried to get the U.N. Security Council to enact sanctions on lawless Sudan similar to what had been done to Libya a few years ago.

In addition to that diplomacy, Egypt was preparing to conduct military operations of their own against Turabi and bin Laden. Clinton asked the Pentagon to formulate plans in case our military joined in. Similar to JFK and the Bay of Pigs disaster, he wanted something small and stealthy to hide our footprint. Weeks later the Pentagon recommended aerial bombing be used.

In the meantime two attempts had been made on bin Laden in Khartoum. More than likely the Egyptians were initiating things on their own rather than wait for the Clinton White House. Or else the Saudis were trying to end the problem.   **Incident # 54**

(It was not known at that time, but those attacks and assassination attempts on bin Laden and al-Qaeda were affecting their terror operations. Bin Laden and his cohorts were being watched and tracked constantly, so no one in al Qaeda could make the finishing touches for implementing the East African Embassy bombings. But that was not all they worked on.)

On the never ending Terror Front more attacks occurred.

July 4, 1995 Kashmiri terrorists kidnapped and murdered six westerners. Indian troops hunted down and killed four of them. **Incident # 55**

July 25, 1995 Algerian terrorists detonated a gas bomb on a Paris train killing eight and wounding eighty. **Incident # 56**

August 17, 1995 Another bomb exploded at the Arc de Triumphe in Paris wounding seventeen. **Incident # 57**

On August 26 a large bomb was found next to the tracks of a high speed train near Lyon, France. **Incident # 58**

On September 3, 1995 Another bomb was discovered in a Paris square. It misfired. **Incident # 59**

September 7, 1995 A bomb exploded near a school in Lyon wounding fourteen. Additional bombs were found nearby and deactivated. **Incident # 60**

October 6, 1995 Another gas bomb detonated in a rail station near Paris wounding thirteen. **Incident # 61**

October 17, 1995 Yet another gas bomb exploded in a rail station wounding twenty-nine. *At this point the FBI was assisting the French and followed leads to a mosque in Sweden.* **Incident # 62**

The only good news on the Terror Front concerned the "disappearance" of the Egyptian leader of their Muj in Bosnia in mid-October. **Abu al-Qasimy** had a long history of work in "relief organizations" beginning in Peshawar in the mid-80s. After that he had been working with **Ayman al-Zawahiri** in Denmark setting up EIJ operations there. His sudden loss was a big setback to the terrorists. **Incident # 63**

In retaliation for the above loss, Islamic terrorists tried to drive a truck bomb into a police station in Croatia on October 20. When they failed to get into the building they detonated the bomb outside wounding twenty-seven. The CIA traced that attack to a **Hassan al-Saad,** a Canadian. Croatian forces found and killed him days later. **Incident # 64**

In light of the recent events the FBI officially opened a case on Bin Laden. JTTF agents Coleman and Liguori were sent to the CTC (Counter-Terrorism Center) to examine their terrorist files. They were amazed by the amount of raw data that had been compiled, but most was what you would pick up at the beginning of an investigation. Since the CIA had no boots on the ground chasing after bin Laden, and no dedicated unit going over the intel, the information was not being collated.

One of the separate files they found concerned a name known to the JTTF, **Wadi el-Hage**. As shown before Hage had come to the attention of investigators in Tuscon and during the Shalabi murder. He flew from Arizona to Texas to NYC to take over the Alkifah Center the day Mustapha Shalabi "disappeared". Then he too seemed to disappear. What they now learned was that el-Hage had gone on to the Afghanistan and the Sudan, and was working with bin Laden. From there he moved south to Nairobi and was running an NGO called the Help Africa People. Naturally those combined movements were suspicious, and it was felt that he might be able to help the bin Laden investigation if he could be leveraged.

Khalid Sheikh Mohammed (KSM) just missed being arrested with Yousef in Pakistan. He too returned to the Sudan, but after a short time was told to move on by the Mukhabarat, Sudan's Intelligence agency. Sudan was trying to improve their image with America, and since KSM was wanted for questioning he was potential problem. He then worked his way east to Qatar.

Unknown to him the Sudanese informed the Cairo based FBI liaison of Sheikh Mohammed's new location.

In October 1995 KSM and another major terrorist **Shawqi Islambuli** were tracked to an exact apartment building. Qatar had a long standing extradition treaty with the U.S., and it should have only taken a day or so to process the paperwork. But weeks went by with no end to the scamming. Again neither Clinton nor any of the principals got involved. Khalid and Shawqi Islambuli secretly moved on to Prague, Czech Republic. While staying there Khalid used the alias Mustafa Nasir, and the pair escaped detection for years.

Khalid Sheikh Mohammed the head of the Philippines Bojinka operation and the future 9/11 attacks would escape because of Clinton's failure to act, and help from sources inside the government of Qatar.   Incident # 65

(In his book *Ghost Wars,* Steve Coll writes that some in the Administration were trying to get a covert operation approved to go and get KSM, but were stopped by "legal and administrative concerns" from up high.)

Soon after that unfathomable screw-up the Clinton administration courted Qatar into allowing us to build a secret airbase known as *Al Adid*. It is one of the largest in the region with storage for 100 warplanes and 15,000 foot runways. They were built to handle our B-52s and the B-1 bombers, and the base was pre-stocked with the munitions and supplies for a full brigade of troops costing the U.S. taxpayers $1.5 billion. (??)

Then on November 13, 1995 a car packed with 250 pounds of C-4 was used to destroy the three story **Saudi National Guard Office in Riyadh**. This non-descript building was staffed with U.S. personnel who were there to help train the Saudi military. They flew no flag and were not demonstrative in their tours, but (as shown earlier), they were being watched the past two years.

No one saw the car pull up, and no one saw the driver run away. This building was on a busy street of fashionable shops and buildings, but at 1130 am the streets were normally empty. The terrorists scheduled this attack for the time of the mid-day prayer to avoid causing casualties to true Muslims. After the driver ran off a strong explosion ripped through the structure killing seven and wounding forty of the American personnel stationed there. **Incident # 66**

An hour before the bomb was set off bin Laden had given his final approval via his satellite phone from his farm near Khartoum, Sudan. The NSA, the National Security Agency intercepted that call and knew the coded phone message was ominous. But there was no way to pinpoint the target.

Over the next few days the electronic trail led to bin Laden. NSA satellite evidence was overwhelming, and the many previous pieces fit right into this puzzle. Bin Laden had opened his war against America in the December 1992 attacks in Yemen. He helped finance the 1993 WTC attacks, was a big part of the Somalia fighting, authorized and supported the Bojinka plot, and now was a key part of this attack in Saudi Arabia. Inside the CIA's CTC the deputy director Vincent Cannistraro warned that more attcks would follow. **Incident # 67**

Clinton responded with a weak speech to *increase our efforts to deter terrorism*, to bring those responsible to justice, to isolate countries that support terrorism and *to spare no effort to make sure our law enforcement officers* have what they need to protect our citizens. There was no mention of stopping or killing the terrorists, of using the CIA or military to retaliate, or at least efforts to tighten our anti-terror security!

What made these terrorists so dangerous was their patience. Al Qaeda attacks were well planned and took years to strike. One of their training chants is, "I will be patient until patience is worn out from patience". They had scouted numerous other targets in

Riyadh, but both the French and British Embassies were rejected as too secure and vigilant. The U.S. Embassy had actually been the desired initial target, but at a meeting of the al Qaeda executive council the Egyptian branch led by number two Ayman al-Zawahiri was overruled by bin Laden as being too difficult. A softer target was desired and found in the Guard office.

(The EIJ branch wanted to just ram a bomb truck into the embassy building as was done in Beirut at the Marines barracks in 1983. And despite the Murrah bombing in Oklahoma and the security warnings afterwards, there were no barricades in place to protect any of our overseas delegations!)

Unknown to U.S. intelligence the Saudis had tried to talk bin Laden into returning to the fold. When that did not work he was threatened and finally they tried to kill him. Sometime in late 1994 Prince Turki al-Faisal had approved bin Laden's execution. Their first attempt was poorly done and only civilians and bodyguards were wounded. However Bin Laden was changed by the attempt and became more isolated and enraged. One reason for the bombing/ attack in Riyadh was to show the Saudi Royals what was possible if they did not back off.

The Saudi's purposely restricted the FBI's access to the Guard Office terrorist site and any suspects that they rounded up. The trail went cold when the "bombers were caught and beheaded" before anyone from the FBI could interrogate them. One of those suspects was al Qaeda's Ali al-Shamrani who had been operating inside Bosnia. (FBI agents did watch the confessions and executions on Saudi TV. Three of the four suspects stated that they were acting on and were inspired by the faxes and fatwa's issued by bin Laden and his organization.)

The only tangible thing that was learned from an intelligence standpoint was that most of those suspects had trained in bin Laden camps in Afghanistan.

Clinton did not press the Saudi's over the matter.

(Another issue that Clinton kept quiet was the refusal by the Saudi's to turning over Imad Mughniyah. He was the bomb maker in the 1983 bombings in Beirut, and numerous other attacks including the murder of Navy Diver Robert Stetham.)

Unhappy that their truck bomb idea was not accepted or just eager to strike at anything in the Egyptian Government, EIJ decided to car bomb the Egyptian embassy in Islamabad, Pakistan On November 19, 1995 a large explosion murdered seventeen and wounded dozens. **Abu Hafs** was the Islamabad raid leader, as their terrorists used gunfire and grenades to kill the protective security guards. Then a car-bomb destroyed the security gates and a jeep-bomb was used to demolish part of the building.

In addition to the embassy building the plotters had also wanted to target the Khan el-Khalili marketplace knowing it would be full of civilians. (EIJ leader Ayman al-Zawahiri had again wanted to attack the U.S. embassy, but the new one was too well protected.)

By December sixteen of those terrorists had been arrested and Pakistan's PM Benazir Bhutto began a clampdown on extremist groups in her country. Bin Laden was unhappy with the attack because they needed Pakistan's permission to get their people back and forth to Afghanistan. **Incident # 68**

As always, the Clinton Administration learned nothing and did even less.

The CIA had been quietly investigating Osama bin Laden since the December 1992 attacks in Yemen. The FBI learned of him a few weeks after the February 1993 WTC attack, but his network called al Qaeda remained in the shadows here because no one would listen to the knowledgeable sources like Steve Emerson or Congressman McCollum. With those continuing terrorist attacks and plots, more and more of bin Laden and his growing network of Islamic terrorists was being revealed.

Clinton's National Security Advisor Tony Lake stated that he was first briefed about bin Laden in 1994 and again in 1995 when an FBI counter-terrorism team had returned from the Philippines with the details of the deadly Bojinka Plot.

Richard Clarke the Counter-Terrorism Czar was also briefed by the CIA and FBI. Clarke states in his book *Against All Enemies* that in mid-1993 he, Lake and others were pestering the CIA to get information about this bin Laden.

The U.S. State Dept. was also well aware of what had been happening overseas and of what group was involved. *By 1995 the Sudan had allowed over twenty terrorist training camps to open in their country.*

The only thing Clinton had done so far on terrorism was to apply some sanctions and diplomatic pressure on the Sudanese to expel bin Laden.(??) After the Guard Office bombing the Saudi's joined the effort to expel him, but in reality what was to be gained by doing so? There was irrefutable evidence that bin Laden and his terrorists were at war with America and killing our people. It was time to act.

Revelations had come in that the terrorist organization PIJ, Palestinian Islamic Jihad had been active in the Tampa area. It was causing a domestic stir, and Federal investigators showed up. In short order they were scouring the records of the Islamic charity groups, ICP and WISE plus their members. *Two bank accounts were found that belonged to a former USF professor **Ramadan Abdullah Shallah**. He was the new head of the PIJ!*

On November 20 agents and officials searched the campus offices and home of previously mentioned **Sami al-Arian**. Records showed that he had called the Sudanese Embassy at the time of the prior terrorist attempt to kill Egypt's Pres. Mubarak. Arian had also called the Iranian Interest Section, a lobbying group used to promote Iran since they have no embassy here. Both nations were on terrorist watch lists, and U.S. citizens cannot contact them.

With their search warrants in hand, agents uncovered the largest collection of terrorist fundraising and propaganda material ever seized, by them. (Steve Emerson's group had uncovered more.) **Both WISE and ICP had deep and longstanding links to terrorist groups all over the world.** Sheikh Omar Rahman had been a guest speaker at their conferences as had other terrorist leaders. It was learned that WISE board member **Tarik Hamdi** had personally delivered a satellite telephone and battery pack to Osama bin Laden. **Incident # 69**

Despite the overabundance of evidence found in this raid, this Administration did not prosecute any of those suspects. (Why?)

Instead Clinton signed a Presidential Directive in mid-1995 directing the CIA to undertake an "aggressive program of foreign intelligence collection, analysis, counter-intelligence and covert action in a Counter-Terrorism effort. The CIA was thus authorized to arrest terrorists and return them for trials in the U.S." * (146) This directive was legally binding for making arrests anytime, but the CIA does not make arrests, the FBI does. (Were they included, or was this just more Clinton scamming?)

Bin Laden was becoming the major target in the anti-terrorism intelligence world. The CIA station in the Sudan was sending in dozens of reports detailing his extensive terrorist ties. In addition the CTC was receiving reports from Egypt, Tunisia, Israel, Algeria and other sources. All were referencing bin Laden. A bin Laden station was established, (finally), and a section of CIA analysts would concentrate just on him.

Funding for anti-terrorism slowly went up to $5.7 billion in late 1995. Overall the FBI's anti-terror budget went up 280%, but that was due to the fact it was so low to start with.

With Clinton specifically trying to get bin Laden expelled from the Sudan, and his Presidential Directive #30 being issued, it again proves that he was well aware of who our enemy was and that he had been involved in the previous terrorist attacks.

All attempts by Clinton to say he did not know about bin Laden was a lie.

Around this same time a Sudanese intelligence officer attempted to gain entry into the U.S with a false passport. His mission was to expand the terrorist capabilities of the NIF, National Islamic Front inside America. **Incident # 70**

Clinton decided to replace the annoying and always correct James Woolsey at CIA with John Deutch in late 1995. (Shortly after Woolsey was fired a small plane crashed into the west lawn of the White House. White House Staffers thought it amusing and joked that it was Woolsey still trying to get in to see Clinton.)

Deutch was another unqualified political hack who further eroded morale at a service that was falling. Because of the constant negativity, retirements were at an all time high, and in late 1995 there were only a dozen agents in the CIA training program. *Deutch was so alien to the world of intelligence that he would illegally e-mail top secret notes to his home computer via AOL!* Some of those sensitive e-mails were found on his home computer two years after he left the CIA. (He too would soon be under investigation and indicted.)

Acting on a "complaint" from Democratic Senator Torricelli, Deutch fired two senior CIA officers and restricted the recruitment of new sources, especially within other countries. Over one thousand potential sources were let go during this politically motivated sweep. *Deutch's new rules on recruitment of foreign assets insisted that the source had to be clean and have a good history.* That inane rule prevented our agents from obtaining new supplies of intelligence worldwide. And this was most acute in the Middle East since that area was the new hot spot.

Deutch wanted to promote analysts and bureaucrats instead of field agents. Among the bureaucrats he brought in were; George Tenet a Democratic Congressional staffer and Michael O'Neil a staff member of leftist Congressman Edward Boland. Boland had a pathological hatred for the intelligence community, and had worked against all of Pres. Reagan's intelligence operations in Central America, (the Boland Amendments.)

O'Neil would continue that insidious work from inside the CIA.

Nora Slatkin was another hack who was appointed to the position of Executive Director at the agency. She was told to change the culture of the Operations Directorate. None of those people had any idea about intelligence or on how any of that work was vital to national security.

They were simply democratic staffers appointed to vital jobs that they had no business going to.

George Tenet would eventually take over at CIA in 1998 **when Deutch was indicted.** He would be the fifth director in six years and continued the downward slide in the CIA's capabilities and morale. *Slatkin and O'Neil would later be reprimanded for "mishandling the internal investigation of Deutch", but then that was how things were done in the crooked Clinton Administration.* (Deutch was later pardoned by Clinton when he left office.)

Yassir Arafat the terrorist leader of the PLO had been banded about by the Democrats as a "statesman" for over a decade. In reality he was a cold blooded terrorist who had ordered the murders of the Israeli athletes in 1972, the American Ambassador Cleo Noel and his charge` d'affaires G. Curtis Martin in Khartoum on March 1, 1973, and Leon Klinghoffer, a disabled American tourist on the cruise ship *Achille Lauro* who was shot multiple times and thrown overboard in his wheel chair by PLF terrorists in 1985.

There were dozens of similar murders, yet Clinton invited Arafat to the White House numerous times. Never in all of those visits was Arafat arrested, threatened with arrest, or pressured to give up the PLO murderers who committed those terrorist acts.

In late 1995 the U.N. was celebrating their 50th anniversary when Arafat showed up at a concert. NYC Mayor Rudy Giuliani ordered Arafat and his minions out of the building. Liberals were aghast at his stance, and Clinton was harsh in his inane criticism. None of them or the media remembered or cared about the innocents the PLO had killed throughout the Middle East the past decades, including the destruction of Lebanon. And their death toll included hundreds of Americans. ** (147)

More Corruption

It had been three years since the Travel-gate firings. A year after congressional investigations began an Independent Counsel was tasked to look into it. They had served subpoenas on the White House for travel-office documents, but it took months for the Clinton's to comply. Then a shocking memo finally surfaced.

A nine page communication written by former aide David Watkins to his then superior Chief of Staff Mack McLarty was given to the special counsel. *It revealed that Hillary was the one pushing for the Travel Staff firings even though she had claimed to have no role at all in the affair.* Judge Kenneth Starr was the Independent counsel and he was incensed that this lie was just being revealed. **Congressman William Clinger who was chairman of the Reform Committee stated that this showed evidence of a White House cover up.**

On January 9, 1996 columnist William Safire wrote his now famous column denouncing Hillary Clinton as a habitual liar going back to her being fired during the Watergate investigations, and including the investigations of the Madison S&L failure. Travel Office manager Billy Dale finally spoke up for himself in an article for the Washington Post. He stated how all of the latest revelations released to the public showed the abuse of power by the Clinton's, their false statements and the outright lying that had come from the Clinton White House.

To hide their crimes from scrutiny the Clinton's often used executive privilege and outright stonewalling to hamper any investigation. It was during this time that Ken Starr first learned that Vince Foster had gone to see attorney James Hamilton for legal advice over the Travel-Gate fiasco! Hamilton had taken three pages of handwritten notes, and Starr wanted them to prove Hillary's guilt and perjury.

Starr had to go to court to obtain those notes, wasting more time. But then the court conveniently ruled that the notes were attorney-client protected even though Foster had been murdered / died nine days after that meeting. (With the former client now dead who was the court trying to protect??)

After the Republicans won the mid-term election in November 1994 Clinton and his team were panicking. They smelled their own ouster in the next presidential election. To prevent that horror Clinton went on a money quest to equal no other. Democratic National Committee (DNC) finance chief Terry McAuliffe came up with a plan to raise tons of money, *Clinton would sell access to him!* Both knew that big money liberal donors would line up to "spend time with their guy Clinton."

Their plan would involve "renting out" the Lincoln bedroom for $50,000 a night. To lure additional but less well off "contributors" they could also rent seats on Air Force 1 & 2, and get access to special White House events, dinners and photo ops. Also instituted were White House coffees for donors with less deep pockets. The "best donors" would also get special access to and be placed on government boards, commissions and obtain various political appointments. **(This was a clear return to the days of corruption ala Tammany Hall - and the NYC Democrats.)**

In all **938 people** stayed overnight at the White House. All of those "renters" were a "donor and friend of Bill". With those scams in place ever more donors were coming in, and ever more money was changing hands. Clinton, Gore and their staffs kept detailed reports on the money they were generating. In the three weeks from Jan. 17 to Feb. 6, 1996 they raised $1,600,000!

As the days and weeks went by their cash cow grew to millions. **However most of those activities were illegal as well as unethical.** As always White House intransience, the party spin doctors and helpful media prevented any judicial action. Keeping watch was Janet Reno, Clinton's Attorney General.

It turns out McAuliffe was also a key player in the Ron Carey-Teamsters conspiracy and embezzlement scandal. As usual the Teamsters were big boosters to the DNC and Clinton campaigns. But as was evidenced at the trials, the money they sent over was illegal. Not until 2000 did those convictions "finally come down".

(Somehow McAuliffe "escaped being indicted" and became governor of Virginia. One of the most important changes that needs to be made to our system of government is that the Congress should pick the Attorney General. *In that way the president has less ability to act illegally or to corrupt investigations. Janet Reno was the key to keeping Clinton in power.* And just look at the way Obama and company obstructed the six major investigations that he was a part of and should have been investigated over.)

In late 1992 and into the summer of 1993 Communist China, (PRC), was buying a large stake in a company owned by the **Lippo Group**. The Chinese purchasing company was the innocuous sounding China Resources Holding Company, CRCH. **However U.S. intelligence agencies knew that the CRHC was a front company for the PRC.**

CRCH used a James Riady as one of their main lobbyists in Washington D.C. *In a strange piece of luck, it turns out that Bill Clinton had extensive ties to the Riady family going back to the mid-1980s.* And in another uncanny coincidence, the Lippo companies were the single largest donors to the 1992 Clinton campaign. They even used "straw donors" to hide the source of the money! (Illegal money.)

Then in another mysterious twist of fate, the Lippo Group was the company that had hired (the disgraced and fired) Clinton appointee and longtime friend Webster Hubbell. Hubbell was "hired by the CRHC" in the dangerous period between his resignation as assistant attorney general in the Reno Justice Department and the time when he was to go to jail in 1994 for his corruption charges. *Hubbell was somehow paid $100,000 up front, but did almost no work for the company because he was in jail.*

In addition to those "connections", James Riady and a Chinese citizen named John Huang had also raised a lot of money for Democratic Senatorial campaigns during 1988. That was when they "met" Al Gore, John Breax and other Democrats in need of cash. John Huang was soon hired by Riady as a lobyist, but he also continued his work in Hong Kong. **Every time Lippo executives James Riady or John Huang came to Washington D.C., large contributions went to the Clinton's or the DNC, (Democratic National Committee).**

Both men had unprecedented access to Clinton, though neither was given the required FBI background check and security clearances! That was "done by the White House staff".

In the fall of 1993 Pres. Clinton offered Huang a position with the Commerce Department. To help "move things along" Commerce Sec. Ron Brown "approved a special clearance" for Huang on January 31, 1994. Huang did not officially leave the Lippo Group **(run by the PRC)** until July 1994, over six months after getting into our government and having that special Top Secret clearance!

During 1994 and 1995 Huang attended 109 Top-Secret briefings at the Commerce Department, which many times involved classified information. In addition to those briefings he went to the White House seventy-eight times!

During September 1995 Huang became an official fund raiser for the DNC at the insistence of Bill Clinton. This occurred even though Huang had already engaged in illegal fundraising and his bosses at Lippo Group had made over $1 Billion from deals negotiated through the Clinton Commerce Dept. Throughout the 1996 election period Huang raised over $3 million dollars, though again much of the money was from questionable sources. One group of Asian business people who dined with Clinton gave him $500,000!

Many on the Congressional Reform Committee suspected Huang was an agent for the PRC. When he was questioned directly by that Committee, Huang who was not a U.S. citizen took the 5th amendment and refused to answer. (He should have been deported immediately, and Sec. Brown terminated for giving him that special clearance.)

Clinton also used Huang to lobby the Congress so he could renew the MFN status, (Most Favored Nation Trade Status) with China. In one day Huang "convinced" four congressmen to vote yes, which insured the renewal. But in late 1995 investigations began.

Caught up in this latest investigation, Clinton again refused to abide by any of the subpoenas from the House Reform Committee. For months the investigation looking into the Lippo-China connection was delayed. Clinton, his staff and democratic officials repeatedly delayed sending information to the committee.

Full reporting of the facts did not come in until December 1996, after the election was over and Clinton got back in! Vice President Al Gore was on *Meet The Press* repeatedly lying that there was no wrongdoing in their hunt for money.

In addition to Lippo-Huang's money and influence peddling, South Korea had also "donated $250,000 to the DNC", which eventually had to be returned when the investigations drew near. Their offices of Cheong Am American Inc. were quickly vacated as their senior executive Kyung Hoon, (John Lee) "disappeared".

Around that same time the "Buddhist Temple" disaster broke in the *Washington Post* as an additional $150,000 dollars were donated. And then a Johnny Chung brought in a $50,000 donation and was granted a private meeting with Clinton. In tow were five Chinese businessmen who wanted to lease the Long Beach Naval Station in California!

Yet another illegal affair was exposed from India. Yogesh Ghandi of California had recently paid only a $10,000 fine for back taxes and other civil penalties. Out of the blue he donated $325,000 to the DNC buying thirteen tickets to a DNC fundraiser at $25,000 each. *It turns out his technology business had been doing quite well thanks to John Huang.*

And throughout this dishonest affair Huang who was involved in most of those suspicious dealings, was still receiving Top Secret briefings. As soon as possible after the meetings ended he would then make calls to China -Lippo.

During December 1995 a **Wang Jun** appeared on the radar. He was the head of a weapons-trading company owned by the Chinese military. Wang had been invited to one of the White House coffees because **Charles Trie,** another friend of Clinton's from Little Rock had arranged the meeting. *Trie had raised $640,000 for the Clinton's, and visited them in the White House over thirty times in 1994-95.* Since Trie was "such a good friend", the meeting with Wang Jun was quickly approved.

During this time the Pentagon was investigating the two U.S. firms that had given vital missile technology to China. Loral Space and Communications based in Manhattan and Hughes Electronics based in LA had been "helping the Chinese" investigate why one of their rockets carrying a Loral satellite had crashed. During their investigation both companies had shared Top Secret information on rocket guidance technology. Those secrets were dual use, civilian and military, and could greatly improve Chinese ballistic missile capabilities. And if the Chinese sold or gave away those secrets to Iran or N. Korea, (which they did repeatedly), America and the world would be in serious strategic jeopardy from different directions at the same time.

Clinton stepped in to end the investigations. It turned out that both companies had contributed to his campaign and were therefore to be left alone!

Just by coincidence, Loral's CEO Bernard Schwartz was the largest individual contributor to the DNC since 1995.

A classified Pentagon assessment concluded that our national security had been seriously harmed by this incident. In an effort to undercut the investigation into this treasonous action, **Clinton recommended and approved** for Loral to "legally export" this technology to the Chinese! And to insure his action passed, Clinton tried to rush the trade waiver through the bureaucracy.

As thanks for this "help", Schwartz gave another $100,000 to the DNC to avoid any direct link to Clinton. *(Jeff Gerth of the NY Times finally broke this story on April 4, 1998, two years after it had come into the light.)*

In the interim the Commerce Dept. Inspector General began their own investigation. **Two months later 40 subpoenas were issued, one was for John Huang.**

More indictments were in the wind. But on April 3, 1996 **Sec. of Commerce Ron Brown**, his female assistant and many others were killed when the jet they were in fortunately crashed near Dubrovnik, Croatia.

As shown before Brown had been the former head of the DNC. When Clinton was elected in 1992 Brown was given the spot as the Commerce Secretary. He took fifteen top staffers from the DNC and placed them into senior positions at the Commerce Dept. Charges of corruption and illegal donations quickly surfaced and followed Brown around during the past years. But with the recent corruption and other charges involving John Huang, the FBI began a serious investigation into the Commerce Department as did the Inspector General.

After many weeks of investigations Brown and his assistant were about to be indicted, and if so there was a good chance Clinton would be investigated and indicted.

Knowing that their arrests were on the table, Clinton had Brown and the others take a "Commerce Dept. trip to get away from the media". Without warning their USAF 737 jetliner "somehow" crashed in the hills near Dubrovnik killing 34.

Reports claimed that bad weather was the cause of the crash, yet five other planes had landed before Brown's with no problems. *Forensics people who analyzed Ron Brown's body noticed a bullet wound to his head, yet no autopsy was performed. And strangely the x-rays of his skull were lost.*

(The investigations were ended.)

Conspiracy theorists thought navigation aides at the airport may had been sabotaged just before the jet landed resulting in the crash. They may have been correct. A backup navigation system had been stolen the day before and was never recovered. And in another one of those strange coincidences, the Croatian maintenance chief at the airport died from gunshot wounds three days later. His death was ruled a suicide.

Between 1993-1998 an additional 10 Clinton people were killed. That included many from the Commerce Dept. who were involved with John Huang. It also included three Marines from the HMX-1 helicopter unit that ferries the president around.

Then in August 1996 *The Chicago Tribune* reported that the Lum family had hosted a presidential gala raising $2.5 million. It turns out that federal authorities were investigating them for buying influence in the Commerce Dept. (Just like everyone else.)

Sec. Brown had been deeply involved with this pair and their questionable dealings going back to 1991 when he ran the DNC.

On October 21, 1996 the DNC hosted a fund raiser in Detroit picking up an additional $800,000. Much of the money came from Iraqi's who were lobbying the president to end sanctions on their country. Clinton kept the money but did not end the Iraqi sanctions.

Nordex, a Vienna based company had been formed by the KGB. They were suspected of helping transfer **nuclear materials** to North Korea and Iran. They too donated large amounts of money to the Democrats.

Roger Tamraz was an Egyptian-American oil financier was wanted in Lebanon on an embezzlement charge. *He too had special access to this White House as he had contributed $300,000.* His play was to get "administration help" in constructing an oil pipeline from the Caspian Sea.

The Teamsters Union had already joined the ranks in trading money for favors, and even a Miami drug kingpin joined the money-influence circuit.

Just before the 1996 election was held the LA Times revealed that over $450,000 went to the DNC from "Indonesian contributors". *It turned out they too were associated with the Lippo Group.* One of their revelations was that the years of lobbying by those sources was directed to get Clinton to improve relations with Vietnam. (Always happy to get donations Clinton had normalized relations with Communist Vietnam in 1994.)

Another bombshell piece of evidence concerned a Eric Hotung, a Hong Kong exec who had ties to the Chinese government. He gave $100,000, and soon after was given access to the White House and met privately with Sandy Berger, Director of the NSC. Of course the White House denied all of those reports, and became quite upset over this increased FBI activity and scrutiny.

Then Charlie Trie the longtime Clinton pal and financial backer had come back to town. China was threatening Taiwan to rejoin their nation and they wanted Clinton and America to step back and stay out of it. **Trie showed up and deposited $460,000 into Clinton's legal defense fund! Somehow that was not illegal.**

(Due to his mounting legal problems the Clinton's needed a legal fund to stay out of jail.)

As National Security Advisor Tony Lake worked on the Administration's limp reply over the latest PRC artillery shelling hitting Taiwan, an additional $180,000 showed up. Clinton decided not to make a show of support for Taiwan! What actually caught everyone's attention in this latest Clinton scandal was that all of this recent money had come from Foreign sources.

FBI agent Jerry Campane stated that Trie was illegally laundering money from foreign patrons to Clinton's re-election and legal funds. Much of it came from Ng Lap Seng, another Chinese Government official. During his previous 23 trips to the White House, investigators believed over $ 1 Million had changed hands! **Again all of this was illegal.**

Except for a few media outlets this story was kept in the background. And even after the new year complaints of illegal fund raising continued to come in.

From all of this corruption, intelligence was showing that Communist China had committed to buying influence in the Clinton White House and the Congress!

Howls of protests from Republicans and a few Democrats could not sway Janet Reno to appoint an Independent counsel. *Not until mid-November, again after the election was over and they stayed in power, did she agree to forming a special task force.* It was weeks before they would even meet, and as usual documents and witnesses disappeared.

In February 1997 after a review of the original investigation FBI Director Freeh assigned twenty-five agents to concentrate on this case and the potential espionage that could involve Bill Clinton.

Their early investigation was showing that China was actively trying to buy influence with this president since 1992! Clinton then sent a letter to Deputy Attn. General Jamie Gorelick to intercede. To his credit Freeh refused to listen to Gorelick's politically based appeal because this was an active investigation into potential espionage.

In addition to this **Attempted Obstruction of Justice**, Clinton demanded to be informed of the results of the FBI search. Freeh again refused, stating that we do not inform bank robbers of what we are doing, and we will not inform the president, who is basically a crook. The media refused to cover this vital storyline and harangue Clinton out of office. *(Impeachment should have been considered for obstruction of justice.)*

But Clinton was not the only recipient of those illegal foreign funds. Democratic House and Senate leaders Gephardt and Daschle scooped up tons of money too. At times Al Gore was so offending to his financial targets, (aka donors), people referred to his donation tactics as shakedowns. The leftist media also kept these important stories off the air.

Democrats, they're the best politicians that money can buy.

(During May 1998 it was learned from intelligence sources that China was indeed interested in influencing the 1998 U.S. elections. Gerth again got that scoop.)

Historical Note: As shown before Pres. Truman and Sec State George Marshall stopped the Nationalists from defeating Mao and his Communists in Manchuria. The Chinese Communists forces were lavishly supported by Stalin, and renewed with North Korean reinforcements. In 1947 they counter-attacked and defeated the Nationalists in two major battles which led to their collapse. The surviving Nationalists escaped to Taiwan and became a separate nation protected by the U.S. The Peoples Republic of China, PRC made repeated attacks against those islands over the decades, and have threatened us with nuclear war now if we intercede!

Our 7th Fleet had operated from the Philippines many times stopping the PRC's attempts to invade. One of the reasons we still have substantial forces based on Okinawa was to protect Taiwan. Those forces were in turn protected by the Navy and Air Force units in the Philippines. But as shown before, the eruption of Mount Pinatubo and the change in government in Manila forced the closing of those bases. Okinawa is now isolated and exposed. Since Japan will not build up their forces, **(It is time for us to relocate our Military from Okinawa to Guam. They are sitting ducks for the numerous, advanced Chinese weapons of today.)**

Sudanese Offers

In January 1996 Clinton signed off on that NSC report that bin Laden was a threat to National Security. *The CIA and FBI were mandated to work together to find, gather evidence, arrest and prosecute bin Laden in a U.S. court.* **Alec Station** was setup by the CIA, and in NYC the JTTF assigned six agents to find bin Laden.

On February 6, 1996 Ambassador Tim Carney and longtime diplomat David Shinn met with Sudan's Foreign Minister Ali Osman Taha at his home, just a half-mile from bin Laden's farm / compound. While they spoke about terrorists Taha stated that Sudan wanted to improve their relations with America.

"If you want bin Laden, we will give him to you." ******(148)

It was decided to continue this line of dialogue in the U.S. and a meeting was organized. *But the next day all U.S. personnel were suddenly ordered out of Khartoum. The Administration considered the city to be "too dangerous to maintain any personnel". Ambassador Carney would have to shuttle in from far off Nairobi.*

Weeks later U.S. officials delivered a memorandum listing what Sudan needed to do to repair relations with the America. First on the list was getting rid of bin Laden and his terrorists. **There was no mention of following up on the Sudan's offer to arresting bin Laden, or on having the FBI arrest him as Clinton"signed off on"!** Incident # 68

Sudan's President Hassan al-Bashir met with Saudi officials to discuss bin Laden. It was well known how the Saudis felt about him, and Sudan was becoming eager to get rid of him. Sudan's only condition was that he not be prosecuted. (Which in Saudi Arabia probably meant beheading.) The Saudis refused to take custody of bin Laden for he was still looked upon as a Jihadist hero from his efforts in Afghanistan. A trial and execution was a surefire way to incite their people into rebellion.

Because the schools in much of the Middle East are religious in nature, their children are indoctrinated in those beliefs from a young age. At the same time those schools do little to prepare their young people for this modern world and the electronic age. Most of the young Muslims are unemployed or underemplyed, and all are easily angered and manipulated. And religion is used by many to control the thoughts of the people. All crimes are considered anti-Islamic, and that includes complaining about the Saudi regime. Any who do are quickly rounded up and imprisoned.

Non-Muslim tourists were not allowed into the Kingdom, and any travelers are strictly controlled. Even photography is not permitted. Saudi Arabia is as sealed up as any Fascist or Communist state ever was. And similar to how the Communist Party members ruled, the Saudi Royals live extravagant and well supplied lifestyles. A complete opposite from what the common citizens have. Hence the Saudi Royals need for extreme controls, just like the Communists used.

On March 3, 1996 Ambassodor Tim Carney, David Shinn and a representative from the CIA met secretly with Sudan's Minister for Defense Elfaith Erwa in a hotel in Virginia. Erwa and the CIA had worked together during the 1980s with Pres. Reagan. He had also helped Israel spirit out persecuted Jews from Ethiopia back in

1985, and he had even helped MI-6 a few times. For all of those efforts he was trusted by many.

Those talks were strictly "back-channel", and designed to "open the door for further action". Erwa was presented with a list of demands from the White House based on input from the CIA, State Dept., the Pentagon and the National security Council (NSC). Their two page proposal was titled Measures Sudan Could take To Improve Relations with the U.S.

Minister Erwa stated to the group that he could provide America with tons of information about bin Laden and his operations. CIA believed that there were two hundred al Qaeda operatives in the Sudan. In actuality there were *almost six hundred!* Among other topics the group discussed was closing the door to Hamas and Hezbollah. Erwa stated that that was not possible as both organizations were looked upon in their world as Islamic charities, while al Qaeda was clearly not.

When Erwa asked where he should send bin Laden, Carney stated anywhere but Somalia. **Incident # 69**

Five days later at a second secret meeting Erwa was surprised that the two diplomats were not present! **He stated that he was approved by his government to arrest bin Laden and hand him over to America!** *(149) (Sudan had turned in terrorist Carlos the Jackal in 1994 to the French, with CIA help.)

The Sudanese government was pleased to send bin Laden wherever the U.S. wanted, **or the CIA could come to Khartoum and pick him up.** The CIA agent present had not been given any prior authority for taking action. According to the Administration principals there was "nothing to hold bin Laden on"! (What happened to Clinton's Presidential Directive??)

In reality Clinton and his State Dept. did not want bin Laden brought to America for trial. That could cause him and the Democrats, Islamic problems, this was an election year.

Erwa then spoke of when Hassan al-Turabi welcomed bin Laden in 1992 things were much different and he had been welcomed. But with their recent "problems with Egypt", America and Saudi Arabia, bin Laden was causing much harm to their country. It was time for bin Laden to go. **Incident #70**

(Egypt and the Sudan were mortal enemies and as stated earlier, Egyptian forces had moved up to their common border. That was in addition to the power struggle between Turabi and President Bashir.)

Over the next few months additional diplomatic offers that were formal and informal were made from the Sudan. But this innane Administration did not want bin Laden. What they wanted was to try to push bin Laden off on the Saudis or Egyptians. Neither of those countries wanted him for fear of an extremist backlash.

Erwa warned the Administration staff that if bin Laden was evicted from the Sudan, he would just go back to Afghanistan and operate from there. And in that land it was doubtful anyone could ever get to him. * (150)

Erwa offered to keep bin Laden in place, and have his secret police the Mukhabarat keep a close watch on him and his group. Any potential terrorist actions could be observed and prevented. *Sudanese intelligence had penetrated all of bin Laden's shell and front companies, and they had extremely detailed records and photographs.* With CIA's help they were sure none of his terrorist efforts could succeed. But Clinton and his people wanted him evicted in the absurd hopes his terrorism would end. **Incident # 71**

After months of those empty meetings nothing was done by the Clinton Administration with those Sudanese offers. If the Administration had just taken the files on al-Qaeda the intelligence windfall could have destroyed them back in 1996! A July 1996 top-secret memo from the CIA to the NSC detailed how little they really knew about bin Laden and his al Qaeda terrorists. Those Sudanese files would have been gold. *(After the 9/11 attacks had devastated our nation the corrupt and deceitful Bill Clinton and his principals insisted that they never knew of those offers from the Sudan.)*

By this point our intelligence officials also knew of the active Saudi role in funding terrorism. **In a classified report the CIA identified fifty Islamic charities that were involved in dubious activities, and one third of those were linked to terrorist groups.** Yet the Clinton Administration turned a blind eye to those issues to promote commerce and "other policy interests".

The U.S. Intelligence Community issued a series of public NIEs, (National Intelligence Estimates), warning about the pending threats from ballistic missiles, illegal immigration, infectious diseases, etc. However Islamic Terrorism was never mentioned in any them, as per Clinton Administration's directives. **Incident # 72**

In late March 1996 Congressional oversight committees had hearings about Islamic terror networks and bin Laden. (Possibly leaks from the Sudanese efforts.) Both Democrats and Republicans on the House and Senate Intelligence Committees recognized the dangers bin Laden posed, and were surprised by the Clinton Administration's failure to act the past months.

(An advisor to Pres. Bush saw the files from the meetings with Minister Erwa after 9/11 had occurred. There was more than enough evidence to have arrested and convicted bin Laden.)

Afghanistan

Back in Afghanistan an Islamic coalition attempted to form a government. Ahmed Massoud had become the Defense Minister in the fractioned country. His northern alliance tribes returned to smuggling heroin, while everywhere else the local tribal warlords wanted a return to the old ways where each leader ruled his own area. Afghanistan remained a strife torn basket case.

As shown before our Afghan embassy was shut in 1990 as a trade off for Russia's military exit. In 1994 the U.S. Agency for International Development was shut down by Clinton. Thus we had no one on the ground to observe what was going on, no aid to offer those poor people. In reality no one in this Administration cared a bit, Afghanistan was so yesterday.

Pakistan viewed the new Afghan coalition government as being too pro-India. Their ISI had been using the Afghan terrorist camps to train their fighters for battles in Kashmir against India. This coalition was complicating things.

Their intelligence service (ISI) had been arming and training a group callled the Taliban. Their efforts to take power began in late 1994, and were heavily propagandized to help them succeed. They were slowly advancing in the southern part of the country. PM Benazir Bhutto and her generals soon realized that they could not control the Taliban as the Saudi's provided funding directly to Taliban leader **Mullah Mohammed Omar**.

(The Saudi's cut the funding to Afghan warlord Hekmatyar and gave it to the Taliban.)

Omar was another religious zealot, and a Fundamentalist who knew bin Laden well. He wanted bin Laden and his followers to return to Afghanistan, and bring his money and fighters. Bin Laden's training camps had continued to run, and his followers had been assisting the *Taliban*. Once they seized control of an area the Taliban invoked restrictive Islamic law, which was fine with bin Laden and his confederates. But the hardships and plight of the people was dramatically increased. Like the former Communist rulers, the Taliban eliminated everyone who stood against them.

What few people know even today was that the Clinton Administration was helping the Taliban! Benazir Bhutto had visited Clinton and staff in Washington in the spring of 1995 to discuss the region. Bhutto was pushing for new trade routes from Central Asia, and naturally she wanted them to go through Pakistan. She also wanted the U.S. sanctions on Pakistan ended, (over their nuclear research). She lied about the nature of the Taliban, claiming they were benevolent and religious.

From late 1994 into 1998 U.S. support was given to the Taliban because naive *Administration officials "saw them as do-gooders, similar to our bible belt Christians"*. The Clinton Administration overlooked any wrongdoings as "just part of their civil issues", and that included the especially hateful way women were treated. (Strange how the Democrats overlooked those humanitarian issues with the Taliban but not the from the more beneficial rule of the Shah or from Somoza.)

As always behind the scenes there was a key stimulus that promoted the Administration's unusual foreign policy, money. *They were backing the Taliban so energy companies could begin a huge commercial project.* Vast areas of the former Soviet dominion were now open to western companies for exploration. Unocal Energy Company wanted to build an energy pipeline from Turkmenistan through Afghanistan to Pakistan. With the collapse of the Communists those energy sources could now be transported out for the worlds use, and great profits. Russia owned the existing regional pipelines, and they were at extreme odds with Turkmenistan over their use and pricing. As a result those oil and gas fields were shut down.

But if Turkmenistan could get new, private routes out, it would mean no more Russian interference. For Unocal getting those energy supplies around hostile Iran and to the sea was the hard part. Political stability in Afghanistan that came from the Taliban running things was something the Administration felt "we could live with", to get the fuel and money flowing.

Turkmenistan was another isolated dreary nation, forgotten by most of the world. Unocal's proposals brought incredible possibilities, for if they succeeded the European Capitalists would not be long in coming. And Pakistan was in dire need of energy, so this Unocal project could solve all kinds of problems. *Unocal gave readily to the Democratic political campaigns.*

Former CIA agent Robert Baer knew the region well. This Unocal affair was a corrupt "sea of self absorption". *(151) **This White House and National Security Council became houses of commerce, where the interests of big business and**

money outweighed any thoughts on national security. NSC's Sandy Berger held $90,000 of stock in one company that "won contracts there". Clinton readily assured those corporate donors that "his Administration" would listen to their concerns.

The four freed countries of Turkmenistan, Uzbekistan, Azerbaijan and Kazakhstan sat on 50-100 Billion barrels of oil reserves, and 250 Trillion cubic feet of natural gas. The policy was to "promote the independence of those nations, and break Russia's monopoly on the energy supplies". *(152) Multiple oil pipelines that avoided Iranian and Russian control were a good thing regardless of the Islamist threat. (And any donations were always appreciated.)

Even with so much administration support the State Department still sent a warning memo to the NSC in 1996 advising that the Iranians, Russians and India were all against the Taliban taking control in Afghanistan. *All of those countries feared a Sunni-Fundamentalist regime taking over in their region, and would probably back any alternative to the Taliban.*

For Iran, Shia extremists were a good thing, but the Sunni Taliban were fiercely anti-Shia so Iran naturally feared them. Russia was alarmed at the Taliban spreading their influence into central Asia and southern Russia, so they could not allow them to win. And India fought the Taliban takeover as a way to deny Pakistan a game-changing potential ally. Hostilities flared anew.

By the late spring of 1996 Benazir Bhutto was convinced the ISI was running the Taliban without her approval. To her it seemed that some in the ISI wanted the Taliban to take over the country and become a separate entity instead of being Pakistan's ally. U.S. officials spoke with Pakistani generals who felt they were trapped by the momentum of what they had created.

Saudi Arabia

After months of doing nothing over the November 1995 attack in Riyadh, and after months of doing nothing over the Sudan's offers to had bin Laden over, it was decided by Clinton and his staff that bin Laden would just be pushed off on some other nation. With the next presidential election just six months away it was too close for Clinton to take any political risks. **Clinton insisted bin Laden be kicked out of the Sudan instead of arresting him.**

The many months of U.S and Egyptian diplomatic pressure had convinced the Sudanese it was time. They subtly warned him it was no longer safe in the Sudan. Egypt's President Mubarak had mobilized his forces and stationed them on the Egyptian-Sudan border. If Sudan did not expel bin Laden soon Egypt was going to go in and get him. Bin Laden's "unanticipated" expulsion from the Sudan was ordered in late May 1996, and he began making his plans to escape. **Incident # 73**

Iran

Iran was still supporting their own terrorists and ordered terror attacks throughout the world. They used their front group Hezbollah as an attacking force first in Lebanon against the West especially America, and of course against Israel. They were effective at taking hostages for ransom, and opened chapters in numerous countries. Because of their terrorist actions, sanctions against Iran had continued and were made worse.

During March 1996 over a period of nine days four suicide bombings took place inside Israel killing sixty two and wounding over two hundred. *Clinton's reaction was to orchestrate a summit in Egypt so the Arab governments could reject terrorism.*

In the Persian Gulf more and more of the small islands became bases for Iran's newest anti-ship missile systems. With the constricted access into and the limited size of the Persian Gulf those missiles were a real threat to all shipping. And as shown before, Iran was upgrading their weapons systems by using the latest N. Korean ballistic missile. The only major enemy the Iranians had in the region was us, operating out of Bahrain. But the Administration did nothing over that threat.

Back in 1970 the Shah had tried to lay claim to Bahrain but was refused by the U.N.. Over the years their attempts at taking Bahrain had continued, *but the Shah did take three other islands near the UAE in 1971.*

Bahrain holds 700,000 people, and is ruled by a Sunni Moslem family. But half of Bahrain's population was comprised of Iranian Shia. (The UAE has over 20% Shia.) Since 1979 the Ayatollahs also **insisted on taking Bahrain back**. During 1993 the Iranians even tried to stage a coup to take over. For them, the Persian Gulf is named that way for a reason.

As a result of that 1993 action Bahrain offered their main port as a permanent stopover for the U.S. Navy, and by 1996 Bahrain had become the home port for the U.S. Fifth Fleet. Having little oil or gas wealth they had turned their country into a Western-style destination of banking, resorts, entertainment and shops. A perfect getaway for rich Muslims looking for some western style fun. In doing so they were despised by the Islamists, especially those in Iran. And with thousands of Americans now based there, it was a haven of hatred.

Recent Hezbollah plots against the Bahrainian Royal family had been uncovered inside Saudi Arabia where the terrorists were based. *One of their strikes was to be directed at the U.S. Navy port facility.* Follow up FBI investigations into that plot came up short as the Saudi's again would not cooperate. As always nothing was done about it by the Administration. **Incident # 74**

In May 1996 Belgium authorities intercepted a shipment that had been destined for Germany. Inside a container marked "pickles", was the largest military mortar ever seen. This weapon was designed to lob a heavy explosive charge a short distance. The height generated by the mortar would easily clear any protective walls and drop the large shell into buildings/ compound. **That shipment was traced back to Iran.   Incident # 75**

Khobar Tower Bombing

On June 25, 1996 the **Khobar Towers** residence in Riyadh, Saudi Arabia was attacked with a massive truck bomb. One military guard saw the vehicle pull up, park, and its occupants run to a waiting car. Sentries on the roof called in a warning and an alarm was sounded, but only three floors could be evacuated before the explosion. Nineteen more U.S. service members were murdered with 515 injured! In what was becoming a common side show Clinton was once more on TV shaking his limp fingers, (from never working a day in his life), at the cameras and saying unconvincingly that the guilty would be punished.

Four terrorists had smuggled the explosives into Saudi Arabia from Lebanon. They bought a gasoline tanker truck and converted it into a huge mobile bomb. Unable to get next to the Tower itself because of barricades, they parked on a side road about 25 yards away. This blast was equivalent to 20,000 pounds of TNT and was felt 20 miles away. Six other buildings were severely damaged. **Incident # 76**

During the past weeks USAF personnel had reported that they were under constant surveillance. But the Saudi security people refused to take any action on the potential suspects. *They also prevented the U.S. personnel from acting on them.*

After the bombing the Saudi's were again reluctant to pursue the case, and showed no intention of cooperating. They denied any American access to the investigation. Again Clinton did nothing to force them to.

Saudi Intelligence chief Turki al-Faisal was thought to be an ally, especially after our efforts in Afghanistan and Desert Storm. But al-Qaeda had many supporters inside the kingdom.

Eleven suspects were eventually rounded up by the Saudi's. *They were given a secretive trial and executed. No notice was given to the FBI or State Dept. prior to the trial and execution.* (To lesson the danger from further attacks all U.S. personnel were relocated to the remote Prince Sultan air base deep in the Saudi desert.)

A day after the blast bin Laden received a congratulatory call from EIJ leader Ayman al-Zawahiri praising him. Another call from the Palestinian Islamic Jihad, PIJ, came from **Ashra al-Hadi**. Though our intelligence services had trouble finding the source of the bombing, the other terrorist groups apparently did not.

The CIA had unquestionably connected bin Laden to the attack in Saudi Arabia, but again Clinton did nothing.

Four days later bin Laden secretly left Port Sudan aboard an unmarked jet and landed in Khartoum, Sudan. Greeting him was **Nafi ali Nafi** from the Sudanese National Islamic Front. After the greeting bin Laden returned to his farm compound near Soba to finish his affairs. His escape plans had been completed and his antagonists punished. Soon after Bin Laden and staff made his secretive flight out of the Sudan and safely relocated to Afghanistan. He was welcomed back as a hero. **Incident # 77**

Because of Bill Clinton's incompeence and stupidity, the last easy chance to get bin Laden had just slipped away. This unwanted relocation and break-in period with the Taliban again delayed their plans to bomb our embassies in East Africa.

One interesting historical **What If** now comes up.

What if al Qaeda had bombed our East African embassies before the election as they had wanted too? If Clinton stayed true to form and did nothing would he have been defeated in the 1996 election? He won with just 49% of the vote against a weak candidate, again thanks to the dispersive effect of Ross Perot.

It was discovered over a year later, that in early 1996 the Saudi's had used bomb sniffing dogs to uncover explosives hidden inside a vehicle at their border. Under "interrogation" the driver gave up his terrorist cell **Hezbollah.** More arrests followed, and the investigation uncovered a plot to destroy a U.S. Military facility there. *The targeted location was kept secret and the Saudis never passed on any of that vital information. Was it the Kobar Tower?*

Bin laden was angry when he returned to Afghanistan in late June 1996 with his al Qaeda army. His finances were in tatters and his group was having a hard time finding new recruits. But he and al Qaeda assisted the Taliban's efforts, and bin Laden even swore an oath of loyalty to Mullah Omar the Taliban leader. That insured he was safe from any betrayal.

As the weeks went by bin Laden was able to reconnect to the golden chain of jihadist money that came from the countries of the Middle East. And he became more determined to enact large scale violence against America. *That August he issued an open call for war against the U.S.* **Incident #78**

Ayman al-Zawahiri did not return to Afghanistan with bin Laden. He decided to travel to Chechnya to resurrect his own brand of Jihad. For him small continuous attacks were just as effective as a few large ones. He was quickly arrested in Dagestan by the Russians who threw him in prison. But al-Zawahiri had wisely traveled with false papers and it was not discovered who he was. Months later he was released, reuniting with bin Laden in Afghanistan. Big plans were coming.

On July 17, 1996 TWA Flight 800 took off normally from JFK airport headed to Paris. Minutes later at 17,000 feet it exploded and was destroyed. The wreckage (and passengers 230) fell into the sea. Smaller debris and the remains of many victims floated on the surface while the larger pieces sank just off of Fire Island, NY. The largest recovery effort ever was directed to recover the parts of the plane to determine what had happened. **Incident # 79**

(This incident was very similar to the bombing of Pan Am Flight 103, Philippines Flight 434, and what was supposed to have happened to our airliners in the **Bojinka Plot** that was stopped in Januaray 1995.)

Over 100 eye-witnesses who were at or near the shore that night were interviewed. They viewed the event from an arc of 270 degrees, and *many reported seeing a rocket-type object rise-up from the sea and strike the passenger plane.*

Their reports were quickly discounted by the "Federal authorities", and eventually under political pressure the FBI and NTSB claimed a "fuel-tank explosion" had occurred from a short circuit. Those witnesses strongly objected to that claim.

That "fuel-tank event" had never happened in the forty previous years that passenger jet aircraft had been flying. It has not happened afterwards either, even in tests that were conducted. Strangely no safety changes or inspections were instituted on any existing plane, or on any new ones being built, to "prevent that catastrophe from ever happening again".

(Not until I highlighted this event in my first book, *My Turn on the Firelines* in 2009 did the government suddenly decide to "order safety changes for aircraft fuel tanks". Any connection??)

One of the competing theories on this explosion suggested an accidental missile launch by the military had occurred. Operating close by the day of the explosion was a joint training exercise with the Coast Guard and Navy. Perhaps a missile was accidently launched as had happened to the Iranian jet in 1988. For others this was a deliberate terrorist missile attack from a small vessel sailing off-shore. (Which was also possible.)

There was one other possibility that was totally ignored, or covered up by the Administration. That terrorists had gotten Ramzi Yousef's home-made nitro glycerin onto the airliner and placed it over the main fuel tank as Ramzi tried to do in the Philippines in 1995. That would explain the extensive fireball that was seen. (Toiletries were banned on Pacific overseas flights, but not on flights from here until 2006! Why??)

In any case all of those other possibilities were dismissed by the authorities to allow for the "accidental fuel tank scenario" to take hold. This Administration did not want anything to distract from the upcoming election. And to use this tragedy to his electoral advantage, Clinton went to New York to meet with the families. His perceptibly insincere "I feel your pain" facade garnered good press from the complicit media.

(Scamming Bill Clinton never met with the World Trade Center bombing victims or families, and never ever spoke or met with any of the military victim's or families from the other attacks!)

As so often happens with the Democrats and calamity, a lot of critical information was withheld from the public.

Explosive residue was found by the FBI inside the plane at three separate locations. And there was no evidence of any fire damage inside the aircraft in the area of the fuel tank.

While at that public relations event Clinton proposed new air travel safety regulations. Under this new policy passengers would have to show a government issued ID to board an aircraft, random passenger and baggage checks would be made, there was no more vehicle parking /standing near the terminals, and curbside check-in would be suspended.

Here is where some vital questions needed to be asked by the media. *Just what did those safety measures have to do with an accidental fuel tank explosion caused by an electrical short-circuit?*

Not much. But they meant a lot to stopping another terrorist bombing against an airliner.

It was also announced that V.P. Al Gore would head a Commission on Aviation Safety. Earlier that year a ValuJet aircraft had caught fire and crashed into the everglades in Florida because it was carrying hazardous cargo that ignited. Over one hundred had died in that unnecessary crash. The mechanic who mishandled the oxygen tanks took off and is still at large. He is on the FBI's ten most wanted list. *(And maybe that was another terrorist attack?)*

A key point governing "this commission" was that it was "non-binding". That meant that nothing they recommended had to be implemented! *Another important point "missed by the media", was that the Commission findings would not be completed until "after the election". In that way they would have no impact on the election results.*

Al-Qaeda

Not long after bin Laden left the Sudan the previously mentioned **Jamal al-Fadl** turned himself in and sought protection. He had been stealing money from the terrorist network in reprisal for his perennial low pay. Now feared for his life.

Al-Fadl was Sudanese, and had immigrated to America in the mid-80s and lived in Brooklyn. Like so many he had helped out at the Alkifah Refugee Center and worked with Mustafa Shalabi. His main job had been to raise money and find recruits to send to Afghanistan. After a while he too went to fight, and months later was introduced to bin Laden. After a few weeks of refitting he went back to the fighting until he was sent to Khost where Jamal trained at numerous bin Laden camps.

For his dedication to the cause he began meeting the senior people who would form al Qaeda. That list included Ayman al-Zawahiri, Mohammed Atef, and Abu al-Banshiri (whose Egyptian name was Amin al-Rashidi). After weeks of discussions Jamal became the third member who signed up for the duration of their Fundamentalist cause. Not long after the Afghan war ended.

Afghanistan had been destroyed by the fighting and Jamal told investigators that Azzam wanted to rebuild the country and then move on to help the Palestinians. Bin Laden only wanted war. He wanted to strike at the "head of the snake", meaning America. The terrorists among them eventually won the argument, and as shown earlier Azzam was murdered with two of his sons.

The winners of that infighting knew they needed a better place to run their Jihad than landlocked and desolate Afghanistan. Sudan had been taken over by the NIF, National Islamic Front in 1989, so it was decided to relocate there. A small group led by one **Abu Hajer** was sent over with al-Fadl to evaluate the prospects.

While all of that was being organized bin Laden had gone back to his home in Jeddah, Saudi Arabia. Though he worked in the family construction business his heart was for revolution. Soon after Iraq invaded Kuwait and the Americans showed up in Saudi Arabia. That outrage gave bin Laden his next targets and reason for war.

Al-Fadl returned to the Sudan in 1990 with **Abu Abdullah**, (a bin Laden son) and **Mamdou Salim** to find houses and farms to rent and buy. Once that was done Al-Fadl personally smuggled four crates of explosives into Yemen from bin Laden's new Sudanese farm at Soba. On another smuggling operation he led a camel train into Egypt full of AK-47 assault rifles. By late 1991 Jamal was a rising star in al Qaeda, and bin Laden was living in the Sudan after his banishment from Saudi Arabia.

At a later meeting with bin Laden and Salim, the al Qaeda leaders decided the continued presence of Americans in Saudi Arabia had to be stopped. They knew that even into 1992 they could not yet strike into his old homeland, but they could easily get at the Americans who were in Somalia on their "humanitarian mission". Bin Laden sent a team back to Afghanistan to retrieve the *Stinger* and *Milan missiles* they had hidden in caves. A cargo plane was used to bring foods to Afghanistan, and then secretly returned full of arms and ammunition.

*That "Sudanese cargo plane" had actually been purchased in Arizona by one **Essam al-Ridi** an American Muslim.* Al-Ridi had previously worked with the Mujahedeen in Afghanistan, and also with bin Laden as a supply agent. His former partner from his Afghan days was the well known **Wadi al-Haj.** It was Haj who called Essam saying that they were in great need of a cargo plane.

Ridi located, bought and flew the plane from Arizona to the Sudan himself. He then met up with Haj who was in the process of taking over as bin Laden's aide. Jamal al-Fadl had been bin Laden's aide the past months, but weeks before al-Banshiri told Jamal to keep his workload light as they would be going to Somalia soon to fight the Americans, (Black Hawk Down).

He verified that the U.S. Army units in Somalia had been fighting bin Laden's terrorists, and why el-Haj had been summoned from America. (However al-Fadl did not go to Somalia, Mohammed Atef did.)

After bringing the plane back from Afghanistan, al-Ridi met with bin Laden for a face to face meeting. He turned down Bin Laden's job offer due to the low pay, and returned to the U.S. with no one the wiser.

From Jamal's detailed, cooperative statements the CIA and the Administration learned about al Qaeda's size and shape and how pervasive the network was. *(The same information they could have obtained from the Sudanese files the past year and a half!)*

Al-Fadl next admitted that Ramzi Yousef and the blind sheik Omar Rahman were part of al Qaeda, and that many of their members had trained with Iran's Hezbollah in Lebanon to learn how to make effective truck bombs!

With cells in over 50 countries bin Laden was not just a financier. He was the mastermind of a huge terrorist organization financing terrorists and smuggling arms and jihadists throughout Africa, Europe and the Middle East.

Al-Fadl also informed the CIA that Bin Laden had an old Saudi business friend open up the innocuous sounding *Advice and Reformation Committee* (ARC) in London. **Khaled al-Fawwaz** used that office to complain about the Saudi Royals, but its main function was as a **secret communication center for al Qaeda!**

While in the Sudan Jamal was assigned to the unit to produce chemical weapons. He had made contacts inside the Sudanese Army, and in a $1.5 million dollar deal tried to get a canister with weapons grade uranium. (The prior story of the red mercury.) Al-Fadl was the key everyone had been looking for to cracking al Qaeda.

As stated before the CIA had no human assets within bin Laden's sphere and with Clinton's rules on recruiting it was doubtful they ever would. Most of the human intelligence we had been getting came from foreign intelligence services. The high-tech gizmos that America relied on were somewhat effective in the trials of the Cold War, but were of limited use against this enemy. Similar to organized crime of the 1930s-60s, those terrorists only worked with others from that region, people they actually knew or referrals from others in their world. No outsiders could get access to them.

Thanks to al-Fadl the CIA now knew that bin Laden was working with other terrorists, including Iraqis, Kuwaitis, Egyptians, Palestinians and the Iranians. New cells had been established in Indonesia and the Philippines, and recent warnings highlighted Iraqi contacts in the development and training in chemical weapons.

(Documents captured after the Iraq War in 2003 highlighted Saddam's efforts at supporting numerous terrorist organizations including EIJ and Ayman Al-Zawahiri.)

No matter how many times Clinton and company claim they did not know, with these sources their lie is visible.

In December 1995 a large arms cache had been discovered by the Kuwaiti's in Al Wafrah. Bin Laden told his supporters not to worry about that loss for there were many others. Those arms had originally been stolen from the Kuwaiti's during the Iraqi occupation. Some of those weapons ended up in Bosnia promoting that war, that was how well organized and supported al Qaeda was.

In a 1996 report the CIA learned of the incident above, and *confirmed that in August 1995* bin Laden had met with an Iraqi intelligence agent, a Sudanese army officer, an Egyptian terrorist, a Palestinian explosives expert and a Bahraini agent. Their targets were thought to be in eastern Saudi Arabia, and bin Laden had **20 Tons** of C-4 shipped into the Sudan from Poland! Two tons of that C-4 went to his former homeland, while the rest went to Qatar. (It was probable that some of those explosives had been used in the previous bombings.) **Incident # 81**

Nuclear Threats and Corruption

Throughout 1996 the U.N. weapons inspectors had gone over half of the half-million pages of documents they had been given by the defection of Saddam's son in law Gen. Hussein Kamil al-

Majid. In those pages the inspectors were learning on how France was helping Iraq with their long range ballistic missile program. *Those upgraded Iraqi missiles would soon be able to carry a crude nuclear warhead that the Iraqi's had designed. All they needed was the uranium.*

(Saddam's invasion of Kuwait actually hurt him more than he realized. Had he not invaded them in all probability Iraq would have had nuclear weapons by 1992.)

In 1997 Hillary Mann of the Institute For Near East Policy wrote how those documents revealed Saddam's true intentions. He was actively sending their best students abroad, especially to America to study at our universities and nuclear labs in order to develop their own WMD programs. (The story of our nuclear labs.)

Echoing the warnings from the Dept. of Energy Security Chief Edward McCallum, she highlighted the poor security procedures which allowed almost anyone into our sensitive schools and labs. None of those students are monitored once they do come in. *(153)

During this time Clinton repeatedly lied to the American people about potential threats from the increasingly militaristic China. He told the nation that for the first time since the dawn of the nuclear age not a single nuclear weapon was pointed at us. *No one in the media jumped on this obvious lie, as everyone including the naive Clinton knew that China and Russia still had weapons targeting the U.S.*

Secretly Clinton had signed off on additional export control waivers to allow even more sensitive missile technology to be sold to China! And he never mentioned that the import company was a big donor to his fund raising.

But that was not all.

Clinton also shifted satellite technology controls, (COCOM system) from the State Dept. to the Commerce Dept. because they had less stringent oversight. More fund raising money came in. **All of those actions by Clinton had occurred despite the recent Chinese theft of our most advanced warhead designs!** That theft was discovered in April 1995, and Clinton was told of it months later. Burt even with such a dangerous episode of espionage he was unmoved and the issue was "kept quite". He had an election to win and that required money.

Thanks to "Bill's actions", Communist China now has missile technology the equal of ours, and they are sharing that knowledge with N. Korea and Iran.

(Communist China began copying Iran's moves, claiming the small islands in the S. China Sea. Nothing was done to stop them, and by 1999 China greatly increased their threatening presence by **creating small islands** in the open water! Then they placed their flag and some missiles on them to keep everyone else out and control the sea lanes for hundreds of miles around. **Again the Clinton Administration said and did nothing about it, and that situation is far worse today**.)

Sudan's Files

Mansour Ijaz an American-Muslim businessman was a self-made multimillionaire. Well educated he had developed the CARAT computer system that enabled his clients to make fortunes. Like many he fell under the allure of being a "friend to Bill Clinton" and raised almost a million dollars for him and the Democrats. That enabled him to enter the high society of the Administration, and he met with many of the principals over the past years.

Terrorism was a serious issue in Pakistan and his father wanted his son Ijaz to continue his work to help them. Ijaz traveled back to his father's home a few times which gave him a feel for bin Laden and his vast appeal to the unhappy masses. Ijaz also decided to travel to Sudan to meet with their national leaders.

Sudan has suffered from civil war since it was founded from the British in 1956. They are the largest nation in Africa, but also one of the poorest. Before he could go there he had to visit the State Dept. and be briefed. As a friend of Bill it was all arranged for him to travel in July 1996. Senior Sudanese officials were still anxious to have the U.S. sanctions removed from their country, **as nothing had been done with their previous offers from February and March and the expelling of bin Laden.**

Meeting with **Hassan Turabi** and his aide **Sanousi**, Ijaz and his business partner Luftur Khan were lectured about the many threats the Sudanese had gotten from the Clinton Administration. Their "diplomacy" was not going well and the men met five more times over the next week. Ijaz advised the Sudanese to make a direct appeal to the U.S. government.

A letter on Hassan Turabi's letterhead was addressed to Pres. Clinton proposing full cooperation with America to stop global terrorism. It was faxed to Ambassador Carney's temporary office in Kenya. Carney was completely surprised by the offer and immediately sent three faxes. One went to the State Department, one to the CIA and the third to the White House at the National Security Council, (NSC) and Sandy Berger.

As usual, there was no response. Incident # 82

Ijaz returned home and on August 21, 1996 was summoned to the White House. Deputy National Security Advisor **Sandy Berger** and **Susan Rice** then in charge of the African Affairs section angrily met with Ijaz. *They were upset that he had succeeded.* Turabi had again offered to let the FBI come to Khartoum to examine their al-Qaeda files in an effort to show how much they wanted a new relationship with the U.S. However both bureaucrats refused to believe the letter sitting in front of them. Ijaz returned to the Sudan to get more proof.

A few days later he was taken to the office of **Gutbi al-Mahdi,** the great grandson of the famous Mahdi who had led the Sudanese rebellion against the Europeans in 1885. In 1996 Gutbi ran Sudan's intelligence service, and produced a copy of a threatening letter the administration had sent to Sudan in 1994. A similar threatening letter was made in 1995. Is this how America seeks friendship?

Ijaz sent the copy of the letter to Berger's office on September 13, 1996. *Berger called Ijaz a few days later and told him we will talk about this after the election. Ijaz needed to continue with the vital work of fund raising!* At that point in time the only thing Clinton and his staff were interested in was buying time and votes to win the election.

A month later Ijaz again returned to the Sudan and met with **President Bashir** who told Ijaz his efforts were appreciated. Pres. Bashir informed the well meaning civilian that they had made repeated offers to America but all had been refused. **Bashir even told Ijaz about the earlier negotiations with the Administration to send bin Laden to the Saudi's or the U.S., and of how those were also refused!** And even after Sudan had expelled bin Laden your government sanctions were still in effect.

After more discussions Bashir reluctantly allowed Ijaz to meet again with Mahdi to see their vast intelligence files on bin Laden. Upon his return to the U.S., Ijaz sent another letter to Berger. He repeated Pres. Bashir's and al-Mahdi's concerns and their problems with the Administration. Ijaz also spoke of the Sudan's frequent anti-terrorist offers that go unanswered. Berger repeated his former line, nothing will be done until after the election.

But nothing ever happened, even after Clinton got back in. Incident # 83

Around this time a **Janet McElligott,** a lobbyist and consultant had a meeting with **Mohammed Ibrahim** Sudan's Ambassador to the U.S. He invited her to lunch to discuss helping the Sudanese with the Administration. Despite their many previous attempts to improve ties, Berger and Rice showed no interest in advancing the relations between their nations. Sudan had been unable to secure any meeting with any senior Administration official, and Ibrahim hoped McElligott could help as they were desperate.

McElligott had worked in the U.S. Senate and for the Bush Administration. (She had helped secure the release of some hostages months earlier.) It was thought that she could explain to the Sudanese how Washington worked. During February she became a paid consultant /lobbyist for the Sudan.

As she learned the workings of the Sudan she too became educated about bin Laden and his group. **Bakri Salih** Sudan's Minister of the Interior spoke with her for hours about the terrorist leader. He also spoke of their vast intelligence files. The Sudanese decided to use her as a courier to get information out to the Administration, and FBI agent David Williams who worked counter-terrorism. Soon after the Sudanese issued repeated warnings. **Another al Qaeda attack was coming, and McElligott passed on the messages.** Incident # 84

The 1996 Olympics

With the summer 1996 Olympics being hosted in Atlanta Counter-Terrorism Czar Clarke and his staff which included most of the federal agencies visited the site and pre-planned for security concerns. *Alerted by the intelligence from the 1995 Philippines Bojinka Plot and the terrorist attack a few months ago in Paris, Clarke worried that somehow a passenger jet would be blown up over the stadium, or hijacked and flown into the stadium.*

(Again proof that the intelligence from those prior attacks had been seen by the Administration.)

Admiral Flynn who was a retired Navy Seal and the head of FAA security warned Clarke that even if they had a no fly zone established over the city a hijacking / attack on a jetliner could still occur. He also warned him that our Air Force fighters would not be able to respond in time to a hijacking unless they were already airborne and flying CAP, (combat air patrol.)

He further warned him that if the terrorists turned off the planes radar transponder our civilian aviation radar systems would not be able to see the plane at all!

Our Civilian Air Traffic Control system works by being told from *the planes equipment* where and how high up the plane is. Without that signal the aircraft becomes invisible to civilian radars. Only military radar systems would be able to find a hijacked jet from among the hundreds of aircraft in the air. But in 1996 none of those systems were in operation inside our nation. A military representative then explained that by law the military could not shoot down a civilian plane inside the U.S. unless we were at war.

After a lengthy debate on the problem the FBI agent present told Clarke it would be best to not let a plane get hijacked.

Additional security concerns centered on the multitude of rail lines that run in, around and under the city of Atlanta. Fears of the Paris and Tokyo railroad terrorist attacks were discussed. Surveillance and security were daunting tasks in their own right, but responding to an attack in a rail tunnel was a nightmare. Intense security for the Olympics was finally organized with a lot of effort by Clarke and the other services. Hundreds of extra agents from many different agencies were brought in.

Despite their efforts, a lone bomber was able to place a small bomb in a bag that went off on July 27, 1996. The FBI wrongly zeroed in on a security guard, and after discovering their mistake were unable to catch the real bomber Eric Rudolph. **Incident # 85** *(Rudolph was finally apprehended by local police in 2003, but only after he had committed other terrorist acts.)*

This episode illustrates just how hard counter-terrorism efforts are. Even on full alert Rudolph slipped through and struck. For Clarke that episode highlighted just how easy it would be to strike anywhere inside America. But he could not persuade Clinton that terrorism was a serious threat.

Bin Laden

Osama Bin Laden made a second public decree for War against America on August 23, 1996. He called for all Islamic groups to kill Americans wherever they were found. His master plan was to drive the Americans from the Middle East, destabilize and take over Saudi Arabia. After Israel was destroyed, Bin Laden truly believed that their efforts would bring on the apocalypse, which would then be followed by the triumph of Islam. (Nostradamus)

He mocked America and the hollow words emanating from Washington. "Where was your supposed bravery in Beirut after the attack in 1983? Where was your bravery in Aden where you fled after two small attacks? And again in Somalia you fled after one night of battle. You were disgraced by Allah and you withdrew. Your impotence and weakness became very clear". *(154)

From Bin Laden's propaganda machine,

"The Hadith, (a saying from the prophet), says if you see Black Banners coming from Khurasan, (the original Caliphate from central Asia), all Muslims should join that army as no power will be able to stop you." *(155)

Bin Laden picked black as al Qaeda's flag, because it was the flag of Khurasan. Agents assigned to the JTTF and the CTC analyzed this latest call to war and knew this was not an idol threat. Clinton had no reaction. **Incident # 86**

Reports went to the White House that terrorists were plotting to use airliners as weapons. (Was this is the original intelligence from the Philippines Bojinka plot and the Murad interrogations, or did some new Intel come in like the hijacking in Paris?) Again nothing was done. **Incident # (87)**

In September 1996 the CIA sent Gary Schroen to Kabul on a secret mission to reestablish contact with Ahmad Massoud. Massoud was skeptical because after the Soviets left all of America's help went too. Schroen told him the new enemy was terrorism. Within a year the CIA would be back in operation in Afghanistan. Many in this CIA were skeptical about Massoud's reliability. They had not dealt with him during the war years, and felt he could become a "problem for the Administration". * (156) In any event Ahmed Massoud was the only non-Fundamentalist game in town, and the Bin Laden Unit wanted some kind of operation started.

(For the CIA the Soviet defeat in Afghanistan was their proudest achievement.* (157) Throughout the Cold War we had been involved in numerous wars and affairs trying to stop the subversive communist expansion across the globe. In Afghanistan the CIA actions had won a victory over the source of forty five years of world conflict.)

One serious fallout from the Soviet-Afghan War was that some 600 hundred of our Stinger missiles were missing from the 2,000 plus we had sent to fight the Russians. *Many had turned up in Iran.* A program had been started in 1991 to "buy back" as many of the unused missiles as possible. Schroen told Massoud if he joined the program in retrieving missing Stingers he could expect a lot of aid. He showed Massoud the list of serial numbers of the 2,000+ missiles, but incredulously Massoud told him all he was given were eight, near the end of the war. Schroen reported that fact back to Langley and was informed it was true.

Massoud had been the best Afghan commander in the war. For that reason Pakistan's ISI was reluctant to give him and his northern tribes any missiles, lest they fight against them. *(158)

Schroen and Massoud next discussed bin Laden and the Fundamentalist Taliban taking over the country. CIA needed Massoud to develop reliable information and sources to get a handle on what was going on. As it was they were in the dark, and Massoud replied he would help. *(This is why Clinton allowing bin Laden to leave the Sudan was so idiotic. Now we had to try to reacquire him and setup shop in distant landlocked Afghanistan.)*

A week after Schroen left Kabul the Taliban, awash with bin Laden's money, weapons and fighters handed Massoud a harsh defeat as they approached Kabul from Jalalabad. Equipped with four-wheel drive pickups armed with rockets and machine guns the Taliban's mobile forces encircled the city's defenses. Showing true generalship and skill Massoud successfully withdrew to save his embattled forces. (Live today, fight again tomorrow.)

Clinton had no reaction to the looming Taliban takeover, he was still running for re-election. His State Dept. produced a sickening statement of emptiness and vagueness.

Once the Taliban surged through the city they invoked their extremist religious views and punishments upon the people. Women could no longer be seen in public, they had to be covered head to toe, girls could no longer work or go to school, and all western style influences like flying kites, haircuts or magazines were banned. Punishments were severe for having anything not approved by them.

Schroen met with a few Taliban officials to encourage them to join the Stinger missile return program. They refused to turn them in because they intended to fight Iran as soon as they finished off Massoud. No one was completely sure about the Taliban intentions, but it was well known that the Sunni Afghans did not like the Shiite Iranians. *(During this time period bin Laden moved his base of operations into the Kandahar region.)*

By the end of September 1996 the Taliban had completed their two year fight to take-over Afghanistan. Only in the northern provinces were local warlords able to keep them at bay. Fighting in that region was tough and the Taliban reluctantly gave up the quest. Former Afghan Pres. Najibullah and his brother who lived in the U.N. compound were both castrated, dragged through the streets and hanged. Huge statues of the Buddha which were carved into a mountain over 1000 years ago were blown up. For those extremists only Islamic teachings and images would be allowed.

To their south Benazir Bhutto was suddenly removed as Pakistan's Prime Minister, and returned to exile in London. Pakistan was heading towards the extremists.

On October 12, 1996 bin Laden again publicly declared war on America. With the election just weeks away the Administration again ignored this call for an Islamic Jihad against America. **Incident # 88**

America

Throughout the past months the 1996 elections were in full swing with senior Republican Senator Robert Dole a WWII vet running against Clinton. As with Ford, the media used every slip or fall as a way to promote Clinton. Dole was a poor choice to oppose the incumbent, even one so tainted by misconduct and scandals which many felt were criminal / treasonous acts.

(The Vince Foster case, Whitewater, Travelgate, Healthcare fraud, FBI-Filegate, campaign finance fraud, using the IRS to audit his "enemies", HUD's secretary's lies to the FBI about payoffs, the Utah Grand Staircase Monument Act, the secretary of Agricultures acceptance of gifts from companies he regulated, and hush money sent to help his friends, the Ron Brown affair at the Commerce Dept. and the numerous Campaign contributions affairs and spying scandals.....)

During this time Saddam Hussein was continually scheming and winning the fight against the U.N. sanctions. Clinton would appear tough for the sound bites, but continually gave in.

One instance involved Iraq trucking oil into Turkey and Jordan. Another was the 1996 agreement to allow him to sell oil for food. Clinton agreed with the Oil for food plan, while Dole had warned the deal would give Saddam a large source of revenue to make and purchase weapons. "Piously the Administration claimed the accord had stringent controls". But as always the Administration was lying and they knew it. Saddam got around all of the controls and inspectors, and had Billions to spend on weapons. *(159)

In reality Clinton wanted the extra Iraqi oil to hit the marketplace as it would lower the rising price of crude just in time for the election. During one of their debates Dole asked Clinton if he would pardon the growing list of former partners and friends who were now in jail. As always Clinton dodged the question, but that is just what he did.

In addition to the constant help from the media, (they repeatedly showed video of Dole falling at an event), the Democrats made sure they loosened the immigration laws to naturalize one million aliens just in time for the election. Of those new residents, over 75,000 had criminal records that should have disqualified them for citizenship. But they voted row D, so that was overlooked

And once again Ross Perot became a disingenuous third party candidate stealing needed independent votes away from the Republican candidate. When the ballots were cast, Clinton got 49%, Dole 40.7%, and Perot took 8% of the vote. That was less than half of what he took from Bush in 1992, but it was still enough to hand the win to Clinton.

Islamic Terrorism and Support

In late 1996 **Khalid Sheik Mohammad, (KSM)** was indicted by a New York Federal Grand Jury for supporting terrorism. Those charges reflected his complicity in the **1993 WTC bombing,** and his direct involvement in the 1995 **Bojinka Plot**. KSM was now a wanted fugitive, though at that time it was not known that he was the real mastermind of al Qaeda. (Here again was proof that the Clinton Administration knew of and understood the full story of the Bojinka Plot and the long term implications.)

Ethiopian Flight 961 from Nairobi to Addis Abba was hijacked on November 23, 1996 when three attackers **simply kicked in the door to the cockpit**. Determined to escape from Africa, they demanded to be flown to Australia. However the air liner was not fueled for such a trip and hours later the pilots were forced to try to ditch the plane near a tourist island. Just before they completed the dangerous move they ran out of fuel and lost control. (The crash was videotaped by shocked tourists.)

One hundred twenty innocents died, but fortunately dozens survived thanks to quick action from those ashore. Afterwards the survivors spoke of the simplistic takeover and of what they had witnessed. The airline industry and the governments of the world were informed on how insanely easy the hijacking had been. **But the real crime was that after this unnecessary disaster no security enhancements were forced upon the airlines! Incident # 89**

On December 3, 1996 Algerian terrorists placed an IED on the southbound tracks of a Paris bound commuter train. Four were murdered with one hundred seventy wounded. **Incident # 90**

In Bosnia the ceasefire had worked and was enforced by the U.N and 15,000 U.S. troops. Free elections were held with a 70% voter turnout, and all three ethnic groups were represented by the new government. *As usual it was military action which forced the ceasefire, not diplomacy.*

A new "Charity" was operating within Bosnia, called *the Saudi High Commission for Bosnia and Herzegovina.* (SHCBH) It was setup in Sarajevo by the Saudis, and was a state funded charity receiving 30% of their income directly from the Saudi government. (This "charity was run by Prince Salman, who in 2004 would become the Saudi King.)

What the SHCBH also did was to secretly help fund al Qaeda terrorists and provide jobs and cover stories. That enabled many al Qaeda fighters to get into and fight in Bosnia. And Bosnia was used as a way station for the Islamic terrorists to infiltrate into Europe. Washington knew of the SHCBH connections to al Qaeda, but as always Clinton took no action.

(Two weeks after the attacks of September 11, 2001, NATO raided the offices of SHCBH. They found hundreds of incriminating documents, maps and diagrams of facilities in Washington D.C. They also found details on how to fake U.S. State Department badges and IDs, and before and after photos of the World Trade Center. The 9/11 Commission would state that Saudi charities did fund al Qaeda, but there was no direct ties back to the Saudi leaders. (Wrong, or just lying.)

In early 1997 **Ali Hamadi** setoff a large car bomb in Bosnia in an effort to destroy the ceasefire and reignite the war. The bomb was purposefully targeted to kill only non-Muslims. **Incident # 91 (In a 2008 video confession Ali Hamadi highlighted his efforts in Afghanistan and Bosnia. It also shows that the Saudi's knew who they were helping.)** *(160)

Back in 1980 a large influx of Muslims began entering Europe. They continued their exodus, and by 2007 their population topped 25 million. **Unlike previous immigrant groups, the Muslims did not try to integrate into their host countries.**

Instead they formed their own communities, spoke only their languages and their children attended Islamic schools run by them. No mixing of the races was allowed, nor was the learning of English. Sharia law predominated and was based on the old principal of an eye for an eye. Those who drank or gambled got the whip, thieves lost their hand, adulterers were stoned, homosexuals were killed and men could hit women for any offense. Sharia demands that Muslims never integrate, they are to convert the land they go into. Any who stray from Islam are to be killed.

(In London some sections of the city are now Islamic, and recently the nation's laws were changed to promote Sharia principals! Basically they are creating a state within the host country. By 2005 France alone was home to 818 Islamic dominated areas. Muslims have been doing the same thing here, and in many states such as Michigan, our towns are now Islamic.)

Throughout the 1980s and 1990s Islamic groups also took up residence in America. They learned how to use our laws and system against us. As the Communists had done in the 40s and 50s, they became a "Fifth Column", to weaken our institutions.

In June 1994 *CAIR*, the Council on American-Islamic Relations was formed. Other groups were; The American-Arab Anti- Discrimination Committee, the Arab American Institute, the American Islamic Group, AIG, The Islamic Cultural Workshop ICW, the National Association of Arab Americans, MAYA the Muslim Arab Youth Association, the American Muslim Council AMC, the Islamic Circle of North America ICNA, the Muslim Public Affairs Council MPAC, the American Muslim Alliance AMA, the Islamic Society of North America ISNA, and the Association of Arab University Graduates.

All of those lobbying groups were purportedly formed to "enhance and protect" Muslim Americans. A main emphasis for these groups was to stop U.S. foreign policies they did not like. But they also raised funds, provided propaganda venues and in some cases directly supported terrorist organizations.

Another group that was mentioned earlier was called the *Islamic Association for Palestine, IAP*. IAP and CAIR had **extensive ties to Hamas and other terrorist groups including al Qaeda**. In 1989 the IAP dedicated their annual convention to the late **Abdullah Azzam**. He and his top aide Sheikh Tamin al-Adnani had visited the U.S. many times in the 1980s speaking in over fifty cities! Palestinian **Ghassan Dahduli** served as the IAP's vice president, and this active lobbying group worked constantly on their causes. (Dahduli's name would soon show up in the fallout from the bombing of the U.S. embassies in East Africa.)

The Muslim Armed Forces & Veterans Council was a spinoff of the *American Muslim Council.* Formed in 1993 by **Abdurrahman Alamoudi**, he created the entire Muslim chaplain corps for the Pentagon.

The Institute for Islamic and Arabic Sciences in America worked to "train imams" in American Mosques. That center was funded by the Saudi's, and set up by Alamoudi to teach and distribute the Wahhabi propaganda. *It is virulently anti-American.*

The *Graduate School of Islamic Social Sciences* was also funded by the Saudi's and used as a front for terrorist financing and training.

The *Islamic Society of North America* is another Saudi led group that also had ties to terrorists. During the winter of 1998 **Abdurrahman Alamoudi** would summon the heads of ISS and ISNA to a meeting to lobby the American political system to stop support for Israel and to weaken U.S. anti-terrorism laws.

One thing you the reader must understand, **you can not go into a Middle eastern nation and practice any religion other than Islam. Nor can you insult Islam.** Yet they can and do go anywhere they want, say anything they want, and demand their freedom of religion and speech from that country.

As the hunt for terrorist funding continued it became evident that much of the money was originating from Saudi sources. They were not cooperating, and Clinton did not push them to.

Anti-Terror Czar Clarke learned from a non-governmental source that al Qaeda was using a front organization to assist the travel needs of their terrorists. MAK, or **Makhtab Al Khidamar** was the "travelers aid organization".The director of the Counter-Terrorism Center discounted it as just an Islamic travelers group, but Clarke proved that it was being funded by bin Laden.

Active offices were found in New York and Arizona, both had active Islamic centers and Mosques used by the terrorists in those previous attacks. **Incident # 92**

(Later it was discovered that al Qaeda used the Islamic *Hawallahs* system to move their money around. Hawallahs are financial agents that keep strict ledgers on the groups finances. There were Hawallahs operating across New York, and terrorists also used Western Union offices to send money around making it even harder to track their funding.)

During 1997 a letter bomb campaign was started by terrorist friends of the WTC bombers. Most were identified before exploding, however two of the bombs did detonate in the offices of Al-Hayat in London injuring a dozen. Again Clinton did not react and his State Dept. feebly referred to the letter bombs as "possible acts of international terrorism". **Incident # 93**

In a February 1997 Arabic television interview bin Laden stated it was a moral obligation for Muslims to kill Americans, especially their soldiers. Again Clinton did not respond. **Incident # 94**

That same month a Palestinian schoolteacher opened fire on the observation deck of the Empire State Building in NYC. One person was murdered with six others wounded before the gunman shot himself. **Incident # 95**

During March 1997 bin Laden had a televised interview with CNN. He accused the Saudi Royal Family of treason to Islam by allowing Americans on their soil. The Saudi's were upset over his words and complained to Mullah Omar since they were funding the Taliban. He ignored their complaints.

On April 5, 1997 Sudan's President Bashir wrote a no-strings letter to Democratic Congressman Lee Hamilton on the foreign affairs committee. *"Come to Khartoum and see our files on bin Laden".* *(161)

Since there had been no reaction from the White House on any of their earlier offers, Bashir hoped the Congress would choose to intervene. Ijaz Mansour hand delivered this letter to Hamilton on April 16, 1997. He also sent a copy to Sandy Berger. Again there was no response from the Administration. **Incident # 96**

In early May 1997 the NSA picked up an important intercept that was forwarded to senior Administration officials on May 7. The report stated that "unnamed" authorities had arrested a top al Qaeda official in the Sudan. *He was the head of the financial committee of bin Laden's Islamic army.*

This al Qaeda paymaster had tons of valuable intelligence as his committee managed the finances and oversaw the audits of all of their members. **No one from the Administration pursued this intelligence bonanza either!** **Incident # 97**

(The only fallout from this important arrest was the capture with FBI help, of four members of EIJ operating in Albania.) **Incident # 98**

On May 21, 1997 Ijaz met with Clinton at another "fund raiser" and told him personally about the Sudanese offers the past two years and the urgent need to see their files on al Qaeda. Clinton dismissingly told him Berger will get me a full report. Sometime in the fall a weak attempt was made to "send eight diplomats" to Khartoum. But it never happened.

In those files were passports, dates, phone numbers, travel logs, pictures, aliases and names of all of the al Qaeda confederates Sudan knew of. Incident # 99

Not until July 2001 was that failure addressed, but by then it was too late.

(After 9/11 occurred Ijaz realized that two of the hijackers who flew into the World Trade Center were names he had heard about from his meetings with the Sudanese back in 1996. **The two White House officials who had repeatedly discounted his claims were Sandy Berger and Susan Rice.** The same Susan Rice who was complicit during the Obama-Clinton disasters.) *(161A)

On June 8, 1997 a U.S. grand jury finally indicted Osama bin Laden with conspiracy charges and found him guilty as the head of al Qaeda. (A lot of evidence had come from the interviews with Jamal al-Fadl.) **Clinton now had the complete legal right to pursue, arrest or target him at any time. Incident # 100**

Mir Amal Kansi the shooter at the CIA roadway back in 1993 was finally tracked to Pakistan. On June 15, 1997 an informant was required to identify the room he was in and called to him to come out for prayers. Kansi was then arrested and his identity confirmed. It was decided that the assets used to find and arrest Kansi would be transferred to the bin Laden unit to find him. With their legal warrants in place, Satellites and other technology were now being used to track his movements. **Incident # 101**

The NYC Subway Bombing Plot

On July 30, 1997 one Abdel Rahman Mussaba walked up to a patrol officer in the NYPD and reported on a suspicious group he felt were secretly making bombs. He showed the officer a derelict building that was in an empty part of Brooklyn. NYPD used a surveillance team to scout the location and they determined that Mussaba was correct, something illegal was going on inside.

In the early morning hours of the 31st, the NYPD stormed the structure. Realizing they were going to be caught one of the suspects pushed a handle on a large suitcase. Inside the suitcase was a large bomb, big enough to have killed most in the building. However his bomb did not detonate, because they had not made the last connection. That was to be done in a few hours.

Caught up in this raid were two more Islamic terrorists, **Ghazi Abu Mezer** and **Lafi Khalil. Their mission had been to ride the subways under the East River and detonate their suitcase bombs while the trains were in the cramped underground tunnels.** Those terrorists had done their homework. The subway lines they targeted had no emergency escape systems. Each pipe-bomb they had was lethal to over 25 feet, and each travel bag had four of them wired together plus black powder. At least one train car would have been destroyed per bomb.   **Incident# 102**

(The carnage in those trains would have been terrible, and would occur in Spain and England just a few years hence.)

Both terrorists were Palestinians, both had ties to Sheikh Rahman and both were here illegally. **Mezer had been apprehended three times over the past year by INS for illegally entering the U.S. through Canada.** The last time he was caught he was allowed to be free while awaiting a hearing trying to get asylum! He was also a member of **Hamas**, and Israel wanted to question him. NYC Mayor Rudy Giuliani was seething over why those known terrorists were still here and free on bail to plan and attack us.

(Many in our government wanted INS to change the way those types of legal procedures were handled. But even today that stupidity still exits as the liberals, Democrats, some Republicans and special interest groups refuse to enact any changes.)

Most do not know this, but Hamas is deeply entrenched inside America, and often had people go to the U.S. to funnel money and cargo back to the Palestinian areas. One **Mohammad Salah** was a naturalized citizen (by marriage), who could travel with a U.S passport even to Israel. He was often used as a courier bringing money from **Musa Abu Marzook** the head of the Hamas Political Bureau into the U.S.

Salah also organized trips into the U.S. for Palestinian youth so they could receive a weekend of terrorist training outside of Chicago. *There they were given instructions on car-bombs and other terrorist type activities.* (He had been arrested in 1993 but was released. He was later imprisoned by the Israelis.)

Similar to the foiled June 1993 NYC day of terror attacks, and the Bojinka Plot, **this "subway incident" was kept low key by the Administration.** Again their failed thinking was since the attack had been stopped there was no use riling up the public with unnecessary details.

(Months later we in the FDNY began drilling in those same subway tunnels. They were tight and constricted with limited access and no ventilation. Many of us felt that dozens of firefighters would die during any fire operations in them. Civilian deaths would be extreme. *At our training academy members of the U.S. military began (quietly) practicing operations on urban terrorism. Attacks all of us knew were coming.*)

More Democratic Disasters

After the election was over Clinton decided to begin a new liberal program called *Partners in the American Dream*. HUD, Housing and Urban Development which was run by NY leftist Democrat Andrew Cuomo Jr., "placed housing goals" on the Federal Housing agencies Fannie Mae and Freddie Mac. This socialistic goal was setup to increase the availability of mortgage credit to low income borrowers, especially minorities. But in mandating that action the Federal Government was *forcing the lenders to "make loans" based on the "quotas" that the Democrats wanted, not what was financially or economically sound.*

That required lenders to loosen the financial standards for those applying for a loan by cutting the normal safety factors out. This policy also forced our "federally insured depository institutions" deeper into the low-income lending program. *Which meant that the taxpayers would be on the hook for any bad loans.*

At first that program mandated the large quota of **30% of all mortgages** purchased by Fannie and Freddie **to be made** to borrowers at or below the median income in the places they lived. By 2000, HUD Sec. Cuomo had increased the number to an astonishing **50%!** And because the financial standards had to be reduced even further to insure those new quotas could be met, many of the loans were considered low quality. In non-Politically Correct terms low quality meant will probably default!

Once again a ludicrous Democratic program was to cause grave damage to our country. *Those low quality loans built up over the years and in 2007 caused the financial collapse that struck us full force in 2008.* Like most of their disasters, it did not cause a crisis until those who started it had left office. And as always, none of them were ever held accountable.

Soon after Clinton made another of those innocuous but incredibly wrong decisions, **he repealed Section 936 of the U.S. Tax Code.** That tax law (called Operation Bootstrap), *was initially enacted by Pres. Eisenhower as a way to help Puerto Rico* grow economically without the U.S. having to give direct financial aid. It provided tax breaks to corporations that setup shop in our territories like Guam and Puerto Rico.

Eisenhower's plan worked out fine as multiple companies opened up businesses on the islands increasing employment opportunities. *In 1976 Pres Ford, another Republican, extended the tax break.*

By 1980 that Republican promoted Tax law had increased total GDP, Gross Domestic Production in Puerto Rico ten fold, and had raised personal income by a factor of 1600!

But in late 1996 that same tax break came up for renewal. Since the election was over, Clinton refused, ending the program! **In the twenty years since Clinton repealed Section 936, jobs in Puerto Rico have fallen over 50%, GNP went down over 40% and the island's debt has gone through the roof to $123 Billion!** There has been no infrastructure upgrades since 2000, and the country has been run by a pack of thieves who have destroyed the once prosperous island. But you will never hear of that inconvenient truth by the major media.

And then Bill Clinton was caught up in yet another scandal. It was finally revealed, **(again after the election),** that the administration had been "renting" the Lincoln bedroom in the White House to big money donors. In addition to that serious law breaking, it was found that "impoverished Buddhist monks," who were not even citizens, had somehow contributed multiple thousands of dollars to Clinton's reelection campaign. Once more the administration was on non-stop damage control.

But ever more issues were coming.

During the 1990s the Clinton-Reno Justice Dept made sweeping changes to law enforcement procedures by banning any type of "racial profiling". Their ruling makes sense in basic traffic and minor criminal offenses, but would cripple our efforts at stopping terrorism. FBI profilers are among the best in the world at spotting criminal trends. As anyone with a clear mind knows, the most reliable way to predict future behavior is to examine past behavior. And that is what profiling does, it examines the behavior, actions and pasts of suspects. In the case of terrorism, certain traits and signs are indicative of potential attackers. (*162A)

To make our counter-terror operations even harder, this inane Administration also imposed restrictions on the information flow between the Intelligence and Law enforcement agencies and within agencies. **The Foreign Intelligence Surveillance Act, FISA had been written to help investigate potential spies and terrorists.** But Janet Reno and her liberal Justice Dept. went out of their way to stop those types of investigations and any information flow that would help catch potential terrorists!

Because of those Democrat mandated rules our Law Enforcement agencies could not attend or (survey) any services at social groups, or local mosques unless a direct lead or a crime had occurred. They could not even print web pages distributed from potential terrorist groups unless a crime was in progress. Contained within those pages was information that could have been useful in learning what was going on within those groups. (And as shown before vital information provided by Steve Emerson's group was also ignored.)

But terrorism was not the only issue the corrupt Clinton Justice Department fouled up. Prosecutor Randy Bellows severely criticized Attn. Gen. Reno and FBI director Freeh for fatally botching the espionage case of Chinese scientist Wen Ho Lee. Lee was a Taiwanese born scientist who was employed at the Dept. of Energy. *It was during 1996 the CIA reported that Communist China had acquired classified data from our nuclear weapons, specifically the W-88 warhead,* (mentioned earlier.)

The FBI was supposed to investigate this as it was considered a seious domestic espionage case. But for some reason they were agonizingly slow in doing so.

And Janet Reno refused to authorize a wiretap on Lee because of his connections to Bill Clinton. (This was the only wiretap she denied out of 2,700 that were issued!) Lee was finally accused of spying for China in 1999, but by then he had copied millions of lines of computer code that encompassed fifty years of our research. And it included our research on the neutron bomb. His most active years of effort were from 1994-96.

In a much needed investigation a 700 page report came out and revealed that known Chinese spies were operating in the U.S. through 3,000 front companies! Security at our nuclear installations had been reduced to an extremely poor state as a result of Clinton appointees ending security protocols. **And no one is monitoring the vast e-mail exchanges that are leaving our nuclear sites. Janet Reno should be held accountable.**

(Four Democrats and five Republicans on the committee signed this harsh report!)

Bellows complained often about the "self-imposed restrictions" being emplaced by "our leaders". "Their actions" constantly prevented rapid and thorough investigations of these most serious activities. *But again that was normal in the crooked Clinton Administration.*

But China was not our only powerful enemy.

Russia was still a nuclear power, and even though the Communists were gone from power and Boris Yeltsin was in charge, their hardliners were still spying on us. The effective, old "Russian Trawlers" had been replaced by updated Russian "merchant ships that were not as noticeable".

Thanks to Bill Clinton, those Russians had been given permission to enter vital sea- ports that their ships could never enter before. Seattle was one of those restricted ports, due to the presence of our Submarine Group Nine which was based there. Clinton's meddling and collusion allowed Russia's Far East Shipping Company called FESCO to send two of their spy-ships into the sea approaches off Alaska and then Seattle.

One Russian ship, *Kapitan Man* was known as a spy ship. (A 1993 search had found special sonar equipment hidden in a forward compartment.)

Those ships routinely placed "sea-buoys" into our shipping lanes, and used them to record and track our missile submarines as they came and went. Tense warnings were forwarded to ONI, Office of Naval Intelligence that the Russians were seeding the sea floor of Puget Sound with these sensors! (In the event of war they could track and sink our subs as they came and went in or out of the base.)

In addition to that issue those Russian spy ships spent an inordinate amount of time near our naval facility at Adak Island and the USAF radar post on Attu, Alaska. The CIA and NSA were alerted to those issues, but again this Administration allowed it!

On April 4, 1997 those Russian ships again arrived in the waters north of Puget Sound. A Canadian military surveillance helicopter arrived and began taking photos spotting numerous suspicious objects on the deck. Unknown to the crew, the Russians were using a powerful laser to blind the pilots, crew and their cameras. *(The Russians had timed their visit perfectly, the USS Ohio was passing close by. Another lucky coincidence.)*

After the flight ended a debriefing was held and it was realized that the crew had been lasered. Within a day both pilots had serious eye injuries. During the Cold War the Soviets had often used lasers on NATO and SEATO pilots and crews flying near Russian ships, border posts and around the Iron Curtain. Word of the attack made its way to the White House and State Dept. *Both were upset, not of the injuries and the attack, but that any negative publicity could cause policy problems.*

The DOD (Department of Defense) investigation quickly proved that the laser attack had indeed occurred, and the Coast Guard was directed to detain the *Kapitan Man.*

To prevent a "potential problem", Clinton's State Dept. actually notified the Russian Embassy in Washington to warn them that the Coast Guard was on the way to their ship!!

By the time the CG arrived all of the suspicious equipment was hidden or disappeared, and the crew was most unhelpful. The Russian ship was allowed to leave U.S. waters and the issue was "decided closed by this crooked Administration". **As always the Clinton spin machine downplayed the incident and ordered all personnel involved that they had to keep silent.**

It was soon leaked that the special laser used on the crew of that aircraft was a type capable of recording the *Ohio's* acoustic propeller signature. That capability would make it easier to track and destroy them using the special acoustic torpedoes the Russians now have. **That type of torpedo is programmed to attack that particular sound signature**. It eliminates wrong turns and wrong attacks, and if a sea mine is so programmed it can sit there waiting for that particular sub to pass by for years and detonate only when it hears that submarine.

One possibility for this latest Administration cover up was to protect the investments being made under the Gore-Chernomyrdin Commission. Once again the Clinton White House viewed money as more valuable than protecting our country or people.

As shown earlier Vice Pres. Al Gore headed the "1997 Committee on Airline Safety". This Commission was created in reaction to "recent air disasters of Flights 800 and 592". (*No mention was ever made of the prior and exponentially more devastating Philippine Bojinka bombing plot, the interrogations of Murad, the Paris hijacking or the Ethiopian hijacking!*)

After those U.S. airline disasters passengers overwhelmingly approved having extensive x-ray and bomb detection machines, Federalizing airport security personnel, using computerized passenger screening and photo identification requirements. But this Commission's directive was that they would only "recommend" safety changes. They did that in February 1997, after the election was over.

However word had leaked out that some on the committee wanted to enact a passenger profiling system to take into account a passenger's origin, background, travel history and ethnicity. (All legitimate concerns.)

Over the past forty years, 95% percent of the attacks on airliners were perpetrated by Islamic males.

Yet the ACLU, liberal groups, Muslim front and political action groups all went into high gear lobbying to prevent any such plan. The FAA, Dept. of Justice, the White House and the Congress were all contacted repeatedly. Democratic congressman David Bonoir of Detroit was a key ally for those Muslim groups.

As a result of their lobbying, they stopped all of the human profiling criteria needed to prevent terrorists from getting onto the planes!

But the Islamic groups were not the only ones lobbying. The ATA, Air Transport Association spent over $16 million lobbying against those increased safety concerns. Their actions were done to keep "airline costs down" and profits up. All of the safety issues and prior intelligence from the FBI and Airline Security Personnel were disregarded. Only minor safety recommendations were made to the airlines by the Committee.

There was no increase to the Federal Air Marshall program, no installing of smoke or heat detectors for the cargo areas, no increased locking mechanisms on the cockpit doors, no updates to the aircraft security systems or repositioning the airline transponders.

The Committee also avoided the tough issues like federalizing airport security. The only security enhancements were increased baggage screening, photo ID for passengers, "training for screeners, and hiring a few more security agents". **Incident # 103**

(After all was said and done the DNC picked up a big donation from the airline industry Political Action Committee, (PAC) which probably explained the Why.)

At that time the airlines "were in charge of their own security", and they contracted that security out to the lowest bidder. In his book, *Against All Enemies*, Richard Clarke states on page 130, "It was clear even at that time that the Gore Commission had not been sufficiently ambitious about the job of airline security." (162)

(A politically correct way of saying Gore and his commission were at fault for 9/11.)

Our airlines operated based on regulations from the Dept. of Transportation. Administration lawyers and officials made it clear that no racial profiling was to be used in any security checks as per Clinton's politically correct rules.

Asst. General Council Sam Podberesky stated at a September 16, 1997 meeting that if three people of the same ethnicity were in line for additional screening the airline would be shut down for discrimination. All of the civil rights attorneys and Janet Reno were on the same page, No hassles for potential terrorists!

An Israeli security consultant was staggered at the idiocy of Clinton and his Administration's PC rules. For Israel the only safe option was not letting a potential risk on the aircraft.

(This civil rights / politically correct inanity continued with the Bush administration and went so far that in early 2001 Fran Lozito the head of FAA air operations e-mailed all of the airlines to stop showing the anti-terrorism video based on Steve Emerson's 1994 video "*Jihad in America*", because it was offensive to Muslims.)

More Islamic Trouble

In the summer of 1997 George Tenet appeared before a Senate panel which would decide if we still needed the CIA. He testified that the nation did need the agency, to guard against the growing threats of terrorist groups, and the WMD's that Iraq's Saddam Hussein, N. Korea and Iran were trying to build and hide.

During August 1997 al Qaeda suffered three serious reversals. The first involved the pickup of one **Maddani al-Tayyib** by the Saudi government. He was a finance official for al Qaeda and one of bin Laden's brothers in law. Tayyib wisely asked for asylum and agreed to cooperate, but only to the Saudi's.

His interrogations should have been passed around, but once more our "allies" were hiding vital information from everyone who needed it. **Incident # 104**

(This story was broken by the British Press a month later, but the Saudi's still refused to share what they had learned.)

Their second problem involved **Ali Mohamed.** The former Egyptian soldier Ali knew he was living on borrowed time as the

U.S. authorities had been getting increasingly suspicious of his movements. **Incident # 105**

Their third problem was **Wadi al-Haj**. A wiretap had been placed on the phone of this suspected terrorist in Nairobi. Over the past weeks enough evidence had been learned to pick him up. (It was the interrogations of Jamal al-Fadl that gave them Wadi al-Haj and the Nairobi cell. That highlights why it is so important not to kill the terrorists.)

As shown earlier al-Haj had been sent to Nairobi to lead that cell. He was running a few businesses to complete their cover stories, and one was a gem trading company that did business in Hamburg, Germany. (After the 9/11 attacks that office was also linked to the 9/11 terrorists.)

Haj traveled the globe moving money, supplies and arms to the various al Qaeda locations that needed support. His aide **Haroun Fazul** and he were the main members in the Nairobi cell, and **Mohamed Saddiq Odeh** was one of the others.

(*Fazul and Odeh had been among the terrorists who had trained the Somali's and provided some of the weapons used against us in Mogadishu in 1993.*)

The wiretap and intensive surveillance were being conducted, and after the arrest of al-Tayyib by the Saudi's, calls to and from Nairobi went up dramatically. **NSA and the CIA picked up follow on calls to and from Germany, London, Pakistan, Afghanistan and Mombasa.** Analysts could hear the desperation in the voices from some of the callers, though the CIA could not decipher the calls as they spoke in Arabic and in code.

Abu Khadija who lived in Hamburg was warned by Fazul to stop calling them in case the lines were bugged. He was so nervous he kept calling anyway. **All of the numbers and locations called were traced, and they were definitely part of bin Laden and al Qaeda!**

After weeks of intelligence gathering the FBI met al-Haj on August 21, 1997 as he returned to Nairobi from yet another trip to Afghanistan. JTTF agents met him at the airport and made it clear they knew what he was doing. He was given a chance to return to the U.S. and roll on his comrades. At the same time search warrants on his home and business gave them his laptop, date books, diaries etc. (They also warned Haj's wife it was not safe for her to remain behind.) But al-Haj declined the offer and the pair returned to the U.S to hide out. Haroun Fazul took over in Nairobi. **Incident # 106**

Though the authorities did not arrest Haj yet, they went over his laptop and papers. Many other al Qaeda phone numbers and names were uncovered such as Nawawi from the Sudan, (al-Ridi's cargo plane copilot.) Names of terrorist supporters inside the U.S. were also uncovered in the files on Haj's computer. One prominent name in his address book was the previously mentioned **Ghassan Dahduli** *of the IAP, Islamic Association of Palestine.*

Also found on Haj's computer was a letter from **Fazul** who worked often with Banshiri. This letter was addressed to al Qaeda's communications director **al-Fawwaz in London.** Fazul warned that **the security of their operation** had been endangered by the prior arrest in May of the al Qaeda paymaster in the Sudan, and by the Saudi arrest of al-Tayyib who the British press reported was now cooperating. Their members needed to go underground, and communicate by using the Internet to keep ahead of the Kenyan, U.S. and Egyptian Intelligence and Security services.

"Our efforts to "Re-establish a Muslim State" is a collective one and not based on any individuals. We are all part of it." Fazul wanted al-Fawwaz to get the word out in case they were caught so any other plans being implemented were not compromised. His letter also stated that the Americans know that we had been involved in the attacks in Somalia. (A clear reference to the Blackhawk Down attacks in 1993, and Al-Fadl's information.)

"Our "sheikh" (an alias of bin Laden), is committed to the war against America, and their cell was just one part of it. "We the East Africa cell members do not need to know everything about operational plans, for we are just the implementers." This eight page letter not only admitted to the existence of their Nairobi cell, but Fazul's admission to being a part of it.

Unknown at that time, that cell had been planning the bombings of the U.S. African Embassies with the prior help from Ali Mohamed since 1994. Those bombings had been postponed multiple times because of pressure from Egypt, bin Laden's 1996 expulsion from the Sudan and the May 21, 1996 death of Banshiri.

(Banshiri and 800 others were on Lake Victoria when the ferry they were on suddenly sank. Wadi el-Haj was sent to investigate the incident with one **Fazul Abdullah Mohammed,** but they could not determine what had happened.)

In addition to the above information, the letter also mentioned a group of "partisans" operating in Mombasa, Kenya and the anticipated arrival of "engineers" to Nairobi.

Having confirmation of the prior arrests in the Sudan and Saudi Arabia, the words; **security of their operation,** and that final sentence about being **the implementers**, should have triggered a full investigation and arrests of all of those suspected terrorists. Obviously something was being planned by a group who were at war with us. But unbelievably this invaluable intelligence was never put to use! **Incident # 107**

When el-Haj left Africa, the "legal reason" for the wiretaps went with him. **Incredulously no new ones were emplaced on anyone else in the group. All of the surveillance on them ended too!** In a year hundreds more would die needlessly.

(That al-Qaeda address book proved that al Haj not only knew bin Laden, he was his personal secretary. Al-Haj is serving a life sentence for the 1998 Embassy bombings, attacks that clearly should have been stopped.)

Also found in Haj's computer files were communications to and from Ali Mohamed and Osama bin Laden! Ali Mohamed was arrested a week later. **Incident # 108**

During September 1997 **Mohammed Atef**, al Qaeda's military chief was visiting Nairobi checking up on their preparations for the overdue attacks on the U.S. embassy. *Since the investigation and surveillance had stopped, Atef was not spotted or arrested!*

Atef and all of the terrorists he met with were in the files the Sudanese had offered Clinton during the past years. **But since Clinton and his Administration made sure we never saw those files, all of the terrorists were able move around freely and continue with their plan.** (Atef was killed in Afghanistan in 2002)

Soon after that visit one **Mustapha Mahmoud Said Ahmed** walked into the U.S. embassy in Nairobi and informed the intelligence officers on a plot to bomb the embassy. He had done this before, and the CIA officials present did not give this November 1997 report any credence as he had been wrong about the other claim. **What they so dismissingly ignored, was the fact he had been off on his timeline because of Banshiri's death!**

By not checking properly into this lead, those officials never realized that Ahmed worked for one of bin Laden's front companies in Nairobi. *He had came across irrefutable evidence of the embassy plan and tried to warn us at great risk to himself.* **Incident # 109**

Highest Level Subversion

In a secret directive known as a PDD, (Presidential Decision Directive), **Bill Clinton unilaterally changed our nuclear response policy from "launch on warning of a Russian attack", to launch after we are attacked!** Basically Clinton would allow the U.S. to suffer nuclear attacks killing millions, before we would or could strike back.

And Clinton arrogantly issued additional PDDs to further delay our missile launches by directing the removal of the circuit boards from the missiles to "prevent accidental launches"! As always this Administration kept those vital policy changes secret even though we were still in great danger and he knew it.

(On January 25, 1995 Russia went on alert over a Norwegian rocket that had been launched to study the aurora borealis. In that episode the Russians had been told of the launch weeks before, but still they panicked the same way they had during Reagan's years, and came close to launching their missiles.)

Clinton next ordered the end of the Energy Department's Special Intelligence Program that monitored Russia's nuclear arsenal. He also ordered all of their records to be destroyed! (For what possible reason would he order this?!!)

The CIA had warned everyone in 1996 that post-Soviet Russia was losing control of their vast stockpiles of nuclear weapons. Records were lost, control was lost, and it was unsure who was in command of what. **This crisis included numerous small and easily moved Soviet suitcase nuclear bombs!**

During the Cold War the Soviets had secreted dozens of those weapons throughout the West with the intent of detonating them inside the target nation if war came. The CIA closed their report by saying we are at great risk! Even so Bill Clinton ordered those detrimental changes anyway. *(This CIA report was also kept quite for as long as possible, until Bill Gertz finally exposed it!)*

And despite the continued construction of their underground city escapes, production of a new mobile ballistic missile the Topol-M, the modernization of their submarine fleets, their strategic bomber forces and long range cruise missiles, Clinton continued to lie to the public claiming we were safe from nuclear weapons. Following the methods of LBJ, Clinton packed the nations top military officers for their political loyalty to him and his ideology. Ability was never considered, nor were the risks to our country.

To insure the public and the Congress had trouble learning about those actions, the ever dishonest Clinton Administration concocted the words "Secret/ Prose" on all documents related to their negotiations with Russia on arms control.

That policy of self-classification was illegal. None of those Administration classifications were allowed under our federal secrecy rules. But because of the weakness in our Congress, Clinton's illegal policys prevented public scrutiny of what his administration was doing. This was most acute as it concerned ending Pres. Reagan's SDI initiative for missile defense

(Though the Russians were allowed to build and sell theirs!)

Instead of calling him out publicly the Congress mandated the Rumsfeld Commission in 1997 to "discuss the pending threats to America". **That Commission unanimously declared Bill Clinton's nuclear policies dangerous and "unwise".** Even so Clinton continued to underfund our ABM research which prevented any progress on our SDI program crippling our future safety from enemy weapons.

And Clinton still provided Communist China with all manner of sensitive military technology. Between November 1997 and November 1998, 192 high-speed supercomputers were allowed to be sold to China. Supercomputers are a necessity for anyone trying to build nuclear weapons and modeling scenarios. Those sales were supposed to be monitored, but as usual only a few (16) inspections had been allowed. **Clinton continued to approve those computer sales and it reached 350 by 1999.**

Communist China has and is working with the North Koreans, Pakistan and Iran in helping them build up their nuclear and ballistic missile programs. Each time the facts of their activities was exposed, Clinton and his administration worked hard to cover it up and or ignore them. In effect he was rewarding the Chinese for arming our enemies, as long as their contributions and "other support" continued to come in. It is a certainty that the gifts that Clinton gave them will eventually be used against us. (Just look at how far along the missile programs being produced in Iran and N. Korea now are in 2019.)

Deceiving and placing the American public in great danger seemed to be the Administration's overall objective.

More Islamic Threats

One year after the conviction of Sheikh Rahman for his "1993 day of terror trial", Islamic militants from EIJ attacked western tourists in Luxor, Egypt. In November 1997 their brutal mid-morning attack killed sixty two with dozens wounded. The terrorists even mutilated the dead women in an effort to chase all westerners out of Egypt. Because of their brutality, public opinion in Egypt turned against the extremists. **Incident # 110**

Pres. Mubarak struck back with extreme force. Hundreds of EIJ members were arrested, and eight were killed in the fighting with two others dying in prison. EIJ was severely weakened, and no longer a threat inside Egypt. Four other members were tracked down and arrested in Albania.

In reaction to that unexpected turn of events, on February 23, 1998 EIJ and al Qaeda declared war upon Egypt, the U.S. and other governments they despised. Americans were to be killed wherever they were found. Clinton again did nothing Soon after Bin Laden invited the western media to come to Khost, Afghanistan to a well staged propaganda event. **Incident # 111**

With Clinton's Politically Correct rules in place Police Depts. could not ask Immigration and Naturalization, INS, about the status of anyone they stopped or had in custody. Police and the FBI were forbidden from cooperating with the CIA or INS. Reports began coming in about numerous unqualified Middle Eastern men going to U.S. flight schools to learn how to "fly passenger jets". Since no crime had been committed the FBI could not investigate them, and they could not check on the immigration status of those person(s) or ask if the CIA knew who those people were.

It turns out that many were terrorists.   Incident # 112

CIA Director George Tenet testified before a closed door session of the Senate Appropriations Committee in May stating, *"I think we are already at war with terrorism, we have been on a war footing for a number of years now."*

A recently released CIA Daily Briefing report prepared for the president stated that bin Laden was seriously interested in hijacking airliners! Still Clinton did nothing.   **Incident # 113**

As Edmund Burke said two hundred years ago, "All that is needed for evil to succeed is for decent men to do nothing." *(163)

During the past years the tense firestorm of Islamic Fundamentalism was sweeping the Middle East and south Asia. Algeria and Egypt had succeeded in beating them down, but in Afghanistan, Iran and the Sudan the Islamists controlled those nations. Inside Pakistan and Saudi Arabia the Islamists exerted increasing control, but faced a strong military in the former and the extensive ruling family in the latter.

By 1998 NATO's southern anchor Turkey was also in serious trouble. Their seventy year secular government was being threatened by the right-wing Islamists. Turkey's modern founder Kamel Ataturk did not want an Islamic nation, he wanted a secular one that could grow and catch up to their European neighbors.

As the decades went by his secular dream was constantly being challenged by the Fundamentalists. And since the Iranian revolution and the Afghan-Soviet War, the Fundamentalists were slowly taking over. They made extensive gains after the death of the pro-west Pres. Ozal. (Gulf War)

In S. Asia, the Philippines and Indonesia were struggling as Islamists were also growing stronger and their terror attacks grew.

And as shown earlier, in Bosnia, al Qaeda had penetrated the country in 1992 and 1993. They organized money men, logisticians and "charities" and then waged war. By 1998 Allied Intelligence services were tracing a lot of the finances back to bin Laden and the many "Islamic charities" that were being used to launder their money. Many of the senior al Qaeda operatives were identified while operating in Bosnia.

French troops successfully raided a Muj facility filled with explosives and arms. In that raid the French also uncovered plans for multiple terrorist attacks upon U.S. and other western military units in Europe. **Incident # 114**

During a follow up raid they stopped a large shipment of C-4 that was bound for an Egyptian Islamic Jihad cell in Germany. That C-4 was to be used against U.S. military installations. Intelligence from that second raid and arrests led to the "disappearance" of a second EIJ cell was based in Albania. That group had been led by **Abu Hajir,** and their target was the U.S. Embassy. **Incident # 115**

Because of the multiple links uncovered between Bosnia and Islamic terrorists, the State Dept. warned the Bosnians to eject the remaining ones or face possible sanctions. Pres. Izetbegovic deceptively claimed there were no terrorists left, but not until 2000 did he actually force the last ones out.

However Bosnia was not alone in allowing terrorists to operate freely. London had the Finsbury Park Mosque, (future terrorists Zacarious Moussaoui & Richard Reid), while Milan had their Islamic Cultural Center. Both were home to large cells of Islamic terrorists.

Authorities in the Netherlands arrested the last Muj leader in Europe, one **Abu al-Ma'ali**. But undetected al Qaeda cells still remained. **Incident # 116**

Soon after Sudan's Interior Minister Salih warned the FBI that al Qaeda was preparing to make a major attack somewhere in the horn of Africa. Incident # 117

As shown earlier Janet McElliot the consultant and lobbyist was still working in the Sudan and still actively trying to get information out to the highest levels of our government. She regularly passed warnings onto the FBI liaison, but supposedly her information never made it to the Administration principals. And to make this situation even worse, the Administration did not want her "butting in" anymore. She was ordered to cease and desist.

During December 1997 even the State Department's Bureau of Intelligence and Research, INR, reported on the growing evidence of bin Laden's involvement in Middle Eastern terrorism. *They too warned of the "broader threats".* **Incident #118**

For some reason the State Dept. did not have a representative at the Counter-Terrorism Center, (CTC) as required. The personnel at the Center were well aware that potential terrorists were operating inside Kenya from the prior arrests of the al-Qaeda money man, Ali Mohamed and the expulsion of Wadi al-Haj. But since Dept. of State was not represented the other agents were not aware they had not hardened all of their Embassies as had been directed. Some of the ones most at risk were in the horn of Africa.

By 1998 over one hundred agents and analysts were working in the CIA's CTC unit. With help from foreign sources, forty former Yugoslavian Islamic terrorists were captured and turned over to Arab governments. *Egyptian security tortured some of them, and uncovered al Qaeda cells in Albania, Bosnia and elsewhere.* The data collected from those destroyed cells would fill up a highway billboard. With those successes the CTC believed that they were knocking out the enemy. In truth they were only scratching at the surface. **Incident # 119**

Their investigations also revealed that the terrorists had increased their use of encrypted communications and fiber-optic networks. That made the "electronic eavesdropping by the NSA much less effective. Covert CIA teams had recruited some informants in Pakistan, Uzbekistan and Afghanistan, and the limited intelligence from those sources was shared with our allies. But it was not enough. We were still operating in the dark.

Near the Syrian/Lebanon border former CIA senior agent Bob Baer met with a former Qatari police official. The information the official gave detailed how his government, (their religious minister), had allowed al Qaeda's **Khalid Sheikh Mohammed** and **Shawqi Islambuli,** their **"expert on airline hijacking"**, to escape the year before despite being wanted by the FBI.

(The 1995-96 stonewalling incident.)

Even though he was out of the agency Baer sent the information to a CIA friend who forwarded it to the CTC. This important information was ignored because Baer had been the one who sent it. **Incident # 120**

Baer had been one of the last of the old hands, and as shown before in late 1986 he had been a founding member of the CIA's Counter Terrorism Center. That was the high point for him, hunting down the terrorists instead of reacting to them. But after Reagan left office the CTC and the CIA began drifting back into turf battles and risk aversion. And the Clinton years were the worst of the worst as the leftist political rulers were chasing more agents out. Baer had been maligned without cause by the present Administration and his own superiors in 1995-96. He left the increasingly politicized agency.

His Qatari source was burned and "quietly disappeared". Someone high up in the agency, or the Administration, had notified the Qatari's of what Baer had been learned. They picked up Baer's friend and he was never seen again.

Nuclear Threats

A huge intelligence failure occurred at CIA which again cast them in a negative light. India and Pakistan both successfully conducted nuclear tests in May 1998. Neighboring nations that had one of the most volatile relationships on the planet had succeeded in testing nuclear explosions within a month of each other. (Pakistan had started their atomic work in the 1980s)

This nuclear arms extension was due to the inanity of the Clinton Administration in allowing foreigners into our nuclear

programs, and by allowing China to sell and barter our advanced technology to other nations.

China, Iran and Pakistan had signed the nuclear non-proliferation Treaty. Anyone who violated the treaty faced automatic sanctions. Yet Clinton continually overlooked the Chinese efforts to help Pakistan with nuclear technology and their M-11 ballistic missiles. And China was also helping Iran with their nuclear advancements.

"At a White House speech Clinton complained that legislation which automatically triggers sanctions to punish dangerous arms sales forces his Administration to fudge the facts about such sales! He was stating to that audience that his administration lies to cover up and ignore unwelcome intelligence about foreign arms sales" to prevent lawful sanctions!   * (164)

For years the NSA and CIA were monitoring those dangerous arms sales by China, and they notified senior officials at the White House, Pentagon, and State Department. Ron Brown at Commerce led the fight against punishing China. His "help extended back as far as 1993, and continued until his "untimely death". Then his successor took over. Bill Gertz repeatedly broke these strategically dangerous stories for the *Washington Times*. However the Administration lied away his breakthroughs each time. New loans to China were made from the U.S. Export-Import Bank, to the tune of $10 Billion dollars.

After watching both India and Pakistan ride out the limited sanctions that had been emplaced to prevent this exact scenario, N. Korea and Iran knew they could proceed with their nuclear programs without fear of American action.

As time went by Clinton never followed up or insisted on enforcement of the treaty provisions he had made with **N. Korea**. For him once the papers were signed the public relations benefit was over and it was time to move onto something else.

On February 12, 1996 a Hwang Jang-yop defected to the South Korean embassy in Beijing. Hwang was the chief ideologist for the N. Koreans, and privy to all of their most vital secrets. A major confrontation ensued over his defection. Hwang willingly spoke of the intense hatred the North had for the South, and that they planned on turning the South into a sea of flames if they did not give up. He also warned that the North already possessed nuclear weapons. **(Once again those revelations were kept secret by the Clinton Administration.)**

Other North Korean defectors from 1995-98 echoed Hwang's claims that Pyongyang already had nukes and wanted a war. They also admitted that the North had an extensive WMD program, numerous secret missile factories, and were improving on the older Russian designs like the Scud and Frog series. To make money the N. Koreans were selling their improved missiles to countries like Iran, Syria, Egypt and Libya.

In 1997 North Korean Colonel Choi Ju-hwal defected to the West. He warned a Senate subcommittee that North Korea had produced two or three atomic weapons, and stockpiled over 5,000 tons of toxic gases. "By having WMD's N. Korea can keep at bay all of the major powers and gain the upper hand in any negotiations". North Korea could decimate S. Korea and Japan with missile attacks, and America could do nothing to stop it.

(An armistice was signed ending the Korean War in 1953. But the ruling Kim's say the fighting ended, the war did not. Only when the peninsula is rejoined on their terms would peace be attained. Until then war was always on the doorstep.)

After his information came out U.S. spy satellites took photos of a huge tunnel complex inside a mountain, similar to what the Soviets had been building back in the 1980s and again in the 1990s. This vast network was 25 miles from the Yongbyon complex and employed 50,000 workers! Even the liberals at the NY Times and Washington Post reported on this serious episode. But Clinton did not inform the Senate of those dangerous developments (as required by law) until July 1998.

Our intelligence services had specifically and repeatedly warned Clinton in the spring of 1997 that N. Korea had reneged on his treaty, and were making weapons in secret underground locations. They estimated N. Korea to have over 8,000 heavy artillery pieces, and hundreds of medium range missiles. *Seoul the capitol of the South holds twenty-five million inhabitants, and is only forty miles from the DMZ.* They are within range of many of those cannon and all of those missiles. Armed with WMD chemical (Sarin gas, VX) or biological munitions such as anthrax or the plague, Seoul could be destroyed or contaminated within an hour of launch killing millions. And if a bio-weapon is used the panicked refugees would spread the disease everywhere they went. The only defense to threats from the North had been the risk of a crushing strike from our forces in the region. But a nuclear armed N. Korea equipped with ICBM's is a different peril altogether.

On March 19, 1997 Bill Clinton gave a false certification to the Congress about N. Korea's conduct. His formal declaration

was "North Korea is complying with the agreed framework and not diverting any of the U.S. supplied fuel oil". * (165)

(Clinton and Albright's deceptions were common procedures among the Democrats, and were done all down the hierarchy even down to James Rubin and Strobe Talbert's level as Deputy at State. Bill was following his Democratic predecessors who created the "Great Shining Lie of Vietnam." (166) And he maintained the fiction that everything was alright.)

N. Korea had some 8,000 plutonium fuel rods sitting in a cooling pool at the Yongbyon reactor complex. That supply alone was enough to make between 5-7 nuclear weapons. One of the worst case scenarios for everyone was that the N. Koreans would make and sell nuclear bombs to other terrorists or terrorist sponsored countries. **One thing was sure, they were trying to make nuclear weapons themselves.**

At a Senate hearing on July 26 Sec. State Albright was called a liar for her previous deceptions. When questioned by the Senators she claimed she had just been made aware of the problem. When proven wrong she stayed quiet. (She should have been terminated and arrested on the spot.) Trying to cover for themselves, the State Dept. finally reported in late 1998 that they had evidence that 10,000 metric tons of our oil had been diverted from Korea to Communist China in a barter arrangement for China's extra "help".

Then in another shocking event N. Korea launched a multi-stage ICBM during August 1998. Kim Jung Il was following on his father's plan, to acquire the means to strike and destroy America. At their rate of their advancement it would not be long before a N. Korean ICBM was capable of delivering nerve gas or other WMD upon Alaska, Hawaii or the West Coast.

(And by not having an anti-missile shield in place there was nothing that could stop that scenario from happening.)

Clinton was quite unhappy that the "great nuclear freeze he and Carter had negotiated" and trumpeted for years was proven to be a lie, just as the Republicans said it was.

The Administration complained to the U.N. about the "infractions", and wanted them to inspect the site. But the intransient N. Koreans demanded we give them $300 Million in order to get a peek!

In 1999 the U.S. Dept of Energy reported that the N. Koreans were secretly using a trading company to acquire gas centrifuge technology. Those devices are used to make nuclear weapons by enriching uranium. **Clinton ensured that report also stayed a secret claiming their "diplomacy" and "arms controls" were**

keeping the peace. He and his principals continued to inform the Congress that all was well.

Once again a totalitarian ruler is a grave threat to the planet. The only way to stop that scenario is to attack first with ruthless, overwhelming force, or by having an effective ABM system in place. As with Russia, there is no guarantee that we can take out all of their weapons. And what would a militarily strong China do if we tried to attack North Korea? The only safe option for us is to have an effective and extensive defensive capability, like Pres. Reagan's SDI program. **But Bill Clinton shut ours down.**

(In October 2002 N. Korea would stun the world after the Bush Administration found evidence of their illegal activities. Confronted by this proof, N. Korea admitted to making nuclear weapons at secret underground locations. All of their sites are located in deep underground lairs inside their mountains.

In 2003 N. Korea officially renounced Clinton's earlier agreement, and the Nuclear Non-proliferation treaty. They admitted they were running a covert program to enrich uranium, and they would cast off the moratorium on testing ballistic missiles. In 2006 N. Korea detonated a nuclear weapon. During Obama's years they tested four more, and long range missiles too. In our time of 2018 they test fired ICBM's often.)

Clinton and Russia's Boris Yeltsin had met in 1996, and Clinton promised that the U.S. would do nothing to hurt Russia's interests as both men had elections coming up. (Similar to the 2012 meeting with Obama and the Russians.) They met again in 1997, but still nothing concrete was being done to help our Cold War foe become a democratic ally. Clinton was his usual self using the meetings to attend to his political and money dominated agenda. His aides notably Strobe Talbott, "often spoke of the rise of Russia's reformers, giving them time and a hands off approach to make things work."

But the Administration non-policies were a disaster as the Russian reformers were pushed aside by corrupt officials, criminals and hardliners. Those groups plundered the no strings attached Western aid to the tune of $20-60 Billion dollars!

Because of those policy failures, hardliner Yevgeni Primakov replaced Yeltsin in 1999. He returned to power many of his old cohorts from the KGB, which included Vladamir Putin. Much of the stolen Western aid was actually being used to build their nuclear-proof underground cities and to restore their military production and capabilities.

Yeltsin's efforts to bring democracy during would fail as Bill Clinton and his administration stood idle along the sideline. That inexscusable breakdown was what allowed Putin and his crew of ex-Communists to take over. In 2018 Putin would start his forth six-year term. *He is the longest sitting Russian leader since Stalin! Russia has renewed their thirst for conquest as evidenced by their battles and annexing of portions of Georgia, the Crimea and eastern Ukraine.*

Their military capabilities are now approaching the dangerous levels of 1986. And we have no defensive shield to protect us.

During February 1999 CIA's Tenet testified to the U.S. Senate that Russia had not stopped the flow of missile technology to Iran. Both countries tried to claim the work was being done to enable "space cooperation. The Congress passed sanctions on Russia, but Clinton vetoed it, and offered the Russians $Billions in aid. "Clinton's policies were all based on carrots, and no sticks." *(167)

(For some reason as I researched the eight years of Clinton's scams and schemes the word traitor kept popping up.)

Iran also stunned the world by test firing their Shahab-3 medium range missile. That missile could carry a 750 kilogram payload and hit a target 1300 kilometers away. Their Shahab-4 was larger and could fly 2,000 kilometers. Iran could now strike most of central Europe with their WMD warheads. *(Mossad confirmed the connections to Russia's defense plants and scientists.)*

This is the legacy of Bill Clinton, more wars and vastly more danger to the worlds inhabitants, especially America.

Russia's illegal help was not limited to Iran. They were a great source for Saddam's Iraq as they worked to rebuild their military and WMD programs too. In 1997 the CIA's National Intelligence Dailey reported the Russians had concluded ventures worth over $10 Billion dollars. Those agreements included Russian oil companies, arms exporters and industrial ministries.

Throughout this time Saddam and his minions worked around the clock using fleets of Mercedes trucks moving, hiding and obstructing the UNSCOM inspectors in their search for his missile and WMD programs. During late 1997 Saddam declared five categories of sites off limits to inspectors. Tensions built up and Clinton saw a chance to take the heat off of himself from the growing Monica Lewinsky scandal. He would get tough on Iraq.

Bin Laden

In January 1998 Saudi security forces arrested several al Qaeda followers who had secreted shoulder fired anti-air missiles into the Kingdom. (Probably Stingers.) Interogations and investigation enabled them to secure a defector, **Mohammed bin Moisalih,** who was bin Laden's Afghanistan treasurer. He revealed the names of prominent Saudi's who were helping bin Laden, which was not good for them. **Incident # 121**

All during that time bin Laden was constantly on television and internet broadcasts denouncing the Saudi Royals. Crown Prince Abdullah sent Prince Turki to Afghanistan in June 1998 to see Mullah Omar. As always the negotiations over bin Laden went on for months accomplishing nothing.

Investigative reporter John Miller learned from a friend that Bin Laden had been indicted in secret in a U.S. court as he had been involved in the previous attacks. (Somalia, the World Trade Center, the Bojinka Plot in the Philippines and the Saudi Arabia bombings.) Miller used a good contact, Vince Cannistraro to get his own information on Bin Laden. Cannistraro was former CIA, and set in motion an attempt to get in contact with Bin Laden's "public relations apparatus". After two weeks word came in to pack for London. They would have a meeting with **Khalid al-Fawwaz** of the ARC.

Khalid had operated in Afghanistan with bin Laden in the early 1980s. After the war ended he was sent to Nairobi to help organize that al-Qaeda cell. Khalid was replaced by Wadi al-Haj when he was dispatched to London to setup the aforementioned ARC propaganda front. Miller and his producer Len Tipper made the trip to London to speak with Khalid, and in their interview they asked if they could speak to bin Laden and present his case to the world. Surprisingly they were approved to go to Islamabad, Pakistan during May 1998 and await instructions.

While in their Islamabad hotel they were visited by a few men at different times. Their belongings and bags were searched and they were sized up to see if they were a threat. A day later they were approved to continue on and were directed to the airport. Their flight took them to Peshawar and more waiting. A day later a van took them deep into the wilderness to Bannu. From there they had to sneak into Afghanistan past Taliban patrols. After a day of hard hiking a truck took them to the first of three camps. There the reporters met with Zawahiri and Atef. Their gear was taken away to be searched again. Days later they were taken to see bin Laden at another camp. Fighters and weapons were everywhere, and weapons firing was staged to scare the news people.

Miller then conducted a televised interview with bin Laden who warned that there were many more Ramzi Yousef's ready to strike, and the next one would be in a few weeks.

Bin Laden spoke of how shocked they were to see how poor your soldiers fought. (Somalia) "We are sure of our victory. Our battle with the Americans is larger than the one with the Russians, but we predict a black day for the United States." Bin Laden complained that everywhere Americans went Muslim children die as you try to take over. They (al-Qaeda) do not differentiate between military or civilians, any American should die. America must end their help to the Jews otherwise war and death will be the result.

This story aired in the U.S. on June 10, 1998 causing a only a mild stir in our government. The State Dept. warned all U.S. travelers of potential terrorist threats, but Clinton did nothing. **Incident # 122**

Days later Bin Laden publicly declared war on America for the 5th time in the past two years. This time he did so at the press conference in Khost, Afghanistan. Pakistani and Chinese press were invited to the secret event to witness the May 1998 gathering. Bin Laden declared that Muslims must kill Americans any time they get the chance to. He also stated on how they had joined with other Islamic groups to wage a Jihad against the crusaders and Jews. It was vital to kill Americans and be rid of them. **Incident# 123**

One of the faithful who listened to the speech was **Rashid al-Owhali**. He was on his way to Nairobi.

As shown earlier, to help their efforts in Afghanistan the CIA had setup a station called **Alec**. They ran a team called *Sisterhood* that was tasked with trying to find bin Laden.

That spring the CIA picked him up, through the use of his satellite phone, at a 300 acre farm known as Tarnak. Tarnak was three miles from an unused airport, and offered no challenging terrain or defenses. It had a ten foot high mud wall that surrounded eighty, one and two story structures. *This was a perfect place to go after bin Laden when he spent a night with one of his wives.*

A CIA team was sent in with Afghan commandos from **Massoud's** Northern Alliance. His Afghans plotted and mapped the entire complex, and devised a meticulous raid. Thirty Afghans would crawl through the flat plains and the minefields approaching the compound from a drainage ditch. They would gain entrance to the farm through the drainage opening in the wall. They had identified the houses where bin Laden usually stayed, and planned on searching them until he was found and captured.

A second team would take out the guards at the main gate. The raiding party would then exit in vehicles that would be hidden close by. It was known that civilians were inside the complex, and the CIA agents in the field understood that casualties could occur. Especially when dealing with the Afghans.

At Langley the higher ups and lawyers worried and asked for detailed explanations and statements that that would not happen. No inane assurances like that could be given. (Few people outside of the CIA knew about this raid, so what was the issue.)

During May Richard Clarke and "another White House official" went to Langley to be briefed at the CTC. CIA officials had to review the proposal raid, set for June. Discussions were then held at the White House. Most all of the administration principals were against the raid "because of the civilians".

Clinton called off the attempted capture.   Incident # 124

Since Clinton had no backbone, the CIA should have been allowed to help finance the Northern Alliance. They were anti-Taliban and anti-Osama bin Laden. At that time their financial needs were around $10-12 million per year. They raised most of their money in various illegal ways which included selling opium. An additional $1-3 million from the CIA might well have dealt a death blow to al Qaeda's senior leadership, and they could have acted when they wanted to. But their was no leadership from this useless White House.

Abu Ayman Zarqawi was a Jordanian street thud who was greatly inspired by bin Laden. During 1997 he traveled to Afghanistan to meet with the terrorist leader who was also impressed. Zarqawi wanted bin Laden to strike more often, and since he was of a like mind Zarqawi was sent to train at one of their Afghan camps to learn. *He excelled, and in 1998 was sent to NW Iraq to another al-Qaeda camp for additional training.* Zarqawi was told to be patient, that his time would come. Over the past months the CIA had learned of that Iraqi camp and they began monitoring it.

(After the attacks of 9/11/01 it was learned that the camp was experimenting with WMDs using dogs and goats as bio-weapon carriers. The CIA wanted to destroy the camp, but Pres. Bush wrongly decided not to. He did not want to alert Saddam Hussein that we were observing. This was yet another tragic mistake as Zarqawi became the leader of the Sunni rebellion in Iraq in 2004 when he went out on his own. Zarqawi's group survived his death and mutated with al-Qaeda and other remnants to form ISIS after the Obama mandated withdrawal in 2009. And the interconnected web of history continues.)

Clinton's Perjury

At this crucial time Pres. Clinton was consumed with non-stop scandals. This latest one involved witness tampering, lying under oath, obstruction of justice and illegal campaign donations. His lawyers were filing endless legal motions in their effort to further obstruct justice and prevent an array of government officials from testifying!

This latest major scandal began when an intern, Monica Lewinsky filed a false affidavit at a hearing on January 7, 1998, claiming she never had a sexual relationship with Clinton. In fact she had, and a friend named Linda Tripp turned over secret tapes revealing that Lewinsky had lied. *When questioned Lewinsky stated to the investigators that she lied at the behest of Bill Clinton.* (Witness tampering and obstruction of justice.)

Bill Clinton had testified on the 17th that he did not accept sexual favors from her, thereby committing perjury too! (Those charges together led to impeachment proceedings.)

On February 3, 1998 yet another Democratic campaign contributor was arrested by the FBI in the ongoing Buddhist scam. Then another one named Maria Hsia was indicted on the 18th. John Chung struck a plea deal in March bringing more illegal contributions to light when he started talking.

Then on March 15 Kathleen Wiley appeared on 60 Minutes claiming that Clinton had groped her many times. Her revelation backed up the long-time claim by another woman named Paula Jones who stated that Clinton sexually harassed her in Arkansas years before.

The Internet site *The Drudge Report* was one of the first to highlight this storyline, something the major media including

Newsweek tried to ignore and bury. Hillary Clinton complained at a press conference that there was too much free speech allowed on the Internet. *There needs to be governmental controls and editing.* *(168)

Monika Lewinsky re-testified before a Federal Grand Jury on **August 6, 1998** and recanted her January affidavit. She stated she had lied to the court in January because the president asked her to. Talk of impeachment began spreading. (Removal by impeachment would require a vote in the House and a 2/3s vote in the Senate.)

Because of this legal trouble no one was *leading* the U.S. intelligence octopus despite the plethora of information coming in. If you do not act on the intelligence you pick up it was of limited use. But Clinton's only concern was just trying to stay in office. **To conceal his serious legal problems Clinton again fired all 90 U.S. attorneys.** He hoped that during the transition of finding and approving new attorneys the people would lose interest.

The 1998 Embassy Bombings

On August 4, 1998 two apprehensive Arabs from Afghanistan arrived in Khartoum, Sudan on a flight from Kenyan Airways. They were trailed by Sudan's intelligence officers. The pair, **Nossair Abbas** and **Skander Suliman** had Pakistani passports, were questioned, and claimed they were going to see the manager of one of bin Laden's factories. (According to Sudan's intelligence he too had been acting apprehensive for weeks.) The pair claimed that when they were finished with their "visit" in the Sudan they were going on to Libya. Looking at their travel documents it was suspicious that the two men had been traveling to and from countries known to harbor terrorists.

Those Sudanese agents checked in with Pakistan's intelligence service, and were informed that the pair normally carried cash into areas just before large attacks occurred. As the two suspects moved through the city they were continually watched.

(Here was a heads up effort by a Foreign intelligence service, checking in with a similar agency in a far away country to confirm information on potential terrorists. *Meanwhile in the U.S., Clinton and his DOJ would not let our intelligence agencies talk to each other!* And as stated before Richard Clarke was the "White House counter-terrorism czar". He had to try to coordinate with forty governmental agencies! It was insane that so much bureaucracy existed, but that was how Clinton wanted it.)

Weeks earlier Ambassador Prudence Bushnell in Nairobi had sent an urgent dispatch to the State Department that the embassy was being targeted and extra security was needed.

The State Dept. refused her request! Incident # 125

(Exactly what happened in Benghazi in 2012 with Hillary Clinton.)

Bushnell had been appointed by Clinton in July 1996. She was a career diplomat and recognized that this embassy located near one of the busiest intersections in Nairobi was a security nightmare. As soon as she arrived she had asked for funds to improve things, but was told there were no funds available. Months later she even contacted Sec. State Albright with a direct appeal via a letter. Still nothing was done.

Her suspicions were not hers alone. *A few months before Kenya's Intelligence service also warned the CIA of an imminent plot on the embassy!* (According to author Paul Muite the CIA conferred with Mossad who discounted the information. Despite the alerts from the previous arrests, the information from Al-Haj's computer, John Miller's interview with bin Laden and these latest warnings nothing was done to tighten security, and prevent this needless calamity. **Incident # 126** (168A)

While John Miller was in Afghanistan interviewing bin Laden, **Haroun Fazul** was renting a gated villa in an expensive neighborhood in Nairobi, less scrutiny. There the terrorists mixed approximately 2,000 pounds of aluminum nitrate and aluminum powder. Packed into six wooden boxes, the explosives were loaded into a Toyota cargo truck. To increase the blast effects, tanks of oxygen and acetylene were added to the cargo.

With everything proceeding as planned, on August 1 senior al-Qaeda member **Saddiq Odeh** was told it was time for him to escape. He made his way to Pakistan.

Mohammed Rashid al-Owhali had been one of the terrorists in training in Afghanistan when Miller did his interview. He arrived in Nairobi on August 2 for his part in the plan, and was teamed up with Jihad Ali who had trained in the camps with him. They were shown the truck, the bomb and how to work the detonator. The next day Fazul showed them their target and route.

By the August 6 all of the important al Qaeda members had escaped the area. **Haroun Fazul** stayed on to make sure nobody got lost. *(Somehow he was never picked up from the prior arrest of Ali Mohamed, the deportation of Wadi al-Haj, or his letter to Fawwaz and the intelligence on the computers.)*

On August 7, 1998 two massive explosions destroyed the U.S. Embassies in Nairobi, Kenya and Dar es Salam in Tanzania. Incident # 127
(This date was the anniversary of Operation Desert Shield.)

The two truck bombs were detonated within minutes of each other killing over 230 and injuring over 5,000. Most of the casualties were innocent civilians, and most of them were Muslim. There was no longer any doubt of the ruthlessness of these enemies, but there should never have been any doubt after the 1993 World Trade Center attack. Bin Laden gave a short statement that the people of Islam were pleased and that this was just the beginning of their war. (The one he had already declared five times.) He then went off the grid using couriers to get and give his communications.

In the CTC the analysts were seething that the recent Tarnak raid had been stopped by Clinton. They were hard at work establishing the ties they already knew would lead to bin Laden. But finding him now would be almost impossible. His satellite phone number was 873-682-505-331. Since 1996 he had placed 2,200 minutes of phone calls to allies and media representattives. That phone was active just before the bombings, but was now turned off. As was the normal routine, it would stay off for weeks.

An analysis of the faxes sent to and from that number in the minutes after the bombing confirmed it was bin Laden's phone. **The location was traced, but since it was now off he could be anywhere.** (By tracing his phone at other times the CIA and NSA knew where he was, but nothing had ever been done with that information!)

One of the faxes mentioned the deaths of the martyrs in Africa, an Egyptian in the Tanzania bombing and the two Saudis in Kenya. *At the time of those messages no one knew that one terrorist was still alive.*

One vital thing went wrong with the embassy bombings, the terrorists in the Nairobi attack could not bring the vehicle completely inside the compound. Their truck was obstructed near the guard gate, and after some shooting the "bodyguard" **Rashid al-Owhali** ran off. Tragically the shooting caused hundreds of people to go to their windows to see what was happening.

Jihad Ali attempted to move further into the lot to destroy the entire building but could not. He then hit the detonator and the blast sent shrapnel and debris flying at 21,000 mph shredding everything and everyone near by, or near the windows. That included wounding Ambassador Bushnell. Incredulously Albright called Bushnell to demand to know "How this happened".

Since Owhali was running away when the bomb went off his injuries were in his back. Over the past hours the doctors at the local hospitals had been treating hundreds of victims whose injuries were everywhere but their backs. When Owhali finally came in for medical treatment the doctors grew suspicious. He had obviously gone somewhere to cleanup as his freshly changed clothes showed no sign of the blast effects. He was treated, but remained in the hospital under surveillance.

It was during that time Owhali called al Qaeda's emergency phone number in Yemen to arrange finances for his escape. But before he could leave the hospital local authorities arrested him. **Incident # 128**

CIA response teams and FBI forensic specialists and investigators arrived in East Africa to conduct the investigations and comb the sites for evidence. The FBI learned of Owhali's phone call and *realized that the CIA had already been monitoring that Yemeni number and house!* A series of calls had been made to and from the house, and many were to and from bin Laden's satellite phone. Further proof that bin Laden had directed the attack, but again pinpointing his previous location.

Investigators interviewed hundreds of victims and workers, and they also took charge of Owhali. Under interrogation he disclosed a telephone number which was traced to their al Qaeda safe house in Nairobi. Bomb residue was found in the villa despite the fact Fazul had hired cleaners to sanitize the place. They also uncovered documents, phone numbers and numerous photographs.

An alert hospital janitor had recovered some ammo and truck keys from one of the trash bins. Owhali's fingerprints were on them. The keys fit a lock from the bomb truck. Like so many others al-Owhali went to NYC and was convicted of the bombing getting a life sentence. But that hardly seems like justice.

Back in the Sudan the suspicious pair **Nossair Abbas** and **Skander Suliman** were clearly interested in the American Embassy building. After the bombings on the 7th Sudanese Minister Gutbi el-Mahdi had seen enough and ordered them arrested. Both suspects were taken to Kober prison and "interrogated". In all seven hours of video were made plus hundreds of pages of transcripts. The men admitted who they were and that they had come to deliver money to several al Qaeda cells. **There was going to be a second wave of attacks on U.S. Embassies throughout Africa and Central Asia.**

Our Embassies in Tirana, Albania, Uganda and Rwanda were all closed and security increased. **Incident # 129**

Minister el-Mahdi telephoned Janet McElligott and cryptically told her that he "had something for the boys", but they had to come to Khartoum to get it." McElligott phoned her FBI contacts (Williams) and gave them the message that the Sudan had arrested al-Qaeda terrorists.

But in typical Clinton bureaucracy, the State Department refused to grant the FBI permission to go into the Sudan claiming the FBI never sent in the "proper paperwork"! This absurdity was going on during the time we had dozens of agents operating in Kenya and Tanzania at those bombing sites!

In Pakistan their immigration officials detained a man who seemed suspicious. His Yemeni passport showed a man with a full beard, but this person was clean shaven. And he had traveled from Nairobi to Dubai to Karachi. They had **Mohammed Saddiq Odeh** in their custody.

Under "questioning" he too admitted he was trained in explosives in Afghanistan, was the al Qaeda leader of the Mombasa cell, and had participated in the Nairobi bombing. He gave up the address of the bomb factory villa and the names of the other bombers. **Khalfan Mohamed**, Ahmed Sweden, Mustafa Fadhil, and others had gathered in Dar es Salaam to grind TNT. They were joined by Fahid Msalam, Ahmed Ghailani, and Ahmed the German in house 213 in the Ilala district for final preparations. It was a **Mamdou Salim** who told them when to leave, and Sheikh Ahmed Sweden and Mustapha Fadhil left first. The others left as the days directive dictated. Odeh also told them about al Qaeda's code system and how it worked! **Incident # 130**

With Odeh's confession and intelligence in hand the FBI and CIA knew for certain that Hezbollah was not the only terrorist group capable of large scale truck bombings. Kenyan authorities continued the interrogations, as a report was sent to Pres. Clinton. Additional arrests were made including Wadi al-Haj residing in the U.S., Mamdou Salim in Kenya and Khalfan Mohamed who was one of the main terrorists from the Tanzania bombing.

And thanks to Odeh's communications-code conversations, agents could re-analyze many prior computer files and letters which allowed for more information to be uncovered.

From that information a cell in Uganda was broken up and those members arrested. **Incident # 131**

In London Khaled al-Fawwaz of the **ARC** was also picked up, with two EIJ terrorists, Adel Bary and Ibrahim Eidarous. U.S. authorities had wanted those three to be arrested before, (Haj's computer), but at that time the British claimed they needed more evidence of terrorism. (The British nearly released those men in 1999 despite a ton of evidence picked up from their offices and computers.) Additional intelligence led to Sudan, Albania, Pakistan and Azerbaijan.

The al Qaeda / EIJ cell in Albania caught a month earlier was planning to bomb the U.S embassy in Tirana, Albania. Caught up in the Balkan War, Albania like most of the region had suffered greatly. Hundreds of terrorists had gone there over the past years and it became a hot bed of Islamic terrorism. Michael Sheehan at the State Dept. wanted to destroy all of al Qaeda and the countries harboring them. "You have to drain this swamp", but Bill Clinton was not interested. **Incident # 132** *(169)

Several other plots were disrupted, and a computer had files of hundreds of locations around the world that had been scouted and targeted. Hundreds of lives were saved. The EIJ terrorists picked up in the Albania raid were transferred to Egypt. There they were "interviewed", and tried for crimes in their country. EIJ leader Zawahiri was very unhappy about that, and promised retribution.

Days after the Embassy bombings Clinton sent U.N. Ambassador Bill Richardson to Pakistan *for a secret diplomatic offer.* A meeting was to be held with the Taliban to cut a deal. *Like the Great Deceiver LBJ,* Clinton the *Great Appeaser* felt he could make a deal with anyone, even the Taliban. Our sanctions were hurting them and tensions in the country were growing.

At their meeting Richardson claimed he had definitive proof that bin Laden was behind the attacks in Africa. Clinton wanted to trade the sanctions for bin Laden being "expelled". Naturally the Taliban refused.

Incredulously Richardson told the Taliban that NSA intercepts from bin Laden's cell phone had confirmed he had ordered the attacks, and Clinton wanted him expelled. *(170) They refused. In the Sudan bin Laden was a guest. In Afghanistan run by the Taliban, he was family.

(What did Clinton expect from this ridiculous request, and what was to be gained? Bin Laden's previous expulsion from

Sudan had accomplished absolutely nothing as he simply setup shop in Afghanistan, **as was warned by the Sudanese. And by informing the Taliban about the cell phone intelligence it showed them that we were intercepting bin Laden's calls).**

A week after the bombings intelligence (probably from Pakistan), had come in stating that bin Laden would be having a meeting near Khost on August 20 to discuss the African attacks and plan their next wave. Pakistan also sent over information as to who had left Africa and who had returned there. It was common knowledge that all of the al-Qaeda people passed through Pakistan to get to their camps in Afghanistan.

At the White House, CIA's Tenet told Clinton that the Embassy attacks were definitely al Qaeda. We had been "going after" al Qaeda for two years, but now was a chance to strike a heavy blow. **Sandy Berger** was put in charge of the operation to strike back.

All of the administration principals knew we had to cross Pakistani airspace to get to Afghanistan. Many of them worried that Pakistan had to be told of any strike in advance or they might assume an attack was coming from India. Others argued that Pakistan had been infiltrated by many agents from al-Qaeda and other terrorist groups. If we gave any warning word would get out and bin Laden would escape.

After much "discussion on how to respond to the terrorist bombings of our Embassies", the military fired 80 cruise missiles at suspected terrorist bases in Afghanistan in the early morning hours on August 20.

(None of the JTTF or CTC people were told of this pending action, even though we had agents and assets on the ground there trying to collect intelligence. And Islamic protests over the missile strikes would spring up all across the region endangering dozens more of our people.)

Three hours prior to the launch, Pakistan was notified by the Administration what was coming. Because of that warning, Bin Laden and all of his lackeys escaped the missiles. They could be seen on a satellite video driving off an hour before the missiles arrived. Two undercover Pakistani intelligence officers who had penetrated the camps did not.

According to Richard Clarke's book, "the military decided" to use cruise missiles instead of a Stealth bomber because they feared something might go wrong. "Supposedly the White House was never told on how the mission would be run, even though Berger

was in charge of the strike. It was all left up to the Pentagon".
Incident # 133

According to John Miller's fine work *The Cell*, *it was the Administration principals who wanted the missile strike used.*

(Just how would the Taliban bring down a Stealth bomber when the Bosnians could not?)

A separate missile strike into a "suspected site" in the Sudan destroyed a pharmaceutical plant. Infuriated with the Clinton Administration's repeated failures, McElligott pulled some strings with the Sudanese to let an NBC news crew inspect the aspirin plant. They filmed and released the footage of the destroyed legitimate factory, which made the Administration look even more second-rate.

After the missile strikes failed Ayman al-Zawahiri proudly telephoned a Pakistani reporter and told him that bin Laden still lives. His "escape" added to the terrorists allure as America was again foiled. And to make this screw up even worse, two of the cruise missiles failed to detonate. *They were recovered by the enemy and sold to Communist China.*

To try to cover up their most recent failures the Administration spin doctors claimed that bin Laden was not the intended target, the camp was. The timing of the missile strikes a few days after the damaging Grand Jury testimony caused even more complaints against Clinton. He appeared to be "wagging the dog", contriving a military crisis to try to take media coverage away from his personal legal problems. *But this wagging was not just in Afghanistan and the Sudan, he was bombing Iraq too.*

And to cap off this implausible failure, the continued bureaucratic inanity and inaction by the Clinton administration forced the Sudan to release the two al-Qaeda suspects they had picked up, *Abbas and Suliman* on September 2, 1998.

They were evicted and flown to Pakistan and taken into ISI custody. CIA learned of the pending transfer and wanted to question them, but when our agents arrived at the airport the two terrorists were "already gone". (It was suspected that they were traded for Islamist support so that prime Minister Sharif could stay in power one more year.)   **Incident # 134**

Because of Bill Clinton and his incompetent administration, two high ranking al Qaeda suspects were allowed to escape. They were still at large as of 2005. *(171)

(And no one went to the Sudan to get copies of the video confessions or the transcripts of those two terrorists!)

More Terrorist Plots and Missed Chances

A NY Times article came out in September of 1998 and reported that Clinton was told during recent meetings (in August) that Bin Laden was trying to obtain WMDs to use against U.S. installations. The White House was more upset that the story had leaked out, than they were over al Qaeda's quest. We also learned that bin laden had met with Pakistani nuclear scientists in an effort to procure one or more nuclear weapons.   **Incident # 135**

FBI Terrorism Chief Dale Watson reported to the Congress on the growing threat of Global terrorism. He stated that those affiliated groups were moving around the world using the Internet and advanced technologies to plan and support their activities. *And all of them were trying to acquire Weapons of Mass Destruction.*

A nuclear blast, even a small one would cause incredible casualties and destruction. Depending on the weapon, the incineration zone could be a few blocks to several square miles. Emergency responders who survived the blast would be unable to move their equipment because the electromagnetic pulse would disable all types of circuitry. Communications in the area would also break down and the fires would burn unchecked. Casualty lists would increase as the disaster worsened.

But the attack does not have to be a nuclear weapon, just unleashing nuclear wastes could cause a severe crisis.

It is paramount that all of our citizens and leaders understand this reality. Being pro-active and preventing this calamity is far better than trying to react to one. That factor was and still is why our agencies must work to stop the terrorists before they can strike. That means they must be legally able to do whatever is necessary to accomplish that goal. As Machiavelli stated long ago, *The End Justifies the Means.*

Even in late 1998 there were only two Arabic speaking FBI agents available for counter-terrorism. And despite the many previous attacks, the FBI not concentrate on the Islamic terrorism threat until November 1999. Director Freeh was unable to get Clinton to see the clear threat facing us.

In 1998 the NSA, (National Security Administration), picked up bin Laden at a known base location in Afghanistan. With help from Clarke, Special Forces troops and strike aircraft were readied for the mission. *But Clinton was at a golf outing and refused to be distracted.* The raid was cancelled because he would not take the call from Berger. **Incident # 136**

With the latest revelations on al Qaeda even the liberal media finally pressed Clinton about why nothing was being done. At a press conference an annoyed Clinton stated that "we can find bin Laden any time we want from his satellite cell-phone".

Naturally that phone was never used again .

Bin Laden was using a Inmarsat Mini-M satellite telephone system, one of the first portable units that allowed communications anywhere on the globe. Over 2,200 minutes of calls had been made in the past 18 months, and numerous calls went to and from the al-Qaeda operations center in Yemen, the place Owahali had called from Kenya.

(The leftist Washington Post quoted a "former intelligence official" as the one who spoke of bin Laden's phone, but I remember watching that press conference on the news.)

Since 1995 the NSA had eavesdropped on every call made by bin Laden and his close circle of terrorist assistants. As shown earlier, through those intercepts bin Laden's location had been known every time it was used. But now that link was permanently lost.

In the past weeks a number of calls had gone to bin Laden's phone. It was not known then, but those calls were in preparation for the coming attack on the *USS Sullivans*.

(After the 9/11 attacks that same Yemeni phone number was called again. **Ahmad al-Hada** made the call, he was father in law to **Khalid al-Mihdhar,** one of the terrorists flying Flight 77. Apparently a lot of Muslims knew that number. Why during all of that time did Clinton not order a strike??)

Agents assisting us from the Northern Alliance in Afghanistan could only report on where bin Laden had been. But after the Embassy bombings, those missile attacks, and the inane announcement about his satellite phone, it was becoming extremely difficult for anyone to pinpoint him.

Without having 100% verification on Bin Laden's location, CIA Director Tenet (the former Senate staffer), would not recommend taking action. And using that as his out, our miserable president would not authorize any.

That happened three times in few months.

(As per Clinton's directives, Tenet had hundreds of senior operations people retired, just as we needed their services. He also promoted staffers into positions they could not handle or comprehend. As was done at the FBI.)

One problem that was not completely Clinton's fault, was the bureaucracy inside the military. Chairman of the JCS Gen. Henry Shelton, like so many regular officers disliked the Special Forces type operations. He would counter-offer a large force attack. Naturally the Administration would object to any "large scale attacks", and the plan would be scrubbed. Which was just what Shelton wanted. The only way out of that catch-22 was for Clinton to personally order the special ops mission in. But that type of command courage never was Bill Clinton.

Throughout this same time period U.S. aircraft were repeatedly bombing southern Iraq and Serbia. Why was Afghanistan different??

One air strike in Belgrade had accidently destroyed the Chinese Embassy garnering much intense negativity and bad press. When a similar operation was proposed later on, the principals would stop it because "Clinton could not tolerate any more bad press". And the military was becoming unhappy with our new moniker the Mad Bomber.

Beginning with Pres. Reagan, the standing policy against terrorists was to use lethal force against them if the strike was necessary to stop an imminent attack. As always in the Clinton White House the lawyers spoke up asking what did "imminent" mean? Do we need to know an exact date and time? Because of their irrational "legal outlook" they became paralyzed over any potential action.

But his command cowardice and inanity was not just about al Qaeda and bin Laden. The CIA also knew the locations of many Hezbollah terrorists who had murdered our people in Lebanon. They were hiding out in Beirut, but Clinton refused to allow any missions there either. *(172)

Ali Mohamed the long running EIJ / al Qaeda spy was tried and convicted for the Embassy bombings. Also indicted for aiding terrorism was Khaled al-Fawwaz of the ARC.

The Administration finally went after the terrorist funding. As shown earlier the administration knew the Saudis were a part of that funding, but as always they were less than helpful. *Pressure needed to be maintained on them, but Bill Clinton did not.*

Another terrible mistake by the Administration was not fully aligning with the anti-Taliban, anti-al Qaeda forces fighting in Northern Afghanistan. Those tribes were of Uzbek ethnicity, and regularly supplied information about bin Laden to *Alec Station.* However no American attempts to intercept al-Qaeda convoys were made because the lawyer saturated White House insisted on "absolute legal proof that bin Laden was present".

But the **Fatal Flaw** in that way of thinking was that al Qaeda was just bin Laden. *By this point in time it was known that al Qaeda had cells in fifty countries.*

During the past months of hostilities Northern Alliance fighters would track and attack bin Laden's convoys and kill dozens of al Qaeda fighters. At times they placed bombs under trucks or in their buildings. After one battle their forces found an al Qaeda training manual. This find was also offered to the U.S., but the CIA "did not want it". **Incident # 137**

Massoud often complained to the field agents and his people about the lack of effort by the U.S. in eliminating this dangerous threat. Weeks after the Embassy bombings he wrote a letter to the U.S. Senate. *Massoud urged that America help in this new war in Afghanistan. His people were fighting the extremists of the Taliban, the ISI and bin Laden.* He admitted that governing mistakes were made after the Soviets left, but his people had never known a free government in their history and needed help in that attempt. (But as he had done with Russia, Clinton stayed out of it.)

At present Pakistan and the Arab governments had committed over 25,000 men to aid the Taliban. He warned that Afghanistan has been delivered to fanatics, extremists, terrorists and mercenaries. **America had to aid them, no one else could.**

But the Clinton Administration especially those in the State Dept. remained skeptical. And they wanted those pipelines built.

The CIA knew full well the links from ISI to the Taliban and bin Laden. By the fall of 1998 a massive flow chart was covered with al Qaeda information similar to how organized crime was identified and charted. Administration principals could see that a well led unholy alliance was in place. It was mostly directed at us, and used to try to start a war with India over Kashmir.

Not only did Clinton make no strategic moves that could have hurt any of those potential enemies, he released over $500 million more in aid to the Pakistani's!

"At a meeting in the White House on December 2, 1998 Pakistani Prime Minister Nawaz Sharif met privately with Clinton to discuss sending a CIA-ISI team into Afghanistan to capture bin Laden. During the luncheon Sharif joked that America spends too much money on missiles, when a few men with briefcases of money would have done the job more quickly." *(173)

The CIA did not believe this offer was genuine. All the ISI had to do was tell them when and where bin Laden was, but that never happened. And the only thing Sandy Berger and Albright ever spoke of was expelling bin Laden. That was never going to happen either.

That same day December 2, 1998 U.S. prosecutors finally unsealed the documents seeking the extradition of **Khalid al-Fawwaz** to the U.S. As head of the ARC, the Advice and Reformation Committee in the United Kingdom, that group was used as a front to use propaganda efforts to hurt Saudi Arabia. However terrorist communications was their real purpose. (During the investigation of ARC, Bin Laden was listed on their articles for incorporation. ARC had addresses in Denver and Kansas City.)

Iraq

Saddam and his minions had been lying to the U.N. for years, as they constantly interfered and obstructed the efforts of the WMD inspectors. Iraq had also been skirmishing with our units the past eight years. During that time our military had been flying 30,000 sorties each year keeping the peace and tabs on Iraq.

In November 1997 Saddam barred Americans from the UN inspection teams, and soon after refused to allow any more inspections. In an expensive show of force 18,000 military personnel and dozens of ships and aircraft were sent back to the Persian Gulf. Saddam appeared to give in, but in the Clinton years looks were always deceiving. *Clinton had made a back-room deal which allowed Saddam more oil sales if he would stop "misbehaving".*

Seeing Clinton's weakness, two weeks later Saddam refused to allow any oil sales, unless all restrictions on Iraq were loosened. To placate Saddam, the U.N. upped his allowed sales to one million barrels a day. U.N. Inspectors returned, but as before their access was obstructed contsantly. Almost a year had gone by when Saddam suddenly chased all of the inspectors out.

They had uncovered stores of deadly VX nerve gas, botulinus and anthrax toxins. Saddam had violated all seventeen U.N. resolutions passed against him.

To take the heat off of himself, Clinton decided "we needed to strike at Iraq too". He would invoke the 1991 law.

On December 16, 1998, **(the day the Congress was voting on his impeachment),** our ships fired **415** cruise missiles into Iraq. That was more than had been used in Operation Desert Storm! An additional 600 plus bombs were also dropped by aircraft, striking a total of 97 "suspected WMD sites".

(Strange how air attacks in the populated cities of Iraq could be used regardless of civilian casualties, but not in bin Laden's Afghan camps where everyone present was al Qaeda.)

Clinton's *Wag the Dog* show did not accomplish much. The destroyed structures were rebuilt and Saddam continued with his WMD programs. (At this same time additional U.S. directed air attacks were also occurring in the populated Balkans.)

Clinton is Impeached

Judge Kenneth Starr was returned as the special prosecutor assigned to the Clinton investigations. This latest one had originally centered on a sex scandal. Back in January 1998 three Federal Judges authorized Starr to expand the investigations because it appeared that Clinton had suborned perjury, gave false statements under oath, and obstructed justice.

As they had done to Whittaker Chambers and Senator Joe McCarthy in the 1950s, the media attacked the messenger instead of the one who rightfully stood accused. Democratic house leader Gephardt was one of those demanding the law giving independent counsel power was wrong and needed to be changed quickly.

(It was passed by the Democrats in 1978 when they had full control of our government. They renewed it in 1982, 1987 & 1994, and the law was upheld by the Supreme Court. But now that it was threatening one of their own they wanted it ended.)

Senior Democrats Lanny Davis, Sydney Blumenthal, James Carville and Rahm Emanuel all worked for the White House, and all were vociferous in ending the investigation. The Democrats and their friends in the media did all they could to obstruct and throw off the Starr staff that were now looking into felony charges. *Clinton himself gave six and half months of lies and excuses not to answer questions or to testify. And Reno announced that she was going to investigate Starr!*

Starr released 18 boxes of evidence, and outlined the case for impeachment on eleven legal grounds which included witness tampering, lying under oath and abuse of power.

Despite the numerous liberal obstructions, the House correctly voted to impeach Bill Clinton based on the proven criminal charges.

Only five House Democrats voted for impeachment, though many Democrats and political aides actually wanted Clinton to resign. (As had Nixon.) They felt he had lost the public trust forever and was hurting their party.

But the Senate's actions bordered on betrayal. They refused to seriously consider the impeachment process, and the Republican Senate leader inanely proposed a toothless censure instead.

The Senate needed a 2/3 vote for impeachment, but could not come close to that number as none of the Democrats would vote yes. Still they should have held the public hearings to show who was who. Following their Party's rules, every Senate Democrat voted to keep that corrupt figure in office. As a result of their collusion a dangerous and incompetent criminal was allowed to remain in office.

Clinton was so guilty, that the entire Supreme Court boycotted his State of the Union address. (An historical first.) They also disbarred him.

One Special Note: **Only after the Senate kept Clinton in office were the interviews by Juanita Broderick finally aired describing how she was raped by Clinton. Even though they knew, those scheming Democrats still kept him in office.**

Nixon's illegal maneuvers during Watergate were not tolerated, so why were Clinton's illegal actions allowed to pass? Back in 1974 the Supreme Court ruled that executive privilege only applied to matters of diplomatic, military or national security issues. Pres. Reagan used the privilege three times in his eight years, while Ford, Carter and Bush Sr. used it only once during their single term.

But Clinton had already used it ten times in just six years in his never ending effort to deny information to grand juries and Congressional investigations. That inconvenient truth was never reported on by the "mainstream media" either. (Clinton also used executive privilege multiple times during the Lewinsky investigation in his effort to thwart Starr's investigation.)

Another interesting What If note needs to be addressed. (If Clinton had been correctly impeached by the Senate and removed from office, or if he had resigned, V.P. Al Gore would have taken over. Would he have been so timid to act against bin Laden and al Qaeda? And what would have been the results in the 2000 presidential election if Gore ran as an incumbent?)

On January 7, 1999 **Sheikh Muhammed Hisham Kabbani** appeared in front of a State Department forum on Islamic Extremism; A Viable Threat to National Security. *Kabbani showed true bravery by speaking at the open meeting and announcing that 80% of all Mosques and Islamic charities in the U.S. have been taken over by the extremists! He also stated that bin Laden was an imminent threat to America.* *(174)

The meeting became filled with threats and shouts from Muslim groups and individuals who opposed his viewpoint. Many threats were made on his life, but not until September 11 did anyone listen. **Incident # 138**

(Kabbani's warnings were actually preceded by one **Seifeldin Ashmawy,** an Egyptian cleric and peace activist. For years Ashmawy had disputed and fought against the extremists. He even debated Omar Rahman in Egypt highlighting his tale of lies. Because of his anti-extremist work Ashmawy was killed in a car accident in 1998. That was what prompted Kabbani to come forward.)

Afghanistan-Pakistan

Weeks after Pakistan's Sharif left Washington, the CIA station in Islamabad received promising intelligence on bin Laden. Agents reported him to be in western Afghanistan on a hunting party with wealthy Arab Sheikhs. A CIA team equipped with communication and sighting gear traveled the isolated nomadic roads towards Herat. After a few days they found the secluded camp which was near an old runway that could handle C-130 cargo planes. Generators provided refrigeration and lighting for the numerous well equipped tents that lined the camp. It was known that the rulers of Abu Dhabi in the UAE hosted many of those hunts.

During February 1999 the CTC directed satellite coverage to that site as their recon team called TRODPINT stayed hidden. Images were sent to Islamabad and the White House as Berger and Clarke were kept updated. Days passed, and the White House insisted on an absolute location for bin Laden inside the camp. CTC-CIA officers were certain he was there and pressed the principals to strike. If anyone was there with him that was just too bad. Again George Tenant was not 100% certain and the White House refused to attack claiming that UAE royals may have been present. **Incident # (138)**

(If their concern for the UAE Royals was real, then why didn't the White House just order an ambush as bin Laden was leaving the camp? Many in the CIA blamed Clarke for his close ties to the UAE.)

Fallout from allowing bin Laden to escape again was quick in coming. He and the Taliban had been aiding the rebels in the new republic of Uzbekistan. On February 16, 1999 a well conceived assassination attempt was made on their autocratic ruler Islam Karimov. As a former communist Karimov was used to harsh rule and danger, but that day the rebels detonated six large car bombs as he was on his way to a meeting in the capitol of Tashkent. He survived, sixteen others did not.

Karimov retaliated and ordered over two thousand arrests of known and suspected Islamic activists. **He described his actions as war against bin Laden and his terrorists. Incident # 140**

Seeing an opportunity the CIA suggested to Karimov that we work together on this problem. The CIA would train his fighters and commandos, and he would allow our use of his air bases, covertly of course. Our nations services got along fine, but the Clinton lawyers were up in arms over every little thing.

Since 1997 CIA teams had been bringing money and equipment to Massoud's headquarters near Barak village. When CTC teams went in through Dushanbe, the former capitol of the Soviet republic of Tajikistan, they were codenamed JAWBREAKER. When Near East Division teams were used they were called TRODPINT. Teams remained for a week or two and their equipment allowed Massoud's people to monitor Taliban radio transmissions. If bin Laden was picked up they could alert Langley. (For what good it would do. The teams were never allowed to act on a tip themselves.)

Massoud told them that bin Laden spent most of his time near Kandahar with visits to Kabul or Jalalabad. He was difficult to pinpoint, and Massoud felt their effort was myopic, concentrating on just bin Laden and not his principal associates. Massoud also warned them that al-Qaeda was much bigger than they realized, and would carry on attacks against the West even if bin Laden was killed. *They needed to shut down all of his support from Pakistan, Saudi Arabia and the Taliban.*

The fighting in Afghanistan was changing with the recent murder of the family of Abdul Haq by the Taliban in early 1999. The Karzi clan joined the opposition, as they too desired to work with Massoud. For their efforts the elder Karzi was ambushed and murdered in Quetta. Hamid Karzi the eldest son was filled with vengeance, as the Taliban were brutal killers and tortuers. They had even mudered Iranian diplomats and civilians, earning the hatred from Iran's leaders and intelligence agency MOIS.

Resistance to the Taliban was growing throughout Afghanistan, but not in Washington. There the Clinton team and lawyers insisted we remain neutral, even if they were harboring bin Laden and al-Qaeda.

For Pakistan, the Taliban and bin Laden were considered allies. Islamists were very active in Kashmir, frightening, and killing the hated Hindus. Their work was vital to Pakistan because they tied up ten divisions of Indian troops. Pakistani Gen. Pervez Musharraf was happy with their work thus far, and as shown before his troops were fighting with the Taliban against Massoud.

And Musharraf was secretly planning a raid into Kashmir using a few hundred commandos to take and hold a 15,000 foot peak called Kargil. It dominated the only road in the region, and if they succeeded India would lose a section of Kashmir called Ladakh. He briefed PM Sharif who approved.

Neither man realized how aggressive India would get as they launched counterattacks and air strikes. Indian politicians were even recommending additional attacks to finish off the Pakistani army. Sharif returned with his family to Washington for talks, and was berated for potentially starting a nuclear war. Upon his return home he pulled their forces back, though he was now at risk for a coup from their army.

Sharif tripled the threat when he fired Musharraf and promoted an unknown. This happened just as the CIA-ISI commando unit was ready to go after bin Laden. When word of the potential coup got around the commandos disappeared into the crowds unsure of what was coming next.

Around this time four young Arabs were infiltrated into Kandahar, Afghanistan with help from the Taliban. They were there to learn Jihad from bin Laden. **Mohammed Atta, Ramzi Binalshibh, Marwan al-Shehhi and Ziad Jarrah** were young educated men, and would become the implementers of the 9/11 plot. After two months of terrorist training they returned to Hamburg and began their plan to infiltrate into America. They had applied to U.S. flight schools to learn the skills needed to make the 9/11 attack. Bin Laden had been looking for people such as these.

Khalid Sheik Mohammed had expanded this idea from their discussions in the Philippines during the **Bojinka Plot**. In 1996 Mohammed Atef produced a feasibility study on hijacking U.S. flights and blowing them up over various targets. (As had been tried in France at the Eiffel Tower.) KSM recommended they fly planes filled with explosives into America's noteworthy buildings. **It was bin Laden with his engineering knowledge who realized they would need large commercial aircraft for their plan.**

The ease of taking over a jetliner and flying it where they wanted was revealed by the hijacking of the Paris and Ethiopian flights in 1996. This could be a devestaing strike, with the right dupes and some convienent help.

America

CAIR, the Council for Arabic Islamic Relations won another court case in their never ending Muslims vs America legal challenges. This latest one was called **the Argen-Bright Case,** and involved a security company that manned checkpoints for United Airlines.

The case overview concerned Muslim women wearing headscarves, (hijabs) while they worked as security screeners at Dulles Airport near Washington D.C. After the bombings of the Embassies in Africa passengers and flight crews complained that Muslims were working as security screeners at vital checkpoints. Argen-Bright told the women that they could not wear head scarves at work, but they refused to take them off and were fired soon after. CAIR sued and won major concessions that benefitted Muslims, and **Argen-Bright had to rehire those Muslim workers.** (Christians never get that treatment.)

(After the 9/11 attacks had gone off the foolish "pro-Muslim feelings" passed for a while. Investigations of suspects were actually being made. **It turned out that many of the people hired as airport screeners were in the U.S. illegally!** Most only spoke

Arabic, and many of them had been forced on the U.S. security companies under the federal EEOC rules passed by the Democrats.)

By 2000 CAIR had moved out of their original cramped office and into their own multi-story building near the U.S. Congress. They aggressively went after any "anti-Muslim" speech, radio, video or advertising. *US News and World Report* was deluged with protests, and electronic and physical demonstrations after their truthful news reports. Nike Corp and radio legend Paul Harvey also caved in to their aggressive actions. The leftist media, (entities like CNN and the NY Times), gave their help to the Islamic activists which furthered their subversive plans. No one from the U.S. government interceded to stop their illegal policies.

Around this time a **National Commission on Terrorism** was setup by Congress, and tasked with learning about and offering solutions. This bipartisan panel was led by Ambassador Paul Bremmer, and they issued a sixty-four page report covering all aspects of the terror threats facing America.

Forty specific recommendations were made to the Congress including; Revoking Clinton's restrictive directives on the CIA as to recruiting "unsavory sources", Relaxing Dept. of Justice rules for surveillance on suspected terrorists, Creating a joint task force from IRS, Treasury and Customs to find and stop the terrorist fundraising, and placing Pakistan and Afghanistan on watch lists for terrorism. (That would restrict their ability to travel.)

They also recommendrd numerous changes on the policies allowing foreign students to come here. Eyyad Ismoil, one of the 1993 WTC bombers, had come in on a fake student visa F-1. Once he entered our country, he never went to a school and simply remained here illegally. *Because INS is so poorly managed, and our colleges and universities refuse to notify INS of any problems about foreign students, no one knew Ismoil was still here!*

Since then over one million illegal aliens had used this entry method to come in and stay. The Commission recommended creating a national database for all foreign students applying and living within our country. They showed how Fed-Ex Corporation was able to track the arrival and delivery of three million packages a day, yet our government has no idea who is here a day after they enter. That insanity had to end. Their report received little support from the Administration or the media. **Incident # 141**

Former CIA Director James Woolsey was on that Commission and was perplexed with the lack of action. Sen. John Kyl of Arizona was one of the most ardent supporters of the reforms, and he too was stunned at the lack of response by the Administration. His state was one of the first places where al-Qaeda set up shop in the early 1980s in Tuscon.

(Former Senators Warren Rudman and Gary Hart worked on a separate civilian panel. Their findings were almost identical to Bremmer's panel, and they were liberals!)

It turns out the proposed reforms were blocked primarily by the Democrats in Congress. *Led by Sen. Leahy of Vermont, these obstructionists objected to any relaxation of rules they had placed on the FBI or INS.* Representatives Bonoir of Michigan, John Conyers and John Dingall also objected to the rule changes as "anti-Islamic". Because of the them another clear chance to make headway against the terrorists was lost.

(All of those legislators accepted donations from Muslim leaders and political groups.)

Back in 1995 then Energy Secretary Hazel O'Leary was speaking with a reporter and she just gave him a diagram of our new W-87 nuclear warhead! Even though the documents she exposed were classified Top-Secret, the reporter gladly took them and published all. (Both should have been instantly arrested and imprisoned.)

From 1996 onward O'Leary increased the numbers of "foreign students" allowed into our most secret nuclear facilities. Many came from unstable countries which included, **Iran, Syria, Iraq and Pakistan. By 1998 there were 3,100 foreign visitors and academic assignees inside our most sensitive nuclear labs.**

At Los Alamos alone the number quickly increased to 107 by 1997, and by 1999 the number of foreign employees working there reached 182. (Which is why Pakistan and India both made nukes.)

O'Leary made repeated junkets to Africa, India and Pakistan to recruit those potentially dangerous foreigners. Her inane pitch was that we have technology to share. During her years Top-Secret laptops disappeared, nuclear material disappeared and security protocols were ended. Tired of the insane situation the head of security Edward McCallum reported this "lack of safekeeping" to the Congress.

O'Leary "was quietly moved on to another appointed job", and long time Democrat Bill Richardson took over as Energy Secretary. *He then forced McCallum out to end his complaints, and worked tirelessly to prevent him from appearing before Congressional inquiries.*

(When Richardson left the Dept. of Energy in 2001, Pres. George Bush appointed an Arab-American into the Energy post, one Spencer Abraham. Abraham was a senator from Michigan who represented one of the largest Arab constituencies in America. He had repeatedly received money from the *Arab American Leadership* PAC. **Abdurrahman Alamoudi** was one of the top contributors to his campaigns! In appreciation for that money Abraham introduced a bill in 2000 to end the use of classified evidence when deporting Arabs! That would prevent the intelligence agencies from testifying against someone because they would have to reveal their source. Even into 2003 hundreds of Iranians went to our nuclear labs to learn how to make bombs! **If anyone wonders at how Iran or any of the other terrorist groups were able to make nuclear weapons, it was the incredible inanity of the Clinton and Bush Administrations.**)

During June 1999 Bill, Hillary and many others were hard at work organizing his "Clinton Foundation" for when he left office. *They claimed the purpose of his "charity" was humanitarian work, but it was much more, it was a huge money maker.*

On October 6, 1999 Anheuser-Busch Companies gave the first of five payments to the Clinton Library Foundation. *Just by coincidence,* a month earlier Clinton's FTC (Federal Trade Commission) had stopped a law regulating advertising on underage drinking.

Back in May one William A. Brandt gave one million dollars to the same foundation. He just happened to be under investigation for perjury in one of the previous cases that addressed Clinton's illegal fundraising. *By sheer luck the DOJ dropped his case in September.*

Then a Dr. Richard Machado Gonzalez lobbied Clinton to support increasing the Medicare payments for Puerto Rican hospitals that he was invested in. After a donation of $1.1 million was made, Clinton increased the Medicare payments to those hospitals.

A Martin Anderson had worked at the DOJ as a policy planner/advisor for international law training programs. In 1997 he blew the whistle on numerous instances of gross security failures, ethical lapses and favoritism in the top levels of DOJ. He was immediately demoted and vilified by the administration. Anderson was then forced to fight the administration in the courts, and was backed by the U.S. Office of Special Council. He later won an award for his assistance to our country by placing himself at great risk. But the corruption continued.

Kosovo

Since late 1997 the Islamic population in Kosovo which was mostly Albanian, began fighting with the repressive regime of Slobodan Milosevic and his Serbians. Like the other republics inside Yugoslavia, the people in Kosovo wanted autonomy. As always the Serbians were brutal in their repression.

This time the United Nations was not asked to intercede as there was growing opposition to the Democracies by Russia and China. In the early spring of 1999 NATO decided to became involved in the Civil War, without asking the U.N.

Operation Allied Force would be a NATO air campaign directed against the forces of Slobodan Milosevic. At that time U.S. General Wesley Clark was in command at NATO. This was a first, NATO attacking another nation without a war being waged against a NATO nation.

France had backed the Serbs against Croatia two years earlier, but joined this allied effort sending over one hundred planes. This was the first French participation with NATO since De Gaulle kicked the allies out in 1965-66. Similar to Clinton, France's Chirac was using war as a way to detract from the many personal and corruption problems he faced at home.

Chirac did not ask the U.N. when France helped organize a coup in the Congo killing over 15,000 in order to back the Marxists who promised to sell France oil. And Chirac did not ask the U.N. for permission when in 1994 he sent $400 million in arms to Angola to back those Marxists against the U.S. backed UNITA forces.

But on May 13 Chirac met with Russian President Boris Yeltsin in Moscow to discuss the growing problems in the world. *International Law was needed and Chirac felt it should be based in the U.N. and the Security Council.* Yeltsin was having his own problems trying to stay in power and could not intervene.

Clinton seemed to be following LBJ's footsteps in Vietnam by ordering our planes into action. Like Johnson, Clinton had no grasp of foreign policy, and was committing our forces to a fight as a bargaining tool. He hoped that with the right amount of force the tyrants would negotiate. But these Serbs were absorbing their losses, as had the Viet Cong 30 years earlier. If this bombing did not work the choice would be committing ground forces or admitting failure. Either way it could be a disaster for Kosovo.

Kosovo's population of 1.8 million had been cut by 30%. Civilians were desperately trying to escape the carnage and the capitol city of Pristina was nearly empty. Thousands jammed trains and all manner of vehicles in the rush to escape. Neighboring nations were being overwhelmed with refugees, and Macedonia closed their borders. No one could guess at the actual civilian losses. (Just like Syria suffered in 2014-17 when Obama did nothing.)

The Serbs were trying to hold onto the last province of old Yugoslavia which had significance for them. Their orthodox church considered some of Kosovo as sacred, and the ground was the site of many famous Serbian battles. Intelligence was picking up signs that Serbian units were moving helicopters and jets into underground bunkers near Podgorica the capitol of Montenegro. And Serbian forces were using civilians as human shields to prevent NATO air strikes, while Milosevic` was using Montenegro's neutrality as a shield even as he shelled neighboring Albania. Numerous conferences and meetings were held to decide how to act. In the end even the French agreed with NATO's Gen. Clark's view that aerial bombing must begin. (That is how you respond to threatening situations, someone takes charge.)

On March 24, 1999 NATO airstrikes began hitting Serbian targets. Well planned air attacks went on for eleven weeks. One mission destroyed the national TV station to prevent Serbian propaganda. (This operation was run quite similar to the successful *Operation Linebacker I & II* in Vietnam and *Desert Storm* in the Gulf War.)

At times this effort took on the feeling that this was a NATO war of aggression, as strikes even occurred in Belgrade the capitol of Yugoslavia. Fortunately the key feature to the overall success of the mission was that it was run by the NATO command, and not the White House or some other politician. Smart weapons were used to take out specific high value targets and limit collateral damage. Facing this power, the aggressors sued for peace in June 1999. *(Tragically, once more it was military action that decided the issue, not diplomats and discussions.)*

It is extremely disturbing that bombing near civilians in multiple populated cities was not a problem for Clinton in 1999. **But he had repeatedly refused to allow any strikes against bin Laden's known terrorist camps the past four years because there might be civilian supporters inside.** The Serbs were not a threat to us, while bin Laden and al Qaeda certainly were.

More Terrorist Issues

During June Clinton was presented with another clear chance to get bin Laden. He was known to be in Kandahar, and intelligence knew what building he was in. Again he refused to allow any action. **Incident # 142**

Between May 1998 to May 1999 there were 10 chances to get to bin Laden. Each time the White House refused to act. Three of those chances concerned submarine launched cruise missile attacks. Each time as the subs were ready to launch CIA's Tenet stated he was "unconvinced". He wanted two sources of intelligence to confirm where bin laden was, which was impossible to get in Taliban ruled Afghanistan. Given that out, Clinton always refused to act.

FBI agents investigating terrorism in Albania followed a lead to Turin, Italy in mid-1999. They were after one **Abdul al-Masri**, a family member to Mohammed Atef. This lead exposed an EIJ cell in Italy, and that gave them a new lead, Ali Mohamed's accomplice in scouting the East African embassies, **Nazih al-Ruqai'i,** (aka Anas al-Liby). He was tracked down and found residing in Manchester, England. He was arrested, but somehow the Brits again felt there was not enough evidence and he was released quickly disappearing. A day later FBI agent Ali Soufan found an al Qaeda training manual inside Ruqai'i's flat on the tradecraft needed to wage terrorist operations and evasion techniques. It was highly detailed, well researched and their "road map". **Incident # 143**

Weeks later another lead turned up. **L'Houssaine Kherchtou** had been a long time al Qaeda member, had trained in many camps and was part of the East African Embassy bombings. As was common among the non-Egyptian members, he was in dire need of funds to care for his family. Abu al-Masri (Mohammed Atef) had refused him the needed funds, and Kherchtou fell away from the group. In the early summer of 1999 the FBI sent Ali Soufan and others to bring him in. He became a star witness against al Qaeda at the embassy trials and in providing additional intelligence. **Incident # 144**

On October 10, 1999 Egyptian Air Flight 990 was deliberately crashed into the Atlantic Ocean off of Nantucket. The second officer took the controls just after takeoff and shouted in Arabic that he put his faith in Allah, *as he deliberately flew the passenger jet into the sea killing everyone.*

On board were over forty Egyptian military officers who had been in the U.S. on training missions. (EIJ retaliation??) Because of where the crash occurred Egypt asked the U.S. to conduct the investigation. But they were unhappy when the NTSB announced that **the relief pilot had deliberately crashed the airliner into the sea.** Little was mentioned of this brutal terrorist attack, and as usual nothing was learned from it by this useless administration. **Incident # 145**

In early 1998 our intelligence agencies had learned that al Qaeda was using a telephone number in Yemen. Monitoring that number the NSA and CIA learned the identities of some of the al Qaeda terrorists. That list included a **Khalid al-Mihdhar,** who was also linked to the embassy bombings in Africa. **Even though the FBI was after bin Laden and al Qaeda, Mihdhar's name was not passed around after this information came to light. Incident # 146** (Again that was as per Clinton's DoJ rules.)

The al-Mihdhar name appeared again in a terrorist attack that occurred in Yemen on December 28, 1998. That time one **Abul al-Mihdhar** who was part of the terrorist Army of Aden, kidnapped sixteen tourists. Twelve were Britons, two were Americans and two were Australians. Those terrorists wanted to exchange the Western hostages for nine Islamists. A rescue force was sent in. Yemeni soldiers fought the terrorists who used the hostages as shields. Many of those terrorists were caught, and Abul al-Mihdhar was executed on October 7, 1999 for that attack.

Then a **Zein al-Mihdhar** was executed in Yemen for his part in another terror attack against other Western tourists. Yet even with this information, Khalid al-Mihdhar was not placed on a watch list. **Incident # 147**

According to Richard Clarke, the CIA knew that two known al Qaeda terrorists, the above mentioned **Khalid al-Mihdhar** and a **Nawaz al-Hamzi** were currently inside the U.S. They never notified INS, Dept. of State or the National Coordinator for Security and Counterterrorism (Clarke) that they were here. **Had Clarke been warned, he could have made the notifications to the other agencies and stopped 9/11 from happening.** (Since Mihdhar was wanted for questioning on the Embassy bombings, the FBI should have been told he was here.)

Both names had been given to the CIA by the Saudi's two years before, and both of them should have been on terrorist watch lists and no-fly lists. * (175)

But the CIA decided they wanted to follow them around to see who they talked to. If either was a listed terrorist they would have been stopped somewhere. Knowing that Mihdhar had a valid U.S. visa, the CIA then expanded on their failure by not having the visa revoked so he could not come back. **Incident # 148**

Calls from that Yemeni phone were soon made to Kuala Lumpur, Malaysia to setup a terrorist meeting. NSA & CIA knew that Khalid al-Mihdhar would be going. CIA would follow.

This storyline was just beginning, and it gets worse.

A well conceived plot by al Qaeda to destroy a U.S. consulate in India was discovered and broken up. Once again this attempt received little coverage and no scrutiny. **Incident # 149**

Clinton finally "approved" a series of covert operations to "gather information in Afghanistan". A four man team was sent to the Northern Alliance. Their mission was technical, to setup listening equipment for the collection of al Qaeda communications only. **No attempt was being made to attack or get to bin Laden or his confederates.** (This collected data was of little use without it being acted upon, but that was the idea, to give the Administration the appearance of doing something.)

Massoud could see that the Americans were not serious about bin Laden, so he had his people made their own attacks. *Over the past weeks they just missed bin Laden twice, but might have gotten him if they had been given more and better resources.* (Intel, money, aerial support, weapons etc.)

They also killed and captured a large number of bin Laden's people. But none of them were picked up by the CIA and interrogated. The CIA liaison to the Northern Alliance was a man named **Amrullah Saleh**. He briefed CIA officials in Washington on their overall efforts in December 1999 and was rebuked for their "harsh work" against al Qaeda. **Incident # 150**

During an American West flight from Phoenix to Washington DC two Arabic looking men repeatedly asked flight attendants about flight procedures and security. Twice they tried to force their way into the cockpit. This flight occurred on November 19, 1999, and the men were **Mohammed al-Qudheein** and **Hamdan al-Shalawi. Both were Saudi government employees, and both had had their tickets purchased by the Saudi embassy.** Pilots notified the FAA of the threatening actions, and made an emergency landing in Ohio. The pair were arrested by the FBI, but hours later both were "released for diplomatic immunity". **Incident # 151**

Just a week later the FBI learned that a suspect in another terrorism investigation was observed driving Shalawi's car in Phoenix. That incident resulted in opening an FBI investigation into Shalawi. **Not until late 2000 was it was learned that Shalawi had trained in terrorist camps in Afghanistan.**

Yet he was here as a Saudi employee.

Meanwhile the furtive Qudheein was often observed meeting with Saudi officials in secret locations. At a recent conference of the IASA, (Islamic Arabic Sciences in America), which both men attended the main speaker was a suspected terrorist supporter, American Cleric **Anwar al-Awalaki.** No further investigation was done.

On December 2, 1999 security agents in Amman Jordan **arrested thirteen al-Qaeda members**. They were planning massive terror attacks against Americans, Westerners and Christian Piligrims at Mt. Nebo and the Radisson Hotel. Included in the catch was one Khadr Abu Hoshar. Two other known terrorists, Raed Hijazi and **Abu Zubaydah** escaped to Pakistan.

The Jordanian surveillance and investigations actually started in late October. They began watching a man named **Khalil Ziyad.** and listened to the phone calls of **Abu Zubaydah**. Both were known terrorists. Intelligence was obtained and the Jordanians did a fine job with those arrests.

As had happened in the Bojinka Plot, a few computers were also seized. Those devices contained large files that were encrypted with a high level of security, Military grade security. Translation was difficult, but Jordan sent copies of all of their work to the FBI, and that included the files from every computer found in the arrests. *Intelligence revealed that the head of this cell had recently been a cab driver in Boston!*

The Jordanians uncovered the locations of the terrorists arms caches and a bomb factory located in an upper middle-class home and at a farm near Amman. Their stockpile was so large the Jordanian King immediately declared a state of emergency and flooded the streets with soldiers. The amount of weapons and ammo found was not for a terrorist attack, it was for a revolution. **Incident # 152**

Under one false floor were 71 containers of nitric and sulfuric acids, which would create an explosive blast the equivalent of **16**

Tons of TNT. That was powerful enough to destroy a large hotel or an entire neighborhood.

More suspects would be arrested, including an al Qaeda member who was from Pakistan, and another American. It was learned that he had lived near the Los Angeles International Airport. This American was located and arrested in Pakistan. His name was **Khalil al-Deek,** and he was one of the main planners. Investigators were stunned when they examined his past.

Deek was an American-Palestinian of Jordanian descent who had had close ties to the imprisoned cleric Sheik Omar Rahman. Because of his U.S. passport Deek had traveled freely with links to terror groups in Gaza, Turkey, Pakistan, the U.K. and other countries. He had often worked with **Khalid al-Fawwaz** of the ARC, and he had put out a Jihadist encyclopedia to use for propaganda. Deek had also been involved in a plan to attack sites in Los Angeles back in 1992 but left to fight in Bosnia and the plot collapsed without him. Deek had first been noticed and arrested in Bosnia in 1993, but had been released.

Current investigators then realized that his name was on the computer disks found in the arrests during the 1995 Bojinka Plot. He was one of the bombers, but somehow he too was never placed on a terror watch list!

Now that he was arrested Deek was returned to Jordan with his face covered so he could not see anything. When the goggles and duct tape came off, he was sitting in a room staring at a picture of Jordan's King Abdullah II. (King Hussein had died ten months earlier.) His face went pale as he realized the jig was up. He talked freely about their activities, and another plot was uncovered. That plan was to unleash cyanide inside a crowded movie theatre filled with tourists. **Incident # 153**

As the investigating teams decrypted the many computer files and chased leads, they exposed plans for a massive terror spree upon regional tourist sites. Multiple machine gun and grenade attacks would be used to cause heavy civilian casualties. Once the seriousness of this threat was learned, all U.S. Embassies in the region were put on high alert.

With all of this intelligence work completed, Clinton was briefed by Richard Clarke and George Tenet on December 8, 1999. Tenet warned him we have to assume their there is more than what was found. CIA believes there was an additional five to fifteen plots in the works! **Incident # 154**

Finally Clinton was convinced he had to act.

(Why was no one fired for those watch list failures?)

At a follow on meeting of the NSC, **Clarke stated that there would be no more concern over evidence or trials.** Anyone captured would be turned over to the "regional intelligence services for interrogation", and Egypt was destination number one. (The State Dept. did not like the wording of the new rules or of even issuing an alert to western or U.S. travelers. It was bad PR.)

In any event on December 14, 2000 a plan was "finally in place" and agents from the CIA, FBI and intelligence services from eight countries were officially sent after bin Laden. Or so it seemed.

Hours later on December 14, (two weeks after the Jordanian arrests), an alert U.S. customs agent spotted a suspicious man coming in from Canada. Agents were giving him a second go over when he tried to run off. He was arrested and they had him open the trunk of the car. When he did the group was staring at a large bomb. Customs officers had unknowingly caught one **Ahmed Ressam** as he tried to exit a ferry from Vancouver in a car packed with explosives. In the trunk were two canisters of nitro-glycerin, 118 pounds of urea and timers.

He was investigated and arrested for plotting to detonate this large bomb at LAX airport on the turn of the Millennium. Incident # 155

(That bomb would have destroyed one section of the airport.)

It was soon learned that Ressam was a well trained Algerian terrorist who had taken part in many of the terrible bombings that had occurred in Algeria and France. At present he was part of an al Qaeda sleeper cell based in Montreal, and run by **Fateh Kamel**.

Ressam had traveled there on a false passport in 1994 and demanded political asylum, which was given. Because of his fake passport, Canadian authorities did not realize he had been in Afghanistan and trained in bin Laden's camp at Derunta near Jalalabad. *Ressam was yet another terrorist who had trained under Abu Zubaydah.* He had uncomplainingly waited six years for his chance to strike a great blow. **Patience.**

But Ressam was not alone.

As investigators followed his trail it led to the exposure of an entire Algerian cell based in Montreal and others in Europe. One of his accomplices was indicted but not found, while another Algerian terrorist was one **Abu Doha.** His mission was to facilitate travel for other terrorists into the U.S. (He may have been a replacement facilitator for the arrested Ali Mohamed.) **Incident # 156**

During his interrogations Ressam gave up the familiar name of **Abu Zubaydah**. Since the 1998 embassy bombings Abu had been in charge of the recruiting and placement of all of their terrorists. He knew who everyone was, and where they were located. Abu however remained hidden after his close call in Jordan.

Another of those arrested was one **Fateh Kamel**, an al Qaeda terrorist who had been active in Bosnia. *From his interviews additional leads led to Boston and Brooklyn NY.*

Their al Qaeda contact in Brooklyn was a phone number for one **Abdel Ghani Meskini**. The JTTF placed him under surveillance and found that all of his phone calls were in code.

No one knew what was being discussed, but to cover all bases he was arrested on December 30 for his conspiracy with Ressam. **Incident # 157**

As more information was uncovered it was found that the Algerians were actively infiltrating people, (terrorists), into Boston by "stowing away" on the Algerian LNG tankers that came into the port weekly. **Incident # 158**

Again these incidents were kept quiet from the public.

(LNG is Liquefied Natural Gas. Liquefying is an efficient way to transport a massive quantity of gas, but to do so it must be kept super cold. *The volume of gas contained in the large refrigerated tankers is the blast equivalent of a small nuclear weapon if it explodes.* NYC stopped allowing those shipments in the mid-70s out of the fear of a cataclysmic accident.)

French Counter-Terrorism **Judge Jean-Louis Bruguie`re** was again instrumental in providing corroborating intelligence against the Millennium bomber Ahmed Ressam. He testified at his trial sending him to jail for life.

(Twice before this Judge had tried to warn the Clinton Administration of imminent terror threats from al-Qaeda networks inside the U.S. He was waved off both times.) Incident # 159

In reaction to those disrupted Millenial Plots the Administration announced the strengthening of security at the nation's airports and shipping ports. But as usual this was just another Clinton bureaucratic dodge to pretend to be doing something. **No real security enhancements were made until after the attacks on 9/11.**

(In his fine book, *Off With Their Heads* Clinton's political guru Dick Morris states that Bill Clinton left three ticking time bombs for his replacement, Al Qaeda, Iraq and N. Korea. Morris stated that Clinton knew full well what was going on, he just had no desire to act, and no clue or concern to the long term picture.)

On December 29, 1999 Jordanian authorities decided to arrest the previously mentioned **Khalil Ziyad, aka Ziyad Khaleel.** Ziyad was another U.S. passport holder who freely traveled the region. The Jordanians suspected him of being a purchasing agent for bin Laden, and had been watching his suspicious movements for a while. Their worries were confirmed as he was sent to pickup computers, satellite telephones, and surveillance equipment.

His addresses in the U.S. went from Orlando, Detroit, Columbia, and Denver. He was eventually released by the Jordanians, but was picked up here for administering a variety of radical Islamic websites. He even lectured at our colleges. **Incident # 160**

U.S. Navy ships were routinely being refueled at Aden harbor in Yemen. *Albright's State Department was sending our navy ships and crews into Yemen for commercial interests, even though it was a known al Qaeda / terrorist hotbed.* They also insisted the ships display minimal security so they did not insult the Yemenis.

Ever since that 1997 agreement had been made al Qaeda members had been watching the comings and goings, and began plotting on how to strike the vulnerable targets.

January 3, 2000 was bin Laden's original target date. Al Qaeda terrorists in Yemen led by **Mohammed Omar al-Harazi** had rigged a small boat with a large bomb. Their plot was to ram the U.S. Navy destroyer the *USS Sullivan's* with the explosive. Fortunately their boat was too small and flimsy for the weight of the explosive and it sank. Like the Viet Cong in Vietnam, those terrorists would learn from their mistakes and return. U.S. intelligence did not learn of that attempt for almost a year. By the time they did, it was too late to stop the next one.

Many in al Qaeda did not want to strike in Yemen since it was their place of refuge, and for others their homeland. To protect themselves from any "retaliatory attacks", the day of the *Sullivan's* attempt bin Laden emptied all of his terrorist camps. Soon after that failure, two of those bombers, Taha al-Ahdal and Salman al-Adani were killed. Ahdal was fighting in Afghanistan, and Adani in Yemen. *New bombers needed to be found and trained, and that would take time.*

As was expected Khalid al-Mihdhar (aka Midhar) and Nawaf al-Hamzi traveled to Malaysia in early January 2000, and met with known and suspected terrorists at a swank golf club. A CTC- CIA officer had finally picked up that Mihdhar's name was in the file from the Embassy bombings, so now they knew who he was.

Since the pair were traveling the agent requested the local security forces photograph everyone who met with them which they did. Though their movements were photographed and videoed, somehow their conversations were not recorded. All of the men were acting suspicious as they met with the other suspects, and used only pay-phones to make and receive calls.

It was arranged to copy Mihdar's passport with the help of Malaysian authorities. Once his passport was copied agents noted stamps for previous entry into the U.S. His original visa had been approved from our embassy in Jeddah, Saudi Arabia. Since the CIA had never "listed him as a terrorist" he had been able to travel and move around freely inside the U.S. for years!

After a few days in Malaysia both Mihdhar and Hamzi traveled to Thailand. **Inanely while in Thailand the suspects were not followed. Both later boarded a United Airlines flight to LAX on January 15, 2000.** Since they still had not been placed on a watch list, they waltzed through immigration and disappeared inside our shores to continue their plans for 9/11. (As will be discussed later that meeting was a vital part of the attacks.)

Even after observing this terrorist meeting, the CIA still did not place him on the *terrorist watch list* or the *do not enter list*. They had a well developed program to make those notifications, and had done so over one hundred times with other terrorists. Yet here they did not. Once it was learned that those terrorists were in Los Angeles an FBI agent in the CTC asked permission to tell his superiors that two known terrorists were at large in California. **His request was denied by the CIA, as this was considered "their operation".** Incident # 161

Moving around Los Angeles, al-Mihdhar and al-Hamzi met up with a Saudi national named **Omar al-Bayoumi.** He set them up in a San Diego residence and began receiving monthly income which he relayed to the them. *Bayoumi's employer was a Saudi company that did contract work with the Saudi Government.*

On February 2, 2000 CIA Director Tenet told the Senate Intelligence Committee that al Qaeda was an intricate web of alliances and cells spread throughout the world. Those Sunni extremists hailed from N. Africa, the Middle East, Pakistan and

Central Asia. The Taliban aids them with profits from their opium trade and protects them from intrusion. **"They are determined to strike further blows against America."** *(176)

Those Senators were still trying to get information about former director John Deutch and his illegal activities, and they somehow missed the warnings Tenet was giving. **Incident # 162**

A CIA cable on March 5, 2000 finally highlighted that two known terrorists had entered the U.S. on their watch. Still Mihdhar and Hamzi were never placed on a terrorist watch list! **It also slipped past our intelligence services that both Mihdhar and Hamzi had trained in U.S. flight schools.** **Incident # 163**

At the White House Richard Clarke, (who was also not aware of this latest failure), was convinced that al Qaeda had active cells inside the U.S. He formed an after action group to go over the previous plots to determine if the intelligence people had missed something.

Inside the IRS, (Internal Revenue Service), their capabilities were finally being used to help track down the terrorist's funding. *But even at this late date administration politics ruled, and the Treasury Dept.* **refused to shut down** *any of the "Islamic Charities that were clearly involved in terrorism."* **Incident # 164**

Not until after 9/11 would this bogus source of funding be ended.

By this point in time there was mounting evidence that Iran was actively aiding bin Laden. Many of the al Qaeda terrorists were being routed through Iran on their way to other locations as a way to clean their itineraries. (Instead of moving through the known dubious sites of Pakistan or Afghanistan.)

While at the previous listed meeting, Malaysian security agents had tracked some of those suspects to and from **the Iranian Embassy.** Those suspects included Mihdhar and Hamzi. **Incident # 165**

It was then discovered that both had stayed with a former Malaysian Army Captain **Yazi Sufaat**. Investigators realized that he was their al Qaeda link in Southeast Asia. Sufaat was suspected of helping Ramzi Yousef during his 1995 failed Bojinka Plot in the Philippines. Months later Sufaat met with a **Zacarias Moussaoui,** and a Bin Laden bodyguard **Tawfiq bin Attash.** At that meeting Sufaat gave Moussaoui $35,000.

(It was not known at that time, but that money was to be used to help finance the coming 9/11 attacks. Had the CIA notified

Clarke of those meetings in Malaysia he could have directed that all of those suspects be picked up as per the new terrorism rule change that had been implemented. *But he was never told.*)

During February 2000 the trials of those arrested for the African Embassy bombings began, and by May all had been convicted and given life in jail. **Iran was officially named in the indictment as Hezbollah had provided the training needed to construct and use that type of truck bomb.** That training had begun back in 1993 in Lebanon's Bekaa Valley and inside Iran.

Al Qaeda's **Saif al Adel** was the senior member who was trained, and he oversaw the bomb making in Africa.

Incredulously on March 17, 2000 Sec. State Albright actually gave an apology to Iran for our involvement in the 1953 Mossadegh affair. Two weeks later Bill Clinton stepped out even further with another apology that was close to groveling. "Iran has been the subject of a lot of abuse from various western nations and has the right to be angry with America and others for the past one hundred years of treatment." (??)

Both Clinton and Albright conveniently forgot all of the aid and protection we and Britain had given to Iran in keeping the Soviets out. They also forgot all of the progress the Shah had given to his country during his years. And this pair of liberal politicos totally ignored all of the murders, terrorism and hostage taking those Revolutionary Iranians had perpetrated in the past twenty one years that the mullahs had been in power, thanks to Carter.

(Once the post 9/11 war in Afghanistan was under way many al Qaeda leaders escaped into Iran. Saif Al-Adel was one of those.)

This episode was one of the best examples of the lack of judgment and downright inanity of Bill Clinton and everyone in his Administration. Is there any wonder why our enemies continue get stronger and threaten us.

(Obama followed the same pathetic and dangerous path when he took over, apologizig to terror states and giving Iran $150 Billion with his fake Iran deal. Look how that has turned out.)

The CTC picked up intelligence that bin Laden was at the Derunta camp near Jalalabad. This camp had been on their radar for a while. As was typical it was crudely built and furnished, sitting in a deep valley protected by ridges. Massoud's sources had informed the CIA that for security no Afghans were allowed near the camp, only Arabs. *From the many interrogations of terrorist* captives the past weeks it was learned that this camp was an al Qaeda terrorist graduate school.

Clarke's work group learned that this camp was experimenting with chemical weapons. (The Defense Intelligence Agency had reported on that a year ago.) Satellites were re-routed to take photos, and the CIA did get some local sources in the area. They established a recon site that overlooked Derunta, though the images obtained were not conclusive.

Since the CTC was certain bin Laden was at the camp they informed Massoud. He sent a team out with mules and missiles to try a strike. *Langley learned of this a day later and their lawyers convulsed in alarm. The White House had not given them permission to kill bin Laden, only to watch.* Scarred of the legal outcome the CIA recalled the mission. This episode was also kept under wraps. **Incident # 166**

(What happened to the kid gloves were off policy??)

After that screw-up Clarke's office "officially approved of lethal force", "but only if the mission was sent to try to capture bin Laden or his principals first"! When Massoud and his lieutenants learned of "those rules of engagement" they were outraged. Captures meant extreme danger to the teams going in. In one recent hard battle with brigade 55, (bin Laden's private Arab mercenaries), Massoud's people had them trapped. But just before Massoud's men could finish them off and capture some, those Arabs committed mass suicide using multiple grenades. That was how dedicated to their cause they were.

Sources on bin Laden were always hard to come by, and only in Kandahar did the CIA have a network that could know when he was there. However Kandahar was Taliban central, and because of Clinton's policies they were not to be targeted. Spying in Kabul was easier, and the CIA learned the location of a few al-Qaeda safe-houses where bin Laden, Mohammed Atef and Ayman al-Zawahiri stayed. But everyone was afraid to act in the crowded city. (??) Even when the out of place cluster of expensive SUVs packed a location and alerted the CTC that someone important was present, no one wanted to act because of the restrictive rules issued by the Administration.

To try to "garner some good relations" in the region Clinton made a trip to India and Pakistan. But Clinton had zero standing among the world's rulers, and nothing was accomplished.

Pervez Musharraf had taken over Pakistan in their recent coup, and he decided to quietly allow the Kashmiri radicals who had close ties to the ISI and al-Qaeda to reorganize and expand their recruitments, even as Clinton was flying in. (What a coup the Islamists could have made had they shot down Air Force One.)

Because of security concerns the Secret Service had a Clinton look alike fly off in AF-1 while Clinton and his aides flew to Islamabad in a CIA G-5. The double walked around, drew no fire and the entourage drove off. To prevent any trouble the Secret Service even had Musharraf clear the streets completely. Many Pakistanis were highly insulted over this high handed and meaningless visit.

A month later Gen. Mahmoud the new head of the ISI was invited to America for a visit. Relations seemed cordial and he visited many sites. Just before he left Thomas Pickering attempted a bluff by having a chat with the general. He insisted that time was running out for the Taliban. They had to hand over bin Laden or face a war with the Northern Alliance backed by U.S. and Russia. Mahmoud did not react, but Pickering's foolish bluff may have doomed Massoud.

By showcasing and threatening our support for Massoud the Administration gave the Pakistanis, the Taliban and bin Laden reason to eliminate him. His tragic murder in 2001 may have doomed Afghanistan to perpetual instability, more fallout from this hopeless administration.

Musharraf returned and met with Omar's deputies to discuss numerous issues. Hurting bin Laden was not one of them. Pakistani volunteers were pouring across the border in the war against Massoud. Weeks later Musharraf delivered a policy speech, he had decided to continue helping the Taliban.

(In post 9/11 documents found in Afghanistan, Gen. Mahmoud discussed his American trip with Mullah Omar. Omar saw the warning for the bluff it was and refused to hand over anyone. The threatening information on Massoud was passed on to bin Laden.)

Iran's Plan

Because of the continuous cross-border fighting, Israel had been forced to go back into southern Lebanon in 1985. At that time they were fighting Islamic militants led by Hezbollah and supplied by Syria and Iran. A fifteen year low-level war was waged. There were periods of quiet and periods of harsh bombardments as the IDF (Israeli Defense Force) tried to keep the terrorists at bay. But aided by Syria and Iran, the Islamic militants were capable of fighting forever. There was always another group of young willing to fight Israel.

Unknown by all was that Hezbollah was able to crack the IDF communications codes, which enabled them to fight smarter and safer. Hezbollah's Imad Mughniyah and Hassan Nasrallah were active in southern Lebanon routinely ambushing IDF patrols. By March 1996 the latest cease-fire was breaking down as Hezbollah killed seven IDF soldiers in addition to shelling Israeli border towns. In mid-April 1996 Israel began shelling southern Lebanon again killing over one hundred with another hundred being wounded. The Islamists and the media labeled the counter-shelling as "The Qana Massacre", but as always the insidious terrorists were hiding out among the civilians. Israel was branded as the aggressor while Hezbollah won another political victory among the Muslim masses.

Throughout the next years the fighting and dying went on accomplishing nothing at first glance. During May 2000 the Israeli Army left Lebanon as part of the latest peace process. To the Islamists this was a great victory, for they were still in control of what was left of Lebanon.

For Iran this was their blueprint on how to defeat the West. Since the early 1990s Hezbollah and the Revolutionary Guard had been converting and building up. Their competent military forces were capable of defeating every one of the lesser nations in the Gulf region. All of their members had been well trained, and most had seen battle. *They were intensely motivated to achieve their objective, Khomeini's Shia Islamic Caliphate across the region.* Shia followers line the entire Persian Gulf region and would probably be joined by the Kurds and the Muslims of Central Asia (Azerbaijan is mostly Shia), to defeat the Sunni nations.

Unlike most of the world, the Iranians are not against "creating Kurdistan" from the Kurdish populations living in Syria 8%, Iraq 18%, southern Turkey 20% and northern Iran 7%. The Kurds are the largest ethnic group in the world without a country, 25-35 million strong. A promise of a nation could work wonders.

After the Gulf War ended in 1991 Saddam Hussein kept the problematic Kurds close to starvation. Iran opened their border and provided the Kurds with everything they needed, earning much gratitude. Iran also funded and armed the rebel Kurdish PKK, (Kurdistan Workers Party) as a way to destabilize Turkey. PKK members are Turkish Kurds intent on creating a socialist state. Their only refuge from the Turkish military is in the remote mountains of northern Iraq. Inciting them with a reward of statehood inside an Iranian run Caliphate would greatly serve Iran's interests in destabilizing its neighbors. (Should Iran succeed they would control over 50% of the worlds oil supplies and the Strait of Hormuz where much of that oil has to pass.)

Islamist Iran is following in the footsteps of the Soviets, using chaos to promote their interests. They are subtly applying pressure on everyone along the Gulf and Caspian Sea. Though their oil supplies are dwindling, they can still control the oil trying to move through pipelines or by sea. And if Iran can build or get atomic weapons, (thanks to the inanity of Bill Clinton and his people, help from Pakistan, Russia, China and N. Korea, and the failures of Bush and Obama to stop them), no one would be able to do anything about it.

A nuclear armed Iran would be a perilous threat to the region and the world. In all probability a nuclear war will result from them having those weapons.

(I feel that should they acquire those weapons, they should be directly warned by the president that they are now a nuclear target for our weapons. Any use of a nuclear weapon by their leaders would result in a nuclear reprisal against their country. The superpowers understood that reality, and that is why those weapons have never been used. A rogue state however is another story, and may be insane enough to try.)

Iran's 1979 Islamic Revolution has morphed from a religious upheaval to an economic and political one. They have the capability to grow stronger, and start their own Domino Theory by knocking off one Middle Eastern country at a time. *Using Hezbollah, Lebanon became Iran's first domino.* Bahrain is definatly a target as they have no military to speak of and no "country to rally behind". Only America's support and military has prevented anyone else in the region from falling.

(After the 2003 defeat of Saddam and his Ba'thists, Iraq fell apart with plenty of help from Iran, and mistakes by the U.S. command. One of our major problems was Bush's decision in 2001 and 2004 not to destroy the al-Qaeda camp where Zarqawi was operating. His terror network caused tremendous damage to our peacekeeping and nation building efforts as we faced two separate insurgencies at the same time. By 2006 Iraq was close to becoming Iran's second domino. Better inteligence and the surge of our forces won the day. But after Obama pulled us out of Iraq in 2009, the power vacuum that followed allowed ISIS to form. They almost conquered Iraq and Syria, which resulted in the Syrian civil war and the refugee crisis that swamped Europe. Obama then snuck in over 200,000 unvetted refugees here.

And the interconnected web of history continues.)

Islamic Influence

Back in 1980 there were just 481 official mosques in the U.S. But throughout the 1980s and 1990s mosques were springing up all over America. As of 2003 there were over 1,200, and the vast majority were financed and controlled by Saudi Arabia. *Their clerics preached Saudi Wahhabism, which is inherently against Judaism and Christianity.*

Unlike the various religions in America, Islam is a political entity. Islam was founded as a way of life, not a spiratual faith. It was spread by force, and all captive subjects had to convert.

Though most Mosques here were in use as houses of worship, many were used to convert and preach jihad. It was (and still is) common to find anti- Israel or anti-U.S. speeches being given in those mosques. Some of those buildings also provided protected housing and secretive meeting places for the terrorist cells already in place. The *Dar al-Hijrah mosque* in Falls Church Virginia and the previously mentioned ones in Brooklyn and Jersey City are examples of the latter. The al-Hijrah Mosque hosted over a dozen militant Islamists, and a mosque in San Francisco was where future Taliban recruit John Lindh was worshiping. But with the Democratic and Clinton rules still in effect no one could or would check into what was going on inside them. Despite ample warnings, none of the other worshipers have ever come forward with any alerts about was being said in those Mosques.

During the fall of 1999 Ali Mohamed had finally given up the names of all of the senior al Qaeda ranks. On October 20, 2000 he pleaded guilty to all charges and talked freely of being a bin Laden supporter, a member of al Qaeda and EIJ, and of being the one who had trained OBL's bodyguards. He also admitted to surveilling numerous civilian targets which included British, French, Israeli and American.

And Ali had organized security for a meeting between bin Laden and Hezbollah's military leader **Imad Mughniyeh** as they planned future operations. Ali's arrest and conviction revealed to those blinded over the past years that his "intelligence to us had been tainted", he was in fact a double agent.

For him and so many other Islamic extremist / terrorists, America and the West were to be destroyed so Islam could take over. His confessions revealed that America was caught up in an interconnected world of terrorists. Those radicals are not just motivated by religious zeal, they are personally motivated and in many cases well schooled to resurrect a new "Ottoman Empire". *But this one would be a strict Fundamentalist regime.* A well thought out and coordinated response was needed to fight this war, but Bill Clinton was not that person.   **Incident # 167**

Over the past weeks the Intelligence services began picking up "chatter" that another attack was coming. FBI agent Jack Cloonan decided to go over the files of the debriefing of Ali Mohamed. **In those sessions Ali had superficially spoken of using jetliners as flying missiles.** Cloonan passed that information over to the CIA. But as had happened with the Filipinos and the Bojinka Plot debriefing, it fell on deaf and secretive ears.   **Incident # 168**

Back on May 1, 1998 Iraq had warned of dire consequences if the U.N. did not leave their country. As shown earlier USAF bombings in southern Iraq were occurring more and more as Saddam tested our resolve. **Congress even passed a resolution in 1999 allowing Clinton to "liberate Iraq" if his WMD programs constituted a pending threat to America.**

The nonprofit group Indict was funded by the U.S. Congress in 1998 to help the Iraqi's organize an international conference on the human rights abuses that were commonplace. During April 2000 witnesses and victims were brought in and showcased for the world to see the horrors of Saddam's Iraq. Videos of brutal interrogations and executions were added to the vast evidence against the Ba'thists rule.

And Iraq was also helping al Qaeda with arms and training. Iraqi security officers met repeatedly with al-Qaeda seniors in the Sudan, Turkey, Afghanistan and in Prague. Scores of defectors had attested to that linkage. The most infamous Iraqi terrorist camp was their facility southeast of Baghdad called *Salman Pak*. That vast training ground was run by Iraq's intelligence service. *At that location the terrorists trained on how to hijack commercial aircraft with knives, and they practiced on a full scale Boeing 707.*

Iraqi **Salah Suleiman** was arrested near the Afghan border by Pakistani authorities during October 2000. He admitted he too had trained in bin Laden's camps. His interrogations discussed Salman Pak and the joint training going on.   **Incident # 169**

That same month the FBI became aware of a bin Laden plot to hijack a Boeing 747. This source was a walk-in to the FBI's Newark, NJ field office. Niaz Khan claimed that he had trained in a Pakistani camp on how to hijack airliners as part of a team that would meet up in the U.S. They would have pilots among their ranks to takeover the controls after the hijacking. Khan passed a polygraph. Again the FBI leadership allowed this vital lead to slip away. **There was no follow up investigation because no "crime had been committed".** (At the least they should have contacted the CTC or Richard Clarke at the White House to let them know about this visit.) **Incident # 170**

During the past year an American defense analyst twice smuggled herself into Afghanistan to gather intelligence from the hundreds of al Qaeda prisoners being held by the Northern Alliance. This civilian, Ottilie English was the sister of Congressman Phil English. She worked as a commercial representative for the Northern Alliance and traveled often to Afghanistan in 2000 and 2001. *(She too was ordered to stop her activities by the Administration.)*

After one trip she returned with over seven hours of video conversations with the al Qaeda prisoners. One repeatedly told her, "We are coming to America to attack you!" She also met with the CIA agent in Tajikistan and showed him the pile of data she had been given. He complained that he had sent that same information out repeatedly, but no one at the top ever listens. **Incident # 171**

Over the past months numerous ideas had been discussed for striking bin Laden, but all were scrapped as being too difficult or causing too many civilian casualties. Clinton feebly asked the United Arab Emirates to get involved, and twice Clarke carried letters from Clinton to **Sheikh Zayed**. The UAE put their country at risk in taking out a few al Qaeda people, providing some intelligence, and in negotiating with the Taliban to turning bin Laden over. Yet in the end all of the offers were rejected by the Administration.

Then in July 2000 a CIA informant revealed that a terrorist group was planning to attack a U.S. naval ship, possibly in the eastern Mediterranean. Lebanon was considered the most likely area, but the CIA and DOD discounted the threat because the Navy had no ships in that area.

But we did have ships in the Persian Gulf region.

CENTCOM and the State Dept. both knew of that fact as they had sent the ships there. Apparently they never told the White House of that fact. Again Clarke could have reacted if he knew we had ships in Yemen. And the DOD did not connect the dots because they were not kept informed of the all of the incoming threats. No additional safety directives or warnings were made to increase the security at our bases or on any of our ships. **Incident # 172**

In late July 2000 FBI agents in Charlotte, North Carolina arrested eighteen people in a smuggling ring that was providing currency, financial services, training, false documentation, communication equipment, explosives and other items to Hezbollah. Two of the terrorists were **Youssef Hammoud** and his brother **Mohammed.** Both had married American women in order to get Green Cards. **Incident # 173**

This marriage fraud issue has been out of control for decades. *One woman who worked in the NC state DMV was murdered soon after those arrests because of her knowledge of the false identities she had previously given out.*

FBI agents working in Arizona became aware of a group of Middle Eastern men who were enrolled at Embry Riddle Aeronautical University in Prescott, Arizona. Those students had openly expressed an intense hatred for America, and were interviewed by agent Ken Williams. To Williams it was clear that they could be part of a coordinated plan.

One of the students was an al Qaeda sympathizer who kept a photo of bin Laden. Another suspect had made a call to **Abu Zubaydah**, the known and sought after Palestinian terrorist who ran terrorist training camps for bin Laden!

But as before, no investigations could be mounted because no "crime" had been committed. **Incident # 174**

Kie Fallis an analyst for the DIA, Defense Intelligence Agency was a former Army interrogator and was fluent in Farsi. He was one of the few who had a good understanding of Iran and had recently finished a year with the FBI investigating the Khobar Towers and the African Embassies terrorists bombings. Working with computers and his own investigative mind he realized that the people involved in the earlier attacks were planning new strikes. Fallis had caught on to the warning signs of impending al Qaeda attacks, mainly the video releases by bin Laden. With the latest intelligence warnings coming in, and bin Laden videos being played on Qatari television, Fallis and others with him began warning of a pending attack. Their superiors brushed them off, and no alerts were issued. **Incident # 175**

Afghanistan

Massoud and his forces were again weathering the latest Taliban-Pakistani storm. He had established supply lines into Iran, had commercial deals to buy Russian weapons, and even India kicked in $10 million to help him out. CIA intelligence was of value to him, but his fighters were growing weary of battling the never ending supply of Pakistani volunteers and al-Qaeda suicide platoons.

Famed 1979 Afghan leader Ismail Khan had escaped into Iran to stir revolts against the Taliban. Pashtun tribal leaders staged protests against the forced conscription being done by the Taliban. Abdul Haq, King Zahir Shah and Hamid Karzai met with Massoud associates to create a grand anti-Taliban alliance to unite the north and south.

Encouraged by those efforts, Massoud planned an offensive by having anti-Taliban rebellions ignite in defensible mountain areas all around northern and western Afghanistan. Once they succeeded in controlling those pockets, Massoud would send his stronger forces to link up on the roadways trapping Taliban units inside various cities and towns. After they were defeated, those initial base areas would supply his fortified alliance, which would then be able to help out the south. He wanted the southerners to follow his lead and establish similar base areas to complete their victory.

But Massoud needed arms, trucks, jeeps and helicopters to enact his plan. *His organizers traveled to Washington to meet with our leaders, but no one was interested.* Few congressional staffers would even make an appearance, let alone administration or elected officials. The State Dept. offered some limited aid, but this Administration refused to make a stand. **Incident # 176**

A Special Forces recon team had checked out an unused airfield near Kandahar. After mapping out the area it was determined that a team could use the site to slip in and get to bin Laden when he showed up. But each time a potential chance came up Gen. Shelton would insist on a 1,000 man total force instead of small covert teams. Since no one in the Administration knew anything about the military they would not overrule Shelton'. And the Navy was tired of keeping ships and submarines on standby in the Iran/Pakistan area for months on end. It was taking a toll on the ships and crews.

In the 1980s the CIA had begun experimenting with small airplane model kits mounted with cameras while they were in

Beirut. The CIA also tried to mount rockets to the units as a way to arm them, but the weapons of that time were inaccurate.

(As shown in Fatal Flaws Book 2, an Israeli intelligence officer had done this on his own in the early 1970s as a way to get photos of Egypt. He warned an invasion was coming, but no one listened.)

Around the mid- 90s a novel idea was begun using the new Predator surveillance drone in place of human assets. In that way the intelligence community could observe large areas unseen and risk little. This technology was still new and most of the initial units were operating in the "hot" areas of Bosnia, Kosovo and Iraq. *(It was former CIA director James Woolsey who saw the value of having those drones watching over suspect areas, and he had arranged for them to be purchased.)*

With our closer ties to officials in Uzbekistan, Clarke (with help from analyst Charlie Allen), was able to get two Predators assigned there to do fly-overs of Afghanistan. Clinton approved of a limited number of "proof of concept" flights only in September 2000. Pres. Karimov insisted on absolute secrecy as we would operate from one of the former Soviet air bases.

(Russia was not happy about NATO's operations in Kosovo. They were even more upset that America was setting up operations just to their south. We had done some training exercises in Uzbekistan in 1998, and to the resurgent Russian hard-liners, they irrationally saw all of this as a threat to them.)

Despite the political tensions numerous Predator flights did go over the known terrorist camps. **Upgrades in video capability had improved the imaging so well, that Richard Clarke was certain he saw bin Laden walking around at least three times!** * (177)

Clarke and some of the anti-terror principals would watch the flights and videos live from Langley. They compared the video to watching live traffic reports. As they watched bin Laden walking around his Tarnak farm, a Taliban MiG fighter went up to intercept the drone but flew past it causing the viewers to instinctively duck. Besides the great views, there was a critical factor these drone flights and footage provided.

The "legal-requirements"from Tenet and Clinton on having their second source verification! Now they could visually confirm that bin Laden was there.

But since there were no CIA assets in the area ready to strike, and no military operations would be approved by Clinton, all the intelligence people could do was watch as bin Laden and his followers moved around their camps!   **Incident # 177**

Then Clarke heard of the program to arm the Predator drone with the fire-and forget hellfire anti-tank missile. Bureaucratic infighting and administration lawyers argued strongly against the idea, but Clarke pushed the program through. The first flight of an armed Predator took off in late September 2000, and flew eleven armed missions in those first weeks.

(Was bin Laden spotted again? Clarke convienently leaves that little secret out of his books.)

A few weeks later one of the Predators crashed from severe weather. With winter coming to the tall hills the missions were stopped because of high winds.

But now we knew bin Laden was at Tarnak, and the video feed gave solid evidence as to which building he was in! The military worked on the "mathematics" of blowing the whole place up. Bin Laden plus bodyguards and staff were present, and so were "some civilians". A child's swing was visible in one video, but no children were ever seen near it.

Again Clinton refused to allow the strike. Incident # 178 (One of the main issues that stopped this attack was Clinton's fear that it would fail and hurt Al Gore's election chances. The election was just two months away.) *(178)

The Air Force did not want the armed-predator program because it could signal the end of human pilots, while CIA's Tenet was nervous about *"the legality"* of shooting a missile from the drone. **As a result of those "inane issues" this program was shut down until the attacks of 9/11/01 proved them fatally wrong! Incident # 179** \

After months of waiting, Huffman Aviation Flight School in Venice, Florida filed requests for M-1 student visas for a **Mohamed Atta** and **Marwan al-Shehhi** in August 2000. Their current visas had to be changed from non-immigrant visitor to student if they were going to attend the year long flight school. *INS, Immigration and Naturalization Service did not actually approve Atta's request until July 17, 2001. It was August 9, 2001 before al Shehhi's form was officially approved.*

A year had passed for the paperwork to get through!

All that time they were allowed to remain in our country and go to the flight school. Their official notification letters did not go to the flight school until March 11, 2002.

That was six months after they flew the hijacked aircraft into the World Trade Center. But Atta and Shehhi were not the only 9/11 terrorists to use this scam. Hani Hanjour and Ahmed Alghamdi also used the student visa program to enter and stay here illegally.

The USS Cole

Jamal al-Badawi had waited over two years for his chance to strike. Like so many al Qaeda followers he was naive but eager. At a bin Laden camp he had been approached and befriended by the previously mentioned **Tawfiq al-Attash**, who was a veteran from the war in Afghanistan and a bin Laden's bodyguard. Al Qaeda camps were always segregated, Saudis trained with Saudis, Yemenis with Yemenis, etc. In that effective way no spies could infiltrate the camps as everyone knew or could cross-check on any newcomers. After his training Badawi was sent home to Yemen to wait for instructions.

In June of 2000 two men visited him with directives to go to Saudi Arabia and buy a small boat. Later a letter from bin Laden arrived with instructions on how to sink a larger ship. Jamal was going to get his chance.

Multiple safe houses were setup with identity cards and other documents prepared for them. Corrupt / sympathetic police and officials made sure the cells were left alone to do their work. As usual various cells were involved in this attack with some making parts, some purchasing equipment etc. But all of the **sixty terrorists** in that project had a dedicated purpose, to kill Americans. It was a classic bin Laden plot as few of the workers knew what the overall objective was.

Attash and al-Harazi (from the failed Sullivan's plot) were the senior al-Qaeda members. They had assembled their attack team, but as always those senior members would escape. Badawi and the others were the sacrificial lambs.

It was during this time frame a high ranking member inside EIJ came forward with a warning that a U.S. Navy ship was going to be attacked soon. His story was passed through the intelligence bureaucracy but was again discounted. (The intel from Kie Fallis.) **Incident # 180**

Inside the harbor at Aden was the *USS Cole*, a guided missile destroyer. The day before the ship had passed through the Suez Canal and the Red Sea en-route for Aden. Their commanders had contacted the Embassy by radio telling them they would come in to take on fuel and provisions, a normal routine for ships in that area.

Their visit would last ten days, and the locals prepared for their port call.

Two months earlier during a similar visit a Yemeni national had come aboard the ship for a "goodwill tour" and meet with the crew. He insisted that he eat in the crew mess instead of the normal meal with the officers. This Muslim male was convincing as a curious local, but in actuality he was casing the ship and the layout. He took note of the time of breakfast chow call.

As shown before, Clinton and his Administration wanted to make a diplomatic effort in the region for "good will". One of their proposals was having navy ships refuel in Aden harbor. Djibouti had been the refueling port for over a decade, and despite the terrorist dangers in Yemen, the Administration made this dangerous and moronic change.

All of our security agencies including NCIS warned against this. But Sec. Albright arrogantly ignored them and sent our ships into harms way.

Normally the harbor shoreline of Aden was deserted except for those at work. But on the 12th the shoreline was packed with "well wishers". The fueling operation was going fine with 2,200 gallons per minute being taken into the fuel bunkers of the ship.

A small speedboat approached with one **Abd al-Taifi** at the helm. *He was another terrorist who was wanted in connection for the bombing in Nairobi.* A second Muslim male was in the boat, but he was distracted by repeatedly calling **Jamal Ba Khorsh**, (aka al-Quoso). Khorsh was supposed to be filming their attack, but he overslept. There were other similar small craft nearby, some taking off trash while others brought in food. Those small boats were a common sight in the harbor, and this one drew no unusual attention as they slowly approached the anchored and peaceful navy ship. But their boat had been packed with several hundred pounds of C-4.

When the small craft reached the mid-line of the ship they were in line with the mess deck. It was time for chow, and the deck was filling up with hungry sailors. The terrorist boat then sped up. Unarmed sentries called out a warning as the craft struck the unprepared destroyer.

On October 12, 2000 the al Qaeda terrorists were successful as a massive explosion rocked the *USS Cole*.

A 30x40 foot hole was blown through the 1/2 inch thick steel hull causing fearsome damage within and nearly sinking the ship. Power went out and high test fuel was leaking into the water around and inside the ship. Incredibly it did not ignite.

Damage Control, a staple skill that the U.S. Navy excels at went into high gear. Corpsmen rushed to the wounded while others tended to their wounded ship. Their work saved both as many more could have died. **Seventeen Americans were murdered with thirty-nine seriously wounded.   Incident # 181**

(Had they struck a few yards more astern, or had a larger explosive been used the terrorists could have caused a catastrophic explosion and fire sinking the Billion dollar ship and murdering the entire crew.)

Within hours of the attack the FBI sent dozens of agents to investigate, led by John O'Neil from the NYC office. However most of the team including O'Neil were not allowed into the country for days because the Ambassador, Barbara Bodine refused to grant them an entry visa!!

After she reluctantly relented, they stayed in the same hotel bin Laden tried to attack back in December 1992. She met the FBI team and insisted they follow the directives from the useless Clinton State Dept. *She told them to go slow and "not ruffle any feathers", Aden was not Nairobi.* Her negative attitude was apparent to all, even the poor sailors from the Cole.

(Bodine had stopped a 1993 report from analyst Marvin Cetron because it gave a harsh warning of the coming Islamist terrorist threats.)   *(178A)

Back in 1998 the Kenyans and Tanzanians were quite helpful and amazed at the effectiveness and skill of the FBI team. But Aden had been harmfully influenced by the Soviets and their anti-western work for decades. Throw in a terrorist mindset armed to the teeth, and the country was a tense place to be. Due to the hostility of the ambassador and the locals, the FBI could do little direct investigating.

Meetings were held in the White House. **With the exception of Clarke, none of Clinton's hand picked principals wanted to strike back.** Clarke suggested a <u>bombing</u> mission be mounted to take out every terrorist camp we know of in Afghanistan plus hitting some Taliban buildings and positions. Most in the room felt that retaliation was "old hat".

All Clarke heard from the administration principals were objections and reasons not to do anything. The lawyers stated that we did not know "definitively" who attacked us so we could not act. And Albright foolishly complained that any retaliatory strike would hurt our negotiations in the region. As usual Clinton was on

TV shaking his limp hand at the camera. The terrorists saw that even when they attacked our ships nothing was done.

Bill Clinton, the world's most **infamous appeaser again did nothing.** He no longer cared. He was on his way out and did not want to cause Democrat nominee Al Gore any potential foreign policy troubles with the election just weeks away. Bin Laden would simply become someone else's problem.

Sandy Berger stated that our "intelligence agencies" could not agree on if bin Laden was behind the attack, and as usual he was lying. And Clinton repeated that lie during the 9/11 hearings to cover himself. **(In John Miller's fine work *The Cell,* Miller wrote that within 48 hours of the attack the initial investigators were certain of the links to bin Laden.)**

DOD Analyst Kie Fallis was disgusted. He had warned of this pending attack, but as always no one listened. He quit in protest that day writing to Admiral Thomas Wilson the head of the DIA citing the poor quality of his superiors. He warned Wilson that more attacks were coming, and that Iran was helping the terrorists. As always the bureaucrats treated him as an enemy because he knew they had failed. It was and is a common theme with all bureaucrats, blame others and cover your butt.

(Fallis was the one who wrote the report in May 2000 in which he connected all of the major terrorist groups together, Al Qaeda, EIJ etc. That included Iran's Ali Khamenei one of their key terrorists. Fallis was also the one who realized the terrorists had gotten together with Iran in Malaysia in January 2000.)

During that first week our Ambassador remained indifferent and the Yemini's unhelpful, and that included their president Ali Abdullah Saleh. Saleh had used many of the Afghan veterans in his army to defeat the socialists in S. Yemen. *In return for their help he looked away at some of their doings, as long as it wasn't a threat to him or Yemen.*

The Yemeni's had insisted they do the investigation. Work was slowly being done by a reluctant Yemini intelligence service the PSO, Political Security Organization. However leads were coming in, and within a few days of the attack Yemini Intelligence found a crucial witness. A small boy had observed the suicide bombers drive up and lower their boat into the water. Their Nissan truck and trailer were still there, and an address was traced to a middle class neighborhood near Aden.

Investigators quickly saw the similarities between this bomb factory/safe house and the one used in Nairobi two years earlier.

Two men were arrested for being the renters of the house. Inside DNA and physical evidence was obtained, and the woman who sold the truck was also arrested.

Within a month over one hundred people had been "arrested", though only six were actual bombing suspects.

One of the renters of the house was the aforementioned **Jamal al-Badawi**. He admitted that he had trained in bin Laden's camps in Afghanistan, and that he had fought in Bosnia with al-Qaeda in 1994. He also admitted buying the boat and bringing it to **Fahd al-Quoso** another long time al Qaeda member, (aka Khorsh). Al-Quoso was the one who was supposed to be filming the attack, and was soon located and arrested. He gave up another al Qaeda terrorist named **Abu Jandal** who had once been a bin Laden body guard. **Al-Harazi, (aka al-Nashiri)** had left Yemen as per the usual al Qaeda timeline of 24 hours before the attack. (Before he left Harazi gave final instructions to al-Badawi and al-Quoso.)

As had happened in the Saudi Arabia attacks, the FBI had no direct access to the suspects. They could only ask questions through the Yemini's. Again the FBI and CIA found the Clinton-Reno DOJ rules on sharing information prevented those agencies from being able to cooperate and collate their information. Agent John O'Neil was so annoying to Ambassador Bodine he was declared persona-non-grata and could never return.

Former CIA agent Bob Baer also uncovered evidence on the bombing of the USS Cole from his former sources inside Lebanon. *His report exposed a listing of some 600 Islamic extremists linked to al Qaeda. As had happened in 1998, this vital information was disregarded because he was the one who sent it.* **Incident #182**

On October 29, 2000 the severely damaged *USS Cole* was placed aboard a Norwegian heavy lift- recovery ship and removed from the harbor. The gaping hole was still visible, proof to the terrorists that their efforts would work. Most of the American investigators had left the city and those remaining moved offshore to the *USS Tarawa* where it was safer. Every time a U.S. helicopter came near the city anti-air missiles were trained on it.

The Yemeni's refused any thought that their suspects would be tried in America. Links to bin Laden were everywhere, including phone call records back and forth. Yet the Administration continued to stonewall any type of response.

But the Clinton Administration's inanity continued.

During the Yemeni investigations it was learned that **Khalid al-Mihdhar** was one of the plotters in the USS Cole attack.

Yemini Prime Minister al-Inyani actually named Mihdhar as one of the senior plotters in the attack. Incident# 183

As investigators traced his recent movements it was learned that Mihdhar had recently met with the radical American cleric **Anwar al-Awlaki** in San Diego. The FBI team investigating showed the CIA-CTC officers pictures and listed phone numbers of the many suspects. Even though they knew about Mihdhar, the CIA again said nothing about him!

Implausibly this known terror suspect Khalid al-Mihdar (aka Mihdhar) was again able to return to the U.S. by plane!

(After the attacks of 9/11 happened, **it was learned that 60 CIA officials knew that Mihdhar and Hazmi had been moving around the U.S., but no one said a thing.** And no one went to jail.)

Anwar Awalaki had already been the subject of a 1999 FBI investigation in San Diego. During that probe they found links from Awalaki and the terrorist cleric Sheik Omar Rahman (WTC, Day of Terror Attacks 1993), and a money man for al Qaeda.

Saudi **Osama Bassnan** was another potential terrorist who often showed up with Awalaki. Bassnan had a file on him from years earlier because he had hosted a celebratory function for Rahman. But with the Clinton DOJ rules in effect and the Congress refusing to enact the legal changes needed to go after the terrorists those inquiries were again stopped. (More on this story to follow.)
Incident # 184

Clinton had used the Oklahoma City bombing to push the FBI into concentrating their investigations on "right-wing causes". *At this late date only 6% of the FBI's manpower was assigned to counterterrorism, about 1300 agents.* And only a few of their analysts were actually assigned to investigate al Qaeda. So poor was the effort from senior management that they did not believe there were terrorist web sites inside America.

In Afghanistan Massoud's Northern forces came under well delivered attacks using artillery and mortars. The Pakistani's were lending their expertise in an attempt to drive Massoud out. His forces lost Taloqan and with it went their supply lines. The planned anti-Taliban offensive was ended before it began.

More Clinton Politics and Disasters

At home the Welfare Reform Act of 1996 cut the number of people from the welfare rolls, but the Democratic law promoting disabilities in 1993 allowed many of those people to end up on the

Social Security rolls instead. And most of those transferred had not paid a dime into the Social Security system.

Their disability act also resulted in the obscene giveaway that the ones who transferred received more money on SS, than they had gotten on Welfare. And once your "disability", (which included drug addicts and alcoholics) was approved, there was no review process to get the person back to work.

In his propaganda sessions with the compliant media Bill Clinton tried to claim that he had cut the *total numbers* of Federal personnel to save money. But in reality all of his manpower cuts were from the Department of Defense.

At the end of the 1991 Gulf War the Army had 710,821 active duty soldiers. By the time Clinton left office in Jan 2001, the Army was down to 478,918 troops. *A reduction of 45%.*

He also cut hundreds of aircraft from the Air Force, and over 100 ships from the Navy. *The Air Force cuts hit 40%, the Navy went down by 37%.* (Clinton's short-sighted work eliminated the fighter aircraft in the New York City and Washington D.C. regions that might have been able to stop the attacks into the South Tower and the Pentagon on 9/11.)

This incompetent, liberal lawyer worked tirelessly to break down our military in an effort to gain a "peace dividend" from the fall of Soviet Communism. Our senior military leadership was cut and rendered ineffective, and he cut the funding for military pay, health insurance and upkeep to housing and living quarters.

Yet despite those cuts, Clinton the Vietnam War draft dodger increased the number and length of the military deployments which further undermined morale and effectiveness.

Next to go were large reductions in military research and development. Like all of the Democrats, Clinton and Gore were completely against Reagan's SDI program. During his Senate years Gore voted against SDI 24 times!

During Clinton/Gores first year in office the SDI program was ended, and their party line was "we were safe for at least 15 years". CIA chief Woolsey heartedly disagreed and said so in Congressional testimony. (He was fired soon after.)

A July 1998 Congressional report contradicted the White House in every aspect of their defense cuts. Still he continued. His defense budget levels for 1996 were the same as the dangerously low levels of 1975. His 1997 budget levels would approach those of 1955! His 2000 budget had fallen to just 3.4% of our gross domestic product, the level of 1947!

Verification of Clinton's stupidity came quickly for on August 31, 1998 North Korea launched their first ballistic missile. In response to that critical event Clinton and Gore complained, but did not enact any defensive upgrades or sanctions. Congress did it on their own in 1999, 345-71 in the House, 97-3 in the Senate.

Still not interested in our national defense the Clinton-Gore team insisted we had to comply with the ABM treaty signed with the USSR back in 1972. SDI was a "legal issue we had to comply with". **No on SDI**.

The previously mentioned SOSUS system of deep ocean hydrophones had protected our shores from enemy submarines since the mid-50s. This worldwide sensor system had been crucial in helping the navy locate the Russian subs during the Cuban Missile Crisis of 1962, and aided in preventing a nuclear war. When it was completed it had cost just $ 16 Billion. Not a bad price for keeping the nation safe. Because of SOSUS the Russians could not simply creep up on our shores and destroy us. But with a stroke of his pen Bill Clinton was putting our entire national security and our population at risk, as that system was being disbanded. (And they say the Democrats care about the little guy.)

Clinton also helped our next potential superpower enemy every time he could. Communist China had been given and sold every hi-tech piece of equipment and technology they wanted during his eight years in office. *Thanks to Clinton, Chinese rockets were launching U.S. satellites into space. With each launch more and more science and technology was changing hands.* China now possesses a serious nuclear threat.

Just a few years earlier at the Tiananmen Square protests the Chinese military had serious trouble communicating because their radio systems were outdated. Thanks to Bill Clinton that shortfall was also erased. And China transferred a lot of this illegal knowledge to North Korea, Pakistan and Iran.

During the last few years the Chinese repeatedly threatened to invade Taiwan. **If the U.S. intervened, China stated they would use nuclear weapons upon us and obliterate LA!** Instead of enacting sanctions or some sort of penalty, Clinton constantly downplayed their words saying it was just rhetoric!

As the decade progressed the Chinese began building missile capable submarines, and never deactivated their Bio-weapons programs. China was (and still is) building up their blue water navy to rival ours, including advanced submarines.

After the Vietnam War ended China invaded the Paracel Islands in the S. China Sea and took them from Vietnam. They militarized those islands and began exploiting the resources.

The nearby Spratly Islands are claimed by Malaysia, the Philippines and Vietnam. Those islands are **800 miles** from China's shores, and just **140 miles** from the Philippines.

Yet China aggressively invaded some of them in 1995 and began emplacing defensive weapons to ensure no one tried to challenge them. Clinton said and did nothing over that international theft. By 1999 they had built fuel bunkers, new airbases equipped with new SU-27 Russian built fighter-bombers, and several warships patrolled the seas around the islands.

No one in the Clinton Administration ever complained or sought to force an end to this dangerous precedent, and that includes the useless United Nations.

To ensure the region stays under their control, China ordered two Russian destroyers that carry missiles designed to destroy U.S. built Aegis-class warships, as well as purchasing four Russian Kilo-class subs. They are constructing their first aircraft carrier and three new types of aircraft. With Clinton in office, China and the world saw that America was a dwindling world power just as the Soviets did during the reign of Jimmy Carter. As always the Chinese are taking the "long view". In twenty or so years they will be ready to strike.

(In 2018 China unveiled a Stealth Bomber. Why would China need such a weapon? The reader is directed to Bill Getz's outstanding works, ***Betrayal and The China Threat.***)

As shown earlier, in 1998 numerous indictments came down over the illegal contributions scandals which included money from Communist China. Even though a few lower level officials had been indicted, Clinton conveniently was not.

FBI agents were assisting four separate investigations into the White House, and Director Freeh wanted a fifth one organized to look at the China connection! **But Janet Reno again obstructed things by refusing to appoint a special counsel who would have total control on all of it.**

Director Freeh wrote a scathing 27 page report to her telling her she was obstructing the overall issue. "It is a conflict of interest for the Attorney General to control an investigation into her superiors, meaning Clinton and Gore". We must go after the major players of Clinton and his top aides. Still she refused.

Freeh briefed Senators Fred Thompson and John Glenn over the matter, but Clinton again escaped.

A month later the NY Times reported that the special Task Force chief Charles La Bella had recommended the same thing. **But La Bella also wanted Al Gore to be the subject of a deeper investigation.** He stated that Reno was not "looking at the issue properly". She was claiming them as independent misconducts, when the investigators had shown and asserted that all of this was a major concerted effort of corruption and influence peddling. **La Bella recommended independent counsel investigations with subpoena power to go after Bill and Hillary Clinton, Al Gore, and Harold Ickes!**

The stench from this corruption was never rectified, and all of the guilty got away to do more harm as is evident in the Obama years. *But the treachery continued in other areas too.*

On December 31, 1999 control of the Panama Canal was transferred to Panama ending all U.S. reins. The person overseeing that transfer was none other than disgraced former president Jimmy Carter. (Vladimir Lenin called people who are so dumb that they do your bidding without question, "Useful Idiots") *(179)

Secretly Clinton-Carter then approved the Communist Chinese front group Huchison-Whampao to take operational control of the Panama Canal and four of the ports!

In addition to that strategic sellout Clinton allowed Huchison-Whampao to operate and build a sea-air container port in the Bahamas. Their operational control includes Grand Bahamas Airport, Freeport Container port and the Freeport Harbor Company. *As a result of those approvals Communist China has military capable ports just 80 miles from our shores!* (179A)

As of this writing China also has control of the Buenos Aires container terminal in Argentina, a terminal at the Port of Manta in Ecuador, a terminal at the Port of Veracruz, the Ensenada Cruiseport and the Ensenada International terminal on our Pacific border with Mexico. Again those operations give Communist China unfettered shipping and air access all along our southern border. *(The perfect way to secretly bring in medium range nuclear or EMP weapons that could take us out with almost no warning.)*

Most people do not know this but Bill Clinton also gave Communist China the highest point of land overlooking the Pentagon to build their new Hi-rise Embassy.

Our next superpower enemy has been spying on our entire military command structure and much of our Capitol from this convenient site. Imagine the results if the Chinese brought in a suitcase nuke via the "diplomatic pouch" and suicide attacked us from their embassy. There would be no warning, just a substantial nuclear explosion that would decimate the area.

And if it was done correctly our Government and Military Command would be gone in that flash.

(In return for his help, China insisted our new embassy be just two stories high, and far removed from any of their vital installations.) **As usual all of those inconvenient facts were ignored by a compliant media and State Dept.**

Historical Note: Over the past two centuries millions of ethnic Chinese had emigrated across the globe but especially around the Pacific rim. One result of that migration is that China began making territorial claims to many areas in the Pacific, and seems determined to take them. What will the world do over China's claims of sovereignty? China does not have a large population of pacifists, not that the Communist government would listen to them anyway.

After the Communists took power in China in 1949 (thanks to Harry Truman), they successfully stopped newly independent India from exerting any control in their region. That effort continued throughout the 1950s and 1960s.

It was China that did the invading, first in Tibet and then in India in the Kashmir province. After winning their one month war with India in 1962, China then built roads and railways to dominate the area. *They also promoted revolution in Burma and Indochina in a successful effort to undermine the Europeans.*

Once the Europeans exited China assisted the Communist regimes that took over. Though they have recently acted to "help control North Korea", secretly they aid them. And China continues to sell advanced weapons and technology to Pakistan as a way to destabilize and threaten India. One of the unstated reasons why India developed nuclear weapons was to fight off the encroaching Chinese, if it came to that. *(In 2017 China was still trying to claim more land there, this time in Bhutan.)*

On December 31, 1998 the Cox Committee released an exhaustive report on Chinese espionage in America. For political reasons they agreed not to release the full report to the public until Clinton could go over it. For five months the Administration sat on it.

Their report stated; During the past twenty years China has been actively acquiring sensitive American military technology including nuclear weapons and research. While the committee explained that the effort began under Carter, *it had become a flood under the Clinton Administration.* Clinton and his people had knowingly and purposefully reduced and limited the background checks to foreign visitors to classified areas, as highlighted before with Hazel O'Leary. Sandy Berger claimed he notified Clinton of this problem back in July 1997, but as always Clinton publicly denied ever having been told anything.

Among the issues in this report,

(1) China had three thousand front companies operating in the United States.

(2) China stole all seven of our nuclear warhead designs, including the W-88 advanced and miniaturized one.

(3) China has acquired information on our re-entry vehicles which shield the warheads.

(4) China has acquired information from us on missile-guidance. (Loral-Hughes)

(5) China has acquired our research on electro-magnetic weapons.

This committee believed that while the other administrations did not realize the extent of the Chinese espionage, the Clinton Administration most certainly did.

During the 19th century China felt violated by the aggression of the colonial powers, (The Boxer Rebellion.) Are they beginning to seek payback as they purchase every commodity possible across the globe? The only potential hold over them may be their intensive worldwide commercial ties. As shown before their military is growing rapidly to protect their interests, and to attack if needed. Their efforts are greatly assisted by their hundreds of spies in the West and dupes like Bill Clinton. At present China could not defeat the U.S. or its SEATO allies. But China is less than a decade away from being able to project a dominating military presence across the seas. The coming years are full of new dangers, dangers created by yet another Democratic president.

Throughout the Clinton Years non-communist Russia was virtually ignored. The fledgling democracy should have been assisted by the U.S. to ensure its survival and progression. But as shown earlier Clinton had no knowledge or desire to be involved in foreign affairs. VP Al Gore, Strobe Talbott at State and Lawrence Summers at Treasury were given the task to help Russia. But in a 200 page report it was revealed they did just the opposite. Over

$20 Billion of our tax money (through the IMF) was squandered. Their poor effort helped Russian criminals to prosper in all manor of illegal activities including arms sales. And that turned their political landscape into a source of patronage and power.

Ultimately the hardliners took over, led by former KGB officer Vladimir Putin. Along with Putin's ascension the Russian military and spying services were renewed with money and upgrades! *Russian GRU Col. Stanislav Lunev revealed in the summer of 2000 that almost half of the Russian journalists in the West are spies.*

And in following their successes from the 1930s-1960s they are finding hundreds of simple minded Americans to turn. Sec. Albright refused to believe the numbers he quoted, because "none of them ever came forward to identify themselves as spies." (??)

FBI Director Freeh warned in November 1999 that the Russians have weapons scattered around our country, and it includes "suitcase nuclear weapons". Of the one hundred plus suitcase nukes Russia produced in the years past, only 48 are accounted for inside Russia. The rest are "unknown".

Col. Lunev also stated that their weapons were always deployed in anticipation of a war with America. Europe also has hidden Russian weapons scattered around their capitols. And as a hedge against the West, Russia has been aiding the Iranian WMD programs in an effort to find allies.

(Obama did little about Iran's nuclear program for seven years, and refused to help their dissidents in 2009. As he was leaving office he came up with that ridiculous arms proposal that greatly benefitted Iran. **Why do all of the Democratic presidents aspire to destroy this nation?)**

To highlight how little Clinton understood or cared about National Security, in 1998 he lost his key-card that contained our nuclear launch codes. Every two weeks the keys are replaced. When the time came to turn in his old card Clinton nonchalantly replied that the last time he had seen it was two weeks ago. He had placed our entire country at risk, and in his arrogance did not even report the loss so it could be rectified.

For two weeks the U.S. nuclear response capability was unusable. Had an enemy learned of that loss, our nation could have been destroyed in a pre-emptive attack killing most of us. Clinton cared not.

It was revealed in June 2000 that numerous smaller islands from the Arctic chain just west of Alaska were being given to Russia with no Congressional debate or discussions.

The islands in question, Wrangell, Herald, Bennett, Jeanette and Henrietta were the western most islands of the Aleutians chain. Back in 1991 those boundaries had been set under then Pres. George H. Bush.

Yet in 2000 Clinton and his State Dept. were now giving them to the Russians. And that included the U.S. citizens who had been living on them! Economically we lost vital oil / gas and mineral rights and important fishing grounds. Strategically the Russians could now base weapons and surveillance systems just a few miles from Alaska. (Clinton also gave away four islands in the central Pacific!)

More Islamic Threats

As shown before one of the 1993 World Trade Center bombers Eyad Ismoil had come in on a student visa and then disappeared until the bombing. In 1996 the Congress had ordered the INS (Immigration-Naturalization Service) to update their computer tracking of foreign students to prevent what had happened in 1993. But INS administrators were so poor that they failed to meet the deadline of 2001. (Naturally none of them were fired and none of them lost their pensions.)

Inside our nation's colleges and universities liberal administrators refused to help INS by supplying any requested data. They claimed that an updated tracking system would be "unfair to foreign students." In reality they did not want to cooperate because foreign students are big money. By 2000 there were 547,867 foreign students going to U.S. schools bringing in $Billions.

"Between 1989 and 1995 over one hundred Middle East "students" paid bribes to community college teachers and administrators in San Diego to "get classes and grades" so they could have "student visas". This scam was later revealed, and Iranian-American Sam Koutchesfahani pled guilty to visa fraud along with officials from six area colleges. They had been paid $350,000 to perpetrate their part of the fraud.

None of those students could be found! * (180)

(To force compliance of our standing Federal Laws, school administrators who break the law should be arrested and imprisoned. The offending school should be penalized by taking them out of all Federal education programs. That would include any federal backed student loans, grants and studies etc.)

A report issued in 2000 by the National Commission on Terrorism warned that the large numbers of foreign students in the U.S. posed a serious risk to our security.

"The U.S. lacks the nationwide ability to monitor the immigration status of so many students, and some of them could be used to support terrorist activity."

In addition to the foreign student problem, some **two million foreign visitors** entered this country on valid visas, but remained in our country illegally after they expired. That included thousands from countries that are designated as sponsors of terrorism.

In 1998 alone over 11,000 special visas for "charitable and Islamic religious workers were allowed into our country. Those visas have almost no scrutiny or background checks!

Of the forty eight Islamic terrorists that have operated inside our shores since 1992, twenty-one had violated our immigration laws which enabled them to stay here to attack us or try to attack us!

From January 2000 to September 11, 2001, over 4,000 Arab / Muslim men from countries with strong ties to al Qaeda were given legal visas by our State Dept. to enter the U.S.

After the 9/11 attacks had occurred the Justice Dept. was able to track down less than half of those men. The rest had disappeared inside our shores! (181)

One **Hesham Hadayet** entered our country on a six month visa in July 1992, but remained here well after the visa expired. Even though he was an illegal immigrant, it was not until 1997 that the court ruled he was to be deported. He then married an American and was able to stay here.

On July 4, 2002 his terrorist side finally was revealed as he murdered two people at the El Al airline counter at LAX! This is indicative on how broken our country is, but even in 2019 the liberal politicos refuse to fix it.

The security task facing us is daunting. America has 7,500 miles of border, much of it shared with Mexico and Canada. Each year over 500 million people enter the U.S. Over 11 million trucks, 2 million rail cars and 7,500 foreign ships also enter our nation each year. There was virtually no anti-terrorist security at those sites, and there were no planned upgrades to that security. **Despite the (184) prior terrorist attacks, plots, warnings and incidents of the past decade, Bill Clinton and his administration did nothing to keep the nation safe.**

During 2000 our "friends" the Saudi's began a series of suspicious activities. (Most of this work has been covered up by the Bush Administration and redacted from official reports.) It was found that numerous Saudi consulate employees had been placed on terrorist watch lists! Yet they too somehow entered our nation. (As of 2016 twenty eight pages of intelligence had been covered up. Some of it was recently released, but it was heavily redacted to protect the identities of our enemies! Hundreds of additional pages of intelligence are still kept secret.)

Open sources have reported that Saudi consulate official **Fahad al-Thumairy** allegedly arranged for an advance team to help two of the 9/11 terrorists.

As shown earlier, known terrorists **Khalid al-Mihdhar** and **Nawaf al-Hazmi** were met at a restaurant at LAX by a suspected Saudi intelligence agent **Omar al-Bayoumi.** He and another suspected Saudi agent **Osama Bassnan** had setup a safe house for those terrorists in San Diego. They provided rooms, money and burn phones, and threw them a party. (All of this was part of the previously mentioned setup work al Qaeda spy Ali Mohamed had organized before his arrest.)

Mohdar Abdullah was an associate of Bayoumi and Thumairy. He too was here illegally, and was the assigned driver for the terrorists they were helping. Mohdar helped them get drivers licenses, and into local flight schools. He had an assistant named **Osama Awadallah**. After 9/11, his phone number was found in Hazmi's abandoned Toyota at Dulles airport. Mohdar's phone number was also found among other Hazmi evidence. And a notebook was found that had references to the 9/11 plot. All of those supporters were guilty under the law, but instead of being arrested they were deported!

Saudi Prince Bandar and his wife had sent checks totaling $130,000 to Bassnan to "help his ailing wife". After the 9/11 attacks investigations uncovered that the money was used to aid the 9/11 terrorists!

While living in San Diego Mihdhar and Hazmi met with hostile cleric **Anwar al-Awalaki** at a Saudi funded Mosque he ran. Awalaki allowed those terrorists to use his bank account to launder a $5,000. check from Dubai. Awalaki had worked with Bayoumi often during the past months as multiple phone calls confirmed their ties. Awalaki was also known to be a close associate of a member of the Muslim Brotherhood, as well as being connected to **Zacarias Moussaoui,** the Algerian terrorist who was at the previously mentioned terrorist meeting in Malaysia. Additional funding from the Gulf region was provided to the terrorists hiding in San Diego, and was later shown to be linked to al Qaeda.

Just before the September 11, 2001 attacks came off the Saudi's conveniently recalled Bandar, and Bayoumi left. Al-Thumairy was later deported. None have returned. (Not until 2004 did the Riggs Bank in DC finally drop the Saudi's as clients.)

Though considered friendly, the UAE was another supporter of the terrorists. Money for 9/11 was moved through UAE banks and two of the terrorists were Emiratis. Bin Laden was reportedly treated for kidney ailments in Dubai in secret, and al Qaeda funds were frequently laundered in the UAE.

More Politics

On August 11, 1999 Bill Clinton had suddenly decided to commute the sentences of sixteen FALN terrorists who were responsible for a series of bombings in the Wall Street area in the early 1980s. (Fraunces Tavern, four murdered over sixty wounded. Prior to this event Clinton had only pardoned three of the thousands of cases that came to him. Eleven of those FALN convicts were released from prison, two had their sentences reduced and he lowered the fines on three who had already been released. *The reason for his clemency was crystal clear, cheap and dirty politics.*

Hillary was running for the empty Senate seat in NY with the retirement of Patrick Moynihan, and Gore would be running for the White House. They would need the support of the Puerto Rican voting bloc. Naturally the bombing victims, their families and Law enforcement groups strongly criticized Bill Clinton, but it did not matter since he was leaving office. The media ensured the incident died quickly. (The Clinton's used Jimmy Carter to "recommend the clemency action" before the pardon was given.)

In another inane political move on April 22, 2000 more than twenty federal agents raided the Florida home of one Lazaro Gonzalez. Firing multiple rounds of pepper-spray and tear gas into the home, the agents crashed through the fence and front door seizing a small boy named Elian Gonzalez.

His news-worthy story had been covered for weeks as his family had tried to escape from Communist Cuba. Sadly he was the lone survivor, and had been staying with his uncle in Florida. Anyone else seeking sanctuary, which included terrorists like Sheik Rahman, would be given refuge. But not in this case.

Months of legal maneuvering and threats from Fidel Castro convinced the weak willed Clinton to steal this child away during the night and send him back to Cuba.

Outrage was quick and vocal over the U.S. government's kidnapping of this child, and it possibly hurt Gore in the Florida election vote. Clinton was terrified of Castro and what he might do just before this election. (Bill lost his reelection bid in Arkansas in 1980 because of Mariel Boatlift refugees escaping from a holding area in Arkansas. Carter also lost.)

The Supreme Court refused to hear this case. On June 23, 2000 the captured Elian was forcibly returned to Cuba.

Every ten years the nation conducts a census to analyze our population and social statistics. Back in 1900 there were 76 million people living in our country. Listed in the minority category were Native-Americans 260,000, Orientals 210,000, and Black Americans at 8.8 million. By 2000 we had grown to 281 million, and the minority populations had greatly expanded in the past century. There were now 34 million African-Americans, 35 million Hispanics, 2 million Native Americans, and 10 million Orientals. *The numbers of the first two groups had grown so high they should no longer be listed as minorities. (In fact those "minorities" now make up over 40% of our population.)*

All of the statistical social-living categories in that census saw a dramatic increase in the life experience from what people had endured just a century ago. As a nation, America was still the best place to live on the planet, though if you listened to the leftists we were the worst.

Historical Note: Slavery, or indentured servitude was a common condition throughout human existence. In America's colonial years thousands of people emigrated from Europe as indentured servants. They served for many years in a contract, under a hard existence before being freed. They then became citizens. But the Africans did not volunteer for their servitude, they were captured by Black and European slave traders, and cruelly sold as a commodity. They were shipped to the Americas, sold and used throughout the region. Freedom was never a term-option. Those slaves worked the plantations and investments of the wealthy in every country that they were sold for almost two hundred years.

After America became a separate nation lawmakers and citizens demanded the practice end. **In the early 1800s the forerunners of today's Democrats were the slave owners and racists that controlled the South. It was they who refused to end the vile practice of slavery.** The northerners and the forerunners of the Republicans argued for decades against slavery. Numerous delaying tactics and compromises were tried, but all failed. That was what led to the brutal American Civil War of 1861-1865, which the southerners/ Democrats lost.

President Lincoln had approved of various reparation and citizenship programs to get the now freed Blacks into our society. One of his plans was to give each slave ten acres from the plantation holdings they had been forced to work. But Lincoln was murdered for his efforts and Democrat Vice-President Andrew Johnson replaced him.

Johnson eliminated all of Lincoln's ideas and programs. His one-sided control of the post-Civil War Reconstruction 1866-1872 did not heal the nation as was hoped. **Instead Johnson pardoned all of the southerners who had fought in the Civil war, and eliminated all of their debts and penalties!**

As a result of his rulings the land owners and southern political leaders retained their wealth and political power, and would fight every effort to allow the former slaves to be free as equal citizens. It was during those years the likes of the KKK, poll taxes and other anti-African-American efforts were instituted to keep them as second class citizens with no voice or rights.

In the northern states no such actions were instituted, (though some racism began as the cultures clashed). Blacks slowly became integrated into the U.S. military and were leaders in combat units during the Indian and Spanish- American Wars.

As shown earlier, in 1913 Democrat Woodrow Wilson became president. **He was a southerner from Virginia, instituted segregation into all of his administration's actions. He re-segregated the military and our society, turning back 40 years of progress.** For the next forty years no advances were made for African-Americans until Pres. Truman desegregated the military and black athletes entered team sports.

It was Dwight Eisenhower and the Republicans who began legislating Civil Rights programs in 1957 and 1960. The vast

majority of Democrats fought against those laws, and few voted for them! Pres. Eisenhower even called in federal troops to enforce the new Civil Rights Laws that he and the Republicans had worked so hard on. Still the Democrats refused to allow black citizens full rights into our society.

Protests continued into the 1960s as three Civil Rights workers were murdered in Misisippi. The nation watched this travesty on the nightly news prompting changes.

In 1964 Democrat Lydon Johnson was running for election, and he decided to embrace Civil Rights to garner votes and liberal support to insure his win. Even so, all of the Republicans voted for the 1964 law, but only half of the Democrats did!

In 1965 LBJ, (the great Deceiver), used his party's majority in Congress to force his "Great Society programs" upon the nation. **Johnson claimed he was ending poverty, but in actuality he and the Democrats were re-enslaving the poor which included a lot of black America.**

Sociologist Daniel Moynihan co-wrote a book on why the Negros in America were failing to advance. His research showed it was from a lack of education and the instability in Black homes. Liberals despised his book, even though he was one of them.

In 1964 **20%** of black children were born into single mother homes, which was twice as high as white single parent homes. Moynihan felt jobs and education were the keys to success, but Johnson and the Democrats refused that path. Instead they handed out money to the poor through their jaded Welfare programs. They actually increased the breakup of the poorer families.

After 40 years of their lies and disastrous social programs the number of black children born into single mother homes had skyrocketed to **over 70% of the total born!** Every social index shows that the single biggest factor that ensures poverty was growing up in a household with only a mother.

In Homes with income over $75,000, 92% have two parents. Eighty percent of homes with incomes under $25,000 are single parent. Our "modern world" necessitates a two income family unit to have a middle class lifestyle. Those underclass single parent family's have almost no chance to make that socio-economic jump. Unless they are on a "Great Society" program like Welfare, the single mom must work full time which disrupts the child's early experiences and development.

Statistics show that whether the single mother works or is on welfare, single parent children are five times more likely to live in poverty and nine times more likely to drop out of school.

It is well known that education is the key to economic success. But with their high drop-out rate those poor children have lost their chance to become educated and advance.

Since LBJ and the Democrats passed those Welfare Laws violent crime has soared over 500%, and Illegitimate births have increased over 400%. How are those poor children supposed to succeed?

Another of their inconvenient truths came out in 1969 when Pres Nixon and his administration put forth *The Philadelphia Plan. That plan required goals and timelines for increasing minority hiring in federally funded construction projects.* It was crafted to crack open the white-only construction unions, not with quotas but with goals. He wanted minorities to gain entrance into construction apprenticeship programs, and eventually union memberships. *(That is the proper type of affirmative action, based on equal opportunity not equal outcome.)*

Nixon's program enabled minority workers to enter the construction fields and learn trades and vocations for life! That type of program was never instituted or even thought of by the Democrats. Nixon never received the credit he should have for starting that program, as few have ever learned of it.

As shown in *Fatal Flaws Book 2*, the increasingly high taxes, crime and other social issues of the late 1960s into the 1970s forced many small businesses to close their doors and leave the older cities in the north for the South and the West. With them went most of the low-education jobs. At the same time low-paying competition from overseas was strangling our manufacturing and industrial production costing us millions more blue-collar jobs.

The election of Ronald Reagan resulted in a 10 year boom time, as millions of jobs were created and returned to our shores. But In 1993 Clinton and the Democrats enacted NAFTA, (North American Free Trade Agreement). That disaster and other world trade agreements have sent millions of our low-education jobs overseas, making it even harder to get a start in the job market.

NAFTA was an attempt by our leftists to spread our wealth around by sending American jobs overseas. That first year over 700,000 manufacturing jobs left the U.S. Most of those who lost their jobs here were never able to recover that income level. Using NAFTA, employers were then able to reduce wage levels by threatening the workers that their jobs would go overseas if they made any job/wage actions or problems.

This multi-front issue virtually ensured that the poor and under-educated never penetrated the job market into anything but menial jobs. Young African-American males are sitting on the sidelines, while educated immigrants from India, China and other nations that do not have our poor social structure get and keep high paying technical jobs.

Presently our social breakup is hitting white families at a higher rate than Black families suffered through forty years ago. Our government must address this issue if our nation is to survive. *Even in Bangladesh they understand that the unleashing of human energy and creativity is the best answer to beating poverty. To accomplish that requires a solid family structure and education.*

Throughout the 1990s our economy grew at an incredible rate and created millions of jobs thanks to the R&D from the 1980s. *But most of those higher paying jobs required advanced degrees or technical knowledge.* Again the majority of our poorest children were left out of the field.

Though there are hundreds of black millionaires in America, **more than in any other nation in the world**, most succeeded through athletics and entertainment. Few used their wealth to open schools for the poor, or to help them succeed in business or the trades with scholarships and training.

In this computer driven world hands-on skills are still needed to thrive. But with our ineffectual public education system, Designed and run by the Democrats, the sad plight continues for the poorest children. *At the same time the children of the wealthy go to the top schools, step into high paying jobs and live a lavish life.* For the rest of us it is a huge struggle.

Professor Daniel Patrick Moynihan and all of the minority Republicans warned about this situation back in 1964-65. They tried to stop Johnson and the Democrat's and their ruinous Welfare programs. Back then Moynihan's thesis on the importance of family ties was dismissed as was the warnings from the Republicans that Welfare would destroy the work ethic of the poor.

Even Jesse Jackson agrees with Moynihan's thesis now.

As the 2000 election cycle began the Republican Party faced a two-man race in the quest for the Presidential Nomination. Senator John McCain from Arizona a decorated Navy pilot from the Vietnam war and a former POW, ran against Gov. George Bush from Texas who was a pilot in the Air National Guard and son from the former president. The race became heated and acrimonious as Bush won the nomination. For many it was not the best choice. (His father lost in 1992.)

Al Gore the V.P. for Clinton became the designated choice for the Democrats, since no investigations on him had been allowed to take place. Following their standard play-book the media claimed Gore was "too smart to be president, while Bush was just a mental lightweight. (This ploy had been used by the media before, with Clinton, and when they claimed that Adlai Stevenson was "the thinking man's president". In fact he was just the opposite, and when he died the only book found in his bedroom was the *Social Register.)* *(182)

As he had learned from eight years at Clinton's side, being shady was fine as long as you denied it. Gore's campaign was using over $600,000 of illegal money that had not been returned. All of the money in question had come from John Huang and Jim Riady's efforts. Both had been indicted, but Gore and his people refused to stop spending it. When pressured over this issue Gore claimed his e-mails were lost and he "could not remember" where the funds came from.

Since they had nothing to campaign on, the Democrats inserted racism, Nazism and every type of complaint possible against Bush to gain some traction in the polls. Gore's campaign manager Donna Brazile claimed that conservative Black Republicans Colin Powell and J.C. Watts were the proverbial uncle Tom. She vowed that "she would not let the white boys win this election."* (183) (A racial crime everywhere but among liberals.)

(Black Democrats are actually the real Uncle Toms. They are the ones who go along with everything their Master Democrats tell them to do.)

To help Gore, Bill Clinton decided to release 30 million barrels of oil from the strategic petroleum reserve as a quick way to lower oil prices just before the election. By law that reserve is not supposed to be tapped unless there is a severe restriction in our supply. But since there is no law Bill won't break, he released the oil to the detriment of our nation.

The race for the White House was neck and neck all through the campaign. *On the night of the election numerous illegal events occurred, all to help Gore.* One was the announcement at 7:49 PM by NBC that Al Gore had won the state of Florida. All of the other major media outlets claimed the same thing minutes later.

This announcement was illegal, because it was made before all of the polls in Florida had closed!

Florida is a state with two time zones, and in the western panhandle those ten counties are on Central Time. To further their fraudulent/criminal action the major networks repeated multiple times that the polls in Florida were closed, even though they were not. CBS alone made that announcement 18 times.

As a result of their "oops announcements", voter turnout in those ten conservative panhandle counties fell over 10% from the 1996 election totals. But their populations had increased by over 10% since 1996. One examination of their fraudulent actions placed the lost votes to Bush at between 10,000-37,000 votes! (Even liberal Democrat and former Carter aide Bob Beckel stated Bush lost at least 8,000 votes.)

The same thing happened in Missouri. And in heavily Democrat St. Louis their voters were "allowed to cast ballots forty minutes" after the polls were supposed to be closed! *(Since their people ran the polls they did what they wanted.)* No one could guess at how many votes Gore gained and Bush lost from those illegal actions.

In Wisconsin, video evidence showed Democrats bribing homeless men to go to the polls (for free smokes), while polls in Milwaukee also remained open too long.

In every state that Gore was ahead the networks called him the winner within minutes of the polls closing. In the case of Bush states the time lag ran into two or more hours. That was done to help Gore by "creating momentum" that he was ahead.

In the case of Florida, despite the major media's scam, Fox News called Bush the winner after 2am. (By that point 90% of the voting results were in.) After a short interval all of the other networks followed suit as Gore could not catch up. *Florida was the deciding state, so Bush was the electoral vote winner and thus the president elect. Gore conceded the election around 3am.*

Then claims of recounting in Florida came up. Florida law has a statue that gives the Secretary of State seven days to certify an election. Thus the Democrats had seven days to figure a way to steal it. The major media quickly showed their prejudice and joined the Gore camp demanding a recount.

As the days went by the complicit media tried to claim that the election was rigged by Bush and the Republicans. Gore's election chief Bill Daley repeatedly claimed the will of the people was being thwarted and they would fight for each vote. (Bill was the son of Chicago's Mayor Daley, the one who had insured JFK won there in 1960. So he knew how that scam worked.)

Historical Note: Back in 1960 the Democrats had stuffed the ballot boxes in Chicago giving Kennedy the lead (8,400 votes) he needed to win the city and as a result the state of Illinois. Most people don't know this, but a larger margin of fraud had also happened in LBJ's Texas in 1960, by over 50,000 votes, stealing the election.

Richard Nixon could have asked for a manual recount, and the process would have uncovered those illegal votes. He was urged by Congressional leaders, and even Pres. Dwight Eisenhower to contest the results and win the election. But Nixon wrongly refused to do so, believing the uncovering of election fraud would hurt the nation's morale and belief in the system. As a result of his (honorable but totally misplaced feelings), the Democrats under JFK and LBJ took over.

Their dismal administrations and legislative actions nearly destroyed our country with Vietnam, and still threatens us today with their ruinous Welfare policies, deficits and the theft of the original Social Security trust funds.

Forty years after that "coup", Al Gore and his team were trying everything they could to steal this election. Claims of racial bias sprang up that Florida's black voters were "disenfranchised". *That too was proven wrong, as over 900,000 black voters had gone to the polls, up 65% in just four years!* (The Democrats drove their voters to the polls to make sure they voted.)

Gore and his people next had an injunction issued to stop the Florida military absentee ballots from counting in the recount. Most military people are conservative, so the absentee military votes would more than likely help Bush.

Because of his injunction, approved by a liberal Federal Judge, the right to vote for over 1,500 Floridians serving our country was taken from them! (Obama pulled the same scam in 2012.)

In Democratic Broward County a poorly labeled and manufactured paper ballot caused an uproar when the initial recount reveled that some ballots did not perforate properly. The insane case of the "hanging chads" became worldwide news as the Democrats desperately fought to get every vote possible including making claims that minorities in that county were "specifically disenfranchised".

(It turned out those same ballots had been used in the 1996 election, with 15,000 invalidated for the same reason. Yet the Democrat who ran Broward's elections did not fix them!)

It also turned out (but was kept quiet), that two of the seven Florida Supreme Court justices overseeing the recount had made multiple donations to the DNC and/or Democratic candidates. Both should have been disqualified, but were not. And the Clinton/Reno Justice Dept. even dispatched the illegally appointed Bill Lee to begin "investigating the civil rights violations in Florida."

As the Florida recount continued ballots became damaged and then misplaced. *But after three recounts (the last one was illegally ordered by the Florida Supreme Court), George Bush was officially certified as the winner in Florida, and thus the Presidency by 500+ votes.* (Green party candidate Ralph Nader had picked up 1% of the total votes.)

The Clintons / Democrats were so incensed over this loss they left piles of trash inside the White House and disabled many of the vital cable and computer connections when they left. (*It took days to fix the damages, imagine if something bad had happened like an attack.*)

Foolishly Bush downplayed this damage saying it was just some pranks in a wasted effort to appease the Democrats.

(This same power-psychosis affected the Democrats after Trump won in 2016. And in 2018 the Broward election office was again involved in a voter fraud/recount crime.)

In keeping with their shameful history the Clintons also illegally removed, (looted), dozens of housekeeping items and furniture from the White House as they left. They were forced to return some of it.

And in a final dishonorable display of his lack of character, during his last night in power Bill Clinton pardoned dozens of convicted criminals, many who had assisted his, his wife's or other democratic political campaigns. One of those pardoned was Marc Rich, an oil trader with ties to many bad people such as Fidel Castro, Libya's Qaddafi, and the Ayatollah Khomeini. Rich had been smuggling commodities in and out of countries that had U.S. sanctions on them as well as other illegal dealings. To escape prosecution Rich had fled the U.S. owing $48 million in back taxes. *Rich had been placed on the FBI's Ten Most Wanted List.*

To "help the Clintons", Rich's wife had made (illegal) large donations to Hillary's campaign to the tune of $400,000, another $450,000 went to Bills Foundation, and $ 1 million to the DNC. Strangely Rich was given a pardon.

Even the media was dismayed. (Again, the Senate was at fault for not impeaching Clinton and ridding us of him.) A House Committee investigating the pardon could not finish their work because, *once again the Clinton's and the DNC delayed turning over the records.* Unless these corrupt politicos are placed in jail with no bail, they will continue to obstruct every investigation that is made. (Just look at how Obama, Hillary and the State Dept. hid the truth on the embassy attacks in Benghazi, or on her illegal private server, money laundering and the Russia-gate probe, etc.)

In addition to Rich and some drug dealers, Bill also pardoned four NY Hasidic Jews who had swindled millions. Those pardons, with Hillary being present at the meeting, helped her to win over 99% of the Jewish vote in New Square, NY. She won Moynihan's open Senate seat. (What a sad tradeoff.)

Another uninvestigated issue was that the Clinton's were given a house in the all-white, liberal and wealthy town of Chappaqua in Westchester County. (Where was the IRS?) That gift made them state residents (and not just carpet-baggers), so she could run for the open Senate seat.

More Terrorism

Algerian terrorists planned to strike a savage blow at the Strasbourg Christmas market in December 2000. That market was near a famous Cathedral, and the attackers expected to kill dozens of tourists and Christians. French and German police learned of the attack days before it went off and arrested ten more Islamic terrorists. As he had done the past eight years, Bill Clinton had no reaction to those latest attacks.   **Incident # 185**

On December 24 a series of **(20)** anti-Christian bombings occurred in Indonesia. Those attacks were carried out by the local Islamists of Jemaah Islamiah and al-Qaeda. Eighteen were murdered with over a hundred wounded.   **Incident # 186**

(One major suspect **Abu Bashir** was arrested, but wrongly not convicted. He was a founder of JI, and had fought in Afghanistan where his forces trained with al-Qaeda. In 2002 he was a principal member of the group that bombed Bali, killing almost 200 more innocent westerners.)

Al-Qaeda terrorists Hanjour and Hazmi left San Diego and began their drive across our country. In Arizona they attended yet another flight school to brush up on their few skills. A Rayeed Abdullah was there, one of the ten Muslim men that FBI agent Ken Williams had warned his superiors about. As before, there was no crime, so there was no folowup. In the spring of 2001 those terrorists began moving east.

Section Six

The Bush Administration   January 2001

Since 1995 the Republicans had controlled both houses of the Congress. They had done little to keep the country safe. In January 2001 they also had the White House. Pres. Bush did not have a mandate from the populace, and he kept his administration's goals limited and cordial. During the campaign George Bush never mentioned terrorism or bin Laden. He was more interested in strategic threats and missile defense to thwart rogue states from striking us. China and Iraq were on his list.

In their transition period the Bush team was briefed on al-Qaeda and other terrorist issues. George Tenet was kept on at CIA, Gen. Shelton as the chairman of the JCS and Clarke in his anti-terror role. Clarke was unhappy with their lax mindset, but as had happened for eight years under Clinton he was unable to change it. Tenet briefed the principals showing videos of bin Laden walking around Tarnak. (Again proof that Clinton could have taken out bin Laden.) He warned the new administration that additional terror attacks were imminent.

National Security Advisor Condoleezza Rice met with Pakistan's Ambassador Maleeha Lodhi to discuss terrorism. The two accomplished women had risen far in male dominated societies, and appeared to mesh well. *Pres. Bush sent a confidential letter to Pres. Musharraf that linked our aid and support for a resolution on bin Laden and the Taliban.*

George Tenet secretly traveled to Islamabad to speak with Gen. Mahmoud. His attitude was still unmoving over their Taliban position, and he insisted on tight control over any Americans working in his country. (Proof they were not serious about getting Bin Laden.)

Over the past months Musharraf had consolidated his rule. Dissidents in his government began warning it was in Pakistan's interests to break with the Taliban. They had shown their true intentions by destroying the two immense statues of the Buddha that had been hewn 1500 years ago. Months of negotiation were attempted to stop the wonton destruction, but Omar refused saying only Allah will judge me. Strangely the world condemned the Taliban over their vandalism to those statues, but never said a word over the years of torment to the Afghan civilians.

(To the liberals of the world who are keeping their heads in the sand, this is exactly what will happen to all of the western world's

art and architecture when the Islamists take over. For them only images of Islam will be allowed.)*

Back in May 2000 the French government had allowed a sale of "oil well logging equipment" to Iraq. In actuality this gear contained neutron generators which could be used to build a crude implosion-nuclear device. Even though they were well aware of the danger this posed, the equipment was sold and shipped anyway. France also upgraded Iraq's military communications. It was becoming harder and more dangerous to patrol over Iraqi airspace, so Pres. Bush authorized additional air attacks on communication hubs and air defense sites inside Iraq.

After a few months in office the first big problem for the Administration occurred. *A U.S. EP-3 recon aircraft flying in the South China Sea was deliberately set upon by Chinese fighter jets and rammed by one of them.* The U.S. pilot wrongly landed his damaged plane on Hainan Island, a large island just off of northern Vietnam that had been stolen by Red China back in 1979.

The airfield he landed on was a Communist Chinese air base. *By landing the aircraft instead of ditching it at sea the pilot enabled the Chinese to access the plane and steal all of the latest technology it carried.* The Chinese kept the plane and equipment for 10 days in a direct challenge to the new President. Bush failed the test as he took no actions against them. Stealing our equipment was the main point of this incident, and similar to the takeover of the USS *Pueblo* in 1968 by North Korea. back then the Russians had wanted the equipment on that ship.

(*Most people are not aware of this, but since LBJ did nothing over the Pueblo theft, the N. Koreans also shot down a U.S. Navy recon plane murdering two dozen crewmen in 1969.* That unarmed plane was flying **over eighty miles out to sea** when it was callously attacked. Pres. Nixon was outraged over that murderous incident, and directed the JCS to provided a target list for a retaliatory tactical **nuclear strike** on the airfield the enemy fighter flew from. Cooler heads prevailed, but some sort of retaliatory attack should have been made.)

During his first months in office Sec-Defense Donald Rumsfeld was trying to turn the military around from the destructive cutbacks enacted by Clinton. *Our military needed to plan against a potential major enemy, and for Rumsfeld and many others that enemy was China, as evidenced by this latest episode.*

The major weapons advances China had made during Clinton's years, (from treason and corruption), meant their military was becoming an increasingly dangerous and probable enemy. With the loss of our bases in the Philippines the far Pacific was at risk from conventional war, and we were at risk for WMD attacks.

Our SDI program had to be re-started, but we had lost eight years of R&D thanks to Clinton.

While those issues were worked out the search for bin Laden continued. Most of the Bush principals would say they had been unaware of the extent of al Qaeda's operations, but according to Richard Clarke they were not interested either.

Pres. Bush and his administration made No Changes to the Clinton rules on airline security, racial profiling, DOJ investigative rules or inter-service communications. (The first major meeting on terrorism occurred in early September 2001.)

Northern Alliance leader Ahmad Massoud retained a lobbyist in Washington in the hopes of allowing meetings with his Panjshiri advisors. He wrote a letter to Vice President Cheney urging the reexamination of the U.S.-Pakistani relations.

To repair his supply lines Massoud traveled to Russia and Iran. In Moscow the tycoon-ruled country was still in flux, but their defense officials were very worried over bin Laden and the Islamists as they had made much progress inside Chechnya and Central Asia. *(Russia and Chechnya were fighting their second war. The Chechans had won the first one, but the Chechans had broken up into warlords. Russian hardliners were intent on defeating the growing Wahabbist movemnet as terror attacks were growing.)*

Massoud was invited to speak in Strasbourg, France, the seat of the European Parliament. He accepted knowing he could not defeat the Taliban by himself as they were funded by bin Laden and the Saudis, and reinforced by Pakistani-madrassas. They needed the support of America and the West to win this fight.

Massoud warned all, "If President Bush does not help us these terrorists will soon cause great damage to the U.S. and Europe."* *(184)

Otilie English, his Washington advocate met with him in northern Afghanistan. Massoud pressed English to push for U.S. humanitarian aid directly to him, not wasted in Pakistan or the U.N. He also needed financial assistance to buy weapons, and wanted the U.S. to reopen their Embassy. He explained that the Taliban have used up their welcome in Afghanistan and the people are challenging them. With help from the Afghan southerners Massoud felt the Taliban could be defeated in a year.

(Peter Tomsen the former U.S. ambassador had retired, but spoke at lectures denouncing the Pakistani's and the Taliban. He felt the CIA had failed Afghanistan in this second war. *Massoud wanted Tomsen to go to Rome and convince the exiled Afghan King Zahir Shah to join their effort in full, as the Afghan people would support the King as their new ruler.*)

On March 15, 2001 a Russian airliner was hijacked as it left Istanbul, Turkey. On board were 174 passengers and crew. The Islamic hijackers were Chechen rebels who demanded to be flown to Afghanistan, and for Russia to stop fighting in Chechnya. This was the 24th successful airline hijacking since 1968! **Incident # 187**

By the spring of 2001 our intelligence services had begun picking up increased "chatter" that something large and destructive was going to happen. Al Qaeda cells were disrupted in Bosnia, Albania, Italy and in the Middle East. Tragically a major cell in Belgium escaped detection.   **Incident # 188**

In April of 2001 **Mohamed Atta** was at a meeting in Prague with **Ahmed al Ani**, the second secretary of the Iraqi consulate. Al-Ani also worked for Saddam's foreign intelligence service. Their multi-hour meeting was watched by the Czech security, but no reports were available. They had met there many times since 2000, but since they were not wanted for anything criminal nothing other than routine surveillance had been done.

But Mohammed Atta had been identified by Ressam, the millennial bomber. Atta was one of those he had trained with in Afghanistan. **Once again intelligence officials failed our country by not placing him on a terrorist watch list.   Incident # 189**

(Atta had had a better life than most in Egypt. But after Pres. Sadat was assassinated he began listening to the propaganda from the Islamists. Islam was better than the West, and has suffered humiliations from the British Colonial occupiers, their spawn in Israel and the American capitalism that keeps them poor. His homeland in Egypt was rife with corruption and nepotism, he believed Fundamentalism offered a change.)

During that time frame Ambassador Robert Gelbard closed the U.S. embassy in Jakarta, Indonesia. He had received credible reports that a six man al Qaeda team had been dispatched from Yemen. Gelbard pressured the Indonesian government to take action against them and **Jemmah Islamiyah**. It appeared to Gelbard the Indonesians were turning a blind eye to the incessant infiltration and subversion going on. (The prior Christmas attacks.) He increased security at his embassy which must have worked for the attack was stopped. **Incident # 190**

(Incredulously Gelbard was removed by Bush administration officials for being "too aggressive". In 2002 the people he had been worried about blew up a night club in Bali killing 202 innocents. In 2003 they attacked a Marriot Hotel murdering 13 more.)

That same month *a longtime Iranian asset* who had worked for the Shah and was an informant for the FBI came in with a dire warning from his sources inside Iran. Meeting at a residence near Washington the asset, an interpreter named **Behrooz Sarshar** and two FBI agents sat down. Speaking at Sarshar, **the asset revealed from his sources still alive inside Iran that a major terrorist-suicide attack involving airplanes was going to strike America.** (Europe was also mentioned as a possible target.)

He also stated that the al-Qaeda terrorists were already in America and were trained as pilots. *(185)

Agent Tony Orefice took detailed notes and forwarded a report to his supervisor Thomas Fields. Incredulously the tip was filed as a simple report, and nothing was done with the information!! **Incident # 191**

Later that summer in a follow up interview that same asset repeated his warnings, still the FBI ignored it. And they never mentioned this or the previous meeting to the CTC or to Clarke. **To make this needless failure even worse, it turns out the FBI had heard this story the year before.**

As shown before, a year earlier in April 2000 Niaz Khan, the British citizen of Pakistani descent informed the FBI of a bin Laden plot to hijack a jumbo jet. Khan had trained at a terrorist camp in Pakistan, and told of how they worked in teams of 5-6 men perfecting their technique on hijacking an airliner.

Trained pilots would be in the team to take over the flight once the aircraft was hijacked. To verify his information he was subjected to a polygraph, he passed.

(What did the FBI do with that information?)

(How many screw-ups does it take before someone goes to prison? *FBI Director Robert Mueller was never asked about these issues during the 9/11 Commission hearings. It was all hushed up.* The senior agents involved in that story all retired and refused to discuss it. During the 9/11 hearings the FBI insisted they had no advance warning of the plot. *FBI translator Sarshar wrote a ten-page report to Mueller over this disaster. He was terminated and told to stay quiet.*)

On April 30, 2001 Stephen Hadley chaired a committee for the administration deputies on al-Qaeda. They reviewed the options from the Clinton years and discussed the latest intelligence. **Richard Armitage set an outline for a new policy, the destruction of al-Qaeda in South Asia.** The CIA was told to dust-off its plan for aiding Massoud. They also continued the testing of armed drones. After the last two terrorist incidents Pres. Bush had decided to make bin Laden a priority.

Paul Wolfowitz the deputy secretary of defense knew that the anti-terror policy had to be a national effort using all of our resources and offices. He told everyone that al-Qaeda could not be stopped with the Taliban in control of Afghanistan. But before any serious actions could be taken, NSC staff had to figure out what impact Pakistan would have on our efforts.

In May cleric **Awalaki** showed up in Falls Church, Virginia to run another mosque built by the Saudi's. This mosque was the Dar al-Hijrah Islamic Center, which was purposely built west of the Pentagon. Awalaki was tasked to set the incoming terrorists up with rooms and IDs. Over the past years he had advanced high up the Saudi ladder going on trips to Mecca and to other state functions. Upon returning from his most recent Saudi trip in April, Awalaki greeted two Middle-Eastern men. One was **Nawaf al-Hazmi** and the other was **Hani Hanjour**. They had just made their way across the U.S. from San Diego.

Hazmi had remained hidden at the San Diego mosque after Awalaki left for Mecca. Reunited with his pilot partner Hanjour, they were the swine who would crash their hijacked flight into the Pentagon. This group of terrorists was comprised of all Saudi's, Bin Laden had hand picked this gang. *(After the 9/11 attacks Awalaki would flee the U.S. on a Saudi jet.)*

To ensure these terrorists would not get stopped by INS they sought out false papers. The best place to find a source was the groups of illegal immigrants looking for work. Hanjour and

Khalid Alimihdhar went to a local 7-11 and spoke with a few Central American illegal's. They found one, Luis Martinez-Flores, who had been here illegally since 1994 after leaving El Salvador. **He took the pair to a Virginia DMV office and falsely certified them as being residents. That DMV office then issued the pair state ID cards!**

The next day they returned to the same office and repeated the process for **Majed Moqed** and **Salem Al-Hazmi** so they could have ID's! Hanjour then returned a third time to get an ID for Ziad Jarrah, the terrorist pilot for Flight 93.

Abdulaziz Alomari and **Ahmed Alghamdi** used the same scam in Arlington, Va. Two illegal's from El Salvador and a legal secretary named Kenys Galicia helped them get their Virginia ID cards.

During April Tennessee legislators under pressure from immigrant groups decided to abolish the requirement that people wanting a drivers license had to show a valid Social Security number. Within weeks their DMV offices were deluged with thousands of out of state applicants, most of whom were illegal immigrants. Among them was one **Abdelmuhsen Mahmid Hammad** and his cousin **Sakhera Hammad**. After the 9/11 attacks those two and five others were arrested for immigration fraud. Found in Sakhera's affects was a World Trade Center repair pass that gave access to the lower levels of the complex. It was dated September 5, 2001.

(During the post-9/11 investigations it was also uncovered that those Muslim suspects had been helped by a Tennessee examiner, one Katherine Smith. She was also arrested, but before she could appear in court she burned to death in her car on February 10, 2002. FBI forensic examiners found evidence of gasoline in her clothing, but not in the car. The car was barely damaged.) *(186)

This crisis with illegal immigrants is not new. Hollywood produced two movies in the early 80's showcasing this issue on our southern border. *Since 1979 Los Angeles has been active in not enforcing Federal Immigration statutes, and became the first Sanctuary city. When liberal Democrat Diane Feinstein was mayor of San Francisco, she instituted a citywide policy of sanctuary for illegal's. Ed Koch did the same in NYC.*

Every time someone tries to protect our country the Democrats -liberals and special interest groups stop the protective policy. Thus our borders remain porous and open to infiltration. And when the political need arises, the Democrats pass a blanket amnesty program to everyone who had slipped in. That allows potential enemies to become legal citizens with no way to remove them.

World Trade Center bomber Mahmud Abouhalima used that process to go from an illegal alien to a citizen. In 1993 he struck.

Border Patrol Officers Mark Hall and Robert Lindemann both testified in 1999 before Congress on the terrible state of our border protection. They spoke of how in 1990 during the Gulf War they worked the Detroit area and were under constant alerts for potential terrorists being smuggled in. Their office was terribly understaffed and unable to provide much security. They too were maligned by their superiors for "speaking up". **Incident # 192**

In the decades since conditions have not gotten better, and "basically our northern and southern border have been abandoned by the government". * (187)

In May Mohamed Atta and two other Middle-Eastern men were observed videotaping and testing airport security at Boston's Logan Airport. Security was alerted to the activity, but the suspects were not detained or questioned as per the Clinton DOJ rules on profiling. Those terrorists knew what they were doing, as there were no security cameras in the area they tested, so no photos or video were available to identify them. Brian Sullivan an FAA Agent had warned his bosses about the security lapses at Logan before, but no actions were ever taken to fix them. **Incident # 193**

In early June 2001 a CIA report warned that **KSM, Khalid sheik-Mohammed** was actively and openly trying to recruit new terrorists who would travel to America to stage attacks with cells already in place. **Incident # 194**

KSM had been photographed in Kuala Lumpur meeting with members of the 9/11 plot. Even though he was a wanted fugitive, no attempt to arrest him was made. And the photos of who he met were never passed around! Yet another chance to breakup the 9/11 plot was missed. **Incident # 195**

(One of KSM's cohorts was a **Mustapha Ahmed al-Hisawi**. After the 9/11 attacks it was learned that Hisawi laundered tens of thousands of dollars from Dubai to Mohammed Atta and the others. On September 10 the remaining money was sent back to that account and it was emptied by KSM as he went into hiding.)

Bin Laden issued a televised decree that America and Israel would be attacked within the next weeks.   Incident # 196

Soon after INS agents caught one **Nabil al-Marabh** coming in from Canada hiding inside a tractor-trailer. He had a false Canadian passport, and was remanded to jail pending his deportation hearing. Upon investigation it was learned that he was a suspected associate of bin Laden, and the Boston Police had an arrest warrant out for him! **Incident # 197**

Despite both issues, he was released on $10,000 bond and disappeared. Not until September 19, 2001 was he located by the FBI near Chicago. He had been issued a new commercial driver license, to carry Hazardous materials! After this second arrest and investigation it was believed he had given $15,000 to the 9/11 terrorists. And he helped three of them enter our country from Canada, possibly bringing them in the way he tried to enter.

Residents from Marabh's Toronto apartment complex recognized Atta and Shehhi from their news photos!

One **Ahmed al-Haznawi** was treated for an infected black lesion on his left calf at a medical facility in Ft. Lauderdale, Florida. *The ER doctor, Christos Tsonas consulted with experts and concluded he had* **coetaneous anthrax**. Unbelievably nothing was done over this bio-hazard incident. **Incident # 198**

Ahmed was one of the hijackers of Flight 93.

Soon after **Mohamed Atta** went to a pharmacy in Delray Beach, Florida looking for medication to treat a strange skin condition on his hands. His symptoms were also consistent with exposure to anthrax. **Again there was no follow up investigation!**

How and where did these two pickup an exposure to anthrax?? Did the hospital notify the CDC? If nothing else was done both should have been quarantined by the local authorities, the CDC notified and an investigation conducted. But Nothing was done! **Incident # 199**

(Weeks after the attacks of 9/11, envelopes began showing up around the country containing anthrax. Those terrorists had stuffed the envelopes with this bio-weapon, and left them behind for future mailings. That meant that someone(s) was still here mailing them out!)

From the late spring into July the NSA reported thirty-three intercepts indicating an imminent al-Qaeda attack! Classified threat warnings ricocheted through our governmental agencies security message systems every day.

(According to author Steve Coll, the FBI sent out warnings about airline hijackings, but nothing was done.) **Incident # 200** *(188)

CIA's Tenet had accomplished little during his years with Clinton in office. Now he was urging *this White House* to see the terrorist threat. Meetings with the NSC highlighted the web, but as always there were few exact targets. Tenet expected mass casualties would come of the next strikes. Recently rockets and explosives had been recovered in Jordan, another plot to attack Americans in Yemen had been stopped, and a recent report warned of *terrorists crashing a plane into our Nairobi Embassy.* **Incidents # 201 & 202**

(Six specific warnings of terrorists plotting airline crashes into buildings were picked up from 1995-2001!) *(188A)

Soon after the CTC reported they had interviewed a source who had recently come in from Afghanistan. That source stated an impending attack would occur inside America. Agents were being overwhelmed with the amount of intelligence coming in, and they knew they were missing clues. **Incident # 203**

Intelligence from the December 2000 arrests in Frankfurt was providing new evidence that led to the follow-on arrests in Milan, Italy, France and then in London. The terrorists in France were led by one **Jamal Beghal**. His cell was targeting the U.S. Embassy in Paris. **Incident # 204**

From those interrogations there was a reliable threat to our Navy based in Bahrain, and the G-8 Summit meeting set for late July in Genoa, Italy when Pres. Bush would attend.

Egyptian Intelligence then sent a warning that Islamic terrorists were planning on flying an aircraft into one of the buildings in Genoa. This plot was so credible that our military ringed the site with surface to air missiles! **Incident # 205**

(Yet no one thought it might happen here!)

Then a cell in Germany was caught using advanced chemicals and explosives, with radio equipment for remote detonations. Intelligence was suggesting a possible Hiroshima type attack, and it had been close to happening. **Incident # 206**

From all of these successes FBI's John O'Neil and others grew alarmed. Al Qaeda was everywhere, and they were well equipped. We were not winning this war.

Clinton appointee Louis Freeh had remained in charge at the FBI until June 30, 2001. His temporary replacement was Thomas Pickard, a veteran FBI agent. Instead of keeping Pickard as director, Bush announced on July 5 that Robert Mueller a U.S. attorney as the next FBI director.

On July 10, 2001 FBI Agent Ken Williams sent a five page memo to Langley, with the names of eight al Qaeda members / sympathizers on it. **He wanted the agency to investigate them further as a number of them had been at Arizona flight schools.** He also wanted the FBI to get a listing of all civil aviation schools around the country. They needed to cross-check the rosters to see if any known terrorists were or had been enrolled. He felt that a coordinated plot was taking shape that would breach security within the U.S. civil aviation system. **Incident # 207**

(Again this vital report was not passed around to the other Field Offices, or to Clarkes office at the White House or the CTC. That failure was crucial, for had the information been disseminated Clarke and the Minneapolis FBI field office would have gotten it.)

This Gets Worse.

During July **the FAA** stated in the *Federal Register* that there was an increasing threat to civil aviation from terrorist hijackings. **In a slide show for airline executives it was disseminated that Islamic Fundamentalists might hijack airliners to commit spectacular suicide attacks.** It was stated clearly, the dots are connected, and they are large. *(189A) **Incident # 208**

The FAA had recently been alerted by the White House that al Qaeda was probably going to strike sometime during the summer and to be prepared. Yet even with the above slide show there still there was no order to upgrade security at the airports or on the aircraft! Just a simple solution like stronger locks or blocks on cockpit doors would have prevented the 9/11 attacks!

Admiral Cathal Flynn the former head of security for the FAA stated he was never told that the State Department had a list of 61,000 suspected terrorists. His list only had 12 names on it! Flynn also stated that he had asked the FBI about hijacking threats and was told there was none! *(189)

Clinton's PC rules preventing any profiling were still in force, and Saudi citizens were given undue deference. Fifteen of the 19 hijackers were Saudis. Despite the poor quality of their passports and other papers, incomplete visa applications, obvious lies during their interviews, and blatant violations of our immigration laws those 19 terrorists received 23 visas and traveled to the U.S. on those visas 33 times before the attacks.

The last time he entered our country terrorist **Khalid Almihdhar** listed his visa address as the Marriot Hotel in NYC. There was no room number, no phone number or street address on the form. But following those PC rules, harried INS agents at JFK allowed him in, not realizing he was wanted for questioning over the 1998 Embassy bombings and the 2000 USS Cole attack! * (190) Days later his name popped up in a suspect database. It was then the FBI began hunting for him. Two months later he was still on the loose.   **Incident # 209**

He was the terrorist pilot who crashed into the Pentagon.

Actor James Wood was on a flight from Boston to San Francisco on August 1, 2001. In the first class section he was joined by four Middle-Eastern men who seemed suspicious and dangerous. He felt they would hijack the plane and alerted the flight crew who remained vigilant. Upon landing the flight crew reported the event to the FAA.

The FAA had just warned the airlines about suicidal hijackings, and here was a potential one that a flight crew observed and warned about. All four of those men should have been investigated and at a minimum placed on the no-fly list. **But after they landed nothing was done and they walked off!**

As to the four suspicious passengers from the Wood's flight; they were among the hijackers on September 11. Each one was on a different aircraft. *(191)   **Incident # 210**

That same day on a flight from Las Vegas to New York one **Abdulaziz Alomari**, a former cleric at the al-Qaeda camp in Khalden, Afghanistan cajoled his way into the cockpit claiming to be a student pilot. He tried to remain in the cockpit during the takeoff but was made to return to his seat. A short while later he tried to regain access to the cockpit claiming he had left a pen. After the 9/11 attacks it became clear he was casing out the cockpit and their safety procedures. *(192)   **Incident # 211**

Once again nothing was done.

On August 6 the CIA give a briefing on potential domestic threats, one of which was hijacking an airliner to ransom hostages. Unlike Clinton, Pres. Bush had daily briefings from the CIA. (But he did not go after terrorist funding nor did he change any of Clinton's failed policies.) Even after this briefing he did not order increased security for the airlines.

Despite the past two months of meetings there were no updated plans on getting to bin Laden. Sec-Def Rumsfeld was still concentrating the DOD efforts on a missile defensive shield, and not until mid-August did Bush ask for a dedicated strategy to neutralize bin Laden.

On August 15, 2001 an employee at the Pan Am Flight Academy in Eagan, Minnesota called the FBI office in Minneapolis. The call centered on a **Zacharias Moussaoui**, a foreign student from Morocco. Moussaoui had a belligerent attitude, and had paid for the flight course in full and in cash. It was quickly realized that he was not qualified for this advanced training, and seemed only interested only in learning how to steer the aircraft. **School staff felt he was a potential hijacker.**

Moussaoui was questioned by FBI agent Rapp and an INS agent. They continued investigating him and uncovered large amounts of cash transactions with no legal source of income. Moussaoui also made numerous phone calls to a suspected terrorist suspect in Hamburg, Germany.

Those agents believed that he was in the school to learn how to fly a passenger airliner in a terrorist act. (He was following the same script as agent Williams had noticed in Arizona. But his report was never passed around.)

The FBI supervisor in Minneoplis was so certain of the danger, he wrote a report stating; "This guy might be part of a plan to take control of an jet and fly it into the World Trade Center!" *(193)   Incident # 212

Incredulously the FBI principals were so blind and politically correct, (as Clinton had wanted), they actually fought against the Minneopolis office in getting search warrants!! They did the same to the FBI agents in Phoenix.

Claiming discrimination Moussaoui was let go by the FBI bureaucrats. Attempts to get a search warrant were refused for "lack of probable cause".

Back in 1978 the **Foreign Intelligence Security Act (FISA)** was passed to help speed investigations in cases of potential espionage and foreign terrorists. Cases such as this one would be heard first in a secret security court to determine if the case was valid and legal. If it was search warrants would secretly be approved. **But the lawyer ridden and politically correct FBI refused to even bring this case to that court!**

The agents in the Minneapolis FBI office were so unhappy with the bureaucratic roadblocks that continued to come up that they (correctly) notified the CTC unit directly. The CTC recieved information linking Moussaoui with other terrorist suspects. **That should have convinced the FBI higher ups of probable cause and they should have gone to court.** Incident # 213

After his release Moussaoui continued attending the Pan Am Flight Academy in Minneapolis. He was re-arrested on August 17 by INS agents because of his suspicious activity. But their immigration case was losing ground because of the politically correct rules in place. Then an ally returned from France.

French Counter-terrorism judge Jean-Louis Brugui`ere again came over and provided vital evidence of terrorist activities against Moussaoui who was now refusing to speak.

Jean-Louis told Attorney General John Ashcroft a week after the arrest that Moussaoui was a dangerous terrorist capable of any type of attack. He also told them that Moussaoui kept all of his important information on his laptop, and that the FBI must check it.

Back in France, Moussaoui had left a long trail of terrorist activities and Jean-Louis Brugui`ere was determined to help his friends across the pond. *Their file on him was a foot high and filled with phone calls, contacts, transcripts, documents and other intelligence they had gathered on this known terrorist.*

On August 23 French authorities officially informed the FBI that Moussaoui was linked to Islamic rebels operating in Chechnya, and that those terrorists were linked to bin Laden and al Qaeda.

Even after all of that follow on intelligence the FBI leaders inanely continued to follow the Clinton DOJ rules which prevented the INS, police or FBI from getting access to his computer files. **Inside those files was vital information on the 9/11 attacks.** Incident # 214

After two plus weeks of legalistic nonsense Moussaoui was to be deported back to France. **At this point the failures all belonged to George Bush and Robert Mueller.** Why did they not overturn Clinton's stupid rules? Was Bush or Rice alerted to this particular case? Was Clarke? If they were why didn't they step up and force the issue. They had been warned about pending attacks?

After the 9/11 attacks had occurred FBI agent Coleen Rowley wrote a critical letter to FBI Director Robert Mueller. **She stated that the FBI bureaucratic roadblocks had fatally hampered the Moussaoui investigation allowing the terrorist attacks to succeed.** It was also explained that the Minneapolis FBI office had notified the CTC directly because nothing was being done by the FBI higher-ups. (Since they went "over the heads of their FBI supervisors, all of the agents involved were stupidly reprimanded by Mueller.)

Mueller tried to minimize this missed chance away. His effort was unconvincing, and most felt he was completely out of his league being in charge of the FBI. But Bush had picked him over Pickering, and somehow he escaped any blame for the 9/11 attacks. He should have been fired and disgraced over this inane failure to think. But this "lawyer" was never even reprimanded for allowing those attacks to succeed. (In 2016 he was put in charge of the phony Russian probe harrasing President Trump.)

(During October 2001 the socialist French Government refused to turn over their complete files. Moussaoui was a French citizen who was now facing a death penalty in America for the 9/11 attacks. **His computer files had been analyzed in France, proving Moussaoui was to have been the 20th hijacker**.)

The FBI failures to get FISA search warrants during the Moussaoui case and the fact that the FBI was in charge of the case instead of the CTC was a major part of the 9/11 plot success. His phone and email records should have been checked out, as some of the other hijackers might have been found and caught.

Mohammed Atta was one of those in his call log!

What is worse, the FBI's Islamic Radicals Unit did see the memos from Phoenix and Minneapolis. Even they somehow failed to connect the two cases. Also found inside Moussaoui's computer files were a commercial flight simulation program, data on U.S. wind currents and general information about commercial jetliners and crop dusters. A bio-attack was coming.

(How was it possible that none of the senior FBI leaders joined the Bojinka intelligence with the Williams memos, the FAA alerts and this latest event. Did Clarke know of Moussaoui's arrest??)

Two other events sums up the insane legalistic bureaucracy established by Clinton and the piles of useless governmental lawyers who are ruining this nation.

In the early summer CIA officers met with the JTTF in New York. They finally showed the JTTF-FBI agents four surveillance photos from the previous Malaysia meeting and asked what they knew of the men in the photos. Several suspected terrorists were visible, but the CIA agents refused to elaborate on what or why they wanted the JTTF help. (They claimed their information was classified, so they could not elaborate.)

At this time the NSA and CIA were routinely monitoring calls to known al Qaeda phones across the globe. However they could not monitor any call that came or went through America. Only the FBI could do that, but only if they had a court order. But they could not get that order without probable cause, and the CIA would not give them the evidence!!

The human element was and is the most vital factor in stopping terrorists. On August 24, 2001 Orlando airport inspector Jose Melendez-Perez relied on his intuitive experience to refuse entry to one **Mohammed al-Qahtani. (aka Kahtani)**

Perez worked for U.S. Customs Service screening airline passengers who were trying to enter our country. He had served two tours in Vietnam and knew what bad felt like. As he interrogated Qahtani he was certain this man was not who he tried to claim, just an ordinary Saudi citizen seeking entry.

"Qahtani gave me the chills" stated Perez.

Perez was spot on as Qahtani had trained for months in the terrorist camps in Afghanistan. He was a dedicated follower of Bin Laden and their extremists views of the world. After two hours of interviews Perez refused Qahtani entry, forcing him to fly back to Dubai. He angrily warned Perez that he would be back. *(193A)

It is thought Mohammed Atta and Ziad Jarrah waited for Qahtani to finish his entry talk. Qahtani was the hand-picked replacement hijacker for Zacarious Moussaoui. After hours of waiting both al Qaeda terrorists left Orlando. Jarrah probably argued that his group could not accomplish their mission without their fifth thug. All of the other teams have five, but his flight would only have four.

Because of his correct actions Perez saved the White House or the U.S. Congress, since they were the intended target for the Flight 93 terrorists. (Qahtani watched the 9/11 attacks from the Tarnak terrorist camp with KSM and others.)

Tensions were rising in Washington. The repeated warnings of terrorism finally struck a nerve at the CIA. **In mid-August "they remembered" that al-Mihdhar and al-Hazmi were on their list, but they had never told the FBI!** In a panic they contacted INS to find out if they were still around. Days later they were told that according to their passports they were still here.

On **August 23** the CIA contacted the State Dept. and placed both men on the terrorist watch list. They then asked the FBI to track them down. **Incident # 216**

Al-Mihdhar purchased two tickets for Flight 77 from Washington to LA on **August 25**. Somehow that purchase escaped detection even though they were now on a watch list and the FBI was on the hunt for him!

Terrorist operations contain five basic elements; target selection, surveillance, operational planning, the attack and then the escape. Due to the open nature of the free Western societies it is extremely difficult to prevent these attacks.

The target nation needs to be in control of all of its access points, it needs solid intelligence to stop the terrorists from entering the nation and its security units must have unfettered access to any and all intelligence and be able to respond quickly to any intelligence picked up. None of those capabilities were in place before 9/11, though the warning signs of the pending attack certainly were.

A State Dept intelligence analyst stated that al Qaeda is a disciplined enemy that lives a clandestine lifestyle. They rarely travel in groups and always have false documents and disguises. They live and stay quietly, and have limited exposure. Due to their extreme ideology and procedures al Qaeda is almost impossible for any westerners to penetrate. They are willing to die for their cause and are good at using the West's weakness to their advantage.

Back in 1993 one of the WTC bombers was clearly heard conversing on a JTTF surveillance tape a month before the attack. They were talking about the explosives they were constructing, but the bomber was speaking in Arabic and the message was not translated until after the attack had occurred!

Despite all of the prior years of multiple, large attacks and threats, U.S. intelligence capability was still hampered by a lack of translators for the enemy languages of Farsi, Pashto, Arabic and Urdu. More warnings were missed.

Throughout the spring and early summer of 2001 all of the 9/11 terrorists had been moving around for their entry into the U.S.

They travelled in pairs from various cities and stayed under the radar. Seven of them arrived here in May, six more came over in June. **Most of the muscle hijackers had transited through Iran on their way to the U.S.** Curiously a few continued moving around the country going to places like Las Vegas, New York and San Francisco instead of just hiding out. Many were in contact with known Islamic suspects, fourteen of them.

Still they slipped by the authorities.

All of those terrorists had trained inside Afghanistan during 1999-2000. For most it was their first and only trip there. Mohammed Atef and Khalid Sheikh Mohammed had decided early on they did not want to use known al-Qaeda terrorists for this attack in case they were spotted before pulling it off.

A main U.S. entry point and hiding spot seemed to be in south Florida. None of those terrorists held jobs, and money was sent to them from U.S. contacts who laundered the al-Qaeda funds as they came in. At least six of the terrorists moved to Prince George County in Maryland in the towns of Laurel, Bowie and Greenbelt. Five of them were the ones that would take Flight 77 from Dulles Airport. They were Nawaq Alhazmi, Salem Alhazmi, Hani Hanjour, Khalid al-Mihdhar and Majed Moqed.

The sixth terrorist in that pack was Ziad Jarrah who would fly United Flight 93. (Jarrah had convinced a martial arts trainer in Florida to take him on as a student. He became proficient at hand to hand fighting in an effort to ensure his success.)

Laurel has two mosques and one resident who was definitely on the watch list, **Moataz al- Hallak.** *He was a known fundraiser for Islamic causes, and was linked to Wadi al-Hage the former cell leader in Nairobi.* Once again the guidelines limiting counter-terror investigations were in effect and no surveillance was being done. **Incident # 215**

In Herndon, Virginia **another top Saudi official** named **Saleh Hussayen** checked into a Marriot Residence Inn near Dulles airport. Inside were three of the Flight 77 hijackers, Hazmi, Hanjour and Mihdhar. It was learned later that Hussayen had checked out of another hotel in order to stay at that one.

(After the attacks the FBI "could not prove" that he had actually met with those terrorists. When questioned Saleh "feigned a seizure" and went to a hospital. *He too left the country days later in the Administration's obscure release of Saudi nationals.*)

FBI investigations also showed that Atta and some of the other terrorists had stayed at a home in a gated community in Sarasota Florida. **That home was owned by Esam Ghazzawi, a Saudi**

advisor to the Royal family. (After 9/11 the home was abandoned by the Saudis along with vehicles and expensive furnishings.)

In mid-August Ahmed Massoud sent his advisor Abdullah to Washington to try to meet with U.S. leaders. Their lobbyist Otilie English was able to cobble together a few appointments, but most of the Congress had lost interest in region and the meetings were became demoralizing.

However the White House was becoming interested in overthrowing the Taliban as it fit in with their recent decisions. Hamid Karzai had been one of the representatives at the latest meetings. His anti-Taliban stance and his visits to Washington had struck a nerve with Pakistan's ISI. He was given an order from the ISI to leave Pakistan by the end of September or he would be arrested. Pakistan was staying with the Taliban and Mullah Omar. Karzai spoke with Massoud via a satellite phone and was warned to come into Afghanistan from the north.

Massoud then contacted the CTC and reported that two Arab journalists had crossed into his territory. Anytime Arabs came into the region suspicions were aroused. This pair held Belgium passports, though they were from Morocco. They had entered Kabul from Pakistan and appeared to be reporters. *In actuality they were part of that Belgium cell that had been missed months before.*

With no warning and with no reason given, Prince Turki al-Faisal was removed as the head of Saudi intelligence. This was a position he had held since 1976, and during those years he had worked with many world leaders and their intelligence services. His replacement was one Nawaf Aziz, a man who knew nothing of the intelligence services or any of the main players. Saudi intelligence was in turmoil for weeks, another one of those strange coincidences.

(It is interesting to speculate on way this was done at this time. Did Turki learn something? Or did he object to something? Or both.)

Mohammed Atta called his former roommate in Hamburg, **Ramzi Bin al-Shibh** on August 29, 2001. In a coded message he alerted Ramzi to report to bin Laden with the date of the attack. Their work had been kept highly secret and need to know only. Their training had started in Germany's flight schools, but all realized they had to go to U.S. flight schools to succeed.

After the attacks it was uncovered that Bin al-shibh was an important member of al-Qaeda, a conduit for funds and a liaison with al Qaeda seniors KSM and bin Laden. He had also met with Moussaoui twice in London during December 2000 as they worked to get him into the U.S. for flight training. Atta had met up with al-Shibh in Berlin during January 2001, and in Madrid in July to keep him updated. This latest call was their final contact.

Khalid Sheikh Mohammed's nephew Ammar al-Baluchi applied for a visa to the U.S. on September 4. His exit date was listed as September 11, but his entry was also denied. Was he a final attempt to replace Moussaoui? Ammar had also helped the 9/11 plotters with money and support.

(He was later captured in Pakistan and interrorgated with EIT, Enhanced Interrogation Techniques. He talked, and his information helped locate KSM and bin Laden.)

At a meeting of the National Security Council on September 4 a new policy was set down. The goal was to eliminate bin Laden and his organization. Massoud was to be given the covert funding and weapons he needed to fight his war against the Taliban. Their wish list of needs was to be fully funded. Not since the early 1990s was such aid to be provided. This Administration had finally made a decision, now it was time to act.

At the CTC Cofer Black and his bin Laden unit wanted to keep armed predator drones in the region to strike opportune targets. As always the lawyers worried over the legality, especially Tenet.

On September 9th the well planned Taliban- al-Qaeda attack killed the pro-western leader of the Northern Alliance in Afghanistan, Ahmed Massoud.

Two al Qaeda terrorists claimed to be Belgium journalists wanting an interview with Massoud. They were in fact Tunisian members of al Qaeda and were assisted in this plot by Ayman al-Zawahiri. Their video-camera battery was filled with explosives, and when they were close enough to Massoud they blew themselves up killing him.   **Incident # 217**

Planning for this attack had begun back in May when Zawahiri had created a false letter of introduction claiming that two journalists from the Islamic Observation Center in London requested an interview with Massoud. They used former Afghan Islamist Abdurrab Sayyaf as the intermediary. He was aged and no longer fighting, but he had contacts with the northern tribes. Their plan worked to perfection, Patience.

Massoud was well known and respected in his world. Even the hostile cleric Abdullah Azzam felt Massoud was the true jihadist figure they could all unite behind. His death was a vital component of the 9/11 attack plan. Bin Laden knew that Massoud was helping America, and keeping the northern alliance of tribes against the Taliban. With him out of the way al-Qaeda and the Taliban would weather the coming storm.

Bin laden was sure that they would be attacked after their strikes on September 11. "He called his mother warning her that big news was coming and she would not hear from him for a while." *(194)

Amrullah Saleh called the CTC from Tajikistan and gave them the fatal news. For the Bush Administration this was a decisive blow. They had planned on striking al Qaeda and the Taliban using Massoud as the leader of the alliance. Now what would they do?

Belgium authorities reacted quickly and arrested several of the al-Qaeda members who had assisted this cell. They also captured **Tarek Maaroufi,** a Tunisian who was planning to bomb the U.S. Consulate in Milan. **Incident # 217**

Taking advantage of the chaos in Massoud's death the Taliban launched a well planned attack against the northern alliance on September 10. (It was obvious this offensive had been pre-planned months in advance.)

Bin Laden and his most important conspirators began moving from Khost to Kabul to Jalalabad. *It was time to hide.*

On September 10, 2001 U.S. intelligence intercepted another message in Arabic, **Tomorrow is Zero Hour.**

FAR STRETCHING ENDLESS TIME
BRINGS FORTH ALL HIDDEN THINGS AND BURIES
THAT WHICH ONCE DID SHINE
THE SACRED OATH IS SHATTERED
THE HIDDEN TRUTH REVEALED,
AND LET NONE SAY IT CAN'T HAPPEN HERE

          Sophocles

September 11, 2001

All of the pieces of this complicated attack were in place and the terrorists were traveling to get to their scheduled airports. Mohammed Atta and another dangerous looking middle-eastern male approached the ticket counter at the Portland, Maine airport. The ticket agent realized that those two were potential trouble. He wanted to refuse them a boarding pass and have security take them away, but due to Clinton's rules on profiling they were allowed to take a plane to Boston. There they boarded planes at Logan Airport for a flight to the west coast.

Sitting on American Airways Flight 11 Atta made a last minute cell call to Marwan al Shehhi who was on United Airlines Flight 175 a few planes away on the taxiway. It is presumed they were confirming their plans. *Both airliners were flying cross-country to LAX, so both had full loads of fuel. Just as they had planned.*

At 0758 **United Flight 175,** a Boeing 767 took off heading westward. At 0802 **American Flight 11** which was also a 767 took off on a similar path. Everything on the two flights appeared normal and the sky was crystal clear. American Flight 11 from Boston was on a more northern course on a path closer to Albany, NY. United Flight 175 took a more southern route and was heading towards Newburgh, NY.

It had been almost two years since that legal case with Argen-Bright. Five young Muslim men brought box cutters past the security checkpoint at Dulles Airport. **In the security video you can observe that the Muslim screeners did not stop, question or remove any suspicious items from those men even after they set off the metal detectors! Nawaf al-Hazmi and Majed Moqed set off the alarms for both the first and second detector they passed through. Yet no further investigation was done even though Moqed's ticket had been flagged for further screening.** They boarded Flight 77.

At 0810 **American Airlines Flight 77** took off from Dulles airport near Washington D.C. on their usual run to LAX. It too was full of fuel and headed west as was normal.

At 0814 Flight 11 failed to answer instructions to increase their altitude.

At 0821 Flight 11's aircraft transponder was suddenly turned off. *After Atta turned off Flight 11's transponder the aircraft became lost in the crowded skies, just as was warned back in 1996 in Atlanta.*

At 0824 Flight Controllers heard a garbled sentence and then the voice of Atta saying "Stay quiet and you will be okay, we are returning to the airport."

Air Controllers determined the flight had been hijacked.

Around 0825 one of the surviving Flight attendants on Flight 11, Betty Ong contacted her office on one of the plane's cellphones. She reported on the violent hijacking, that two of the crew had been stabbed, and that she was unsure of where they were.

At 0828 strange messages from an accented voice came from the cockpit stating "we have more planes". Controllers tried to contact the flight but there was only silence.

Despite all of the prior attacks, the warnings, the plots, attempted attacks and the intelligence windfalls, the cockpit doors on the aircraft were easily breeched by the well trained terrorists. The aircraft transponders which transmitted the vital flight data were still accessible inside the cockpits, and were turned off. Through Clarke's eight plus years in charge of anti-terror and the knowledge of the Bojinka Plot, the security concerns from the Olympics, the recent hijackings, the discussions during the past and present Administrations, and the recent hijacking alerts, nothing was done by anyone to prevent the scenario that so many had worried about.

Once the terrorists on hijacked Flight 11 spotted their navigation beacon the Hudson River, they turned due south towards NYC. Flying on their normal route was Flight 175. As Flight 11 headed south they began flying towards the other aircraft. Warnings were radioed to Flight 175 that another flight was approaching them. The pilots of Flight 175 radioed back that they saw the other jet and were safe from impact.

(By a strange twist of fate the two planes might have collided near Newburgh, NY. They were just 3,000 feet apart. If only they had.)

FAA protocols called for immediate notification of a hijacking to the military so that fighter planes could be scrambled to catch up to and follow the hijacked aircraft.

Inanely the FAA waited thirteen minutes before reporting this confirmed hijacking to the Air Force, which was done at 0837!

Boston Center contacted (NEADS), Northeast Air Defense Center based in Rome, NY with the hijacking report. At one time the airbase in Rome housed a major unit of our air defense and attack capability. But the base had been virtually shut down by Bill

Clinton and his defense cuts. All they had now was a small headquarters and staff. They called NORAD (North American Aerospace Defense Command) based in Colorado to appraise them of the situation.

At 0840 Flight Attendant Mary Ann Sweeny called in informing the home office that four Middle Eastern men took the aircraft using box cutters. She also gave them the seat assignments of the hijackers. That enabled the FBI to begin the investigation and understand what was happening.

At 0842 **United Flight 93** took off from Newark Airport heading west to Cleveland. Everything there appeared normal.

Around this time Air Controllers became aware that something was wrong on Flight 175.

Then the same thing happened with Flight 77 as all contact with that aircraft ended.

Because of the Clinton cuts to the Department of Defense, the closest fighter aircraft were now based at Otis AFB Air Force Base near Boston. At 0846, NORAD authorized the launch of two armed F-15 fighters. It had been nine minutes since being notified.

Around that same time Mary Sweeny on Flight 11 reported that they were flying over some water and many buildings, and were flying dangerously low. Then she screamed.

At 0846 Flight 11 kamikazied into the north face of the North Tower. The impact was dead center into the north side of the building.

A few blocks north of the World Trade Towers there was an active fire call for a gas leak. Two French brothers were filming a documentary at the local firehouse on Duane Street, making a video on life in a firehouse. All of the units in that firehouse responded to that gas leak together, Engine Co 7, Ladder Company 1 and Battalion 1. As was usual one of the French brothers filmed the scene of the gas leak while the other stayed at the firehouse.

While the companies checked around the location for the gas leak an unexpected roar of a jet aircraft was heard approaching the site. All of the firefighters looked up to watch a passenger jetliner pass just overhead and very low. Not knowing what was happening the filmmaker pointed his camera skyward and captured the image as the jet passed them. It went behind another hi-rise building, and then reappeared crashing seconds later into the north face of the North Tower. All present were stunned as Battalion 1 called in second alarm and reported that the jet airliner flew into the building on purpose. Filming as they responded the one brother captured the horrible scene from outside and then inside the lobby of the North Tower. Injured and burning civilians littered the lobby and sidewalk as did debris from the building.

Because the aircraft penetrated through the exterior columns it left its outline on the face of the building as it destroyed almost half of the supporting columns of that side.

After hitting the exterior columns and entering the structure the aircraft became shredded and the nearly full fuel tanks carrying some 10,000 gallons of aviation fuel ruptured and exploded into a massive fireball. The fragmented aircraft and fireball continued through the open floor area striking and devastating the center core area and then exiting out of the south face of the North Tower.

Numerous supporting columns in the core were also destroyed and damaged, but those were more valuable because there were fewer of them. (Their interior location prevented anyone from seeing that destruction from the exterior.)

As described earlier, building elevators were located in the core area between the rows of center core columns. Many of those elevator cars had their cables severed, plunging them into freefall. Some fell the height of the building and crashed into the lower levels killing all aboard. Others stopped when the emergency brakes engaged. Most had ignited in the jet-fuel based fireball incinerating the occupants.

Also severed in the crash were the fire suppression water mains and all three of the building stairways that were wrongly grouped together in that core area.

As shown earlier, when the Port Authority insisted on the construction of these towers the FDNY Commissioner and senior chiefs were against it. One of the FDNY's reasons was the fact that the Port Authority had grouped all of the stairways in one area to make it easier and cheaper to construct.

The NFPA (National Fire Protection Agency) has long decreed that you must have at least two fire exits remote from each other for safety. In that way if one exit is inaccessible the other one (s) should still be clear. By using their cheaper core-system all of the stairways were destroyed at the same time. Everyone above the crash site was now trapped.

One of the most vital features a Fire Department does for the community is Fire Safety. In NYC the FDNY and others had fought long and hard to have a fireproof stairway built in all commercial buildings.

Back in 1911 the infamous Triangle Shirtwaist Fire needlessly claimed the lives of 146 young women. In that uncalled for tragedy the exit doors had been locked to prevent theft, and the only stairway was unprotected from fire and led directly onto the factory floor itself. Once the fire and smoke entered that stairway it was inaccessible for anyone who was above the fire. Most of those who died had to jump to escape the flames. Fallout from that preventable disaster was a series of worker (Labor Laws) and Fire Safety laws, one of which was to legislate a **Fire Tower** in all commercial buildings over 75 feet high. (At that time the fire-ladders in use only reached 75 feet.)

A Fire Tower, (NYC code) is a fire-proof stairway located in a separate area of the building, usually in a corner. The Fire Tower is enclosed in 8 or more inches of reinforced concrete to make it super-strong, self supporting and fireproof.

To access the fire tower stairs, the floor occupants have to pass through fireproof doors that lead to a vented hallway. In that way any smoke that entered the hallway would not build up, keeping the stairway egress safe and clear. After traveling those few steps in the hallway the occupants then pass through another set of fireproof doors into the fire tower stairway itself. Any occupant who enters the Fire Tower can easily and safely descend to the street. All of the tall buildings built after the Triangle Shirtwaist Fire had that Fire Tower including the Empire State Building, Chrysler Bldg etc. *All of them except the (WTC) World Trade Towers, and those that were built after them when the code was changed!*

When the Port Authority presented the proposals for those Trade Towers then FDNY Fire Commissioner John O'Hagen was totally against the project. He warned that the towers were too big, (110 stories), the open floor area to large, (200x200), and the safety features too few. There were no sprinklers in the buildings, and with the open floor plan the Port Authority insisted upon there was no compartmentation of the floor areas. Hence any fire that started would have a free run of the entire floor since there were no sprinklers to knock it down and no interior walls to help contain it.

With that massive open floor area on fire, our biggest interior attack hoselines (2 1/2 inch diameter) would be no match for the heavy fire condition that would quickly develop. (You would need a minimum of four hose teams to fight that fire. An extremly difficult task to organize in high heat and smoke.)

Firefighting is a manual skill based on science and manpower. A fire will give off a certain amount of heat at any given time. You must be able to reduce the heat level to put the fire out. If you don't the fire will spread and grow exponentially. It is almost impossible to "catch up" to a fire. You either have the forces, (manpower), equipment and water capacity to defeat it or you will lose the building/s and lives.

(Never allow the useless politicos or bureaucrats to cut your Fire Service.)

Those buildings were a disaster waiting in the wings as the PA administration and the politicos ensured that the World Trade Center Towers went up the way they wanted. Fire safety was not a priority.

The Towers had been engineered to withstand the lateral pressure of hurricane force winds, and the impact of a 707 jetliner coming in at 200 mph. (The speed of an aircraft trying to land and lost in fog, at that time the 707 was the heaviest jet in service.) **But the airliner that had just crashed into the North Tower was a monstrous 767 that weighed 137 tons empty, almost three times the weight of the 707.**

The impact of Flight 11's airliner flying close to 500 mph was so violent that the 110 story building swayed almost six feet. Even the lobby sustained serious damage as dozens of heavy sections of marble broke free of the walls crashing to the floor. Large glass windows also shattered all around the lobby area of the acre sized building. Those elastic dampers the PA had used to reduce the sway of the towers from high winds worked fine to control the swaying caused from the impact of the jet.

Occupants caught in or near the elevators were burned when the vaporized fuel detonated into a multi-story fireball inside the elevator shafts, stairways and floors. *Everyone who had been in the impact area of floors 93-98 were mercifully killed in an instant as were the passengers and flight crew of Flight 11.*

Despite their many years of schooling and designing, none of the PA engineers or designers gave a single thought on the vast fire potential which would be created by the jet fuel an airliner would be carrying. They also missed how the fire potential of the occupied acre sized floors would affect the stability of the structure.

Both were Fatal Flaws.

Modern furnishings are mostly plastic based, and that means oil based. And oil based means high heat and heavy smoke production in a fire. The fireball from the 10,000 plus gallons of jet fuel ignited five full floors into a searing blast furnace. Tons of aircraft seats, oils, luggage, carpets, office paper, desks, furniture, wall coverings, computers and everything else in the offices added to the heavy fire load. And with the open floor plan of the Towers those fires filled each floor in seconds. The minimal fire protection that had been sprayed on the trusses and floor decks was incapable of standing up to that much heat.

Most people know that fire can destroy a wooden or brick building, but few (except firefighters and engineers) realized that fire can also weaken and destroy a steel one too.

When steel is heated in a fire that heat is conducted throughout the beam. When steel reaches the temperature of 1100 degrees it weakens, and losses 40% of its load carrying capacity. In addition to weakening, the steel softens and will actually expand 1 inch for every 10 linear feet. In other words a 100 foot long piece of steel will expand 10 inches when heated to that temperature. If the I-beam hits an obstruction (like a strong wall) which prevents it from expanding, it will warp. If that happens the re-shaped steel can fall off from its support position and / or be incapable of supporting the load it was carrying.

When structural steel cannot carry its load whatever depended on it for support will collapse. There are no exceptions, gravity always wins.

(Watch some of the videos of highway overpass fires that are online. Those videos repeatedly show overpasses that collapse after a high heat fire burns under them. What you the reader needs to realize is the fact that those heavy weight steel I beams holding up the roadways were holding no weight other than their own and the road. Yet all collapsed within an hour after the fires had heated and weakened the steel.)

All normal fires will follow a similar time/temperature graph. **Within five minutes an uncontrolled fire will reach 1000 degrees Fahrenheit. After 10 minutes an uncontrolled fire will reach 1300 degrees, and within an hour 1700 degrees.** (This fire graph does not factor in 10,000 gallons of jet fuel.) Though that high temperature will not melt the steel, it will weaken it and cause it to fail.

The special structural steel used for the WTC columns was of high strength, (and was produced at mills all over the nation.) Those buildings were basically a hollow tube of steel columns with a second tube of columns in the center core area.

As stated earlier to save weight the PA used lightweight open-web metal trusses to span the open floor area from the perimeter columns to the core columns. Those trusses sat on small metal ledges attached to the columns by spot welding. For the engineers that "tied the building together from exterior sides to the center core". *Those lightweight trusses supported the floors, and were vital to the overall support and stability of the Towers.*

But it is normal for light-weight steel bar-joist trusses to fail from the heat of a fire within 5-10 minutes. Those trusses were so poorly rated the FDNY changed our operations around 1992 so that no one would operate above or below them if the fire involved the structure. (Versus a contents fire).

Lightweight corrugated metal decking had been placed on top of those trusses forming the floor base/mold, and was simply tack welded to the lightweight metal trusses. About 3 and 1/2 inches of light concrete was spread over the metal decking creating the actual floor slabs. With this heavy fire condition attacking them, the trusses and floor decking began to soften and fail.

All three stairs in the North Tower were destroyed by the crash. They were not enclosed by concrete, but regular interior walls, which in this case was just sheetrock. Since the stairways had been grouped together and breeched by the crash, everyone who was above the impact floors 93-98 was cutoff. The only way out was getting to the roof or using a parachute, and the PA had locked the roof.

Contrary to the flawed 9/11 Commission report the FDNY has had a helicopter roof rescue plan since 1984. It was practiced regularly, and updated a few months ago. The last update on that roof operation, (AUC 269) was done the summer of 2001 and released as a training film.

Despite that needed life-safety operation, none of the swine politicos would give us the funds to have a dedicated FDNY helicopter unit. Almost every city in the country has FD helicopters, Los Angeles and Tokyo have fleets. Even tiny Flagler County in Florida has a FD helicopter. But not the FDNY.

Back in 1970 at the infamous Sao Palo office building fire over 300 were saved from the roof by helicopters. In 1972 a dozen trapped civilians were saved in New Orleans at their tragic office fire. And in 1983 helicopters saved dozens at the MGM Grand fire in Las Vegas. But the scheming politicos in NYC ignorantly and arrogantly told us to borrow one from the NYPD.

PD helicopters are too small for the heavy lift needs of FD roof rescues, and none of their people would take orders from the

FDNY, ever. Every time there were drills on that roof operation cross-departmental issues constantly came up. And PD helicopters were based close to JFK airport, miles away from our units.

The logical need of roof rescues is in Manhattan, where most of the hi-rise buildings are. And that was where that dedicated helicopter unit needed to be based!

Ladder Co. 21 in my firehouse on W38street was the Roof Rescue Company for fires in lower Manhattan. Ladder Co. 15 near he seaport was the roof company for mid-town fires. Each unit had a heliport within blocks of the firehouse.

Dozens upon dozens of civilians could have been saved if we had had our own helicopter unit based in Manhattan. They would have responded to the crash as the FDNY units always do, quickly.

If you watch the videos of the North Tower you can see that the roof area was in a light smoke condition during those first 15 minutes. That was the time to get a team on the roof and force open the locked roof doors. Our members could have evacuated and rescued as many as possible from the top floors to the roof. Then it would be in the hands of the helicopter pilots and crews to lower the harness/seat and pull them up. And they could have tried to use the same method to rescue people trapped at windows.

But the FDNY Roof Rescue operation was never called in.

(Had the Port Authority not deleted the FDNY required Fire Tower, those not killed or seriously injured in the actual crashes could have found that stairway to make their escape. Most of them would have survived.)

I was supposed to be on duty that morning as the Captain of Engine Co. 34 based at W 38 street and 9th Ave in Manhattan. Just before I was going to drive in from my home in Newburgh, one of my Lieutenants' called me to swap the shifts. For that reason I am still alive.

Both of those hijacked airliners flew over us in the lower Hudson Valley. Flight 11 was on their way south to attack the World Trade Center, while Flight 175 continued westward after that near-miss.

After dropping my daughters off at school I returned home and heard a frantic message on my answering machine. It was that lieutenant calling about the first crash. As I turned on the TV thoughts were racing through my head. I knew the sky was crystal clear, and felt that this was not an accident. *When the TV went on there was the proof, a dead center hit into the north face of the building.* I called the firehouse to warn them that this was a terrorist attack and that more would come, but my company and my guys had already been sent down on the 3d alarm. Engine Co. 26 and Ladder 21 were also based at my firehouse, and both would be responding soon.

At the WTC complex the French filmmaker remained at the North Tower Fire Command Post (CP) with Battalion 1, Division 1, and the senior operations chief. That CP was on the 1st floor at the NW corner of the North Tower, and he filmed the mornings trials from that unique location. His brother had run down from the Duane Street firehouse and was filming from the streets until he was ordered away by the police.

In the neighboring South Tower Cyril Ric Rescorla was at work as vice-president for security at Morgan Stanley Dean Witter. Rescorla was a highly decorated Vietnam Vet, and had worked for British intelligence after the war. He was a good man to have around, and he understood the meaning of security.

For people like him intelligence and security are symbiotic.

When he joined the investment company back in 1990 Ric Rescorla was weary of the WTC complex because it was an easy and obvious target. The terrorist bombing in 1993 proved him tragically correct, and he tried to get his bosses to leave the WTC for a safer location. They could not because of their lease.

Unable to escape from the potential danger Rescorla prepared everyone for it. He held evacuation and escape drills for all 3,700 employees regularly. Everyone had to attend and practice. When debris and flames shot out from the North Tower, Rescorla sprang into action getting his people moving. Practice makes perfect, and the Morgan Stanley staff moved like experts down the stairs to safety.

Unbelievably down in the main lobby WTC staff tried to get everyone to return at work claiming the problem was "at the North Tower". However Rescorla brushed them aside and his people did as they had practiced, they escaped and survived. (Some people did listen to those inane directives and returned upstairs. Many of them died when caught by the second crash.)

Senior FBI agent John O'Neil had retired after a solid career. He had just taken over as the head of security at the WTC. As shown many times, his last eight years had been spent in counter-terrorism in the NYC office. Like many of us he complained often that we were going to be attacked again by Islamic terrorists, but none of his supervisors would listen. As he left his new office in the S. Tower to get a handle on what was happening the sights and sounds were crippling. People were already jumping from the top floors to escape the flames.

The F-15 fighters scrambled from Boston were not told what was happening. *They took off at 0852 and went out to sea to fight an approaching enemy as was their protocol. They were redirected a minute later for NYC, but had lost irreplaceable time and distance.* That inexcusable time delay in the notification to NEADS was not a detrimental factor for Flight 11, because no one knew what was going to happen. But the nine minute delay by NORAD before alerting Otis AFB to send up the fighters and by not telling them what was going on was detrimental.

Those Boston F-15s would not have been abe to stop Flight 11, but they could have intercepted Flight 175.

An unexpected lapse by the terrorists on Flight 175 had delayed their assault. They struck the cockpit sometime after the near miss with Flight 11. Air Controllers were unable to contact Flight 175 after 0851, five minutes since the first crash. But by waiting to strike the terrorists had inadvertently allowed enough time for their flight to fly past their Hudson River navigation landmark. Flight 175 continued to fly south-westward, while the terrorists looked around trying to figure out where they were. As before, their transponder was turned off.

Within minutes of the crash the North Tower fires emitted a huge plume of smoke skyward. It drifted with the slight breeze to the southeast and continued to grow as the minutes ticked by. Television coverage showed a thirty story plume of smoke escaping from the tower and drifting slowly away.

At American Airlines Operations Center in Texas the FAA helped them reconstruct the radar data on Flight 11. They watched it head south, but could not fathom that the plane had crashed into the WTC.

Around 0855 Flight 175 made a sudden 200 degree turn from their inadvertent south-westward course. My belief is that they spotted the smoke plume, realized their location and turned the aircraft towards NYC. At that point Flight 175 was located at the junction of middle New Jersey near the Pennsylvania border, and they had many miles to make up.

That simple mistake provided the occupants of the South Tower with a 16 minute divine reprieve. Most took advantage of it. Lead by people like Rescorla and the memory of the 1993 attack, the South Tower had already began emptying. Thousands were saved each minute that went by.

At 0854 Flight Controllers in Indianapolis realized that Flight 77 had also deviated from their flight plan, and they lost all contact with the Flight.

At 0858 the FAA reported another 'possible" hijacking, that of Flight 175. Seven minutes had gone by!

At 0900 the FAA reported that Flight 77 was now missing and possibly crashed.

A few blocks from Tower 2, NYPD Commissioner Kerick and his staff had arrived on the scene from Police HQ. From their initial location near the WTC Plaza, they too witnessed the horrible sights and sounds of people falling from the buildings. He directed his staff to setup a PD-CP north of the towers on Barclay Street. Seconds later a massive explosion erupted from the South Tower forcing everyone to dive for cover as thousands of pieces of debris headed their way. The second plane had struck Tower 2.

As a result of the FAA delays in notifying the Air Force, the severe cutbacks to the military during the Clinton years, and the needless failures by those in charge, there were still no fighter planes near NYC. **The F-15s from Boston were 50 miles away.**

Since there was no air cover, at 0903 Flight 175 kamikazied into the South Tower at the south-east corner at a 38 degree angle. Realizing their mistake, the terrorists had sped up to over 500 mph to prevent their being shot down. The passenger jet struck the 78 floor near the south-east corner and crashed through the eastern face of the building. **As a result of that angle most of the fatal structural damage was to the columns on the south-eastern and eastern side of the building.** A lot of fuel and debris exited the eastern side of the building creating a huge fireball and covering the WTC plaza and nearby streets with destruction. (Parts of the aircraft ended up in the streets and on the roof of WTC-5.)

As before the vaporized jet fuel created by the high speed crash resulted in heavy fire conditions on multiple floors. With the reprieve in the timing of the second crash it is believed that only nineteen people above the crash area died.

However Ric Rescorla was tragically killed with two of his aides because they went back in searching for three missing employees. Out of 3,700 workers, Morgan Stanley lost only those six! That is what true leadership is, not the self-serving scheming by useless lawyers and politicos.

Incredulously the FAA again waited to contact NEADS on the hijacking of Flight 175 until 0903. (By that point Flight 175 had already struck Tower 2.)

With this second crash additional FDNY units were ordered to respond. All of them reacted to the attacks with their usual hard-charging style of interior operations. In a high density environment like NYC, our fire operations were based on an **aggressive interior attack.** That type of operation places the firefighters in extreme peril, but that's what is needed to protect the civilians. Get between them and the fire.

However in this case errors by the senior commanders in planning and understanding what they faced gave them a false confidence. Since the FDNY was the busiest fire department in the world only a few of us studied other city's fires to learn. Most of those senior chiefs had worked in the FDNY during the busiest years of service, the 1960s & 1970s. They had all been to thousands of fires in tenements, stores and residences, but no one had ever seen something like this. (One of my haunts is that I did have a good understanding of those fires. I had gone to John Jay College for Fire Science, and fought over a dozen Hi-rise office fires. I knew a problem was coming if a plane crashed into one of those buildings, and tried a couple of times to get the chiefs to answer my questions. But each time it was brushed aside and I wrongly did not pursue the issue.)

In NYC our strict building code mandated extra fire protection to help contain the fire in Hi-rises. Most of the time fires in those office buildings would destroy only one floor. However those types of fires were always hard to fight because of the height of the building, difficulty in getting access, difficulty in getting fresh troops into the fight, the tangled layouts, intense heat and dense black smoke.

The last major office fire in NYC was in 1993 at the Bankers Trust Fire at E 48 and Park Ave. I was there as the Lt. in the second due Engine company, E-54. It was brutally hot. All attempts at entry were pushed back with burned members.

Fortunately that fire could be reached with exterior streams from tower ladders and was eventually knocked down. (Like the WTC fire in 1973.) Once that was done we returned to the fight with handlines and finished it off.

After the fire was out some three hours later, I saw that many of the smaller I-beams that held up the floor slab above had failed. About a dozen of them looked like pretzels as they deformed from the intense heat. During the fire Rescue-1 had called on the radio repeatedly that fire was coming through the concrete floor onto the floor above where they were operating. **That is not supposed to happen, and was not believed by some of the Chiefs.** I tried to bring my hoseline up to them, but was stopped by the sector chief.

This building was built in the 1950s, and was not as solidly built as earlier ones. I vividly remember at the post-fire critiques that there was no critical discussion of the failures of the floor I-beams or the concrete floor. All of us younger officers were basically ignored. None of those senior chiefs asked; What would have happened if the fire had been higher up in the building and out of range of the tower ladder streams? We would probably have lost multiple floors, but what about the building?

Los Angeles in 1989, and Philadelphia in 1993 suffered similar serious office building fires. Both of their fires had gotten out of control because of water problems, and both had multiple floors burned out. *To their credit both Fire Departments realized that they needed input from structural engineers to determine if the buildings could collapse. In both cases the structural engineers inspected while the firefight was still going on!*

At the LA fire the building was very well built and the fire damage to the five floors of the building were not considered a collapse threat. **But in the Philadelphia fire, that engineer warned that a serious collapse could occur.** That building was not as well built as the one in LA, and they had more floors damaged (14) by the intense fire. Philly FD wisely pulled their people out and let the fire burn. (Still three firefighters died there.) Though that building did not collapse, multiple floors had serious localized collapses. (The previoisly mentioned major fires in Brazil and New Orleans did not collapse either.)

Because there had never been a total collapse of a steel and concrete Hi-rise office building no one in the FDNY gave it much thought. And the fact that the Towers did not collapse from the initial impacts gave the commanders a false sense of security. (It was actually amazing that they stayed up as long as they did with the terrible structural damage they had suffered.)

The buildings of the World Trade Center were not the normal Hi-rise. Unknown to our commanders they had been critically damaged by the impacts of the aircraft, before the fires finished the devil's work.

(One of the WTC head engineers saw the first crash and drove through the Holland Tunnel to try to warn the Police and Fire Departments that the buildings would collapse. He was stopped by the police at the NYC side of the tunnel and forced to leave the city. He was never able to get out a warning.)

The other two companies in my firehouse, Ladder 21 and Engine 26 had responded on the following alarms after the second plane struck. Even then no call was made for a helicopter rescue, and Ladder 21 responded as a regular ladder company.

At my home near Newburgh I watched the second crash as it happened with my wife who had worked in those same Towers for the Port Authority. We were fighting mad at what we were watching, and around 0910 a call came in from the firehouse. All off-duty personnel were ordered in on a total recall and report to their firehouses and await instructions. Minutes later I left in uniform not knowing if I would see my family again.

Around 0923 NEADS was still unsure of the status of Flight 77. They realized that the aircraft did not crash, and was heading back towards the Washington D.C. area.

At 0924 NORAD scrambled F-16 fighter jets from Langley Air Force Base in Virginia to find it. Both aircraft were airborne by 0930, but they were not armed. Instructions to the pilots was to prevent the airliner from crashing into another building.

Their only option was to crash their fighter into the airliner!

At 0929 Cleveland based Controllers heard the unmistakable sounds of a struggle from the cockpit of Flight 93. Screaming was heard and the worst was feared. But no notification went out.

At 0932 Flight 77, a Boeing 757 reappeared on radar flying in at 600 mph past Dulles Airport heading towards Washington D.C. The Secret Service was notified as the White House was evacuated. *Communications between the federal agencies was still poor, and the fighter planes from Langley were again headed in the wrong direction for intercept.* (They were near Ronald Reagan Airport.)

At 0934 Flight 93 began climbing erratically and controllers moved several other aircraft out of the way. NEADS was still not notified of this hijacking!

At 0937 Flight 77 crashed into the Pentagon.

An unarmed National Guard aircraft had been enlisted to help find them. A minute later at 0938 they reported that the airliner had already crashed into the Pentagon.

Because no fighters were in the area the terrorists had time to overfly the Pentagon and then turn back to crash into it at 500 miles per hour. The impact destroyed the aircraft as the crash created a 80 foot opening. Unlike the WTC Towers, the Pentagon was constructed of masonry exterior, and had substantial columns placed inside the building. Both factors prevented the extensive penetration as seen in the Towers, though some debris was ejected out of the C ring structure leaving a sixteen-foot diameter hole. Heavy fire erupted in the impact floors of the outer E-ring. Fire sprinklers helped control the fires from spreading which helped the rescue efforts. *Despite its strong construction, after a short while the façade and the five burning floors of the E-ring collapsed.*

At 0939 a transmission came in from Flight 93 confirming the plane had been hijacked. As with the other airliners the weak cockpit door was quickly breeched and the pilots murdered. **Again NEADS was not notified of this attack and hijacking until 1007!** (Was anyone fired?)

Surviving passengers and crew of Flight 93 were forced to the rear of the airliner. Passengers and crew used the air phones to call home and speak to loved ones explaining that the hijackers had stabbed and killed the flight crew. *They then learned of the fate of the other hijacked aircraft, and decided to fight back and retake their jet from the terrorists.*

President George Bush had traveled to Sarasota, Florida and was sitting in a classroom at the Emma Booker Elementary School for a reading by the children. Just before entering the classroom the President was told by Chief of Staff Andy Card that a plane had hit the World Trade Center in NYC. Bush spoke to National Security Advisor Condoleezza Rice on the phone and then entered the classroom. Minutes later Chief of Staff Card whispered into the President's ear that a second plane had hit the other tower, we were clearly under attack. The president struggled with his emotions for he was in a classroom with thirty second grade children. Around him his aides were speaking into radios and cell-phones. This school trip had to end.

At 0930 Pres. Bush spoke to the nation describing that terrorists were behind the attacks. After that quick statement Air Force One prepared for an abrupt take off. The Secret Service was worried that the terrorists could even be targeting the President, so many of those who flew down on the presidential jet were left behind.

At 0957 Air Force One took off and then climbed high, up to 45,000 feet. (The S. Tower was collapsing at that time.) That altitude was out of range of smaller aircraft and most anti-aircraft weapons. The mood on the plane was tense, **and with the prior cutbacks to the military there were no fighter jets immediately available for escort duty!** Air Force One was on its own as it flew north above Florida. News of the attack on the Pentagon reached them.

Back in New York each Tower at the Trade Center was given a 5th alarm assignment. WTC 3 was the hotel, and they had a 3d alarm assignment as did the rest of the complex as a whole. Hundreds of on-duty and multiple dozens of off-duty firefighters had already responded to the WTC in that first hour.

In addition to the FDNY firefighters there were dozens of FD-EMS, NYC Police, Port Authority Police and security agents, plus Federal agents from many offices. All went into the buildings getting as many out as they could.

The PD had setup their separate command post near Barkley Street, while the FDNY commanders took over the corner of West and Vesey streets. When the FDNY setup their Command Post (CP) only the North Tower was on fire. That location gave the best visibility and access to it, and there was also an open underground parking garage right behind the CP. (I'm sure that that potential egress was part of the decision to setup there.)

After the second plane struck the South Tower, PD and FD commanders stayed in place organizing the movement of their units and material. As always there was little cooperation between the two services. Personnel from all agencies were trying to get into the buildings, but they had to be watchful of falling debris and victims. Falling from that great height their impacts sounded like explosions as they struck overhangs, roofs, sidewalks, street and site lights and vehicles. Multiple dozens decided to jump, rather than face the intense heat and smoke.

When the second crash occurred some of the units getting ready for operations in the North Tower were reassigned over to the South Tower. *Battalion 7 Chief Orio Palmer, Ladder 15 led by Lt. Joe Leavey and Fire Marshall Ron Bucca moved quickly, and actually made it up to the crash floors of the S. Tower around 0945* Their radio messages spoke of a terrible scene and the need for more troops. All three were friends, and all three would soon die.

Because of the speed and direction of Flight 175 when they crashed, one of the Tower 2 stairways had actually survived. Sadly only 18 additional people found it and made it out of the building in time. One elevator had also survived the impact, and was put to use ferrying the FDNY brothers up and survivors down from the sky lobby area near floor 45. Just before the fatal collapse a firefighter from Ladder-15 who was running the elevator car called in that the elevator had stopped somewhere in a blind elevator shaftway. Sadly the car was filled with casualties who were just minutes from safety.

(As the weakened Tower increasingly swayed more than likely the elevator safety interlocks activated locking the elevator in place. They did not escape.)

Since 0900 Police helicopters had been orbiting the WTC complex taking photos. None tried to land on the roofs. **Ten minutes before the collapse of the South Tower they reported on their radios that they could see the Tower actually swaying and leaning eastward.** Numerous Police radios echoed their warning, and those police personnel that could escape did. **However the FDNY was on a different radio network, and was never told.** (194A)

The structural damage from the crash had greatly weakened the building. No one overbuilds anything anymore, (as was done in the Empire State Bldg,). Everything was and is engineered to perfection to save money. But that too is a **Fatal Flaw**, because without some structural redundancy there is no room for loss. Those uncontrolled fires continued to weaken the structural steel by conduction, convection and radiation. Unprotected steel rapidly picks up heat, and the above processes ensured that even the heaviest of the steel was fatally heated almost uniformly along its entire span.

With the intense fires free burning on numerous floors localized floor collapses occurred as the lightweight trusses failed. That reduced the ties between the interior-exterior columns, and pushed others outward as the floor sections collapsed.

In the South Tower the angled crash was centered on floors 78-82. Most of the physical damage striking the columns was on the southern and eastern faces. Over two dozen of the heavy vertical steel columns had been ruptured in the crash and explosive exit, and more were physically damaged but had seemingly remained in place. Because of the heavy smoke condition the structural damage they had suffered was unseen from the street. As had happened with the North Tower, the unbroken steel columns of the S. Tower had to pickup the weight that the ruptured and damaged columns had been carrying.

In the case of the S. Tower, those undameged columns had to support all of the weight of the thirty two stories above the crash, some 100,000 tons. (The North Tower was struck at floors 93-98. Those damaged columns only had to support the 15 floors above, some 45,000 tons.)

The intense heat from the fires was nearing 1,700 degrees. As shown earlier, steel losses 40% of its carrying capacity when heated past 1,000 degrees. As those structural columns were further degraded, they finally reached a point of no return.

The time was 0958.

Since much of the structural damage had occurred along the eastern face of the South Tower, that was the side that failed first. If you watch the videos you can see the top quarter of the building shift eastward.

That shift happened near the crash damage, and was quickly followed by the eastern facing columns bending inward as they weakened and failed.

When that happened the massive weight of the thirty two stories above crushed downward onto the floor below. Naturally the columns on that floor could not support that momentous shifting weight or impact, so they too failed. And that collapse fell onto the next floor which also failed. The successive collapses crashed downward from floor to floor. As this "pancake" type of collapse continued, it picked up speed and momentum. It took just eight seconds to destroy the building killing everyone still inside.

When the debris struck the ground it was traveling at 120 MPH, and seismic shock waves were felt over 20 miles away.

An outstanding film was shot from Broadway.

The videographer was filming from the east, and something caught his attention. What he spotted was debris falling from the S.

Tower. *He raised his camera to capture the east face of the Tower, and as he filmed he caught what engineers call the "moment of failure".* You can clearly see the columns of the east face bending as the massive weight of the thirty-two floors above overstressed the damaged columns in the crash zone. Then the pancake collapse begins and he filmed that for a few seconds too. Once he realizes what is happening he instinctively retreats.

(Watch the video *Seven Days in September.*)

Video shot near the main FDNY CP on West Street also captured the collapse of the S. Tower. The fifty or so FDNY members present which included Chief of Department Peter Ganci and my company Engine 34 rushed into the nearby parking garage trying to escape the collapsing mountain that was heading towards them. All who went into the garage survived, but many of those who sought shelter elsewhere died.

As the Tower collapsed massive sections of the destroyed building fell away and onto the adjoining streets, sidewalks, and buildings crushing everything it hit. Pieces of debris also scattered about killing dozens who were in the open. Multiple firefighters who were searching the hotel were killed inside the building, not realizing that Tower 2 was collapsing onto them. The 28 story WTC-3 had been perilously sited between those massive towers. When the collapse occurred a large area of debris struck the hotel like a giant tomahawk. After the dust cleared only the ends of the hotel were still recognizable.

The French Brother who was filming inside WTC-1 at the Fire Command Station recorded the collapse from that vantage point. As one all present heard a strange sound high above them. The sound grew stronger, and turned into a growing, roaring type noise. Sensing danger all tried to run away from the sound into the nearby lobby of WTC-6. They did not get far before the horrific crashing and crushing sounds were upon them. This was where the FDNY's Chaplain Father Mychal Judge was killed. (He was given death certificate #1.)

In addition to the debris that fell there was a tremendous dust cloud that was composed of all of the pulverized building materials, office furniture, supplies and people. That dust cloud had mass, as it contained all of the above elements. Many unusual events occurred from that cloud such as 60,000 pound fire vehicles being flipped over but not struck by any large pieces of debris. Heavy steel doors inside the Firehouse that housed Engine Co. 10 and Ladder Co. 10, (the 10 House), on Liberty Street were buckled inward, and dozens of firefighters were picked up by the cloud and thrown 20-30 feet from where they had been. Again none were struck by any physical debris, just the dense dust cloud.

(Watch the videos and photos of the Mt Saint Helens volcano eruption in 1981, and then watch the video *American Vesuvious*.)

That dense cloud rapidly moved through the nearby concrete canyons like a grey tidal wave, killing and injuring many more. It covered everything in the area like an evil blanket.

It took over ten minutes for the FD personnel inside Tower 1 CP who had survived the collapse to exit the damaged lobby. On the French Brother's film you can watch their movements as they found Father Judge, and then crossed the northern footbridge exiting on the west side of West Street into the World Financial Center. *As he pans his camera around his film clearly shows the crippled hotel structure, and the devastated site where the South Tower had been.*

Numerous uniformed members and civilians had been in the area around the WTC complex, and were caught in the collapse of the South Tower. Amazingly some were still alive, but trapped under or within heavy debris. As the brothers in the FDNY recovered from the first collapse and the dust cloud moved away, they returned to those victims to try to save as many as possible. For many of those rescuers it would be fatal decision, including Chief Ganci. *The clock was already ticking for Tower 1.*

At 1003 the forth known hijacked jet Flight 93 crashed near Shankesville, Pennsylvania. Jeremy Glick, Todd Beamer, Mark Bingham and Tom Burnett become the first Americans to jump into this fight against the Islamic terrorists.

As those four took out the terrorists guarding the cockpit, the swine flying the jet crashed the airliner into the ground to prevent the passengers from taking it back. The actions of those brave passengers saved the Capitol Building or the White House from destruction. Their sacrifice was just the beginning of a long and preventable war.

All commercial flights were ordered grounded and any aloft ordered to land immediately. At 1018 Vice-President Cheney asked Air Force One if the military had permission to shoot down any other hijacked aircraft. Pres. Bush agreed. It was not a hard choice, we were at war and innocent lives were at stake. Sec of Defense Rumsfeld ordered a mobile command post be flown up in case more attacks occurred, and AWACS radar and control planes and flights of F-16s and F-15s were also sent aloft to fly CAP, (combat air patrol).

All military bases and embassies were placed on high alert and the Defense Readiness condition was raised from Defcon 4 to Defcon 3. The highest level it had been since the 1973 Yom Kipper War when Pres Nixon placed our units on alert to fight the Russians. To his credit Pres. Putin of the Russian Federation was one of the first world leaders to call Pres. Bush. Putin clearly understood the situation, and ordered Russian forces to stand down. Tensions were high enough already.

During his years in office Bill Clinton had refused to support Russia and help them stop the al-Qaeda operations in Chechnya and the Balkans. Russia had lost over 7,000 killed in the past few years, and Pres. Bush had recently reduced Russian intelligence operations inside the U.S.

Even so Putin and his advisors decided they would support future U.S. operations against al-Qaeda. That meant allowing U.S. military use of bases in Uzbekistan and Tajikistan, giving intelligence support and logistical help. In return we would allow the Russians a free hand in Chechnya. Without Russia's help, our operations against the Taliban and al-Qaeda would have been extremely difficult.

Around 1015 firefighters I knew and (later interviewed) told me that the Police personnel in the North Tower began exiting in a mad rush. One firefighter from L-18 asked what was going on and was told "get the hell out now". The police officer did not elaborate nor stop his escape. They knew another collapse was near as the orbiting Police helicopters were again reporting that the N. Tower was swaying and leaning to the north.

Again the FDNY was not informed of that sighting.

A fixed camera was filming the North Tower from a position to the north. As you watch that video you can observe the heavy fire condition as it climbed upward through the floors. A minute before the end a blast of dark smoke rises from the west side of the roof area where the Hat Truss was sited. Those of us in the Fire Service know that strange occurrences like that always mean bad news. I believe a partial collapse occurred at the roof /top floors that further and fatally stressed the center core columns.

At 1028 the same terrible sequence of events befell the North Tower. A sudden bending of the exterior columns visibly occurs on the video, followed by blasts of fire venting out of the windows. That fire blast was a normal event, for as the ceilings /

floors above collapse downward they physically push the interior air / fire / smoke outward. In this case out of the windows.

Unlike the S. Tower, the impact area was not the area that failed first! This collapse started higher up and dropped a few floors near the roof onto the one below. As before the columns there could not accept that weight or impact, and they failed onto the floor below in a replay of the deadly pancake collapse of Tower 2. Dozens of first responders were still operating inside the Tower, dozens more were lined up in the stairway waiting to escape, while others were in the exterior kill zone. Some of those caught outside were attempting to rescue other firefighters and civilians who had been injuted and pinned in the first collapse. (Chief Ganci was one of those killed.)

On one video a 40-story section of steel falls away from the collapsing tower almost intact. It spread like a deadly blanket across West Street from the north footbridge to the south one, crushing everything under it. After the collapse was over a second dense and deadly dust cloud permeated the area as it raced through the streets. This second shock-wave was also picked up over twenty miles away.

(For more stories of the FDNY and 9/11 the reader can look for my first book, *My Turn on the Firelines 1980-2003.*)

My ride into the city was clear of traffic as everyone was off of the roads except for those of us trying to get in. I was at 230 Street in the Marble Hill section of the Bronx, and panic was everywhere. On the radio I heard a reporter state they were flying over the site where the Trade Towers used to be. It was then a cold chill struck as I realized we had probably lost 500 guys. And that most likely included my guys.

By the time Air Force One reached the border with Georgia images of the collapsing towers were watched repeatedly on the nations television screens. Flight 93 was down in Pennsylvania, the Pentagon was on fire and had suffered a partial collapse.

Initial reports believed that three more commercial planes were still unaccounted for. Amidst the confusion a report came in to V.P. Cheney that "Angel was the next target." Angel was the code word for Air Force One, and it was decided to divert them to another location. Washington D.C. was in a lockdown with hundreds of thousands of workers trying to get out.

NYC was also in a lockdown, and the entire area of lower Manhattan was ordered evacuated. Mayor Giuliani had just missed being killed in the first collapse, and his small staff slowly made their way northward. He setup a temporary office in the quarters of Engine Co-24 and Ladder Co-5 at Houston and Sixth Ave. As things stabilized they relocated to a better site, but NYC was in chaos.

I had continued driving through the mayhem in Washington Heights, found the streets deserted in Harlem and the West Side getting into my firehouse on W 38 street around 1050. After getting my gear and checking the status of those who had gotten in ahead of me we reported to our Battalion 7 firehouse on W19 Street. That firehouse also housed Engine-3 and Ladder-12. All of the off-duty officers and firefighters of our Battalion had collected there awaiting orders on what to do next. (No one knew if another attack was coming to hit another Hi-rise building.)

While there we critiqued the TV replays of the collapses and could clearly see the structural failures that caused the buildings to come down. Watching the pancake type collapses most of us knew that few would still be alive.

Battalion 7 Commander Chief Byrnes told the assembled officers that multiple dozens of companies were MIA, missing in action and presumed dead. It included all of the companies in our Battalion, (mine), and Chief Palmer and his aide Steve Belson.

Surviving members of Ladder Co. 24 had just been brought back from the WTC and was missing two guys. They had seen two of my guys, and I pressed my case to go to the WTC and learn the fate of Engine Co-34, Ladder 21 and Engine Co. 26. It was approved and four of us were sent down.

Far away in Kandahar and Kabul, Afghanistan dozens of terrorist swine rejoiced over a day of attacks against America. However two of them were not pleased and another one was crying. News reports told the story of Flight 93 and of how the passengers had fought back preventing the aircraft from crashing into its target. Bin Laden and Khalid Sheikh Mohammed cursed Mohammed Qahtani for his failure to get entry into the U.S. They had recruited, trained and trusted him, and he failed. **Because of his failure, that flight did not make its target.**

(That one missing terrorist may have made a difference. But it is also possible that our people would have killed that one too. The other flights did not fight back because they did not know what was going on. Those on Fl-93 did know what was going to happen, so they attacked, hard.)

During those tense post-collapse hours Air Force One continued on to Barksdale AF base in Louisiana. It had been two hours since the president had been seen and newscasters began demanding to know his location. While he was there the President gave another small talk to the nation. "Make no mistake, The United States will hunt down and punish those responsible for these cowardly acts". (Bill Clinton had said the same thing six times but never acted when he should have.)

Speaking to the Sec. of Defense the president told him to get the military together for our counterattacks. Air Force One next headed west to Nebraska and Offutt AF base. (The liberal talking heads condemned the president for staying away for ten hours. They did not believe that he had been a potential target.)

With the correct shutdown of our air space the FAA had landed over four thousand aircraft. Planes inside our borders landed at whatever field was nearest to them. Flights from Europe were forced to land, and some made it to Canada. They landed on whatever airfield they could, but there were not enough hotels for the influx, and the gracious Canadian citizens opened their homes.

During and after the collapses FDNY fireboats and civilian craft began and completed the evacuation of over 500,000 people from lower Manhattan. That included emergency workers, civilians and the injured. Their hours-long flotilla crossed the Hudson River into New Jersey, crossed the East River into Brooklyn and lower New York Bay into Staten Island. That outstanding water borne evacuation resembled and even surpassed the incredible British effort at Dunkirk in WWII!

September 11 was the most massive sea-going evacuation in recorded history.

Behind the flotilla of boats the fires and dense smoke billowed unabated from the burning buildings and dozens upon dozens of burning vehicles. Once the life threat was over, the fireboats returned to the World Financial Center complex which was directly across West Street from the Trade Center Complex. Tethered to the eastern shore of the Hudson River, the boats began a duty they were built for, pumping tremendous quantities of water. It was that water that was used by the brothers to attack the fires consuming the WTC area.

But by the time all of those efforts had been organized, it was too late to try to save WTC 7.

While Air Force One flew westward an army of recalled firefighters, including me, reported for duty at the various staging areas. My small group had been dropped off behind the 47 story WTC-7. Serious fires had erupted on multiple floors when super hot debris and I-beams had fallen into and crashed through Tower 7 from the collapse of Tower-1.

As we walked behind the building, we saw heavy fire conditions on at least ten floors, and extension into another ten.

(Because WTC-7 had been chosen as the site for the City's Emergency Operations Center, auxillary generators held over 6,000 gallons of diesal fuel. That added to the intense fires and heavy black smoke condition all observed and many filmed.)

As my group walked around the block there was a deadly silence. There were no sounds, no birds, no traffic, no horns, no talking, just the roar of the flames destroying Building 7. Even our footsteps were muffled by the four inches of that deadly grey dust. Everything was coated in it, every vehicle, sidewalk, road, trees, and buildings. Paper, that bane of modern society was stuffed into every crevice you could see. Whatever had been written down, was no longer important.

Once we turned the corner and neared West and Vesey Streets victims and remains yet unrecovered could just be seen as coated shadows in the dust. Some were marked with traffic cones so they could be quickly found and removed when operations started.

At the main intersection of West and Vesey streets the site was indescribeable. The World Trade Center had occupied 16 acres with its gleaming towers. Now wreckage covered 30 acres, and in the center was a ten story pile of twisted debris and steel. Fire and smoke vented skyward from multiple places and cast a dark pall over the area. Debris was everywhere, as were dozens of crushed FDNY rigs and burned out vehicles from every department. Damaged buildings surrounded the site, and so were the dangers of falling debris.

Then the saddest sound began to be heard. It was the sound of multiple dozens of safety alarms going off, alarms that all firefighters wear. Normally the alert sound is annoying and extra loud to get your attention. But these sounds were muted and muffled. Their wearers lay buried under the debris.

The unfathomable destruction from the total collapse of two 110 story buildings had also taken out the area's utilities. Thousands upon thousands of tons of debris had fallen onto the roadways crushing the water mains, phone lines, electrical cables and gas mains that had been hidden under the streets.

(Almost 200,000 tons of steel alone was used in the construction of those towers. Add in the thousands upon thousands of tons of concrete, paper, desks, chairs, rugs, cabinets, furniture, windows etc, and you can imagine the weight that fell. One report stated over a billion pounds of debris was removed.)

Our group went to a small CP setup near the World Financial Center buildings on the west side of West and Vesey. After being updated by the sector chief we began moving around questioning and surveying the few survivors that were there to get a head count. While there I found three of my guys among the striken and shocked firfighters. Most of the brothers were searching for companies or missing members. Very seldom was the answer, yeah I saw him over there.

Due to the multiple emergencies, the major life hazards at the scene, the waterborne-evacuation and the extreme losses the FDNY had taken, **(almost 90 companies were missing and presumed buried in the massive debris piles),** no firefighting effort could be mounted for WTC-7. By the time any regrouping and firefighting efforts could be organized, it was decided the building was too far gone to risk any more or our units. We would allow it to burn and collapse, and around 1400 hrs all rescue and search operations had been suspended until WTC-7 came down.

Around 1600 myself and a few others were looking east at the heavy fire condition destroying WTC-7. As was normal with buildings we suspected were a collapse hazard, the FDNY had setup teams to watch the building with surveyors transits. Our people would observe a certain point on the structure and use the graduated markings to denote any deviations in the building's stability. Movement was noted and logged in the notepads and radioed out. Dozens of firefighters and I stood about 175 yards away from the crippled building. Collapse would be soon as our teams were reporting increased swaying. Around 5 PM large sections of marble facade began breaking free as the increasing movement of the tower fragmented and separated the heavy stone. The loose sections crashed heavily into the ground. Windows began shattering as the glass was incapable of withstanding any type of lateral movement. (Photos from the north show the incredibly thick smoke condition that existed along the lower floors. Some of that was from the diesal fuel in those tanks.)

We heard a loud crack around 5:45 PM, and watched as WTC 7 appeared to break in the middle and rapidly collapse. Unlike the other Towers, this one did not pancake, it collapsed almost intact. The earstern half seemed to go first and pulled the western half down in the now common dust cloud. I think it took just three seconds for it to drop, as I moved about that many steps away from it. Then it crashed into the gound.

As stated before, the 47story WTC-7 had been built over a Con-Edison sub-station. In order to support the building over that eequipment an unusual truss system was designed and constructed. Trusses are effective structural elements, but must stay intact for it to function. More than likely that was what had failed, as the collapse I witnessed (and heard) began in the lower floors. Once that something had failed, all of the floors above that truss were unsupported, and the building appeared to break in the middle and collapsed rapidly towards its center in a V shape. There was no pancaking, the building just collapsed.

And unlike the Towers, there was no impact damage first. This building was destroyed by the fire and the cheaper construction methods used to build it.

With the collapse threat from WTC 7 now ended hundreds of firefighters went back to work. Nearby rigs that had been crushed or burned were stripped and canabilized of anything still usable. Destroyed hoses were cut loose and new hoselines laid out. Ladder companies were sent into the debris piles to begin search and rescue. A few construction rigs had appeared and they were a big help in clearing the access roadways and main intersection at West and Vesey. Lines of responders soon formed into bucket brigades passing debris from an area being searched to an open one for removal. Reports of missing planes continued, and USAF fighters flew over us. (I warned the brothers nearby that if they here any strange sounds from above find a hole and pray.)

With the skies cleared of air traffic Pres. Bush insisted they had to get back to DC. At 1636 hrs they were airborne and they landed back at Andrews AF base two hours later. At 2030 Pres. Bush gave a short speech on TV that was meant for the entire world. One of his statements was; *"We will make no distinctions between the terrorists who committed the attacks and those who harbor them"*. The talk was well received.

Immediately afterward Bush went to the situation room for another briefing on the attacks and what was going on worldwide. Sleep at the White House was hard to come by when all were hurriedly awakened and brought to a bomb shelter. An F-16 flying CAP (Combat Air patrol) was misidentified.

The extensive destruction zone was hard to describe. Someone called it the pile, for the massive multi-story pile of debris that once made up the towers. Others called it Ground Zero. To those of us who were there it was a place of deep sadness and heartbreak.

Of the 343 members we lost, one hundred five of them were friends that I had known. In some cases for over twenty years.

(It is a certainty that I would have joined that long list had that Lieutenant not swapped the tour. Our rig was one of nine designed to pump water to the top of the tallest Hi-rise buildings. I would not have gone to the CP as he had, I would have grabbed a hydrant and prepared to use our high pressure pump for the fires. Then we would have gone inside as Eng-26 had done.)

At a small press conference Mayor Giuliani was asked if everyone had escaped the towers. As expected his answer was no. Initial panicked estimates were ranging as high as 20,000 dead. When asked about the losses he graciously stated, *our losses are more than we can bear no matter what the number.*

My group of firefighters reinforced with some on and off-duty guys were assigned to the Verizon Building on the N/E corner of West and Vesey. When WTC-7 collapsed sections of the building struck the Verizon bldg knocking large holes into the eastern face. There were four separate teams of firefighters inside the building using handlines in an effort to keep the flames from WTC-7 from entering those breeches. We remained on the seventh floor operating in the toxic smoke with no air masks for hours. (All of our air masks were buried with the brothers caught in the collapses.) I vividly remember watching the last rays of light fade on that ghastly scene, and knowing that few would be found alive.

From our vantage point in the Verizon Building we watched WTC 5&6 become total losses as their fires advanced mostly unchecked. We used one of our hoselines to hit WTC-6, but could not make much headway with a handline from across Vesey Street. Around 2230 hrs my group was relieved. Most of us were shot from the smoke we had to endure as we crawled around the past hours. After slowly making our way down the black stairway we hit the street and saw some headway had been made in darkening down the fires and in clearing the main intersection.

We hitched a ride back uptown and returned to the firehouse on W38 around 2300. As I walked up the stairs to the office a young firefighter followed. I could tell he wanted to speak, and we discussed how bad he felt that he was still alive. I listened to this young mans anguish as he described the days horrors. My advice was to him was simple, *we were not in the Big Book today.* You and the rest of Eng-34 performed as ordered, saved a few lives, (they found two seriously injured civilians on top of the debris pile near the N. footbridge), and put out a lot of fires. We both survived today because those other guys were the ones meant to die. They had been in the Big Book.

He seemed unconvinced, and I told him who knows Pat, *perhaps tomorrow you will be in the Book.* With that thought his eyes opened, he nodded his head and seemed more at ease.

Since our founding in 1865, the FDNY had lost 790 officers and firemen in the Line of Duty. During the past twenty years that I had been on the job we lost 44 additional brothers. In the FDNYs 135 years of service, that averaged to over six men per year. A high price to help your fellow citizens.

I continued down the hall going past the offices of Ladder 21 and Engine 26. Their officers were deep into duties I was glad not to have. Both companies were missing and presumed lost. Since Ladder-21 was not used in the Roof Operations they responded in as a regular unit. They entered the complex and were lost in the first collapse. Eng-26 was using their High Pressure rig on Vesey Street, and only the pump operator survived, though seriously injured. (Like so many others, he was never able to return to duty.)

A chance popped up to call my home and I spoke briefly with my wife and daughters who were stricken by the day's events. A minute later Battalion-7 called and wanted all of the members still on duty to go back to the WTC. (Hundreds of guys were waiting in the outer Boros, but there was no way to get them in.)

An empty city bus was sent to pick us and some other units up. We rode in silence along the darkened and empty streets. Along the way we saw squads of armed soldiers posted every few blocks. We returned to West and Vesey around 0030 hours and worked until 0830, removing victims, putting out fires and uncovering voids that could be searched. We were so exhausted by morning that none of us could remember what we did after 0300hrs, or how we got back to the firehouse.

Since my rig was one of 91 destroyed in the attacks, (another 100 rigs were damaged), *we worked on the pile for the next few days 24 hours on and 24 off.*

On the 15th an old, barely working wreck was dropped off for us to use. I formed two crews, one worked at the pile for twelve hours, while the other responded to calls on that pile of junk. Then we switched places. By the end of September a dedicated recovery unit was organized from the firehouses and the line units retured to normal duties, unless a KIA from your company was found. *It is a tradition in the FDNY that a fallen brother is always recovered and removed by the guys of his company.* We never got that call, because the 12 missing men from Ladder -21 and Engine -26 were among those never found.

The terrorist attacks on September 11, 2001 resulted in the murder of 2,753 people at the World Trade Center. That included those on the aircraft, 343 Officers and Firefighters of the FDNY, 2 FDNY EMS medics, 23 NYPD, and 37 Port Authority Police.

At the Pentagon 184 military personnel and civilians were murdered in that attack.

Flight 93 from Newark to San Francisco crashed at Shanksville, Pennsylvania when the passengers rose up to fight the hijackers. Just as they were about to retake the aircraft the scum terrorists flew the jet into the ground. Forty more died.

For just $500,000 in costs, the terrorists had caused over $100 Billion in economic damages, sickened forty thousand people, and ruined thousands of lives and families.

In all nineteen hijackers were involved, 15 of them were Saudi nationals. And as shown earlier, **Zacharias Moussaoui** was supposed to have been the 20th hijacker but had been picked up two months earlier. His replacement **Qhatani** had been refused entry in Orlando a month ago because an Immigration agent correctly refused him entry.

September 11, 2001 was an event similar to August 19, 1914, September 1, 1939, or December 7, 1941.
It was a crossover point that heralded war.

Those attacks would finally bring World War IV into focus, and Islamic Extremism was the enemy. Most of the world leaders which included George Bush, but principally Bill Clinton, had ignored the significance of the dozens of previous Islamic attacks throughout the past years. They failed to see them for what they really were, the opening shots in this new world war.

That same failure had happened in the 1930s with Japan's militarists invading Manchuria in 1931 and China in 1937, Germany's military buildup and takeovers under Adolph Hitler, and Mussolini's buildup and invasion of Ethiopia. Britain's Prime Minister Neville Chamberlain would be vilified for appeasing Hitler during his years in office, but he was not alone for there were many appeasers during the 1930s.

There was another one in the 1990s.

The WTC Bombing in February 1993 was the first major Islamic Terror attack inside America. **Those terrorists had tried to murder 50,000 people, and Bill Clinton did nothing.**

That June additional large scale attacks were broken up in NYC just hours before the terrorists struck, thanks to an FBI informant. Those attacks would also have murdered thousands, and crippled the NYC region. **Again the potential carnage from this well planned attack was dismissed by Democrat Bill Clinton.**

In the Philippines yet another well planned and violent series of attacks, **(Bojinka)**, was narrowly averted because of an accidental fire. Multiple thousands of innocent lives were spared, which included Clinton and the Pope. **Yet despite the arrests and uncovering of vast quantities of intelligence, which included the initial ideas for the 9/11 attacks, Bill Clinton did nothing.**

The two bombings in Saudi Arabia claimed 50 more Americans murdered with over 600 wounded. Clinton again did nothing.

The Sudanese had offered to arrest bin Laden, but they were ignored by the administration. Numerous intelligence and policy failures followed, and Bin laden escaped to Afghanistan, helping the Sunni extremists take over.

In 1998 the bombings at the U.S. Embassies in Africa went off with 200 plus murdered and over 1,000 wounded. Clinton wrongly sent cruise missiles into the Afghan camps, but warned the Pakistanis three hours before the launch. Word of the coming strike was relayed out and Bin Laden and his senior people escaped. Over the next months bin Ladens location was discovered a few times, but Clinton refused to act.

Then came the Millennium plots at LAX and in Jordan. Both were broken up just before those attacks came off, or else hundreds more would have died with hundreds wounded. Multiple attacks were being thwarted, but still Clinton did nothing.

Last was the attack on the USS Cole, with 17 killed 50 wounded. Again nothing was done.

As had happened in Europe and the Pacific in the 1930s, hiding your head in the sand did not stop the trouble,

It made things far worse.

Albert Einstein who escaped from the Nazi's in Germany said, *"The world is a dangerous place not because of those who do evil, but because of those who look on and do nothing."* *(195)

There are no negotiations that can stop or curtail this war against Islamic Terrorism. It must be fought with full intensity and effort to its terminus. **Either the Western Judeo-Christian world will prevail, or it will fall.**

For the Islamic Fundamentalist-terrorists the West must be destroyed, which means America must be destroyed. They despise our freedom loving way of life, and our loss of discipline and religion to guide that life. Europe is awash with churches and Cathedrals, but most are empty except for he tourists who crowd them to enjoy the artwork, not for spiritual guidence. One of the major reasons the Muslims believe they defeated the Russians was that Communists are athiests. They believe fully in Allah and Islamic paradise, while the people of the West believe in nothing. Those who are not slaughtered will have to convert to Islam.

Since 2000 there have been 31,000 terrorist attacks worldwide! In those attacks over 140,000 people have been killed by Islamic Extremists. Most who have died were Muslims who were innocent tagets or those who refused to convert. (In Europe thousands of attacks go unreported by the insanely PC governments there. Those assaults include gang rapes of uncovered, single western women by groups of Muslim men. No one is allowed to tell or report the truth on any of those assaults!)

During three thousand of those attacks a dozen or more people have been murdered. Europe alone has suffered 800 deaths by those terrorists within their borders, and another 1,100 who were killed in other continents. Recent attacks have used trucks to run over hundreds of civilians in Nice, bombings and gunfire in Paris and Belgium, and the Easter Sunday bombings in Sri Lanka.

Despite these viscious attacks, the liberals of the world continue to downplay the carnage. And that includes Hillary Clinton, Barak Obama and dozens of other Democrats. These inane liberals fight and complain of our efforts to prevent victory, yet they will be among the first who will suffer from those new masters.

A century ago Lord William Beveridge stated;

"Ignorance is an evil weed that Dictators depend among their willing dupes. But no Democracy can afford such a trait among its citizens." (195A)

As shown throughout these three books, no other nation on this earth has tried to help the rest of humanity more than the United States. And we never took anything from the lands and people we helped, except for one small request,

A place to bury our fallen. * (195B)

We are the standing power that the Islamists must defeat in order to create their worldwide Islamic Caliphate. Once we are gone none of the Western Democracies will long survive.

As was clearly shown on September 11, 2001, the long-lasting safety of our ocean moats was breeched.

We have to take the fight to the enemy's shores and defeat them and their radical ideas. Anything less will only allow them more time to strengthen and to spread. Our young people are the inheritors of America and our freedoms,

But only if they survive.

Over sixty years ago T.R. Farhenbach aptly predicted this assertion in his outstanding 1959 memoir of the Korean War, ***This Kind of War***.

" He stated that America would be forced to fight *Wars of Policy*, because the world seethes with revolt and dissatisfaction. Until mankind has freed itself from tyranny, greed and ruthlessness, war will always be close at hand."

"Although Military force cannot possibly solve the world's problems, without using such force, all will eventually be lost. However repugnant this premise is to the liberals of the world, it is also incredibly true. "

And the man who will go to the fringe to fight those wars, who will face and endure incredible hardships and death is still what he has always been, *He is the stuff from which Legions are made*." (196)

If nothing else remember this one phrase,

There are Tigers in this World, (2)

                            and They are Always Watching.

End of Book 3

Final Thoughts

Though some may discount these pages as too political or anti Democrat-Liberal, the historical truth is what it is, **the truth.** Through twelve plus years of research using hundreds of books, periodicals and documentaries, the historical record is clear. History is littered with mistakes, treason and tragedy, which have shaped our world more than our successes. It was not the citizen or common person who made those grievous errors, it was the politicos and bureaucrats in power. **And in the past century it was the Democrats who caused the most damage.**

Since the Great Depression the Democrats had become the majority party. They expanded governments reach into all aspects of our lives, even though it took away our freedoms. They relied on their "spoils system" to reward allies and punish foes. Patronage is their glue. Terrible mistakes by FDR and Truman created the Cold War, causing the trials that followed.

"Watching those years of failure, the Republican Party turned conservative, while the Democrats became more liberal and socialistic. Republicans repeatedly tried to warn the American people about the Democrats use and abuse of power. Democrats became addicted to power and control." *(198)

Their obsession was so extreme they stole the 1960 Presidential Election by stuffing the ballot boxes in Illinois and Texas. Richard Nixon was pressed to demand a manual recount. **The New York Herald Tribune was planning a 12-part expose on that fraud, which would have destroyed JFK and LBJ.** But Nixon wrongly refused both efforts, "for the good of the country".* (197) The results were the Vietnam war and all of the strategic and social problems that followed.

Even though he did not get the Republican nomination in 1976, Ronald Reagan exposed the Democrats as frauds and a threat to our society. Jimmy Carter's election in 1976 proved him right as Carter the Democrat's held all of the reigns of power. Those liberals made multiple, terrible mistakes allowing Soviet Communism to advance unchecked across the globe. And Carter also worked to help the Islamists take over in Iran. Despite the fact the radical clerics executed more people in one year than the Shah had in twenty-five, the liberals rejoiced over that innane outcome.

On April 1, 1980 the Ayatollah Khomeini controled Iran, and proclaimed that this was the first day of the government of Allah as all western influences were gone. (197A)

Islamic Extremism was unleashed upon the world. Israel was their main target, for their proximity, and for what they stand for, Western influence in a Muslim Sea. Soon after Iraq invaded Iran, and Russia invaded Afghanistan. Both events seriously curtailed the expansion of Khomeini's radical Shia Islam. Still millions of innocents died from that one grievous and inane decision by Jimmy Carter.

Watching the fallout from those disasters our people elected Ronald Reagan in a landslide in 1980. He stood fast to his ideals, and defeated Soviet Communism despite the eight years of Democrat obstructions. Congressman Jack Kemp would call Pres. Ronald Reagan the last Lion of the 20th Century". (198A)

His efforts to promote freedom also caused a growing revolt inside Communist China. Their hardliners observed the collapse of Communism occurring in Russia and Eastern Europe, and worked ruthlessly to stop any move towards Democracy there.

George Bush became president in 1988, but was unable to help the Chinese protestors in 1989. **Had they waited just one more year, Deng would have retired and moderate Zhao Ziyang would have been Premier. Those factors may have ended Communism in China too.** (Yet another tragic, What If.)

Though Pres. Bush stopped Saddam Hussein's invasion and takeover of Kuwait, in 1992 Democrat Bill Clinton connived his way into power. As shown in these pages his liberal and corrupt administration allowed the continued growth of Islamic Extremism which culminated in the attacks of 9/11.

It may never be ascertained what the real truth is on the deceitful Clinton Administration. After the September 11 attacks occurred calls went out to uncover the cause, and a "bipartisan" Commission was formed to investigate. Two Clinton lawyers were foolishly assigned to the case to keep things bipartisan.

Knowing that an in-depth investigation would be starting, **Sandy Berger, Clinton's former NSC Director,** and one of those deep in the decision making the past years repeatedly entered the National Archives while he could still gain access with his security clearance. Inside the Archives, Berger was able to operate illegally. **He worked alone in a room with the door closed. On each visit he was stealing and destroying dozens of classified documents from the files.** All of the stolen documents were vital to the work of the 9/11 Commission, and all of them were essential pages of the Clinton failures.

One of the senior workers at the Archives repeatedly complained of this illegal activity to his superior, who refused to stop Berger's actions. (That supervisor had been appointed to the position by Clinton.) Berger was finally caught outside the building with classified papers hidden in his socks and underwear. *Inanely Pres. Bush did not insure he confessed and testified on what he had destroyed, (or given life in prison).*

Instead Berger got a slap on the wrist as America and the world were cheated from the truth.

Only Fox News covered this vital story in a special report!

In 2006 a two-night documentary on 9/11 was directed by Cyrus Nowrasteh. Just before the film was to be released a private viewing was given to some of Clinton's former staff. The director of the film did not have an agenda, just presenting the facts they had obtained. When the Clinton people saw the show they went into panic mode and called the heads of Disney, ABC and the advertisers to have the show stopped. It was still shown on TV, but was heavily edited (to protect Bill), as that film highlighted two serious failures. Because of that interference, the original version was buried along with the evidence of Bill Clinton's failures.

Unhappy with what had been done to his truthful film the director released a short video called ***Blocking the Path to 9/11***. It highlights how the deep state worked to protect the Clinton's at all costs. Michael Barrone the editor of USNWR, (another former Democrat), warned Cyrus that the Democrats would attack him over his effort to get the truth out. (They did.)

Word however did get out, for on page 111 of the 9/11 Commission Report it was revealed that Ahmed Massoud's forces and the CIA team had bin Laden trapped, **but Clinton refused to allow the attack.** Another inexscusable failure was witnessed by Lt. Col Buzz Patterson the White House Military Aide. In 1998 they had a two-hour window to strike bin Laden. **Clinton refused to take the call from Berger because he was playing golf!** (When Berger testified before the 9/11 Commission he repeatedly lied about those missed chances.) (199, 200)

To help our anti-terror efforts the Republican led Congress had approved a new terror-court in the spring of 1996. The Alien Terrorist Removal Court was tasked with deporting suspected terrorists and their supporters. **But in the five years since it opened not a single case was ever presented by Janet Reno's Justice Department.** Or Ashcroft in the months after he took over.

Jaime Gorelick, who "was appointed" to the 9/11 Commission, was the Clinton Justice Dept official who wrote the legal blocks that prevented our intelligence agencies from being able to communicate with law enforcement during the 1990s. **That rule is what allowed 9/11 to happen.**

Throughout his eight years Bill Clinton refused to see or care about that truth of Islamic Extremists, and did nothing to stop them. Thousands died needlessly, and over 200,000 would die in the post-9/11 wars that did not have to be fought if Bill Clinton had done what the Oath of Office demands, his job.

Clinton, the world's most Infamous Appeaser and turncoat still lives a life of luxury adored by millions of dupes. Only time will tell if his treason will result in our deaths. (In the past two years Berger and Reno have died, and the truth died with them.)

George Bush decided that we would not treat the attacks of September 11, 2001 as a "civilian crime", this was War. Even the liberal media understood that fact with some of their headlines. Pres. Bush planned on treating any terrorists we caught or captured as POWs. Their treatment would be humane as always, but they were going to be interrogated repeatedly. Senior terrorist leaders would get extra treatment to try to get them to talk.

In 2002 the CIA hired psychologists to develop rough but humane ways to get those terrorist leaders to talk during their interrogations. Dr. James Mitchell was one of those psychologists, and he wrote an in depth book called *Enhanced Interrogation.*

One of the terrorists who was given the maximum treatment (of "water-boarding") was **Abu Zubadyah, al Qaeda's training director.** He had been located in Pakistan in 2002. After a short battle most of his assembledge had been killed and he was wounded. Thanks to the EIT techniques, Abu gave up the location of **Ramzi bin al-shibh,** the contact in Germany Atta had used.

Ramzi was also captured in Pakistan, on September 11, 2002 while organizing a new 9/11 type attack at London's Heathrow airport and buildings in their financial district. Ramzi was also questioned under the EIT tactics, and from both of those interrogtions the CIA learned where other high placed al-Qaeda terrorists were. Many were killed, some were captured.

One who was caught was KSM, Khalid Sheikh Mohammad. Discovered in Pakistan too, he was the driving force behind the **Bojinka and 9/11 attacks.** He was the one who had escaped from Qatar in 1995 because Bill Clinton refused to compel the Qataris to arrest him. He too gave up information.

During his "talks", KSM revealed that he was shocked by our aggressive reaction to the 9/11 attacks. After eight years of passivity and appeasement by Bill Clinton, America was striking back, hard. In just two months of fighting the Taliban were beaten and Afghanistan subdued. Al Qaeda was on the run having lost hundreds of their terrorists, supporters and followers.

Had Bush followed Clinton's failures with more inaction, KSM admitted that a second wave of attacks would have struck us. The U.S. war in Afghanistan stopped that from happening saving thousands of lives and untold suffering.

(KSM's original plan for 9/11 was to use ten airliners, and to poisonus us through our water supplies.)

Despite their imprisonment for life, Zubadayah and KSM are certain that Islam will eventually win because the liberal people in the West are weak and stupid. **America may not be in a religious war with them, but the Islamic terrorists are with America.** For them terror attacks against you are always good, and there are no innocents. Everyone is a target, including babies.

KSM admitted he dreamed of crippling America with large attacks like 9/11. But small ones such as the Beltway snipers Muhammed and Malvo did a fine job in terrorizing your nation. He admitted that the practical way to defeat you was through Immigration and breeding. We will come into your countries and expand our reach. **Islam will breed you out, and hide behind your laws until we are strong enough to rise up and overthrow your countries from within. Eventually America will expose her neck to us and be slaughtered.** *[201]

Abd al-Rahim al-Nashiri, the cell leader of the Cole Attack was caught in the United Arab Emirates while planning a kamikaze attack on another US naval ship. Abd also knew of a pending attack on our consulate in Riyadh, (which was not stopped in 2003 killing dozens), and an attempt to sink multiple oil tankers in the strait of Hormuz. They struck only once, and sunk a French tanker the *Limburg* in October 2002.

Another terrorist was *Jafar al-Tayyar*. With his US passport he could travel with ease as he surveiled numerous targets in the U.S., such as presidential residences, nuclear power plants, landmarks, dams, subways and bridges. Jafar was far along in his plot to attack the NYC subway system when he had to go into hiding. (It is believed he was killed in Pakistan in 2014.)

Hassan Ghul, a bin Laden courier and a link to OBL was yet another terrorist given up by the senior al-Qaeda terrorists who went through EIT. He too disappeared, but was later caught.

Pakistani *Saifullah Paracha* and his son Uzair were caught trying to smuggle in explosives they needed for their planned attacks on gas stations along the U.S. East Coast.

One *Iyman Faris* was planning to blowup the suspension cables on the Brooklyn Bridge during rush-hour to collapse it.

Another disrupted plot involved cell leader Hambali. He had led the Bali attack weeks earlier, and his latest plot was to duplicate 9/11 using *Non-Arab Student pilots.* His targets were the Library Tower in California, The Plaza Bank in Seattle, the Sears Tower in Chcago and other high value targets.

This latest enemy speaks in the difficult languages of Arabic and others from the region. That gives them a big advantage over the Western world. Muslim clerics recruit willing dupes from our prison system in the same secretive way they do in their mosques. They switch the sermons from English to Arabic so few outsiders can understand. As stated earlier, many warning signs were present before their prior attacks, but few could decipher the information. Arabic is considered a level 4 degree in difficulty, similar to Chinese. Add in regional variations and dialects, and this enemy has a perfect code for passing information. (Similar to our use of the Navajo code talkers in the Pacific in WWII)

The Federal Govt. should offer full scholarships to students to learn Arabic and related languages. Those students would then have guaranteed jobs translating the vast amount of material that is picked up to help us win this war.

The Islamic calendar is complex and different than ours. That disparity makes it difficult to converse or transcribe information accurately. And this enemy has differing names available because of how they use the compound name. With that factor they have numerous aliases already built in. The spelling can be differed by just a letter allowing even more name variations which vastly complicates our efforts to track and arrest them.

(Which is why it is paramount that everyone traveling be finger-printed and photographed into a scanner system.)

This enemy comes from a world so closed off and insular it may well be impossible to get informants into their highest circles. It took decades for law enforcement to infiltrate the Mafia. It may never be possible in this immoral world of Islamic terrorists. They recruit only their own for important assignments.

Their senior leaders are highly educated, and most studied in western universities. They know how to manipulate our liberal media and the dopey and corrupt politicians at will. Their financial capabilities are unlimited because of oil revenues, and expertly hidden within a maze of shell companies and "charities."

Since the mid-80s the Saudi's have spent dozens of Billions to spread their Wahabist Fundamentalist sect worldwide. They have setup their Islamic schools all over the world, and it is common to hear the most vituperative anti-America- anti-Jewish propaganda and speech from Arizona to England to Germany. *The Saudi's have been quietly waging and winning the propaganda war against the West.*

After the 9/11 attacks the Saudi Embassy demanded our State Department allow dozens of Saudi nationals to exit from the U.S. to "prevent any retaliation". Nine flights flew out carrying a total of 142 Saudis. **The FBI was not able to interview most of them, so no can say who actually escaped.**

The Islamists in our midsts use our freedom of religion laws to hide and shield their terrorist activity and fund raising. Saudi backed Islamists infiltrated the charitable sector by masquerading as philanthropists and clerics. They used and enjoyed our religious Tax-exempt status to escape scrutiny and move their funds around. And the deep pockets of the Saudi's are there to lend legal or financial support when needed. The true terrorist believers are not materialistic, they are spiritually driven. It is not possible to get them to help us by offering bribes.

Even though we had saved Afghanistan from the Communits with our support, and saved over 200,000 Kuwaitis and even more Saudis from Saddam's invasion, the Islamic extremists cared not. **They are determined to rule the world, and have worked for over three decades to set up their U.S and European infrastructure.**

Europe is now awash with Muslim immigrants and refugees.They will not assimilate, and thousands of crimes and attacks occur each year but are unreported by the media and governments. Barak Obama and the Democrats helped hundreds enter our country every month with no supervision or restrictions. Some towns in this country are now Islamic, even the street signs are in Arabic.

Americans must react to the threat from Islamic extremists by forcing the politicos to enact laws to protect us, and enforce the laws we already have to catch them. If you do not, they could strike a crippling blow the next time they make a major attack. They have the numbers and political protectors here to succeed.

All across the globe the terrorists have reverted back to small, simple attacks that are hard to stop. (Using trucks to run civilians over, small bombs, etc.) Their plan is to continue to attack and weaken the resolve of the masses. Their efforts are the same as the stages of revolutionary war used by the Communists.

Questions must be asked such as why do we allow Islamic schools and mosques to be built here while the Muslim world refuses those rights to Christians and Jews? The Muslim world routinely persecutes anyone not of their faith. If that practice is not stopped, then they should not be allowed to emigrate here to enjoy our freedoms.

Why are Immigrants allowed to keep their original citizenship and passports? As Teddy Roosevelt said one hundred years ago, if you come here to be a citizen, this is your only loyalty. Otherwise stay out.

The outstanding work *Infiltration* lists many needed changes;

All Muslim travelers must be profiled until the War on Terror has been won.

Islamic Charities must release all information about them, and must pass an annual forensic audit.

No Governmental agency or member should be allowed to meet with or be lobbied by any Islamic organization until the War on Terror has been won.

The secret twenty-seven page report detailing the Saudi government's support of the 9/11 plot must be completely declassified and read by the American people. Inside that report is clear evidence that Saudi Arabia is an enemy, even though we saved them from Saddam in 1990-91.

(Jean-Charles Brisard an investigator hired by the United Nations reported that during the 1990s Saudi Arabia provided over $500 Million to al Qaeda alone.) *(202)

No anti-U.S. clerics or agents should be allowed in this country. And none should be allowed to speak out against us. If they do they should be deported immediatly. Our Govt. needs to stop Islamic activism and all anti-U.S. propaganda that is being promoted within our nation by any group. If any of it occurs, the activist(s) should be deported and the facility closed.

No non-citizen should have any Top-Secret clearance.

China's famed military philosopher Sun-Tzu's first rule of war is to Know Your Enemy. Yet even after the attacks of 9/11 America's pathetic liberal political leaders will not confront the cold, hard, fact that Islam is our enemy. Because of their failed policies and beliefs in political correctness, there are few Democrats in our government who will admit to this truth. And those who try to bring this to light are hounded and branded by liberal activists and a turncoat media that perversely seek to destroy the very nation that has given them life.

These Islamic terrorists are driven by their faith that they must destroy the infidels and will be rewarded in paradise. For them this is the Apocalypse foretold in the Bible and by their prophet. **This is a war of religions, one that they expect to win. Americans need to accept that this war against Islamic Extremism will be bloody and exhaustive. Patience and propaganda are some of the main tools of the Islamic extremists, just as it was and is for the Communists.**

Al-Qaeda training manuals specifically counsel that patience is necessary to defeat the infidels. **Ayman al-Zawahiri,** the number two man in al-Qaeda preached that they are a nation of patience, and will continue to fight us until their last hour.

The planning for the 1998 Embassy bombings began in 1993, the attacks of 9/11 in 1995. They are a determined enemy.

In our Congress there are many in power who worked hard to protect their Muslim supporters. Cynthia McKinney was the biggest booster of the Islamic lobby, and profited greatly. Two of her donors were the terror suspects **Alamoudi, and al-Arian.**

Jim Moran from Virginia took cash from many of the same Muslim sources as McKinney. His district has a large Muslim population, and he worked hard for them. Other cash-flow Democrats included David Bonior, John Conyers, **Nancy Pelosi**, Dennis Kucinich, John Bryant and **Hillary Clinton**. And Bonoir lobbied to have al-Arian's brother in law Mazen al-Najjar released from jail, he is being held on terrorist charges.. Najjar had attended North Carolina A&T State University's engineering school at the same time as Khalid Sheikh Mohammed, KSM.

Hillary Clinton's efforts to accept money from a Hamas front was almost criminal. She tried to hide and cover it up, and refunded the money only after the NY press reported the incident. Hillary even invited Alamoudi to the White House for a Muslim holiday reception! While there he argued for Hamas, though it had been officially listed as a terrorist group in January 1995 by our own government! **As always the Clinton pattern of deceit was in high gear.** (Had she won in 2016 our strategic situation would be much worse than it is.)

Republican turncoats included Tom Campbell, Spencer Abraham, Dana Rohrabacher and Paul Findley. All of those listed accepted money from groups that worked against America's interests. And the Muslim PAC even worked on the Bush team to secure favor. During the campaign Bush repeated the standard line of no profiling and no secret evidence gathering! His campaign also accepted funds from Islamic groups. Just before 9/11, his advisors were working to stop anti-Muslim legislation.

The depth of the Muslim influence in our government is alarming and too lengthy to include here. For more information the reader is directed to ***Infiltration*** by Sperry.

Russia's Lenin had wisely noted and made use of a philosophy he believed back in 1917-18. For him it was the unseen changes in economics that led to the rise and fall of specific powers. If a nation underwent a steady economic decline it would be followed by erosion of that nation's military and political power. And that would lead to shifts in the world's political and military balance, shifts that could be taken advantage of.

It appeared to those of us who were living during the 1960s and 1970s that he was right. As a college lad I watched the news each night and could see that America and the world was collapsing. *Only the election of Ronald Reagan stopped that event by causing the fall of the Soviet Union.*

(A Gallup Poll conducted in February 2001 placed Ronald Reagan as the greatest president our nation ever had.) *(203)

The Cold War lasted 45 years before our victory.

This World War against Islamic hegemony may last 100 years, but only if the West has the fortitude to fight. *We lost more of our civilians on 9/11, than we did during the entire Cold War.* But many of the Western liberals in today's world already seek to surrender, to be nice and not offend Muslim sensibilities. What they inanely fail to realize is that if we lose this fight, most of them will be killed by the Islamists. Their westernized, liberal way of life will be ended, and after surviving many torments the few who survive will wish for salvation.

But if America is defeated there will be no savior.

Nowhere in the Western world is there any nation or group of nations that would work together to face and defeat this menace. All we see among the West's leaders are more Clinton-Obama clones, appeasers and cowards.

Our country is being overrun with liberal dupes and subversives who do not, or refuse to see what is coming. And America's education system has been prostituted by the leftists into a non-educating scam. Few of our young know anything of truth or of our actual history. I hope that those who read these books can remedy that treasonous failure.

> "America is the only country in human history that was founded on an idea, of liberty for all.
>
> This is our gospel, and it works.
>
> America is the most flourishing and powerful nation on earth.
>
> We are exceptional, because those brilliant minds of the 1770s created an unprecedented nation of free people from the tyranny of a Kings rule."

Charles Krauthammer (204)

The Revolutionary War was fought to create America.

The Civil War was fought to to save America.

The World Wars and the Cold War were fought to protect America, as is The War on Terror. (205)

But in the shadows a new war is being waged from within,

A War of Ideas.

Designed and directed by well placed liberal subversives and traitors, their efforts are calculated to destroy America, quietly.

Then they will control whatever remains, under their rules.

Our only hope is to vote all of the liberal Democrats out of poltical office. As shown by these books, they cannot be trusted with our childrens future.

In Afghanistan the terrorist jubilation over 9/11 had ended, and panic set in at bin Laden's camps. The Americans were invading, and what was worse they were winning. Dozens of Al-Qaeda principals scurried to find a place to hide as they sent their terrorists and lackeys into battle to postpone their defeat.

Days later al Qaeda terrorist **Mohammed Qahtani,** who had failed in his 9/11 mission to get in and join Flight 93, was sent to Tora Bora to fight the attacking Americans and Northern Alliance forces. He failed in that effort too, as he was captured and imprisoned in Guantanamo Bay.

Trying to stay to the terrorist cause he refused to talk to any of the investigators. But after ten months in prison Qahtani's fingerprints came back from a search of Customs records in Orlando, Florida. Investigators then realized that he had been the replacement 5th hijacker for Zacharias Moussaoui.

Inside a CIA black site staff received permission to use EIT, Enhanced Interrogation on him. **Qahtani revealed a name, one Abu Ahmed al-Kuwaiti, a supposed computer instructor / courier for al Qaeda.**

The CIA then re-questioned all of the prisoners they had, and could see through the prisoners attempts to shield and protect that potential suspect.

They hunted for that name for seven years, and finally got a hit on an intercepted communication. The message was speaking about a courier, a Sheik al-Kuwati. His position was triangulated and Abbottabad, Pakistan came up. Satellites photographed and highlighted a large walled compound on the outskirts of town.

Months of additional investigations and analysis examined every conceivable lead, written, personal, electronic and biological. They unearthed what was almost impossible to find.

At 0200 hours on May 2, 2011 **Seal Team Six** landed quietly by stealth helicopter at the suspicious site. They moved into the buildings, killing Abu Ahmed, a few body-guards and male relatives who tried to fight them.

Seal Team Six then found, shot and killed Osama bin Laden.

Patience goes both ways.

References

A Bright Shining Lie   by   Neil Sheehan
             Random House   1988
A Century's Journey   by Robert A. Pastor
             Basic Books   1999
A Fellowship of Valor   by Col. Joseph H. Alexander
    The History Channel and Lou Reda Productions
             Harper Collins Publishers   1997
A History of the Twentieth Century by Martin Gilbert
             W. Morrow and Co.   1997
A History of the Twentieth Century Volumes Two and Three
       by   Martin Gilbert
             William Morrow and Co.   1998
A World Transformed   by George Bush and Brent Scowcroft
             Alfred Knopf   1998
About Face by Colonel David Hackworth and Julie Sherman
             Simon and Schuster   1989
Above Hallowed Ground   Photos from the NYPD   2002
Absolute Power: The Legacy of Corruption
by David Limbaugh   Regnery Publishing   2001
Absolute Power   by Rush Limbaugh
             Hyperion Books   2002
Against All Enemies   by Richard Clarke
             Free Press   2004
Al Gore; America in the Balance by Kerri Houston
             & Patricia Fava   ACU   2000
Alien Wars   by Gen. Oleg Sarin and Col. Lev Dvoretsky
             Presidio Press   1996
American Jihad: The Terrorists Among Us
   Steven Emerson   The Free Press   2002

America's Secret War   by George Freidman
               Doubleday   2004
An Inconvenient Book   by   Glen Beck
Betrayal   by   Bill Gertz
             Regnery Publishing   1999
Beyond Peace   by   Richard Nixon
           Random House   1994
Beyond the Wild Blue   by Walter J. Boyne
               St. Martin's Press   1997
Bin Laden   by Yossef Bodansky
               Prima Publishing   1999
Bitter Legacy   by Christopher Ruddy & Carl Limbacher
             Newsmax.com   2001
Black Book of Communism   by   Stephane Courtois Harvard
              University Press   1999
Blackhawk Down   by Mark Bowden   1995

Blind Mans Bluff   by Sherry Sontag and Christopher Drew
               Public Affairs   1998
Breakdown   by Bill Gertz
              Regnery Publishing Inc.   2002
Chronicle of the Twentieth Century   by Time Life Books
                                                    1990
Clinton Cash   by Peter Schweizer
               HarperCollins   2015
Closing Pandora's Box   by Patrick Glynn
               Basic Books   1992
Cold War   by James R. Arnold and Roberta Wiener
               ABC-Clio   2012
Collapse of Burning Buildings   By Chief Vincent Dunn
               PennWell Publication   1988
Conflict: The History of the Korean War   Robert Leckie
               Putnam   1962

Danger and Survival by McGeorge Bundy
                Random House   1988

Days of Infamy   by Michael Coffey and A&E Television
                Hyperion   1999

Debunking The 9/11 Myths   Popular Mechanics   2006

Deep Black   *by* William E. Burrows
                Random House   1986

Dereliction of Duty   by H.R. McMasters
                Harper Collins   1997

Dereliction of Duty   by Lt. Col. Robert Patterson
                                                               2004

Devil's Game   by Robert Dryfuss
                Metropolitan Books   2005

Dictators and Double Standards   by   Jeanne Kilpatrick   .
                Simon & Schuster   1983

Enhanced Interrogation   By James Mitchel Ph.D &
    Bill Harlow   Crown Forum   2016

Energy   by   Carol and John Steinhart
                Duxbury Press   1974

Exceptional   by Dick & Liz Cheney
                Threshold Editions   2015

Extortion   by Peter Schweizer   2013

Farenhype 9/11   by   Dick Morris

Fatal Victories   by William Weir
                ArchonBooks   1993

FDR's Last Year   by   Jim Bishop
                William Morrow and Co.   1974

Fighting Back,   *Winning the War on Terror*
    by   Neil C. Livingstone and Terrell E. Arnold.
                Lexington Books   1986

First Due   by Alexander Donchin   1980

From a Dark Sky   by   Orr Kelly
          Presidio Press   1996
From Hiroshima to Glasnost   by   Paul H. Nitze
          Grove Weidenfeld   1989
From the Shadows   by   Robert M. Gates
          Simon and Schuster   1996
General of the Army   by Ed Cray
          WW Norton and Co.   1990
Ghost Wars   by   Steve Coll   PenguinPress   2004
Godless   by Anne Coulter   Crown Forum   2006
Guests of the Ayatollah   by Mark Bowden
          Atlantic Monthly Press   2006
Guilty   by   Ann Coulter   Crown Forum   2008
Harry S. Truman: Memoirs Vol. 1 & 2
          Doubleday   1955-56
High Crimes and Misdemeanors   by Ann Coulter
          Regnery Publishers   1998
History's Worst Decisions   by Stephen Weir
          Metro Books   2008
Holy War Inc. by Peter L. Bergen   Simon & Schuster   2002
Honorable Men: My Life in the CIA   by   William E. Colby .
          Simon &Schuster   1978
Incursion   by J.D. Coleman   St. Martins Press   1991
Into Laos, The Story of Operation Dewey Canyon
  by Keith William Nolan   Presido Press   1986
Into Cambodia   by Keith William Nolan   Presidio   1990
In The Arena   by   Richard Nixon   Simon & Schuster   1990
Infamy   by John Toland   AnchorPublishers   1982
Infiltration   by Paul Sperry   Nelson Current   2005
Inner Circles: How America Changed the World
      Gen. Alexander Haig Jr.   Warner Books   1992
Inside al Qaeda   by Rohan Gunaratna
          Columbia University Press   2002

Inside Terrorism by Bruce Hoffman
Columbia University Press 1998
Inside The PLO by Neil C. Livingstone and David Halevy
William Morrow & Company 1990
Invasion by Michelle Malkin
Regnery Publishing 2002
Jawbreaker by Gary Berntsen & Ralph Pezzullo
Crown Publishers 2005
Jimmy Carter The Liberal Left and World Chaos
by Mike Evans Time Worthy Books 2009
Just Cause by Malcolm McConnell St. Martin's Press 1991
Kennedy's Wars by Lawrence Freedman
Oxford Press 2000
Kuwait by Gustavo Ferrari Sipa Press 1992
Lies the Government Told You by Judge Andrew Napolitano
2014
Losing Bin Laden by Richard Miniter
Regnery Publishers 2003
Merchants of Treason Thomas B. Allen & Norman Polmar
Delacorte Press 1988
Military Lessons of the Gulf War by Bruce W. Watson
Presidio Press 1991
Miracles and Massacres by Glen Beck
Simon and Schuster 2014
My Turn on the Firelines by Capt. Richard A. Meo Ret FDNY
MRK Publishing 2014
Off With Their Heads by Dick Morris
Regan Books 2003
Power Faith and Fantasy by Michael B. Oren
Norton & Company 2007
Preachers of Hate by Kenneth R. Timmerman 2004
Three Rivers Press

Presidents Under Fire by James R. Arnold
            Orion Books   1994
Reagan's Revolution   by Craig Shirley
            Random House   2005
Reilly: Ace of Spies   Robin Bruce Lockhart   (1928)
            reprinted Penguin Books   1984
Russia and the West Under Lenin and Stalin
       by George Keenan   Little, Brown & Co.   1960
See No Evil   by Robert Baer   Three Rivers Press 2002
Shut Up and Sing by Laura Ingrham   Regenery   2003
Silent Warrior   by Charles Henderson
            Berkley Publishing   2000
Slander   *by* Ann Coulter   Crown Publishing   2002
Slouching Towards Gomorrah by Robert Bork
            Regan Books   1996
SOG   by John L. Plaster   Simon &Schuster   1997
So Others Might Live by Terry Golway   Basic Books 2002
Stealth Fighter Pilot   by D.M. Giangreco
            Motorbooks International   1993
Strategy For Defeat   by Admiral U. S. G. Sharp
            Presidio Press   1978
Study of Revenge   by Laurie Mylroie   AEI Press   2000
Sun Tsu's Art of War   by General Tao Hanzhang
            Sterling Publishing Co.   1987
Tactical Genius in Battle   by Len Deighton and
    Simon Goodenough   Phaidon Press   1979
Target America   by Yossef Bodansky
            Shapolsky Publishing   1993
Target Patton   by Robert K. Wilcox
            Renemy Publishing   2008
The 1950s   by Richard A. Schwartz
            Facts on File Inc.   2003

The 1993 World Trade Center Bombing by Charles Shields Chelsea House Publishers 1994
The Age of the Secret Terror by Daniel Benjamin & Steven Simon Random House 2002
The Base by Jane Corbin Simon and Schuster 2002
The Black Banners Ali H. Soufan W.W. Norton & Company 2011
The Blood Road by John Prados John Wiley and Sons 1998
The Brotherhood by Erik Stakelbeck Regnery Publishing 2013
The Building of the Panama Canal by Ulrich Keller Dover Publications 1983
The Bureau and the Mole by David A. Vise Atlantic Monthly 2002
The Case for Democracy by Natan Sharansky Public Affairs 2004
The Cell by John Miller, Michael Stone, and Chris Mitchell
The Death of Outrage by William J. Bennett Simon and Schuster 1998
The Devil We Knew by H.W. Brands Oxford Press 1993
The Devil We Know by Robert Baer 2008 Crown Publishers
The Enemy At Home by Dinesh D"Souza 2007 Doubleday
The Eve of Destruction by Howard Blum 2003 Harper Collins Publishers
The Final Days by Barbara Olsen Regenery Publ. 2001
The French Betrayal of America by Kenneth R. Timmerman Crown Forum 2004
The Generals by Thomas E. Ricks Penguin Press 2012
The Giants by Richard J. Barnet Simon and Schuster 1977

The Great War   by Jay Winter and Blaine Baggett
         Penguin Studio   1996
The Haunted Wood   by Allen Weinstein and Alexander Vassiliev   The Modern Library   1999
The Hillary Trap by Laura Ingrham   Encounter Books   2000
The Illusion of Peace   by Tad Zulc   Viking Press   1978
The Korean War by Max Hastings   Simon & Schuster   1987
The Linebacker Raids by John T. Simith   Arms&Armors   1998
The Memoirs of Richard Nixon   by Richard M. Nixon
         Sidgwick and Jackson   1978
The Middle East   by   Bernard Lewis
         Oxford University Press   1995
The Real America   by Glen Beck   Pocket Books   2005
The Real War   by   Richard Nixon   Simon & Schuster   1980
The Real Watergate Scandal   Geoff Sheppard
         Regnery Publishing   2015
The Rise and Fall of the Great Powers by   Paul Kennedy
         Lexington Books   1987
The Root   by Eric Hammel
         Harcourt- Brace Jovanovich   1985
The S&L Debacle Lawrence J. White   Oxford University Press   1991
The Timelines of History   by Bernard Grun
         Simon & Schuster   1991
The Vast Left Wing Conspiracy   by   Byron York
         Crown Publishing   2005
The White House Years   by Henry Kissinger
         Little & Brown   1979
Then and Now   by Tad Zulc
         William Morrow and Co.   1990
Theodore and Woodrow   by Judge Andrew Napolitano
         Thomas Nelson Publishers   2012
This Kind of War   by T. R. Fehrenbach   Brassey's   1963

Throw Them All Out　　　　by Peter Schweizer
　　　　　　Harper Collins　　　　　　2011
Treachery　　by Bill Gertz　　　Crown Forum　　2004
Treason　　by Ann Coulter　Three Rivers Press　2007
Triumph in the Desert　　Peter David　　　1991
Useful Idiots　　by Mona Charen　Regnery Publishing　2003
Victory and Deceit　by James F. Dunnigan and Albert A. Nofi
　　　　William Morrow and Company　　　1995
Vietnam at War　　by Phillip B. Davidson
　　　Sidgwick and Jackson　　　　　1988
Vietnam, Decisive Battles　　by John Pimlott
　　　Barnes and Noble　　　　　　1990
Vietnam: A History　Stanley Karnow　Viking Press　1981
Warthog　by William L. Smallwood　　Brassey's　1993
We Were Soldiers Once and Young　Lt. Gen. Harold G. Moore and Joseph L. Galloway　　Random House　1992
What If　Robert Crowley　Essays by Carr, Lucas, Ambrose, and Keegan　　PuntamBooks　　1999
Your Government Failed You　by Richard Clarke　2008
　　　Harper Collins

Periodicals

American Heritage Magazine
Atlantic Monthly
Fire Engineering
New York Post
U.S. News & World Report
WNYF
The Weekly Standard
Bloomberg Business Week

Video Sources

Afghanistan PBS		2001
Age of Tanks French Documentary		2016

America, Imagine A World Without Her
        Dinesh D'Souza   2014

American Experience: New York The Center of the World
    PBS & Ric Burns   2003

    Blackout New York 1977   2015

American Experience:

Harry Truman	PBS	1991
JFK	PBS	1990
LBJ	PBS	1991
FDR	PBS	1994
Nixon	PBS	1990
Ronald Reagan	PBS	2006
General Douglas MacArthur	PBS	1999
George H. Bush	PBS	2003
Gerald Ford	PBS	2006
American Vesuvious	PBS	2010
Archives of War		2006
Astro Spies	Nova	2008
Bin Laden	PBS	2002
Bin Laden; In the Name of Allah	A&E	2004
Black Hawk Down	The History Channel	2003
Blocking the Path to 9/11	ABC	2006
Blood and Oil	Mary Callaghan	2006
Chappaquiddick Revealed	Fox News	2018
Chosin	Brian Iglesias	2016
CIA Declassified	The History Channel	2008-14
Codes and Conspiracies	American History Channel	2016
ColdWar: TheSeries		2012
Evolution of Evil Series	American History Channel	2015

Faith of the Century, A History of Communism
   Patrick Barberis   1999
First to Fight: The Marines   The Military Channel 2008
Flight 800   The Discovery Channel
Fox News
Fox News Specials   Sandy Berger,   2007
Frontline, the Al Qaeda Files   PBS
George Marshall and the American Century   2007
Great Blunders of WWII   The History Channel
Hijacked   PBS   2006
Hillary's America   DineshD'Souza   2016
History Channel; A New Age in Terror   2017
History Exposed; Secrets of the Gulf War   2002
History Rediscovered   Why We Fight, the Series
                 Frank Capra   1955
Horror in the East   The BBC   2001
In Memoriam; New York City 9/11/01   2002
In Memoriam; The World Trade Center   2002
Inside 9/11   National Geographic   2006
Inside North Korea   National Geographic   2006
Iran; The Bomb At Any Cost   Newsmax   2014
Israel; Birth of a Nation   The History Channel   1997
Israel's War History   2009
JFK From the Solomon Islands to the Bay of Pigs
                History Channel   2009
JFK – A Legacy in Blood   2011
JFK'sWomen, TheScandalsRevealed   NewssMax   2007
Korea   The History Channel   2005
Last Days in Vietnam   PBS   2014
Lawrence of Arabia: The Battle for the ArabWorld PBS 2003
Lessons of Darkness   by Walter Herzog   1992
Liberating a Continent, Pope John Paul II   2016
Medal of Honor   PBS   2008

Title	Source	Year
Michelle Malkin Investigates	NewsMax	2019
Modern Marvels; Stealth Technology	the History Channel	
Modern Warfare the Series		
Modern Warfare; Iran-Iraq War, Russia in Afghanistan		2003
Momo, The Same Giancans Story	Newsmax	2007
New Age in Terror	NewsMax	2014
9/11	Jules and Gideon Naudet	2002
Nobody Listened, Castro	Nestor Almendros	1984
One America News		
Oklahoma City		2017
Panama Canal; Prized Possession		2010
Red Files; Secrets of the Russian Archives	PBS	1999
Remembering 9/11	Marilyn Higging	2011
Ronald Reagan, An American Journey	NewsMax	2016
S-21; The Khmer Rouge Killing Machine	Rithy Panh	2003
Saudi Arabia Uncovered	David Henshaw	2016
Sea Spies; Secrets Beneath the Waves	Robert Ballard	2003
Secret Sex Files of the KGB	Newsmax	2000
Secret KGB Files, JFK's Assasination	NewsMax	2000
Secrets of the Gulf War		1998
Seven Days in September		2004
Six Days in June	PBS	2007
Spies Declassified	The History Channel	2008
Stories of the SAS		2008
The 50 Years War Israel and the Arabs	PBS	1998
The Atomic Café		1982
The Balkans		2006
The Century of Warfare	The History Channel	1994
The Fires of Kuwait	IMAX	1992
The Great War and the Shaping of the 20th Century	PBS	1996
The Iran-Iraq War	The History Channel	1996

The Manhattan Project	The History Channel	2002
The Men Who Killed Kennedy	A&E	1988
The Nuclear Option	Nova	2017
The Road to 9/11	PBS	2005
The Saint of 9/11	Glen Holsten	2006
The Secret War Series	The History Channel	2012
The Tank Man	PBS	2006
The Vietnam War	The History Channel	2008
The Wall; A World Divided	PBS	2010
The War Zone: The Series		
The World at War	The BBC	1974
The World Trade Center Anatomy of the Collapse	Discovery Channel	2002
Triple Cross; Bin Laden's Spy in America	National Geographic	2006
TimMcVeigh, InDefense BillSieli	NewsMax	2014
United Flight 93 The Flight that Fought Back		2005
Under Surveillance	One American News	2016
Vietnam A Television History American Experience PBS		1983
Vietnam in HD	The History Channel	2011
Vietnam The Ten Thousand Day War	PBS	1998
Winston Churchill	The History Channel	1991
World War I	The History Channel	
Worlds Greatest Mysteries Series	Newsmax	2015

Source Notes

Page 9 Real Scandal xx-xxvi, 2-7

Pages 13-14 Then& Now 463-64, Useful Idiots 55-63, 64-72

Pages 15-16 Useful Idiots 49-51,64-71,75-76, USNWR, Then &Now 463

Pages 17-20 Vietnam Vizual Encyc. 184,390, Guilty 119-20, Gerald Ford; Appoit. With History, Useful Idiots 259, Breakdown 91,96,105-10

Pages 21-23 From the Shadows 64-68, CIA Declassified, Closing Pandoras Box 269-71, Useful Idiots 173-80, Then&Now 366-71

Pages 24-25 Real War 10-12,82, A Centurys Journey 33-34, Americas Secret War 6-7, Secrets of the SAS

Page 26 A Centurys Journey 152-54, Devil We Know 31-33,55-56

Pages 27-30 Memoirs of Harry Truman 242-44, American Jihad 229-30, Inside the PLO 60-62,65-83,150-53, Devils Game 108-122,131-32, Ghost War 77-79,131, Black Banners11, JCarter & the Liberal Left 131

Pages 31-33 Then&Now 370-75, Inside the PLO 82-84,94-99

Pages 33-35 French Betrayal of America 39-50

Pages 35-39 Deep Black 2-8,10-13, From the Shadows 62-6384-89,106-08,161, Rise& Fall of Great Powers 401-04, A Centurys Journey 118-23,154-55, Closing Pandoras Box 269-71, Devil We Know 135-37

Pages 40-42 Closing Pandoras Box 269-72, Devil We Know 135-37, Then&Now 47

Pages 44-46 Deep Black 19-20,57,174-81,185-92, Hillays America, G. Ford; Appot. History, Theodore& Wilson 17-21,58-6075-81,102-04,206-23, 227-29, Useful Idiots 85-89,99-104, Merchants of Treason 1-42, JCarter& Liberal Left 29-34,38-46

Pages 49-50 Useful Idiots 77-79, Exceptional 76-77, Vietnam Vizual Encly. 45, Closing Pandoras Box 275-80, JCarter&Liberal Left 52-55, Deep Black 225-30, From the Shadows 136-39

Pages 50-52 Blackout-NYC, WNYF magazine, First Due FDNY

Pages 53-54 French Betrayalof America 30-36,

Pages 54-56 Alien Wars 126-35, Closing Pandoras Box 286-89, Useful Idiots 104-06, From the Shadows 73-74,

Pages 57-58 JCarter&Liberal Left 54,57-61, Breakdown 63, Fox News-Chappaquiddick,

Pages 59-62 Power Faith& Fantasy 538-40, Devils Game 131-33, Then& Now 378-79,382-83, JCarter&Liberal Left 63-68, Useful Idiots77-78,81-85

Pages 63-64 Secrets of SAS, Devils Game 131-33,138-46, Then &Now 383-84, American Jihad 162-63, From the Shadows 77,82-83, Power Faith Fantasy 519-21,528

Pages 65 From the Shadows 74-80

Pages 65-73 Real War78,83-85,272-75 JCarter&Liberal Left78-84,95-106,112-123,127,130-32,136-41,163-65,186-87,211-13, From Shadows149-50, Inside PLO 153-55, An Inconvenient Book 40, Then&Now144, The Enemy at Home 68-95,97-118, Iran; The Bomb t Any Cost

Pages 73-74 Devils Game 191-201, Devil We Know78-80,

Pages 74-76 JCarterLiberalLeft90-95, Building The Panama Canal

Pages 77-78 Rise&FallGreatPowers 407-10, RealWar10, Then&Now385

Pages 78-83 JCarterLiberalLeft 415-16,454-55, AlienWars21-30,37-38,55-65, Devil WeKnow 14-21,29-31, The Generals330-39, UsefulIdiots153, Hiroshima-Glasnost 360,366-67, From Shadows108-110, Exceptional77-78, The Enemy at Home 195-207

Pages 85-89 JCarterLiberalLeft88-90,336-41,354-59,364,433, Then&Now 384-87,DevilsGame146-56,PowerFaithFantasy528-30,539-41,EveofDestruction, USNWR10/8/07,

Pages89-91 JCarterLiberalLeft 95-110,163-65,197-200211-13,225-29, ACenturysJourney 121-23, Then&Now388-90, ClosingPandorasBox 299-301

Pages 91-92 From Shadows110-13, ACenturys Journey 121-23, Then&Now 388-90, JCarter Liberal Left229-30,237-39,246-48

Pages 93-95 Black Book of Communism xv,xvii, Real War 121, Vietnam Vizual Encyl. 182,314,318,398, The Killing Fields, S-71, Silent Watrrior 131-32,

Pages 95-97 Then&Now 389-91,402-03, OffWith Their Heads 125-26, Beyond Peace 122-25, Vietnam Decisive Battles 186,188-90, Closing Pandoras Box 291-300, Hiroshima-Glasnost 361-63, From Shadows 119-20,123

Pages 98-103 InsidePLO 153-55, Devil We Know 11,34,106, JCarterLiberal Left 110, 153-55,167-69,174-79,219-21,239-41,249-51,253-64,270-75, The Enemy at Home 199-2011

Pages 103-04 French Betrayal of America 52-56

Pages 104-05 An Inconvenient Book 94-100, Black Banners 11, From Shadows 135-37, JCarter Liberal Left 95-99, 178-79

Pages 106-07 From The Shadows 123-26,143,150-52

Pages 107-09 Victory&Deciet 298-99, HiroshimaTo Glasnost 361-63,368-69, Closing Pandoras Box 291-303, Devil we Knew 159, From Shadows 110-12Devil We Know 156-62, JCarter&Liberal Left 98

Pages 110 Freeing A Continent, Exceptional 79-82

Pages 111-12, Real War 39, From Shadows 126-28,151, Inside PLO 156-57, Useful Idiots 193-95,205-06, JCarterLiberal Left 89-91

Pages 113   Real War 122,239, Then&Now 390-93, Devil We Knew 156-60

Pages 113-15   Ghost war 38-42,47-49,57, Real War 11

Pages 115-16   Rise & Fall Great Powers 423-26, In The Arena 52-53, A Centurys Journey 51-56,

Pages 116-19   JCarter& Liberal Left 266,270,279-81,289-93,297-99, Devil we Know 52-53, 59-61,77-78, Real War 38, Inside PLO 155, From The Shadows 128-31

Pages 119-27   Devils Game 125,252-55,260-69, Real War 38, JCarterLiberal Left 305-06, 378-84, 506-07, Ghost War 27-37,47-5266-67,79-81, Blacck Banners 22, Shut Up and Sing 73, From Shadows 130-33, Afghanistan, Devil We Knew 160-62, Closing Pandoras Box 304-05,

Pages 127-31   Alien Wars 120-30, Then& Now 390-93, Devil We Knew 156-60, Treason 157, Ghost War 92,97,100, Closing Pandoras Box 289-92, Devils Game 247-49, The Cell 130-31, Americas Secret War 7-12

Page 131   In The Arena 70-71

Pages 132-33   Devil We Knew 180-82, Hiroshima-Glasnost 364, Rise & Fall Great Powers 416-21, 425-37, Then & Now 360-62, An Inconvienent Book 100-01

Pages 133-36   Freeing A Continent

Page 136   Americas Secret War 12-13, Ghost War 82-85, JCarter& Liberal Left 401-06, From The Shadows 115-16

Pages 136-37   Inside PLO 127-28, The Cell 34-35,

Pages 137-39   JCarter& Liberal Left 305-09, 316-20, From Shadows 113-15, Devil We Know 52-54, Rise & Fall Great Powers 395-94, Power Faith&Fantasy516-18

Pages 140-43   The French Betrayal America 56-61,124, JCarterLiberal Left 282, Iran-Iraq War, Devil We Know 69-74

Pages 143-46   From Shadows 151-53,155-61, Then&Now 450-52, Useful Idiots 184-87, 195,209-13

Pages 146-47   From The Shadows 163-69, Freeing A Continent

Pages 147-48   JCarter Liberal Left 323-26,408-09,507

Pages 148-52   Days of Infamy 272-75, JCarter 329-332, From Shadows 190-95, Closing Pandoras Box 138-39,145-48,154-57162-71,309-11, Treason 165, Exceptional 43-50

Pages 152-54   Exceptional 43-50, From Shadows 196-98, Useful Idiots 195,204-08,217-19, JCarter Liberal Left 330

Pages 154-56   Exceptional 43-50, From Shadows 226-35, Freeing A Continent

Pages 156-58   Iran-Iraq war, The French Betrayal of America 63-71

Pages 158-59   Inside PLO 128-29, Freeing A Continent, Devil we Knew 165,

Pages 159-60   French Betrayal America 66-67,71-77, Power Faith Fantasy 528

Pages 160-63   Devil We Knew 165, Ghost war 57-68,89-91, Against All Enemies 38-39

Pages 163-64   Then&Now 362-63, A Centurys Journey 248-55,

Page 165   Devils Game 202-05

Pages 165-70   In The Areana 275-76, French Betrayal America 78-83

Pages 170-72   French Betrayal America 63-71, Iran-Iraq War

Pages 172-75   JCarterLiberal Left 284-85,397-99, Devils Game 127-29,162-65,169-72

Pages 175-89   Then&Now 144, Freeing A Continet, From Shadows 234-39,260-62, Closing Pandoras Box 313-19, Hiroshima-Glasnost 366-99, Useful Idots 141-43, Blind Mans Bluff 212-14,

Pages 179-80   JCarterLiberal Left 387, Inside PLo 129

Pages 180-82   Deep Black 286-96, From Shadows 244-49, Inside PLO 156-58

Pages 182-84   French Betrayal America 89-95

Pages 184-95   JCarter&Liberal Left 368-69, Inside PLO 21-25,83-84,129-30,140-41,262-65, 269-71, Devils Game 205, The Root 3-9, 12-16,23-29,33-49, Your Government Failed You 23-25, Devil We Know 60-69,75-76,213-17, Power Faith&Fantasy 533-35, Eve of Destruction Devil We Knew 165-67, French Betrayal America 100

Pages 196-200   Treason 160, Exceptional 43, From Shadows 256-57,280-81, French Betrayal America 97-101, Useful Idiots 107-09,124-33, Hiroshima-Glasnost 368, Ghost War 38-40, A Centurys Journey 11-12, Against All Enemies 47-48

Pages 200-01   Treason 160, Ghost War 69-70, Breakdown 127-28

Pages 201-02   The Root 53-57,70-75, Deep Black 234, From The Shadows 253-55

Pages 203-06   Useful Idiots 14,17-20,131,221-24, Blind Mans Bluff 220-21, Treason 165, From Shadows 260-66, Hiroshima-Glasnost 401-02, Closing Pandoras Box 328-29

Pages 207-09   Inside The PLO 265-67, Ghost War 98, The Root 77-83,93-95,110-14

Pages 209-210   Closing Pandoras Box 326-38, Treason 161

Pages 210-215   French Betrayal America 101-03,117, Devil We Knew 170, Treason 161,175-76,   JCarter&Liberal Left 468, The Root 93-95,110-14, 117-35,138-40,146-68,174-94,211-25, Closing Pandoras Box 334, Useful Idiots 124-26, From Shadows 266-68

Pages 215-219   Devils Game 184-89, The Root 200-24,227-29,248-85,288-378,381-82,399-419 French Betrayal America 100,   Devil We Know 11-15,37, Against All Enemies 39-40, Your Government Failed You 29-32, JCarterLiberal Left 468

Pages 219-222   About Face 818-20, Just Cause 204, From A Dark Sky 266-69, Then&Now 452-53, Treason 179, Closing Pandoras Box 334, Useful Idiots 187-93 From The Shadows 274-76

Pages 222-223   The Root 420-26, From The Shadows 289

Pages 223-226   Secrets of the Russian Archives, Closing Pandoras Box 332-33, Blind Mans Bluff 222-23, From The Shadows 270-73

Pages 226-227 French Betrayal of America 100-05, Inside PLO 274Against All Enemies 49

Pages 229-232 The Root 420-26, French Betrayal America 109-111, Inra-Iraq War, From The Shadows 293-301,304-08,311-15, Hiroshima-Glasnost 401-03

Page 232-233 Inside The PLO 311-15,130-33

Pages 233-238 From Shadows 319-321, Devils Game 277-79,283-87, Treason 160, Ghost War 69-70,101-06,120-23,

Pages 238-240 Treason 180-81, In The Arena 271, Death of Outrage 35-37

Pages 241 Inside The PLO 102-24, Devil We Know 43

Pages 241-244 Blind Mans Bluff 226-27, A World Transformed 3-5, Hiroshima-Glasnost 400-06, In The Areana 69, From Shadows 335-39,346-48,337-39,381

Pages 244-247 Inside The PLO 32-36,39-41,48-58,102-24, Devil We Know 78-80

Pages 247-252 Devil We Knew 184, Blind Mans Bluff 168-210, 227-29, USNWR 2/3/03, From The Shadows 327-28,357-369,382-85, Merchants of Treason 50-76,89-139,160,262-75,256-58,288-319,323,336-45,

Pages 252-256 Rise & Fall Great powers 488-502, From The Shadows 327-28,340-45,382-85, Useful Idiots 162-66, Deep Black 258-62,276-83,329-32,

Pages 256-259 Ghost War 3-5,122-24, Afghanistan, Deep Black 331, Devils Game 277-79,283-87, Ghost War 3-5,122-24, 131-35, 149-58, From The Shadows 346-50, Historys Worst Decisions 219-23,

Pages 259-261 Rise & Fall Great Powers 449-52, Beyond Peace 105,212-23,

Pages 261-266 Inside The PLO 145-48,239-47, 249-61, From Shadows 351-53, French Betrayal of Americ 123-25, Losing Bin Laden 5-6, Ghost War 136-43, Deep Black 18

Pages 266-268 Hiroshima-Glasnost 418-23, Then&Now 406-07, 454-56, Treason 177, From The Shadows 381,

Pages 268-270 Inside The PLO 143-49, Breakdown 91, French Brtrayal America 124-27, From The Shadows 353-54,

Page 270 Iran-Iraq War, Against All Enemies 42-43, French Betrayal 128-30

Page 271-274 Then&Now 480-82, Historys Worst Decisions, Nuclear Option

Pages 273-274 City For Sale

Pages 274-277 French Betrayal Of America 132-35,139,142-44, Hiroshima-Glasnost 422-438, Blind Mans Bluff 232-35, Useful Idiots 167-70, From Shadows381,404-09 Ghost War 158-60

Pages 277-278 Devil We Know 145, CIA Declassified

Pages 278-79 From The Shadows 390-405,408-14,, Ghost War 161-62

Pages 279-287 French Betrayal of America 140-45, Then&Now 456, Against All Enemies 45-47, Hiroshima-Glasnost 440-43, From The Shadows 383-89,421-23,427 ,430-31, Blind Mans Bluff 236-39, Freeing A Continent, Ghost War 167-69, A World Transformed 2-9, Deep Black 19-20,57,174-81, 332-334, Your Government Failed You 101-03,

Pages 285-286 Ray Kerrison NY Post, In The Arena 281-82

Pages 287-290 Devils Game 205-09, USNWR 12/15/03, American Jihad 28,62,81-85,109-16

Pages 290- 293 Iran-Iraq War, French Betrayal America 393-94, Then&Now460-61,464-65, Devil We Know 80-85,97-99

Pages 293-295 Inside The PLO 212-16,223-26, 235-37, Against All Enemies 50-51, Then&Now 20, Ghost War 178-79, Losing Bin Laden 10-11, Black Banners 44-48

Pages 295-298 From The Shadows 433-37, In The Arena 268-69, 281-82, Useful Idiots 83

Section 4 page 298

Pages 298-305 Ghost War 165-67, 172-79, 181-83,190-99, Your Government Failed 103-18, French Betrayal America 150-52, 157-58, A World Transformed 8-16,27-31, 134, Merchants of Treason 334-35, Flight 103, Losing Bin Laden 10-14, Against All Enemies 50-51

Pages 305-307 A World Transformed 94-98,105

Pages 307 Breakdown 88-91,94-95

Pages 307-311 A World Transformed 86-113, Liberating A Continent, Exceptional 85-89, Then&Now 126-27,144,292-94,465-67, From Shadows 438-43, The Tank Man,

Pages 311-314 Then&Now 409-414, A World Transformed 113-23,140-41, Liberating A Continent,

Pages 314-325 Then&Now 51,75,79,188,191-93,288-292,423-35,439-448,457-468,484-485,494, A World Transformed 14-15,36-39,46-48,51-54,137-39,145-154,159-165,179,183, From The Shadows 205-07,441-443,450-451,464-70, USNWR2/2/03, A Centurys Journey 108-113,229, Useful Idiots 179-181,233-38,

Pages 325-327 Then&Now 457-464, The Cell 50-52, American Jihad 28, Devil We Know 107-108,

Pages 327-330 Losing Bin Laden 7-13, JCarter&Liberal Left 399, Against All Enemies 52-54, American Jihad 62, Americas Secret War 16-17, Devils Game 287-292, The Cell 130-132, Ghost War 205-07, Bin Laden, Devil We Know 110

Pages 330- 336 Breakdown 115-116, Panama , Just Cause 29-32,52-72,78-91,94-110,120-132,144-52,205-217,238-240,245-249,251-274 Devils Game 29-32,42-43, Then&Now 485-490, From A Dark Sky 278-286,

Pages 337-340 A World Transformed 186-203,206-207, Power Faith&Fantasy 307-348,378-382

Pages 340-343   Ghost war 211-221, French Betrayal America 158-160, Against All Enemies 103,

Pages 343-346   Then&Now 42, A World Transformed 214-18,222-27, From Shadows 492,512-516

Pages 346   The Cell 52-53, Invasion 10, The Burea & The Mole

Pages 347-351   Devil We Know 187-191, Military lessons Gulf War 16, Triumph in the Desert 42-45, A World Transformed 308-313, Americas Secret War 19-21, French Betrayal America 157

Pages 351-371   French Betrayal America 157-163, A World Transformed 302-305,314-328,331-341, 344-353 A Centurys Journey 191-205,235-237   Your Government Failed You 95-97, Triumph in the Desert 45-46, Military lessons Gulf war 16-20, Beyond Peace 166, The Generals 371, Bin Laden, Losing Bin Laden 13-15, Ghost war 221-224, American Jihad 230, Devils Game 312-316, A Fellowship of Valor 370

Pages 371-372   Lessons of Gulf War 57, A World Transformed 362-368,377, Then&Now 22, 185, A Centurys Journey 157-160,174-76,

Pages 371-373   Exceptional 92, French Betrayal Of America 157-164,170-72, The Generals 372-375,

Pages 373-378   Invasion 12-13, 1993 WTC Bombing, Breakdown 27-28, The Cell 42-56, Black Banners 46-47, American Jihad 43-44,54-56, Enhanced Interrogation 8-11, Black Banners 46-49

Pages 379-408   A World Transformed 382-392, 403-419,425-427,432,437-439,444-446, 455-459,476-479,483, Devil We Know 137,190-94, JCarter& Liberal Left 385-387, The Generals 371-78, 381-384, The Art of War, Just Cause 276-278, From A Dark sky 289-295, The Generals War 381-382,442-457, Your Government Failed You 33, French Betrayal America 182-183, Americas Secret War 246-251, Linebacker Raids 204-210,

Pages 409- 416   Lessons of the Dark, Kuwaits Oil Well Fires, A World Transformed 489-492, The Generals 386, French Betrayal America 182-184, Against All Enemies 66-71, Your Government Failed You 97-99, A Centurys Journet 228-229, Devil We Know 101-108,172-173, Ghost War 226-231

Pages 416- 418   American Jihad 132-35, The Cell 57-66,196-199, Black Banners 47-48, Invasion 10

Page 418- 422   A World Transformed 497-503,509-512,539-545,556-561, Your Government Failed You 100-101, From The Shadows 510-526, Useful Idiots 114-117, Beyond Peace 43-55, Alien wars xii-xiv,70-79,88-118   Blind Mans Bluff 242-243,

Pages 423-429   Ghost war 231-235, Americas Secret War 27-28,31-36,46,54, 141-144 Weekly Standard8/5/11, Fighting back 141-143, Against All Enemies 52-54,135-139, Bin Laden, Losing Bin Laden American Jihad 138-147, The Cell 130-32, Devils game 289-292,

Pages 429   A Centurys Journey 59-60

Pages 430-431   JCarterLiberal Left 382-383, Alien Wars 129-134,

Pages 432-434   The 1993 WTC Bombing, The Cell 71-74, 141-143, Triple Cross, American Jihad 56-59,

Pages 434-438   Death Of Outrage 2-4,59-62,68, Bitter Legacy 193-94, JFK Mistresses Revealed, NYPost 7/28/93, The Hillary Trap 80, Guilty 33-36, Jcarter&Liberal Left 437,445,450-459,

Pages 438-445   JCarterLiberalLeft 263, 437-440,450-453, Devils Game 330-333, The Cell 75-80,82-86, The 1993 WTC Bombing, American Jihad 5-7,44-46, Against All Enemies 67-69, Losing Bin Laden 1-6,

Pages 445-449   JCarter&LiberalLeft 465-467, Death of Outrage 45-47, Beyond Peace 2-15,30-35, Theodore &Wilson 14-18, USNWR 10/2/2000,12/25/2000, BitterLegacy

Pages 450   Losing Bin Laden 1-6,

Pages 450-452   Against All Enemies 67-69, French Betrayal America 183-189, Losing bin Laden 25

Pages 452- 469   Losing Bin Laden 3-5,15-16,19,26-39,236-237, The Cell 89-93,96-113, Ghost War 241-246,255-256, Against All Enemies 73-74,77-79,   The 1993 WTC Bombing, Fire Engineering 12/1993, WNYF , Exceptional 95, American Jihad 28-29,44-47, Invasion 10

Pages 469   Absolute Power 1-38   In Defense, Tim McVeigh

Pages 469-470   Readers Digest 12/99 Bitter Legacy

Pages 470- 472   The Cell 111-116, American Jihad 43-51,121,142-144, The 1993 WTC Bombing, Invasion 10, Against All Enemies 80-81, Losing bin Laden 53-55, Triple Cross, Black Banners 48-51

Pages 473-475   French Betrayal of America 184-189, Against All Enemies 80-81, Losing bin Laden 53-55, Ghost War 262-265

Page 476   Losing bin Laden 36, The Cell143-145, Triple Cross

Pages 476-485   NYPost 2/3/1999, Absolute Power xii,66-69,74-82, Guilty 184-193, Bitter Legacy xi, High Crimes and Misdemeanors, Death of Outrage, Making Waves,

Pages 485-488   Triple Cross, Loisngbin Laden 38-39, Ghost War 267-269, Devils Game 318-324, 1993 WTC Bombing, The Cell 116-117, Breakdown 94-101, A Centurys Journey 228-229

Pages 488-493   Losing bin Laden 39,41-44,49-58, 61-69, Triple Cross, Fighting Back 144, Blackhawk Down, American Jihad 7-8, From A Dark Sky 308-311, Against All Enemies 87

Pages 494-495   American Jihad 7-8,136-137, Triple Cross, Black Banners 41-45

Pages 495-497   NYPost 1/13/1994, Bitter Legacy 15-16, Losing bin Laden 69-70,

Pages 498-500   The Cell 139-140, American Jihad 156-158, Ghost War 275-76, Losing bin Laden 17-18, Against All Enemies 90-92,96

Pages 501- French Betrayal of America 187-196, JCarter&Liberal Left 416-417, Beyond Peace 30-33, Treason 236-237, Breakdown 114-115, Betrayal 108-117,125-127 Useful Idiots 132-137, Weekly Standard 11/12/12, A Centyrys Journey 283-287, Infiltration 216-220, BitterLegacy 85-87, Nuclear Option

Pages 506-507 NYPost 2/14/94, Guilty 35-39

Pages 507-518 Triple Cross, American Jihad 10-14,52,61, The Cell 120-128,134-139 Losing Bin Laden 71-73,76-79,83-85,92-95, Breakdown 21-24,52-55,88-90,149, Against All Enemies 93-94,98-105,158-162 Ghost War 271-275, Off With Their Heads 89-91, French Betrayal America 6-9, 200-202

Pages 519- 522 Readers Digest 12/1999, Against All Enemies 98-105, The Cell 133,-138, Losing Bin Laden 89-91, Breakdown 52-55,88-90, French Betrayal America 200-202, USNWR 8/04, Blindmans Bluff 200-202

Pages 523-525 Oklahoma City Bombing, Tim McVeigh, In Defense, Against All Enemies 127

Pages 525- 528 Breakdown 25-27, Ghost War 278-279,511-513, Against All Enemies 97, Farenhype 9/11, American Jihad 16-23,

Pages 528-529 Venona Project, Black Book of Communism, The Haunted Wood, Treason, USNWR 2/3/2003, Codes & Conspiracies

Pages 529-530 French Betrayal America 187-198,334-338

Pages 530-538 American Jihad 62-63,120-123, Devils Game 324-325, Against All Enemies 138-141, Losing bin Laden 82-88,93-98,107-112, The Cell 144,148-150, Ghost War 318-320,326-327, Breakdown 7-8,55-58,

Pages 538-539 Breakdown 63-74, Ghost War 314-318,

Pages 539-540 JCarter&Liberal Left 453-454

Pages 540-548 Absolute Power 85-91,169-181,190-201,205-208,225-230,241-245, High Crimes & Misdemeanors 213-256, Death of Outrage 49-50, Bitter Legacy 3-4, 132-137, Betrayal 82-85, NYPost 7/30/1997, USNWR 9/6/1999, Making Waves

Pages 548-552 Your Government Failed You 200, Losing bin Laden 103-110,115-123, The Cell 151-153, Ghost War 321-325, Inside Saudi Arabia, Breakdown 2, USNWR 12/15/2003,

Pages 552- 555 Against All enemies 141-142, Losing bin Laden 125-126, Ghost War 5-7,281-284,283-295, 298-307,331, Devils Game 326-329

Pages 555- 559 Against All Enemies 101-104,111-118,141-142, Devil We Know 137,147-149, Breakdown 8-9, Americas Secret War 235-237, Devils Game 326-329, Black Banners 68-69, Losing Bin Laden

Pages 559- 561 Flight 800, Against All Enemies 121-124, Off With Their Heads 108-114

Pages 561-564 The Cell 154-165, Black Banners 25-37,67-69, Against All Enemies 147-148, Ghost War 11,366-367, Breakdown 10-12, American Jihad 144-145, Exceptional 112-113,

Pages 564-565   French Betrayal of America 206-212,259-263, Exceptional 113, Invasion 44-46, Bitter Legacy 94-100

Pages 565-568   Losing bin Laden 127-145,151-160

Pages 568-569   Against All Enemies 104-110

Pages 569-571   Ghost War 8-15,332-341,348-349, Black Banners xvii,13-15, 58-61, Exceptional 97-98 Losing bin Laden161

Pages 571-573   Theodore & Wilson 157-161, High Crimes &Misdemeanors 294-300, NYPost 11/2/2000,6/23/2000, Off With Their Heads 116-119

Pages 573- 580   Saudi Arabia Uncovered, American Jihad 31-32,80-108,183-220,231 An Inconvienent Book 40-47, Your Government Failed You 133-134, Americas Secret War 238-239,   Infiltration 87-92,212-214,233-237,249-251, Losing bin Laden 146-147,161,165,   Black Banners 69-70,   Ghost War 374-376,   Breakdown 15,28-29,96, Invasion 65-68,

Pages 580-586   USNWR 5/10/1999,5/25/1999, Bitter Legacy 13-14, Breakdown 29-30, The Cell 3, Betrayal 1-30, Off With Their Heads 110-114, Infiltration 238-245 Against All Enemies 129-131, Bureau & the Mole 180-191

Pages 586-589   Ghost War 359-360, Triple Cross, American Jihad 32-33,59-60,137-139, The Cell 194-204, Breakdown 16-17,   Black Banners 49-50   Infiltration 239-245,249-250

Pages 589-592   Betrayal 33-79,82-89,98-104, The Atlantic Monthly Magazine July-August 2017 66-77, Bitter Legacy 65-99350-362, Readers Digest 12/1999,

Pages 592-596   Against All Enemies 137-140,152-154, Ghost War 380-381, JCarter 445, Devils Game 329-330, Breakdown 53-58, The Cell 152, Losing bin Laden 165-166, Preachers of Hate 304-312

Pages 596-600   Betrayal 1109-149,158-205, USNWR 2/6/1994,2/3/2003, Off With Their Heads 85-90, A Centurys Journey 155-156,175-177,

Pages 600-603   Ghost War 397-402, The Cell 4,175-194, 204-209, Losing bin Laden 161-164,172-174, Exceptional 112-113, New Age of Terror, CIA Declassified, Triple Cross

Page 604   Slander 119, High Crimes &Misdemeanors 272-280

Pages 605- 612   Triple Cross, The Cell 193-194,204-206,212-216, Losing bin Laden 172-174, 177-188, Black Banners 85-96, 101-103,111-116, Against All Enemies 184-187, Off With Their Heads 69-71,85-88, The Enemy at Home 214-218

Pages 613-621   Exceptional 93, The Bureau& the Mole 187-191, Deriliction of Duty, Breakdown 94-101,129-131,   Your Government Failed You   172,219-222, Losing bin Laden 165-173,   Against All Enemies 200-203,209-210, The Cell 163, Ghost war 430-432,439-444,456-4562,466-471,476-479, American Jihad 38-41, 159-168,

Pages 622-627   Infiltration 135-140,233-237, 246-250,   Absolute Power 96-138,158-160, Slander 6,20, High Crimes &Misdemeanors 285-294, Death of Outrage 2-4,16-

17,49,59-60,73-82,84-91,95-98, The Cell 332-333, Invasion 21,161-162,197-201, Clinton Cash 12-14,

Pages 627-629   French Betrayal of America 216-218, A Centurys Journey 11, USNWR 4/10/99, Preachers of Hate 305-308

Pages 629-642   CIA Declassified, Black Banners 95-96,101-103,111-116,142-144, 150-152,260-264, The Cell 212-213, 224-226,270, 323-326,335, Your Government Failed You 165-167, Ghost war 480-496,499-503,506-511, Losing bin Laden 187-190,194-196, American Jihad 33-35,153-155, Against All Enemies 138,211-212, French Betrayal America 5-9, Breakdown 165, JCarter Libera Left 71-73, Weekly Standard 8/15/2011, Devil We Know 238-240,

Pages 642-644   Devil We Know 51-56,123-135,150-152,163-165,

Pages 644-648   Infiltration 100-102,106-132, 194-195, Against All Enemies 216, Triple Cross, American Jihad 35-36,59-60, Weekly Standard 8/15/2011, Losing bin Laden 199-200,215-216,233-238, Invasion 10-11, Breakdown 39-49

Pages 648-651   Ghost war 510-519, Against All Enemies 220-221, Losing bin Laden 201-205, Americas Secret War 143-145,

Pages 651-655 Losing bin Laden 213-221,224-226, The Cell 129,225-237, Infiltration 120-125, Against All Enemies , Black Banners 154-158,180-222,230-238, prologue, Ghost War 531-537, Breakdown 39-58,

Pages 656-664   Infiltration 120-125,141-143, Against All Enemies Black Banners 286-292, Your Government Failed You 167-170, Invasion 69, Sea Spies, Off With Their Heads 69, Making Waves 174-176, Death of Outrage 44-46, Bitter Legacy 272-273,281-295,302-307,325-326,330-332, Betrayal 100-107, Absolute Power 250-275, A Centurys Journey 300-331, Bloomberg Buisness Week 8/14/2017, NYPost 9/24/2000, USNWR 12/6/1999, JCarter&Liberal Left 92-93, Bureau and the Mole 179-182

Pages 665-667   Invasion 15,21-23,30,   Breakdown 143,   Infiltration 106-108,119-121,129,255-259,

Pages 668-677   Absolute Power 293-305,   307-331,   USNWR 8/5/2001, 11/5/2007,10/23/2006, Beyond Peace 174-178, NYPost 1/13/1994, Black Banners 358-364, Momo, The Sam Giancana Story, Secrets of the KGB

Page 677   Against All Enemies 233

Page 678-680   Ghost War 544-552, Americas Secret War 87-91, French Betrayal America 238-241, USNWR 4/5/2004,

Pages 680-681   Ghost War 553-558, Americas Secret war

Pages 681-696   Ghost war 559-564, Against All Enemies 230-235, Infiltration 127-131,175-177,191-195,239-240, Losing bin Laden 86-87,193-195,239, The Cell 242-245,261-262,283-301-305,322,   Invasion 33-38,45-55,63-68,76-77,162-166, NYPost 2/13/2002, USNWR 8/5/2004, 2/4/2004, Breakdown 31,37,83-88,131-132,146-148, French Betrayal America 6-8,221, Miricles & Massacres 239-252, Black Banners 248-252,

767

Pages 696   Ghost War 565-566

Pages 697-698   Infiltration 175-177, Ghost war 572-574 Black Banners 271-279, Americas Secret War 237-239

Pages 699-731   Infiltration 233-237, The Cell 8-15, Breakdown 139-141, Fighting Back 90-137, Collapse of Buring Buildings 136-142, In Memorium, 9/11, The World Trade Center, Fire Engineering Sept. 2002, NYTimes Magazine Sept. 8,2002, WNYF Magazine, Americasa Secret War 146-149, USNWR 10/8/2001,9/24/2001 CIA Declassified, The Cell 7-13, One America News

Final Thoughts 732-743   Against All Enemies 184-187, Fox News Specials, Blocking The Path To 9/11, USNWR 6/3/2002, 6/2/2003, Enhanced Interrogation, Off With Their Heads 96, Infiltration 128,263-294, Miracles & Massacres 239-259, The Enemy At Home 30-32,205-220, Enhanced Interrogation 70-79, CIA Declassified, Enhanced Interrogation 74-77,80-88,98-104,132-147, 161-164,178-189,194-210, 217-219, Black Banners xvii-xix, Infiltration

Page 743   Miracles and Massacres 239-259

Quotes

Quote	Page	Source	
1	6	Secrets of the Russian Archives	
2	9	This Kind of War	page 59
2A	10	Years of Upheaval	
3	14	From Movie Title, The Killing Fields	
4	14	Useful Idiots	page 62
5	14	Against All Enemies	page 48
6	15	Useful Idiots	page 49
7	16	Useful Idiots	page 36
7A	16	The French Betrayal of America	page 28
8	18	Guilty	page 119
8A	17	JFK's Women – The Scandals Revealed	
9	20	Useful Idiots	page 259
10	23	Then and Now	page 371
11	24	From the Shadows	page 69
12	28	American Jihad	page 229
13	30	Devils Game	page 131
14	33	Closing Pandora's Box	page 270
15	37	Beyond Peace	page 89
16	40	Closing Pandora's Box	page 271
17	41	Closing Pandora's Box	page 272
18	46	Jimmy Carter and the Liberal Left	page 31
19	46	Jimmy Carter and the Liberal Left	page 31
20	61	Useful Idiots	page 78
21	62	Useful Idiots	page 82
22	62	Useful Idiots	page 83
23	64	Devils Game	page 133
24	79	Devil We Know	page 21
25	83	Useful Idiots	page 153
26	83	Jimmy Carter and the Liberal Left	page 416
27	86	Jimmy Carter and the Liberal Left	page 90
28	88	Power, Faith and Fantasy	page 530

Quote	Page	Source	
29	90	Jimmy Carter and the Liberal Left	page 211
29a	93	Jimmy Carter and the Liberal Left	Fr- Flap
30	95	The Black Book of Communism	page xv
31	97	From the Shadows	page 120
32	97	Off With their Heads	page 126
32A	99	The Enemy At Home	page 207
33	102	Jimmy Carter and the Libera Left	page 260
34	102	Jimmy Carter and the Liberal Left	page 129
35	103-04	Devil We Know	page 11
36	104	Jimmy Carter and the Liberal Left	page 174
37	106	From the Shadows	page 135
38	109	Devil We Knew	page 159
39	109	Jimmy Carter and the Liberal Left	page 98
40	110	Jimmy Carter and the Liberal Left	page 276
41	111	Jimmy Carter and the Liberal Left	page 242
42	113	Useful Idiots	page 205
43	113	Jimmy Carter and the Liberal Left	page 90
44	113	The Real War	page 122
45	115	Ghost Wars	page 57
46	116	A Century's Journey	page 282
47	118	Jimmy Carter and the Liberal Left	page 291
48	119	Jimmy Carter and the Liberal Left	page 289
49	119-20	From the Shadows	page 128
50	123	Shut Up and Sing	page 73
51	126	Closing Pandora's Box	page 304
2	127	This Kind of War	page 59
52	129	Treason	page 157
53	132	Devil We Knew	page 182
54	136	From the Shadows	page 116
55	140	Devil We Know	page 54
56	140	The French Betrayal of America	page 124
57	141	ibid	page 124

Quote	Page	Source	
58	145	Useful Idiots	page 210
59	147	From the Shadows	page 168
59a	147	Jimmy Carter and the Liberal Left	page 329
60	147	Jimmy Carter and the Liberal Left	page 507
61	149	Jimmy Carter and the Liberal Left	page 329
62	149	From the Shadows	page 194
63	152	Shield of the Republic	
64	152	Treason	page 165
65	153	Useful Idiots	page 217
66	153	Useful Idiots	page 216
67	154	Useful Idiots	page 195
68	157	From the Shadows	page 194
69	157	Closing Pandoras Box	page 311
70	161	Power, Faith and Fantasy	page 528
71	162	Devil We Knew	page 165
72	162	Ghost Wars	page 63
73	163	Ghost Wars	page 68
74	174-75	Devils Game	page 171
75	182	From the Shadows	page 249
76	185	Inside the PLO	page 141
77	193	Devil We Knew	page 166
78	195	From The Shadows	page 256
79	195	Exceptional	page 43
80	198	Useful Idiots	page 128
81	198	The French Betrayal of America	page 99
82	199	Useful Idiots	page 129
83	199	A Centurys Journey	page 12
2	199	This Kind of War	page 59
84	203	Useful Idiots	page 14
85	203	Treason	page 165
86	204	From the Shadows	page 263
87	205	Closing Pandora's Box	page 329

Quote	Page	Source	
88	210	Closing Pandora's Box	page 327
89	210	Devil We Knew	page 170
89A	215	Jimmy Carter And The Liberal Left	page 217
90	220	Useful Idiots	page 193
91	236	Treason	page 181
92	242	From The Shadows	page 339
93	255	Ghost Wars	page 131
94	258	Beyond Peace	page 105
95	258	Ibid	page 123
96	267	From the Shadows	page 381
97	274	From the Shadows	page 409
98	277	The French Betrayal of America	page 145
99	279	From The Shadows	page 389
100	280	Liberating A Continent (video)	
101	281	From The Shadows	page 431
102	284	From the Shadows	page 385
103	287	Ray Kerrison NYPost	
104	303	Ghost Wars	page 177
105	312	A World Transformed	page 121
106	318	A World Transformed	page 183
107	328	Devil's Game	page 287
108	337	Power, Faith and Fantasy	page 330
109	337	Power, Faith and Fantasy	page 331
110	338	Power, Faith and Fantasy	page 333
111	338	Power, Faith and Fantasy	page 335
112	339	Power, Faith and Fantasy	page 348
113	349	Triumph in the Desert	page 44
114	349	Triumph in the Desert	page 45
2	350	This Kind of War	page 59
115	352	A Century's Journey	page 202
116	358	Military Lessons of the Gulf War	page 20
117	384	Sun Tzu, The Art of War	

Quote	Page	Source	
118	391	*A World Transformed*	page 457
119	413	*The Generals*	page 386
120	421	*Beyond Peace*	page 55
121	421	*Beyond Peace*	page 55
122	422	*Useful Idiots*	page 114
123	423	*Alien Wars*	page xiii
124	424	*Ghost Wars*	page 233
125	425	*Americas Secret War*	page 28
126	437	*Death of Outrage*	page 68
127	437	*Jimmy Carter and the Liberal Left*	page 437
128	438	*Jimmy Carter and the Liberal Left*	page 450
129	439	*Jimmy Carter and the Liberal Left*	page 263
130	445	*Death of Outrage*	page 47
131	447	*Beyond Peace*	page 8
132	447	Ibid	page 8
133	447	Ibid	page 9
134	448	Ibid	page 9
135	448	Ibid	page 33
2	450	*This Kind of War*	page 59
136A	457	*The World Trade Center* video	
136	485	*Bitter Legacy*	page xi
137	487	*Devils Game*	page 320
138	493	*Losing Bin Laden*	page 67
139	501	*Against All Enemies*	page 92
140	505	*Betrayal*	page 127
141	508	*American Jihad*	page 14
142	515	*Ghost Wars*	page 271
142A	517	*The French Betrayal of America*	page 7
143A	521	*The Cell*	page 134
143	525	*Ghost Wars*	page 278
144	526	*Ghost Wars*	page 279
145	530	*Devils Game*	page 324

Quote	Page	Source	
146	537	*Ghost Wars*	page 318
147	541	*Jimmy Carter and the Liberal Left*	page 453
148	548	*Losing Bin Laden*	page 110
149	550	*Losing Bin Laden*	page 105
150	552	*Losing Bin Laden*	page 105
151	553	*Ghost Wars*	page 307
152	555	*Ghost Wars*	page 305
153	564	*Invasion*	page 46
154	568	*Exceptional*	page 98
155	568	*Black Banners*	page 15
156	569	*Ghost Wars*	page 15
157	569	*Ghost Wars*	page 14
158	569	*Ghost Wars*	page 15
159	571	*Off With Their Heads*	page 117
160	573	*Saudi Arabia Uncovered* (video)	2016
161	576	*Losing Bin Laden*	page 147
161A	577	*Breakdown*	pages 28-29
162 A	581	*The Cell*	page 3
162	584	*Against All Enemies*	page 130
163	591	*Jimmy Carter and the Liberal Left*	page 445
164	595	*Betrayal*	page 137
165	596	*Betrayal*	page 129
166	596	*A Great Shining Lie*	
167	599	*Betrayal*	page 188
168	603	*Slander*	page 119
168A	605	*The Cell*	page 194
169	609	*The Cell*	page 213
170	609	*The Cell*	page 215
171	611	*Losing Bin Laden*	page 181
172	614	*Jawbreaker*	page 33
173	615	*Ghost Wars*	page 442
174	619	*American Jihad*	page 167

Quote	Page	Source	
175	629	Your Government Failed You	page 167
176	636	Ghost Wars	page 485
177	648	Against All Enemies	page 221
178	649	Ghost Wars	page 530
178A	652	The Cell	page 333
179	659	Jimmy Carter and the Liberal Left	page 453
179A	659	Jimmy Carter And The Liberal Left	page 92
180	663	Invasion	page 21
181	664	Invasion	page 15
182	672	Slander	page 152
183	672	Slander	page 11
184	679	Ghost Wars	page 555
185	681	Infiltration	pages 191-93
186	683	Invasion	pages 35-38
187	684	Invasion	page 165
188	686	Ghost Wars	
188A	686	US News & World Report	2/04/2004
189A	687	US News & World Report	2/04/2004
189	687	US News & World Report	2/04/2004
190	688	Invasion	pages 65-66
191	688	The Cell	pages 294-95
192	688	The Cell	page 295-96
193	689	America's Secret War	page 2
193A	692	Miricles and Massacres	page 239-40
194	697	America's Secret War	page 2
194A	718	Fire Engineering September 2002	page 15
195	729	Jimmy Carter and the Liberal Left	page 445
195B	730	Hillary's America (video)	2016
195A	730	Jawbreaker	page 311
196	731-32	This Kind of War	pages 59-84
2	732	This Kind of War	pages 59-84
197A	732	Jimmy Carter And The Liberal Left	page 15

Quote	Page	Source	
197	732	*The New York Post*	10/10/2000
198	732	*Reagan's Revolution*	page xxvii
198A	733	*Reagan's Revolution*	page 346
199	734	*Bllocking the Path To 9/11*	
200	734	*Jawbreaker*	page 211
201	736	*Enhanced Interrogation*	pages 189, 216
202	739	*Saudi Arabia Uncovered* (video)	2016
203	741	*Slander*	page 134
204	742	Charles Krauthammer	
205	742	Dinesh D'Souza	

Index

al Banshiri, Abu Ubaidah 489,494,560-61,587-88

Alamoudi, Abdurrahman 573-74,625,735-36

al-Arian, Sami 290,472,536,735-36

al-Assad, Hafez 31-32, 62,74, 166, 187, 192, 203, 222, 263, 280, 314, 359, 380,

al-Fawwaz, Khaled 494, 562, 586-87, 600, 608, 616-17, 633

al-Fadl, Jamal 494, 560-64, 577, 585-86

al-Haj, Wadi 289, 416, 493-94, 561, 585-88, 594, 600, 604-05, 608

al-Mihdhar, Khalid 629-30, 636-38, 655-56, 666, 683, 688, 694-95

al-Turabi, Hassan 423-25, 526, 530, 549, 565

al-Zawahiri, Ayman 175, 314, 328, 474, 489, 531, 534-35, 557-63, 593, 600, 608-10, 640, 654, 697, 737

Andropov, Yuri 111, 114, 198, 206, 210-11, 215, 223, 229, 243, 247, 253, 271-72

Arafat, Yassir 28-32, 90-91, 98, 112, 119, 187-92, 233, 245, 261-62, 280, 288, 414, 424, 486, 538-39

Atta, Mohammed 516, 620, 685, 692-93, 696, 698, 700

Awalaki, Anwar 632, 656, 666, 683

Azzam, Abdullah 173-75, 288-89, 314, 328-29, 365, 377, 415-16, 424, 433, 440, 560, 574, 697

Berger, Sandy 546, 553, 565-66, 576-77, 609-10, 613, 617-18, 653,662, 731-32

bin Laden, Osama 29, 63, 120, 124, 136-37, 162, 237, 259, 268, 289, 328-30, 341, 363, 372, 376, 415-17, 423-28, 433, 440-41, 449-52, 461-62, 465-68, 473-74, 484, 488-90, 493-500, 506-08, 514-17, 522, 525, 530-37, 546-54, 557-66, 568-70, 574-77, 585-88, 592-94, 599-623, 628-41, 644-55, 677-85, 689-93, 696-98, 721, 728-31

Brezhnev, Leonid 36, 40, 53, 61, 128-29, 147, 152, 161, 182, 198, 200, 210, 253, 260, 311, 321

Bush Sr., George 37, 50, 132, 148, 160, 170, 203, 229, 242, 285, 297-301, 303-19, 324, 327-330, 343, 348-66, 368-71, 374-75, 378-83, 389-90, 394-97, 400-21, 427-31, 445-51, 472-74, 477, 487-90, 496, 515, 550, 566, 571, 623

Bush, George 585, 601, 611, 625, 642-43, 663-65, 672--81, 687-92, 698, 719-20, 725-27, 731-33, 736

Carter, Jimmy   32, 43-50, 52-65, 67-78, 82-86, 89-93, 96-115, 117-23, 126-33, 137-41, 144-49, 153, 155, 161-64, 177, 194, 202, 210, 227, 236, 246, 277, 293, 296, 302, 315, 331-32, 349-50, 355, 366, 380, 411, 429, 438, 444-47, 453, 464, 473, 477, 485-86, 493, 501-03, 530, 537, 597, 623, 639, 659-62, 667-68, 727-28, 737

Casey, William   Director CIA   156, 163, 170, 183, 205-07, 230-35, 241, 257, 263, 279

Castro, Fidel   20-23, 55, 83, 107, 111-12, 144-45, 152, 181, 221, 302, 316, 325, 328, 331, 667-68, 675

Clarke, Richard   201, 499, 507, 512-19, 523, 536, 567-68, 575, 584, 602-04, 610, 613, 618-19, 630, 633, 637-39, 645-49, 653, 677-82, 688, 691-92, 700

Clinton, Bill   3, 5, 20, 49, 61, 411, 434-36, 441, 444-49, 452-53, 460-69, 472-89, 492-508, 510-24, 530-46, 548-59, 562-85, 588-92, 595-604, 607-29, 631-35, 638-68, 671-81, 685-92, 699-701, 710, 720-21, 727-33

Emerson, Steve   433-44, 493, 506-07, 521, 524-27, 535-36, 581, 584

Fazul, Haroun   586-87, 605, 607

Ford, Gerald   9, 13-22, 33-52, 54, 89, 105-06, 241, 298, 300, 322, 570, 580, 623

Foster, Vincent   479-84, 495, 540, 571

Gorbachev, Michel   187, 206, 242-44, 252-53, 256, 266, 272, 275-76, 280-87, 299-300, 303, 306-18, 321-27, 330, 337, 343-46, 368, 371-72, 389, 394, 418-22, 445

Huang, John   541-45, 550-51, 672

Hussein, Saddam   34-35, 66, 91, 104, 141-44, 158, 171-73, 181, 203, 217, 230, 233, 260, 270, 274, 293, 301, 314, 330, 341-42, 347-51, 356-74, 378-86, 389-414, 423-24, 442, 445, 450-51, 468, 472-73, 501, 519-20, 528-29, 563, 571, 585, 599-601, 613-14, 642—45, 681, 735

Ijaz, Mansour   564-66, 576-77, 632

Jaruleski, General Wojciech   155, 176, 282

Johnson, Lyndon LBJ   8, 36, 45-47, 53, 366, 627, 669-71

Kennedy, John JFK   17-20, 53, 64, 129, 152, 435, 471, 492, 674

Khalifa, Mohammed Jamal   426, 497, 507-08, 511

Khomeini, Ayatollah   29, 70-73, 89-93, 98-03, 109-113, 117-120, 125-27, 141-43, 172-75, 190, 213, 292-93, 311, 424, 438, 675, 727

Massoud, Ahmed Shah   235, 256-58, 301, 313, 329, 415, 422, 551, 568-70, 602, 616-20, 631, 639-41, 647-48, 655, 679-81, 695-98, 731

Mohamed, Ali   377, 432,-33, 474, 484, 488, 493-94, 506, 585-87, 594,

605, 616, 628, 634, 644, 650, 666

Mugniyah, Imad Fayez   190, 193-95, 237, 245, 265, 291, 535, 641, 644

Salameh, Mohammed   326, 376-77, 416, 441-42, 454, 464-65, 471, 487, 514

Mohammed, Khalid sheik, (KSM)   426, 467, 508-09, 514, 523, 532-33, 572, 594, 621, 685, 694, 696, 721, 732, 736

Moussaoui, Zacarias   638, 666, 689-93, 696-97, 727, 739

Mubarak, Hosni   175, 278, 314, 342, 347-49, 359, 364, 375, 425, 434, 438, 466, 470, 473, 485-86, 517, 529-30, 536, 554, 591

Murad, Abdul Hakim   507-14, 525, 568, 583

Nidal, Abu   180, 216, 246, 262-65, 268-70, 277-78, 293-94

Nitze, Paul   108-09, 177, 275

Nixon, Richard   8-9, 15-19, 25, 33-40, 44, 48-49, 53-54, 60, 64-68, 87, 105-06, 123, 127, 132, 149, 152-53, 161, 173, 193, 198, 254, 260, 268, 274, 278, 297-300, 312, 354, 375, 388, 419-20, 446-48, 471, 477, 502, 527, 622-23, 670, 674, 679, 720

Nosair, Sayeed   326-27, 346, 375-78, 416-17, 432-34, 440, 445-47, 470-471

Omar, Mullah Mohammed   552, 557, 576, 600, 640-41, 678, 696

Pope John Paul II   111, 134-35, 156-57, 197, 282, 308, 510-12

Prince Turki al-Faisal   30, 121, 124, 136, 259, 330, 415, 534, 556, 600, 696

Qaddafi, Momar   62, 91, 155, 159, 203, 213, 237, 243, 265, 269 280, 675

Reagan, Ronald   43, 83, 109, 132-33, 139, 148-63, 166-73, 176-90, 193-219, 221-43, 251-56, 260-70, 273-90, 296-307, 314-18, 329-31, 344-46, 350, 355, 358, 364-66, 382, 385, 390, 407, 420, 426, 429, 436, 441, 446, 453, 458, 462, 474-77, 483-85, 492, 496, 503, 507, 538, 548, 589, 594, 615, 623, 653, 657, 713, 728, 737

Reno, Janet   468, 480-83, 495, 499, 540-41, 545, 580-81, 5585, 622, 655, 659, 675, 732

Riady, James   541, 672

Sadat, Anwar   60, 86-89, 93, 120, 132, 138, 173-75, 328, 364, 414, 432-33, 438, 471, 485, 681, 728

Salem, Emad   433-34, 440, 443-44, 464-66, 469-71

Schultz, George   Sec. State   194, 197, 215-16, 226, 230-32, 242-44, 253, 276, 281-83, 296, 302, 329

Schwarzkopf, General Norman   360-61, 365-67, 370, 374, 379-86, 390, 393-99, 403-06, 521

Shah Mohammed Reza Pahlavi   25, 29, 49, 65-74, 85, 89-93, 99-105, 110, 117-19, 124-27, 132, 138, 141-42, 173-75, 293, 342, 356, 429, 438, 473, 552, 555, 639, 682, 737

Shalabi, Mustafa   326-27, 377, 415-16, 432-33, 442, 532, 560

Sheikh Omar Abdul- Rahman   175, 290, 377, 416, 432, 438-39, 454, 465, 469, 475, 486, 526, 536, 562, 618, 656

Somoza, Anastasio   20, 49, 57, 71, 85-86, 106, 111-13, 146, 204

Starr, Kenneth   539-40, 622-23

Tenet, George   538, 585, 592, 599, 609, 615, 628, 633, 636-37, 649-50, 677, 686, 697

Thatcher, Margaret   116, 155-57, 183-84, 221, 224, 299, 312, 324, 337, 352, 357-59, 363-64, 378, 406, 419

Truman, Harry   5-7, 17, 20, 26, 67, 79-80, 85, 106-08, 135, 150-54, 180, 305-06, 312, 354, 435, 445, 463, 485-87, 496, 502, 527-30, 545, 661, 669

ul-Haq, Mohammed Zia   122-26, 131, 162-64, 234, 277, 294, 301, 304, 428-29

Walesa, Lech   39, 136, 147, 156, 176, 238, 315, 373

Wilson, Woodrow   45-47, 133, 338-40, 354, 448, 669

Woolsey, James   453, 462-63, 485-86, 498, 518-19, 537, 624, 648, 657

Xiaoping, Deng   96, 145, 259-60, 305-09, 353

Yousef, Ramzi   289, 426, 441, 453, 462, 465-67, 471, 497, 507, 511, 523-25, 532, 559, 562, 583, 600, 638

Locations and Events

Afghanistan   61, 73, 77, 91, 114-15, 123-32, 136, 141, 161-63, 174, 187, 198, 201, 204, 212, 221, 234-35, 239, 243, 253, 256-58, 276-77, 283, 285, 288-89, 294, 300-06, 311-14, 324-30, 333, 340-41, 363, 366, 372, 415-16, 421-29, 433, 439-42, 446, 450-54, 474, 498-99, 510, 516, 520, 524, 535, 547-53, 556-61, 569-70, 573, 586, 592, 595, 600-05, 608-20, 624, 628, 631, 634-41, 645-50, 653-55, 678-82, 686, 689, 693-97, 721, 128, 733, 739

Angola   21-23, 40, 56, 61, 78, 128, 201, 232, 239, 243-44, 258, 298-96, 311, 314, 324, 627

Baltic States   312, 343-44, 371-72, 420

Bulgaria   156, 181, 319-320

Chad   62, 203, 213, 237, 243, 279-80, 327

Chechnya   426, 500, 529, 558, 679-80, 691, 720

Croatia   373, 430-32, 500, 532, 550-51, 627

Cuba   17-23, 36, 40, 55-57, 60-65, 76-78, 83-85, 98-100, 107, 111-13, 127-28, 144-46, 151-52, 155, 161, 178, 181, 187, 212, 219-22, 232, 243, 258, 267, 284, 295-96, 302, 314, 324-25, 331-36, 352-53, 414, 429, , 446, 492, 658, 667-68

Czechoslovakia   31, 125, 160-62, 308, 311, 320-21, 371, 379, 422, 533, 645, 681

Egypt   8, 27-29, 57, 60-64, 74, 86-89, 93, 99, 120, 129-32, 138-40, 162-64, 173-75, 187-89, 193, 203, 223, 261-65, 278-80, 288-90, 314, 328, 341, 347-49, 359, 362-66, 373-77, 383, 401, 424-28, 432, 439, 465-66, 469, 473-75, 485-86, 489, 517, 529-32, 535-37, 544, 549, 554, 560-63, 585-87, 591-97, 608, 618, 629, 633, 648, 681-82, 687, 728

El Salvador   113, 145, 154, 182, 201, 204, 211, 231-32, 238, 246, 314, 683

Eritrea   23, 55-56

Ethiopia   23, 41, 55*56, 60-63, 83, 97, 128, 237-29, 311, 324, 429, 517, 529, 548, 572, 583, 621

France   4-7, 24-29, 32-34, 53-54, 59, 70, 73, 89-93, 100, 104, 116-18, 134, 141, 144, 157-61, 170-71, 180-85, 190, 193, 198-99, 213, 229-32, 237, 264-70, 275, 279-80, 285-86, 289, 301-02, 305, 318-19, 327, 337, 340-41, 344-45, 349-52, 356-59, 373, 379, 396, 403, 424, 440, 451, 475, 500-01, 510, 529-31, 563, 575, 621, 627, 634, 678-80, 687, 690-91

Germany   6, 25-26, 29, 37-38, 59, 74, 79-83, 92, 104, 108, 113, 116, 133-34, 157-61, 165, 172, 178, 184, 197-99, 224, 244-46, 250, 268, 283, 289, 294-95, 299, 316-19, 323, 337-40, 344-46, 352, 356, 367-69, 372-73, 379, 442, 445, 486, 494, 529, 554, 586, 593, 687, 690, 696, 727, 729, 732, 734

Grenada   61, 107, 128, 219-23, 239, 333-35

Hungary   26, 147, 186, 307, 312-16, 340, 371

Iran   8, 25-26, 29-30, 33, 49, 57, 64-73, 77, 85, 89-94, 98—106, 109—10, 115—32, 137-43, 148-49, 152, 158-62, 165, 171-76, 181, 188-90, 194-96, 202-03, 207, 212, 216—18, 222-23, 227-30, 235-37, 241, 263-66, 268-70, 278-87, 290-96, 299, 302, 311, 321, 330, 334, 342-44, 347-50, 356-57, 362, 366-69, 372, 380, 386, 391-93, 407, 414-15, 421—29, 438-39, 475, 485, 498-502, 518-19, 525, 530, 536, 543-44, 553-55, 559, 562-64, 569-70, 585, 590-92, 596-99, 609, 620, 625, 638-43, 647-48, 653-54, 658, 663-64, 679, 682, 694, 727

Iraq   24, 27-29, 33-35, 54, 62, 66, 72-73, 88-91, 103—04, 122, 141-44, 157-59, 171-72, 181, 187, 196, 202-03, 217-18, 223, 227, 230, 233-36, 241, 262, 270, 290-93, 301, 311, 341-42, 347-75, 379-415, 424, 442, 445, 450-52, 463, 467, 472-73, 489, 500-01, 516, 520, 528-29, 544, 561-63, 571, 585, 599-601, 613-15, 625, 635, 642-45, 655, 677-78, 681, 728

Israel   7, 16, 20, 25-28, 31-35, 39, 59-60, 66, 70-74, 86-90, 98-99, 103-04, 112, 119, 123, 129-32, 138, 158-59, 165, 171-75, 180-81, 185-93, 196, 202-03, 208, 213-18, 223, 229-33, 238, 243-45, 260—63, 268-70, 278-80, 288-95, 301-02, 325, 342-43, 347-48, 355-56, 364, 368, 373, 377-83, 389-91, 410, 413-14, 425, 432, 450-11, 467, 471, 475, 486, 497-98, 501, 507, 514, 537, 548, 554-55, 574, 578, 585, 641-44, 648, 682, 685, 727-28

Kuwait   24, 66, 69, 143, 164, 137, 216-17, 223, 226-27, 235, 241, 269, 290-91, 330, 347-74, 378-85, 388-89, 392-42, 415, 423-24, 441-47, 463, 468, 472, 501, 509, 528, 561-63, 728, 739

Lebanon   9, 27-35, 74, 88, 98-99, 112, 122-23, 132, 142, 165, 174, 181, 185-96, 202, 207-19, 222-23, 229, 233, 237, 241, 245, 262-65, 268, 291-95, 311, 331, 348, 364, 368, 380, 414-15, 425-26, 438, 472, 487-88, 494, 539, 544, 554-56, 562, 594, 638, 641-43, 646, 655, 727

Libya   62, 70, 91, 99-100, 117, 121-22, 130, 155, 159, 182-83,, 203, 213, 222, 236-37, 243, 263-65, 268-69, 279-80, 293-95, 299, 327, 364, 423, 510, 530, 597, 604, 675, 728

Los Angeles   632-33, 637, 68, 712

Manila   236, 261, 417, 507-08, 511-13

Mogadishu   449, 484, 489-92, 494, 586

New York   41, 50, 273, 287, 375, 455, 462, 467-69, 478, 486, 513, 559, 572, 575, 657, 689, 692-94, 712, 722

Nicaragua   20, 29, 33, 49, 57, 61, 71, 85-86, 106, 109-13, 127-28, 145-46, 154, 161, 181-83, 201, 204, 212, 220-21, 230, 237-39, 243-44, 267, 274, 280, 296, 314-15, 324, 464, 485

Oklahoma City Bombing   520-24

Operation Boot Strap   580-81

Pakistan   40, 54, 66, 77, 120-26, 131, 140, 161-64, 216, 234-35, 243, 256-59, 276-79, 283-85, 293-96, 301-04, 314, 328-30, 340-41, 363-64, 396, 415-16, 427-29, 432-33, 441-42, 453, 462-64, 468-70, 484, 488, 492, 499, 507-16, 524, 529, 532, 535, 551-54, 564, 569-70, 577, 586, 590-96, 599-601, 604-12, 615-20, 624-25, 632-33, 637-41, 645-48, 655, 658, 661, 677-82, 696, 729, 732, 739

Panama   75-77, 85, 181-82, 212, 235, 324, 330-36, 353-54, 387, 660

Philippines   7, 49, 124, 131-32, 153, 236-37, 260-61, 289, 353, 362, 471, 424-26, 497-99, 507-14, 522-25, 532-33, 536, 559, 562, 567-68, 583, 593, 600, 621, 638, 659, 728

Poland   6, 38-40, 61, 79, 111, 134-36, 147, 155-57, 161, 176, 196-98, 211, 238, 282, 295, 307-08, 312-16, 337, 345, 371-73, 422, 563

Rumania   31, 321

Russia   5-6, 21, 24-26, 31-40, 43-45, 54-56, 60-61, 66-66, 73, 77-82, 87-88, 91-92, 96, 104, 107-08, 114-15, 119-21, 124-36, 140-43, 151-57, 160-66, 170-72, 176-79, 182-85, 188-89, 197-201, 205-06, 209—11, 215-17, 220-26, 230-31, 234-35, 242-60, 264-66, 269, 275-86, 291, 299-308, 311-12, 318-19, 322-24, 327-29, 333, 337-39, 343-47, 350-58, 368, 371-72, 387-89, 397, 415, 418-29, 433, 437-39, 445, 476, 492, 500-02, 508, 516, 519-20, 524, 527-29, 551-53, 558-60, 564, 582-83, 588-91, 597-601, 626-27, 640-42, 647-48, 658-59, 662-64, 679-80, 692, 720, 728, 736-37

Saudi Arabia   26, 30, 57, 63, 69, 86-87, 104-05, 111, 119-24, 130-31, 136, 164, 171, 174, 257, 285, 291, 328-30, 351, 357, 360-64, 367, 370, 373, 379, 384-86, 389-92, 396, 401, 407, 423, 426, 465, 475, 496-98, 501, 534, 547-49, 555-57, 561-63, 568, 586-87, 592, 600, 617-19, 630, 643, 650, 655, 666, 695, 728, 735

Serbia   373, 430-31, 497, 500, 615, 626-28

Somalia   55, 60, 129, 239, 364, 429-30, 449, 484, 487-96, 529, 534, 548, 561-62, 568, 587, 600, 728

Sudan   55-57, 62, 122, 203, 213, 237, 243, 264, 268, 311, 364, 423-25, 432-33, 441, 454, 464, 469-72, 484, 488-89, 493-96, 514-17, 526, 530-33, 536-37, 546—50, 554, 557, 560-66, 569, 576-77, 586-88, 592-94, 604, 607-12, 645

Syria   27, 30-32, 36, 43, 60-64, 74, 86-88, 101, 104, 122-23, 145, 165-66, 186-89, 192-96, 203, 207, 211, 214-18, 222-23, 229, 233, 236, 261-64, 268-70, 280, 294-95, 314, 337-39, 348, 355-56, 359, 364, 368, 373, 380, 594, 597, 625-27, 641-43

Tiananmen Square   307-309

Turkmenistan   552-53

Uzbekistan   115, 371-72, 422, 553, 595, 616, 619, 648-49, 720

Yemen   31, 61-66, 69, 78, 100, 104, 121-22, 183, 192, 207, 239-30, 241, 363-65, 449-52, 466, 493, 499, 534-35, 561, 606-07, 614, 629-30, 636, 646, 650-51, 654-55, 681, 686

Air France Flight 8969   512

Alkifah Refugee Center and the Al-Farook Mosque   288-89, 377, 418, 434-35, 440, 467, 495, 527, 533, 562, 595

Al-Qaeda 328, 433, 441, 497, 523, 531, 556, 560, 563-65, 594, 600-01, 605, 609-20, 624, 632, 635-37, 640, 643-47, 651, 654, 676-77, 681-82, 686, 689, 694, 697-98, 720, 737

Argen Bright Case 622

Bojinka Plot 510-518, 523-25, 532-36, 558, 567-68, 572, 583, 600, 621, 632-33, 638, 644, 692, 700, 728, 732

Contras 181-82, 204, 212, 231, 238-41, 267-68, 274, 278-79, 296,

Clinton Scandals and Coorruption 433-436, 474-483, 539-546, 570, 579-582, 601-602, 655-662,

Clinton is Impeached 623-624

Day Of Terror Plot 471-74, 524

Desert Shield 380-86

DesertStorm 387-410

Druze 211-12, 216, 222

Egypt Flight 990 630

Flight 800 559-561

Grand Mosque Attack 119-21

Hezbollah 123, 174, 190, 194-96, 203, 207, 217-18, 227, 237, 241, 245, 265-68, 278, 292, 327, 343, 347-48, 380, 414, 424, 441, 494, 498, 548, 554-57, 562, 608, 615, 638, 641-46

IAEA - International Atomic Energy Agency

Iran-Iraq War 141, 230, 235, 241, 270, 290

Iraqi Nuclear Reactor 171

Iraq-Kuwait Invasion 350-51, 355-62

Israeli Defense Force IDF 187, -89, 195-196, 202, 213, 215-17, 222, 229, 380, 641

Khobar Tower 556-57, 649

Lebanese Armed Forces LAF 194, 202, 211, 213-15

Lippo Group 542-44

Millenial Plots 633-637

MNDF - Multi National Defense Force - Lebanon 193- 96, 202 207-19, 222-23, 229

Mukhabarat 534, 552

Muslim Brotherhood 28-31, 74, 87, 120, 124, 165-66, 173-75, 187, 193, 259, 288, 301, 328, 428, 432, 440-41, 485-86, 493, 529-30, 666

1993 World Trade Center Bombing 455-65

National Commission on Terrorism 623-24, 666

Operation Urgent Fury 220-23

Panama Canal 75-76, 181-82, 354, 660

Partners in the American Dream 580-581

PLO 27-34, 59, 73-74, 90, 98-104, 112, 123, 137, 145, 159, 165, 181-82, 185-96, 203, 223, 233, 245, 262, 265, 269, 278-80, 288, 293-95, 325, 347, 364, 414, 424-25, 486, 501, 538-39,

Project Independence 105-06

Revolutionary Guards 99-102, 110, 141-43, 159, 172, 181, 188-90, 237, 241, 294, 380, 415, 425, 475, 642

Sandinistas 20, 29, 85-86, 106, 111-13, 145-46, 154, 161, 181-82, 204, 222, 237-38, 264, 267, 274, 296, 314, 336

Saudi National Guard Office 534-536

Saudi-GID 30, 64, 121, 136, 163, 257, 301, 415

Section 936 US Tax Code 579-580

Subway Plots 500, 578, 578-80, 739

Tarnak 603, 607, 651, 679, 695

Terrorism 3-5, 8-9, 20, 27-38, 42, 59, 61, 66, 69, 73-74, 85-87, 90-95, 98-101, 106, 112-15, 119-26, 135-37, 145-46, 153-55, 159, 174-75, 180-82, 185-96, 202-03, 207-09, 214-18, 222-23, 226, 229-33, 237, 241-46, 253, 257-65, 268-70, 277-80, 284, 288-95, 299, 304, 318, 321-23, 325-26, 332, 346, 354, 363, 376, 380, 404, 408, 414-17, 423-29, 432-34, 438-44, 449-54, 460-74, 484-90, 493-501, 504-26, 530-39, 547-51, 554-68, 572-81, 585-89, 591-96, 601, 604-20, 623-25, 628-39, 641-56, 664-66, 676-98

U.S. Embassy Attacks 100-01, 118-122, 137-39, 154, 159, 207-08, 214, 216, 226-27, 237, 494, 515-16, 587-88, 604-609

USS Cole 452, 650-52, 655, 688, 729

Wahabbism 30, 63, 174, 259, 289, 328, 426-28, 500, 547, 574, 643, 734

www.ingramcontent.com/pod-product-compliance
Lightning Source LLC
Chambersburg PA
CBHW050146130526
44591CB00033B/696